Literacy
for the 21st Century

Teaching Reading and Writing in Grades 4 Through 8

Gail E. Tompkins

California State University, Fresno

PEARSON

Merrill
Prentice Hall

Upper Saddle River, New Jersey
Columbus, Ohio

Library of Congress Cataloging-in-Publication Data
Tompkins, Gail E.
    Literacy for the 21st century: teaching reading and writing in grades 4 through 8/by Gail
    E. Tompkins.— 1st ed.
        p. cm.
    Includes bibliographical references and index.
    ISBN 0-13-098654-2
        1. Language arts (Elementary) I. Title: Literacy for the twenty-first century. II. Title.

LB1576.T6574 2004
372.6—dc21

2003049875

Vice President and Executive Publisher: Jeffery W. Johnston
Editor: Linda Ashe Montgomery
Editorial Assistant: Laura Weaver
Development Editor: Hope Madden
Production Editor: Mary M. Irvin
Design Coordinator: Diane C. Lorenzo
Text Design: Grannan Art and Design
Cover Designer: Ali Mohrman
Cover Image: Christy Terry
Photo Coordinator: Valerie Schultz
Production Manager: Pamela D. Bennett
Director of Marketing: Ann Castel Davis
Marketing Manager: Darcy Betts Prybella
Marketing Coordinator: Tyra Poole

This book was set in Galliard by Carlisle Communications, Ltd. It was printed and bound by Courier Kendallville, Inc.
The cover was printed by Phoenix Color Corp.

Photo Credits: Gail E. Tompkins: 2, 30, 66, 136, 200, 233, 242, 269, 282, 294; KS Studios/Merrill: 9; Anne
Vega/Merrill: 19, 40, 361; Scott Cunningham/Merrill: 53, 100, 172, 259, 302, 326, 372, 401; Karen
Mancinelli/Pearson Learning: 77; Anthony Magnacca/Merrill: 91, 108, 166, 206, 314, 332, 350, 380, 388; Tony
Freeman/Photo Edit: 129, 144; Tom Watson/Merrill: 186; Frank Siteman/PhotoEdit: 223.

Pearson Prentice Hall™ is a trademark of Pearson Education, Inc.
Pearson® is a registered trademark of Pearson plc
Prentice Hall® is a registered trademark of Pearson Education, Inc.
Merrill® is a registered trademark of Pearson Education, Inc.

Pearson Education Ltd.   Pearson Education Australia Pty. Limited
Pearson Education Singapore Pte. Ltd.   Pearson Education North Asia Ltd.
Pearson Education Canada, Ltd.   Pearson Educación de Mexico, S.A. de C.V.
Pearson Education—Japan   Pearson Education Malaysia Pte. Ltd.

10 9 8 7 6 5 4 3 2 1
ISBN: 0-13-098654-2

For Jayne Marlink,
Interim Director of the California Writing Project,
in recognition of your resolute leadership and
in celebration of the CWP's 30th anniversary

About the Author

Gail E. Tompkins is a Professor at California State University, Fresno, in the Department of Literacy and Early Education, where she teaches courses in reading, language arts, and writing for preservice teachers and students in the reading/language arts master's degree program. She directs the San Joaquin Valley Writing Project and works regularly with teachers, both by teaching model lessons in classrooms and by leading staff development programs. Recently Dr. Tompkins was inducted into the California Reading Association's Reading Hall of Fame in recognition of her publications and other accomplishments in the field of reading. She has also been awarded the prestigious Provost's Award for Excellence in Teaching at California State University, Fresno.

Previously, Dr. Tompkins taught at Miami University in Ohio and at the University of Oklahoma in Norman where she received the prestigious Regents' Award for Superior Teaching. She was also an elementary teacher in Virginia for eight years.

Dr. Tompkins is the author of five other texts published by Merrill/Prentice Hall: *Literacy for the 21ˢᵗ Century,* 3rd edition (2003), *Language Arts: Content and Teaching Strategies,* 5th edition (2002), *Teaching Writing: Balancing Process and Product,* 4th edition (2004), *50 Literacy Strategies,* 2nd edition (2004), *and Literacy for the 21ˢᵗ Century: Teaching Reading and Writing in Pre-kindergarten through Grade 4,* (2004). Dr. Tompkins is also a contributing author to two Merrill texts: *Sharing the Pen: Interactive Writing with Young Children* (2004) and *Teaching Vocabulary: 50 Creative Strategies, Grades K–12* (2004). She has written numerous articles related to reading and language arts that have appeared in *The Reading Teacher, Language Arts,* and other professional journals.

Preface

Founded on the principles and research that have made *Literacy for the 21st Century* the best selling literacy text in the market, my new text, *Literacy for the 21st Century: Teaching Reading and Writing in Grades Four Through Eight,* focuses on the literacy needs and development of 4th through 8th grade learners. My aim is to present, clearly and thoroughly, the theory, application, examples, and strategies prospective teachers need to fully understand teaching and assessing reading and writing in these grades.

Created for core literacy courses that have been split to meet a growing demand for credentialing teachers with more in-depth knowledge of upper elementary literacy strategies, this text provides a solid foundation for teaching and using vocabulary, content area reading, the reading and writing connection, narrative text, and print skills with middle grade students. Of particular importance is the strong focus on the needs of struggling readers.

Middle grade teachers have special concern for their struggling readers. By the middle grades, students are no longer learning to read, but reading to learn. If students are uncomfortable, or unfamiliar, with the basics of reading and writing by the time they reach grade four, all their learning will suffer. For that reason, middle grade teachers need the understanding, strategies, and skills to best address the needs of struggling readers. A special feature in each chapter addresses the needs of struggling readers and writers, culminating in a complete chapter addressing the topic.

This comprehensive text presents sound approaches to literacy instruction and guides teachers toward best practice in teaching strategies as well as skills. The principles of effective reading instruction outlined in Chapter 1 provide a strong, easily understood foundation for the entire book. I have culled and created minilessons and assessment tools geared specifically toward teaching and assessing strategies and skills in grades 4–8; the authentic classroom activities and student artifacts included spotlight a number of middle grade teachers who illustrate how they plan for and engage their students in literacy activities; English Language Learner margin notes address the specific concerns of this audience of learners; and the accompanying CD-ROM of classroom footage, along with a full-color CD insert within the text, further establish what is best practice for literacy teachers working with students in this age range.

DRIVING PRINCIPLES

My goal in this text is to show beginning teachers how to teach reading and writing effectively in middle grades, how to create a classroom climate where literacy flourishes, and how to empower the diverse array of readers and writers in today's classrooms to function competently as literate adults in the twenty-first century. To that end, I have based the text on four contemporary theories of literacy learning: constructivist, interactive, sociolinguistic, and reader response theories.

You will learn how to implement a reading program with strategies and skills taught in context using a whole-part-whole organizational approach. The approach I take can, I believe, best be described as balanced and comprehensive. You will learn how to teach vital strategies and useful skills within the context of authentic reading and writing experiences. I have carefully selected the principles, strategies, skills, and examples of literature that will empower the beginning teacher to get up to speed quickly with their early adolescent readers. In creating this textbook, I used knowledge I gleaned from a host of teachers who have been students in my reading courses over the years, and I also sifted through the array of practices and procedures proven effective in today's classrooms and with today's diverse student populations. Although there are many other useful ideas and strategies that can accomplish the goal of producing literate students, I have deliberately and painstakingly chosen research-based, classroom-tested ideas—the best of the best—as the focus of this textbook.

THEMES OF THIS BOOK

These special features increase the effectiveness of the text and address the most current resources in the field of literacy.

Struggling Readers and Writers

One essential focus for middle grade teachers is supporting the learning of struggling readers. You will find insights and ideas embedded in each chapter, as well as one complete chapter dedicated to the topic.

Struggling Readers and Writers Feature: Throughout chapters this feature provides guidelines that will help you address the needs of the struggling reader and writer.

Chapter 11: Working with Struggling Readers and Writers: The chapter-by-chapter look at supporting struggling readers culminates in a complete chapter, addressing the spectrum of needs facing this group of readers. I address the needs of English language learners and unmotivated readers and writers, cover interventions and strategies, and focus teachers' attention, again, on best practice.

English Language Learners: Throughout the text are ELL margin notes specifying which strategies and methods are most appropriate for English language learners and how to adapt teaching to benefit all students.

Real Classrooms

My texts have always been grounded in real classroom teaching and learning. I want readers to experience the effective instruction that takes place in classroom communities, so I always provide as many examples from real classrooms as I can, to model best practice and teacher decision-making.

- Starting with Chapter 2, I begin each chapter with a vignette in which you will see how a real teacher teaches the topic addressed in the chapter. These vignettes are rich and detailed, with photos, dialogue, student writing samples, and illustrations. Readers will be drawn into the story of literacy instruction in an actual classroom as they build background and activate prior knowledge about the chapter's topic. Throughout the chapter, I refer readers to the vignette so that they can apply the concepts they are reading about and make connections to the world of practice.

- The CD-ROM and full color CD insert provide concrete illustrations of real classroom teaching and connections between chapter content and teaching.

Instructional Procedures

Components of a Balanced Literacy Program: In each chapter you will find a figure outlining the components of a balanced literacy program, and explaining how the topic of that chapter fits into a balanced literacy program. This piece makes it easy for prospective teachers to see how to address each component, no matter the content they are addressing with their students.

Mini-lessons: This feature presents clear information showing how to teach strategies and skills within reading and writing classrooms in grades 4 through 8.

Assessment Resources: This feature builds on the discussion and examples in Chapter 3, providing ideas and illustrating tools for meaningful assessment.

Compendium of Instructional Procedures: The easily accessible Compendium of Instructional Procedures at the back of the book offers clearly articulated instructional methods, an invaluable resource and quick reference. When the procedures are mentioned in the text, they are marked with [c] to alert readers that they can turn to the Compendium for more information.

Technology

I have taken an integrated approach to technology in this text, highlighting resources and applications within the text and including technological resources as part of the text package.

CD-ROM: A free CD comes with my text. The CD, *Literature Circles: Responding to Literature in an 8th Grade Classroom* contains footage of a master teacher in her eighth-grade reading and writing classroom. You will have the opportunity to observe the classroom footage, hear from the teacher and students involved, listen to my feedback, and consider the research behind the teacher's decisions. Margin notes in appropriate chapters and a full-color insert in Chapter 8 walks you through using the CD to the fullest.

Technology Links: You will learn about innovative uses of technology in teaching reading and writing through the Technology Links. Among the topics I present in these special features are electronic dialoguing to write back and forth to a reading buddy to respond to literature, videotape portfolios to document student learning, and computer programs that middle grade students can use as they create writing projects.

Companion Website: Margin notes and chapter-ending features provide full text integration with the robust Companion Website that accompanies my text. Providing more ways to use technology effectively as a teaching tool, the Companion Website, available at *www.prenhall.com/tompkins,* offers opportunities for self-assessment; analysis, synthesis, and application of concepts; regularly updated links to web addresses; and special information for teachers required to pass state tests in teaching reading in order to obtain credentials.

ACKNOWLEDGMENTS

Many people helped and encouraged me during the development of this text. My heartfelt thanks go to each of them. First, I want to thank my students at California State University, Fresno, who taught me as I taught them, and to the Teacher Consultants of the San Joaquin Valley Writing Project, who shared their expertise with me. Their insightful questions challenged and broadened my thinking.

Thanks, too, go to the teachers who welcomed me into their classrooms, showed me how they taught reading and writing effectively, and allowed me to learn from them and their students. In particular, I want to express my appreciation to Laurie Goodman, an eigth grade teacher at Pioneer Middle School, who appears in the CD-ROM, and to these teachers who along with Laurie are featured in the vignettes: Jill Peterson, Mickey Cox Elementary School; Charles King, Washington Intermediate School; Kacey Sanom, John Muir Elementary School; Robery Wyatt, Washington Irving Middle School; Tony Abrams, Martin Luther King, Jr., Elementary School; Jessica Bradshaw, Rocky Hill Elementary School; Eileen Boland, Tehipite Middle School; Arlene Lee, Oakton Elementary School; Stacy Shasky, Fairmead Elementary School; and Christina Torres, Lawless Middle School.

I appreciate so many other teachers who shared children's writing samples with me and allowed me to take photos in their classrooms, including: Kimberly Clark, Aynesworth Elementary School; Bob Dickinson and Whitney Donnelly, Williams Ranch School; Peggy Givens, Watonga Middle School; Sandy Harris, Anadarko Middle School; Dawna Lantz, Liberty Middle School; Carol Ochs, Andrew Jackson Elementary School; Judith Salzberg, Charles Wright Elementary School; Jo Ann Steffen, Nicoma Park Junior High School; Cecilia Uyeda, Eaton Elementary School; and Susan Zumwalt, Andrew Jackson Elementary School.

Thanks to R. Carl Harris, Brigham Young University, for creating such an innovative CD-ROM design and successfully showcasing Laurie Goodman and her expert teaching techniques in the CD-ROM that accompanies this text. I want also to thank the reviewers of my manuscript for their comments and insight: Judy A. Abbott, West Virginia University; Sister Regina Alfonso, Notre Dame College, Cleveland, Ohio; Joanne E. Bernstein, Brooklyn College; Jean M. Casey, California State University, Long Beach; Hollis Lowery-Moore, Sam Houston State University; Carolyn L. Piazza, Florida State University; Thomas C. Potter, California State University, Northridge; Cheryl Rosaen, Michigan State University; Sam Sebesta, University of Washington (retired); and Sharyn Walker, Bowling Green State University.

I'd like to thank Hellen Hoffner for her masterful work with the Instructor's Manual and Companion Website for this text, as well as Abigail Garthwait for her insights into the use of technology in teaching in the middle grades.

Finally, I am indebted to Jeff Johnston and his team at Merrill/Prentice Hall in Columbus, Ohio, who produce so many high-quality publications. I am honored to be a Merrill author. Linda Montgomery is the guiding force behind my work, and Hope Madden is my cheerleader, encouraging me every step of the way and spurring me toward impossible deadlines. I want to express my sincere appreciation to Mary Irvin, who has done a fine job supervising the production of this book; to Melissa Gruzs, who has so expertly copy edited the manuscript; and to Jenifer Cooke, whose careful attention to detail makes the text look so good. Thank you all.

DISCOVER THE COMPANION WEBSITE ACCOMPANYING THIS BOOK

The Prentice Hall Companion Website: A Virtual Learning Environment

Technology is a constantly growing and changing aspect of our field that is creating a need for content and resources. To address this emerging need, Prentice Hall has developed an online learning environment for students and professors alike—Companion Websites—to support our textbooks.

In creating a Companion Website, our goal is to build on and enhance what the textbook already offers. For this reason, the content for each user-friendly website is organized by chapter and provides the professor and student with a variety of meaningful resources.

For the Professor

Every Companion Website integrates **Syllabus Manager**™, an online syllabus creation and management utility.

- **Syllabus Manager**™ provides you, the instructor, with an easy, step-by-step process to create and revise syllabi, with direct links into Companion Website and other online content without having to learn HTML.
- Students may logon to your syllabus during any study session. All they need to know is the web address for the Companion Website and the password you've assigned to your syllabus.
- After you have created a syllabus using **Syllabus Manager**™, students may enter the syllabus for their course section from any point in the Companion Website.
- Clicking on a date, the student is shown the list of activities for the assignment. The activities for each assignment are linked directly to actual content, saving time for students.
- Adding assignments consists of clicking on the desired due date, then filling in the details of the assignment—name of the assignment, instructions, and whether or not it is a one-time or repeating assignment.
- In addition, links to other activities can be created easily. If the activity is online, a URL can be entered in the space provided, and it will be linked automatically in the final syllabus.
- Your completed syllabus is hosted on our servers, allowing convenient updates from any computer on the Internet. Changes you make to your syllabus are immediately available to your students at their next logon.

Common Companion Website features for students include:

For the Student

- **Chapter Objectives**—Outline key concepts from the text.
- **Interactive Self-quizzes**—Complete with hints and automatic grading that provide immediate feedback for students.

After students submit their answers for the interactive self-quizzes, the Companion Website **Results Reporter** computes a percentage grade, provides a graphic representation of how many questions were answered correctly and incorrectly, and gives a question-by-question analysis of the quiz. Students are given the option to send their quiz to up to four email addresses (professor, teaching assistant, study partner, etc.).

- **Web Destinations**—Links to www sites that relate to chapter content.
- **Message Board**—Virtual bulletin board to post or respond to questions or comments from a national audience.

To take advantage of the many available resources, please visit the *Literacy for the 21st Century: Teaching Reading and Writing in Grades 4 Through 8* Companion Website at

www.prenhall.com/tompkins

Contents

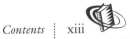

9   *Teaching With Content-Area Textbooks*   282

Vignette: Ms. Boland's Students Study Medieval Life   *283*

10 *Connecting Reading and Writing*   *314*

Vignette: Fourth-Grade English Learners Read and Write About Pilgrims   *315*

11 Working With Struggling Readers and Writers   *350*

12 Becoming Lifelong Readers and Writers   *380*

Compendium of Instructional Procedures   *408*

Glossary   459

Index of Authors and Titles   463

Subject Index   474

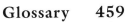

SPECIAL FEATURES

Guidelines for Struggling Readers and Writers

How Effective Teachers . . .

Technology Links

Assessment Resources

Minilessons

chapter 1

Becoming an Effective Teacher of Reading

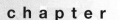

chapter
QUESTIONS

- How do effective teachers teach reading and writing?

- Which instructional practices are most effective for teaching reading and writing?

- How are instruction and assessment linked?

- What is a balanced approach to literacy?

The children of the 21st century will face many challenges that require them to use reading and writing in different forms. As we begin the new millennium, teachers are learning research-based approaches to teach reading and writing that will prepare their students for the future. Teachers make a significant difference in children's lives, and this book is designed to help you become an effective reading teacher. Researchers have examined many teaching practices and have drawn some important conclusions about the most effective ones: We must teach students the processes of reading and writing, as well as how to use reading and writing as learning tools. Bill Teale (1995) challenges us to teach students to think with and through reading and writing, to use reading and writing to get a wide variety of things done in their lives, and to use reading and writing for pleasure and insight.

Let's start with some definitions. "Literacy" used to mean knowing how to read, but the term has been broadened to encompass both reading and writing. Now literacy means the competence "to carry out the complex tasks using reading and writing related to the world of work and to life outside the school" (*Cases in Literacy*, 1989, p. 36). Educators are also identifying other literacies that they believe will be needed in the 21st century (Harris & Hodges, 1995). Our reliance on radio and television for conveying ideas has awakened us to the importance of "oracy," the ability to express and understand spoken language. Visual literacy, the ability to create meaning from illustrations, is also receiving a great deal of attention.

The term "literacy" is being used in other ways as well. For example, teachers are introducing even very young children to computers and developing their "computer literacy." Similarly, math and science educators speak of mathematical and scientific literacies. Hirsch (1987) called for another type of literacy, "cultural literacy," as a way to introduce children "to the major ideas and ideals from past cultures that have defined and shaped today's society" (p. 10). Literacy, however, is not a prescription of certain books to read or concepts to define. Rather, according to Rafferty (1999), it is a tool, a way to learn about the world and a means to participate more fully in the technological society of the 21st century.

This chapter introduces the eight principles of an effective reading program. Each principle is stated in terms of what an effective teacher does. Ernest Boyer, in his book *The Basic School* (1995), explains that we really do know what works in elementary schools. From the research that has been conducted in the last 25 years and the effective practices used in good schools today, we can identify the characteristics of a quality literacy program and incorporate them in our own teaching.

PRINCIPLE 1: EFFECTIVE TEACHERS UNDERSTAND HOW STUDENTS LEARN

Understanding how students learn, and particularly how they learn to read, influences the instructional approaches that effective teachers use. A generation ago, behaviorists influenced how teachers taught reading. According to behavioral theory, students learn to read by learning a series of discrete, sequenced skills (Skinner, 1968), and teachers applied this theory by drilling students on skills and having them complete skills worksheets.

Reading instruction has changed considerably in the past 25 years, thanks to four intertwining theories of learning, language, and literacy: the constructivist, interactive, sociolinguistic,

Figure 1-1   The Four Learning Theories

CONSTRUCTIVIST

Children are active learners.

Children relate new information to prior knowledge.

Children organize and relate information in schemata.

INTERACTIVE

Students use both prior knowledge and features in the text as they read.

Students use word-identification skills and comprehension strategies.

Fluent readers focus on making meaning.

READER RESPONSE

Readers create meaning as they read.

Students vary how they read according to aesthetic and efferent purposes.

The goal is for students to become lifelong readers.

SOCIOLINGUISTIC

Thought and language are related.

Social interaction is important in learning.

Teachers provide scaffolds for students.

and reader response theories. Figure 1-1 presents an overview of these theories. In the figure, the theories are drawn as though they were parts of a jigsaw puzzle in order to show that they are linked.

Constructivist Learning Theories

Jean Piaget's (1969) theoretical framework differs substantially from behaviorist theories. Piaget described learning as the modification of students' cognitive structures, or schemata, as they interact with and adapt to their environment. Schemata are like mental filing cabinets, and new information is organized with prior knowledge in the filing system. Piaget also posited that children are active and motivated thinkers and learners. This definition of learning and children's role in learning require a reexamination of the teacher's role: Instead of simply being dispensers of knowledge, teachers engage students with experiences so that they modify their schemata and construct their own knowledge. The key concepts are:

1. Children are active learners.
2. Children relate new information to prior knowledge.
3. Children organize and integrate information in schemata.

Interactive Learning Theories

The interactive theories describe what readers do as they read. They emphasize that readers focus on comprehension, or making meaning, as they read (Rumelhart, 1977; Stanovich, 1980). Readers construct meaning using a combination of text-based information (information from the text) and reader-based information (information from readers' backgrounds of knowledge, or schemata). These theories echo the importance of schemata described in the constructivist theories. In the past, educators have argued over whether children's attention during reading moves from noticing the letters on the page and grouping them into words to making meaning in the brain, or the other way around, from activating background knowledge in the brain to examining letters and words on the page. Educators now agree that the two processes take place interactively, at the same time.

The interactive model of reading includes an executive function, or decision maker. Fluent readers identify words automatically and use word-identification skills when they come across unfamiliar words so that they can focus their attention on comprehension. The decision maker monitors the reading process and the skills and strategies that readers use. Teachers focus on reading as a comprehension process and teach both word-identification skills and comprehension strategies. The key concepts are:

1. Students use both their prior knowledge and features in the text as they read.
2. Students use word-identification skills and comprehension strategies to understand what they read.
3. Teachers help students become fluent readers.

Sociolinguistic Learning Theories

The sociolinguists contribute a cultural dimension to our consideration of how children learn. They view reading and writing as social activities that reflect the culture and community in which students live (Heath, 1983; Vygotsky, 1978, 1986). According to Lev Vygotsky, language helps to organize thought, and children use language to learn as well as to communicate and share experiences with others. Understanding that children use language for social purposes allows teachers to plan instructional activities that incorporate a social component, such as having students talk about books they are reading or share their writing with classmates. And, because children's language and concepts of literacy reflect their cultures and home communities, teachers must respect students' language and appreciate cultural differences in their attitudes toward learning and becoming literate.

Social interaction enhances learning in two other ways: scaffolding and the zone of proximal development (Dixon-Krauss, 1996). Scaffolding is a support mechanism that teachers and parents use to assist students. Vygotsky suggests that children can accomplish more difficult tasks in collaboration with adults than they can on their own. For example, when teachers assist students in reading a book they could not read independently or help students revise a piece of writing, they are scaffolding. Vygotsky also suggests that children learn very little when they perform tasks that they can already do independently. He recommends the zone of proximal development, the range of tasks between students' actual developmental level and their potential development. More challenging tasks done with the teacher's scaffolding are more conducive to learning. As students learn, teachers gradually withdraw their support so that eventually students perform the task independently. Then the cycle begins again. The key concepts are:

1. Thought and language are interrelated.
2. Social interaction is important in learning.

3. Teachers provide scaffolds for students.
4. Teachers plan instruction based on students' zone of proximal development.

Reader Response Learning Theories

Louise Rosenblatt (1978, 1983) and other reader response theorists consider how students create meaning as they read. These theories extend the constructivist theories about schemata and making meaning in the brain, not the eyes. According to reader response theorists, students do not try to figure out the author's meaning as they read. Instead, they negotiate or create a meaning that makes sense based on the words they are reading and their own background knowledge. Reader response theorists agree with Piaget that readers are active and responsible for their learning.

Rosenblatt (1991) explains that there are two stances or purposes for reading. When readers read for enjoyment or pleasure, they assume an aesthetic stance, and when they read to locate and remember information, they read efferently. Rosenblatt suggests that these two stances represent the ends of a continuum and that readers often use a combination of the two stances when they read, whether they are reading stories or informational books. For example, when students read *Nature's Green Umbrella* (Gibbons, 1994), an informational book about tropical rain forests, they may read efferently to locate information about the animals that live in rain forests. Or they may read aesthetically, carried off—in their minds, at least—on an expedition to the Amazon River. When students read a novel such as *Sarah, Plain and Tall* (MacLachlan, 1985), a story about a mail-order bride, they usually read aesthetically as they relive life on the prairie a century ago. Students are encouraged to step into the story and become a character and to "live" the story. This conflicts with more traditional approaches in which teachers ask students to recall specific information from the story, thus forcing students to read efferently, to take away information. Reader response theory suggests that students read differently depending on their purpose, and if students read only efferently, they do not learn to love reading and may not become lifelong readers. The key concepts are:

1. Readers create meaning as they read.
2. Students vary how they read depending on whether they are reading for aesthetic or efferent purposes.
3. The goal of literacy instruction is for students to become lifelong readers.

PRINCIPLE 2: EFFECTIVE TEACHERS SUPPORT STUDENTS' USE OF THE FOUR CUEING SYSTEMS

Language is a complex system for creating meaning through socially shared conventions (Halliday, 1978). English, like other languages, involves four cueing systems:

- the phonological or sound system
- the syntactic or structural system
- the semantic or meaning system
- the pragmatic or social and cultural use system

Together these four systems make communication possible, and children and adults use all four systems simultaneously as they read, write, listen, and talk. The priority

Type	Terms	Uses in the Middle Grades
Phonological System The sound system of English with approximately 44 sounds and more than 500 ways to spell the 44 sounds	• Phoneme (the smallest unit of sound) • Grapheme (the written representation of a phoneme using one or more letters) • Phonemic awareness (understanding that speech is composed of individual sounds) • Phonics (teaching sound-symbol correspondences and spelling rules)	• Pronouncing words • Detecting regional and other dialects • Decoding words when reading • Using invented spelling • Reading and writing alliterations and onomatopoeia • Dividing words into syllables
Syntactic System The structural system of English that governs how words are combined into sentences	• Syntax (the structure or grammar of a sentence) • Morpheme (the smallest meaningful unit of language) • Free morpheme (a morpheme that can stand alone as a word) • Bound morpheme (a morpheme that must be attached to a free morpheme)	• Adding inflectional endings to words • Combining words to form compound words • Adding prefixes and suffixes to root words • Using capitalization and punctuation correctly • Writing simple, compound, and complex sentences • Combining sentences
Semantic System The meaning system of English that focuses on vocabulary	• Semantics (meaning)	• Learning the meanings of words • Discovering that some words have multiple meanings • Using context clues to figure out an unfamiliar word • Studying synonyms, antonyms, and homonyms • Using a dictionary and a thesaurus • Reading and writing comparisons (metaphors and similes)
Pragmatic System The system of English that varies language according to social and cultural uses	• Function (the purpose for which a person uses language) • Standard English (the form of English used in textbooks and by television newscasters) • Nonstandard English (other forms of English)	• Varying language to fit specific purposes • Reading and writing dialogue in dialects • Comparing standard and nonstandard forms of English

people place on various cueing systems can vary; however, the phonological system is especially important for beginning readers and writers as they apply phonics skills to decode and spell words. Information about the four cueing systems is summarized in Figure 1-2.

The Phonological System

There are approximately 44 speech sounds in English. Children learn to pronounce these sounds as they learn to talk, and they learn to associate the sounds with letters as they learn to read and write. Sounds are called phonemes, and they are represented in print with diagonal lines to differentiate them from graphemes (letters or letter combinations). Thus, the first grapheme in *mother* is *m*, and the phoneme is /m/. The phoneme in *soap* that is represented by the grapheme *oa* is called "long o" and is written /ō/.

The phonological system is important for both oral and written language. Regional and cultural differences exist in the way people pronounce phonemes. For example, people from Massachusetts pronounce sounds differently from people from Georgia. Similarly, the English spoken in Australia is different from American English.

Children who are learning English as a second language must learn to pronounce English sounds, and sounds that are different from those in their native language are particularly difficult to learn. For example, Spanish does not have /th/, and children who have immigrated to the United States from Mexico and other Spanish-speaking countries have difficulty pronouncing this sound. They often substitute /d/ for /th/ because the sounds are articulated in similar ways (Nathenson-Mejia, 1989). Younger children usually learn to pronounce the difficult sounds more easily than older children and adults.

The phonological system plays a crucial role in reading instruction during the primary grades. Children use their knowledge of phonics as they learn to read and write. In a purely phonetic language, there would be a one-to-one correspondence between letters and sounds, and teaching students to sound out words would be a simple process. But English is not a purely phonetic language because there are 26 letters and 44 sounds and many ways to combine the letters to spell some of the sounds, especially vowels. Consider these ways to spell long *e: sea, green, Pete, me,* and *people.* And sometimes the patterns used to spell long *e* don't work, as in *head* and *great.* Phonics, which describes the phoneme-grapheme correspondences and related spelling rules, is an important part of reading instruction. Students use phonics information to decode words, but phonics instruction is not a complete reading program because many common words cannot be decoded easily and because good readers do much more than just decode words when they read.

Children also use their understanding of the phonological system to create invented or temporary spellings. Young children or older, struggling writers, for example, often spell *home* as *hom* or *school* as *skule,* based on their knowledge of phoneme-grapheme relationships and the English spelling patterns. As children learn more phonics and gain more experience reading and writing, their spellings become more conventional. For students who are learning English as a second language, their spellings often reflect their pronunciations of words (Nathenson-Mejia, 1989).

The Syntactic System

The syntactic system is the structural organization of English. This system is the grammar that regulates how words are combined into sentences. The word *grammar* here means the rules governing how words are combined in sentences, not parts of speech. Children use the syntactic system as they combine words to form sentences. Word order is important in English, and English speakers must arrange words into a sequence that makes sense. Young Spanish-speaking children who are learning English as a second language, for example, learn to say "This is my red sweater," not "This is my sweater red," which is the literal translation from Spanish.

Children use their knowledge of the syntactic system as they read. They expect that the words they are reading have been strung together into sentences. When they come

English language learners' grammatical errors are best dealt with through writing activities because students may not hear the errors when speaking.

to an unfamiliar word, they recognize its role in the sentence even if they don't know the terms for parts of speech. In the sentence "The horses galloped through the gate and out into the field," students may not be able to decode the word *through*, but they can easily substitute a reasonable word or phrase, such as *out of* or *past*.

Many of the capitalization and punctuation rules that students learn reflect the syntactic system of language. Similarly, when children learn about simple, compound, and complex sentences, they are learning about the syntactic system.

Another component of syntax is word forms. Words such as *dog* and *play* are morphemes, the smallest meaningful units in language. Word parts that change the meaning of a word are also morphemes. When the plural marker *-s* is added to *dog* to make *dogs*, for instance, or the past-tense marker *-ed* is added to *play* to make *played*, these words now have two morphemes because the inflectional endings change the meaning of the words. The words *dog* and *play* are free morphemes because they convey meaning while standing alone. The endings *-s* and *-ed* are bound morphemes because they must be attached to free morphemes to convey meaning. Compound words are two or more morphemes combined to create a new word: *Birthday*, for example, is a compound word made up of two free morphemes.

During fourth through eighth grades, children learn to add affixes to words. Affixes that are added at the beginning of a word are prefixes, and affixes added at the end are suffixes. Both kinds of affixes are bound morphemes. The prefix *un-* in *unhappy* is a bound morpheme, and *happy* is a free morpheme because it can stand alone as a word.

The Semantic System

The third language system is the semantic or meaning system. The key component of this system is vocabulary. As children learn to talk, they acquire a vocabulary that is

This student uses all four cueing systems as she prepares her presentation and shares it with the class.

continually increasing. Researchers estimate that children have a vocabulary of 5,000 words by the time they enter school, and they continue to acquire 3,000 to 4,000 words each year during the elementary grades (Lindfors, 1987; Nagy, 1988). Considering how many words children learn each year, it is unreasonable to assume that they learn words only through formal instruction. They learn many, many words informally through reading and through social studies and science lessons.

Children learn approximately 8 to 10 words a day. A remarkable achievement! As children learn a word, they move from a general understanding of the meaning of the word to a better-developed understanding, and they learn words through real reading, not by copying definitions from a dictionary. Researchers have estimated that students need to read a word 4 to 14 times to make it their own, and this is possible only when students read and reread books and write about what they are reading.

The Pragmatic System

The fourth language system is pragmatics, which deals with the social aspects of language use. People use language for many purposes, and how they talk or write varies according to their purpose and audience. Language use also varies among social classes, ethnic groups, and geographic regions. These varieties are known as dialects. School is one cultural community, and the language of school is Standard English. This dialect is formal—the one used in textbooks, newspapers, and magazines and by television newscasters. Other forms, including those spoken in urban ghettos, in Appalachia, and by Mexican Americans in the Southwest, are generally classified as nonstandard English. These nonstandard forms of English are alternatives in which the phonology, syntax, and semantics differ from those of Standard English. These forms are neither inferior nor substandard; they reflect the communities of speakers, and the speakers communicate as effectively as those who use Standard English. The goal is for children to add Standard English to their repertoire of language registers, not to replace their home dialect with Standard English.

As children who speak nonstandard English read texts written in Standard English, they often translate what they read into their dialect. Sometimes this occurs when children are reading aloud. For example, a sentence written "They are going to school" might be read aloud as "They be goin' to school." Emergent or beginning readers are not usually corrected when they translate words into nonstandard dialects as long as they don't change the meaning, but older, more fluent readers should be directed to read the words as they are printed in the book.

Effective teachers understand that children use all four cueing systems as they read and write. For example, when students read the sentence "Jimmy is playing ball with his father" correctly, they are probably using information from all four systems. When a child substitutes *dad* for *father* and reads "Jimmy is playing ball with his dad," he might be focusing on the semantic or pragmatic system rather than on the phonological system. When a child substitutes *basketball* for *ball* and reads "Jimmy is playing basketball with his father," he might be relying on an illustration or his own experience playing basketball. Because both *basketball* and *ball* begin with *b*, he might have used the beginning sound as an aid in decoding, but he apparently did not consider how long the word *basketball* is compared with the word *ball*. When the child changes the syntax, as in "Jimmy, he play ball with his father," he may speak a nonstandard dialect. Sometimes a child reads the sentence as "Jump is play boat with his father," so that it doesn't make sense. The child chooses words with the correct beginning sound and uses appropriate parts of speech for at least some of the words, but there is no comprehension. This is a serious problem because the child doesn't seem to understand that what he reads must make sense.

You will learn ways to apply information on the cueing systems in upcoming chapters. This information is applied to spelling in Chapter 4, "Refining Students' Print Skills," to word identification and vocabulary in Chapter 5, "Learning About the Meanings of Words," and to comprehension in Chapter 6, "Facilitating Students' Comprehension."

PRINCIPLE 3: EFFECTIVE TEACHERS CREATE A COMMUNITY OF LEARNERS

Middle grade classrooms are social settings in which students read, discuss, and write about literature. Together, students and their teachers create the classroom community, and the type of community they create strongly influences students' learning. Effective teachers establish a community of learners in which students are motivated to learn and are actively involved in reading and writing activities. Teachers and students work collaboratively and purposefully. Perhaps the most striking quality of classroom communities is the partnership that the teacher and students create. Students are a "family" in which all the members respect one another and support each other's learning. Students value culturally and linguistically diverse classmates and recognize that all students make important contributions to the classroom (Wells & Chang-Wells, 1992).

Students and teachers work together for the common good of the community. Consider the differences between renting and owning a home. In a classroom community, students and the teacher are joint "owners" of the classroom. Students assume responsibility for their own learning and behavior, work collaboratively with classmates, complete assignments, and care for the classroom. In traditional classrooms, in contrast, the classroom is the teacher's, and students are simply "renters" for the school year. This doesn't mean that in a classroom community, teachers abdicate their responsibility to the students. On the contrary, teachers retain all of their roles as guide, instructor, monitor, coach, mentor, and grader. Sometimes these roles are shared with students, but the ultimate responsibility for them remains with the teacher.

Ten Characteristics of Classroom Communities

Classroom communities have specific characteristics that are conducive to learning and that support students' interactions with literature. Ten of the characteristics are:

1. *Responsibility.* Students are responsible for their learning, their behavior, and the contributions they make in the classroom. They see themselves as valued and contributing members of the classroom community.
2. *Opportunities.* Children have opportunities to read and write for genuine and meaningful purposes. They read real books and write for real audiences—their classmates, their parents, members of their community. They rarely use workbooks or drill-and-practice sheets.
3. *Engagement.* Students are motivated to learn and are actively involved in reading and writing activities. Students sometimes choose which books to read, how they will respond to a book, and which reading and writing projects they will pursue.
4. *Demonstration.* Teachers provide demonstrations of literacy skills and strategies, and children observe in order to learn what more capable readers and writers do.
5. *Risk taking.* Students are encouraged to explore topics, make guesses, and take risks.

C See the Compendium of Instructional Procedures, which follows Chapter 12, for more information on terms marked with the symbol C.

6. *Instruction.* Teachers are expert readers and writers, and they provide instruction through minilessons[C] on procedures, skills, and strategies related to reading and writing.

7. *Response.* Children share personal connections to stories, make predictions, ask questions, and deepen their comprehension as they write in reading logs[C] and participate in grand conversations[C]. When they write, children share their rough drafts in writing groups to get feedback on how well they are communicating, and they celebrate their published books by sharing them with classmates.

8. *Choice.* Students often make choices about the books they read and the writing they do within the parameters set by the teacher. When given opportunities to make choices, students are often more highly motivated to read and write, and they value their learning experience more because it is more meaningful to them.

9. *Time.* Children need large chunks of time to pursue reading and writing activities; it doesn't work well for teachers to break the classroom schedule into many small time blocks. Two to three hours of uninterrupted time each day for reading and writing instruction is recommended. It is important to minimize disruptions during the time set aside for literacy instruction, and administrators should schedule computer, music, art, and other pull-out programs so that they do not interfere.

10. *Assessment.* Teachers and children work together to establish guidelines for assessment so that children can monitor their own work and participate in the evaluation. These 10 characteristics are reviewed in Figure 1-3.

Creating an Effective Classroom Community

Teachers are more successful when they take the first 2 weeks of the school year to establish the classroom environment (Sumara & Walker, 1991). Teachers can't assume that children will be familiar with the procedures and routines or that they will instinctively be cooperative, responsible, and respectful of classmates. Teachers explicitly explain classroom routines, such as how to get supplies out and put them away and how to work with classmates in a cooperative group, and set the expectation that students will adhere to the routines. Next, they demonstrate literacy procedures, including how to choose a book from the classroom library to read, how to provide feedback about a classmate's writing, and how to participate in a grand conversation about a book. Third, teachers model ways of interacting with students, responding to literature, respecting classmates, and assisting classmates with reading and writing projects.

Teachers are the classroom managers. They set expectations and clearly explain to children what is expected of them and what is valued in the classroom. The classroom rules are specific and consistent, and teachers also set limits. For example, students might be allowed to talk quietly with classmates when they are working, but they are not allowed to shout across the classroom or talk when the teacher is talking or when students are making a presentation to the class. Teachers also model classroom rules as they interact with students. According to Sumara and Walker (1991), the process of socialization at the beginning of the school year is planned, deliberate, and crucial to the success of the literacy program.

Not everything can be accomplished during the first 2 weeks, however; teachers continue to reinforce classroom routines and literacy procedures. One way is to have student leaders model the desired routines and behaviors. When this is done, other students are likely to follow the lead. Teachers also continue to teach additional literacy

ELL

In a classroom community, social interaction and small-group activities are rich learning opportunities for English language learners.

Figure 1-3   Ten Characteristics of a Community of Learners

Characteristic	Teacher's Role	Students' Role
Responsibility	Teachers set guidelines and have the expectation that students will be responsible. Teachers also model responsible behavior.	Students are responsible for fully participating in the classroom, including completing assignments, participating in groups, and cooperating with classmates.
Opportunities	Teachers provide opportunities for students to read and write in genuine and meaningful activities, not contrived practice activities.	Students take advantage of learning opportunities provided in class. They read independently during reading workshop, and they share their writing during sharing time.
Engagement	Teachers make it possible for students to be engaged by the literature and activities they provide for students. Also, by planning units with students and allowing them to make choices, they motivate students to complete assignments.	Students are actively involved in reading and writing activities. They are motivated and industrious because they are reading real literature and are involved in activities they find meaningful.
Demonstration	Teachers demonstrate what readers and writers do and use think-alouds to explain their thinking during the demonstrations.	Students observe the teacher's demonstrations of skills and strategies that readers and writers use.
Risk taking	Teachers encourage students to take risks, make guesses, and explore their thinking. They deemphasize students' need to get things "right."	Students explore what they are learning, take risks as they ask questions, and make guesses. They expect not to be laughed at or made fun of. They view learning as a process of exploration.
Instruction	Teachers provide instruction through minilessons. During minilessons, teachers provide information and make connections to the reading and writing in which students are involved.	Students look to the teacher to provide instruction on procedures, concepts, strategies, and skills related to reading and writing. Students participate in minilessons and then apply what they have learned in their own reading and writing.
Response	Teachers provide opportunities for students to share and respond to reading and writing activities. Students are a supportive audience for classmates.	Students respond to books they are reading in reading logs and grand conversations. They share their writing in writing groups and get feedback from classmates.
Choice	Teachers encourage students to choose some of the books they read and some of the writing activities and projects they develop.	Students make choices about some books they read, some writing activities, and some projects they develop within parameters set by the teacher.
Time	Teachers organize the class schedule with large chunks of time for reading and writing activities. They plan units and set deadlines with students.	Students have large chunks of time for reading and writing activities. They work on projects over days and weeks and understand when assignments are due.
Assessment	Teachers set grading plans with students before beginning each unit, meet with students in assessment conferences, and assist students in collecting work for portfolios.	Students understand how they will be assessed and graded, and they participate in their assessment. They collect their work in progress in folders and choose which work they will place in portfolios.

procedures as students are involved in new types of activities. The classroom community evolves during the school year, but the foundation is laid during the first 2 weeks.

Teachers develop a predictable classroom environment with familiar routines and literacy procedures. Children feel comfortable, safe, and more willing to take risks and experiment in a predictable classroom environment; this is especially true for students from varied cultures, students learning English as a second language, and less capable readers and writers.

The classroom community also extends beyond the walls of the classroom to include the entire school and the wider community. Within the school, students become "buddies" with students in other classes and get together to read and write in pairs (Morrice & Simmons, 1991). When parents and other community members come into the school, they demonstrate the value they place on education by working as tutors and aides, sharing their cultures, and demonstrating other types of expertise (Graves, 1995).

PRINCIPLE 4: EFFECTIVE TEACHERS ADOPT A BALANCED APPROACH TO LITERACY INSTRUCTION

A balanced approach is also effective for English language learners because they receive direct instruction and have opportunities to participate in authentic reading and writing activities.

In recent years, we have witnessed a great deal of controversy about the best way to teach reading. On one side are the proponents of a skills-based or phonics approach; on the other side are advocates of a holistic, literature-based approach. Teachers favoring each side cite research to support their views, and state legislatures are joining the debate by mandating systematic, intensive phonics instruction in the primary grades. Today many teachers agree with Richard Allington that there is "no quick fix" and no one program to meet the needs of all children (Allington & Walmsley, 1995). Many teachers recognize value in both points of view and recommend a "balance" or combination of holistic and skills approaches (Baumann, Hoffman, Moon, & Duffy-Hester, 1998). That is the perspective taken in this text.

A balanced approach to literacy, according to Spiegel (1998), is a decision-making approach through which teachers make thoughtful and purposeful decisions about how to help students become better readers and writers. A balanced approach "is built on research, views the teacher as an informed decision maker who develops a flexible program, and is constructed around a comprehensive view of literacy" (Spiegel, 1998, p. 117).

Fitzgerald (1999) identified three principles of a balanced literacy approach. First, teachers develop students' skills knowledge, including phonics, their strategy knowledge for comprehension and responding to literature, and their affective knowledge, including nurturing students' love of reading. Second, instructional approaches that are sometimes viewed as opposites are used to meet students' learning needs. Phonics instruction and reading workshop, for instance, are two very different instructional programs that are used in a balanced literacy approach. Third, students read a variety of reading materials, ranging from trade books to leveled books with controlled vocabulary and basal reading textbooks.

Even though balanced programs vary, they usually embody these characteristics:

1. Literacy is viewed comprehensively, as involving both reading and writing.
2. Literature is at the heart of the program.
3. Skills and strategies are taught both directly and indirectly.
4. Reading instruction involves learning word identification, vocabulary, and comprehension.

Figure 1-4 Components of a Balanced Literacy Program

Component	Description
Reading	Students participate in a variety of modeled, shared, interactive, guided, and independent reading experiences using trade books, basal reader textbooks, content-area textbooks, and self-selected books.
Phonics and Other Skills	Students learn to use phonics to decode and spell words. In addition, students learn other types of skills including comprehension, grammar, reference, and study skills that they use in reading and writing.
Strategies	Students use problem-solving and monitoring behaviors called strategies as they read and write. Types of strategies include word-identification, comprehension, writing, and spelling strategies.
Vocabulary	Students learn the meanings of words through wide reading as well as by posting key words from books and thematic units on word walls[C] and by participating in word sorts[C], word maps, and semantic feature analysis[C] activities.
Comprehension	Students choose appropriate reading materials; activate background knowledge and vocabulary; consider the structure of the text; make connections to their own lives, to the world, and to other literature; and apply reading strategies to ensure that they understand what they are reading.
Literature	Students read and respond to a variety of fiction and nonfiction texts as part of literature focus units, literature circles, and reading workshop.
Content-Area Study	Students use reading and writing to learn about social studies and science topics in content-area units. They read content-area textbooks as well as stories, informational books, and poetry, learn to conduct research, and prepare projects to apply what they have learned.
Oral Language	Students participate in oral language activities as they work in small groups, participate in grand conversations and instructional conversations[C], and present oral reports. They also listen to the teacher during read-alouds, minilessons, and other oral presentations.
Writing	Students use informal writing when they write in reading logs and other journals, make clusters and diagrams, and they use the writing process to write stories, essays, reports, and poems.
Spelling	Students apply phonics, syllabication, and morphemic analysis skills to spell words. They learn to spell high-frequency words first, and then other words that they need for writing through a variety of spelling activities that may include weekly spelling tests.

5. Writing instruction involves learning to express meaningful ideas and use conventional spelling, grammar, and punctuation to express those ideas.
6. Students use reading and writing as tools for learning in the content areas.
7. The goal of a balanced literacy program is to develop lifelong readers and writers. (Baumann & Ivey, 1997; McIntyre & Pressley, 1996; Spiegel, 1998; Strickland, 1994/1995; Weaver, 1998)

Figure 1-4 presents a list of 10 components of a balanced literacy program; these components embody the characteristics and recommendations from researchers, professional literacy organizations, and state boards of education. These components are addressed in each chapter of this text to show how the topic of that chapter fits into a balanced literacy program.

PRINCIPLE 5: EFFECTIVE TEACHERS SCAFFOLD STUDENTS' READING AND WRITING EXPERIENCES

Teachers scaffold or support children's reading and writing as they demonstrate, guide, and teach, and they vary the amount of support they provide according to their instructional purpose and the students' needs. Sometimes teachers model how experienced readers read, or they record students' dictation when the writing is too difficult for students to do on their own. At other times, they carefully guide students as they read a leveled book or proofread their writing. Teachers also provide plenty of time for students to read and write independently and to practice skills they have learned. Teachers use five levels of support, moving from the greatest amount to the least as students assume more and more of the responsibility for themselves (Fountas & Pinnell, 1996). Figure 1-5 summarizes these five levels—modeled, shared, interactive, guided, and independent—of reading and writing.

Teachers working with fourth through eighth graders use all five levels. For instance, when teachers introduce a new writing form or teach a reading strategy or skill, they use demonstrations or modeling. Or, when teachers want students to practice a strategy or skill they have already taught, they might use a guided or independent lit-

Figure 1-5   A Continuum of Literacy Instruction

	Reading	Writing
Modeled	Teacher reads aloud, modeling how good readers read fluently and with expression. Books too difficult for students to read themselves are used. Examples: reading aloud and listening centers.	Teacher writes in front of students, creating the text, doing the writing, and thinking aloud about writing strategies and skills. Example: demonstrations.
Shared	Teacher and students read books together, with the students following as the teacher reads. Books students can't read by themselves are used. Example: buddy reading.	Teacher and students create the text together; then the teacher does the actual writing. Students may assist by spelling familiar words. Example: language experience approach[C].
Interactive	Teacher and students read together and take turns doing the reading. The teacher helps students read fluently and with expression. Instructional-level books are used. Examples: choral reading[C] and readers theatre[C].	Teacher and students create the text and share the pen to do the writing. Teacher and students talk about writing conventions. Example: interactive writing[C].
Guided	Teacher plans and teaches small, homogeneous group reading lessons using instructional-level books. Focus is on supporting and observing students' use of strategies. Example: guided reading groups.	Teacher plans and teaches lesson on a writing procedure, strategy, or skill, and students participate in supervised practice activities. Example: class collaborations.
Independent	Students choose and read books independently. Teachers conference with students to monitor their progress. Examples: reading workshop and Sustained Silent Reading[C].	Students use the writing process to write stories, reports, and other compositions. Teacher monitors students' progress. Example: writing workshop.

eracy activity. The purpose of the activity, not the activity itself, determines which level of support is used. Teachers are less actively involved in directing independent reading and writing, but the quality of instruction that students have received is clearest when they work independently because they are applying what they have learned.

Modeled Reading and Writing

Teachers provide the greatest amount of support when they demonstrate or model how expert readers read and expert writers write while students observe. When teachers read aloud to students, they are modeling. They read fluently and with expression, and they talk about the strategies they use while they are reading. When they model writing, teachers write a composition on chart paper or using an overhead projector so that all students can see what the teacher does and what is being written. Teachers use this level to demonstrate how to make small books and how to do new writing forms and formats, such as poems and essays. Often teachers talk about or reflect on their reading and writing processes as they read and write to show students the types of decisions they make and the strategies they use.

Modeling is especially important for English language learners who may have difficulty understanding oral directions.

Four purposes of modeling are:

1. To demonstrate fluent reading and writing.
2. To demonstrate how to use reading and writing strategies, such as connecting, monitoring, and revising.
3. To demonstrate the procedure for a new reading or writing activity.
4. To demonstrate how reading and writing conventions and other skills work.

Shared Reading and Writing

At this level, students and the teacher "share" the reading and writing tasks. Teachers use shared reading[C] to read novels and other books that students could not read independently. The teacher or another capable reader usually reads aloud while the students follow along, reading silently.

Teachers at different grade levels use shared writing in a variety of ways. Upper-grade teachers may take students' dictation when they make K-W-L charts[C], draw story maps[C] and clusters[C], and write class collaboration poems.

The most important way that sharing differs from modeling is that students actually participate in the activity rather than simply observe the teacher: In the shared reading activity, they follow along as the teacher reads, and in shared writing, they suggest the words and sentences that the teacher writes. Three purposes for shared reading and writing are:

1. To involve students in reading and writing activities that they could not do independently.
2. To provide opportunities for students to experience success in reading and writing.
3. To provide practice before students read and write independently.

Interactive Reading and Writing

Students assume an increasingly important role in interactive reading and writing activities. At this level, they no longer observe the teacher read or write, repeat familiar words, or suggest to the teacher what to write. Instead, students are more actively involved in reading and writing. They support their classmates by sharing the reading and writing responsibilities, and their teacher provides assistance when needed. Choral reading and readers theatre are two examples of interactive reading. In choral reading, students take turns reading lines of a poem, and in readers theatre, they assume the roles of characters and read lines in a script. In both of these interactive reading activities, the students support each other by actively participating and sharing the work. Teachers provide support by helping students with unfamiliar words or reading a sentence with more expression.

Interactive writing is a recently developed writing activity in which students and the teacher create a text and "share the pen" to write the text on chart paper (Button, Johnson, & Furgerson, 1996; Tompkins & Collom, 2004). The text is composed by the group, and the teacher assists students as they write the text word by word on chart paper. Students take turns writing known letters and familiar words, adding punctuation marks, and marking spaces between words. The teacher helps students to spell all words correctly and use written language conventions so that the text can be easily read. All students participate in creating and writing the text on chart paper, and they also write the text on small white boards. After writing, students read and reread the text using shared and independent reading. Interactive writing is generally used with young children, but teachers can also use this instructional approach with older, struggling writers who can't write sentences and paragraphs independently and when introducing a new writing form to the whole class.

Four purposes of interactive reading and writing are:

1. To successfully read and write texts that students could not do independently.
2. To teach and practice spelling, capitalization, and punctuation skills.
3. To develop reading and writing fluency.
4. To have students share their reading and writing expertise with classmates.

Guided Reading and Writing

Teachers continue to support students' reading and writing during guided literacy activities, but the students do the actual reading and writing themselves. In guided reading, small, homogeneous groups of students meet with the teacher to read a book at their instructional level. The teacher introduces the book and guides students as they begin reading; then they continue reading on their own while the teacher monitors their reading. After reading, students and the teacher discuss the book, and students often reread the book.

Teachers plan structured writing activities in guided writing and then supervise as students do the writing. For example, when students make pages for a class alphabet book[C] or write formula poems, they are doing guided writing because the teacher has set up the writing activity. Teachers also guide students' writing when they conference with students as they write, participate in writing groups[C] to help students revise their writing, and proofread with students.

Teachers use guided reading and writing to provide instruction and assistance as students are actually reading and writing. Four purposes of guided reading and writing activities are:

1. To support students' reading in instructional-level materials.
2. To teach literacy procedures, concepts, skills, and strategies during minilessons.
3. To introduce different types of writing activities.
4. To teach students to use the writing process—in particular, how to revise and edit.

Independent Reading and Writing

Students do the reading and writing themselves during independent reading and writing activities. They apply and practice the procedures, concepts, strategies, and skills they have learned. Students may be involved in reading workshop or literature circles. During independent reading, they usually choose the books they read and work at their own pace. Similarly, during independent writing, students may be involved in writing workshop or work at a writing center. They usually choose their own topics for writing and move at their own pace through the stages of the writing process as they develop and refine their writing.

Through independent reading experiences, students learn the joy of reading and, teachers hope, become lifelong readers. And, through independent writing experiences, they come to view themselves as authors. Three purposes of independent reading and writing activities are:

1. To create opportunities for students to practice reading and writing procedures, concepts, strategies, and skills that they have learned.
2. To provide authentic literacy experiences in which students choose their own topics, purposes, and materials.
3. To develop lifelong readers and writers.

PRINCIPLE 6: EFFECTIVE TEACHERS ORGANIZE LITERACY INSTRUCTION IN FOUR WAYS

Effective teachers put literature at the center of their instructional programs, and they combine opportunities for students to read and write with lessons on literacy skills and strategies. Teachers choose among four instructional approaches for their reading programs.

Students need daily opportunities to read independently during reading workshop and Sustained Silent Reading.

1. *Literature focus units.* All students in the class read and respond to the same book, and the teacher supports students' learning through a variety of related activities. Books chosen for literature focus units should be of high quality; teachers often choose books for literature focus units from a district- or state-approved list of books that all children are expected to read at that grade level.

2. *Literature circles.* Teachers select five or six books for a text set. These books range in difficulty level to meet the needs of all students in the classroom, and they are often related in theme or written by the same author. Teachers collect five or six copies of each book and give a book talk[C] to introduce the books. Then students choose a book to read from a text set and form a group to read and respond to the book they have chosen.

3. *Reading and writing workshop.* In reading workshop students individually select books to read independently and then conference with the teacher about their reading. Similarly, in writing workshop, students write books on topics that they choose and the teacher conferences with them about their writing. Usually teachers set aside a time for reading and writing workshop, and all students read and write while the teacher conferences with small groups of students. Sometimes, however, when the teacher is working with guided reading groups, the remainder of the class works in reading and writing workshop.

4. *Basal reading programs.* Commercially developed reading programs are known as basal readers. These programs consist of a textbook or anthology of stories and other reading selections and accompanying skill sheets, books, and related instructional materials at each grade level. Instructional manuals and testing materials are also included. Teachers usually divide students into small, homogeneous groups, and then they meet with groups to read selections and teach skills. They use guided reading to scaffold students' reading and monitor their progress. The publishers tout these books as complete reading programs, but effective teachers integrate basal reading programs with other instructional approaches.

GUIDELINE 1

Struggling Students Need to Spend More Time Reading and Writing. Struggling students need more reading and writing practice. Allington (2001) recommends that teachers dramatically increase the amount of time struggling readers spend reading each day so that they can become more capable readers and develop a desire to read. The same recommendation could be made for writers: Besides direct instruction lessons, students need large blocks of uninterrupted time for reading and writing workshop. During reading workshop, students read self-selected books at their own reading level, and during writing workshop, they use the writing process to create compositions on self-selected topics. Practice is just as important when you are learning to read and write as it is when you're learning to ride a bike or play the piano. How much time should students spend reading and writing? Although there is no hard-and-fast rule, it seems reasonable that students spend at least an hour each day reading and an hour writing.

These four approaches are used at all grade levels, from kindergarten through eighth grade, and effective teachers generally use a combination of them. Students need a variety of reading opportunities, and some books that students read are more difficult and require more support from the teacher. Some teachers alternate literature focus units or literature circles with reading and writing workshop and basal readers, whereas others use some components from each approach throughout the school year. Figure 1-6 presents a comparison of the four approaches.

As you continue reading, you will often see the terms *literature focus units, literature circles, reading and writing workshop,* and *basal reading programs* used because they are the instructional approaches advocated in this text. In addition, you will read more about these instructional approaches in Chapter 8, "Teaching With Narrative Texts," Chapter 10, "Connecting Reading and Writing," Chapter 11, "Working With Struggling Readers and Writers," and Chapter 12, "Becoming Life-long Readers and Writers."

PRINCIPLE 7: EFFECTIVE TEACHERS CONNECT INSTRUCTION AND ASSESSMENT

Teachers understand that students learn to read and write by doing lots of reading and writing and by applying skills and strategies in real reading and writing, not by doing exercises on isolated literacy skills. This understanding affects the way they assess students. No longer does it seem enough to grade students' vocabulary exercises or ask them to answer multiple-choice comprehension questions on reading passages that have no point beyond the exercise. Similarly, it no longer seems appropriate to measure success in writing by means of spelling and grammar tests. Instead, teachers need assessment information that tells about the complex achievements that students are making in reading and writing.

Teachers use assessment procedures that they develop and others that are commercially available to:

- monitor students' learning
- identify students' reading levels
- diagnose students' reading problems
- identify strengths and weaknesses in students' writing
- analyze students' spelling development
- document students' learning
- showcase students' best work
- assign grades

Also, teachers use the results of standardized achievement tests as indicators of students' literacy levels and their strengths and weaknesses, as well as to assess the effect of their instruction.

Assessment is more than testing; it is an integral and ongoing part of teaching and learning (Glazer, 1998). Serafini (2000/2001) describes assessment as an inquiry process that teachers use in order to make informed instructional decisions. Figure 1-7 shows the teach-assess cycle. Effective teachers identify their goals and plan their

Figure 1-6   Four Instructional Approaches

Features	Literature Focus Units	Literature Circles
Description	Teacher and students read and respond to one text together as a class or in small groups. The teacher chooses texts that are high-quality literature, either trade books or from a basal reader textbook. After reading, students explore the text and apply their learning by creating projects.	The teacher chooses five or six books and collects multiple copies of each book. Students each choose the book they want to read and form groups or "book clubs" to read and respond to the book. They develop a reading and discussion schedule, and the teacher often participates in the discussions.
Strengths	• Teachers develop units using the reading process. • Teachers select picture books or novels, or use selections from basal reader textbooks for units. • Teachers scaffold reading instruction as they read with the whole class or small groups. • Teachers teach minilessons on reading skills and strategies. • Students explore vocabulary and literary language. • Students develop projects to extend their reading.	• Books are available at a variety of reading levels. • Students are more strongly motivated because they choose the books they read. • Students have opportunities to work with their classmates. • Students participate in authentic literacy experiences. • Activities are student-directed, and students work at their own pace. • Teachers may participate in discussions to help students clarify misunderstandings and think more deeply about the book.
Drawbacks	• Students all read the same book whether or not they like it and whether or not it is at their reading level. • Many of the activities are teacher-directed.	• Teachers often feel a loss of control because students are reading different books. • Students must learn to be task-oriented and use time wisely in order to be successful. • Sometimes students choose books that are too difficult or too easy for them.

instruction at the same time as they develop their assessment plan. The assessment plan involves three components: preassessing, monitoring, and assessing.

Preassessing

Teachers assess students' background knowledge before reading in order to determine whether students are familiar with the topic they will read about. They also check to see that students are familiar with the genre, vocabulary, skills, and strategies. Then, based on the results of the assessment, teachers either help students develop more background knowledge or move on to the next step of their instructional plan. Some preassessment tools are:

- creating a K-W-L chart
- quickwriting[C] about a topic
- discussing a topic with students
- completing an anticipation guide[C]
- brainstorming a list of characteristics about a topic

Reading and Writing Workshop	Basal Reading Programs
Students choose books and read and respond to them independently during reading workshop and write books on self-selected topics during writing workshop. The teacher monitors students' work through conferences. Students share the books they read and the books they write with classmates during a sharing period.	The teacher groups students into small, homogeneous groups for reading instruction and uses commercially developed basal readers that are graded according to difficulty so that students can read selections at their instructional level. The teacher uses guided reading to scaffold students so they can be successful. Students read independently and the teacher provides assistance as needed. The teacher also uses running records[C] to monitor students' reading.
• Students read books appropriate for their reading levels. • Students are more strongly motivated because they choose the books they read. • Students work through the stages of the writing process during writing workshop. • Teachers teach minilessons on reading skills and strategies. • Activities are student-directed and students work at their own pace. • Teachers have opportunities to work individually with students during conferences.	• Students read selections at their instructional level. • Teachers teach word-identification skills and vocabulary words. • Teachers teach strategies and skills and provide structured practice opportunities. • Teachers monitor students' reading. • Teachers are available to reteach strategies as needed. • The instructor's guide provides detailed instructions for teachers.
• Teachers often feel a loss of control because students are reading different books and working at different stages of the writing process. • Students must learn to be task-oriented and use time wisely in order to be successful.	• Students do not select the books they read and thus may not be interested in them. • The reading lesson is very structured. • Programs include many skill workbooks and worksheets.

Monitoring

Teachers often monitor students' progress in reading and writing as they observe students participating in literacy activities. Students might participate in conferences with the teacher, for example, and talk about what they are reading and writing, the strategies and skills they are learning to use, and problem areas. They reflect on what they do well as readers and writers and on what they need to learn next. Here are some monitoring tools:

- listening to students read aloud
- taking running records of students' oral reading "miscues" or errors
- conferencing with students during reading and writing workshop
- listening to comments students make during grand conversations and other book discussions
- reading students' reading log entries and rough drafts of other compositions
- examining students' work in progress

Figure 1-7   The Teach-Assess Cycle

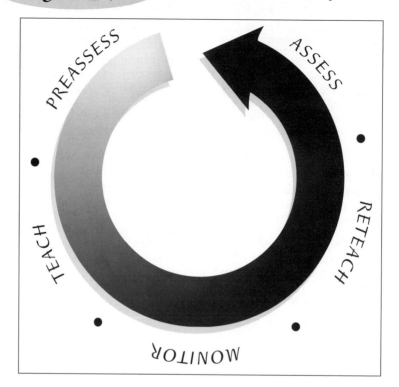

Assessing

Teachers assess and grade students' learning at the end of a unit. Besides grading students' written assignments, teachers collect other assessment information through the following activities:

- observing students' presentation of oral language projects, such as puppet shows, oral reports, and story retellings
- examining students' art and other visual projects
- analyzing students' comprehension through charts, dioramas, murals, Venn diagrams, and other story maps they have made
- examining all drafts of students' writing to document their use of the writing process
- checking students' use of newly taught vocabulary in their compositions and other projects
- analyzing students' spelling using their compositions

Teachers also have students keep track of their progress using checklists that list assignments and other requirements. Then at the end of the unit, teachers collect and grade students' assignments. Figure 1-8 shows a checklist from an eighth-grade literature focus unit on *Holes* (1998), Louis Sachar's Newbery Medal–winning book about a boy named Stanley Yelnats who is sent to a hellish correctional camp in the Texas desert. During the unit, students read *Holes* and participate in a variety of literacy activities, some of which are included on the checklist. Students check off items as they complete them, and at the end they assess their own work before submitting it to the teacher.

Figure 1-8

An Assessment Checklist for a
Literature Focus Unit on *Holes*

Checklist for *Holes*

Name _____ Date _____

Student's   Teacher's
Check _____   Grade

☐ 1. Make 15 entries in your reading log. (30 points)   _____

☐ 2. Make a file-folder word wall with at least 50 key words
        from the story. (10 points)   _____

☐ 3. Make word maps on index cards for 10 words from your
        word wall. (10 points)   _____

☐ 4. Create an open-mind portrait to reveal Stanley's thoughts
        at five points in the story. (30 points)   _____

☐ 5. Draw a diagram to illustrate the plot structure of *Holes*.
        (20 points)   _____

☐ 6. Create a project to extend your learning. (30 points)   _____

☐ 7. Write a letter to the teacher to reflect on the book, your
        use of reading strategies, and your work habits in this unit.
        (20 points)   _____

Total Points (150 points possible)   _____

Assessment Tools

You will learn more about how to monitor, document, and grade student learning in Chapter 3, "Assessing Students' Literacy Development."

PRINCIPLE 8: EFFECTIVE TEACHERS CONTINUE TO LEARN ABOUT READING AND WRITING

As you begin teaching, you will want to continue to learn about reading and writing instruction and ways to become a more effective teacher. Through professional organizations, you can stay abreast of the newest research and ways to implement the research in your classroom. Two organizations dedicated to improving literacy instruction are the International Reading Association (IRA) and the National Council of Teachers of English (NCTE). Both organizations publish journals for classroom teachers, and both also organize yearly conferences that are held in major cities around the United States. In addition, these organizations have state and local affiliate groups you can join. Through these local groups, you can meet other teachers with similar interests and concerns and form support networks.

In addition, teachers learn more about teaching writing by participating in workshops sponsored by the National Writing Project (NWP). Since it began more than

25 years ago at the University of California, Berkeley, the NWP has spread to more than 150 sites located in almost every state; for example, the Gateway Writing Project serves the St. Louis area, and the Capital Writing Project serves the Washington, DC, area. You may be able to attend in-service workshops that are scheduled in school districts near each affiliate group. After you have a few years' teaching experience, you might be interested in applying to participate in a special summer institute. Figure 1-9 provides information about ways to continue learning about teaching reading and writing.

VISIT CHAPTER 1 ON THE COMPANION WEBSITE AT
www.prenhall.com/tompkins

- Complete a self-assessment to demonstrate your understanding of the concepts presented in this chapter
- Complete field activities that will help you expand your understanding of the middle-grade classroom and becoming an effective teacher
- Visit important web links related to teaching middle-grade students to read and write
- Look into your state's standards as they relate to teaching reading and writing and the middle-grade student
- Communicate with other preservice teachers via the message board and discuss the issues of becoming an effective teacher for students in grades 4 to 8
- Complete CD-ROM activities that will help you make virtual field experience connections to becoming an effective teacher

Review

This chapter set out eight principles of effective teaching of reading:

1. Effective teachers understand how students learn.
2. Effective teachers support students' use of the four cueing systems.
3. Effective teachers create a community of learners in their classrooms.
4. Effective teachers adopt a balanced approach to literacy instruction.
5. Effective teachers scaffold students' reading and writing experiences.
6. Effective teachers organize literacy instruction in literature focus units, literature circles, reading and writing workshop, and basal reading programs.
7. Effective teachers connect instruction and assessment.
8. Effective teachers continue to learn about reading and writing.

These principles were drawn from research over the past 30 years about how children learn to read and from the "best teaching practices" used in successful elementary schools. These principles suggest a balanced reading program. In the chapters that follow, you will learn how to develop and implement a balanced reading program for students in fourth through eighth grades.

Figure 1-9 Ways to Continue Your Learning

1. Join these literacy organizations and your state and local affiliate groups:

   International Reading
       Association (IRA)
   800 Barksdale Road
   P.O. Box 8139
   Newark, DE 19711
   www.reading.org

   National Council of Teachers of
       English (NCTE)
   1111 Kenyon Road
   Urbana, IL 61801
   www.ncte.org

2. Attend conferences sponsored by local professional organizations, IRA and NCTE affiliated groups, and national organizations.

3. Subscribe to one or more of these journals and magazines about reading, children's literature, and writing:

   Book Links
   P.O. Box 1347
   Elmhurst, IL 60126

   CBC Features
   Children's Book Council, Inc.
   350 Scotland Rd.
   Orange, NJ 07050
   www.cbcbooks.org

   Language Arts
   National Council of Teachers
       of English
   1111 Kenyon Road
   Urbana, IL 61801

   Primary Voices K–6
   National Council of Teachers
       of English
   1111 Kenyon Road
   Urbana, IL 61801

   The Reading Teacher
   International Reading Association
   800 Barksdale Road
   P.O. Box 8139
   Newark, DE 19711

   Teaching K–8
   P.O. Box 54808
   Boulder, CO 80322

   Voices From the Middle
   National Council of Teachers
       of English
   1111 Kenyon Road
   Urbana, IL 61801

   Writing Teacher
   P.O. Box 791437
   San Antonio, TX 78279

4. Check the International Reading Association's on-line journal, *Reading Online* (www.readingonline.org), which includes articles, an on-line discussion community, and the Electronic Classroom, for ideas and information about applying technology in literacy instruction.

5. Subscribe to a literacy-related listserv, such as RTEACHER at Listserv@listserv.syr.edu.

6. Mine the Internet for other websites about teaching reading and writing.

7. Visit local children's bookstores and libraries to preview newly published children's books and meet children's authors when they visit.

8. Attend writing workshops sponsored by the local affiliate of the National Writing Project (NWP) or apply to participate in a summer invitational institute. To locate the NWP affiliate group nearest you, contact the National Writing Project, University of California, 2105 Bancroft, #1042, Berkeley, CA 94720, telephone 510-642-0963, or www.writingproject.org.

Professional References

Allington, R. L. (2001). *What really matters for struggling readers: Designing research-based programs.* New York: Longman.

Allington, R., & Walmsley, S. (Eds.). (1995). *No quick fix: Rethinking literacy programs in America's elementary schools.* New York: Teachers College Press.

Baumann, J. F., Hoffman, J. V., Moon, J., & Duffy-Hester, A. M. (1998). Where are teachers' voices in the phonics/whole language debate? Results from a survey of U.S. elementary teachers. *The Reading Teacher, 51,* 636–650.

Baumann, J. F., & Ivey, G. (1997). Delicate balances: Striving for curricular and instructional equilibrium in a second-grade, literature/strategy-based classroom. *Reading Research Quarterly, 23,* 244–275.

Boyer, E. (1995). *The basic school: A community for learning.* Princeton, NJ: Carnegie Foundation for the Advancement of Teaching.

Button, K., Johnson, M. J., & Furgerson, P. (1996). Interactive writing in a primary classroom. *The Reading Teacher, 49,* 446–454.

Cases in literacy: An agenda for discussion. (1989). Newark, DE: International Reading Association and National Council of Teachers of English.

Dixon-Krauss, L. (1996). *Vygotsky in the classroom.* White Plains, NY: Longman.

Fitzgerald, J. (1999). What is this thing called "balance"? *The Reading Teacher, 53,* 100–107.

Fountas, I. C., & Pinnell, G. S. (1996). *Guided reading: Good first teaching for all children.* Portsmouth, NH: Heinemann.

Glazer, S. M. (1998). *Assessment is instruction: Reading, writing, spelling, and phonics for all learners.* Norwood, MA: Christopher-Gordon.

Graves, D. H. (1995). A tour of Segovia School in the year 2005. *Language Arts, 72,* 12–18.

Halliday, M. A. K. (1978). *Language as social semiotic: The social interpretation of language and meaning.* Baltimore: University Park Press.

Harris, T. L., & Hodges, R. E. (Eds.). (1995). *The literacy dictionary: The vocabulary of reading and writing.* Newark, DE: International Reading Association.

Heath, S. B. (1983). Research currents: A lot of talk about nothing. *Language Arts, 60,* 999–1007.

Hirsch, E. D., Jr. (1987). *Cultural literacy: What every American needs to know.* Boston: Houghton Mifflin.

Lindfors, J. W. (1987). *Children's language and learning* (2nd ed.). Englewood Cliffs, NJ: Prentice Hall.

McIntyre, E., & Pressley, M. (Eds.). (1996). *Balanced instruction: Strategies and skills in whole language.* Norwood, MA: Christopher-Gordon.

Morrice, C., & Simmons, M. (1991). Beyond reading buddies: A whole language cross-age program. *The Reading Teacher, 44,* 572–578.

Nagy, W. E. (1988). *Teaching vocabulary to improve reading comprehension.* Urbana, IL: ERIC Clearinghouse on Reading and Communication Skills and National Council of Teachers of English and International Reading Association.

Nathenson-Mejia, S. (1989). Writing in a second language: Negotiating meaning through invented spelling. *Language Arts, 66,* 516–526.

Piaget, J. (1969). *The psychology of intelligence.* Paterson, NJ: Littlefield, Adams.

Rafferty, C. D. (1999). Literacy in the information age. *Educational Leadership, 57,* 22–25.

Rosenblatt, L. (1978). *The reader, the text, the poem: The transactional theory of the literary work.* Carbondale, IL: Southern Illinois University Press.

Rosenblatt, L. (1983). *Literature as exploration* (4th ed.). New York: Modern Language Association.

Rosenblatt, L. (1991). Literature—S.O.S.! *Language Arts, 68,* 444–448.

Rumelhart, D. E. (1977). Toward an interactive model of reading. In S. Dornic (Ed.), *Attention and performance* (Vol. 6). Hillsdale, NJ: Erlbaum.

Serafini, F. (2000/2001). Three paradigms of assessment: Measurement, procedure, and inquiry. *The Reading Teacher, 54,* 384–393.

Skinner, B. F. (1968). *The technology of teaching.* New York: Appleton-Century-Crofts.

Spiegel, D. L. (1998). Silver bullets, babies, and bath water: Literature response groups in a balanced literacy program. *The Reading Teacher, 52,* 114–124.

Stanovich, K. (1980). Toward an interactive-compensatory model of individual differences in the development of reading fluency. *Reading Research Quarterly, 16,* 32–71.

Strickland, D. S. (1994/1995). Reinventing our literacy programs: Books, basics, and balance. *The Reading Teacher, 48,* 294–306.

Sumara, D., & Walker, L. (1991). The teacher's role in whole language. *Language Arts, 68,* 276–285.

Teale, B. (1995). Dear readers. *Language Arts, 72,* 8–9.

Tompkins, G., & Collom, S. (2004). *Sharing the pen: Interactive writing with young children.* Upper Saddle River, NJ: Merrill/Prentice Hall.

Vygotsky, L. S. (1978). *Mind in society.* Cambridge, MA: Harvard University Press.

Vygotsky, L. S. (1986). *Thought and language.* Cambridge, MA: MIT Press.

Weaver, C. (Ed.). (1998). *Reconsidering a balanced approach to reading.* Urbana, IL: National Council of Teachers of English.

Wells, G., & Chang-Wells, G. L. (1992). *Constructing knowledge together: Classrooms as centers of inquiry and literacy.* Portsmouth, NH: Heinemann.

Children's Book References

Gibbons, G. (1994). *Nature's green umbrella: Tropical rain forests.* New York: Morrow.

MacLachlan, P. (1985). *Sarah, plain and tall.* New York: Harper & Row.

Sachar, L. (1998). *Holes.* New York: Farrar, Straus & Giroux.

chapter 2

Teaching the Reading and Writing Processes

QUESTIONS

- What are the stages in the reading process?

- What are the stages in the writing process?

- How are the two processes alike?

- How do teachers use these two processes in teaching reading and writing?

Mrs. Goodman's Seventh Graders Read The Giver

The seventh graders in Mrs. Goodman's class are reading the Newbery Award–winning book *The Giver* (Lowry, 1993). In this futuristic story, 12-year-old Jonas is selected to become the next Keeper of the Memories, and he discovers the terrible truth about his community. Mrs. Goodman has a class set of paperbacks of the book, and her students use the reading process as they read and explore the book.

To introduce the book to her students, Mrs. Goodman asks them to get into small groups and brainstorm lists of all the things they would change about life if they could. They write the lists on butcher paper. Their lists include getting $200 for allowance every week, no more homework, no AIDS, no crime, no gangs, no parents, no taking out the garbage, and being allowed to drive a car at age 10. The groups hang their lists on the chalkboard and then share them. Then Mrs. Goodman puts check marks by many of the items, seeming to agree with the points. Next she explains that the class is going to read a story about life in the future. She explains that *The Giver* takes place in a planned utopian, or "perfect," society with the qualities that she checked on students' brainstormed lists.

She passes out copies of the book and uses shared reading^C as she reads the first chapter aloud while students follow along in their books. Then the class talks about the first chapter, and they ask a lot of questions: Why were there so many rules? Doesn't anyone drive a car? What does "released" mean? Why are children called a "Seven" or a "Four"? What does it mean that people are "given" spouses—don't they fall in love and get married? Why does Jonas have to tell his feelings? Why can't he keep them to himself? Classmates share their ideas and are eager to continue reading. Mrs. Goodman's reading aloud of the first chapter and the questions that the students raise cause everyone in the class to become interested in the story, even several students who often try to remain uninvolved in class activities. The power of this story grabs them all.

The class sets up a schedule for reading and discussion. Every 3 days, they will come together to talk about the chapters they have read, and over 2 weeks, the class will read and talk about the story. They will also write in reading logs^C after reading the first chapter and then five more times as they read. In their reading logs, students write reactions to the story. Maria wrote this journal entry after she finished reading the book:

> *Jonas had to do it. He had to save Gabriel's life because the next day Jonas's father was going to release (kill) him. He had it all planned out. That was important. He was very brave to leave his parents and his home. But I guess they weren't his parents really and his home wasn't all that good. I don't know if I could have done it but he did the right thing. He had to get out. He saved himself and he saved little Gabe. I'm glad he took Gabriel. That community was supposed to be safe but it really was dangerous. It was weird to not have colors. I guess that things that at first seem to be good are really bad.*

Ron explored some of the themes of the story:

> *Starving. He has memories of food. He's still hungry. But he's free. Food is safe. Freedom is surprises. Never saw a bird before. Same-same-same. Before he was starved for colors, memories and choice. Choice. To do what you want. To be who you can be. He won't starve.*

Alicia thought about a lesson her mother taught her as she wrote:

> As Jonas fled from the community he lost his memories so that they would go back to the people there. Would they learn from them? Would they remember them? Or would life go on just the same? I think you have to do it yourself if you are going to learn. That's what my mom says. Somebody else can't do it for you. But Jonas did it. He got out with Gabe.

Tomas wrote about the Christmas connection at the end of the story:

> Jonas and Gabe came to the town at Christmas. Why did Lois Lowry do that? Gabe is like the baby Jesus, I think. It is like a rebirth—being born again. Jonas and his old community didn't go to church. Maybe they didn't believe in God. Now Jonas will be a Christian and the people in the church will welcome them. Gabe won't be released. I think Gabe is like Jesus because people tried to release Jesus.

[C] See the Compendium of Instructional Procedures, which follows Chapter 12, for more information on terms marked with the symbol [C].

During their discussions, which Mrs. Goodman calls grand conversations[C], students talk about many of the same points they raise in their journal entries. The story fascinates her students—at first they think about how simple and safe life would be, but then they think about all the things they take for granted that they would have to give up to live in Jonas's ordered society. They talk about bravery and making choices, and they applaud Jonas's decision to flee with Gabriel. They also speculate about Jonas's and Gabe's new lives in Elsewhere. Will they be happy? Will they ever go back to check on their old community? Will other people escape to Elsewhere?

The students collect "important" words from the story for their word wall[C]. After reading chapters 4, 5, and 6, students add these words to their alphabetized word wall:

leisurely pace	bikeports	regulated
invariably	gravitating	rehabilitation
serene	chastised	rule infraction
the wanting	stirrings	reprieve
relinquish	chastisement	assignment

Sometimes students choose unfamiliar or long words, but they also choose words such as *assignment* that are important to the story. Students refer to the list for words and their spellings for the various activities they are involved in. Later during the unit, Mrs. Goodman teaches a minilesson[C] about root words using some of these words.

Mrs. Goodman teaches a series of minilessons about reading strategies and skills as students read the story. The day after students read about colors in the story, she teaches a minilesson on the visualization strategy. She begins by rereading excerpts from chapters 7 and 8 about Jonas being selected to be the next Receiver and asks students to try to picture the scene in their minds. Mrs. Goodman asks students to focus on the sights, sounds, smells, and feelings, and she talks about the importance of bringing a story to life in their minds as they read. Then students draw pictures of their visualizations and share them in small groups.

To review spelling patterns and phonics rules, Mrs. Goodman does a making words[C] activity. She divides the class into six groups and gives each group a different set of letter cards that can be sorted to spell a word from the word wall: *stirrings, release, memories, receiver, fascinated,* or *ceremony.* She asks the students in each group to arrange the letter cards to spell as many words as they can. Letters from *ceremony,* for example, can be used to spell *me, my, on, no, eye, men, more, core, corn, mercy,* and *money.* Then they arrange all of the letters to spell the word wall word.

Another minilesson is about literary opposites. Mrs. Goodman explains that authors often introduce conflict and develop themes using contrasts or opposites. She asks students to think of opposites in *The Giver.* One example that she suggests is *safe* and *free.* Other opposites that the students suggest include:

alive—released	color—black and white
choice—no choice	conform—do your own thing
rules—anarchy	stirrings—the pill
families—family units	memories—no memories

Mrs. Goodman asks students to think about how the opposites relate to the development of the story and how Lois Lowry made the opposites explicit in *The Giver.* Students talk about how the community seemed safe at the beginning of the story, but that chapter by chapter, Lowry uncovered the shortcomings of the community. They also talk about themes of the story reflected in these opposites. Mrs. Goodman ends the minilesson by asking students to look for opposites in other stories they read.

After they finish reading the book, students have a read-around[C] in which they select and read aloud favorite passages to the class. Then students make a quilt[C] about the story: Each student makes a quilt piece from construction paper and writes a favorite quote on the square. One quilt square is shown in Figure 2-1. The students decide to use white, gray, and black for most of the quilt squares to represent the sameness of Jonas's community, and they add color in the center to represent Elsewhere.

Students also choose projects that they will work on individually or in small groups to apply their reading of *The Giver.* One student makes a book box[C] with objects related to the story, and two other students read *Hailstones and Halibut Bones* (O'Neill, 1989) and then write their own collection of color poetry. One student makes an open-mind portrait[C] of Jonas to show his thoughts the night he decided to escape with Gabe. Some students read other books with similar themes or other books by Lois Lowry, including *Gathering Blue* (2000), and they share their books with the class during a book talk[C]. Other students write about memories of their own lives. They use the writing process to draft, refine, and publish their writing. They share their published pieces at a class meeting at the end of the unit.

The reading process that Mrs. Goodman uses represents a significant shift in thinking about what people do as they read. Mrs. Goodman understands that readers construct meaning as they negotiate the texts they are reading, and that they use their life and literature experiences and reading strategies and skills as they read. She knows that it is quite common for two people to read the same story and

Figure 2-1   One Square for a Quilt on *The Giver*

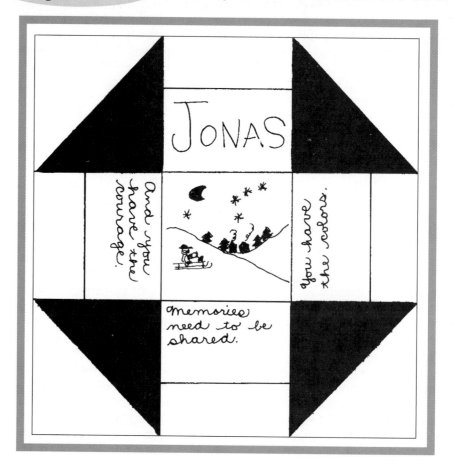

come away with different interpretations, and that their understanding of the story will depend on things that have happened in their own lives. Meaning does not exist on the pages of the book readers are reading; instead, comprehension is created through the interaction between readers and the texts they are reading.

The reading process involves a series of stages during which readers construct interpretations as they read and respond to the text. The term *text* refers to all reading materials—stories, maps, newspapers, cereal boxes, textbooks, and so on; it is not limited to basal reader textbooks. The writing process is a similar recursive process involving a variety of activities as students gather and organize ideas, draft their compositions, revise and edit the drafts, and, finally, publish their writings.

Reading and writing have been thought of as the flip sides of a coin—as opposites; readers decoded or deciphered written language, and writers encoded or produced written language. Then researchers began to note similarities between reading and writing and talked of both of them as processes. Now reading and writing are viewed as parallel processes of meaning construction, and we understand that readers and writers use similar strategies for making meaning with text.

Teachers use the reading and writing processes to organize their instruction and students' reading and writing experiences in a balanced literacy program. The feature on page 35 shows how the reading and writing processes fit into a balanced program. As you continue reading this chapter, you will learn more about the ideas presented in the feature.

The Role of the Reading and Writing Processes in a Balanced Literacy Program

Component	Description
Reading	Teachers use the five-stage reading process to teach reading.
Phonics and Other Skills	Teachers teach phonics and other skills during the exploring stage of the reading process and during the editing stage of the writing process.
Strategies	Teachers teach strategies during the reading and writing processes, and students apply these strategies as they read and write.
Vocabulary	Students learn vocabulary as they read, and teachers involve students in vocabulary activities during the exploring stage of the reading process.
Comprehension	Making meaning is at the heart of both the reading and writing processes.
Literature	Students use the reading process as they read novels in literature focus units, literature circles, and reading workshop.
Content-Area Study	Students use the reading process as they read informational books and content-area textbooks, and they use the writing process as they create projects during content-area units.
Oral Language	Students use talk in both the reading and writing processes to activate background knowledge, clarify their understanding, and share ideas.
Writing	Teachers use the five-stage writing process to teach students to write narrative, expository, poetic, and persuasive compositions.
Spelling	Students focus on correcting spelling errors in the editing stage of the writing process because they learn that conventional spelling is a courtesy to readers.

THE READING PROCESS

Reading is a process in which readers comprehend and construct meaning. During reading, the meaning does not go from the page to readers. Instead, reading is a complex negotiation among the text, readers, and their purpose for reading that is shaped by many factors:

- Readers' knowledge about the topic
- Readers' knowledge about reading and about written language
- The language community to which readers belong
- The match between readers' language and the language used in the text

Figure 2-2   Key Features of the Reading Process

Stage 1: Prereading
- Set purposes.
- Connect to prior personal experiences.
- Connect to background knowledge.
- Connect to prior literary experiences.
- Connect to thematic units or special interests.
- Make predictions.
- Preview the text.
- Consult the index to locate information.

Stage 2: Reading
- Make predictions.
- Apply skills and strategies.
- Read independently, with a partner, using shared reading or guided reading, or listen to the text read aloud.
- Read the illustrations, charts, and diagrams.
- Read the entire text from beginning to end.
- Read one or more sections of text to learn specific information.
- Take notes.

Stage 3: Responding
- Write in a reading log.
- Participate in a grand conversation or instructional conversation[C].

Stage 4: Exploring
- Reread and think more deeply about the text.
- Make personal, world, and literary connections.
- Examine the author's craft.
- Identify memorable quotes.
- Learn new vocabulary words.
- Participate in minilessons on reading procedures, concepts, strategies, and skills.

Stage 5: Applying
- Construct projects.
- Use information in thematic units.
- Connect with related books.
- Reflect on interpretations.
- Value the reading experience.

English language learners benefit from direct experience, concrete objects, and social interaction with classmates as they activate and develop background knowledge.

- Readers' culturally based expectations about reading
- Readers' expectations about reading based on their previous experiences (Weaver, 1988)

The reading process involves five stages: prereading, reading, responding, exploring, and applying. Figure 2-2 presents an overview of these stages.

Stage 1: Prereading

The reading process does not begin as readers open a book and read the first sentence. The first stage is preparing to read. In the vignette, Mrs. Goodman developed her students' background knowledge and stimulated their interest in *The Giver* as they brain-

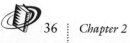

stormed lists and talked about how wonderful life would be in a "perfect" world. As readers prepare to read, they activate background knowledge, set purposes, and plan for reading.

Activating Background Knowledge.   Readers activate their background knowledge, or schemata, about the text they plan to read. They make connections to personal experiences, to literary experiences, or to thematic units in the classroom. The topic of the book, the title, the author, the genre, an illustration, a comment someone makes about the text, or something else may trigger this activation, but for readers to make meaning with the text, schemata must be activated. For instance, millions of readers loved J. K. Rowling's *Harry Potter and the Sorcerer's Stone* (1998) and have continued to read every book in the series. Others like books written by Gary Paulsen or Jack Gantos, and they eagerly read every book written by their favorite authors.

Sometimes teachers collect objects related to the book and create a book box to use in introducing the book to the class. A sixth-grade teacher collected objects related to *Bunnicula: A Rabbit-Tale of Mystery* (Howe & Howe, 1979), the story of a bunny who is thought to be a vampire. She painted fabric vegetables white and added two little "fang" holes in each one and placed them in the box. She also added a small, black-and-white stuffed bunny and a book about vampires. As she introduced the book, she showed students the objects, talked about each one, and asked students to speculate on how they might be related to the story.

Setting Purposes.   The two overarching purposes for reading are pleasure and information. When students read for pleasure or enjoyment, they read aesthetically, to be carried into the world of the text; when they read to locate information or for directions about how to do something, they read efferently (Rosenblatt, 1978). Often readers use elements of both purposes as they read, but usually one purpose is more important to the reading experience than the other. For example, when students pick up *The Sweetest Fig* (1993), one of Chris Van Allsburg's picture book fantasies, their primary purpose is enjoyment. They want to experience the story, but at the same time, they search for the white dog, a trademark that Van Allsburg includes in all of his books, and they compare this book with others of his that they have read. As they search for the white dog or make comparisons, they add efferent purposes to their primarily aesthetic reading experience.

Purpose setting is usually directed by the teacher during literature focus units, but in reading workshop, students set their own purposes because everyone is reading different self-selected books. For teacher-directed purpose setting, teachers explain how students are expected to read and what they will do after reading. The goal of teacher-directed purpose setting is to help students learn how to set personally relevant purposes when they are reading independently (Blanton, Wood, & Moorman, 1990). Students should always have a purpose for reading, whether they are reading aesthetically or efferently, whether reading a text for the first time or the tenth. Readers are more successful when they have a single purpose for reading the entire selection. A single purpose is more effective than multiple purposes, and sustaining a single purpose is more effective than presenting students with a series of purposes as they read.

When readers have purposes for reading, their comprehension of the selection is enhanced in three ways, whether teachers provide the purpose or students set their own purpose (Blanton et al., 1990). First of all, the purpose guides the reading process that students use. Having a purpose provides motivation and direction for reading, as well as a mechanism that students use for monitoring their reading. As they monitor their reading, students ask themselves whether they are fulfilling their purpose.

Second, setting a purpose activates a plan for readers to use while reading. Purpose setting causes students to draw on background knowledge, consider strategies they might use as they read, and think about the structure of the text they are reading. Students are better able to sort out important from unimportant information as they read when they have a purpose for reading. Teachers direct students' attention to relevant concepts as they set purposes for reading and show them how to connect the concepts they are reading about to their prior knowledge about a topic.

Students read differently depending on the purpose for reading, and the instructional procedures teachers use also vary according to the purpose for reading. When students are reading stories, teachers might use the Directed Reading-Thinking Activity[C] (DRTA) to help them predict and then read to confirm or reject their predictions, or have them create story maps[C] to focus their attention on plot, characters, or another element of story structure. When students are reading informational books and content-area textbooks, teachers might use an anticipation guide[C] to activate prior knowledge, or cubing[C] to explore a concept from different viewpoints.

In contrast to teacher-directed purpose setting, students set their own purposes for reading during literature circles, reading workshop, and at other times when they choose their own books to read. Often they choose materials that are intrinsically interesting or that describe something they want to learn more about. As students gain experience in reading, identify favorite authors and illustrators, and learn about genres, they acquire other criteria to use in choosing books and setting purposes for reading. When teachers conference with students, they often ask about their purposes for reading and why they choose particular books to read.

Planning for Reading.   Students often preview the reading selection during the prereading stage. They look through the selection and check its length, the reading difficulty, and the illustrations in order to judge the general suitability of the selection for them as readers. Previewing serves an important function as students connect their prior knowledge, identify their purpose for reading, and take their first look at the selection. Teachers set the guidelines for the reading experience, explain how the book will be read—independently, in small groups, or as a class—and set the schedule for reading. Setting the schedule is especially important when students are reading a chapter book. Often teachers and students work together to create a 2-, 3-, or 4-week schedule for reading and responding and then write the schedule on a calendar to which students can refer.

Students make other types of plans depending on the type of selection they will read. Those who are preparing to read stories, for instance, make predictions about the characters and events in the story. Students often use the title of the selection and the illustration on the cover of the book or on the first page as a basis for their predictions. If they have read other books by the same author or other selections in the same genre, students also use this information in making their predictions. Sometimes students share their predictions orally as they talk about the selection, and at other times, they write and draw their predictions as the first entry in their reading logs.

When students are preparing to read informational books, they preview the selection by flipping through the pages and noting section headings, illustrations, diagrams, and other charts. Sometimes they examine the table of contents to see how the book is organized, or consult the index to locate specific information they want to read. They may also notice unfamiliar terminology and other words they can check in the glossary, ask a classmate or the teacher about, or look up in a dictionary. Teachers also use anticipation guides, prereading plans[C] (PRePs), and the survey step of the SQ3R study strategy[C] as they introduce informational books and content-area textbooks.

Students often make notes in learning logs as they explore informational books and content-area textbooks. They do quickwrites[C] to activate prior knowledge and explore the concepts to be presented in the selection, write down important terminology, and draw clusters[C], data charts[C], and other diagrams they will complete as they read. As they move through the remaining stages in the reading process, students add other information to their learning logs.

Stage 2: Reading

Students read the book or other selection in the reading stage. They use their knowledge of decoding and word identification, sight words, strategies, skills, and vocabulary while they read. Fluent readers are better able to understand what they are reading because they identify most words automatically and use decoding skills when necessary. They also apply their knowledge of the structure of text as they create meaning. They continue reading as long as what they are reading fits the meaning they are constructing. When something doesn't make sense, readers slow down, back up, and reread until they are making meaning again.

Students may read the entire text or only sections of it. When students are reading aesthetically, they usually read the entire text, but when they are reading efferently, they may be searching for specific information and read only until they locate that information. Also, students may decide to put a book down if it does not capture their interest, if it is too difficult to read, or if it doesn't have the information they are searching for. It is unrealistic to assume that students will always read entire texts or finish reading every book they begin.

Outside of school, readers usually read silently and independently. Sometimes, however, people listen as someone else reads. For example, young children often sit in a parent's lap and look at the illustrations as the parent reads a picture book aloud. Adults also listen to books read aloud on cassette tapes. In the classroom, teachers and students use five types of reading: shared reading[C], guided reading, independent reading, buddy reading, and reading aloud to students. Teachers choose the type of reading experience according to the purpose for reading, students' reading levels, and the number of copies of the selection available.

Shared Reading.   Teachers use shared reading to read aloud novels, content-area textbooks, and other books that students can't read independently (Holdaway, 1979). The books that are used for shared reading should be appropriate for students' interest level but too difficult for them to read for themselves. As an instructional strategy, shared reading differs from reading aloud to students because students see the text as the teacher reads.

Teachers distribute copies of the book to all students, and students follow along in the book as the teacher reads aloud. Sometimes students take turns reading sections aloud, but the goal is not for everyone to have a turn reading. Students who want to read and are fluent enough to keep the reading meaningful volunteer to read. Often the teacher begins reading, and when a student wants to take over the reading, he or she begins reading aloud with the teacher. Then the teacher drops off and the student continues reading. After a paragraph or a page, another student joins in and the first student drops off. Many teachers call this technique "popcorn reading."

Guided Reading.   Teachers use guided reading to work with groups of four or five students who are reading at the same level (Clay, 1991). They select a book that students can read at their instructional level, with approximately 90–94% accuracy. Teachers support students' reading and their use of reading strategies during guided reading

In guided reading, small groups of students read and discuss the story with the teacher.

(Depree & Iversen, 1996; Fountas & Pinnell, 1996). Students do the actual reading themselves, although the teacher may read aloud with students to get them started on the first page or two. Struggling readers who are not yet fluent readers may murmur the words softly as they read, but most intermediate grade students read silently during guided reading.

Guided reading lessons usually last 25 to 30 minutes. When the students arrive for the small-group lesson, they often reread, either individually or with a buddy, familiar books used in previous guided reading lessons. For the new guided reading lesson, students read books they have not read before. Beginning readers usually read small picture books at one sitting, but older students who are reading longer chapter books take several days to several weeks to read their books. The steps in a guided reading lesson are listed in Figure 2-3.

Teachers observe students as they read during guided reading lessons. They spend a few minutes observing each student, sitting either in front of or beside the student. Teachers observe the student's behaviors for evidence of strategy use and confirm the student's attempts to identify words and solve reading problems. The strategies and problem-solving behaviors that teachers look for include:

- self-monitoring
- checking predictions
- decoding unfamiliar words
- determining if the word makes sense
- checking that a word is appropriate in the syntax of the sentence
- using all sources of information
- chunking phrases to read more fluently

Teachers take notes about their observations and use the information in deciding what minilessons to teach and what books to choose for students to read.

Teachers also take running records[C] of one or two students during each guided reading lesson and use this information as part of their assessment. Teachers check to

Figure 2-3   A Guided Reading Lesson

1. Prereading

Teachers introduce the new reading selection and prepare students to read. They begin by activating or building background knowledge of a topic related to the selection or the genre. Then they show the cover of the book, say the title and the author's name, and talk about the problem in the story or one or two main ideas in an informational book. They set the purpose for reading, and students often make predictions. They continue with a book walk to give an overview of the selection, but they do not read it aloud to students. Teachers introduce vocabulary words that are essential to the meaning of the text and teach or review a strategy that students should use while reading.

2. Reading

Teachers guide students through one or more readings of the selection. During the first reading, students and the teacher may read the first page or two together. Then students read the rest of the selection independently, usually reading silently. Teachers prompt for strategies and word identification as needed, and they move from student to student, listening in as the student reads. Students often complete a brief writing assignment, such as writing a summary or a reading log entry, after they finish reading and while they wait for classmates to finish.

3. Responding

Students discuss the selection, making text-to-self, text-to-world, and text-to-text connections. Teachers ask inferential and critical-level questions, such as "What would happen if . . . ?" "Why did . . . ?" and "If . . . , what might have happened next?" Students also reread to locate evidence for their answers. After talking about the selection, students usually write in reading logs or share what they wrote earlier.

4. Exploring

Teachers involve students in three types of activities:

- *Strategy instruction.* Teachers review and reinforce the reading strategy that students used in reading the selection. Sometimes teachers model how they used the strategy or ask students to reread a portion of the selection and think aloud about their strategy use.
- *Literary analysis.* Teachers explain genres, present information about story elements or other text structures, and locate examples of literary devices in the selection. Sometimes students create story maps or other graphic organizers.
- *Word work.* Teachers focus students' attention on words from the selection. They review vocabulary words from the selection and teach students to identify words by breaking them into syllables or using root words and affixes.

5. Applying

Students apply the strategies they are learning in independent reading activities such as reading workshop.

see that students are reading books at their instructional level and that they are making expected progress toward increasingly more difficult levels of books.

Independent Reading.   When students read independently, they read silently by themselves, for their own purposes, and at their own pace (Hornsby, Sukarna, & Parry, 1986). For students to read independently, the reading selections must be at their reading level. Many students read chapter books independently, but less capable readers may not be able to read the featured book independently. Students also independently read related books at varied reading levels from the text set as part of these units.

During reading workshop, students almost always read independently. Because students choose the books they want to read, they need to learn how to identify books that are written at an appropriate level of difficulty.

Independent reading is an important part of a balanced reading program because it is the most authentic type of reading. This type of reading is what most people do when they read, and this is the way students develop a love of reading and come to think of themselves as readers. The reading selection, however, must be at an appropriate level of difficulty so that students can read it independently. Otherwise, teachers use one of the other four types of reading to support students and make it possible for them to participate in the reading experience.

Buddy Reading.   In buddy reading, students read or reread a selection with a classmate. Sometimes students read with buddies because it is an enjoyable social activity, and sometimes they read together to help each other. Often students can read selections together that neither student could read individually. Buddy reading is a good alternative to independent reading because students can choose books they want to read and then read at their own pace. By working together, they are often able to figure out unfamiliar words and talk out comprehension problems.

As teachers introduce buddy reading, they show students how to read with buddies and how to support each other as they read. Students take turns reading aloud to each other or they read in unison. They often stop and help each other identify an unfamiliar word or take a minute or two at the end of each page to talk about what they have read. Buddy reading is a valuable way of providing the practice that struggling readers need; it is also an effective way to work with students with special learning needs and students who are learning English. However, unless the teacher has explained the approach and taught students how to work collaboratively, buddy reading often deteriorates into the stronger of the two buddies reading aloud to the other student, and that is not the intention of this type of reading.

Reading Aloud to Students.   In fourth through eighth grades, teachers read aloud to students for a variety of purposes each day. During literature focus units, for example, teachers read aloud featured selections that are appropriate for students' interest level but too difficult for students to read themselves. Sometimes it is also appropriate to read the first few pages of the featured selection aloud before distributing copies of it for students to read with buddies or independently. When they read aloud, teachers model what good readers do and how good readers use reading strategies. Reading aloud also provides an opportunity for teachers to think aloud about their use of reading strategies.

Reading aloud to students is not the same as "round-robin" reading, a practice that is no longer recommended in which students take turns reading paragraphs aloud as the rest of the class listens. Round-robin reading has been used for reading novels aloud, but it is more commonly used for reading chapters in content-area textbooks, even though there are more effective ways to teach content-area information and read textbooks.

Round-robin reading is no longer recommended, for several reasons (Opitz & Rasinski, 1998). First, if students are going to read aloud, they should read fluently. When less capable readers read, their reading is often difficult to listen to and is embarrassing to them personally. Less capable readers need reading practice, but performing in front of the entire class is not the most productive way for them to practice.

Figure 2-4 — Advantages and Disadvantages of the Five Types of Reading

Type	Advantages	Drawbacks
Shared Reading Teacher reads aloud while students follow along using individual copies of book.	• Access to books students could not read themselves. • Teacher models fluent reading. • Opportunities to model reading strategies. • Students practice fluent reading. • Develops a community of readers.	• Multiple copies needed. • Text may not be appropriate for all students. • Students may not be interested in the text.
Guided Reading Teacher supports students as they apply reading strategies and skills to read a text.	• Teaches skills and strategies. • Teacher provides direction and scaffolding. • Opportunities to model reading strategies. • Use with unfamiliar texts.	• Multiple copies of text needed. • Teacher controls the reading experience. • Some students may not be interested in the text.
Independent Reading Students read a text on their own.	• Develops responsibility and ownership. • Self-selection of texts. • Experience is more authentic.	• Students may need assistance to read the text. • Little teacher involvement and control.
Buddy Reading Two students read or reread a text together.	• Collaboration between students. • Students assist each other. • Use to reread familiar texts. • Develops reading fluency. • Students talk and share interpretations.	• Limited teacher involvement. • Less teacher control. • The stronger reader may control the reading.
Reading Aloud to Students Teacher or other fluent reader reads aloud to students.	• Access to books students could not read themselves. • Reader models fluent reading. • Opportunities to model reading strategies. • Develops a community of readers. • Use when only one copy of text is available.	• No opportunity for students themselves to read. • Text may not be appropriate for all students. • Students may not be interested in the text.

Better techniques are for them to read with buddies and in small groups during guided reading. Second, if the selection is appropriate for students to read aloud, they should be reading independently. Whenever the reading level of the text is appropriate for students, they should be reading independently. During round-robin reading, students often follow along only just before it is their turn to read. Third, round-robin reading is often tedious and boring, making students lose interest in reading.

The advantages and drawbacks for each type of reading are outlined in Figure 2-4. In the vignette at the beginning of this chapter, Mrs. Goodman used a combination of these approaches. She used shared reading as she read the first chapter of *The Giver* aloud, with students following in their own copies. Later, students read together in small groups, with a buddy, or independently. As teachers plan their instructional programs, they include reading aloud to students, teacher-led student reading, and independent reading each day.

Stage 3: Responding

During the third stage, readers respond to their reading and continue to negotiate the meaning. Two ways that students make tentative and exploratory comments immediately after reading are by writing in reading logs and participating in grand conversations.

Writing in Reading Logs. Students write and draw their thoughts and feelings about what they have read in reading logs. Rosenblatt (1978) explains that as students write about what they have read, they unravel their thinking and, at the same time, elaborate on and clarify their responses. When students read informational books, they sometimes write in reading logs, as they do after reading stories and poems, but at other times, they make notes of important information or draw charts and diagrams to use in thematic units.

Students usually make reading logs by stapling together 10 to 12 sheets of paper at the beginning of a literature focus unit or reading workshop. At the beginning of a thematic unit, students make learning logs[C] to write in during the unit. They decorate the covers, keeping with the theme of the unit, write entries related to their reading, and make notes related to what they are learning in minilessons. Teachers monitor students' entries during the unit, reading and often responding to the entries. Because these journals are learning tools, teachers rarely correct students' spellings. They focus their responses on the students' ideas, but they expect students to spell the title of the book, the names of characters, and other high-frequency words accurately. At the end of the unit, teachers review students' work and often grade the journals based on whether students completed all the entries and on the quality of the ideas in their entries.

ELL students comprehend better when they connect talk with dramatizing episodes or drawing pictures about what they are reading.

Participating in Discussions. Students also talk about the text with classmates in grand conversations and instructional conversations. Peterson and Eeds (1990) explain that in these types of discussions, students share their personal responses and tell what they liked about the text. After sharing personal reactions, they shift the focus to "puzzle over what the author has written and . . . share what it is they find revealed" (p. 61). Often students make connections between the text and their own lives or between the text and other literature they have read. If they are reading a novel, they also make predictions about what they think will happen in the next chapter.

Teachers often share their ideas in grand conversations, but they act as interested participants, not leaders. The talk is primarily among the students, but teachers ask questions regarding things they are genuinely interested in learning more about and share information in response to questions that students ask. In the past, many discussions have been "gentle inquisitions" during which students recited answers to factual questions teachers asked about books that students were reading (Eeds & Wells, 1989). Teachers asked these questions to determine whether students read and understood an assignment. Although teachers can still judge whether students have read the assignment, the focus in grand conversations is on clarifying and deepening students' understanding of the story they have read. Teachers and students have similar instructional conversations after reading content-area textbooks and informational books.

These grand conversations can be held with the whole class or in small groups. Students can meet as a class, but many prefer to talk with classmates in small groups. When students meet as a class, there is a feeling of community, and the teacher can be part of the group. When students meet in small groups, they have more opportunities to participate in the discussion and to share their interpretations, but fewer viewpoints are expressed in each group. In addition, teachers must move around, spending only a few minutes with each group. Some teachers compromise and have students begin their discussions in small groups and then come together as a class to share what the groups discussed.

Stage 4: Exploring

In the exploring stage, students go back into the text to explore it more analytically. They reread the selection, examine the author's craft, and focus on words from the selection. Teachers also present minilessons on procedures, concepts, strategies, and skills.

Rereading the Selection. As students reread the selection, they think again about what they have read. Each time they reread a selection, students benefit in specific ways (Yaden, 1988). They deepen their comprehension and make further connections between the selection and their own lives, the world, or other literature they have read. Students often reread a basal reader story, a picture book, or excerpts from a novel several times. If the teacher used shared reading to read the selection with students in the reading stage, students might reread it with a buddy once or twice and then, after these experiences, read it independently.

Examining the Author's Craft. Teachers plan exploring activities to focus students' attention on the structure of text and the literary language that authors use. Students notice literary opposites in the story, use story boards[C] to sequence the events in the story, and make story maps to highlight the plot, characters, and other elements of story structure. Another way students learn about the structure of stories is by writing books based on the selection they have read. In sequels, students tell what happens to the characters after the story ends. Stories such as *Jumanji* (Van Allsburg, 1981), a fantasy about a board game that comes to life, suggest another episode at the end of the story and invite students to create a sequel. Students also write innovations, or new versions, for the selection, in which they follow the same sentence pattern but use their own ideas. They also write innovations for patterned books such as *Alexander and the Terrible, Horrible, No Good, Very Bad Day* (Viorst, 1977).

Teachers share information about the author of the featured selection and introduce other books by the same author. Sometimes teachers help students make comparisons among several books written by a particular author. To focus on literary language, students often reread favorite excerpts in read-arounds and write memorable quotes on quilts that they create.

Focusing on Words and Sentences. Teachers and students write "important" words on word walls after reading and post these alphabetized word walls in the classroom. Students refer to the word walls when they write, using these words for a variety of activities during the exploring stage. Students make word clusters and posters to highlight particular words. They also make word chains, do word sorts[C], create semantic feature analysis[C] charts to analyze related words, and play word games.

Teachers choose words from word walls to use in minilessons, too. Words can be used to review phonics skills, such as vowel patterns, *r*-controlled vowels, and syllabication. Other concepts, such as root words and affixes, compound words, contractions, and metaphors, can also be taught using examples from word walls. Teachers may decide to teach a minilesson on a particular concept, such as words with the -*ly* suffix, because five or six words representing the concept are listed on the word wall.

Students also locate "important" sentences in books they read. These sentences might be important because of figurative language, because they express the theme or illustrate a character trait, or simply because students like them. Students often copy the sentences on sentence strips to display in the classroom and use in other exploring activities. Also, students can copy the sentences in their reading logs.

Teaching Minilessons. Teachers present minilessons on reading procedures, concepts, strategies, and skills during the exploring stage. In a minilesson, teachers introduce the topic and make connections between the topic and examples in the featured selection students have read. In this way, students are better able to connect the information teachers are presenting with their own reading process. In the vignette, Mrs. Goodman presented minilessons on the visualization strategy and on root words and affixes using examples from *The Giver*.

Stage 5: Applying

During the applying stage, readers extend their comprehension, reflect on their understanding, and value the reading experience. Building on the initial and exploratory responses they made immediately after reading, students create projects. These projects can involve reading, writing, talk and drama, art, or research and can take many forms, including murals, readers theatre[C] scripts, and reports[C], as well as reading other books by the same author. Usually students choose which projects they will do rather than the entire class doing the same project. Sometimes, however, the class decides to work together on a project. In Mrs. Goodman's class, for example, some students wrote color poems, and others read books and wrote about memories. A list of projects is presented in Figure 2-5. The purpose of these activities is for students to expand the ideas they read about, create a personal interpretation, and value the reading experience.

ELL

Pair ELL students with native English-speaking classmates to create projects. English language learners benefit from social interaction, gain content knowledge, and refine their English skills through collaboration.

THE WRITING PROCESS

The focus in the writing process is on what students think and do as they write. The five stages are prewriting, drafting, revising, editing, and publishing. The labeling and numbering of the stages do not mean that the writing process is a linear series of neatly packaged categories. Rather, research has shown that the process involves recurring cycles, and labeling is simply an aid to identifying and discussing writing activities. In the classroom, the stages merge and recur as students write. The key features of each stage in the writing process are shown in Figure 2-6 on p. 49.

Stage 1: Prewriting

Prewriting is the "getting ready to write" stage. The traditional notion that writers have a topic completely thought out and ready to flow onto the page is ridiculous. If writers wait for ideas to fully develop, they may wait forever. Instead, writers begin tentatively—talking, reading, writing—to see what they know and in what direction they want to go. Prewriting has probably been the most neglected stage in the writing process; however, it is as crucial to writers as a warm-up is to athletes. Murray (1982) believes that at least 70% of writing time should be spent in prewriting. During the prewriting stage, students choose a topic, consider purpose, audience, and form, and gather and organize ideas for writing.

Choosing a Topic. Choosing a topic for writing can be a stumbling block for students who have become dependent on teachers to supply topics. For years, teachers have supplied topics by suggesting gimmicky story starters and relieving students of the "burden" of topic selection. These "creative" topics often stymied students, who were forced to write on topics they knew little about or were not interested in. Graves (1976) calls this situation "writing welfare." Instead, students need to choose their own writing topics.

Figure 2-5   **Projects Students Develop During the Applying Stage**

Art Projects

1. Experiment with the illustration techniques (e.g., collage, watercolor, line drawing) used in a favorite book. Examine other books illustrated with the same technique.
2. Make a diagram or model using information from a book.
3. Create a collage to represent the theme of a book.
4. Design a book jacket for a book, laminate it, and place it on the book.
5. Decorate a coffee can or a potato chip can using scenes from a book. Fill the can with quotes from characters in the story. Other students can guess the identity of the characters. Or fill the can with quotes from a poem with words missing. Other students guess the missing words.
6. Construct a shoebox or other miniature scene of an episode for a favorite book (or use a larger box to construct a diorama).
7. Make illustrations for each important event in a book.
8. Make a map or relief map of a book's setting or something related to the book.
9. Construct a tabletop display of the setting of the book.
10. Construct a mobile illustrating a book.
11. Make a roll-movie of a book by drawing a series of pictures on a long strip of paper. Attach ends to rollers and place in a cardboard box cut like a television set.
12. Make a comic strip to illustrate the sequence of events in a book.
13. Prepare bookmarks for a book and distribute them to classmates.
14. Prepare flannel board pictures to use in retelling the story.
15. Use or prepare illustrations of characters for pocket props to use in retelling the story.
16. Prepare illustrations of the events in the story for clothesline props to use in retelling the story.
17. Experiment with art techniques related to the mood of a poem.
18. Make a mural of the book.
19. Make a book box[C] and decorate it with scenes from a book. Collect objects, poems, and illustrations that represent characters, events, or images from the book to add to the box.

Writing Projects

20. Write a review of a favorite book for a class review file.
21. Write a letter about a book to a classmate, friend, or pen pal.
22. Dictate or write another episode or sequel for a book.
23. Create a newspaper with news stories and advertisements based on characters and episodes from a book.
24. Write a simulated letter from one book character to another.
25. Copy five "quotable quotes" from a book and list them on a poster.
26. Make a scrapbook about the book. Label all items in the scrapbook and write a short description of the most interesting ones.
27. Write a poem related to the book.

(continues)

Figure 2-5 (continued)

28. Write a lifeline related to the book, the era, the character, or the author.
29. Write a business letter to a company or organization requesting information on a topic related to the book.
30. Keep a simulated journal from the perspective of one character from the book.
31. Write a dictionary defining specialized vocabulary in a book.
32. Rewrite the story from another character's point of view.
33. Make a class collaboration book. Each student dictates or writes one page.
34. Create a PowerPoint presentation about the book.

Reading Projects
35. Read another book by the same author.
36. Read another book by the same illustrator.
37. Read another book on the same theme.
38. Read another book in the same genre.
39. Read another book about the same character.
40. Read and compare another version of the same story.
41. Listen to and compare a tape, filmstrip, film, or video version of the same story.
42. Tape-record a book or an excerpt from it to place in the listening center.
43. Read aloud to the class a poem that complements the book.
44. Tape-record a book using background music and sound effects.

Drama and Talk Projects
45. Give a readers theatre presentation of a book.
46. Write a script and present a play about a book.
47. Make puppets and use them in retelling a book.
48. Dress as a character from the book and answer questions from classmates.
49. Write and present a rap about the book.
50. Videotape a commercial for a book.
51. Interview someone in the community who is knowledgeable about a topic related to the book.

Literary Analysis Projects
52. Make a chart to compare the story with another version or with the film version of the story.
53. Make an open-mind portrait to probe the thoughts of one character.
54. Make a Venn diagram to compare two characters.
55. Make a plot diagram of the book.

Research Projects
56. Research the author of the book on the Internet and compile information in a chart or summary.
57. Research a topic related to the book using book and Internet resources, and present the information in a report.
58. Create a multigenre project.

Some students complain that they don't know what to write about, but teachers can help them brainstorm a list of three, four, or five topics and then identify the one topic they are most interested in and know the most about. Students who feel they cannot generate any writing topics are often surprised that they have so many options available. Then, through prewriting activities, students talk, draw, read, and even write to develop information about their topics.

Figure 2-6　　Key Features of the Writing Process

Stage 1: Prewriting
- Write on topics based on personal experiences.
- Engage in rehearsal activities before writing.
- Identify the audience who will read the composition.
- Identify the purpose of the writing activity.
- Choose an appropriate form for the composition based on audience and purpose.

Stage 2: Drafting
- Write a rough draft.
- Emphasize content rather than mechanics.

Stage 3: Revising
- Reread the composition.
- Share writing in writing groups^C.
- Participate constructively in discussions about classmates' writing.
- Make changes in the composition to reflect the reactions and comments of both teacher and classmates.
- Between the first and final drafts, make substantive rather than only minor changes.

Stage 4: Editing
- Proofread the composition.
- Help proofread classmates' compositions.
- Identify and correct mechanical errors.
- Meet with the teacher for a final editing.

Stage 5: Publishing
- Publish writing in an appropriate form.
- Share the finished writing with an appropriate audience.

Asking students to choose their own topics for writing does not mean that teachers never give writing assignments; teachers do provide general guidelines. They may specify the writing form, and at other times they may establish the purpose, but students should choose their own content.

Considering Purpose.　As students prepare to write, they need to think about the purpose of their writing. Are they writing to entertain? to inform? to persuade? Setting the purpose for writing is just as important as setting the purpose for reading, because purpose influences decisions students make about audience and form.

Considering Audience.　Students may write primarily for themselves—to express and clarify their own ideas and feelings—or they may write for others. Possible audiences include classmates, younger children, parents, foster grandparents, children's authors, and pen pals. Other audiences are more distant and less well known. For example, students write letters to businesses to request information, articles for the local newspaper, or stories and poems for publication in literary magazines and e-zines (on-line magazines).

Children's writing is influenced by their sense of audience. Britton and his colleagues (1975) define audience awareness as "the manner in which the writer expresses a relationship with the reader in respect to the writer's understanding"

Figure 2-7 Writing Genres

Genre	Purpose	Activities
Descriptive Writing	Students become careful observers and choose precise language when they use description. They take notice of sensory details and learn to make comparisons (metaphors and similes) in order to make their writing more powerful.	Character sketches Comparisons Descriptive essays Descriptive paragraphs Descriptive sentences Found poems Observations
Expository Writing	Students collect and synthesize information for informative writing. This writing is objective, and reports are the most common type of informative writing. Students use expository writing to give directions, sequence steps, compare one thing to another, explain causes and effects, or describe problems and solutions.	Alphabet books[C] Autobiographies Biographies Brochures Cubes[C] Data charts Interviews Newspaper articles Posters Reports Simulated journals Summaries
Journals and Letters	Students write to themselves and to specific, known audiences in journals and letters. Their writing is personal and often less formal than other genres. They share news, explore new ideas, and record notes. Letters and envelopes require special formatting, and students learn these formats during the elementary grades.	Business letters Courtesy letters Double-entry journals E-mail messages Friendly letters Learning logs Postcards Reading logs Simulated journals

(continues)

(pp. 65–66). Students adapt their writing to fit their audience, just as they vary their speech to meet the needs of the people who are listening to them.

Considering Form.   One of the most important considerations is the genre the writing will take: a story? a letter? a poem? a journal entry? A writing activity could be handled in any one of these ways. As part of a science unit on hermit crabs, for instance, students could write a story or poem about a hermit crab, write a report on hermit crabs with information about how they obtain shells to live in, or write a description of the pet hermit crabs in the classroom. There is a wide variety of writing genres that students learn to use during the middle grades. A list of six genres is presented in Figure 2-7. Students need to experiment with a wide variety of writing forms and explore the potential of these functions and formats.

Through reading and writing, students develop a strong sense of these genres and how they are structured. Langer (1985) found that by third grade, students responded in distinctly different ways to story- and report-writing assignments; they organized the writing differently and included varied kinds of information and elaboration. Similarly, Hidi and Hildyard (1983) found that elementary students could

Figure 2-7 (continued)

Genre	Purpose	Activities
Narrative Writing	Students retell familiar stories, develop sequels for stories they have read, write stories called personal narratives about events in their own lives, and create original stories. They include a beginning, middle, and end in the narratives they write. In the beginning, they introduce the characters, identify a problem, and interest readers in the story. In the middle, the problem becomes worse or additional roadblocks are set up to thwart the main character as he/she attempts to solve the problem. In the end, the problem is resolved.	Original short stories Personal narratives Retellings of stories Sequels to stories Scripts of stories
Persuasive Writing	Persuasion is winning someone to your viewpoint or cause. The three ways people are persuaded are by appeals to (1) logic, (2) moral character, and (3) emotion. Students present their position clearly and then support it with examples and evidence.	Advertisements Book and movie reviews Editorials Letters to the editor Persuasive essays Persuasive letters
Poetry Writing	Students create word pictures and play with rhyme and other stylistic devices as they create poems. As students experiment with poetry, they learn that poetic language is vivid and powerful but concise, and they learn that poems can be arranged in different ways on a page.	Acrostic poems Color poems Found poems Free verse Haiku "I am" poems "If I were in charge of the world" poems Poems for two voices

differentiate between stories and persuasive essays. Because children are clarifying the distinctions between various writing genres during the middle grades, it is important that teachers use the correct terminology and not label all children's writing "stories."

Decisions about purpose, audience, and form influence each other. For example, if the purpose is to entertain, an appropriate form might be a story, script, or poem—and these three forms look very different on a piece of paper. Whereas a story is written in the traditional block format, scripts and poems have unique page arrangements. Scripts are written with the character's name and a colon, and the dialogue is set off. Action and dialogue, rather than description, carry the story line in a script. In contrast, poems have unique formatting considerations, and words are used judiciously. Each word and phrase is chosen to convey a maximum amount of information.

Gathering and Organizing Ideas. Students engage in activities to gather and organize ideas for writing. Graves (1983) calls what writers do to prepare for writing "rehearsal" activities. Rehearsal activities take many forms, including:

Drawing. Young children typically use drawing as a way to gather and organize ideas for writing, and older, struggling writers also like to use drawing as a prewriting activity. Even though drawing can be time-consuming, some students seem unable to rehearse their writing in any other way.

Clustering. Students make clusters (weblike diagrams) in which they write the topic in a center circle and then draw rays from the circle for each main idea. Then they add details and other information on rays drawn from each main idea. Through clustering, students organize their ideas for writing. Clustering is a better prewriting strategy than outlining because it is nonlinear.

Talking. Students talk with their classmates to share ideas about possible writing topics, try out ways to express an idea, and ask questions.

Reading. Students gather ideas for writing and investigate the structure of various genres through reading. They may retell a favorite story in writing, write new adventures for favorite story characters, or experiment with repetition, onomatopoeia, or another poetic device used in a poem they have read. Informational books also provide raw material for writing. For example, if students are studying the rain forest, they read to gather information about the animal and plant life in each layer that they can use in writing a report.

Role-playing. Students discover and shape ideas they will use in their writing through role-playing. Even though you might think of role-playing as something young children do, it is equally effective with students in fourth through eighth grades. During thematic units and after reading stories, students can reenact events to bring an experience to life. Teachers should choose a particular critical moment for students to reenact. For example, after reading *Sarah, Plain and Tall* (MacLachlan, 1985), children might reenact the day Sarah took the wagon to town. This is a critical moment: Does Sarah like the family and their prairie home well enough to stay?

Stage 2: Drafting

Students write and refine their compositions through a series of drafts. During the drafting stage, they focus on getting their ideas down on paper. Because writers don't begin writing with their compositions already composed in their minds, students begin with tentative ideas developed through prewriting activities. The drafting stage is the time to pour out ideas, with little concern about spelling, punctuation, and other mechanical errors.

Students skip every other line when they write their rough drafts to leave space for revisions. They use arrows to move sections of text, cross-outs to delete sections, and scissors and tape to cut apart and rearrange text, just as adult writers do. They write only on one side of a sheet of paper so it can be cut apart or rearranged. As computers become more available in middle-grade classrooms, revising, with all its moving, adding, and deleting of text, is much easier. However, for students who handwrite their compositions, the wide spacing is crucial. Teachers might make small x's on every other line of students' papers as a reminder to skip lines as they draft their compositions.

Students label their drafts by writing *Rough Draft* in ink at the top or by using a ROUGH DRAFT stamp. This label indicates to the writer, other students, parents, and administrators that the composition is a draft in which the emphasis is on content, not mechanics. It also explains why the teacher has not graded the paper or marked mechanical errors.

Instead of writing drafts by hand, students can use computers to compose rough drafts, polish their writing, and print out final copies. There are many benefits of using computers for word processing. For example, students are often more motivated to write, and they tend to write longer pieces. Their writing looks neater, and they can use spell-check programs to identify and correct misspelled words. To learn more about word-processing and other writing-related computer programs for elementary students, check the Technology Link on page 54.

During drafting, students may need to modify their earlier decisions about purpose, audience, and, especially, the form their writing will take. For example, a composition that began as a story may be transformed into a report, letter, or poem. The new format allows the student to communicate more effectively. The process of modifying earlier decisions continues into the revising stage.

As students write rough drafts, it is important for teachers not to emphasize correct spelling and neatness. In fact, pointing out mechanical errors during the drafting stage sends students the false message that mechanical correctness is more important than content (Sommers, 1982). Later, during editing, students clean up mechanical errors and put their composition into a neat, final form.

Stage 3: Revising

During the revising stage, writers refine ideas in their compositions. Students often break the writing process cycle as soon as they complete a rough draft, believing that once they have jotted down their ideas, the writing task is complete. Experienced writers, however, know they must turn to others for reactions and revise on the basis of these comments. Revision is not just polishing; it is meeting the needs of readers by adding, substituting, deleting, and rearranging material. *Revision* means "seeing again," and in this stage, writers see their compositions again with the help of classmates and the teacher. The revising stage consists of three activities: rereading the rough draft, sharing the rough draft in a writing group, and revising on the basis of feedback.

Students share their rough drafts and get feedback from classmates.

Technology Link

Computer Programs for Writers

A variety of word-processing programs, desktop publishing programs, and graphics packages support students who use the process approach to writing (Cochran-Smith, 1991; DeGroff, 1990). Students revise and edit their rough drafts more easily when they use word processors, and they print out neat and "clean" final copies without the drudgery of recopying their compositions (Strickland, 1997). They use digital cameras, graphics packages, and drawing and painting programs to create illustrations. And, with desktop publishing programs, students create professional-looking newspapers, brochures, and books. Here's a list of writing-related computer programs:

Type of Program	*Title*
Integrated packages	Appleworks
	Microsoft Works
	The Writing Center
Word-processing programs	Amazing Writing Machine
	Kid Works II
	Kidwriter Gold
	Mac Write Pro
	Microsoft Word
	Talking Text Writer
	Writer's Helper
Desktop publishing programs	Big Book Maker
	The Children's Writing and Publishing Center
	Make-a-Book
	Newspaper Maker
	Newsroom
	Pagemaker
	Print Shop
	Publish It!

Rereading the Rough Draft. After finishing the rough draft, writers need to distance themselves from it for a day or two, then reread it from a fresh perspective, as a reader might. As they reread, students make changes—adding, substituting, deleting, and moving—and place question marks by sections that need work. It is these trouble spots that students ask for help with in their writing groups.

Sharing in Writing Groups. Students meet in writing groups to share their compositions with classmates. They respond to the writer's rough draft and suggest possible revisions. Writing groups provide a scaffold in which teachers and classmates talk about plans and strategies for writing and revising (Applebee & Langer, 1983; Calkins, 1983).

Writing groups can form spontaneously when several students have completed drafts and are ready to share their compositions, or they can be formal groupings with identified leaders. In some classrooms, writing groups form when four or five students finish writing their rough drafts. Students gather around a conference table or in a corner of the classroom and take turns reading their rough drafts aloud. Classmates in the

Types of Program	Title
	Ready, Set, Go! Toucan Press
Graphics packages	Bannermania PrintShop Deluxe SuperPrint
Drawing and painting programs	DazzleDraw Freehand Kid Pix Studio Deluxe Kid Works Deluxe
Presentation software	Keynote Kid Pix Slide Show PowerPoint
Hypermedia programs	HyperCard HyperStudio MicroWorlds Multimedia Workshop Runtime Revolution
Keyboarding programs	Kid Keys Kids on Keys Microtype: The Wonderful World of Paws Type to Learn
Mapping programs	Inspiration Kidspiration

It's a good idea to make the first writing project a class collaboration so students can review word-processing procedures. The next several writing projects should be short so that students can concentrate on working through the word-processing procedures. Often one or two students will assume an important new status as "computer expert" because of special interest or expertise. These experts help other students with word-processing tasks and using the printer.

group listen and respond, offering compliments and suggestions for revision. Sometimes the teacher joins the writing group, but if the teacher is involved in something else, students work independently.

In other classrooms, the writing groups are assigned; students get together when all students in the group have completed their rough drafts and are ready to share their writing. Sometimes the teacher participates in these groups, providing feedback along with the students. Or, the writing groups can function independently. For these assigned groups, each cluster is made up of four or five students, and a list of groups and their members is posted in the classroom. The teacher puts a star by one student's name, and that student serves as a group leader. The leader changes every quarter.

Making Revisions. Students make four types of changes to their rough drafts: additions, substitutions, deletions, and moves (Faigley & Witte, 1981). As they revise, students might add words, substitute sentences, delete paragraphs, and move phrases. Students often use a blue or red pen to cross out, draw arrows, and write in the space left between the double-spaced lines of their rough drafts so that revisions will show

Struggling Writers Need to Revise Their Writing. Struggling writers often break the writing process as soon as they write a draft of their compositions, thinking their work is finished. They don't realize that they need to revise their writing in order to communicate more effectively with an audience. The key to enticing struggling writers to revise is helping them to develop a sense of audience. Many novice writers write primarily for themselves, but when they want their classmates or another audience to understand their message, they begin to recognize the importance of revision. Teachers emphasize audience by encouraging students to share their writing with classmates from the author's chair, and they model the revision process through minilessons when students work together to revise an anonymous piece of writing. Lots of writing and sharing are necessary before students begin to appreciate revision.

clearly. That way teachers can see the types of revisions students make by examining their revised rough drafts. Revisions are another gauge of students' growth as writers.

Stage 4: Editing

Editing is putting the piece of writing into its final form. Until this stage, the focus has been primarily on the content of students' writing. Once the focus changes to mechanics, students polish their writing by correcting spelling mistakes and other mechanical errors. The goal here is to make the writing "optimally readable" (Smith, 1982, p. 127). Writers who write for readers understand that if their compositions are not readable, they have written in vain because their ideas will never be read.

Mechanics are the commonly accepted conventions of written Standard English. They consist of capitalization, punctuation, spelling, sentence structure, usage, and formatting considerations specific to poems, scripts, letters, and other writing forms. The use of these commonly accepted conventions is a courtesy to those who will read the composition.

Students learn mechanical skills best through hands-on editing of their own compositions, not through workbook exercises. When they edit a composition that will be shared with a genuine audience, students are more interested in using mechanical skills correctly so they can communicate effectively. Studies over the past quarter century suggest that it is more effective to teach mechanical skills as part of the writing process than through practice exercises (Bissex, 1980; Elley, Barham, Lamb, & Wyllie, 1976; Graves, 1983).

Students move through three activities in the editing stage: getting distance from the composition, proofreading to locate errors, and correcting errors.

Getting Distance. Students are more efficient editors if they set the composition aside for a few days before beginning to edit. After working so closely with a piece of writing during drafting and revising, they are too familiar with it to notice many mechanical errors. With the distance gained by waiting a few days, students are better able to approach editing with a fresh perspective and gather the enthusiasm necessary to finish the writing process by making the paper optimally readable.

Figure 2-8 Proofreaders' Marks

Delete	ℓ	Most whales are ~~big and~~ huge creatures.
Insert	∧	A baby whale is ^{called} a calf.
Indent paragraph	¶	¶Whales look a lot like fish, but the two are quite different.
Capitalize	≡	In the United s̲t̲ates it is illegal to hunt whales.
Change to lower case	/	Why do beached W̸hales die?
Add period	⊙	Baleen whales do not have any teeth⊙
Add comma	∧	Some baleen whales are blue whales ̬gray whales and humpback whales.
Add apostrophe	∨	People are the whale's only enemy.

Proofreading. Students proofread their compositions to locate and mark possible errors. Proofreading is a unique type of reading in which writers read slowly, word by word, hunting for errors rather than reading quickly for meaning (King, 1985). Concentrating on mechanics is difficult because of our natural inclination to read for meaning. Even experienced proofreaders often find themselves reading for meaning and thus overlooking errors that do not inhibit meaning. It is important, therefore, to take time to explain proofreading to students and to demonstrate how it differs from regular reading.

To demonstrate proofreading, teachers copy a piece of writing on the chalkboard or display it on an overhead projector. The teacher reads it several times, each time hunting for a particular type of error. During each reading, the teacher reads the composition slowly, softly pronouncing each word and touching the word with a pencil or pen to focus attention on it. The teacher marks possible errors as they are located.

Errors are marked or corrected with special proofreaders' marks. Students enjoy using these marks, the same ones that adult authors and editors use. Proofreaders' marks that elementary students can learn to use in editing their writing are presented in Figure 2-8.

Editing checklists help students focus on particular types of errors. Teachers can develop checklists with six to eight items appropriate for the grade level, such as using commas in a series, indenting paragraphs, capitalizing proper nouns and adjectives, and spelling homonyms correctly. Teachers revise the checklist during the school year to focus attention on skills that have recently been taught.

A sample fifth-grade editing checklist is presented in Figure 2-9. The writer and a classmate work as partners to edit their compositions. First, students proofread their own compositions, searching for errors in each category on the checklist, and, after proofreading, check off each item. After completing the checklist, students sign their

Figure 2-9   A Fifth-Grade Editing Checklist

EDITING CHECKLIST

Author   Editor

☐	☐	1. Misspelled words have been circled and corrected.
☐	☐	2. Proper nouns and adjectives have been capitalized.
☐	☐	3. Punctuation marks have been used correctly.
☐	☐	4. There are no sentence fragments.
☐	☐	5. Paragraphs have been indented.
☐	☐	6. Title has been written at the top of the paper.

Signatures

Author: _____ Editor: _____

Assessment Tools

names and trade checklists and compositions. Now they become editors and complete each other's checklist. Having writer and editor sign the checklist helps them to take the activity seriously.

Correcting Errors. After students proofread their compositions and locate as many errors as they can, they use red pens to correct the errors independently or with an editor's assistance. Some errors are easy to correct, some require use of a dictionary, and others involve instruction from the teacher. It is unrealistic to expect students to locate and correct every mechanical error in their compositions. Not even published books are always error free! Once in a while, students may change a correct spelling or punctuation mark and make it incorrect, but they correct far more errors than they create.

Editing can end after students and their editors correct as many mechanical errors as possible, or after students meet with the teacher in a conference for a final editing. When mechanical correctness is crucial, this conference is important. Teachers proofread the composition with the student, and they identify and make the remaining corrections together, or the teacher makes check marks in the margin to note errors for the student to correct independently.

Stage 5: Publishing

In this stage, students bring their compositions to life by writing final copies and by sharing them orally with an appropriate audience. When they share their writing with real audiences of classmates, other students, parents, and the community, students come to think of themselves as authors.

Making Books.   One of the most popular ways for students to publish their writing is by making books. Simple booklets can be made by folding a sheet of paper into quarters, like a greeting card. Students write the title on the front and use the three remaining sides for their composition. They can also construct booklets by stapling sheets of writing paper together and adding covers made out of construction paper. Sheets of wallpaper cut from old sample books also make sturdy covers. These stapled booklets can be cut into various shapes, too. Students can make more sophisticated books by covering cardboard covers with contact paper, wallpaper samples, or cloth. Pages are sewn or stapled together, and the first and last pages (endpapers) are glued to the cardboard covers to hold the book together. Directions for making one type of hardcover book are shown in Figure 2-10.

Sharing Writing.   Students read their writing to classmates or share it with larger audiences through hardcover books placed in the class or school library, plays performed for classmates, or letters sent to authors, businesses, and other correspondents. Here are some other ways to share students' writing:

- Submit the piece to writing contests
- Display the writing as a mobile
- Contribute to a class anthology
- Contribute to the local newspaper
- Make a shape book
- Record the writing on a cassette tape
- Submit it to a literary magazine
- Read it at a school assembly
- Share it at a read-aloud party
- Share it with parents and siblings
- Display poetry on a "poet-tree"
- Send it to a pen pal or key pal (electronic pen pal)
- Display it on a bulletin board
- Make a big book
- Design a poster about the writing
- Submit it to student e-zines (on-line magazines)
- Read it to foster grandparents
- Share it as a puppet show
- Display it at a public event
- Read it to children in other classes

Through this sharing, students communicate with genuine audiences who respond to their writing in meaningful ways. Sharing writing is a social activity that helps children develop sensitivity to audiences and confidence in themselves as authors. Dyson (1985) advises that teachers consider the social interpretations of sharing—the students'

Figure 2-10 Directions for Making Hardcover Books

1. Fold sheets of 8½ x 11-inch writing paper in half and copy the composition on the paper. List the title and author's name on the first page.

2. Put an additional sheet of writing paper, construction paper, or other colorful paper on the outside of the folded sheets of writing paper to be the book's endpaper.

Add tape along fold.

end-paper

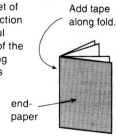

3. Staple the folded papers together with two or three staples on the fold. Use a long-arm stapler to reach the fold more easily.

stapler

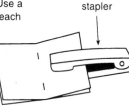

4. Cut a sheet of contact paper, 11 x 15 inches, for the outside covering.

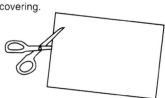

5. Cut two pieces of cardboard, 6 x 9 inches, for the front and back covers.

6. Peel the backing from the contact paper and place the two pieces of cardboard on the contact paper, centering them and leaving ¼ inch between the two pieces.

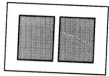

7. Cut off the four corners of the contact paper and place them on the adjacent corners of the cardboard pieces.

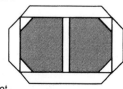

8. Fold the edges of contact paper back onto the cardboard pieces.

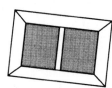

9. Set the stapled booklet inside the contact paper cover so that the stapled edge fits into the space between the two cardboard pieces.

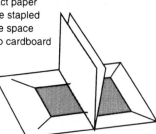

10. Glue the outside of the endpaper to the cardboard pieces. First glue one side, making sure to keep the stapled edge in the space between the two cardboard pieces. Then glue the other side of the paper to the second cardboard piece.

glue →

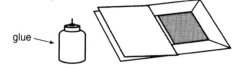

behavior, the teacher's behavior, and the interaction between students and teacher—within the classroom context. Individual students interpret sharing differently. Beyond just providing the opportunity for students to share writing, teachers need to teach students how to respond to their classmates. Teachers themselves serve as a model for responding to students' writing without dominating the sharing.

READING AND WRITING ARE SIMILAR PROCESSES

Reading and writing are both meaning-making processes, and readers and writers are involved in many similar activities. It is important that teachers plan literacy activities so that students can connect reading and writing.

Comparing the Two Processes

The reading and writing processes have comparable activities at each stage (Butler & Turbill, 1984). In both reading and writing, the goal is to construct meaning, and, as shown in Figure 2-11, reading and writing activities at each stage are similar. For example, notice the similarities between the activities listed for the third stage of reading and writing—responding and revising, respectively. Fitzgerald (1989) analyzed these two activities and concluded that they draw on similar processes of author-reader-text interactions. Similar analyses can be made for other activities as well.

Tierney (1983) explains that reading and writing are multidimensional and involve concurrent, complex transactions between writers, between writers as readers, between readers, and between readers as writers. Writers participate in several types of reading activities. They read other authors' works to obtain ideas and to learn about the structure of stories, but they also read and reread their own work in order to problem solve, discover, monitor, and clarify. The quality of these reading experiences seems closely tied to success in writing. Readers as writers is a newer idea, but readers participate in many of the same activities that writers use—generating ideas, organizing, monitoring, problem solving, and revising.

Classroom Connections

Teachers can help students appreciate the similarities between reading and writing in many ways. Tierney explains: "What we need are reading teachers who act as if their students were developing writers and writing teachers who act as if their students were readers" (1983, p. 151). Here are some ways to point out the relationships between reading and writing:

- Help writers assume alternative points of view as potential readers.
- Help readers consider the writer's purpose and viewpoint.
- Point out that reading is much like composing, so that students will view reading as a process, much like the writing process.
- Talk with students about the similarities between the reading and writing processes.
- Talk with students about reading and writing strategies.

Readers and writers use similar strategies for constructing meaning as they interact with print. As readers, we use a variety of problem-solving strategies to make decisions about an author's meaning and to construct meaning for ourselves. As writers,

To see how the reading process is applied in a real classroom, view the CD-ROM titled *Literature Circles: Responding to Literature in an 8th Grade Classroom* that accompanies this text.

Figure 2-11   A Comparison of the Reading and Writing Processes

What Readers Do	What Writers Do
Stage 1 *Prereading*	*Prewriting*
Readers use knowledge about	Writers use knowledge about
• the topic • reading • literature • language systems	• the topic • writing • literature • language systems
Readers' expectations are cued by	Writers' expectations are cued by
• previous reading/writing experiences • genre • purpose for reading • audience for reading	• previous reading/writing experiences • genre • purpose for writing • audience for writing
Readers make predictions.	Writers gather and organize ideas.
Stage 2 *Reading*	*Drafting*
Readers	Writers
• use word-identification strategies • use comprehension strategies • monitor reading • create meaning	• use transcription strategies • use comprehension strategies • monitor writing • create meaning
Stage 3 *Responding*	*Revising*
Readers	Writers
• respond to the text • interpret meaning • clarify misunderstandings • expand ideas	• respond to the text • interpret meaning • clarify misunderstandings • expand ideas
Stage 4 *Exploring*	*Editing*
Readers	Writers
• examine the impact of words and literary language • explore structural elements • compare the text to others	• identify and correct mechanical errors • review paragraph and sentence structure
Stage 5 *Applying*	*Publishing*
Readers	Writers
• go beyond the text to extend their interpretations • share projects with classmates • reflect on the reading process • make connections to life and literature • value the piece of literature • feel success • want to read again	• produce the finished copy of their compositions • share their compositions with genuine audiences • reflect on the writing process • value the composition • feel success • want to write again

Adapted from Butler & Turbill, 1984.

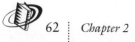

we also use problem-solving strategies to decide what our readers need as we construct meaning for them and for ourselves. Comparing reading to writing, Tierney and Pearson (1983) describe reading as a composing process because readers compose and refine meaning through reading much as writers do through writing.

There are practical benefits of connecting reading and writing. Reading contributes to students' writing development, and writing contributes to students' reading development. Shanahan (1988) has outlined seven instructional principles for relating reading and writing so that students develop a clear concept of literacy:

1. Involve students in reading and writing experiences every day.
2. Introduce the reading and writing processes in kindergarten.
3. Plan instruction that reflects the developmental nature of reading and writing.
4. Make the reading-writing connection explicit to students.
5. Emphasize both the processes and the products of reading and writing.
6. Emphasize the purposes for which students use reading and writing.
7. Teach reading and writing through authentic literacy experiences.

These principles are incorporated into a balanced literacy program in which students read and write books and learn to view themselves as readers and writers.

VISIT CHAPTER 2 ON THE COMPANION WEBSITE AT
www.prenhall.com/tompkins

- Complete a self-assessment to demonstrate your understanding of the concepts presented in this chapter
- Complete field activities that will help you expand your understanding of the middle-grade classroom and teaching the reading and writing processes
- Visit important web links related to teaching the reading and writing processes to middle-grade students
- Look into your state's standards as they relate to the reading and writing processes and the middle-grade student
- Communicate with other preservice teachers via the message board and discuss the issues involved in teaching the reading and writing processes to students in grades 4 to 8
- Complete CD-ROM activities that will help you make virtual field experience connections to teaching the reading and writing processes

Review

Teachers incorporate the five stages of the reading process—prereading, reading, responding, exploring, and applying—in planning for instruction. Teachers incorporate shared reading, guided reading, independent reading, buddy reading, and reading aloud to students in their instructional programs. Teachers also use the five stages of the writing process—prewriting, drafting, revising, editing, and publishing—in teaching students how to write and refine their compositions. The goal of both reading and writing is to construct meaning, and the two processes involve similar activities at each stage. Researchers recommend that teachers connect reading and writing because they are mutually supportive processes. The feature that follows presents guidelines for effectively teaching the reading and writing processes to students.

How Effective Teachers ...

Teach the Reading and Writing Processes

1. Teachers use the five-stage reading process to plan an integrated, balanced instructional program.
2. Teachers and students set purposes for reading.
3. Teachers incorporate different types of reading into their instructional program: shared reading, guided reading, independent reading, buddy reading, and reading aloud to students.
4. Students respond to their reading as they participate in grand conversations and write in reading logs.
5. Students reread the selection, examine the author's craft, and focus on words during the exploring stage.
6. Teachers teach skills and strategies during the exploring stage.
7. Teachers provide opportunities for students to complete self-selected application projects.
8. Teachers view reading and writing as processes of creating meaning.
9. Teachers teach students how to use each of the five stages in the writing process.
10. Teachers involve students in genuine and meaningful reading and writing activities.

Professional References

Applebee, A. N., & Langer, J. A. (1983). Instructional scaffolding: Reading and writing and natural language activities. *Language Arts, 60,* 168–175.

Bissex, G. L. (1980). *Gyns at wrk: A child learns to write and read.* Cambridge: Harvard University Press.

Blanton, W. E., Wood, K. D., & Moorman, G. B. (1990). The role of purpose in reading instruction. *The Reading Teacher, 43,* 486–493.

Britton, J., Burgess, T., Martin, N., McLeod, A., & Rosen, H. (1975). *The development of writing abilities (11–18).* London: Schools Council Publications.

Butler, A., & Turbill, J. (1984). *Towards a reading-writing classroom.* Portsmouth, NH: Heinemann.

Calkins, L. M. (1983). *Lessons from a child: On the teaching and learning of writing.* Portsmouth, NH: Heinemann.

Clay, M. M. (1991). *Becoming literate: The construction of inner control.* Portsmouth, NH: Heinemann.

Cochran-Smith, M. (1991). Word processing and writing in elementary classrooms: A critical review of related literature. *Review of Educational Research, 61,* 107–155.

DeGroff, L. (1990). Is there a place for computers in whole language classrooms? *The Reading Teacher, 43,* 568–572.

Depree, H., & Iversen, S. (1996). *Early literacy in the classroom: A new standard for young readers.* Bothell, WA: Wright Group.

Dyson, A. H. (1985). Second graders sharing writing: The multiple social realities of a literacy event. *Written Communication, 2,* 189–215.

Eeds, M., & Wells, D. (1989). Grand conversations: An exploration of meaning construction in literature study groups. *Research in the Teaching of English, 23,* 4–29.

Elley, W. B., Barham, I. H., Lamb, H., & Wyllie, M. (1976). The role of grammar in a secondary school English curriculum. *Research in the Teaching of English, 10,* 5–21.

Faigley, L., & Witte, S. (1981). Analyzing revision. *College Composition and Communication, 32,* 400–410.

Fitzgerald, J. (1989). Enhancing two related thought processes: Revision in writing and critical thinking. *The Reading Teacher, 43,* 42–48.

Fountas, I. C., & Pinnell, G. S. (1996). *Guided reading: Good first teaching for all children.* Portsmouth, NH: Heinemann.

Graves, D. H. (1976). Let's get rid of the welfare mess in the teaching of writing. *Language Arts, 53,* 645–651.

Graves, D. H. (1983). *Writing: Teachers and children at work.* Exeter, NH: Heinemann.

Hidi, S., & Hildyard, A. (1983). The comparison of oral and written productions in two discourse modes. *Discourse Processes, 6,* 91–105.

Holdaway, D. (1979). *The foundations of literacy.* Portsmouth, NH: Heinemann.

Hornsby, D., Sukarna, D., & Parry, J. (1986). *Read on: A conference approach to reading.* Portsmouth, NH: Heinemann.

King, M. (1985). Proofreading is not reading. *Teaching English in the Two-Year College, 12,* 108–112.

Langer, J. A. (1985). Children's sense of genre. *Written Communication, 2,* 157–187.

Murray, D. H. (1982). *Learning by teaching.* Montclair, NJ: Boynton/Cook.

Opitz, M. F., & Rasinski, T. V. (1998). *Good-bye round robin: 25 effective oral reading strategies.* Portsmouth, NH: Heinemann.

Peterson, R., & Eeds, M. (1990). *Grand conversations: Literature groups in action.* New York: Scholastic.

Rosenblatt, L. (1978). *The reader, the text, the poem: The transactional theory of the literary work.* Carbondale: Southern Illinois University Press.

Shanahan, T. (1988). The reading-writing relationship: Seven instructional principles. *The Reading Teacher, 41,* 636–647.

Smith, F. (1982). *Writing and the writer.* New York: Holt, Rinehart and Winston.

Sommers, N. (1982). Responding to student writing. *College Composition and Communication, 33,* 148–156.

Strickland, J. (1997). *From disk to hard copy: Teaching writing with computers.* Portsmouth, NH: Boynton/Cook.

Tierney, R. J. (1983). Writer-reader transactions: Defining the dimensions of negotiation. In P. L. Stock (Ed.), *Forum: Essays on theory and practice in the teaching of writing* (pp. 147–151). Upper Montclair, NJ: Boynton/Cook.

Tierney, R. J., & Pearson, P. D. (1983). Toward a composing model of reading. *Language Arts, 60,* 568–580.

Weaver, C. (1988). *Reading process and practice: From sociopsycholinguistics to whole language.* Portsmouth, NH: Heinemann.

Yaden, D. B., Jr. (1988). Understanding stories through repeated read-alouds: How many does it take? *The Reading Teacher, 41,* 556–560.

Children's Book References

Howe, D., & Howe, J. (1979). *Bunnicula: A rabbit-tale of mystery.* New York: Atheneum.

Lowry, L. (1993). *The giver.* Boston: Houghton Mifflin.

Lowry, L. (2000). *Gathering blue.* Boston: Houghton Mifflin.

MacLachlan, P. (1985). *Sarah, plain and tall.* New York: Harper & Row.

O'Neill, M. (1989). *Hailstones and halibut bones.* New York: Doubleday.

Rowling, J. K. (1998). *Harry Potter and the sorcerer's stone.* New York: Scholastic.

Van Allsburg, C. (1981). *Jumanji.* Boston: Houghton Mifflin.

Van Allsburg, C. (1993). *The sweetest fig.* Boston: Houghton Mifflin.

Viorst, J. (1977). *Alexander and the terrible, horrible, no good, very bad day.* New York: Atheneum.

chapter 3

Assessing Students' Literacy Development

- Which assessment tools do teachers use to monitor students' learning in reading and writing?

- How do students use portfolios?

- How do teachers assign grades?

Mrs. Peterson Conducts End-of-Quarter Conferences

During the last week of the third quarter, Mrs. Peterson conferences with each of her sixth graders to review and reflect upon their work during the quarter. Students bring their three language arts folders to their conferences. One folder contains students' work from a literature focus unit on *The Watsons Go to Birmingham—1963* (Curtis, 1995), the story of an African American family living in Flint, Michigan, whose lives change drastically after they go to visit Grandma in Alabama in the summer of 1963. During this 3-week unit, students:

- read and responded to the book
- focused on reading skills and strategies through a series of minilessons[C]
- put words on the class word wall[C]
- participated in other exploring activities
- created projects to apply their learning

Students kept track of assignments using an assignment sheet and placed all of their work in their unit folders. At the end of the unit, Mrs. Peterson collected the students' folders, reviewed the work in them, and assigned grades using the point system listed on the assignment sheets.

The second folder contains students' work from literature circles in which students divided into small groups and read and responded to one of six books. The groups chose from these books:

- *The Lion, the Witch and the Wardrobe* (Lewis, 1950)
- *Bunnicula: A Rabbit-Tale of Mystery* (Howe & Howe, 1979)
- *Shiloh* (Naylor, 1991)
- *The Midnight Fox* (Byars, 1968)
- *Julie of the Wolves* (George, 1972)
- *Hatchet* (Paulsen, 1987)

During this 2-week unit, students chose the book they wanted to read after Mrs. Peterson gave brief book talks[C] about each book. Then students divided into literature circle groups. Each group determined its own schedule for the 2 weeks. They read the book, conducted grand conversations[C], and wrote in reading logs[C]. During the first week, Mrs. Peterson taught daily minilessons to the whole class to review the structural elements of stories—plot, character, setting, point of view, and theme—and then asked students to think about how the author of the book they were reading used these elements and what the relative importance of each element was in the book. Mrs. Peterson moved from group to group as students read, responded, and discussed the story elements. At the end of the unit, each literature circle reported to the class on its book and about how the author wove the story elements together. Each group prepared a chart to highlight one of the story elements, and students presented the charts to the class during the sharing time. Students kept track of their work during this unit on assignment sheets, too. After the unit ended, Mrs. Peterson collected students' folders, reviewed them, and assigned grades using the point system listed on the assignment sheets.

To read more about how to implement reading and writing workshop, turn to Chapter 12.

During the last 4 weeks of the quarter, students are doing reading and writing workshop. They are choosing and reading books that interest them. Several are reading other books by Gary Paulsen or other books in C. S. Lewis's Chronicles of Narnia series. Mrs. Peterson encourages students to choose books that are a "good fit" for them—neither too hard nor too easy. During the 4-week unit, students are expected to read at least two books. Students document their reading by writing reactions in reading logs, and they conference once a week with Mrs. Peterson.

During writing workshop, students use the writing process to compose stories, poems, essays, how-to manuals, and other types of writing. Most students use a computer to print out their final copies, and then they bind them into books. Students are expected to complete two books during the 4-week unit. The weekly assignment sheets that Mrs. Peterson's students use during reading and writing workshop are shown in Figure 3-1.

Mrs. Peterson collects other types of assessment information about her students on a regular basis during this quarter. She does the following activities:

^C See the Compendium of Instructional Procedures, which follows Chapter 12, for more information on terms marked with the symbol ^C.

- listens to students read aloud excerpts of books they are reading and takes running records[C] to check their fluency
- reviews students' reading logs to check for comprehension
- listens to comments students make during grand conversations to monitor comprehension
- checks their understanding of story elements as they develop charts during literature circles
- analyzes spelling errors in students' reading logs and on students' rough drafts during editing conferences in writing workshop
- uses rubrics to assess students' compositions
- observes students and makes anecdotal notes each week to monitor their work habits and learning

Mrs. Peterson keeps a literacy folder for each student in which she places the assessment information she collects as well as notes from each conference. She brings these folders to the conferences at the end of the third quarter and will add to them the notes she makes during these conferences.

During the last week of the quarter, Mrs. Peterson conferences with each student. She spends approximately 15 minutes talking with each student about his or her work and making plans for the next quarter. She uses a conference sheet to take notes about these conferences, and both she and the student sign this sheet. A copy of the conference sheet is shown in Figure 3-2. At the conference, Mrs. Peterson accomplishes these things:

- reviews the student's work during the three units and the grades the student received
- examines the items the student has chosen to add to his or her portfolio and asks the student to explain why these items were chosen
- presents some of the assessment information she has collected about the student
- determines the student's reading and writing grades for the report card
- sets goals with the student for the next quarter
- completes the conference sheet

Figure 3-1   Record Sheets Used by Mrs. Peterson's Sixth Graders

Reading Workshop Weekly Assignment Sheet

Name _____   Week _____

1. What books did you read?

2. Did you write in your reading log?

3. Did you conference with Mrs. Peterson?

4. What did you do each day during Reading Workshop?

M	T	W	Th	F

Writing Workshop Weekly Assignment Sheet

Name _____   Week _____

1. What did you write?

2. Did you use the writing process?

☐ prewriting   ☐ drafting   ☐ revising   ☐ editing   ☐ publishing

3. Did you conference with Mrs. Peterson?

4. What did you do each day during Writing Workshop?

M	T	W	Th	F

Figure 3-2   Mrs. Peterson's Assessment Form

End-of-Quarter Conference Sheet

Name _____   Date _____

Unit 1

Unit 2

Unit 3

_____

Items Chosen for Portfolio

_____

Accomplishments

_____

Concerns and Issues

_____

Goals for the Next Quarter

_____

Grades   [   ] Reading   [   ] Writing   [   ] Work Habits

_____   _____
Student   Teacher

Assessment Tools

After the conference, students finish writing reflections to attach to the new portfolio items and then add them to their portfolios. They will take the rest of the unit folders home with their report cards. They will also take home a copy of the conference sheet with their goals for the next quarter.

Today Mrs. Peterson conferences with Ted. They go over his three unit folders and set goals for the next quarter. Ted explains that he really didn't like *The Watsons Go to Birmingham–1963* and didn't work as hard as he usually does. He says that the unit grade he received—B—reflects the grade he would give the book. Ted asks if he can choose five items from the other two units because he really doesn't have anything in this unit folder that he wants to put into his portfolio, and Mrs. Peterson agrees.

Ted participated in the literature circle reading *Bunnicula: A Rabbit-Tale of Mystery* (Howe & Howe, 1979), and he says that this is one of his favorite books. Through his reading log and participation in grand conversations, Ted demonstrated his comprehension of the story and his knowledge of story structure. Mrs. Peterson recalls that Ted asked her about humor and whether or not it was an element of story structure. He says that he now thinks humor is the glue that holds the story together because it is a combination of characters, plot, setting, and point of view. He tells Mrs. Peterson that he has concluded that he prefers stories like *Bunnicula* that are told in the first person.

Ted shows Mrs. Peterson his reading log, written from Harold the dog's viewpoint, and a chart he has made about the humor in the book that he wants to place in his portfolio. Mrs. Peterson agrees. Ted's grade for this literature circle unit is an A on his assignment sheet, and Ted agrees that he deserved it.

During reading workshop, Ted has continued reading Bunnicula sequels, including *Howliday Inn* (Howe, 1981), *The Celery Stalks at Midnight* (Howe, 1983), *Nighty-Nightmare* (Howe, 1987), and *Return to Howliday Inn* (Howe, 1992). He made an audiotape of his reading of excerpts from each of the books, and this is one of the items he wants to put in his portfolio. He is especially proud of the voices he used for each character. Mrs. Peterson praises Ted for his enthusiasm and the number of books he has read in reading workshop. His grade for reading workshop will be an A. She also asks if the Bunnicula books are challenging him, or if they are easy for him. He admits that they are "sort of easy" and agrees to choose some more challenging books during the next quarter.

During writing workshop, Ted has written and mailed a letter to author James Howe. He wants to put a copy of the letter in his portfolio, along with the response he is eagerly awaiting. He became interested in vampires through the Bunnicula books and has researched them. Now he is finishing a book he's calling "What's True and What's Not About Vampires," and he wants to place it in his portfolio, too. He is preparing his final copy on the computer so that it will be neat. Mrs. Peterson talks with Ted about his writing process. He talks about how he draws a series of small boxes representing each page on a sheet of paper during prewriting to plan his book. He tries to plan out the entire book in his head, and then he writes the book straight through, paying little attention to revising. He met with Mrs. Peterson several days earlier to edit his book, and although there were several places where he might have made some revisions, he didn't want to. Mrs. Peterson expresses her concern that he isn't giving adequate attention to revising and that this is affecting the quality of his writing. His grade for writing workshop will be a B.

During the last several minutes of the conference, Ted sets goals for the next quarter. For reading, he wants to read 10 books and agrees to choose more challenging ones. For writing, he reluctantly agrees to take time to revise his work. Because Ted enjoys word processing, Mrs. Peterson suggests that he do his rough drafts and final copies on the computer. Ted also volunteers that he would like to try his hand at writing a play during writing workshop in the next quarter. He had attended a play with his family and learned about scripts; now he wants to write one. He thinks that he may feature Bunnicula, Harold, and Chester in the play.

The conference ends, Ted returns to his desk, and Mrs. Peterson calls another student to the conference table.

ssessing students' literacy development is a difficult task. Although it may seem fairly easy to develop and administer a criterion-referenced test, tests often cannot measure the complex ways students in grades 4 through 8 use reading and writing. Tests in which students match characters and events or write the meanings of words do not measure comprehension very well, and a test on punctuation marks, for example, does not indicate students' ability to use punctuation marks correctly in their own writing. Instead, tests typically evaluate students' ability to add punctuation marks to a set of sentences created by someone else, or to proofread and spot punctuation errors in someone else's writing.

Traditional assessment reflects outdated views of how students learn to read and write, and it provides an incomplete picture of students' literacy abilities. Tests and other traditional assessment procedures focus on only a few aspects of what readers do as they read, and of what writers do as they write. Traditional reading assessment fails to use authentic reading tasks or to help teachers find ways to help students succeed.

Assessment is an integral part of teaching and learning in a balanced literacy program. The purpose of classroom assessment is to inform and influence instruction. Through assessment, teachers learn about their students, about themselves as teachers, and about the impact of the instructional program. Similarly, when students reflect on their learning and use self-assessment, they learn about themselves as learners and also about their learning. The feature on page 73 explains the role of assessment in a balanced program. As you continue reading this chapter, you will learn more about the ideas presented in the feature.

LITERACY ASSESSMENT TOOLS

Teachers use a variety of literacy assessment tools and procedures to monitor and document students' reading and writing development. These tools examine students' ability to identify words, read fluently, comprehend what they are reading, use the writing process, and spell words. Many of these tools are informal and created by teachers, but others have been developed, standardized, and published by researchers. Teachers also use assessment tools to diagnose struggling students' reading and writing problems. Many of these assessments are used with individual students, and even though it takes time to administer individual assessments, the information the teacher gains is useful and valuable. Giving a paper-and-pencil test to the entire class rarely provides much useful information. Teachers learn much more about their students as they listen to individual students read, watch individual students write, and talk with individual students about their reading and writing. Figure 3-3 presents guidelines for classroom assessment and describes how teachers can use assessment tools in their classrooms.

Assessing Students' Phonics Knowledge

Students learn strategies for segmenting, blending, and substituting sounds in words through phonemic awareness instruction and learn about consonant and vowel sounds and phonics generalizations through phonics instruction. Both phonemic awareness and phonics instruction are usually completed in the primary grades, but some older students who are struggling readers have not acquired all of the phonics skills. Cunningham (1990) developed The Names Test to measure older students' ability to decode unfamiliar words. She created a list of 50 first and last names, including both one-syllable and multisyllabic names representing many common phonics elements. Duffelmeyer, Kruse, Merkley, and Fyfe (1994) expanded the test to 70 names in order

The Role of Assessment in a Balanced Literacy Program

Component	Description
Reading	Teachers use assessment tools to regularly monitor students' reading development and plan for instruction. Informal reading inventories (IRIs) are used to determine students' reading levels.
Phonics and Other Skills	Teachers use The Names Test to assess struggling readers' ability to decode unfamiliar words, and running records to analyze students' word-identification errors.
Strategies	Teachers use observation to monitor students' use of reading and writing strategies.
Vocabulary	Teachers monitor students' use of vocabulary through classroom activities, including grand conversations and reading logs.
Comprehension	Teachers ask questions and listen to students' comments in grand conversations and read their reading log entries to assess students' comprehension. They also administer an IRI to determine students' reading levels.
Literature	Teachers assess students' literature experiences through response to literature activities, such as grand conversations and reading logs, and projects.
Content-Area Study	Teachers assess students' learning in content-area units through learning logs^C, classroom activities, and projects.
Oral Language	Teachers use an IRI to determine whether students can understand grade-level books that teachers read aloud.
Writing	Teachers assess students' writing using rubrics, and students can use rubrics to assess their own writing.
Spelling	Teachers assess students' stage of spelling development by categorizing the spelling errors they make in their writing. Many teachers also use weekly spelling tests to monitor students' growth in spelling.

to increase its validity. Teachers administer this test individually. They ask students to read the list of names, and they mark which names students read correctly and which they pronounce incorrectly. Then teachers analyze students' errors to determine which phonics elements they have not acquired in order to plan for future instruction.

Assessing Students' Fluency

Fluent readers read words accurately, rapidly, and automatically, and they read with expression. These readers are better able to comprehend what they read because they have the mental energy to focus on what they are reading. Teachers monitor students'

Figure 3-3   Guidelines for Classroom Assessment

1. Select Appropriate Assessment Tools
Teachers identify their purpose for assessment and choose an appropriate assessment tool. To gauge students' reading fluency, for example, teachers can do a running record, and to judge whether or not students are comprehending, they can examine students' reading logs and listen to their comments during a grand conversation.

2. Use a Variety of Assessment Tools
Teachers learn and then regularly use a variety of assessment tools that reflect current theories about how children learn and become literate, including running records, anecdotal notes, and reading logs.

3. Integrate Instruction and Assessment
Teachers use the results of assessment to inform their teaching. They observe and conference with students as they teach and supervise students during reading and writing activities. When students do not understand what teachers are teaching, teachers need to try other instructional procedures.

4. Focus on the Positive
Teachers focus on what students can do, not what they can't do. Too often, teachers want to diagnose students' problems and then remediate or "fix" these problems, but they should focus on how to facilitate students' development as readers and writers.

5. Examine Both Processes and Products
Teachers examine both the processes and the products of reading and writing. Teachers notice the strategies that students use as well as assess the products they produce through reading and writing.

6. Use Multiple Contexts
Teachers assess students' literacy development in a variety of contexts, including literature focus units, literature circles, reading and writing workshop, and thematic units. Multiple contexts are important because students often do better in one type of activity than another.

7. Work With Individual Students
In addition to making whole-class assessments, teachers make time to observe, conference with, and do other assessment procedures with individual students in order to develop clear understandings of the student's development as a reader or writer.

8. Encourage Self-Assessment
Students' reflection on and self-assessment of their progress in reading and writing should be an integral part of assessment.

fluency as they listen to students read aloud. They check to see that students read with appropriate speed, intonation, and pauses.

Teachers often take running records of students' oral reading to assess their word identification and reading fluency (Clay, 1985). With a running record, teachers calculate the percentage of words the student reads correctly and then analyze the miscues or errors. Teachers make a series of check marks on a sheet of paper as the student reads each word correctly. Teachers use other marks to indicate words that the student substitutes, repeats, mispronounces, or doesn't know. Although teachers can take the running record on a blank sheet of paper, it is much easier to duplicate the page or pages the student will read and take the running record next to or on top of the actual text. Making a copy of the text is especially important for older students who read more complex texts and read them more quickly than younger students do.

After identifying the words that the student read incorrectly, teachers calculate the percentage of words the student read correctly. Teachers use this percentage to determine whether the book or other reading material is too easy, too difficult, or appropriate for the student at this time. If the student reads 95% or more of the words correctly, the book is easy, or at the independent reading level for that child. If the student reads 90–94% of the words correctly, the book is at the student's instructional level. If the student reads fewer than 90% of the words correctly, the book is too difficult for the student to read: It is at the student's frustration level.

Running records are easy to take, although teachers need some practice before they are comfortable with the procedure. Figure 3-4 presents a running record done with a sixth grader in Mrs. Peterson's classroom. This student was reading the beginning of chapter 1 of *Bunnicula: A Rabbit-Tale of Mystery* (Howe & Howe, 1979) when the running record was taken.

Teachers categorize and analyze students' errors to identify patterns of error, as shown at the bottom of Figure 3-4. Then teachers use this information as they plan minilessons and other word-study activities.

Another way to analyze students' errors is called miscue analysis (K. S. Goodman, 1976). "Miscue" is another word for "error," and it suggests that students used the wrong cueing system to figure out the word. For example, if a student reads "Dad" for "Father," the error is meaning-related because the student overrelied on the semantic system. If a student reads "Feather" for "Father," the error is more likely graphophonic (or phonological), because the student overrelied on the beginning sound in the word and didn't evaluate whether the word made sense semantically. The Dad/Father and Feather/Father miscues are both syntactically correct because a noun was substituted for a noun. Sometimes, however, students substitute words that don't make sense syntactically. For example, if a student reads "tomorrow" for "through" in the sentence "Father walked through the door," the error doesn't make sense either semantically or syntactically, even though both words begin with *t*.

Teachers can categorize students' miscues or errors according to the semantic, graphophonic, and syntactic cueing systems in order to examine what word-identification

Figure 3-4 Running Record and Analysis

Text	Running Record
I shall never forget the first time I laid these	✓ *will / shall* ✓ ✓ ✓ ✓ ✓ ✓
now tired old eyes on our visitor. I had been	— / *now* *tie-red / tired* ✓ ✓ ✓ ✓ ✓ ✓ ✓
left home by the family with the admonition	✓ ✓ ✓ ✓ ✓ ✓ ✓ ⌐ / *admonition*
to take care of the house until they returned.	✓ ✓ ✓ ✓ ✓ ✓ ✓ ✓
That's something they always say to me when	✓ ✓ ✓ ✓ ✓ ✓ ✓
they go out: "Take care of the house, Harold.	✓ ✓ ✓ ✓ ✓ ✓ ✓
You're the watchdog." I think it's their	✓ ✓ *wa-wash-watchdog / watchdog* ✓ ✓ ✓
way of making up for not taking me with	✓ ✓ ✓ ✓ ✓ ✓ ✓
them. As if I wanted to go anyway. You can't	✓ ✓ ✓ ✓ ✓ ✓ ✓ ✓ ✓
lie down at the movies and still see the screen.	*lay / lie* ✓ ✓ ✓ ✓ ✓ ✓ ✓ ✓
And people think you're being impolite if you	— / *And* ✓ ✓ ✓ ✓ *impo-impo-⌐ / impolite* ✓ ✓
fall asleep and start to snore, or scratch	✓ ✓ ✓ ✓ ✓ ✓ *scrap / scratch*
yourself in public. No thank you, I'd rather	✓ ✓ ✓ ✓ ✓ ✓ ✓
be stretched out on my favorite rug	✓ *streaked / stretched* ✓ ✓ ✓ ✓
in front of a nice, whistling radiator.	✓ ✓ ✓ ✓ ✓ ✓ *radio / radiator*

Analysis

Total words	128
Errors	11
Accuracy rate	92% (instructional level)

This student read the text with interest, enthusiasm, and good expression. After reading, the student was able to talk about what he had read and to make predictions about Harold's role in the story. The errors are:

Substitution	will/shall	streaked/stretched
	lay/lie	radio/radiator
	scrap/scratch	
Omission	now	and
Mispronounced	tie-red/tired	
Teacher told	admonition	impolite
Prolonged decoding	watchdog	

Most of the errors were multisyllabic words, which the student was unable to break apart. A series of minilessons on breaking apart multisyllabic words to decode them is recommended for this student. The first two substitution errors did not affect meaning, and the two omission errors did not affect meaning either.

Reprinted with the permission of Atheneum Books for Young Readers, an imprint of Simon and Schuster Children's Publishing Division. From *Bunnicula: A Rabbit-Tale of Mystery* by Deborah Howe and James Howe. Text copyright © 1979 James Howe.

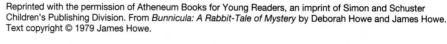
Assessment Tools

Teachers take running records to assess struggling readers' reading fluency.

strategies students are using. As they categorize the miscues, teachers should ask themselves these questions:

- Does the reader self-correct the miscue?
- Does the miscue change the meaning of the sentence?
- Is the miscue phonologically similar to the word in the text?
- Is the miscue acceptable within the syntax (or structure) of the sentence?

Errors that interfere with meaning and those that are syntactically unacceptable are the most serious because the student doesn't realize that reading should make sense. Errors can be classified and charted, as shown in Figure 3-5. These errors were taken from the sixth grader's running record presented in Figure 3-4. Only words that students mispronounce or substitute can be analyzed. Repetitions and omissions are not calculated.

Assessing Students' Comprehension

Comprehension is the goal of reading, and students demonstrate their comprehension in many ways. The comments they write in reading logs and make during grand conversations and instructional conversations[C] provide evidence. Children's interest in a book is sometimes an indicator, too: When children dismiss a book as "boring," they may really mean that it is confusing. Story retelling and the cloze procedure[C] are two informal assessment activities. In a story retelling, teachers ask students to

Figure 3-5 — Miscue Analysis of the Student's Errors From the Running Record

Student __Josh__ Date __Oct. 15__

Text __Bunnicula, a Rabbit-Tale of Mystery__

WORDS			SEMANTICS	PHONOLOGY	SYNTAX
Text	Student	Self-corrected?	Similar meaning?	Graphophonic similarity?	Syntactically acceptable?
shall	will		✓		✓
tired	tie-red			✓	
lie	lay		✓	✓	✓
scratch	scrap			✓	
stretched	streaked			✓	✓
radiator	radio			✓	✓

Analysis:

Josh seems to rely on graphophonic similarities—particularly beginning sounds—more than semantic similarities. Josh did not self-correct any words.

Assessment Tools

retell the story in their own words (Gambrell, Pfeiffer, & Wilson, 1985; Morrow, 1985). In the cloze procedure, teachers take an excerpt of 100 to 300 words from a selection students have read, delete every fifth word from the passage, and replace the deleted words with blanks. Then students read the passage and write the missing words in the blanks. Students use their knowledge of the topic, narrative or expository structure, English word order, and the meaning of the words in the sentences to guess the missing words.

Teachers use commercial tests called informal reading inventories (IRIs) to determine students' reading levels. The reading levels are expressed as grade-level scores—second-grade level or sixth-grade level, for example. The IRI is an individually administered reading test and is typically composed of graded word lists, graded passages from stories and informational books, and comprehension questions. This inventory can also be used to assess students' reading strengths and weaknesses.

The graded word lists consist of 10 to 20 words at each grade level, from first grade through eighth. Students read the lists of words until they reach a point when the words become too difficult for them; this indicates an approximate level for students to begin reading the graded reading passages. In addition, teachers can note the decoding skills that students use to identify words presented in isolation.

The graded reading passages are series of narrative and expository passages, ranging in difficulty. Students read these passages orally or silently and then answer a series of comprehension questions. The questions are designed to focus on main ideas, inferences, and vocabulary. Teachers use scoring sheets to record students' performance, and they analyze the results to see how readers use strategies in context, how they identify unknown words, and how they comprehend what they read.

Students' scores on the IRI can be used to calculate their independent, instructional, and frustration reading levels. At the independent level, students can read the text comfortably and without assistance. Students read books at this level for pleasure and during reading workshop. At the instructional level, students can read textbooks and trade books successfully with teacher guidance. Books selected for literature focus units and literature circles should be at students' instructional levels. At the frustration level, the reading materials are too difficult for students to read, so students often don't understand what they are reading. As the name implies, students become very frustrated when they attempt to read trade books and textbooks at this level. When books featured in literature focus units are too difficult for some students to read, teachers need to make provisions for these students; they can use shared reading, buddy reading, or read aloud to students.

IRIs are also used to identify students' listening capacity levels. Teachers read aloud passages written at or above students' frustration levels and ask students the comprehension questions. If students can answer the questions, they understand the passage. Teachers then know that students can comprehend books and texts at that level when they are read aloud and that students have the potential to improve their reading comprehension to this level.

Assessing Students' Vocabulary

Students need to understand the meaning of words they read; otherwise, they have problems decoding words and understanding what they are reading. Elementary students learn the meanings of 3,000 or more words each year, or 8–10 new words every day, and they learn most of them informally or without direct instruction (Stahl, 1999).

To learn more about vocabulary, see Chapter 5, "Learning About the Meanings of Words."

GUIDELINE 3

Struggling Readers Need Books at Their Reading Levels. Too often, struggling readers choose books that are too difficult for them, and when they attempt to read these "too hard" books, they give up in frustration. In contrast, when students read easier books—books at their independent reading level—they are more successful and view reading more positively. For reading workshop and other independent reading practice, students need books that they can read successfully. A quick way to determine whether a book is at a student's independent reading level is to ask the student to turn to any page in the book and read it aloud. If the student reads it fluently, chunking the words into phrases, and with good intonation and high word recognition (missing three words or less), the book is probably suitable. Teachers need to ensure that their classroom libraries are well stocked with interesting fiction and nonfiction books at their students' independent reading levels.

Teachers monitor students' use of new vocabulary as they talk and write about books they are reading for content-area units. In addition to determining whether students know the meaning of specific words, teachers consider whether students can differentiate among related words, such as *grumpy, surly, crabby, stern, rude, discourteous, snarling, grouchy,* and *waspish.* Another way to examine vocabulary knowledge is to ask students to name synonyms or antonyms of words. Teachers also monitor students' knowledge about root words and affixes. For example, if students know that *legible* means "readable," can they figure out what *illegible* means?

There are very few vocabulary tests available, so teachers often depend on informal measures of students' vocabulary knowledge. Some of the comprehension questions on informal reading inventories focus on the meanings of words, and students' answers to these items provide one indication of their vocabulary knowledge.

Assessing Students' Writing

Teachers assess both the process that students use as they write and the quality of students' compositions. They observe as students use the writing process to develop their compositions, and they conference with students as they revise and edit their writing. Teachers notice, for example, whether students use writing strategies to gather and organize ideas for writing, whether they use feedback from classmates in revising their writing, and whether they think about their audience when they write. They also have students keep all drafts of their compositions in writing folders so that they can document their writing processes.

As students' writing develops, it becomes more complex in a variety of ways. One of the most obvious changes is that it gets longer. Longer doesn't mean better, but as students write longer pieces, their writing often shows other signs of growth, too. Four ways that elementary students' writing develops are:

1. **Ideas.** Students' writing is creative, and they develop the main ideas and provide supporting details. Their writing is tailored to both purpose and audience.

ELL

English learners' writing is assessed using these same criteria, with special attention to their English grammar and vocabulary development.

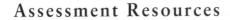

Assessment Resources

Comprehension

The traditional way to check on students' comprehension is to ask literal, inferential, and evaluative questions after reading, but there are better ways to assess comprehension. For example, teachers can examine students' entries in reading logs, note students' comments during grand conversations, and consider how students apply what they have learned in the projects they develop after reading. Two informal assessments are story retellings and the cloze procedure.

Teachers use informal reading inventories (IRIs) to diagnose students' reading levels. A variety of commercially published IRIs are available, including the following:

Analytical Reading Inventory (Woods & Moe, 1999)
Classroom Reading Inventory (Silvaroli, 2001)
English/Español Reading Inventory for the Classroom (Flynt & Cooter, 1999)
Qualitative Reading Inventory—3 (Leslie & Caldwell, 2001)

Other IRIs accompany basal reading series, and teachers can construct their own using textbooks or trade books written at each reading level.

2. ***Organization.*** Writers present ideas in a logical sequence and provide transitions between ideas. The composition is divided into paragraphs. For stories, students organize their writing into beginning, middle, and end, and for informational pieces, topic sentences clarify the organization.

3. ***Language.*** Students use words effectively, including figurative language. They choose language that is appropriate for purpose and audience. Students use Standard English word forms and sentence constructions. They also vary the types of sentences they write.

4. ***Mechanics.*** Students use correct spelling, punctuation, and capitalization. The composition is formatted appropriately for the writing form (e.g., letters, poems, plays, or stories), and the final copy is neat (Tompkins, 2004).

Teachers develop rubrics, or scoring guides, to assess students' growth as writers (Farr & Tone, 1994). Rubrics make the analysis of writing simpler and the assessment process more reliable and consistent. Rubrics may have 4, 5, or 6 levels, with descriptors related to ideas, organization, language, and mechanics at each level. Some rubrics are general and appropriate for almost any writing assignment, whereas others are designed for a specific writing assignment. Figure 3-6 presents two rubrics: One is a general 5-level rubric for middle-grade students, and the other is a 4-level rubric for assessing sixth graders' reports on ancient Egypt. In contrast to the general rubric, the report rubric addresses specific components that students were to include in their reports.

Elementary students, too, can learn to create rubrics to assess the quality of their writing. To be successful, they need to examine examples of other students' writing and determine the qualities that demonstrate strong, average, and weak papers; teachers need to model how to address the qualities at each level in the rubric. According to Skillings and Ferrell (2000), perhaps the most important outcome of teaching students to develop rubrics is that students develop metacognitive strategies and the ability to think about themselves as writers.

Figure 3-6 Two Rubrics for Assessing Students' Writing

Middle-Grade Writing Rubric
5 Exceptional Achievement
____ Creative and original ____ Clear organization ____ Precise word choice and figurative language ____ Sophisticated sentences ____ Essentially free of mechanical errors
4 Excellent Achievement
____ Some creativity, but more predictable than an exceptional paper ____ Definite organization ____ Good word choice but not figurative language ____ Varied sentences ____ Only a few mechanical errors
3 Adequate Achievement
____ Predictable paper ____ Some organization ____ Adequate word choice ____ Little variety of sentences and some run-on sentences ____ Some mechanical errors
2 Limited Achievement
____ Brief and superficial ____ Little organization ____ Imprecise language ____ Incomplete and run-on sentences ____ Many mechanical errors
1 Minimal Achievement
____ No ideas communicated ____ No organization ____ Inadequate word choice ____ Sentence fragments ____ Overwhelming mechanical errors

Assessment Tools

Both teachers and students can use rubrics to assess writing. They read the composition and highlight words and phrases in the rubric that best describe the composition. Usually words and phrases are marked in more than one level. The score is determined by examining the highlighted words and phrases and determining which level has the most highlighted words.

Figure 3-6   (continued)

Rubric for Assessing Reports on Ancient Egypt

4 Excellent Report

____ Three or more chapters with titles
____ Main idea clearly developed in each chapter
____ Three or more illustrations
____ Effective use of Egypt-related words in text and illustrations
____ Very interesting to read
____ Very few mechanical errors
____ Table of contents

3 Good Report

____ Three chapters with titles
____ Main idea somewhat developed in each chapter
____ Three illustrations
____ Some Egypt-related words used
____ Interesting to read
____ A few mechanical errors
____ Table of contents

2 Average Report

____ Three chapters
____ Main idea identified in each chapter
____ One or two illustrations
____ A few Egypt-related words used
____ Sort of interesting to read
____ Some mechanical errors
____ Table of contents

1 Poor Report

____ One or two chapters
____ Information in each chapter rambles
____ No illustrations
____ Very few Egypt-related words used
____ Hard to read and understand
____ Many mechanical errors
____ No table of contents

Assessment Resources

Writing

Teachers use rubrics to assess the quality of students' compositions. Some rubrics are general and can be used for almost any writing assignment, whereas others are designed for a specific writing assignment. Sometimes teachers use rubrics developed by school districts; at other times, they develop their own rubrics to assess the specific components and qualities they have stressed in their classrooms. Rubrics should have 4 to 6 achievement levels and address ideas, organization, language, and mechanics. Search the Internet for writing rubrics. Many examples of rubrics are available that have been developed by teachers, school districts, state departments of education, and publishers of educational materials.

Assessing Students' Spelling

The choices students make as they spell words are important indicators of their knowledge of both phonics and spelling. For example, a student who spells phonetically might spell *money* as *mune,* and other students who are experimenting with long vowels might spell the word as *monye* or *monie.* No matter how they spell the word, students are demonstrating what they know about phonics and spelling. Teachers classify and analyze the words students misspell in their writing to gauge students' level of spelling development and to plan for instruction. The steps in determining a student's stage of spelling development are explained in Figure 3-7. An analysis of a fifth grader's spelling development is shown in Figure 3-8.

To read more about the five stages of spelling development, turn to Chapter 4, "Refining Students' Print Skills."

Teachers can analyze the errors in students' compositions, analyze students' errors on weekly spelling tests, or administer diagnostic tests such as Bear's Elementary Qualitative Spelling Inventory for grades K–6 and his Upper Level Qualitative Spelling Inventory for grades 6–8 (Bear, Invernizzi, Templeton, & Johnston, 2000). These tests include 20–25 spelling words listed according to difficulty and can easily be administered to small groups or whole classes. Other spelling tests are available to provide grade-level scores.

Assessing Students' Attitudes and Motivation

Students' attitude and motivation affect their success in learning to read and write (Walberg & Tsai, 1985). Students who view themselves as successful readers and writers are more likely to be successful, and students whose families value literacy are more likely to be motivated to read and write.

Teachers conference with students and parents to understand students' reading and writing habits at home, their interests and hobbies, and their view of themselves as readers and writers. Teachers can help students select appropriate books when they know more about them and their interests, and they can get parents more involved in reading activities at home.

Researchers have developed several survey instruments that teachers can use to assess students' attitudes about reading and writing. Two surveys designed for third through sixth graders are the Reader Self-Perception Scale (Henk & Melnick, 1995)

Figure 3-7

Steps in Determining a Student's Stage of Spelling Development

1. Choose Writing Samples
Teachers choose one or more writing samples written by a single student to analyze. In the middle grades, samples should total at least 100 words. Teachers must be able to decipher most words in the sample in order to analyze it.

2. Identify Misspelled Words
Teachers read the writing samples and identify the misspelled words and the words the student was trying to spell. When necessary, teachers check with the student who wrote the composition to determine the intended word.

3. Make a Spelling Analysis Chart
Teachers draw a chart with five columns, one for each of the stages of spelling development, at the bottom of the student's writing sample or on another sheet of paper.

4. Categorize the Student's Misspelled Words
Teachers classify the student's spelling errors according to the stage of development. They list each spelling error in one of the stages, ignoring proper nouns, capitalization errors, and grammar errors. Teachers often ignore young children's poorly formed letters or reversed letter forms, but these are significant errors when they are made by older students. They write both the student's spelling and the correct spelling in parentheses to make the analysis easier.

5. Tally the Errors
Teachers count the number of errors in each column to determine the stage with the most errors. The stage with the most errors is the student's current stage of spelling development.

6. Identify Topics for Instruction
Teachers examine the misspelled words to identify spelling concepts for instruction, such as vowel patterns, possessives, homophones, syllabication, and cursive handwriting skills.

Assessment Resources

Spelling
Teachers monitor students' spelling development by examining misspelled words in the compositions that students write. They classify students' spelling according to the five stages of spelling development and plan instruction on the basis of this analysis. Teachers also examine students' misspellings in weekly spelling tests and in diagnostic tests, including the following:

Developmental Spelling analysis (Ganske, 2000)
Elementary Qualitative Spelling Inventory (Grades K–6) (Bear et al., 2000)
Upper Level Qualitative Spelling Inventory (Grades 6–8) (Bear et al., 2000)
Qualitative Inventory of Spelling Development (Henderson, 1990)

After teachers mark spellings on tests as correct or incorrect, they analyze students' errors to determine which skills students use correctly, which skills they are using but confusing, and which skills they are not yet using. Then teachers plan instruction based on the test results.

Figure 3-8   An Analysis of a Fifth Grader's Spelling

My mom is specil to me. She gave me everething when I was small. When she gets some mony she byes me pizza. My mom is specil to me becuze she taks me anywhere I want to get some nike shose. She byes me some.

My mom changed my life. She is so nice and loveble. She cares what I am doing in shool. She cares about my grades. I will do anything for mom. I would get a ceriar. Maybe I could be a polisman. That is why I think she is so nice.

Emergent	Letter Name	Within-Word	Syllables and Affixes	Derivational Relations
	TAKS/takes	BECUZE/because	SPECIL/special	
		SHOSE/shoes	EVERETHING/everything	
		SHOOL/school	MONY/money	
		CERIAR/career	BYES/buys	
		POLISMAN/policeman	SPECIL/special	
			BYES/buys	
			LOVEBLE/loveable	

Data Analysis		Conclusions
Emergent	0	Eugenio's spelling is at the syllables and affixes stage. Based on this sample, this instruction is suggested:
Letter Name	1	• dividing words into syllables
Within Word	5	• compound words
Syllables and Affixes	7	• using *y* at the end of 1- and 2-syllable words
Derivational Relations	0	• homophones
Correctly spelled words	82	• suffixes
Total words in sample	95	

and the Writer Self-Perception Scale (Bottomley, Henk, & Melnick, 1997/1998). On these surveys, students respond to statements such as "I think I am a good reader" and "I write better than my classmates do" using a 5-level Likert scale (responses range from "strongly agree" to "strongly disagree"). Then teachers score students' responses and interpret the results to determine both overall and specific attitude levels.

McKenna and Kear (1990) developed the Elementary Reading Attitude Survey to assess first- through sixth-grade students' attitudes toward reading in school and reading for fun. The test consists of 20 questions about reading that begin with the stem "How do you feel . . . ?" Students respond by marking one of four pictures of Garfield, the cartoon cat. Each picture of Garfield depicts a different emotional state, ranging from positive to negative. This survey enables teachers to quickly estimate students' attitudes toward reading.

Teachers should consider ELL students' attitudes toward English and their English-speaking classmates and teachers as well as their motivation to learn to speak, read, and write English.

Monitoring Students' Progress

Teachers monitor students' learning day by day, and they use the results of their monitoring to make instructional decisions (Baskwill & Whitman, 1988; Winograd & Arrington, 1999). As they monitor students' learning, teachers learn about their students, about themselves as teachers, and about the impact of the instructional program. Four ways to monitor students' progress are:

1. **Observe students as they read and write.** Effective teachers are "kid watchers," a term Yetta Goodman (1978) coined and defined as "direct and informal observation of students" (p. 37). To be effective kid watchers, teachers must understand how children

---

Assessment Resources

Attitudes and Motivation

Students' attitudes, values, and motivation play a significant role in their literacy learning. Teachers monitor students' attitudes informally as they talk with students about books they are reading and compositions they are writing.

Researchers have developed instruments that measure students' perceptions of themselves as readers and writers. They probe students' past literacy successes, students' comparison of themselves with their peers, input students have received from teachers and classmates, and feelings students experience during reading and writing. Five surveys are:

Elementary Reading Attitude Survey (McKenna & Kear, 1990)
Motivation to Read Profile (Gambrell, Palmer, Codling, & Mazzoni, 1996)
Reader Self-Perception Scale (Henk & Melnick, 1995)
Writer Self-Perception Scale (Bottomley et al., 1997/1998)
Writing Attitude Survey (Kear, Coffman, McKenna, & Ambrosio, 2000)

All five instruments are readily available because they have been published in *The Reading Teacher.*

learn to read and write. Some observation times should be planned when the teacher focuses on particular students and makes anecdotal notes about their involvement in literacy events. The focus is on what students do as they read or write, not on whether they are behaving properly or working quietly. Of course, little learning can occur in disruptive situations, but during these observations, the focus is on literacy, not behavior.

2. *Take anecdotal notes of literacy events.* Teachers write brief notes as they observe students, and the most useful notes describe specific events, report rather than evaluate, and relate the events to other information about the student (Rhodes & Nathenson-Mejia, 1992). Teachers make notes about students' reading and writing activities, the questions students ask, and the strategies and skills they use fluently or indicate confusion about. These records document students' growth and pinpoint problem areas for future minilessons or conferences. Mrs. Peterson's anecdotal notes about sixth-grade students in the literature circle reading *Bunnicula: A Rabbit-Tale of Mystery* (Howe & Howe, 1979) appear in Figure 3-9.

3. *Conference with students.* Teachers talk with students to monitor their progress in reading and writing activities as well as to set goals and help students solve problems. Figure 3-10 lists seven types of conferences that teachers have with students. Often these conferences are brief and impromptu, held at students' desks as the teacher moves around the classroom. At other times, the conferences are planned and students meet with the teacher at a designated conference table, as Mrs. Peterson did with her sixth graders in the vignette at the beginning of this chapter.

4. *Collect students' work samples.* Teachers have students collect their work in folders to document learning. Work samples might include reading logs, audiotapes of students' reading, photos of projects, videotapes of puppet shows and oral presentations, and books students have written. Students often choose some of these work samples to place in their portfolios.

IMPLEMENTING PORTFOLIOS IN THE CLASSROOM

Portfolios are systematic and meaningful collections of artifacts documenting students' literacy development over a period of time (Graves & Sunstein, 1992; Porter & Cleland, 1995; Tierney, Carter, & Desai, 1991). These collections are dynamic and reflect students' day-to-day reading and writing activities as well as across-the-curriculum activities. Students' work samples provide "windows" on the strategies they use as readers and writers. Not only do students select pieces to be placed in their portfolios, they also learn to establish criteria for their selections. Because of students' involvement in selecting pieces for their portfolios and reflecting on them, portfolio assessment respects students and their abilities. Portfolios help students, teachers, and parents see patterns of growth from one literacy milestone to another in ways that are not possible with other types of assessment.

Why Are Portfolio Programs Worthwhile?

There are many reasons why portfolio programs complement balanced reading programs. The most important one is that students become more involved in the assessment of their work and more reflective about the quality of their reading and writing. Other benefits include the following:

Figure 3-9   Mrs. Peterson's Anecdotal Notes
About a Literature Circle

March 2
Met with the *Bunnicula* literature circle as they started reading the book. They have
their reading, writing, and discussion schedule set. Sari questioned how a dog
could write the book. We reread the Editor's Note. She asked if Harold really wrote
the book. She's the only one confused in the group. Is she always so literal? Mario
pointed out that you have to know that Harold supposedly wrote the book to
understand the first-person viewpoint of the book. Talked to Sari about fantasy.
Told her she'll be laughing out loud as she reads this book. She doubts it.

March 3
Returned to *Bunnicula* literature circle for first grand conversation, especially to
check on Sari. Annie, Mario, Ted, Rod, Laurie, and Belinda talked about their pets
and imagine them taking over their homes. Sari is not getting into the book. She
doesn't have any pets and can't imagine the pets doing these things. I asked if she
wanted to change groups. Perhaps a realistic book would be better. She says no.
Is that because Ted is in the group?

March 5
The group is reading chapters 4 and 5 today. Laurie asks questions about white
vegetables and vampires. Rod goes to get an encyclopedia to find out about
vampires. Mario asks about DDT. Everyone—even Sari—involved in reading.

March 8
During a grand conversation, students compare the characters Harold and Chester.
The group plans to make a Venn diagram comparing the characters for the sharing
on Friday. Students decide that character is the most important element, but Ted
argues that humor is the most important element in the story. Other students say
humor isn't an element. I asked what humor is a reaction to—characters or plot? I
checked journals and all are up to date.

March 10
The group has finished reading the book. I share sequels from the class library. Sari
grabs one to read. She's glad she stayed with the book. Ted wants to write his own
sequel in writing workshop. Mario plans to write a letter to James Howe.

March 12
Ted and Sari talk about *Bunnicula* and share related books. Rod and Mario share
the Venn diagram of characters. Annie reads her favorite part, and Laurie shows
her collection of rabbits. Belinda hangs back. I wonder if she has been involved. I
need to talk to her.

- Students feel ownership of their work.
- Students become more responsible about their work.
- Students set goals and are motivated to work toward accomplishing them.
- Students reflect on their accomplishments.
- Students make connections between learning and assessing.
- Students' self-esteem is enhanced.
- Students recognize the connection between process and product.
- Portfolios eliminate the need to grade all student work.

Figure 3-10   Seven Types of Conferences

1. On-the-Spot Conferences
The teacher visits briefly with students at their desks to monitor some aspect of the students' work or to check on progress. These conferences are brief; the teacher may spend less than a minute at each student's desk.

2. Prereading or Prewriting Conferences
The teacher and student make plans for reading or writing at the conference. At a prereading conference, they may talk about information related to the book, difficult concepts or vocabulary words related to the reading, or the reading log the student will keep. At a prewriting conference, they may discuss possible writing topics or how to narrow down a broad topic.

3. Revising Conferences
A small group of students meets with the teacher to get specific suggestions about revising their compositions. These conferences offer student writers an audience to provide feedback on how well they have communicated.

4. Book Discussion Conferences
Students meet with the teacher to discuss the book they have read. They may share reading log entries, discuss plot or characters, compare the story to others they have read, or make plans to extend their reading.

5. Editing Conferences
The teacher reviews students' proofread compositions and helps them correct spelling, punctuation, capitalization, and other mechanical errors.

6. Minilesson Conferences
The teacher meets with students to explain a procedure, strategy, or skill (e.g., writing a table of contents, using the visualization strategy when reading, capitalizing proper nouns).

7. Assessment Conferences
The teacher meets with students after they have completed an assignment or project to talk about their growth as readers or writers. Students reflect on their competencies and set goals.

Portfolios are especially effective for English language learners because the artifacts reflect students' learning in ways tests often cannot.

- Portfolios are used in student and parent conferences.
- Portfolios complement the information provided in report cards.

Rolling Valley Elementary School in Springfield, Virginia, implemented a portfolio program schoolwide several years ago. The students overwhelmingly reported that by using portfolios, they were better able to show their parents what they were learning and also better able to set goals for themselves (Clemmons, Laase, Cooper, Areglado, & Dill, 1993). The teachers also reported that by using portfolios, they were able to assess their students more thoroughly, and their students were better able to see their own progress.

Collecting Work in Portfolios

Portfolios are folders, large envelopes, or boxes that hold students' work. Teachers often have students label and decorate large folders and then store them in plastic crates or large cardboard boxes. Students date and label items as they place them in their portfolios, and they often attach notes to the items to explain the context for the ac-

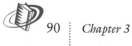

Students conference with the teacher about items they select for their portfolios.

tivity and why they selected this particular item. Students' portfolios should be stored in the classroom in a place where they are readily accessible; students like to review their portfolios periodically and add new pieces to them.

Students usually choose the items to place in their portfolios within the guidelines the teacher provides. Some students submit the original piece of work; others want to keep the original, so they place a copy in the portfolio instead. In addition to the reading and writing samples that can go directly into portfolios, students also record oral language and drama samples on audiotapes and videotapes to place in their portfolios. (To learn more about videotape portfolios, check the Technology Link on page 93.) Large art and writing projects can be photographed, and the photographs can be placed in the portfolio. The following types of student work might be placed in a portfolio:

"All About . . . " books
alphabet books[C]
autobiographies
biographies
books
choral readings[C] (on audiotape)
clusters[C]
drawings, diagrams, and charts
learning log[C] entries
letters to pen pals, businesses, and authors (copies, because the originals have
    been sent)
lists of books read
newspaper articles
open-mind portraits[C]
oral reading (on audiotape or videotape)
oral reports (on videotape)
poems
projects

puppets (in photographs)
puppet shows (on videotape)
quickwrites[C]
readers theatre[C] presentations (on audiotape or videotape)
reading log entries
reports
simulated journal entries
stories
story boards[C]

This variety of work samples reflects the students' literacy programs. Samples from literature focus units, literature circles, reading and writing workshop, basal reading programs, and content-area units should be included.

Many teachers collect students' work in folders, and they assume portfolios are basically the same as work folders; however, the two types of collections differ in several important ways. Perhaps the most important difference is that portfolios are student-oriented, whereas work folders are usually teachers' collections. Students choose which samples will be placed in portfolios, but teachers often place all completed assignments in work folders (Clemmons et al., 1993). Next, portfolios focus on students' strengths, not their weaknesses. Because students choose items for portfolios, they select samples that best represent their literacy development. Another difference is that portfolios involve reflection (D'Aoust, 1992). Through reflection, students pause and become aware of their strengths as readers and writers. They also use their work samples to identify the literacy procedures, concepts, skills, and strategies they already know and the ones they need to focus on.

Involving Students in Self-Assessment

A portfolio is not just a collection of work samples; instead, it is a vehicle for engaging students in self-evaluation and goal setting (Clemmons et al., 1993). Students can learn to reflect on and assess their own reading and writing activities and their development as readers and writers (Stires, 1991). Teachers begin by asking students to think about their reading and writing in terms of contrasts. For reading, students identify the books they have read that they liked most and least, and ask themselves what these choices suggest about themselves as readers. They also identify what they do well in reading and what they need to improve about their reading. In writing, students make similar contrasts. They identify the compositions they thought were their best and others that were not so good, and think about what they do well when they write and what they need to improve. By making these comparisons, students begin to reflect on their literacy development. Teachers use minilessons and conferences to talk with students about the characteristics of good readers and writers. In particular, they discuss:

- what fluent reading is
- what reading skills and strategies students use
- how students demonstrate their comprehension
- how students value books they have read
- what makes a good project to extend reading
- what makes an effective piece of writing
- what writing skills and strategies students use
- how to use writing rubrics
- how the effective use of mechanical skills is a courtesy to readers

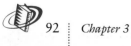

Technology Link

Videotape Portfolios

Teachers can document students' learning using a camcorder in ways that reading logs, lists of books students have read, and conference notes cannot (Herrell & Fowler, 1998). The saying that "a picture is worth a thousand words" really is true! Students each bring a blank VCR tape at the beginning of the school year for their video portfolios. A sheet of paper is attached to each tape case to note dates and topics of the tapings. This sheet becomes the table of contents for the videotape.

When a camcorder is introduced, students are distracted and "mug" for the camera, but after a few days they get used to it. Using a camcorder frequently is the best way to acclimate students. The teacher and student videographers film students as they are involved in a variety of literacy activities:

- Record individual students reading aloud at the beginning of the year and at the end of each grading period.
- Film students during reading and writing workshop.
- Document student-teacher conferences.
- Film oral performances, including puppet shows, readers theatre presentations, book talks, and reports.
- Include group activities such as grand conversations and read-arounds.
- Document students' work on projects—especially projects such as dioramas, book boxes, and murals—that can't be saved in traditional portfolio folders.

Keeping a camcorder in the classroom with batteries charged allows students and the teacher to capture ongoing classroom activities.

Creating video portfolios is too heavy a burden if teachers do all of the videotaping. Students—even second and third graders—can learn how to use the camcorder. Teachers identify guidelines for videotaping and establish routines for regular taping. They also experiment to determine how to get the best sound quality for individual and group activities, how long to film episodes, and how to transition between episodes. Aides and parent volunteers can be enlisted to assist, too.

Video portfolios often have jerky starts and abrupt stops, and sometimes the audio is difficult to hear, but nevertheless they are a meaningful record of students' literacy development and reading and writing activities spanning a school year. Even though video portfolios are rarely polished productions, they are valuable documentation for students, teachers, and parents.

As students learn about what it means to be effective readers and writers, they acquire the tools they need to reflect on and evaluate their own reading and writing. They learn how to think about themselves as readers and writers and acquire the vocabulary to use in their reflections, such as "goal," "strategy," and "rubric."

Students write notes on items they choose to put into their portfolios. In these self-assessments, students explain their reasons for the selection and identify strengths and accomplishments in their work. In some classrooms, students write their reflections and other comments on index cards, and in other classrooms, they design special comment sheets that they attach to the items in their portfolios. A fifth grader's self-assessment of her simulated journal, written from the viewpoint of Benjamin Franklin, is shown in Figure 3-11.

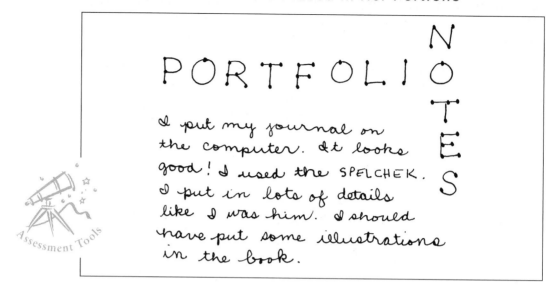

Clemmons et al. (1993) recommend collecting baseline reading and writing samples at the beginning of the school year and then conducting portfolio review conferences with students at the end of each grading period. At these conferences, the teacher and the student talk about the items placed in the portfolio and the self-assessments the student has written. Together they also set goals for the next grading period. Students talk about what they want to improve or what they want to accomplish during the next grading period, and these points become their goals.

Self-assessment can also be used for an assessment at the end of the school year. Coughlan (1988) asked his seventh-grade students to "show me what you have learned about writing this year" and "explain how you have grown as a written language user, comparing what you knew in September to what you know now" (p. 375). These upper-grade students used a process approach to develop and refine their compositions, and they submitted all drafts with their final copies. Coughlan examined both the content of students' compositions and the strategies they used in thinking through the assignments and writing their responses. He found this "test" to be a very worthwhile project because it "forced the students to look within themselves . . . to realize just how much they had learned" (p. 378). Moreover, students' compositions verified that they had learned about writing and that they could articulate that learning.

Showcasing Students' Portfolios

At the end of the school year, many teachers organize "Portfolio Share Days" to celebrate students' accomplishments and to provide an opportunity for students to share their portfolios with classmates and the wider community (Porter & Cleland, 1995). Often family members, local businesspeople, school administrators, local politicians, college students, and others are invited to attend. Students and community members form small groups, and students share their portfolios, pointing out their accomplishments and strengths. This activity is especially useful in involving community members in the school and showing them the types of literacy activities in which students are involved as well as how students are becoming effective readers and writers.

These sharing days also help students accept responsibility for their own learning—especially those students who have not been as motivated as their classmates. When less motivated students listen to their classmates talk about their work and how they have grown as readers and writers, these students often decide to work harder the next year.

ASSIGNING GRADES

Assigning grades is one of the most difficult responsibilities placed on teachers. "Grading is a fact of life," according to Donald Graves (1983, p. 93), but he adds that teachers should use grades to encourage students, not to hinder their achievement. The assessment procedures described in this chapter encourage students because they document what students can do as they read and write. Reviewing and translating this documentation into grades is the difficult part.

One way for teachers to monitor students' progress and grade their achievements is to use assignment sheets. Teachers create the assignment sheet as they plan the unit, make copies for each student, and then distribute them at the beginning of the unit. All assignments are listed on the sheet along with how they will be graded. These sheets can be developed for any type of unit—literature focus units, literature circles, reading and writing workshop, and content-area units. Teachers can also create assignment sheets to use with literacy centers.

An assignment sheet for a fifth-grade unit on *The Sign of the Beaver* (Speare, 1983) is shown in Figure 3-12. Students receive a copy of the assignment sheet at the beginning of the unit and keep it in their unit folders. Then, as they complete the assignments, they check them off, and it is easy for the teacher to make periodic checks to monitor students' progress. At the end of the unit, the teacher collects the unit folders and grades the work.

Assignments can be graded as "done" or "not done," or they can be graded for quality. Teachers of middle- and upper-grade students often assign points to each activity on the assignment sheet so that the total point value for the unit is 100 points. Activities that involve more time and effort earn more points. The maximum number of points possible for each assignment is listed in parentheses in Figure 3-12.

Checklists have the power to enhance student learning and simplify assessment (Kuhs, Johnson, Agruso, & Monrad, 2001). Students tend to be more successful when they understand what is expected of them, and when teachers develop and distribute assignment sheets and other checklists at the beginning of a unit, students are much more likely to understand what is expected of them. Later, when teachers grade the students' assignments, the grading is easier because teachers have already identified the criteria for grading. Grading is fairer, too, because teachers use the same criteria to grade all students' assignments.

Figure 3-12   An Assignment Sheet for a Literature Focus Unit

Checklist for *The Sign of the Beaver*

Name _____   Date _____

Student's Check   Teacher's Grade

_____   1. Read *The Sign of the Beaver.*   _____

_____   2. Make a map of Matt's journey in 1768. (10)   _____

_____   3. Keep a simulated journal as Matt or Attean. (20)   _____

_____   4. Do a word sort by characters. (5)   _____

_____   5. Listen to Elizabeth George Speare's taped interview and do a quickwrite about her. (5)   _____

_____   6. Do an open-mind portrait about one of the characters. (10)   _____

_____   7. Make a Venn diagram to compare/contrast Matt or Attean with yourself. (10)   _____

_____   8. Contribute to a model of the Indian village or the clearing.   _____

_____   9. Write a sequel or do another project. (20)   _____

My project is _____

_____

_____

_____

_____   10. Read other books from the text set. (10)   _____

_____   11. Write a self-assessment about your work, behavior, and effort in this unit. (10)   _____

TOTAL POINTS   _____

Assessment Tools

VISIT CHAPTER 3 ON THE COMPANION WEBSITE AT
www.prenhall.com/tompkins

- Complete a self-assessment to demonstrate your understanding of the concepts presented in this chapter
- Complete field activities that will help you expand your understanding of the middle-grade classroom and assessing students' literacy development
- Visit important web links related to assessing the literacy development of middle-grade students
- Look into your state's standards as they relate to assessing literacy development and the middle-grade student
- Communicate with other preservice teachers via the message board and discuss the issues of assessing literacy development of students in grades 4 to 8

Review

Assessment is more than testing; it is an essential part of teaching and learning. In classroom assessment, teachers examine both the processes of reading and writing and the artifacts that students produce. Teachers use a variety of literacy assessment tools to monitor students' progress, determine students' reading levels, assess students' comprehension, document students' growth as writers, and analyze students' spelling development. Teachers help students collect their work samples in portfolios and document their literacy development. Teachers use assignment sheets to monitor students' work during literature focus units, literature circles, reading and writing workshop, and thematic units, and to assign grades. Effective practices for assessing students' literacy learning are reviewed in the feature that follows.

How Effective Teachers . . .
Assess Students' Literacy Development

1. Teachers use a variety of informal and formal assessment tools to assess students' literacy development.
2. Teachers take running records to assess students' reading fluency.
3. Teachers use informal reading inventories to determine students' comprehension levels.
4. Teachers use rubrics to assess the ideas, organization, vocabulary, style, and mechanics in students' compositions.
5. Teachers analyze students' spellings to determine their stages of development and plan for instruction based on students' developmental levels.
6. Teachers conference with students about their attitudes and motivation for reading and writing, and they also use surveys to better understand their students.
7. Teachers monitor students' learning using observation and anecdotal notes, conferences, checklists, and collections of students' work samples.
8. Teachers have students choose work samples for portfolios to document their literacy development.
9. Teachers encourage students to self-assess their work samples and set goals for future learning.
10. Teachers distribute assignment sheets during units so that students understand how they will be assessed and graded.

Professional References

Baskwill, J., & Whitman, P. (1988). *Evaluation: Whole language, whole child*. New York: Scholastic.

Bear, D. R., Invernizzi, M., Templeton, S., & Johnston, F. (2000). *Words their way: Word study for phonics, vocabulary, and spelling instruction* (2nd ed.). Upper Saddle River, NJ: Merrill/Prentice Hall.

Bottomley, D. M., Henk, W. A., & Melnick, S. A. (1997/1998). Assessing children's views about themselves as writers using the Writer Self-Perception Scale. *The Reading Teacher, 51*, 286–296.

Clay, M. M. (1985). *The early detection of reading difficulties: A diagnostic survey with recovery procedures*. Portsmouth, NH: Heinemann.

Clay, M. M. (1993). *An observational survey of early literacy assessment.* Portsmouth, NH: Heinemann.

Clemmons, J., Laase, L., Cooper, D., Areglado, N., & Dill, M. (1993). *Portfolios in the classroom: A teacher's sourcebook.* New York: Scholastic.

Coughlan, M. (1988). Let the students show us what they know. *Language Arts, 65,* 375–378.

Cunningham, P. (1990). The Names Test: A quick assessment of decoding ability. *The Reading Teacher, 44,* 124–129.

D'Aoust, C. (1992). Portfolios: Process for students and teachers. In K. B. Yancy (Ed.), *Portfolios in the writing classroom* (pp. 39–48). Urbana, IL: National Council of Teachers of English.

Duffelmeyer, F. A., Kruse, A. E., Merkley, D. J., & Fyfe, S. A. (1994). Further validation and enhancement of The Names Test. *The Reading Teacher, 48,* 118–128.

Farr, R., & Tone, B. (1994). *Portfolio and performance assessment.* Orlando: Harcourt Brace.

Flynt, E. S., & Cooter, R. B., Jr. (1999). *English-Español reading inventory for the classroom.* Upper Saddle River, NJ: Merrill/Prentice Hall.

Gambrell, L. B., Palmer, B. M., Codling, R. M., Mazzoni, S. A. (1996). Assessing motivation to read. *The Reading Teacher, 49,* 518–533.

Gambrell, L. B., Pfeiffer, W., & Wilson, R. (1985). The effects of retelling upon reading comprehension and recall of text information. *Journal of Educational Research, 78,* 216–220.

Ganske, K. (2000). *Word journeys: Assessment-guided phonics, spelling, and vocabulary instruction.* New York: Guilford Press.

Goodman, K. S. (1976). Behind the eye: What happens in reading. In H. Singer & R. B. Ruddell (Eds.), *Theoretical models and processes of reading* (2nd ed., pp. 470–496). Newark, DE: International Reading Association.

Goodman, Y. M. (1978). Kid watching: An alternative to testing. *National Elementary Principals Journal, 57,* 41–45.

Graves, D. H. (1983). *Writing: Teachers and students at work.* Portsmouth, NH: Heinemann.

Graves, D. H., & Sunstein, B. S. (Eds.). (1992). *Portfolio portraits.* Portsmouth, NH: Heinemann.

Henderson, E. (1990). *Teaching spelling.* Boston: Houghton Mifflin.

Henk, W. A., & Melnick, S. A. (1995). The Reader Self-Perception Scale (RSPS): A new tool for measuring how children feel about themselves as readers. *The Reading Teacher, 48,* 470–482.

Herrell, A. L., & Fowler, J. P., Jr. (1998). *Camcorder in the classroom: Using the videocamera to enliven curriculum.* Upper Saddle River, NJ: Merrill/Prentice Hall.

Kear, D. J., Coffman, G. A., McKenna, M. C., & Ambrosio, A. L. (2000). Measuring attitude toward writing: A new tool for teachers. *The Reading Teacher, 54,* 10–23.

Kuhs, T. M., Johnson, R. L., Agruso, S. A., & Monrad, D. M. (2001). *Put to the test: Tools and techniques for classroom assessment.* Portsmouth, NH: Heinemann.

Leslie, L., & Caldwell, J. (2001). *Qualitative reading inventory—3* (3rd ed.). Boston: Allyn & Bacon.

McKenna, M. C., & Kear, D. J. (1990). Measuring attitudes toward reading: A new tool for teachers. *The Reading Teacher, 43,* 626–639.

Morrow, L. M. (1985). Retelling stories: A strategy for improving children's comprehension, concept of story structure, and oral language complexity. *Elementary School Journal, 85,* 647–661.

Porter, C., & Cleland, J. (1995). *The portfolio as a learning strategy.* Portsmouth, NH: Heinemann.

Rhodes, L. K., & Nathenson-Mejia, S. (1992). Anecdotal records: A powerful tool for ongoing literacy assessment. *The Reading Teacher, 45,* 502–511.

Silvaroli, N. J. (2001). *Classroom reading inventory* (9th ed.). Boston: McGraw-Hill.

Skillings, M. J., & Ferrell, R. (2000). Student-generated rubrics: Bringing students into the assessment process. *The Reading Teacher, 53,* 452–455.

Stahl, S. A. (1999). *Vocabulary development.* Cambridge, MA: Brookline Books.

Stires, S. (1991). Thinking through the process: Self-evaluation in writing. In B. M. Power & R. Hubbard (Eds.), *The Heinemann reader: Literacy in process* (pp. 295–310). Portsmouth, NH: Heinemann.

Tierney, R., Carter, M., & Desai, L. (1991). *Portfolio assessment in the reading-writing classroom.* Norwood, MA: Christopher-Gordon.

Tompkins, G. E. (2004). *Teaching writing: Balancing process and product* (4th ed.). Upper Saddle River, NJ: Merrill/Prentice Hall.

Walberg, H. J., & Tsai, S. (1985). Correlates of reading achievement and attitude: A national assessment study. *Journal of Educational Research, 78,* 159–167.

Winograd, P., & Arrington, H. J. (1999). Best practices in literacy assessment. In L. B. Gambrell, L. M. Morrow, S. B. Neuman, & M. Pressley (Eds.), *Best practices in literacy instruction* (pp. 210–241). New York: Guilford Press.

Woods, M. L., & Moe, A. J. (1999). *Analytical reading inventory* (6th ed.). Upper Saddle River, NJ: Merrill/Prentice Hall.

Children's Book References

Byars, B. (1968). *The midnight fox*. New York: Viking.

Curtis, C. P. (1995). *The Watsons go to Birmingham—1963*. New York: Delacorte.

George, J. C. (1972). *Julie of the wolves*. New York: Harper & Row.

Howe, D., & Howe, J. (1979). *Bunnicula: A rabbit-tale of mystery*. Boston: Atheneum.

Howe, J. (1981). *Howliday Inn*. Boston: Atheneum.

Howe, J. (1983). *The celery stalks at midnight*. Boston: Atheneum.

Howe, J. (1987). *Nighty-nightmare*. Boston: Atheneum.

Howe, J. (1992). *Return to Howliday Inn*. Boston: Atheneum.

Lewis, C. S. (1950). *The lion, the witch and the wardrobe*. New York: Macmillan.

Naylor, P. R. (1991). *Shiloh*. New York: Atheneum.

Paulsen, G. (1987). *Hatchet*. New York: Viking.

Speare, E. G. (1983). *The sign of the beaver*. Boston: Houghton Mifflin.

chapter 4

Refining Students' Print Skills

chapter
QUESTIONS

- What are print skills?

- Which print skills do students in grades 4 through 8 need to learn?

- How do teachers teach word-identification strategies?

- What are the stages of spelling development?

- How do teachers teach spelling?

Mr. King Teaches Word Work Lessons

The fifth graders in Mr. King's classroom spend 30 minutes each day refining their print skills in word work lessons. He sets out supplies in tubs at each table for students to use. The materials include magnetic letters, white boards and dry-erase pens, plastic letter squares that link together, letter and word cards in small plastic bags, dictionaries and thesauri, sentence strips and marking pens, and overhead transparencies and marking pens. He keeps a similar tub of supplies for himself, but he has added extra-large magnetic letters to his tub. In addition, he has chart paper and pocket charts available in the front of the classroom.

This week and next, the fifth graders are learning about syllables. The teacher begins the series of lessons with an explanation of syllabication and how to count syllables. Mr. King explains, "Syllables are important for two reasons: First, knowing how to break a word into syllables helps you to decode a long, unfamiliar word, and second, you can learn more about spelling patterns when you study syllables." Together the class makes a chart about syllables to post in the classroom. The "Syllables" chart says:

- Syllables are units of language with a vowel sound.
- Some words have one syllable, and others have two, three, or four syllables. Only a few words have five or more syllables.
- You can count syllables by clapping or cupping your chin while you say the word or by checking a dictionary.

Next, students each collect 10 words, some one-syllable words and others multisyllabic, from books they are reading and write them on word cards. They practice clapping or cupping their chins with their hands while they say the words aloud to count the syllables. They sort their cards according to the number of syllables, and Mr. King walks around the classroom to provide assistance as needed. Then the students come together to share their words and arrange them according to the number of syllables in a large pocket chart in the front of the classroom. An excerpt from the chart is shown in Figure 4-1. In addition, they share these five-syllable words that they collected: *vocabulary, superintendent, cafeteria, university, controversial, uncomfortably, congratulations,* and *educational.*

The next day, Mr. King explains that they can draw lines to divide multisyllabic words into syllables, and he demonstrates the procedure using word cards from the chart they made. For example: *free/dom, med/i/cine,* and *re/mem/ber/ing.* "Sometimes it is easy to see where to separate syllables, but sometimes it is much harder," Mr. King continues. "So, there are rules to help us know how to mark syllables." He shows a poster he has prepared with these rules:

1. When there are two consonants together, divide the syllables between them. Examples: *let/ter, rep/tile*
2. When the two consonants are blends or digraphs, divide the syllables to keep the digraph or blend together. Examples: *bank/er, flash/ling*
3. When three consonants come together, divide the syllables to keep the digraph or blend together. Examples: *ar/cher, duck/ling*

Figure 4-1 — A Chart of Words Sorted by Syllable Length

One-Syllable Words	Two-Syllable Words	Three-Syllable Words	Four-Syllable Words
wheels	tourists	transmission	dictionary
bunch	hero	unwanted	intelligent
girls	rascal	continue	invitation
thought	million	property	troublemaker
stage	object	customers	authority
truth	city	suddenly	impatiently
kids	hundreds	average	obviously
scarf	eerie	terrible	macaroni
week	freedom	satellites	conditioning
slow	trample	erupted	remembering
hair	stiffly	permanent	advertisement
couch	awkward	squeakier	experiment
smiles	pungent	embroidered	automatic
worst	believe	amazing	custodian
tricked	kitchen	carefully	transportation
fangs	system	monorail	cameraman
zoom	taxis	complaining	emergency
fifth	turtle	hamburger	America
pale	quiet	commercial	untouchable
milk	huddled	medicine	scientific

4. When there is only one consonant and the vowel before it is long, divide the syllables before the consonant. Examples: *ro/bot, dai/sy*

5. When there is only one consonant and the vowel before it is short, divide the syllables after the consonant. Examples: *mag/ic, sal/ad*

Mr. King explains each rule, and students find examples of words that follow each rule from the words they collected earlier, and they also continue to collect more words from books they are reading.

The next day, the teacher reviews the words, and students work in small groups to complete a word sort[C]—a collection of 25 words with five words that illustrate each rule. Students set out the words and organize them into categories. The completed word sort with words divided into five categories is shown in Figure 4-2.

To provide additional practice with two-syllable words, Mr. King passes out packets of magnetic letters for students to use for spelling practice. The teacher

[C] See the Compendium of Instructional procedures, which follows Chapter 12, for more information on terms marked with the symbol[C].

Figure 4-2 — A Word Sort of Two-Syllable Words According to Syllabication Rules

When there are two consonants together, divide syllables between them.	When the two consonants form a blend or digraph, divide syllables to keep them together.	When three consonants come together, divide syllables to keep the digraph or blend together.	When there is one consonant and the vowel before it is long, divide syllables before the consonant.	When there is one consonant and the vowel before it is short, divide syllables after the consonant.
window	brother	sickness	spider	woman
fossil	freshest	saddle	duty	modern
balloon	cricket	handful	easel	edit
fountain	blinker	hamster	silent	lemon
reptile	trouble	dolphin	future	dragon

pronounces two-syllable words, syllable by syllable, and students use the magnetic letters or white boards and pens to spell the words. As the students work at their tables, Mr. King spells out the words on the chalkboard using extra-large magnetic letters. He chooses words from the word sort activity completed the previous day as well as other words, including *frosting, needle, simple, unreal, whimper, radish, wheelchair, candle, crumble,* and *lettuce.*

Once students become comfortable reading and spelling two-syllable words, Mr. King passes out a pack of laminated word cards with three syllable words. The students work together to read the words and break them into syllables using erasable marking pens. The words on the cards include: *terrible, electric, criminal, catalog, unbuckle, handicap, lemonade, innocent, audiotape, chimpanzee, submarine, attention, origin, patriot, unusual, violent, department, relative, qualify,* and *exhaustion.* Over the next 2 days, students continue to practice with these three-syllable words: reading them, breaking them into syllables, and spelling them.

Finally, students move on to four-syllable words. They practice reading, writing, and breaking these 25 words into syllables: *transportation, geography, community, photography, electronic, astronomer, superhighway, magnificent, librarian, constellations, approximate, satisfaction, separation, relaxation, philosopher, measurable, medication, responsible, invitation, governmental, ecosystem, dishonesty, disappointment, convertible,* and *automatic.* As a final activity, students each choose one of the four-syllable words and design a word card for it showing the word broken into syllables and a drawing to illustrate it. Then Mr. King makes copies of the word cards for each student, and they cut them apart and glue them on index cards so that they can practice reading them. One student's word card for *constellations* is shown in Figure 4-3.

Figure 4-3 One Student's Word Card for *Constellations*

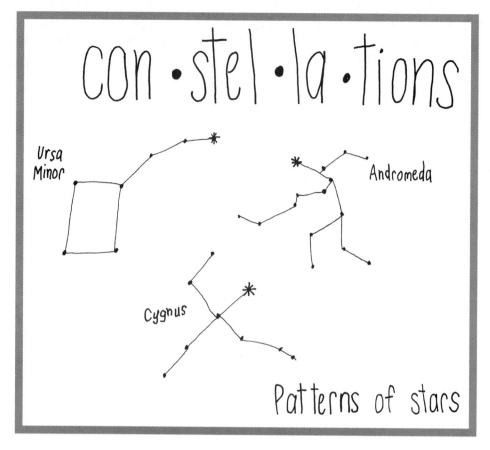

con·stel·la·tions

Ursa Minor

Andromeda

Cygnus

Patterns of stars

The fifth graders' classroom shows evidence of other print skills these students have studied this year. For example, there's a high-frequency word wall[C] posted on one side of the classroom. The word wall is divided into 26 boxes, one for each letter of the alphabet, and word cards attached with Velcro are displayed in each box. Currently there are 92 common words on the word wall, and Mr. King continues to add several more words each week. Some words, such as *school* and *where,* are printed in red ink and others, such as *special* and *through,* are printed in black ink. Micah explains, "The red words are the ones we have to spell right because we already know them, and the black words are harder. Those are the ones we're still learning. We just have to try our hardest to spell them right." In addition, there are small, 9×11-inch laminated word wall cards hung on a nearby hook that students can take back to their desks to refer to while they are writing.

On another wall, capitalization and punctuation posters that the students have made are posted. Charts with sentences students have written or collected from books they are reading are hanging nearby. The capital letters and punctuation marks have been omitted on the laminated charts, and erasable marking pens are clipped to the charts so that students can practice adding capital letters and punctuation marks appropriately. A sheet with the answers is stuck partially out of sight behind the charts so that students can check their work.

Hanging from the ceiling over several bookcases are homophone mobiles made from coat hangers and wooden dowel sticks that students created during a series of lessons on homophones. The mobiles show pictures of homophone pairs and sentences illustrating their meanings. Nearby, on the side of a bookcase, is a chart listing homophone pairs and trios, such as *sun–son, hair–hare, peel–peal,* and *to–two–too.* Several teacher- and student-made homophone games are stored in plastic bags on the bottom shelf of a nearby bookcase along with a stack of well-worn copies of *What in the World Is a Homophone?* (Presson, 1996), an illustrated dictionary of more than 300 sets of homophones. The students continue to have access to the games and dictionaries, and they often return to them during free choice time.

During the remainder of the school year, Mr. King plans word work lessons on root words, prefixes and suffixes, possessives, and parts of speech, other print skills included in his district's curriculum standards. As part of these lessons, too, students will read and spell words, manipulate letter and word cards, participate in word sort activities, and make charts and posters.

During the primary grades, children learn about the alphabetic principle, that there is a relationship between phonemes (or sounds) and graphemes (or letters). Even though that relationship is imperfect in English, students learn to read and write many, many phonetically regular one-, two-, and three-syllable words, such as *pet, slice, morning, tackle,* and *butterfly.* They also learn many other common words that are not entirely phonetic, such as *have, break, of,* and *could.* Students learn these words through a combination of direct instruction and lots of reading and writing practice. The outcome of these experiences is that most students become fluent readers and writers by the end of third grade, but 10–15% have difficulty learning to recognize words, and their learning to read is slowed (Allington, 1998).

At the same time students are becoming fluent readers, they are also becoming fluent writers. Through phonics and spelling instruction and lots of writing practice, students learn to spell many words automatically, apply capitalization and punctuation rules, and develop writing speed. They also develop strategies for spelling longer words. Acquiring print skills is just as important for writers because both readers and writers must be able to focus on meaning, not decoding or spelling words.

Students continue to refine their print skills during fourth through eighth grades. They learn to use syllabic and morphemic analysis in addition to phonic analysis to read and spell unfamiliar words. It is important that students learn how to break words into syllables and identify root words and affixes because older students read and write many, many multisyllabic words as part of literature and content-area study. In addition, struggling readers and writers need special instruction in phonics, high-frequency sight words, and other print skills to help them become more fluent readers and writers.

The feature on page 106 shows how print skills fit into a balanced program. As you continue reading this chapter, you will learn more about the ideas presented in the feature.

The Role of Print Skills in a Balanced Literacy Program

Component	Description
Reading	Students need strong print skills to be able to identify unfamiliar words when reading.
Phonics and Other Skills	Students apply phonics skills in phonic and syllabic analysis to identify unfamiliar words and when spelling unfamiliar words.
Strategies	Students learn three strategies for identifying unfamiliar words—phonic analysis, syllabic analysis, and morphemic analysis—and strategies for spelling words.
Vocabulary	Knowing the meanings of words is important because it is unreasonable to expect students to identify and spell unfamiliar words.
Comprehension	Students must be able to quickly identify unfamiliar words in order to read fluently and comprehend what they are reading.
Literature	In grades 4 through 8, students read longer, more challenging novels, and they need strong print skills so that decoding unfamiliar words does not impede their reading.
Content-Area Study	Students need strong print skills in order to decode and spell multisyllabic words in content-area units.
Oral Language	Students use two phonemic awareness strategies—blending and segmenting—in identifying and spelling unfamiliar words.
Writing	Students apply what they have learned about spelling when they write, and writing is the best way to assess what students know about spelling.
Spelling	Students learn to spell words through wide reading, direct instruction, and word study activities.

WORD IDENTIFICATION

Struggling readers encounter many words that they don't recognize immediately, and more proficient readers also come upon words that they don't recognize at once. Students use word-identification strategies to identify these unfamiliar words. Struggling readers often depend on phonics to identify unfamiliar words, but more proficient readers develop a repertoire of strategies that use phonological information as well as semantic, syntactic, and pragmatic cues to identify words. Three word-identification strategies are:

1. Phonic analysis
2. Syllabic analysis
3. Morphemic analysis

Figure 4-4   Word-Identification Strategies

Strategy	Description	Examples
Phonic Analysis	Students use their knowledge of sound-symbol correspondences and spelling patterns to decode words when reading and to spell words when writing.	*flat* *peach* *spring* *blaze* *chin*
Syllabic Analysis	Students break multisyllabic words into syllables and then use phonics and analogies to decode the word, syllable by syllable.	*cul-prit* *tem-por-ar-y* *vic-tor-y* *neg-a-tive* *sea-weed* *bi-o-de-grad-a-ble*
Morphemic Analysis	Students apply their knowledge of root words and affixes (prefixes at the beginning of the word and suffixes at the end) to identify an unfamiliar word. They "peel off" any prefixes or suffixes and identify the root word first. Then they add the affixes.	*trans-port* *astro-naut* *bi-cycle* *centi-pede* *pseudo-nym* *tele-scope*

Writers use these same strategies to spell words as they write. As with reading, young children depend on phonics to spell many, many words, but as they learn more about words, they apply more of these strategies to spelling. The word-identification strategies are summarized in Figure 4-4.

Eldredge (1995) calls these strategies "interim strategies" because students use them only until they learn to recognize words automatically. For example, fourth graders may break the word *disruption* into syllables to identify the word the first time they encounter it, but with practice, they learn to recognize it automatically. And seventh graders writing a report need to spell the word *bibliography*, which they learn to spell using their knowledge of word parts: *Biblio-* is a Greek word part meaning *books*, and *-graphy*, also a Greek word part, means *writing*. In time, students will write *bibliography* without breaking it into word parts or thinking about the meaning. They will write it automatically.

Phonics

Phonics is the set of relationships between phonology (the sounds in speech) and orthography (the spelling patterns of written language). The emphasis is on spelling patterns, not individual letters, because there is not a one-to-one correspondence between phonemes and graphemes in English. Sounds are spelled in different ways. There are several reasons for this variety. One reason is that the sounds, especially vowels, vary according to their location in a word (e.g., *go–got*). Adjacent letters often influence how letters are pronounced (e.g., *bed–bead*), as do vowel markers such as the final *e* (e.g., *bit–bite*) (Shefelbine, 1995).

Phonemic Awareness Strategies. Phonemic awareness is children's basic understanding that speech is composed of a series of individual sounds or phonemes, and this understanding provides the foundation for developing print skills (Yopp, 1992).

Teachers teach minilessons to introduce and review print skills.

The emphasis is on manipulating the sounds of spoken words, not reading or writing letters or pronouncing letter names. Phonemes are the smallest units of speech, and they are written as graphemes, or letters of the alphabet. In this book, phonemes are marked using diagonal lines (e.g., /d/) and graphemes are italicized (e.g., *d*). Sometimes phonemes (e.g., /k/ in *duck*) are spelled with two graphemes (*ck*).

As students become phonemically aware, they learn to segment and manipulate sounds in several ways, and the two most important strategies they develop are blending and segmenting. In blending, students learn to blend two, three, or four individual sounds to form a word. The teacher says /b/, /ĭ/, /g/, for example, and the students repeat the sounds, blending them to form the word *big*. Students apply the blending strategy when they sound out words while reading. In segmenting, students learn to break a word into its beginning, middle, and ending sounds. For example, students segment the word *feet* into /f/, /ē/, /t/ and *go* into /g/, /ō/ (Yopp, 1992). Students apply the segmenting strategy when they spell words while writing. Learning to blend and segment sounds is extremely important because researchers have concluded that at least some level of phonemic awareness is a prerequisite for learning to read (Cunningham, 1999; Tunmer & Nesdale, 1985; Yopp, 1985). Shefelbine (1995) also emphasizes the importance of blending and suggests that older students who have difficulty decoding words usually know the sound-symbol correspondences but cannot blend the sounds together into recognizable words. Moreover, phonemic awareness has been shown to be the most powerful predictor of later reading achievement (Juel, Griffith, & Gough, 1986; Lomax & McGee, 1987; Tunmer & Nesdale, 1985).

Phonics Concepts, Skills, and Generalizations. Teachers teach sound-symbol correspondences, how to blend sounds to decode words and segment sounds for spelling, and the most useful phonics generalizations or "rules." There is no simple way to explain all of the types of phonics information that students need to learn, nor can they be listed in a clean, sequential order, because they are built on student's foundation of

GUIDELINE 4

Struggling Readers and Writers Need to Be Phonemically Aware.
Teaching struggling students to blend and segment is difficult because once students have some knowledge of reading and writing, they focus on letters, not sounds. Teachers model blending when students decode unfamiliar one-syllable words. Teachers pronounce the individual sounds. Next, they blend the sounds before the vowel (onset) and then the vowel and ending sounds (rime). Then they blend the onset and rime. For multisyllabic words, teachers repeat the process for each syllable and then blend the syllables.

During spelling, teachers reverse the procedure to model segmenting. First they break a one-syllable word into the onset and rime. Next they segment the sounds and spell each part. Teachers draw a series of boxes with one box for each sound, and students write one or more letters to represent the sound in the box. Teachers repeat the process for each syllable when spelling multisyllabic words.

phonemic awareness. However, the most important are consonants, vowels, and phonics generalizations. Most of these concepts are taught in the primary grades, but students continue to refine their knowledge of the phonological system during the middle grades.

1. ***Consonants.*** Phonemes are classified as either consonants or vowels. The consonants are *b, c, d, f, g, h, j, k, l, m, n, p, q, r, s, t, v, w, x, y,* and *z*. Most consonants represent a single sound consistently, but there are some exceptions. *C*, for example, does not represent a sound of its own. When it is followed by *a, o,* or *u,* it is pronounced /k/ (e.g., *castle, coffee, cut*), and when it is followed by *e, i,* or *y,* it is pronounced /s/ (e.g., *cell, city, cycle*). *G* represents two sounds, as the word *garbage* illustrates. It is usually pronounced /g/ (e.g., *glass, go, green, guppy*), but when *g* is followed by *e, i,* or *y,* it is usually pronounced /j/, as in *giant.*

Two kinds of combination consonants are blends and digraphs. Consonant blends occur when two or three consonants appear next to each other in words and their individual sounds are "blended" together, as in *grass, belt,* and *spring.* Consonant digraphs are letter combinations for single sounds that are not represented by either letter. The four most common are *ch* as in *chair* and *each, sh* as in *shell* and *wish, th* as in *father* and *both,* and *wh* as in *whale.* Another consonant digraph is *ph,* as in *graph* and *photo.*

2. ***Vowels.*** The remaining five letters—*a, e, i, o,* and *u*—represent vowels; *w* and *y* are vowels when used in the middle and at the end of syllables and words. Vowels often represent several sounds. The two most common are short (marked with the symbol ˘, called a breve) and long sounds (marked with the symbol ¯, called a macron). The short vowel sounds are /ă/ as in *cat,* /ĕ/ as in *bed,* /ĭ/ as in *win,* /ŏ/ as in *hot,* and /ŭ/ as in *cup.* The long vowel sounds—/ā/, /ē/, /ī/, /ō/, and /ū/—are the same as the letter names, and they are illustrated in the words *make, feet, bike, coal,* and *mule.* Long vowel sounds are usually spelled with two vowels, except when the long vowel is at the end of a one-syllable word (or a syllable), as in *be* or *belong* and *try* or *tribal.*

When *y* is a vowel at the end of a word, it is pronounced as long *e* or long *i,* depending on the length of the word. In one-syllable words such as *by* and *cry,* the *y* is

ELL

English language learners whose native language uses an alphabetic system, such as Spanish, will learn the blending and segmenting strategies and phonics much more easily than students whose native language employs a logographic system of symbols without sound correspondences, such as Chinese.

pronounced as long *i*, but in longer words such as *baby* and *happy,* the *y* is usually pronounced as long *e*.

Vowel sounds are more complicated than consonant sounds, and there are many vowel combinations representing long vowels and other vowel sounds. Consider these combinations:

ai as in *nail*	*oa* as in *soap*
au as in *laugh* and *caught*	*oi* as in *oil*
aw as in *saw*	*oo* as in *cook* and *moon*
ea as in *peach* and *bread*	*ou* as in *house* and *through*
ew as in *sew* and *few*	*ow* as in *now* and *snow*
ia as in *dial*	*oy* as in *toy*
ie as in *cookie*	

Most vowel combinations are vowel digraphs or diphthongs. When two vowels represent a single sound, the combination is a vowel digraph (e.g., *nail, snow*), and when the two vowels represent a glide from one sound to another, the combination is a diphthong. Two vowel combinations that are consistently diphthongs are *oi* and *oy,* but other combinations, such as *ou* as in *house* (but not in *through*) and *ow* as in *now* (but not in *snow*), are diphthongs when they represent a glided sound. In *through,* the *ou* represents the /$\overline{oo}$/ sound as in *moon,* and in *snow,* the *ow* represents the /$\overline{o}$/ sound.

When the letter *r* follows one or more vowels in a word, it influences the pronunciation of the vowel sound, as shown in the words *car, air, are, ear, bear, first, for, more, murder,* and *pure.* Students learn many of these words as sight words.

The vowels in the unaccented syllables of multisyllabic words are often softened and pronounced "uh," as in the first syllable of *about* and *machine,* and the final syllable of *pencil, tunnel, zebra,* and *selection.* This vowel sound is called schwa and is represented in dictionaries with a ə, which looks like an inverted *e.*

3. ***Phonics Generalizations.*** Because English does not have an exact one-to-one correspondence between sounds and letters, linguists have created generalizations or rules to clarify English spelling patterns. One rule is that *q* is followed by *u* and pronounced /kw/, as in *queen, quick,* and *earthquake.* There are very few, if any, exceptions to this rule. Another generalization that has few exceptions relates to *r*-controlled vowels: *r* influences the preceding vowel so that the vowel is neither long nor short. Examples are *car, market, birth,* and *four.* There are exceptions, however, and one example is *fire.*

Many generalizations aren't very useful because there are more exceptions than words that conform to the rule (Clymer, 1963). A good example is this rule for long vowels: When there are two vowels side by side, the long vowel sound of the first one is pronounced and the second is silent; teachers sometimes call this the "when two vowels go walking, the first one does the talking" rule. Examples of words conforming to this rule are *meat, soap,* and *each.* There are many more exceptions, however, including *food, said, head, chief, bread, look, soup, does, too, again,* and *believe.*

Only a few phonics generalizations have a high degree of utility for readers. The generalizations that work most of the time are the ones that students should learn because they are the most useful (Adams, 1990). Eight high-utility generalizations are listed in Figure 4-5. Even though these rules are fairly reliable, very few of them approach 100% utility. The rule about *r*-controlled vowels just mentioned, for example,

ELL

ELL students who are already literate in their first language need to learn phoneme-grapheme correspondences and phonics generalizations, but they do not need as much phonics instruction as nonliterate English learners.

Figure 4-5 The Most Useful Phonics Generalizations

Pattern	Description	Examples
Two sounds of *c*	The letter *c* can be pronounced as /k/ or /s/. When *c* is followed by *a, o,* or *u,* it is pronounced /k/—the hard *c* sound. When *c* is followed by *e, i,* or *y,* it is pronounced /s/—the soft *c* sound.	cat cough cut cent city cycle
Two sounds of *g*	The sound associated with the letter *g* depends on the letter following it. When *g* is followed by *a, o,* or *u,* it is pronounced as /g/—the hard *g* sound. When *g* is followed by *e, i,* or *y,* it is usually pronounced /j/—the soft *g* sound. Exceptions include *get* and *give.*	gate go guess gentle giant gypsy
CVC pattern	When a one-syllable word has only one vowel and the vowel comes between two consonants, it is usually short. One exception is *told.*	bat cup land
Final *e* or CVCe pattern	When there are two vowels in a one-syllable word and one of them is an *e* at the end of the word, the first vowel is long and the final *e* is silent. Three exceptions are *have, come,* and *love.*	home safe cute
CV pattern	When a vowel follows a consonant in a one-syllable word, the vowel is long. Exceptions include *the, to,* and *do.*	go be
r-controlled vowels	Vowels that are followed by the letter *r* are overpowered and are neither short nor long. One exception is *fire.*	car for birthday
-igh	When *gh* follows *i,* the *i* is long and the *gh* is silent. One exception is *neighbor.*	high night
kn- and *wr-*	In words beginning with *kn-* and *wr-,* the first letter is not pronounced.	knee write

Adapted from Clymer, 1963.

has been calculated to be useful in 78% of words in which the letter *r* follows the vowel (Adams, 1990). Other commonly taught, useful rules have even lower percentages of utility. The CVC pattern rule—which says that when a one-syllable word has only one vowel and the vowel comes between two consonants, it is usually short, as in *bat, land,* and *cup*—is estimated to work only 62% of the time. Exceptions include *told, fall, fork,* and *birth.* The CVCe pattern rule—which says that when there are two vowels in a one-syllable word and one vowel is an *e* at the end of the word, the first vowel is long and the final *e* is silent—is estimated to work in 63% of CVCe words. Examples of conforming words are *came, hole,* and *pipe;* but three very common words, *have, come,* and *love,* are exceptions.

Phonic Analysis

Students use what they have learned about phoneme-grapheme correspondences, phonic generalizations, and spelling patterns to decode words when they are reading and to spell words when they are writing. Even though English is not a perfectly phonetic language, phonic analysis is a very useful strategy because almost every word has some phonetically regular parts. The words *have* and *come,* for example, are considered irregular words because the vowel sounds are not predictable; however, the initial and final consonant sounds in both words are regular.

Struggling readers often try to identify words based on a partial word analysis (Gough, Juel, & Griffith, 1992). They may guess at a word using the beginning sound or look at the overall shape of the word as a clue to word identification. However, these are not effective techniques. Researchers report that the big difference between students who can identify words effectively and those who cannot is whether they survey the letters in the word and analyze the interior components (Stanovich, 1992; Vellutino & Scanlon, 1987). Capable readers notice all or almost all letters in a word, whereas less capable readers do not completely analyze the letter sequences of words. Struggling readers with limited phonics skills often try to decode words by sounding out the beginning sound and then making a wild guess at the word without using the cueing systems to verify their guesses (I. W. Gaskins, Ehri, Cress, O'Hara, & Donnelly, 1996/1997). And, as you might guess, their guesses are usually wrong; sometimes they don't even make sense in the context of the sentence.

Once students know some letter-sound sequences, the focus of phonics instruction should become using phonic analysis to decode and spell words. Here are the steps students follow in decoding an unfamiliar one-syllable word:

1. Determine the vowel sound in the word, and isolate that sound.
2. Blend all of the consonant sounds in front of the vowel sound with the vowel sound.
3. Isolate the consonant sound(s) after the vowel sound.
4. Blend the two parts of the word together so the word can be identified. (Eldredge, 1995, p. 108)

For students to use this strategy, they need to be able to identify vowels and vowel patterns in words. They also need to be able to blend sounds to form recognizable words. For multisyllabic words, students break the word into syllables and then use the same procedure to decode each syllable. Because the location of stress in words varies, sometimes students have to try accenting different syllables to pronounce a recognizable word.

Syllabic Analysis

During the middle grades, students learn to divide words into syllables in order to read and write multisyllabic words such as *biodegradable, admonition,* and *unforgettable.* Once a word is divided into syllables, students use phonic analysis to pronounce or spell the word. Identifying syllable boundaries is important, because these affect the pronunciation of the vowel sound. For example, compare the vowel sound in the first syllables of *cabin* and *cable.* For *cabin,* the syllable boundary is after the *b,* whereas for *cable,* the division is before the *b.* We can predict that the *a* in *cabin* will be short because the syllable follows the CVC pattern, and that the *a* in *cable* will be long because the syllable follows the CV pattern.

The most basic rule about syllabication is that there is one vowel sound in each syllable. Consider the words *bit* and *bite.* They are both one-syllable words because they contain one vowel sound. *Bit* has one vowel letter representing one vowel sound. Even though it has two vowels, *bite* is a one-syllable word because the two vowels represent one sound. *Magic* and *curfew* are two-syllable words; there is one vowel letter and sound in each syllable in *magic*, but in the second syllable of *curfew*, the two vowels *ew* represent one vowel sound. Let's try a longer word: How many syllables are in *inconvenience*? There are six vowel letters representing four sounds in four syllables.

Syllabication rules are useful in teaching students how to divide words into syllables. Five of the most useful rules are listed in Figure 4-6. Many rules depend on whether the syllable ends in a vowel or a consonant. Linguists call syllables that end with a vowel, such as the first syllable in *begin* and *rapid*, open syllables; syllables ending with a consonant, such as the second syllable in *begin* and *rapid*, are called closed syllables.

Teachers like Mr. King in the vignette at the beginning of the chapter use minilessons[C] to introduce the concept of syllabication and the syllabication rules. During additional minilessons, students and teachers choose words from books students are reading and from thematic units for guided practice breaking words into syllables. After identifying syllable boundaries, students pronounce and spell the words, syllable by syllable. Teachers also mark syllable boundaries on multisyllabic words on word walls in the classroom and create center activities in which students practice dividing

Figure 4-6 Syllabication Rules

Rules	Examples
1. When two consonants come between two vowels in a word, divide syllables between the consonants.	cof-fee bor-der hec-tic plas-tic jour-ney
2. When there are more than two consonants together in a word, divide syllables keeping the blends together.	em-ploy mon-ster lob-ster en-trance bank-rupt
3. When there is one consonant between two vowels in a word, divide syllables after the first vowel.	ca-jole bo-nus fau-cet plu-ral gla-cier
4. If following the third rule does not make a recognizable word, divide syllables after the consonant that comes between the vowels.	doz-en dam-age ech-o meth-od cour-age
5. When there are two vowels together that do not represent a long-vowel sound or a diphthong, divide syllables between the vowels.	cli-ent du-et po-em cha-os li-on qui-et

words into syllables and building words using word parts. For example, after the word *compromise* came up in a social studies unit, a sixth-grade teacher developed a center activity in which students created two- and three-syllable words beginning with *com-* using syllable cards. Students created these words:

comic	compliment	common
companion	complex	computer
complete	commitment	complain
compromise	comment	compartment

After building these words, students brainstormed a list of additional words beginning with *com-*, including *complement, commuter, company, communicate, compass,* and *committee.* Through this activity, students become more familiar with syllables in words and the vowel patterns in syllables. The syllable cards for the center activity are presented in Figure 4-7.

Morphemic Analysis

Students examine the root word and affixes of longer unfamiliar words in order to identify the words. A root word is a morpheme, the basic part of a word to which affixes are added. Many words are developed from a single root word. For example, the Latin words *portare* (to carry), *portus* (harbor), and *porta* (gate) are the sources of at least 12 words: *deport, export, exporter, import, port, portable, porter, report, reporter, support, transport,* and *transportation.* Latin is the most common source of English root words; Greek and English are two other sources. Some root words are whole words, and others are parts of words. Some root words have become free morphemes and can be used as separate words, but others cannot. For instance, the word *cent*

Figure 4-7 A Syllable-Building Activity

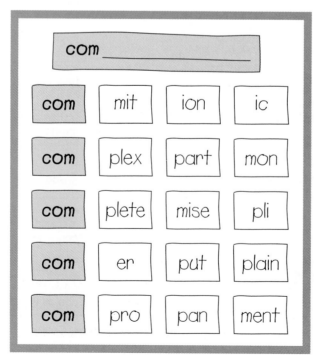

comes from the Latin root word *cent*, meaning "hundred." English treats the word as a root word that can be used independently and in combination with affixes, as in *century, bicentennial*, and *centipede*. The words *cosmopolitan, cosmic*, and *microcosm* come from the Greek root word *cosmo*, meaning "universe"; it is not an independent root word in English. A list of Latin and Greek root words appears in Figure 4-8. English words such as *eye, tree*, and *water* are root words, too. New words are formed through compounding—for example, *eyelash, treetop*, and *waterfall*—but other English root words, such as *read*, combine with affixes, as in *reader* and *unreadable*.

Affixes are bound morphemes that are added to words and root words. Prefixes are added to the beginning of words, as in *replay*, and suffixes are added to the end of words, as in *playing, playful*, and *player*. Like root words, some affixes are English, and others come from Latin and Greek. Affixes often change a word's meaning, such as adding *un-* to *happy* to form *unhappy*. Sometimes they change the part of speech, too. For example, when *-tion* is added to *attract* to form *attraction*, the verb *attract* becomes a noun.

Two types of suffixes are inflectional and derivational. Inflectional suffixes are endings that indicate verb tense and person, plurals, possession, and comparison, and these suffixes are English. They influence the syntax of sentences. Some examples are:

the *-ed* in *walked*	the *-es* in *beaches*
the *-ing* in *singing*	the *-'s* in *girl's*
the *-s* in *asks*	the *-er* in *faster*
the *-s* in *dogs*	the *-est* in *sunniest*

Inflectional suffixes are by far the most common suffixes in English. In contrast, derivational suffixes show the relationship of the word to its root word. Consider, for example, these words containing the root word *friend: friendly, friendship*, and *friendless*.

When a word's affix is "peeled off," what remains is usually a real word. For example, when the prefix *pre-* is removed from *preview*, the word *view* can stand alone, as it can when the suffix *-er* is removed from *viewer*. Some words include letter sequences that appear to be affixes, but because the remaining word cannot stand alone, they are not affixes. For example, the *in-* at the beginning of *include* is not a prefix because *clude* is not a word. Similarly, the *-ic* at the end of *magic* is not a suffix because *mag* cannot stand alone as a word. Sometimes, however, Latin and Greek root words cannot stand alone. One example is *legible*. The *-ible* is a suffix, and *leg* is the root word even though it cannot stand alone. Of course, *leg*—meaning part of the body—is a word, but the root word *leg-* from *legible* is not. It is a Latin root word, meaning "to read."

A list of English, Greek, and Latin prefixes and suffixes is presented in Figure 4-9. Not surprisingly, most affixes are from Latin, as are 50–60% of words in English. White, Sowell, and Yanagihara (1989) researched affixes and identified the most common prefixes and derivational suffixes, and these are marked with an asterisk in Figure 4-9. White and his colleagues recommend that the commonly used affixes be taught to middle- and upper-grade students because of their usefulness. Some of the most commonly used prefixes can be confusing because they have more than one meaning. The prefix *un-*, for example, can mean *not* (e.g., *unclear*) or it can reverse the meaning of a word (e.g., *tie–untie*).

Teaching and Assessing Word Identification

Word-level learning is an essential part of a balanced literacy program (Hiebert, 1991), and teaching minilessons about phonic, syllabic, and morphemic analysis is a useful way to help students focus on words. Minilessons grow out of meaningful literature experiences or thematic units, and teachers use words for minilessons from books students are reading, as Mr. King did in the vignette. The minilesson feature on page 118

Figure 4-8 Latin and Greek Root Words

Root	Language	Meaning	Sample Words
ann/enn	Latin	year	anniversary, annual, centennial, millennium, perennial, semiannual
arch	Greek	ruler	anarchy, archbishop, architecture, hierarchy, monarchy, patriarch
astro	Greek	star	aster, asterisk, astrology, astronaut, astronomy, disaster
auto	Greek	self	autobiography, automatic, automobile, autopsy, semiautomatic
bio	Greek	life	biography, biohazard, biology, biodegradable, bionic, biosphere
capit/capt	Latin	head	capital, capitalize, Capitol, captain, caption, decapitate, per capita
cent	Latin	hundred	bicentennial, cent, centennial, centigrade, centipede, century, percent
circ	Latin	around	circle, circular, circus, circumspect, circuit, circumference, circumstance
corp	Latin	body	corporal, corporation, corps, corpuscle
cosmo	Greek	universe	cosmic, cosmopolitan, microcosm
cred	Latin	believe	credit, creed, creditable, discredit, incredulity
cycl	Greek	wheel	bicycle, cycle, cyclist, cyclone, recycle, tricycle
dict	Latin	speak	contradict, dictate, dictator, prediction, verdict
graph	Greek	write	autobiography, biographer, cryptograph, epigraph, graphic, paragraph
gram	Greek	letter	cardiogram, diagram, grammar, monogram, telegram
jus/jud/jur	Latin	law	injury, injustice, judge, juror, jury, justice, justify, prejudice
lum/lus/luc	Latin	light	illuminate, lucid, luminous, luster
man	Latin	hand	manacle, maneuver, manicure, manipulate, manual, manufacture
mar/mer	Latin	sea	aquamarine, Margaret, marine, maritime, marshy, mermaid, submarine
meter	Greek	measure	centimeter, diameter, seismometer, speedometer, thermometer
mini	Latin	small	miniature, minibus, minimize, minor, minimum, minuscule, minute
mort	Latin	death	immortal, mortality, mortuary, postmortem
nym	Greek	name	anonymous, antonym, homonym, pseudonym, synonym
ped	Latin	foot	biped, pedal, pedestrian, pedicure
phono	Greek	sound	earphone, microphone, phonics, phonograph, saxophone, symphony
photo	Greek	light	photograph, photographer, photosensitive, photosynthesis
pod/pus	Greek	foot	octopus, podiatry, podium, tripod
port	Latin	carry	exporter, import, port, portable, porter, reporter, support, transportation
quer/ques/quis	Latin	seek	inquisitive, query, quest, question
scope	Latin	see	horoscope, kaleidoscope, microscope, periscope, telescope
scrib/scrip	Latin	write	describe, inscription, postscript, prescribe, scribble, scribe, script
sphere	Greek	ball	atmosphere, atmospheric, hemisphere, sphere, stratosphere
struct	Latin	build	construct, construction, destruction, indestructible, instruct, reconstruct
tele	Greek	far	telecast, telegram, telegraph, telephone, telescope, telethon, television
terr	Latin	land	subterranean, terrace, terrain, terrarium, terrier, territory
vers/vert	Latin	turn	advertise, anniversary, controversial, divert, reversible, versus
vict/vinc	Latin	conquer	convince, convict, evict, invincible, victim, victor, victory
vis/vid	Latin	see	improvise, invisible, revise, supervisor, television, video, vision, visitor
viv/vit	Latin	live	revive, survive, vital, vitamin, vivacious, vivid, viviparous
volv	Latin	roll	convolutions, evolve, evolution, involve, revolutionary, revolver, volume

Figure 4-9 English, Greek, and Latin Affixes

Language	Prefixes	Suffixes
English	***over-** (too much): overflow **self-** (by oneself): self-employed ***un-** (not): unhappy ***un-** (reversal): untie **under-** (beneath): underground	**-ed** (past tense): played **-ful** (full of): hopeful **-ing** (participle): eating, building **-ish** (like): reddish **-less** (without): hopeless **-ling** (young): duckling ***-ly** (in the manner of): slowly ***-ness** (state or quality): kindness **-s/-es** (plural): cats, boxes **-ship** (state, or art or skill): friendship, seamanship **-ster** (one who): gangster **-ward** (direction): homeward ***-y** (full of): sleepy
Greek	**a-/an-** (not): atheist, anaerobic **amphi-** (both): amphibian **anti-** (against): antiseptic **di-** (two): dioxide **hemi-** (half): hemisphere **hyper-** (over): hyperactive **hypo-** (under): hypodermic **micro-** (small): microfilm **mono-** (one): monarch **omni-** (all): omnivorous **poly-** (many): polygon **sym-/syn-/sys-** (together): synonym	**-ism** (doctrine of): communism **-ist** (one who): artist **-logy** (the study of): zoology
Latin	**bi-** (two, twice): bifocal, biannual **contra-** (against): contradict **de-** (away): detract ***dis-** (not): disapprove ***dis-** (reversal): disinfect **ex-** (out): export ***il-/im-/in-/ir-** (not): illegible, impolite, inexpensive, irrational ***in-** (in, into): indoor **inter-** (between): intermission **milli-** (thousand): millennium ***mis-** (wrong): mistake **multi-** (many): multimillionaire **non-** (not): nonsense **post-** (after): postwar **pre-** (before): precede **quad-/quart-** (four): quadruple, quarter **re-** (again): repay ***re-/retro-** (back): replace, retroactive ***sub-** (under): submarine **super-** (above): supermarket **trans-** (across): transport **tri-** (three): triangle	**-able/-ible** (worthy of, can be): lovable, audible ***-al/-ial** (action, process): arrival, denial **-ance/-ence** (state or quality): annoyance, absence **-ant** (one who): servant **-ary/-ory** (person, place): secretary, laboratory **-cule** (very small): molecule **-ee** (one who is): trustee ***-er/-or/-ar** (one who): teacher, actor, liar **-ic** (characterized by): angelic **-ify** (to make): simplify **-ment** (state or quality): enjoyment **-ous** (full of): nervous ***-sion/-tion** (state or quality): tension, attraction **-ure** (state or quality): failure

*Indicates the most commonly used prefixes and derivational suffixes (White, Sowell, & Yanagihara, 1989)

Minilesson

Topic: Greek Words for Types of Government
Grade: Sixth Grade
Time: Three 30-minute periods

As part of a social studies unit on ancient civilizations, Mr. Morales introduces the concepts *democracy, monarchy, oligarchy,* and *theocracy* to his sixth graders and adds the words to the social studies word wall; however, he notices that many of his students have difficulty pronouncing the words and remembering what they mean even though they have read about them in the social studies textbook.

1. Introduce the Topic
Mr. Morales reads over the word wall for the social studies unit on ancient civilizations and reads aloud these words: *democracy, monarchy, oligarchy,* and *theocracy.* Marcos volunteers that he thinks that the words have something to do with kings or rulers, but he's not sure.

2. Share Examples
The teacher writes the words on the chalkboard, dividing them into syllables so that the sixth graders can pronounce them more easily. The students practice saying the words several times, but they are puzzled about the meaning of the words even though they learned about them when they listed them on the word wall.

3. Provide Information
Mr. Morales tells the class that he can help them figure out the meaning of the words. "The words are Greek," he says, "and they have two word parts. If you know the meaning of the word parts, you will be able to figure out the meaning of the words." He writes the four words from the word wall and the word parts this way:

democracy = demo + cracy   *monarchy = mono + archy*
oligarchy = olig + archy   *theocracy = theo + cracy*

Then he explains that Marcos was right—the words have to do with kings and rulers; they describe different kinds of government. *Cracy* means *government* and *archy* means *leader.* The first word part tells more about the kind of government; one of them means *gods,* and the others mean *one, people,* and *few.* The students work in small groups to figure out that *democracy* means government by the people, *monarchy* means one leader, *oligarchy* means rule by a few leaders, and *theocracy* means government by the gods.

4. Guide Practice
The next day, Mr. Morales divides the class into four groups, and each group makes a poster to describe one of the four types of government. On each poster, students write the word, the two Greek word parts, and a definition. They also create an illustration based on what they have learned about this type of government. Afterwards, students share their posters with the class and display them in the classroom.

5. Assess Learning
On the third day, Mr. Morales gives students a list of six sentences about the different types of government taken from the social studies textbook and asks them to identify the type of government. He encourages the sixth graders to refer to the posters the class made as they complete the assignment. Afterwards, he reviews students' papers to determine which students understand the four types of government and can use the words correctly.

shows how Mr. Morales teaches his sixth graders about morphemic analysis as part of a social studies unit on ancient civilizations.

Delpit (1987) and Reyes (1991) have argued that learning print skills implicitly through reading and writing experiences assumes that students have existing literacy and language proficiencies and that the same sort of instruction works equally well for everyone. They point out that not all students have a rich background of literacy experiences before coming to school. Some students, especially those from nonmainstream cultural and linguistic groups, may not have been read to as preschoolers or been as successful in the primary grades as mainstream students. Delpit and Reyes conclude that explicit instruction is crucial for nonmainstream students who do not have the same literacy background as middle-class students.

Fluent readers develop a large repertoire of sight words and use word-identification strategies to decode unfamiliar words. Less capable readers, in contrast, cannot read as many sight words and do not use as many strategies for decoding words. Researchers have concluded again and again that students who do not become fluent readers depend on explicit instruction to learn how to identify words (Calfee & Drum, 1986; R. W. Gaskins, Gaskins, & Gaskins, 1991; Johnson & Baumann, 1984).

Many fourth-grade teachers notice that their students seem to stand still or lose ground in their reading development. It has been assumed that the increased demands for reading informational books with unfamiliar, multisyllabic words cause this phenomenon. Now researchers suggest that lack of instruction in word-identification strategies might be the cause of the "fourth-grade slump" (Chall, Jacobs, & Baldwin, 1990). Perhaps more minilessons on identifying multisyllabic words will help eliminate this difficulty.

Teachers informally assess students' ability to use word-identification strategies as they observe students reading and writing and monitor their use of the strategies. They can also assess students' use of word-identification strategies by asking them to read or write a list of grade-level-appropriate words or by asking students to think aloud and explain how they decoded or spelled a particular word. It is also important that teachers check to see that students use these strategies on an "interim basis" and that through practice, they learn to read and write words automatically. Fourth graders, for example, may use syllabic analysis to read or write a word such as *relatives,* but with practice, they should learn to read and write the word automatically, without having to stop and analyze it.

SPELLING

Students' spelling is a reflection of what they are learning about word identification. During fourth through eighth grades, students learn how to spell multisyllabic words and develop a better understanding of the English orthographic, or spelling, system. In the past, weekly spelling tests were the main instructional strategy. Now, they are only one part of a comprehensive spelling program.

The English Orthographic System

The alphabetic principle suggests a one-to-one correspondence between phonemes (or sounds) and graphemes (or letters), such that each letter consistently represents one sound. English, however, is not a purely phonetic language. The 26 letters represent approximately 44 phonemes, and three letters—*c, q,* and *x*—are superfluous because they do not represent unique phonemes. The letter *c,* for example, can represent either /k/ as in *cat* or /s/ as in *city,* and it can be joined with *h* for the digraph /ch/. To further complicate the situation, there are more than 500 spellings to represent the 44 phonemes. Consonants are more consistent and predictable than vowels. Long *e,* for instance, is spelled 14 ways in common words! Consider, for example, *me, seat, feet, people, yield, baby,* and *cookie.* How a word is spelled depends on several factors, including the location of the sound in the word and whether the word entered English from another language (Horn, 1957).

Researchers estimate that words are spelled phonetically approximately half the time (Hanna, Hanna, Hodges, & Rudorf, 1966), and the nonphonetic spelling of many words reflects morphological information. The word *sign,* for instance, is a shortened form of *signature,* and the spelling shows this relationship. Spelling the word phonetically (i.e., *sine*) might seem simpler, but the phonetic spelling lacks semantic information (Venezky, 1999).

Other reasons for this mismatch between phonemes, graphemes, and spellings can be found by examining events in the history of the English language (Tompkins & Yaden, 1986). The introduction of the printing press in England in 1476 helped to stabilize spelling. The word *said,* for example, continues to be spelled as it was pronounced in Shakespeare's time. Our pronunciation does not reflect the word's meaning as the past tense of *say* because pronunciations have continued to evolve in the last 500 years, but few spellings have been "modernized." In addition, 75% of English words have been borrowed from other languages around the world, and many words—especially those acquired more recently—have retained their native spellings. For example, *souvenir* was borrowed from French in the middle 1700s and retains its French spelling. Its literal meaning is "to remember."

The English orthographic system can't be explained by the alphabetic principle alone because it is not merely a reflection of phoneme-grapheme correspondences. Our spelling system includes morphological, semantic, and syntactic elements, and it has been influenced by historical events.

Stages of Spelling Development

Students' spellings reflect their knowledge of the English orthographic system, and their spellings become more sophisticated as their knowledge grows (Read, 1986). A preschool child, for example, might spell *elephant* as L, but by the end of kindergarten, the child would add beginning and ending sounds and spell it as ELT. In first grade, the child would represent more sounds in the word and spell it ELFT or ELFANT. By second grade, the child might spell it ELPHANT before finally adding the schwa sound and spelling it correctly. These unique spellings are called invented spellings.

Based on observations of students' spellings, researchers have identified five stages that students move through on their way to becoming conventional spellers. At each stage, they use different types of strategies and focus on different aspects of spelling. The stages are emergent spelling, letter-name spelling, within-word pattern spelling, syllables and affixes spelling, and derivational relations spelling (Bear, Invernizzi, Templeton, & Johnston, 2000). The characteristics of the five stages of spelling development are summarized in Figure 4-10.

Stage 1: Emergent Spelling.   Children string scribbles, letters, and letterlike forms together, but they do not associate the marks they make with any specific phonemes. Spelling at this stage represents a natural, early expression of the alphabet and other concepts about writing. Children may write from left to right, right to left, top to bottom, or randomly across the page, but by the end of the stage, they have an understanding of directionality.

Figure 4-10   Stages of Spelling Development

Stage 1: Emergent Spelling

Children string scribbles, letters, and letterlike forms together, but they do not associate the marks they make with any specific phonemes. This stage is typical of 3- to 5-year-olds. Children learn:

- the distinction between drawing and writing
- how to make letters
- the direction of writing on a page
- some letter-sound matches

Stage 2: Letter-Name Spelling

Children learn to represent phonemes in words with letters. At first, their spellings are quite abbreviated, but they learn to use consonant blends and digraphs and short-vowel patterns to spell many short-vowel words. Spellers are 5- to 7-year-olds. Children learn:

- the alphabetic principle
- consonant sounds
- short-vowel sounds
- consonant blends and digraphs

Stage 3: Within-Word Pattern Spelling

Children learn long-vowel patterns and *r*-controlled vowels, but they may confuse spelling patterns and spell *meet* as *mete,* and they reverse the order of letters, such as *form* for *from* and *gril* for *girl.* Spellers are 7- to 9-year-olds, and they learn:

- long-vowel spelling patterns
- *r*-controlled vowels
- more complex consonant patterns
- diphthongs and other less common vowel patterns

Stage 4: Syllables and Affixes Spelling

Children apply what they have learned about one-syllable words to spell longer, multisyllabic words, and they learn to break words into syllables. They also learn to add inflectional endings (e.g., *-es, -ed, -ing*) and to differentiate between homophones, such as *your–you're.* Spellers are often 9- to 11-year-olds, and they learn:

- inflectional endings
- rules for adding inflectional endings
- syllabication
- homophones
- contractions
- possessives

Stage 5: Derivational Relations Spelling

Children explore the relationship between spelling and meaning and learn that words with related meanings are often related in spelling despite changes in sound (e.g., *wise–wisdom, sign–signal, nation–national*). They also learn about Latin and Greek root words and derivational affixes (e.g., *amphi-, pre-, -able, -tion*). Spellers are 11- to 14-year-olds. Students learn:

- consonant alternations
- vowel alternations
- Latin and Greek affixes and root words
- etymologies

Adapted from Bear, Invernizzi, Templeton, & Johnston, 2000.

This stage is typical of 3- to 5-year-olds, and as they learn the letters of the alphabet and a few phoneme-grapheme correspondences, they apply their new knowledge in spelling. During the emergent stage, children learn:

- the distinction between drawing and writing
- how to make letters
- the direction of writing on a page
- some letter-sound matches

Stage 2: Letter-Name Spelling.   Children learn to represent phonemes in words with letters. They develop an understanding that a link exists between letters and sounds. At first, the spellings are quite abbreviated and represent only the most prominent features in words. Children use only several letters of the alphabet to represent an entire word. Examples of early Stage 2 spelling are D (*dog*) and KE (*cookie*), and children may still be writing mainly with capital letters. Children pronounce slowly the words they want to spell, listening for familiar letter names and sounds.

In the middle of the letter-name stage, students use most beginning and ending consonants and often include a vowel in most syllables; they spell *like* as *lik* and *bed* as *bad*. By the end of the stage, students use consonant blends and digraphs and short-vowel patterns to spell *hat, get,* and *win,* but some students still spell *ship* as *sep.* They can also spell some CVCe words such as *name* correctly.

Spellers at this stage are usually 5- to 7-year-olds, and they are in the beginning stage of reading and writing development. Their spellings demonstrate their phonics knowledge. During the letter-name stage, students learn:

- the alphabetic principle
- consonant sounds
- short-vowel sounds
- consonant blends and digraphs

Stage 3: Within-Word Pattern Spelling.   Students begin the within-word pattern stage when they can spell most one-syllable short-vowel words; during this stage, they learn to spell long-vowel patterns and *r*-controlled vowels (Henderson, 1990). The focus remains on one-syllable words.

Students experiment with long-vowel patterns and learn that words such as *come* and *bread* are exceptions that do not fit the vowel patterns. They often confuse spelling patterns and spell *meet* as *mete* and learn about less frequent vowel patterns, such as *oi/oy* (*boy*), *au* (*caught*), *aw* (*saw*), *ew* (*sew, few*), *ou* (*house*), and *ow* (*cow*). Students also become aware of homophones and compare long- and short-vowel combinations (*hope–hop*) as they experiment with vowel patterns. They also reverse the order of letters, such as *form* for *from* and *gril* for *girl* as they begin to view spelling as more than just sounding out words.

Spellers at this stage are 7- to 9-year-olds. Most of these children are in the process of becoming fluent readers and writers. During the within-word pattern stage, students learn these spelling concepts:

- long-vowel spelling patterns
- *r*-controlled vowels
- more complex consonant patterns
- diphthongs and other less common vowel patterns

Stage 4: Syllables and Affixes Spelling.   The focus is on syllables in this stage. Students apply what they have learned about one-syllable words to longer, multisyllabic words, and they learn to break words into syllables. They have already learned to use *y* at the end of a one-syllable word, as in *cry* to spell /ī/, and in this stage, they learn that *y* at the end of a two-syllable word represents /ē/ as in *ready*. They also learn that sometimes *ey* is used to spell /ē/ in a two-syllable word (e.g., *honey, monkey*).

Students learn about inflectional endings (*-s, -es, -ed,* and *-ing*) and rules about consonant doubling, changing the final *y* to *i*, or dropping the final *e* before adding an inflectional suffix; for example, *run + ing = running, baby + s = babies,* and *have + ing = having.* They begin to notice some of the more common prefixes and suffixes and experiment with them. A fourth grader, for example, proudly announced that her head was "thinkful," or full of thinking. She invented her new word by analogy—she knew that *beautiful* means full of beauty and *hopeful* means full of hope.

Students also learn several other sophisticated spelling concepts about one- and two-syllable words, including homophones, compound words, and contractions. They begin to consider homophone choices (e.g., *to, two,* or *too*), decide when words are compound and should be spelled as one word (e.g., *flashlight* but not *bright light*), and place apostrophes correctly in contractions and possessives. Although younger spellers often spell *don't* as *do'nt* during this stage, children learn what the apostrophe represents and usually spell the word correctly.

Spellers in this stage are generally 9- to 11-year-olds who are fluent readers and writers. They learn these concepts during the syllables and affixes stage of spelling development:

- inflectional endings (*-s, -es, -ed, -ing*)
- rules for adding inflectional endings
- syllabication
- homophones
- compound words
- contractions
- possessives

Many ELL students omit inflectional endings on words when they write, and they benefit from minilessons drawing their attention to this linguistic feature when they're at the fourth stage of spelling development.

Stage 5: Derivational Relations Spelling.   Students explore the relationship between spelling and meaning during the derivational relations stage, and they learn that words with related meanings are often related in spelling despite changes in vowel and consonant sounds (e.g., *wise–wisdom, sign–signal, nation–national*) (Templeton, 1983). The focus in this stage is on morphemes, and students learn about Greek and Latin root words and affixes. They also begin to examine etymologies and the role of history in shaping how words are spelled. They learn about eponyms (words from people's names), such as *maverick* and *sandwich.*

Most spellers at this stage are 11- to 14-year-olds. Students learn these concepts at this stage of spelling development:

- consonant alternations (e.g., *soft–soften, magic–magician*)
- vowel alternations (e.g., *please–pleasant, define–definition, explain–explanation*)
- Greek and Latin affixes and root words
- etymologies

To learn how to assess a student's stage of spelling development, turn back to Chapter 3, "Assessing Students' Literacy Development."

Students' spelling provides evidence of their growing understanding of English orthography. The words they spell correctly show which phonics skills, spelling patterns, and other language features they have learned to apply, and the words they invent and misspell show what they are still learning to use and those features of spelling they have not noticed or learned about. Invented spelling is sometimes criticized because it may appear that students are learning bad habits by misspelling words, but researchers have confirmed that students grow more quickly in phonics and spelling when they use invented spelling as long as they are also receiving spelling instruction (Snow, Burns, & Griffin, 1998). As students learn more about spelling, their invented spellings become more sophisticated to reflect their new knowledge, even if the words are still spelled incorrectly, and increasingly students spell more and more words correctly as they move through the stages of spelling development.

Teaching and Assessing Spelling

Perhaps the best-known way to teach spelling is through weekly spelling tests, but spelling tests should never be considered a complete spelling program. To become good spellers, students need to learn about the English orthographic system and move through the stages of spelling development. Students develop strategies to use in spelling unknown words and gain experience in using dictionaries and other resources. A complete spelling program:

- teaches spelling concepts, strategies, and skills
- matches instruction to students' stage of spelling development
- provides instruction on spelling concepts and skills
- provides daily reading and writing opportunities
- requires students to learn to spell high-frequency words

When students are engaged in a spelling program that incorporates these components, there is evidence of their learning in their writing. The number of errors that children make becomes progressively less, but more important, the types of spelling errors change; the errors become more sophisticated as students move from spelling phonetically to using morphological information and spelling rules.

Two of the most important ways that students learn to spell are through daily reading and writing activities. Students who are good readers tend to be good spellers, too. As they read, students visualize words—the shape of a word and the configuration of letters within it—and they use this knowledge to spell many words correctly and to recognize when a word they've written doesn't look right. Through writing, of course, students gain valuable practice using the strategies they have learned to spell the words they are writing. And, as teachers work with students to proofread and edit their writing, they learn more about spelling and other writing conventions.

In addition to reading and writing activities, students learn about the English orthographic system through spelling activities and minilessons. The minilesson feature on p. 125 shows how Mr. Silverman teaches his eighth graders about eponyms, people's names and place names that have become words. Then in the following sections, you will read about a number of spelling activities that expand students' spelling knowledge and help them move through the stages of spelling development.

Word Walls. Teachers use two types of word walls in their classrooms. One word wall features "important" words from books students are reading or social studies and science thematic units. Words may be written on a large sheet of paper hanging in the classroom or on word cards and placed in a large pocket chart. Then students refer to

Minilesson

Topic: Eponyms
Grade: Eighth Grade
Time: Three 30-minute periods

Mr. Silverman's eighth-grade students became interested in eponyms after reading a note in their literature anthologies about eponyms, people's names and place names that have become words, such as *candy, bikini, maverick,* and *America.* To expand their interest in word histories, Mr. Silverman plans this minilesson to kick off a mini-research and presentation project.

1. Introduce the Topic
Mr. Silverman reminds students about the note in their anthologies about Samuel Maverick (1803–1870), an unconventional pioneer Texas cattle rancher, whose name became an eponym. He explains that an eponym is a name that becomes a word.

2. Share Examples
The teacher shares copies of a list of 60 eponymous words, words that developed from people's names and place names, that he collected from *Guppies in Tuxedos* (Terban, 1988), *What's in a Name?* (Ehrlich, 1999), and several other resources. The list includes:

America	cardigan	Friday	June	pasteurize
ampere	cheddar cheese	frisbee	leotards	Pennsylvania
April	Chevrolet	Geiger counter	Levi's	pickles
August	Chrysler	Georgia	Louisiana	rugby
beef Stroganoff	Delaware	graham crackers	marathon	sandwich
bikini	derrick	guillotine	March	sideburns
bologna	diesel	guppy	Maryland	teddy bear
braille	Dodge	hamburger	Mason-Dixon Line	tuxedo
Bunsen burner	Fahrenheit	July	maverick	volt

3. Provide Information
Mr. Silverman asks students which words they're most curious about and offers to tell the stories behind them. In response to their requests, he tells about the origin of the *teddy bear,* which honors President Theodore "Teddy" Roosevelt; *hamburger,* which is named for Hamburg, a city in Germany; *cheddar,* which is named for the English city where the cheese was first made; and *July,* which Julius Caesar named for himself.

4. Guide Practice
Mr. Silverman divides the students into small groups to research an eponym and report to the class. The teacher shares the resources that he has available—word history books, dictionaries, and a website about eponyms—and the students research their words and prepare a poster.

5. Assess Learning
Small groups of students take turns reporting the results of their research. They practice their presentational skills as they share what they have learned and display their posters. Mr. Silverman and their classmates assess each group using a rubric they developed that includes credit for research, display, and presentational skills. Afterward, students hang their posters in the classroom for their classmates to reread.

Figure 4-11   The 100 Most Frequently Used Words

A	B	C	D	E
a and	back	came	day	
about are	be	can	did	
after around	because	could	didn't	
all as	but		do	
am at	by		don't	
an			down	

F	G	H	I	J
for	get	had his	I into	just
from	got	have home	if is	
		he house	in it	
		her how		
		him		

K	L	M	N	O
know	like	man	no	of our
	little	me	not	on out
		mother	now	one over
		my		or

P	QR	S	T	U
people		said	that think	up
put		saw	the this	us
		school	them time	
		see	then to	
		she	there too	
		so	they two	
		some	things	

V	W	X	Y	Z
very	was when		you	
	we who		your	
	well will			
	went with			
	were would			
	what			

these word walls when they are writing. Seeing the words posted on word walls, clusters[C], and other charts in the classroom and using them in their writing helps students learn to spell the words.

The second type of word wall displays high-frequency words. Researchers have identified the most commonly used words and recommend that children during the primary grades learn to spell 100 of these words because of their usefulness. The most frequently used words represent more than 50% of all the words children and adults write (Horn, 1926)! Figure 4-11 lists the 100 most frequently used words. Teachers can assist struggling readers by posting the 100 high-frequency words on a word wall in the classroom, or they can make individual word walls for these students. Teachers type up a list of words in alphabetical order and make copies to cut into bookmarks, to glue on a file folder, or to make into personal dictionaries. Teachers who work with students who read and write on grade level can also make word walls to display more difficult common words. Figure 4–12 presents a list of 100 common words that fourth through eighth

Figure 4-12   **100 High-Frequency Words for Older Students**

A	B	C	D	E
a lot	beautiful	caught	decided	either
again	because	certain	desert–dessert	embarrassed
all right	belief	close–clothes	different	enough
although	believe	committee	discussed	especially
another	beneath	complete	doesn't	etc.
anything	between			everything
around	board–bored			everywhere
	breathe			excellent
	brought			experience
F	G	H	I	J
familiar		hear–here	immediately	
favorite		heard–herd	interesting	
field		height	it's–its	
finally		herself		
foreign		himself		
friends		humorous		
frighten		hungry		
K	L	M	N	O
knew–new	language	maybe	necessary	once
know–no	lying		neighbor	ourselves
knowledge				
P	QR	S	T	U
particular	quiet–quite	safety	their–there–they're	until
people	really	school	themselves	usually
piece–peace	receive	separate	though	
please	recommend	serious	thought	
possible	remember	since	threw–through	
probably	restaurant	special	throughout	
	right–write	something	to–two–too	
		success	together	
V	W	X	Y	Z
	weight		your–you're	
	were			
	we're			
	where			
	whether			
	whole–hole			

graders need to learn. Some of the words, such as *himself, finally,* and *remember,* are more appropriate for fourth and fifth graders, and others, such as *independent, foreign,* and *throughout,* are more appropriate for sixth through eighth graders. These are commonly used words that students often misspell or confuse with other words.

Making Words.   Teachers choose a multisyllabic word and prepare sets of letter cards for a making words[C] activity (Cunningham & Cunningham, 1992). Then students use letter cards to practice spelling words and review spelling patterns and rules. They arrange and rearrange the cards to spell one-letter words, two-letter words, three-letter words, and so forth, until they use all the letters to spell the original word.

Struggling Readers and Writers Need to Know High-Frequency Words. Many struggling readers and writers can't read or spell all of the 100 high-frequency words, but because they are so common, it's essential that all students learn them. Teachers test students at the beginning of the year to see which words students can't read or spell and then make a word wall with these words. If only a few students need to work on these words, try making individual word walls on file folders for students to keep at their desks to refer to. Then, plan daily practice activities. Have students search for the words in books they are reading and spell the words using magnetic letters, linking plastic letters, and white boards and dry-erase pens. It's also important to periodically check students' progress to make sure they are learning the words.

Teachers often choose words from thematic units for making words activities. For example, during a unit on the American Revolution, a fifth-grade teacher chose the word *revolutionary,* and the students spelled these words:

1-letter words: I, a
2-letter words: it, in, on, an, at, to
3-letter words: lay, are, not, run, ran, oil, via, toy, tie, lie, urn, lye, rye, our, out, nut, ear, rat, lit, lot, let, vet
4-letter words: rain, tire, year, vote, only, live, love, rule, rely, your, tail, near, earn, liar, turn, tear, rear, note, rate, rein, root, volt, yarn, vary, into, toil
5-letter words: learn, yearn, rerun, royal, relay, you're, early, liter, ultra, ruler, voter, lover, liver, outer, value, untie, until
6-letter words: lotion, nation, ration, turner, return, nearly, lively, tailor, revolt
9-letter words: voluntary
10-letter words: revolution
13-letter words: revolutionary

Students manipulated letter cards to spell the words, and the teacher listed the words on a chart, beginning with one-letter words and making increasingly longer words until students used all of the letters to spell *revolutionary.* As students worked, they consulted dictionaries to check the spelling of possible words and to argue (unsuccessfully) that *litter* was spelled *liter* and *volunteer* was spelled *voluntear* so that the words could be added to the chart. Students manipulated many different spelling patterns in this activity and reviewed prefixes and suffixes, homophones, and rhyming words. Some students were also introduced to new words, including *urn, ration, rye, yearn,* and *volt.*

Word Sorts.   Students use word sorts to explore, compare, and contrast word features as they sort a pack of word cards. Teachers prepare word cards for students to sort into two or more categories according to their spelling patterns or other criteria (Bear et al., 2000). In the vignette at the beginning of the chapter, Mr. King's students sorted word cards according to the number of syllables in a word and syllabication rules. Sometimes teachers tell students what categories to use, and the sort is a closed sort; at other times, students determine the categories themselves, and the sort is an open

Students examine spelling patterns as they sort words.

sort. Students can sort word cards and then return them to an envelope for future use, or they can glue the cards onto a sheet of paper.

Proofreading.   Proofreading is a special kind of reading that students use to locate misspelled words and other mechanical errors in rough drafts. As students learn about the writing process, they are introduced to proofreading in the editing stage. More in-depth instruction about how to use proofreading to locate spelling errors and then correct these misspelled words is part of spelling instruction (Cramer, 1998). Through a series of minilessons, students can learn to proofread sample student papers and mark misspelled words. Then, working in pairs, students can correct the misspelled words.

Proofreading activities are more valuable for teaching spelling than are dictation activities, in which teachers dictate sentences for students to write and correctly capitalize and punctuate. Few people use dictation in their daily lives, but students use proofreading skills every time they polish a piece of writing.

Dictionary Use.   Students need to learn to locate the spelling of unfamiliar words in the dictionary. Although it is relatively easy to find a "known" word in the dictionary, it is hard to locate unfamiliar words, and students need to learn what to do when they do not know how to spell a word. One approach is to predict possible spellings for unknown words, then check the most probable spellings in a dictionary.

Students should be encouraged to check the spellings of words in a dictionary as well as to use dictionaries to check multiple meanings of a word or the etymology of the word. Too often, students view consulting a dictionary as punishment; teachers must work to change this view of dictionary use. One way to do this is to appoint some students in the classroom as dictionary checkers. These students keep dictionaries on their desks, and they are consulted whenever questions about spelling, word meaning, and word usage arise.

Spelling Options. In English, there are alternate spellings for many sounds because so many words borrowed from other languages have retained their native spellings. There are many more options for vowel sounds than for consonants. Even so, there are four spelling options for /f/ (*f, ff, ph, gh*). Spelling options sometimes vary according to the letter's position in the word. For example, *ff* is found in the middle and at the end of words but not at the beginning (e.g., *muffin, cuff*), and *gh* represents /f/ only at the end of a syllable or word (e.g., *cough, laughter*). Common spelling options for phonemes are listed in Figure 4-13.

Teachers point out spelling options as they write words on word walls and when students ask about the spelling of a word. They also can use a series of minilessons to teach upper-grade students about these options. During each lesson, students can focus on one phoneme, such as /f/ or /ar/, and as a class or small group, they can develop a list of the various ways the sound is spelled in English, giving examples of each spelling. A sixth-grade chart on long *o* is presented in Figure 4-14.

Weekly Spelling Tests. Many teachers question the usefulness of spelling tests to teach spelling, because research on invented spelling suggests that spelling is best learned through reading and writing (Gentry & Gillet, 1993; Wilde, 1992). In addition, teachers complain that lists of spelling words are unrelated to the words students are reading and writing and that the 30 minutes of valuable instructional time spent each day in completing spelling textbook activities is excessive. Even so, parents and school board members value spelling tests as evidence that spelling is being taught. Weekly spelling tests, when they are used, should be individualized so that students learn to spell the words they need for their writing.

In the individualized approach to spelling instruction, students choose the words they will study, and many of the words they choose are words they use in their writing projects. Students study 10 specific words during the week using a study strategy; this approach places more responsibility on students for their own learning. Teachers develop a weekly word list of 20 or more words of varying difficulty from which students select words to study. Words for the master list include high-frequency words, words from the word wall related to literature focus units and thematic units, and words students needed for their writing projects during the previous week. Words from spelling textbooks can also be added to the list.

On Monday, the teacher administers a pretest using the master list of words, and students spell as many of the words as they can. Students correct their own pretests, and from the words they misspell, they create individual spelling lists. They make two copies of their study list, using the numbers on the master list to make it easier to take the final test on Friday. Students use one copy of the list for study activities, and the teacher keeps the second copy.

Students spend approximately 5 minutes each day during the week studying the words on their study lists. Research shows that instead of "busy-work" activities such as using their spelling words in sentences, it is more effective for students to use this study strategy:

1. Look at the word and say it to yourself.
2. Say each letter in the word to yourself.
3. Close your eyes and spell the word to yourself.
4. Write the word, and check that you spelled it correctly.
5. Write the word again and check that you spelled it correctly.

This strategy focuses on the whole word. Teachers explain how to use the strategy during a minilesson at the beginning of the school year and then post a copy of the strat-

Figure 4-13 Common Spelling Options

Sound	Spellings	Examples	Sound	Spellings	Examples
long a	a-e	date	short oo	oo	book
	a	angel		u	put
	ai	aid		ou	could
	ay	day		o	woman
ch	ch	church	ou	ou	out
	t(u)	picture		ow	cow
	tch	watch	s	s	sick
	ti	question		ce	office
long e	ea	each		c	city
	ee	feel		ss	class
	e	evil		se	else
	e-e	these	sh	ti	attention
	ea-e	breathe		sh	she
short e	e	end		ci	ancient
	ea	head		ssi	admission
f	f	feel	t	t	teacher
	ff	sheriff		te	definite
	ph	photograph		ed	furnished
j	ge	strange		tt	attend
	g	general	long u	u	union
	j	job		u-e	use
	dge	bridge		ue	value
k	c	call		ew	few
	k	keep	short u	u	ugly
	ck	black		o	company
l	l	last		ou	country
	ll	allow	z	s	present
	le	automobile		se	applause
m	m	man		ze	gauze
	me	come	syllabic l	le	able
	mm	comment		al	animal
n	n	no		el	cancel
	ne	done		il	civil
long o	o	go	syllabic n	en	written
	o-e	note		on	lesson
	ow	own		an	important
	oa	load		in	cousin
short o	o	office		contractions	didn't
	a	all		ain	certain
	au	author	r-controlled	er	her
	aw	saw		ur	church
oi	oi	oil		ir	first
	oy	boy		or	world
long oo	u	cruel		ear	heard
	oo	noon		our	courage
	u-e	rule			
	o-e	lose			
	ue	blue			
	o	to			
	ou	group			

Figure 4-14 Spelling Options Chart for Long *o*

Spelling	Word	Initial	Medial	Final
o	oh, obedient	X		
	go, no, so			X
o-e	home, pole		X	
ow	own	X		
	known		X	
	blow, elbow, yellow			X
oa	oaf, oak, oat	X		
	boat, groan		X	
ew	sew			X
ol	yolk, folk		X	
oe	toe			X
ough	though			X
eau	beau			X
ou	bouquet		X	

egy in the classroom. In addition to this study strategy, sometimes students trade word lists on Wednesday or Thursday or give each other a practice test.

A final test is administered on Friday. The teacher reads the master list, and students write only those words they have practiced during the week. To make it easier to administer the test, students first list the numbers of the words they have practiced from their study lists on their test papers. Any words that students misspell should be included on their lists the following week.

VISIT CHAPTER 4 ON THE COMPANION WEBSITE AT
www.prenhall.com/tompkins

- Complete a self-assessment to demonstrate your understanding of the concepts presented in this chapter
- Complete field activities that will help you expand your understanding of the middle-grade classroom and refining students' print skills
- Visit important web links related to middle-grade spelling and word-identification skills
- Look into your state's standards as they relate to word identification and spelling and the middle-grade student
- Communicate with other preservice teachers via the message board and discuss the issues of refining print skills of students in grades 4 to 8

Review

Too often, teachers assume that students master phonics and print skills in the primary grades, but students continue to refine their print skills in fourth through eighth grades. They learn to read and write more multisyllabic words, and the focus at this level is on using three strategies—phonic analysis, syllabic analysis, and morphemic analysis—to identify and spell new words. As students learn more about the English orthographic system, they increase their ability to spell words. Most students in grades 4 through 8 are at the syllables and affixes and derivational relations stages of spelling development. The feature that follows presents a list of recommended practices that effective teachers use to help students refine their print skills.

How Effective Teachers . . .
Refine Students' Print Skills

1. Teachers teach students the blending and segmenting strategies to use in decoding and spelling words.
2. Teachers check that students know how to read and spell the 100 high-frequency words and also teach students other commonly used words.
3. Teachers teach the high-utility phonics concepts, skills, and generalizations to students who have not already learned phonics so that they can decode unfamiliar words through phonic analysis.
4. Teachers teach students how to divide words into syllables as an aid to decoding and spelling multisyllabic words.
5. Teachers teach students about root words and affixes as an aid to decoding and spelling multisyllabic words.
6. Teachers teach print skills through minilessons and practice activities using words taken from students' reading and writing.
7. Teachers analyze students' spelling errors as a measure of their understanding of the English orthographic system.
8. Teachers recognize that daily reading and writing experiences contribute to students' spelling development.
9. Teachers post word walls in the classroom, involve students in making words and word sort activities, and teach students to proofread and to use the dictionary as part of spelling instruction.
10. Teachers may use weekly spelling tests, but only as part of the spelling program.

Professional References

Adams, M. J. (1990). *Beginning to read: Thinking and learning about print.* Cambridge, MA: MIT Press.

Allington, R. L. (Ed.). (1998). *Teaching struggling readers.* Newark, DE: International Reading Association.

Bear, D. R., Invernizzi, M., Templeton, S., & Johnston, F. (2000). *Words their way: Word study for phonics, vocabu-lary, and spelling instruction.* Upper Saddle River, NJ: Merrill/Prentice Hall.

Calfee, R., & Drum, P. (1986). Research on teaching reading. In M. W. Wittrock (Ed.), *Handbook of research on teaching* (3rd ed.) (pp. 804–849). New York: Macmillan.

Chall, J. S., Jacobs, V. A., & Baldwin, L. E. (1990). *The reading crisis: Why poor children fall behind*. Cambridge, MA: Harvard University Press.

Clymer, T. (1963). The utility of phonic generalizations in the primary grades. *The Reading Teacher, 16*, 252–258.

Cramer, R. L. (1998). *The spelling connection: Integrating reading, writing, and spelling instruction*. New York: Guilford Press.

Cunningham, P. M. (1999). What should we do about phonics? In L. B. Gambrell, L. M. Morrow, S. B. Neuman, & M. Pressley (Eds.), *Best practices in literacy instruction* (pp. 68–89). New York: Guilford Press.

Cunningham, P. M., & Cunningham, J. W. (1992). Making words: Enhancing the invented spelling-decoding connection. *The Reading Teacher, 46*, 106–115.

Delpit, L. (1987). The silenced dialogue: Power and pedagogy in educating other people's children. *Harvard Educational Review, 58*, 280–298.

Eldredge, J. L. (1995). *Teaching decoding in holistic classrooms*. Englewood Cliffs, NJ: Prentice Hall.

Gaskins, I. W., Ehri, L. C., Cress, C., O'Hara, C., & Donnelly, K. (1996/1997). Procedures for word learning: Making discoveries about words. *The Reading Teacher, 50*, 312–326.

Gaskins, R. W., Gaskins, J. W., & Gaskins, I. W. (1991). A decoding program for poor readers—and the rest of the class, too! *Language Arts, 68*, 213–225.

Gentry, J. R., & Gillet, J. W. (1993). *Teaching kids to spell*. Portsmouth, NH: Heinemann.

Gough, P. B., Juel, C., & Griffith, P. L. (1992). Reading, spelling, and the orthographic cipher. In P. B. Gough, L. C. Ehri, & R. Treiman (Eds.), *Reading acquisition* (pp. 35–48). Hillsdale, NJ: Erlbaum.

Hanna, P. R., Hanna, J. S., Hodges, R. E., & Rudorf, E. H. (1966). *Phoneme-grapheme correspondences as cues to spelling improvement*. Washington, DC: US Government Printing Office.

Henderson, E. H. (1990). *Teaching spelling* (2nd ed.). Boston: Houghton Mifflin.

Hiebert, E. H. (1991). The development of word-level strategies in authentic literacy tasks. *Language Arts, 68*, 234–240.

Horn, E. (1926). *A basic writing vocabulary*. Iowa City: University of Iowa Press.

Horn, E. (1957). Phonetics and spelling. *Elementary School Journal, 57*, 233–235, 246.

Johnson, D. D., & Baumann, J. F. (1984). Word identification. In P. D. Pearson (Ed.), *Handbook of reading research* (pp. 583–608). New York: Longman.

Juel, C., Griffith, P. L., & Gough, P. B. (1986). Acquisition of literacy: A longitudinal study of children in first and second grade. *Journal of Educational Psychology, 78*, 243–255.

Lomax, R. G., & McGee, L. M. (1987). Young children's concepts about print and meaning: Toward a model of word reading acquisition. *Reading Research Quarterly, 22*, 237–256.

Read, C. (1986). *Children's creative spelling*. London: Routledge.

Reyes, M. de la Luz. (1991). A process approach to literacy using dialogue journals and literature logs with second language learners. *Research in the Teaching of English, 25*, 291–313.

Shefelbine, J. (1995). *Learning and using phonics in beginning reading* (Literacy research paper; volume 10). New York: Scholastic.

Snow, C., Burns, M. W., & Griffin, P. (1998). *Preventing reading difficulties in young children*. Washington, DC: National Academy Press.

Stanovich, K. E. (1992). Speculations on the causes and consequences of individual differences in early reading acquisition. In P. B. Gough, L. C. Ehri, & R. Treiman (Eds.), *Reading acquisition* (pp. 307–342). Hillsdale, NJ: Erlbaum.

Templeton, S. (1983). Using the spelling/meaning connection to develop word knowledge in older students. *Journal of Reading, 27*, 8–14.

Tompkins, G. E., & Yaden, D. B., Jr. (1986). *Answering students' questions about words*. Urbana, IL: ERIC Clearinghouse on Reading and Communication Skills and National Council of Teachers of English.

Tunmer, W., & Nesdale, A. (1985). Phonemic segmentation skill and beginning reading. *Journal of Educational Psychology, 77*, 417–427.

Vellutino, F. R., & Scanlon, D. M. (1987). Phonological coding, phonological awareness, and reading ability: Evidence from a longitudinal and experimental study. *Merrill-Palmer Quarterly, 33*, 321–363.

Venezky, R. L. (1999). *The American way of spelling: The structure and origins of American English orthography*. New York: Guilford Press.

White, T. G., Sowell, J., & Yanagihara, A. (1989). Teaching elementary students to use word-part clues. *The Reading Teacher, 42*, 302–308.

Wilde, S. (1992). *You kan red this! Spelling and punctuation for whole language classrooms, K–6*. Portsmouth, NH: Heinemann.

Yopp, H. K. (1985). Phoneme segmentation ability: A prerequisite for phonics and sight word achievement in beginning reading? In J. Niles & R. Lalik (Eds.), *Issues in literacy: A research perspective* (pp. 330–336). Rochester, NY: National Reading Conference.

Yopp, H. K. (1992). Developing phonemic awareness in young children. *The Reading Teacher, 45*, 696–703.

Children's Book References

Ehrlich, E. (1999). *What's in a name? How proper names became everyday words.* New York: Henry Holt.

Presson, L. (1996). *What in the world is a homophone?* New York: Barron's.

Terban, M. (1988). *Guppies in tuxedos: Funny eponyms.* New York: Clarion.

chapter 5

Learning About the Meanings of Words

chapter
QUESTIONS

- How do students learn vocabulary words?

- What is the relationship between vocabulary knowledge and reading?

- How do teachers teach vocabulary?

- What are the components of word study?

Mrs. Sanom's Word Wizards Club

rs. Sanom is the resource teacher at John Muir Elementary School, and she sponsors an after-school Word Wizards Club for fifth and sixth graders. The club meets for an hour on Wednesday afternoons. Nineteen students are club members this year, and many of them are English language learners. Mrs. Sanom teaches vocabulary lessons during the club meetings using costumes, books, and hands-on activities. She focuses on a different word study topic each week; the topics include writing alliterations, choosing synonyms carefully, applying context clues to figure out unfamiliar words, using a dictionary and a thesaurus, understanding multiple meanings of words, choosing between homophones, adding prefixes and suffixes to words, and studying root words.

She devised this club because many of the students at John Muir Elementary School have limited vocabularies, and this affects their reading achievement. She has two banners displayed in her classroom that say "Expanding your vocabulary leads to school success" and "Knowing words makes you powerful." In the letters that the Word Wizards club members write to Mrs. Sanom at the end of the school year, they display a new sense of how important vocabulary is in life. They find themselves paying more attention to words an author uses, and they are more successful in figuring out the meaning of unfamiliar words using context clues. Most important, the students say that participation in the Word Wizards Club gives them an appreciation for words that will last a lifetime. Rosie writes:

> I love being a Word Wizard. I learned lots of new words and that makes me smart. I have a favorite word that is hypothesis. Did you know that I am always looking for more new words to learn? My Tio Mario gave me a dictionary because I wanted it real bad. I like looking for words in the dictionary and I like words with lots of syllables the best. I want to be in the club next year in 6th grade. Ok?

At the first meeting of the Word Wizards Club, Mrs. Sanom read aloud *Miss Alaineus: A Vocabulary Disaster* (Frasier, 2000), an outrageous and touching story of a girl named Sage who loves words. In the story, Sage misunderstands the meaning of *miscellaneous,* but what begins as embarrassment turns into victory when she wins an award for her costume in the school's annual vocabulary parade. The students talked about the story in a grand conversation[C], and they decided that they want to dress in costumes and have a vocabulary parade themselves, just as Mrs. Sanom knew they would. They decided that they will have a vocabulary parade at the end of the year, and they will invite their classmates and teachers to participate, too. "I like to dress in vocabulary costumes," Mrs. Sanom explained. "I plan to dress up in clothes or a hat that represents a vocabulary word at each club meeting." With that introduction, she reached into a shopping bag and pulled out an oversized, wrinkled shirt and put it on over her clothes. "Here is my costume," she announced. "Can you guess the word?" She modeled the shirt, trying to smooth the wrinkles, until a student guessed the word *wrinkled.*

The students talked about *wrinkle,* forms of the word (*wrinkled, unwrinkled,* and *wrinkling*), and the meanings. They checked the definitions of *wrinkle* in the dictionary. They understood the first meaning, "a crease or fold in clothes or skin," but the second

C See the Compendium of Instructional Procedures, which follows Chapter 12, for more information on terms marked with the symbol C.

meaning—"a clever idea or trick"—was more difficult. Mrs. Sanom called their idea to have a vocabulary parade "a new wrinkle" in her plans for the club, and then the students began to grasp the meaning.

The borders of each page in *Miss Alaineus* are decorated with words beginning with a specific letter of the alphabet. The border on the first page has words beginning with A, the second page B, and so on through the story. To immerse students in words, Mrs. Sanom asked the students each to choose a letter from a box of plastic alphabet letters, turn to that page in the book, and then choose a word beginning with that letter from the border to use in an activity. The words they chose included *awesome, berserk, catastrophe,* and *dwindle.* Students wrote the word on the first page of their Word Wizard Notebooks, checked its meaning in a dictionary and wrote it beside the word, and then drew a picture to illustrate the meaning. While they worked, Mrs. Sanom wrote the words on the alphabetized word wall[C] she has posted in the classroom. Afterward, the students shared their words and illustrations with the other club members using a tea party[C] activity.

Mrs. Sanom has a collection of vocabulary books in her classroom library, and she gives brief book talks[C] to introduce the books to the Word Wizards Club members. Her library includes alphabet books, word play books, books about the history of English, and novels that range from second- to sixth-grade reading levels. A list of some of her books is presented in Figure 5-1. She explains that the very best way to learn lots of words is to read every day, and she encourages them to choose a vocabulary book or other book from her library each week to read between club meetings. At the end of each meeting, she allows a few minutes for students to choose a book to take home to read.

At today's club meeting, Mrs. Sanom is wearing a broad-rimmed hat with two wrecked cars and a stop sign attached. The students check out Mrs. Sanom's costume because they know that her costume represents a word—and that word is the topic of today's meeting. They quickly begin guessing words: "Is it *crash?*" Oscar asks. "I think the word is *accident.* My dad had a car accident last week," says Danielle. Ramon suggests, "Those cars are *wrecked.* Is that the word?" Mrs. Sanom commends the club members for their good guesses and says that they're on the right track. To provide a little help, she draws a row of nine letter boxes on the chalkboard and fills in the first letter and the last four letters. Then Martha guesses it—*collision.* Mrs. Sanom begins a cluster on the chalkboard with the word *collision* written in the middle circle and related words on each ray. They compare the noun *collision* and the verb *collide.* They also check the dictionary and a thesaurus for more information and write *crash, accident, wreck, hit, smashup,* and *collide* on the rays to complete the cluster. They talk about how and when to use *collide* and *collision.* Ramon offers, "I know a sentence: On 9-11, the terrorists' airplanes collided with the World Trade Center."

Mrs. Sanom explains that ships can be involved in collisions, too. A ship can hit another ship or it can collide with something else in the water—an iceberg, for example. Several students know about the *Titanic,* and they share what they know about that ship's fateful ocean crossing. Mrs. Sanom selects *Story of the Titanic* (Kentley, 2001) from her text set of books about the *Titanic* and shows photos and drawings of the ship to provide more background information. They make a K-W-L chart[C], listing what they know in the K column and questions they want to find answers for in the W column. The students also make individual charts in their Word Wizard Notebooks, small, spiral-bound notebooks that Mrs. Sanom purchased for them.

Next, Mrs. Sanom presents a list of words using an overhead projector— some about the *Titanic* article they will read and some not—for an exclusion brain-

Figure 5-1   Mrs. Sanom's Collection of Books About Words

Agee, J. (2000). *Elvis lives!: And other anagrams.* New York: Farrar, Straus & Giroux.

Amato, M. (2000). *The word eater.* New York: Scholastic.

Brook, D. (1998). *The journey of English.* New York: Clarion.

Brown, R. (1996). *Toad.* New York: Puffin Books.

Cheney, L. (2002). *America: A patriotic primer.* New York: Simon & Schuster.

Clements, A. (1996). *Frindle.* New York: Simon & Schuster.

Edwards, P. D. (1996). *Some smug slug.* New York: HarperCollins.

Edwards, P. D. (2001). *Slop goes the soup: A noisy warthog word book.* New York: Hyperion.

Fakih, K. O. (1995). *Off the clock: A lexicon of time words and expressions.* New York: Ticknor.

Frazier, D. (2000). *Miss Alaineus: A vocabulary disaster.* San Diego, CA: Harcourt Brace.

Graham, J. B. (1999). *Flicker flash.* Boston: Houghton Mifflin.

Gwynne, F. (1970). *The king who rained.* New York: Windmill Books.

Gwynne, F. (1976). *A chocolate moose for dinner.* New York: Windmill Books.

Gwynne, F. (1980). *The sixteen hand horse.* New York: Prentice Hall.

Gwynne, F. (1988). *A little pigeon toad.* New York: Simon & Schuster.

Heller, R. (1987). *A cache of jewels and other collective nouns.* New York: Grosset & Dunlap.

Janeczko, P. (Sel.). (2001). *A poke in the I: A collection of concrete poems.* Cambridge, MA: Candlewick Press.

Kalman, B., & Lewis, J. (2000). *Pioneer dictionary.* New York: Crabtree.

Mammano, J. (2001). *Rhinos who play soccer.* San Francisco: Chronicle Books. (And others in the Rhino series.)

Presson, L. (1996). *What in the world is a homophone?* New York: Barron's.

Scieszka, J. (2001). *Baloney (Henry P.)* New York: Viking.

Scillian, D. (2001). *A is for America.* Chelsea, MI: Sleeping Bear Press.

Terban, M. (1983). *In a pickle and other funny idioms.* New York: Clarion.

Terban, M. (1987). *Mad as a wet hen! And other funny idioms.* New York: Clarion.

Terban, M. (1988). *Guppies in tuxedos: Funny eponyms.* New York: Clarion.

Terban, M. (1989). *Superdupers: Really funny real words.* New York: Clarion.

Terban, M. (1990). *Punching the clock: Funny action idioms.* New York: Clarion.

Terban, M. (1991). *Hey, hay! A wagonload of funny homonym riddles.* New York: Clarion.

Terban, M. (1992). *The dove dove: Funny homograph riddles.* New York: Clarion.

Terban, M. (1996). *Scholastic dictionary of idioms: More than 600 phrases, sayings, and expressions.* New York: Scholastic.

storming[C] activity. The words include *unsinkable, crew, liner, passengers, voyage, airplane, catastrophe, ship, mountain, lifeboat,* and *general.* The students predict which words relate to the article and which do not. The word *general* stumps them because they think of it as an adjective meaning "having to do with the whole, not specific." A student checks the dictionary to learn about the second meaning—a high-ranking military officer (noun). The students are still confused, but after reading the article, they realize that the word *general* is not related: The officer in charge of the *Titanic* (or any ship, for that matter) is called a *captain.*

Mrs. Sanom passes out copies of the one-page article and reads it aloud while students follow along. They discuss the article, talking and asking more questions about the needless tragedy. Then they complete the L section of the K-W-L chart and the exclusion brainstorming activity. Because the students are very interested in learning more about the disaster, Mrs. Sanom introduces her text set of narrative and informational books about the *Titanic,* including *Inside the*

Titanic (Brewster, 1997), *Polar, the Titanic Bear* (Spedden, 1994), *Tonight on the Titanic* (Osborne & Osborne, 1995), *Titanic: A Nonfiction Companion to Tonight on the Titanic* (Osborne & Osborne, 2002), *On Board the Titanic: What It Was Like When the Great Liner Sank* (Tanaka, 1996), and *Voyage on the Great Titanic: The Diary of Margaret Ann Brady* (White, 1998). She invites the students to spend the last few minutes of the club meeting choosing a book from the text set to take home to read before the next club meeting.

Mrs. Sanom wears a different costume or hat each week. Ten of her favorite costumes are:

> *Bejeweled: A silky shirt with "jewels" glued across the front*
> *Champion: Racing shorts, tee shirt, and a medal on ribbon worn around her neck*
> *Hocus-pocus: A black top hat with a stuffed rabbit stuck inside, white gloves, and a magic wand*
> *International: A dress decorated with the flags of many countries and a globe cut in half for a hat*
> *Mercury: A white sheet worn toga style with a baseball cap with wings on each side*
> *Myriad: A dress made of fabric with thousands of tiny stars printed on it and other stars attached to a headband*
> *Porous: A necklace with small strainer hanging on it and a colander for a hat*
> *Slick: A black leather jacket, sunglasses, and hair slicked back with mousse*
> *Transparent: A clear plastic raincoat, clear plastic gloves, and a clear shower cap*
> *Vacant: A bird cage with a "for rent" sign worn as a hat with an artificial bird sitting on her shoulder*

One week, however, Mrs. Sanom forgets to bring a costume, so after a bit of quick thinking, she decides to feature the word *ordinary,* and she wears her everyday clothes as her costume!

For their 17th weekly club meeting, Mrs. Sanom dressed as a queen with a flowing purple robe and a tiara on her head. The focus of the week was words beginning with Q, the 17th letter of the alphabet. They began by talking about queens—both historical queens such as Queen Isabella of Spain, who financed Christopher Columbus's voyage to the New World, and queens who are alive today. Next, Mrs. Sanom began a list of Q words with *queen,* and then the students added words to the list. They checked the Q page in alphabet books and examined dictionary entries for Q words. They chose interesting words, including *quadruped, quadruplet, qualify, quest, quarantine, quintet, quiver, quench,* and *quotation.* After they had more than 20 words on their list, Mrs. Sanom asked each student to choose a Q word, study it, and make a square poster to share what they learned about the word. Afterward, Mrs. Sanom collected the posters, made a quilt[C] and hung it on the wall outside the classroom. One student's square about *quadruped* is presented in Figure 5-2, and it documents the student's understanding of root words.

Last week's topic was homographs, two or more words that are spelled alike but pronounced differently, such as *record, bow, read,* and *dove.* Mrs. Sanom was dressed with a big red ribbon bow tied around her waist and smaller red bows tied on pigtails. At the beginning of the club meeting, she retied the bow at her waist and then she bowed to the students. Ramon quickly guessed that the word was *bow,* but the concept of homographs is new to him and the other club members. Mrs. Sanom introduced the word *homograph,* explained the definition, and offered

Figure 5-2 A Student's Square on
Quadruped for the Q Quilt

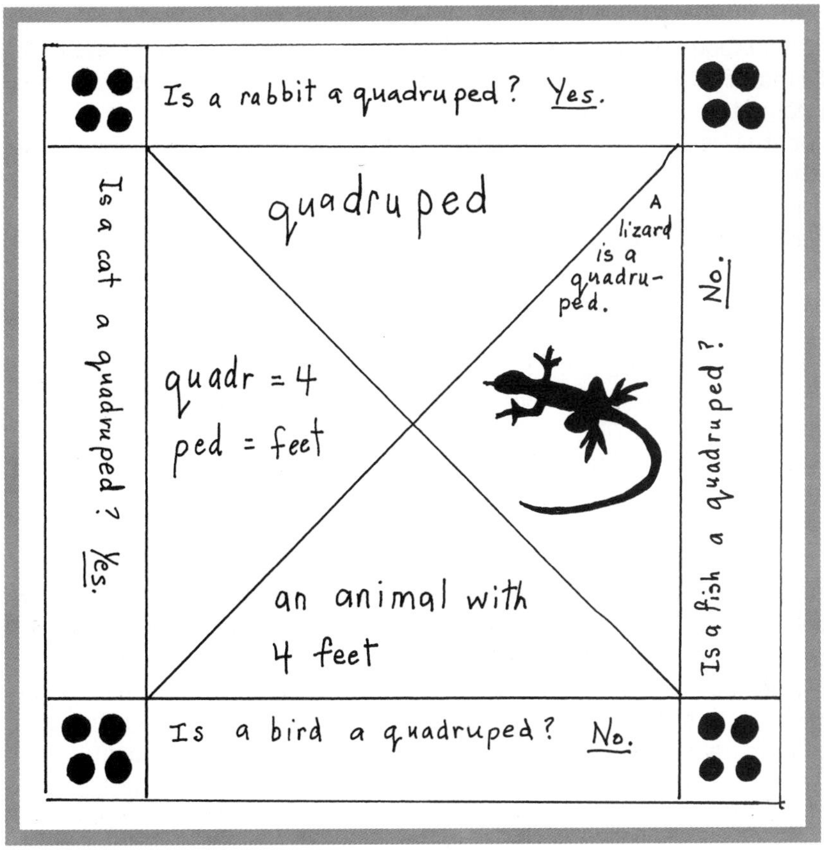

Is a rabbit a quadruped? Yes.

quadruped

Is a cat a quadruped? Yes.

A lizard is a quadruped.

quadr = 4
ped = feet

an animal with 4 feet

Is a fish a quadruped? No.

Is a bird a quadruped? No.

examples. Then she shared several homograph riddles from *The Dove Dove: Funny Homograph Riddles* (Terban, 1992), including "The nurse *wrapped* the bandage around the *injury.*" The students solve the riddle by identifying the homograph that can replace the highlighted words; for this riddle, the answer is *wound.*

Next, Mrs. Sanom divided the students into small groups, and she gave each group a different homograph riddle from Terban's book to solve. Then they shared the riddles with the whole group. As they got more practice with homographs, the students became more confident at solving the riddles, but some of the students were confused about homophones and homographs. Mrs. Sanom explained that homophones are words that sound alike but are spelled differently, such as *wood–would* and *there–their–they're.* The students used the last 10 minutes of the club meeting to write in their Word Wizard Notebooks about homographs. They also chose new books to take home to read before the next club meeting.

The Word Wizards make and wear word bracelets to highlight special words. In October, the students make word bracelets that spell the word they've chosen to describe or represent themselves, such as *genius, ornery,* or *sincere.* Mrs. Sanom's word is *sassy,* and she demonstrates how to make a bracelet using small alphabet beads strung on an elastic string. Then the students follow her steps as they make their own bracelets, which they proudly wear to school and show off to their classmates. In February, they study patriotic words, such as *allegiance, citizen, equality, independence,* and *republic,* and choose a word for a second bracelet. They choose words after reading books with patriotic themes, such as Lynne Cheney's *America: A Patriotic Primer* (2002) and *A is for America: An American Alphabet* (Scillian, 2001). For their third word bracelet, they choose the most interesting word from all the words they've collected on the word wall and in their Word Wizard Notebooks. Some of the words that the club members choose for their third bracelets are *valiant, awesome, phenomenon, plethora, incredulous, cryptic, guffaw, mischievous,* and *razzle-dazzle.*

The vocabulary parade is the highlight of the year. Every club member creates a costume and participates in the parade. Mrs. Sanom dresses as a wizard—a word wizard, that is—and she leads the parade from classroom to classroom in the intermediate wing of the school. The students dress as *camouflage, victory, shimmer, monarch, liberty, uncomfortable, fortune, emerald,* and *twilight,* for example, and they carry word cards so that everyone will know the words they represent. As they tour each classroom, Mrs. Sanom and the students talk about their words and what they are learning. The club members' parents come to school to view the parade, and a local television station videotapes the parade for the evening news.

Teachers use realia—real objects, models, and pictures—to teach vocabulary to ELL students because using language to explain words is often ineffective.

C hildren learn vocabulary by being immersed in words, and Mrs. Sanom engaged her fifth and sixth graders with words as they participated in Word Wizards Club activities. Researchers have reported again and again that reading is the best way for students to learn words. As they read, students learn many, many words incidentally, and teachers reinforce students' learning by directly teaching some difficult words that are significant to the literature or content-area study (Stahl, 1999).

Unfamiliar words are not equally hard or easy to learn; the degree of difficulty depends on what students already know about the word. Graves (1985) identifies four possible situations for unfamiliar words:

1. *Sight word.* Students know the word and what it means when they hear someone say it, and can use it orally, but they don't recognize its written form.
2. *New word.* Students have a concept related to the word, but they are not familiar with the word itself, either orally or in written form.
3. *New concept.* Students have little or no background knowledge about the concept underlying the word, and they don't recognize the word itself.
4. *New meaning.* Students know the word, but they are unfamiliar with the way the word is used and its meaning in this situation.

Of the four categories of word learning, the most difficult for students is the one involving new concepts because they must first learn the concept and then attach a word label to it and learn the definition.

In a balanced literacy program, students meet unfamiliar words every day through literature and content-area study, and teachers recognize that they need to assist students in different ways depending on whether the unfamiliar words are new sight words, new words, new concepts, or new meanings. Sometimes simply pronouncing a new word is all that is needed, and sometimes relating a new meaning to a familiar one will be enough, but sometimes teaching a direct instruction lesson is necessary for students to learn a difficult new word or concept. The feature on page 143 shows how vocabulary fits into a balanced literacy program. As you continue reading this chapter, you will learn more about the ideas presented in the feature.

The Role of Vocabulary in a Balanced Literacy Program

Component	Description
Reading	Reading is the most important way that students learn words.
Phonics and Other Skills	Vocabulary skills include synonyms, antonyms, homophones, idioms, dictionary use, and root words and affixes.
Strategies	Students learn strategies for using context clues, identifying multiple meanings of words, examining etymological information in dictionaries, and studying words.
Vocabulary	Students learn an average of 3,000 words a year through a combination of reading and direct instruction.
Comprehension	Knowing the meaning of words students are reading is a prerequisite for comprehension.
Literature	Teachers post words on word walls and involve students in vocabulary activities and direct instruction lessons to teach key words.
Content-Area Study	Teachers also post word walls as part of content-area units and involve students in word study activities using these words.
Oral Language	Students use the words they are learning orally as they talk about books they are reading, in content-area study, and through direct instruction activities.
Writing	Students apply their knowledge of vocabulary when they use words in writing.
Spelling	Students apply knowledge about words in spelling homophones and other words.

HOW DO STUDENTS LEARN VOCABULARY WORDS?

Students' vocabularies grow at an astonishing rate—about 3,000 words a year, or roughly 7 to 10 new words every day (Nagy & Herman, 1985). By the time students graduate from high school, their vocabularies may reach 25,000 words or more. It seems obvious that to learn words at such a prolific rate, students learn words both in school and outside of school, and that they learn most words incidentally, not through explicit instruction. Reading has the greatest impact on children's vocabulary development, but other activities are important, too. Students learn words through family activities, hobbies, and trips. Television can also have a significant impact on children's vocabularies, especially when children view educational programs and limit the

Reading is the most important way students learn new words.

amount of time they spend watching television each day. Teachers often assume that students learn words primarily through the lessons they teach, but students actually learn many more words in other ways.

Levels of Word Knowledge

Students develop knowledge about a word slowly, through repeated exposure to the word. They move from not knowing the word at all, to recognizing that they have seen the word before, and then to a level of partial knowledge where they have a general sense of the word or know one meaning. Finally, students know the word fully; they know multiple meanings of the word and can use it in a variety of ways (Dale & O'Rourke, 1986; Nagy, 1988). The four levels or degrees of word knowledge are:

1. Unknown word: I don't know this word.
2. Initial recognition: I have seen or heard this word or I can pronounce it, but I don't know the meaning.
3. Partial word knowledge: I know one meaning of this word and can use it in a sentence.
4. Full word knowledge: I know more than one meaning or several ways to use this word. (Allen, 1999)

Once students reach the third level of word knowledge, they can usually understand the word in context and use it in their writing. Students do not reach the fourth level with all the words they learn. Stahl (1999) describes full word knowledge as "flexible": Students understand the core meaning of a word and how it changes in different contexts.

Incidental Word Learning

Students learn words incidentally, without explicit instruction, all the time, and because students learn so many words this way, teachers know that they do not have to teach the meaning of every unfamiliar word in a text. Students learn words from many sources, but researchers report that reading is the single largest source of vocabulary growth for students after third grade (Beck & McKeown, 1991; Nagy, 1988). In addition, the amount of time children spend reading independently is the best predictor of vocabulary growth between second and fifth grades.

Students need daily opportunities for independent reading in order to learn vocabulary words, and they need to read books that are appropriate for their reading levels. If they read books that are too easy or too hard, students will learn very few new words. Two of the best ways to provide opportunities for independent reading are reading workshop and literature circles. Through both of these activities, students have opportunities to read self-selected books that interest them and to learn words in context.

A third way teachers provide for incidental learning of vocabulary is by reading books aloud to students. You may think that students in fourth through eighth grades are too old for teachers to read aloud to them, but they're not. Teachers should read aloud high-quality books that students are interested in but could not read themselves every day, whether during "story time" or as part of literature focus units, reading workshop, or thematic units. Although reading aloud is important for all students, it is an especially important experience for struggling readers who typically read fewer books themselves; also, the books at their reading level have less sophisticated vocabulary words. In fact, researchers report that students learn as many words incidentally while listening to teachers read aloud as they do by reading themselves (Stahl, Richek, & Vandevier, 1991).

To read more about literature circles, turn to Chapter 8, "Teaching With Narrative Texts," and to learn more about reading workshop, read Chapter 12, "Becoming Lifelong Readers and Writers."

Context Clues

Students learn many words from context as they read books (Nagy, Anderson, & Herman, 1987; Nagy, Herman, & Anderson, 1985). Six types of context clues are definition, example-illustration, contrast, logic, root words and affixes, and grammar. The surrounding words and sentences offer context clues. Some clues provide information about the meaning of the word, and others provide information about the part of speech and how the unfamiliar word is used in a sentence. This contextual information helps students figure out the meaning of the word. Illustrations also provide contextual information that helps readers identify words. Figure 5-3 lists six types of context clues that readers use to figure out unfamiliar words as they read sentences and paragraphs.

The six types of context clues do not operate in isolation; two or three types of contextual information are often found in the same sentence. Also, readers' differing levels of background knowledge affect the types of word-identification strategies they can use effectively.

Consider how context clues might help students figure out the italicized words in these four sentences from *The Magic School Bus and the Electric Field Trip* (Cole, 1997):

We must have an unbroken *circuit*—circle—of wire. (p. 12)
Never use appliances with *frayed*, torn, or damaged insulation. (p. 42)
Steam is an invisible gas made of water molecules—the tiniest bits of water. (p. 20)
The *switch* pulled the contacts together, and the electric path was complete again. (p. 41)

Which sentences provided sufficient context clues to figure out the meaning of the italicized words? Which types of context clues did the author use in these sentences? In the first sentence, for example, *circle*—a synonym for *circuit*—provides useful information, but it may not be enough information for students who do not understand concepts related to electricity.

Figure 5-3   Six Types of Context Clues

Clue	Description	Sample Sentence
Definition	Readers use the definition in the sentence to understand the unknown word.	Some spiders spin silk with tiny organs called *spinnerets.*
Example-Illustration	Readers use an example or illustration to understand the unknown word.	Toads, frogs, and some birds are *predators* that hunt and eat spiders.
Contrast	Readers understand the unknown word because it is compared or contrasted with another word in the sentence.	Most spiders live for about one year, but *tarantulas* sometimes live for 20 years or more!
Logic	Readers think about the rest of the sentence to understand the unknown word.	An *exoskeleton* acts like a suit of armor to protect the spider.
Root Words and Affixes	Readers use their knowledge of root words and affixes to figure out the unknown word.	People who are terrified of spiders have *arachnophobia.*
Grammar	Readers use the word's function in the sentence or its part of speech to figure out the unknown word.	Most spiders *molt* five to ten times.

Unfortunately, context clues rarely provide enough information in a sentence to help students learn a word. The clues may seem to be useful to someone who already knows a word, but context clues often provide only partial information—and the information can be misleading. In the third sentence, for example, the definition of *steam* leaves out an important fact—that steam is dangerously hot! Researchers have concluded that context clues are relatively ineffective unless they provide definitions (Baumann & Kameenui, 1991; Nagy, 1988). Nonetheless, researchers recommend that students be taught how to use context clues because some context clues are useful, and they do help students develop word-learning strategies to use on their own (Nagy, 1988).

Nagy, Anderson, and Herman (1987) found that students who read books at their grade level had a 1 in 20 chance of learning the meaning of any word from context. Although that chance might seem insignificant, if students read 20,000 unfamiliar words a year, and if they learn 1 of every 20 words from context, they would learn 1,000 words, or one-third of the average student's annual vocabulary growth. How much time does it take for students to read 20,000 words? Nagy (1988) has estimated that if teachers provide 30 minutes of daily reading time, students will learn an additional 1,000 words a year!

The best way to teach students about context clues is by modeling. When teachers read aloud, they should stop at a difficult word and talk with students about how they can use context clues to figure out the meaning of the word. When the context provides enough information, teachers use the information and continue reading, but when the rest of the sentence or paragraph does not provide enough information, teachers model other strategies (such as looking up the word in the dictionary) to learn the meaning of the word.

It is interesting to note that capable and less capable readers learn from context at about the same rate (Stahl, 1999). Researchers have speculated that the difference in vocabulary growth is due to differences in the amount of words that students read, not the differences in their reading achievement.

Word-Learning Strategies

Capable readers use a variety of effective strategies to figure out the meaning of unknown words as they read. They might check the definition of a word in a dictionary or ask a teacher, classmate, or parent about a word. Sometimes they can use context clues to figure out the meaning of the unknown word. They also figure out a probable meaning by thinking about possible synonyms that make sense in the context of the sentence. Allen (1999) lists these 12 ways students can figure out the meaning of unknown words:

1. Look at the word in relation to the sentence.
2. Look up the word in the dictionary and see if any meanings fit the sentence.
3. Ask the teacher.
4. Sound it out.
5. Read the sentence again.
6. Look at the beginning of the sentence again.
7. Look for other key words in the sentence that might tell you the meaning.
8. Think what makes sense.
9. Ask a friend to read the sentence to you.
10. Read around the word and then go back again.
11. Look at the picture if there is one.
12. Skip it if you don't need it. (p. 23)

Less capable readers, in contrast, have fewer strategies for figuring out the meaning of unfamiliar words. They often depend on just one or two strategies, such as sounding out the word or skipping it.

Why Is Vocabulary Knowledge Important?

Vocabulary knowledge and reading achievement are closely related. Students with larger vocabularies are more capable readers, and they have a wider repertoire of strategies for figuring out the meanings of unfamiliar words than less capable readers do (McKeown, 1985). Reading widely is the best way students develop their vocabularies, and that is one reason why capable readers have larger vocabularies (Nagy, 1988; Stahl, 1999): They simply do more reading, both in school and out of school (Anderson, Wilson, & Fielding, 1986).

The idea that capable readers learn more vocabulary because they read more is an example of the Matthew effect (Stanovich, 1986). The Matthew effect suggests that "the rich get richer and the poor get poorer" in vocabulary development and other aspects of reading. Capable readers become better readers because they read more, and the books they read are more challenging and have sophisticated vocabulary words. The gulf between more capable and less capable readers grows larger because less capable readers read less and the books they do read are less challenging.

Learning vocabulary is a challenge for ELL students because they are often learning the oral and written forms of a word at the same time. Students' lack of English vocabulary often adversely affects their reading development.

TEACHING STUDENTS TO UNLOCK WORD MEANINGS

Vocabulary instruction plays an important role in balanced literacy classrooms (Rupley, Logan, & Nichols, 1998/1999). Teachers highlight important vocabulary words related to literature focus units and thematic units and teach minilessons about multiple meanings of words, etymologies, idioms, dictionary use, and other word-study skills. These lessons focus on words that students are reading and teach students how to figure out the meaning of unfamiliar words (Blachowicz & Lee, 1991). These lessons are even more important to students who are English language learners, because these students rely more heavily on explicit instruction than native speakers do. Figure 5-4 lists guidelines for teaching vocabulary.

Characteristics of Effective Instruction

The goal of vocabulary instruction is for students to learn how to learn new words. According to Carr and Wixon (1986), Nagy (1988), and Allen (1999), effective vocabulary instruction exemplifies five characteristics:

1. *Connections to background knowledge.* For vocabulary instruction to be effective, students must relate new words to their background knowledge. Because learning words in isolation is rarely effective, teachers should teach words in concept clusters whenever possible.
2. *Repetition.* Students need to read, write, or say words 8 to 10 times or more before they recognize them automatically. Repetition helps students remember the words they are learning.
3. *Higher-level word knowledge.* The focus of instruction should be to help students develop higher-level word knowledge; just having students memorize definitions or learn synonyms will not lead to full word knowledge.
4. *Strategy learning.* Not only are students learning the meanings of particular words through vocabulary lessons, they are developing knowledge and strategies for learning new words independently.
5. *Meaningful use.* Students need to be actively involved in word-study activities and opportunities to use the words in projects related to literature focus units and thematic units.

Teachers apply these five characteristics when they teach minilessons about vocabulary. In the vignette, for example, Mrs. Sanom applied these characteristics in the Word Wizards Club activities. Too often, however, vocabulary instruction has emphasized looking up definitions of words in a dictionary, but this is not a particularly effective activity, at least not as it has been used in the past.

Minilessons. Teachers present minilessons to teach key words, vocabulary concepts, and strategies for unlocking word meanings. These lessons should focus on words that students are reading and writing and involve students in meaningful activities. Students make predictions about the meaning of unfamiliar words as they read, using a combination of context clues, morphemic analysis, and their own prior knowledge (Blachowicz, 1993). Later, teachers often ask students to return to important words after reading to check their understanding of the words. The minilesson on page 150 shows how one teacher introduces vocabulary before reading a chapter in a content-area textbook.

Figure 5-4   Guidelines for Teaching Vocabulary

1. Choose Words to Study

Teachers and students choose words for vocabulary instruction from books they are reading and from thematic units. These words should not be high-frequency words, such as *what* or *because,* but content-rich words. Vocabulary instruction grows out of words that students are reading and concepts they are learning about in the classroom.

2. Highlight Words on Word Walls

Students and teachers select important and interesting words to display on word walls during literature focus units and thematic units, and they use separate word walls for each unit. Teachers highlight a few key terms before reading, and then students and teachers choose other words to add during and after reading.

3. Develop Full Word Knowledge

Students need to learn more than just single definitions of words in order to develop full word knowledge. They need to learn multiple meanings of words, how root words and affixes combine to affect meaning, synonyms, antonyms, and homonyms, word histories, and figurative meanings.

4. Teach Minilessons

Teachers teach students the meanings of individual words, vocabulary concepts, and word-learning strategies through minilessons[C]. In a minilesson, teachers introduce the topic, present information, provide a structured practice activity, review, and provide application activities.

5. Plan Word-Study Activities

Teachers plan word-study activities so that students can explore words after reading. Activities include word posters, word maps, dramatizing words, word sorts[C], word chains, and semantic feature analysis[C].

6. Use Dictionaries and Thesauri

Students learn how to use dictionaries to learn about the meanings of words and thesauri to locate synonyms and antonyms. Teachers provide structured opportunities for students to use these books during minilessons and other word-study activities. They don't ask students to copy definitions of words or to write words in sentences or contrived stories.

7. Teach Context Clues

Words in a sentence provide clues to the meaning of other words in the sentence. They may provide definitions, comparisons, examples, or other types of information. Teachers explain the types of context clues and demonstrate how to use context clues so that students can learn words more effectively through independent reading.

8. Promote Wide Reading

Students learn only a small percentage of the 3,000 or more words they learn each year through teacher-directed lessons and activities; wide reading is far more important in developing students' vocabularies. Teachers provide daily opportunities for students to read independently for at least 15 minutes in grades 1–3 and 30 minutes in grades 4–8. They also read aloud stories and informational books to students every day.

Minilesson

Topic: Introducing Content-Area Vocabulary Words
Grade: Fifth Grade
Time: Three 30-minute periods

Mrs. Cramer's fifth-grade class is involved in a social studies unit on immigration. The class has already created a K-W-L chart on immigration to develop and activate students' background knowledge, and students
have written about how and when their families came to the United States. They have also marked their
countries of origin on a world map in the classroom. In this 3-day minilesson, Mrs. Cramer is introducing six
key vocabulary words before students read a chapter in their social studies textbook. Many of her students
are English learners, so she takes more time to practice vocabulary before reading the chapter.

1. Introduce the Topic
Mrs. Cramer explains to her class of fifth graders that after a week of studying immigration, they are now
getting ready to read the chapter in the social studies text about immigration. She places these six words
written on word cards in a pocket chart and reads each one aloud: *culture, descendant, ethnic custom,
immigrant, prejudice,* and *pluralism.* She tells the students that these words are used in the chapter and that it
is important to be familiar with them before reading.

2. Share Examples
Mrs. Cramer distributes anticipation guides[C] for students to rate their knowledge of the new words. The guide
has four columns; the six new words are listed in the left column, and the other three columns have these
headings: I know the word well, I have heard of it, I don't know this word. For each word, the students put a
check mark in the appropriate column. At the end of the unit, students will again rate their knowledge of the
words and then compare the two ratings to assess their learning.

3. Provide Information
Mrs. Cramer divides the students into small groups for a word sort. Each group receives a pack of 12
cards; the new vocabulary words are written on six of the cards and their definitions on the other six cards.
The students work together to match the words and definitions. Then Mrs. Cramer reviews the meaning of
each word.

4. Guide Practice
The next day, the students repeat the card sort activity to review the meaning of each word. Next students
work with partners to complete a cloze[C] activity. Mrs. Cramer has prepared a list of sentences taken from the
chapter and omitted the new vocabulary words. The students write the correct word in each blank. Then the
teacher reviews the sentences with the students, explaining any words students use incorrectly.

5. Assess Learning
On the third day, Mrs. Cramer adds the six new words to the alphabetized word wall on immigration displayed
on a wall in the classroom. Next she models writing a quickwrite[C] using the new words and other
"immigration" words from the word wall. Then the students write quickwrites following the teacher's model
and using at least three of the new words and three other words from the word wall. After they finish writing,
the students use highlighters to mark the "immigration" words they have incorporated in their writings. Later,
Mrs. Cramer reads the quickwrites and uses them to assess the students' vocabulary knowledge.

Using Dictionaries. In traditional classrooms, the most common vocabulary activities involved listing new words on the chalkboard and directing students to write the words and copy the definitions from a dictionary or use the words in sentences. These activities are not effective for developing in-depth understanding and are no longer recommended (Stahl, 1999).

Looking words up in the dictionary without teacher support and guidance usually isn't very effective because definitions do not provide enough useful information for students or because the words used in the definition are forms of the word being defined (Allen, 1999; Stahl, 1999). Sometimes the definition that students choose—usually the first one—is the wrong one. Or, the definition they find may not make sense to them. In addition, many entries don't provide examples of how the word is used in sentences. For example, the word *pollution* is usually defined as "the act of polluting"; this is not a useful definition. Students could look for an entry for *polluting*, but they won't find one. If they continue looking, they might notice an entry for *pollute*, and the first definition is "to make impure." The second definition is "to make unclean, especially with man-made waste." Even this definition provides very little useful information. On-line dictionaries may be more useful to students because the entries often provide more information about words and related words.

Although parents and teachers urge students to look up unknown words in a dictionary, dictionary definitions are most useful after a person already knows the meaning of a word. Therefore, teachers play an important role in dictionary work. They contextualize the definitions that students locate by explaining the meaning of the word in more detail, providing sample sentences, and comparing the word to related words and opposites.

Components of Word Study

Word knowledge involves more than learning definitions. Eight components of word study are:

1. Concepts and word meanings
2. Multiple meanings
3. Morphemic analysis
4. Synonyms
5. Antonyms
6. Homonyms
7. Etymologies
8. Figurative meanings

Students learn a wide range of information about words and make connections between words and concepts. They learn one or more meanings for a word and synonyms and antonyms to compare and contrast meanings. Sometimes they confuse words they are learning with homonyms that sound or are spelled the same as the word they are learning. Students also learn that prefixes and suffixes change the meaning of a word. And, they learn about idioms and figurative sayings involving the word they are learning. A seventh-grade student's investigation of the word *vaporize* is shown in Figure 5-5.

Concepts and Word Meanings. Students use words to label concepts, and they learn words best when they are related to a concept. Consider the words *axle, groundwater, buffalo chips, wagon train, ford, fur trader, dysentery, outpost, guide, mountain men, oxen, Bowie knife, snag, cut-off, cholera, winch,* and *prairie dog.* They all relate to pioneers traveling west on the Oregon Trail. When students read a book about the Oregon Trail, for example, or during a social studies unit on the westward movement, students learn

Figure 5-5 | A Seventh Grader's Investigation of *Vaporize*

Morphemic Analysis	Root Word	Suffix
vapor + ize	vapor	ize
		It is used to change a noun into a verb.

VAPORIZE

To change from a solid into a vapor (gas) (verb)

Word History	Related Words	Figurative Use
It became a word in the 1600's. It came from the Latin word "steam".	evaporate vaporizer vaporous	The boy's thoughts vaporized and he couldn't remember the answer.

many of these words by connecting them to their Oregon Trail schema or concept. It is easier to learn a group of words relating to a concept than a group of unrelated words.

Multiple Meanings of Words.   Most words have more than one meaning, and many common words have five, eight, or more meanings. For some words, multiple meanings develop for the noun and verb forms of the word, but sometimes meanings develop in other ways. The word *bank*, for example, has the following meanings:

> a piled-up mass of snow or clouds
> the slope of land beside a lake or river
> the slope of a road on a turn
> the lateral tilting of an airplane in a turn
> to cover a fire with ashes for slow burning
> a business establishment that receives and lends money
> a container in which money is saved
> a supply for use in emergencies (e.g., a blood bank)
> a place for storage (e.g., a computer's memory bank)
> to count on
> similar things arranged in a row (e.g., a bank of elevators)
> to arrange things in a row

You may be surprised that there are at least a dozen meanings for the common word *bank*. Some are nouns and others are verbs, but grammatical form alone does not account for so many meanings.

The meanings of *bank* come from three sources. The first five meanings come from a Viking word, and they are related because they all deal with something slanted or making a slanted motion. The next five meanings come from the Italian word *banca*,

Figure 5-6   Common Words With More Than Five Meanings

act	draw	lay	place	set	strike
air	dress	leave	plain	sharp	stroke
around	drive	line	plant	shift	strong
away	dry	low	plate	shine	stuff
bad	dull	make	play	shoot	sweep
bank	even	man	point	short	sweet
bar	eye	mark	positive	shot	swing
base	face	measure	post	show	switch
black	fail	mind	power	side	tack
blow	fair	mine	print	sight	take
boat	fall	natural	put	sign	thick
break	fast	new	quiet	sing	thing
by	fight	no	rain	sink	think
carry	fire	nose	raise	sit	through
case	fly	note	range	slip	throw
cast	good	now	reach	small	tie
catch	green	number	rear	snap	tight
change	hand	of	rest	so	time
charge	have	off	return	sound	to
check	head	on	rich	spin	touch
clear	heel	open	ride	spread	tough
close	high	out	right	spring	train
color	hold	over	ring	square	trip
count	horn	paper	rise	stamp	turn
court	hot	part	roll	star	twist
cover	house	pass	round	start	under
crack	in	pay	rule	stay	up
cross	just	pick	run	step	use
crown	keep	picture	scale	stick	warm
cut	key	piece	score	stiff	watch
dead	knock	pipe	send	stock	way
deep	know	pitch	serve	stop	wear

a money changer's table. All these meanings deal with financial banking except for the 10th meaning, "to count on," which requires a bit more thought. We use the saying "to bank on" figuratively to mean "to depend on," but it began more literally from the actual counting of money on a table. The last two meanings come from the French word *banc*, meaning "bench." Words have acquired multiple meanings as society became more complex and finer shades of meaning were necessary; for example, the meanings of bank as an emergency supply and a storage place are fairly new. As with many words with multiple meanings, it is just a linguistic accident that three original words from three languages with unrelated meanings came to be spelled the same way (Tompkins, 2004; Tompkins & Yaden, 1986). A list of common words with more than five meanings is shown in Figure 5-6.

Students gradually acquire additional meanings for words, and they usually learn these new meanings through reading. When a familiar word is used in a new way, students often notice the new application and may be curious enough to check the meaning in a dictionary.

Morphemic Analysis. Students use their knowledge of root words and affixes to unlock many multisyllabic words. For example, *omnivorous, carnivorous,* and *herbivorous* relate to the foods that animals eat; *omni* means "all," *carn* means "flesh," and *herb* means "herbs or vegetation." The common word part *vorous* comes from the Latin *vorare,* meaning "to swallow up." When students know *carnivorous* or *carnivore,* they can use their knowledge of prefixes to figure out the other words.

Many English words are compound words, and the meaning is usually clear from the word parts and the context in which the word or phrase is used, as in the words *toothbrush, breakneck, earthquake,* and *anteater.* The word *fire* is used in a variety of compound words and phrases, such as *fire hydrant, firebomb, fireproof, fireplace, firearm, fire drill, under fire, set the world on fire, fire away,* and *open fire.*

Students can examine words developed from a common root, such as these words from the Latin roots *-ann* and *-enn,* which mean "year": *annual, biennial, perennial, centennial, bicentennial, millennium,* and *sesquicentennial.* Students figure out the meaning of the words by locating the root and identifying prefixes and suffixes. Then they work together to make a cluster[C] to highlight the words and their meanings. A sixth-grade class chart on *-ann/-enn* words is shown in Figure 5-7.

Synonyms: Words With the Same Meaning. Words that have nearly the same meaning as other words are synonyms. English has so many synonyms because so many words have been borrowed from other languages. Synonyms are useful because they provide options, allowing writers to be more precise. Think of all the synonyms for the word *cold: cool, chilly, frigid, icy, frosty,* and *freezing.* Each word has a different shade of meaning: *Cool* means moderately cold; *chilly* is uncomfortably cold; *frigid* is intensely cold; *icy* means very cold; *frosty* means covered with frost; and *freezing* is so cold that water changes into ice. Our language would be limited if we had only the word *cold.*

Figure 5-7   A Class Chart of *-ann/-enn* Words

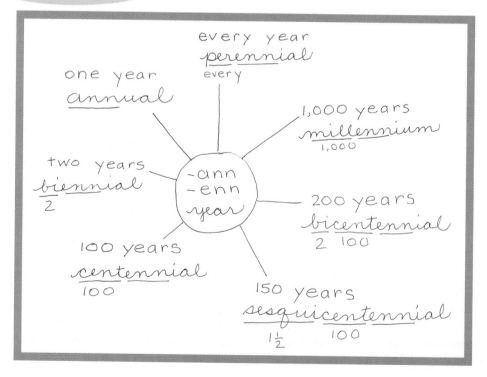

Teachers should be careful to articulate the differences among synonyms. Nagy (1988) emphasizes that teachers should focus on teaching concepts and related words, not just provide single-word definitions using synonyms. For example, to tell a child that *frigid* means *cold* provides only limited information. And, when a student says, "I want my sweater because it's frigid in here," it shows that the student does not understand the different degrees of cold; there's a big difference between *chilly* and *frigid*.

Antonyms: Words That Mean the Opposite. Words that express opposite meanings are antonyms. Antonyms for the word *loud,* for example, are *soft, subdued, quiet, silent, inaudible, sedate, somber, dull,* and *colorless.* These words express shades of meaning just as synonyms do, and some opposites are more appropriate for one meaning of *loud* than for another. When *loud* means *gaudy,* for instance, opposites are *somber, dull,* and *colorless;* when *loud* means *noisy,* the opposites are *quiet, silent,* and *inaudible.*

Students can use a thesaurus to locate both synonyms and antonyms. *A First Thesaurus* (Wittels & Greisman, 1985), *Scholastic Children's Thesaurus* (Bollard, 1998), and *The American Heritage Children's Thesaurus* (Hellweg, 1997) are three excellent thesauri designed for students in grades 4 through 8. Students use these reference books to locate more effective words when revising their writing and for word-study activities.

Homonyms: Words That Confuse. Homonyms, also known as homophones, are words that sound alike but are spelled differently, such as *right* and *write, to, too,* and *two,* and *there, their,* and *they're.* A list of homophones is presented in Figure 5-8. Sometimes students confuse the meanings of these words, but more often they confuse their spellings.

Most homonyms are linguistic accidents, but *stationary* and *stationery* share an interesting history. *Stationery,* meaning paper and books, developed from *stationary.* In medieval England, merchants traveled from town to town selling their wares. The merchant who sold paper goods was the first to set up shop in one town. His shop was "stationary" because it did not move, and he came to be called the "stationer." The spelling difference between the two words signifies the semantic difference.

There are many books of homonyms for students, including Gwynne's *The King Who Rained* (1970), *A Chocolate Moose for Dinner* (1976), *The Sixteen Hand Horse* (1980), and *A Little Pigeon Toad* (1988); Maestro's *What's a Frank Frank? Tasty Homograph Riddles* (1984); *What in the World Is a Homophone?* (Presson, 1996); and *Eight Ate: A Feast of Homonym Riddles* (Terban, 1982).

During the primary grades, students are introduced to the concept of homonyms and learn the easier pairs, including *see–sea, I–eye, right–write,* and *dear–deer.* In the upper grades, teachers focus on the homophones that students continue to confuse, such as *there–their–they're* and the more sophisticated pairs, including *morning–mourning, flair–flare,* and *complement–compliment.*

Intensive study is necessary because homonyms are confusing to many students. The words sound alike and the spellings are often very similar—sometimes only one letter varies or one letter is added: *pray–prey, hole–whole.* And sometimes the words have the same letters, but they vary in sequence: *bear–bare* and *great–grate.*

Teachers teach minilessons to explain the concept of homonyms and make charts of the homophone pairs and triplets. Calling students' attention to the spelling and meaning differences helps to clarify the words. Students can also make homophone posters, as shown in Figure 5-9. On the posters, students draw pictures and write sentences to contrast the homophones. Displaying these posters in the classroom reminds students of the differences between the words.

air–heir	close–clothes	heroin–heroine	pain–pane	seam–seem
allowed–aloud	coarse–course	hi–high	pair–pare–pear	serf–surf
ant–aunt	colonel–kernel	hoard–horde	palette–pallet	sew–so–sow
ate–eight	complement–	hoarse–horse	passed–past	shear–sheer
ball–bawl	compliment	hoes–hose	patience–patients	shone–shown
band–banned	council–counsel	hole–whole	pause–paws	shoot–chute
bare–bear	creak–creek	hour–our	peace–piece	side–sighed
base–bass	days–daze	jam–jamb	peak–peek–pique	sighs–size
based–baste	dear–deer	knead–need	peal–peel	slay–sleigh
be–bee	dense–dents	knew–new	pedal–peddle	soar–sore
beat–beet	dew–do–due	knight–night	peer–pier	soared–sword
bell–belle	die–dye	knot–not	phase–faze	sole–soul
berry–bury	doe–dough	know–no	plain–plane	some–sum
berth–birth	dual–duel	lacks–lax	plait–plate	son–sun
billed–build	ewe–you	lead–led	pleas–please	stairs–stares
blew–blue	eye–I	leak–leek	pole–poll	stake–steak
boar–bore	fair–fare	leased–least	pore–pour	stationary–stationery
board–bored	feat–feet	lie–lye	praise–prays–preys	steal–steel
boarder–border	fined–find	links–lynx	presence–presents	straight–strait
born–borne	fir–fur	load–lode	pride–pried	suite–sweet
bough–bow	flea–flee	loan–lone	prince–prints	tail–tale
brake–break	flew–flu	loot–lute	principal–principle	taught–taut
bread–bred	floe–flow	made–maid	profit–prophet	tear–tier
brews–bruise	flour–flower	mail–male	quarts–quartz	tense–tents
bridal–bridle	foaled–fold	main–mane	rain–rein–reign	their–there–they're
brows–browse	for–fore–four	maize–maze	raise–rays–raze	threw–through
buy–by–bye	forth–fourth	manner–manor	rap–wrap	throne–thrown
cache–cash	foul–fowl	marshal–martial	real–reel	tide–tied
callous–callus	gait–gate	meat–meet–mete	red–read	to–too–two
capital–capitol	genes–jeans	medal–meddle–metal	reed–read	toad–toed–towed
carat–carrot	gofer–gopher	might–mite	rest–wrest	toe–tow
cast–caste	gorilla–guerrilla	mind–mined	right–rite–write	tracked–tract
cede–seed	grate–great	miner–minor	ring–wring	troop–troupe
ceiling–sealing	grill–grille	missed–mist	road–rode–rowed	undo–undue
cell–sell	groan–grown	moan–mown	role–roll	vain–vane–vein
cellar–seller	guessed–guest	moose–mousse	roomer–rumor	wade–weighed
cent–scent–sent	hail–hale	morning–mourning	root–route	waist–waste
chews–choose	hair–hare	muscle–mussel	rose–rows	wait–weight
chic–sheik	hall–haul	naval–navel	rote–wrote	waive–wave
chili–chilly	halve–have	none–nun	rung–wrung	wares–wears
choral–coral	hangar–hanger	oar–or–ore	sac–sack	warn–worn
chord–cord–cored	hay–hey	one–won	sail–sale	way–weigh
chute–shoot	heal–heel	paced–paste	scene–seen	weak–week
cite–sight–site	hear–here	packed–pact	sea–see	wood–would
clause–claws	heard–herd	pail–pale	sealing–ceiling	yoke–yolk

Etymologies: The History of the English Language. Glimpses into the history of the English language provide interesting information about word meanings and spellings (Tompkins & Yaden, 1986; Venezky, 1999). The English language began in 447 A.D. when the Angles, Saxons, and other Germanic tribes invaded England. This Anglo-Saxon English was first written down by Latin missionaries in approximately 750 A.D.

Figure 5-9   A Sixth Grader's Homophone Poster

Soared

Sword

The rocket soared through space.

The golden knight's sword was the most perfect sword in the land.

The English of the period from 450 to 1100 is known as Old English. During this time, English was a very phonetic language and followed many German syntactic patterns. Many loan words, including *ugly, window, egg, they, sky,* and *husband,* were contributed by the marauding Vikings who plundered villages along the English coast.

The English of the second period of development, Middle English (1100–1500), began with the Norman Conquest in 1066. William, Duke of Normandy, invaded England and became the English king. William, his lords, and the royals who followed him spoke French for nearly 200 years, so French was the official language of England. Many French loan words were added to the language, and French spellings were substituted for Old English spellings. For example, *night* was spelled *niht* and *queen* was spelled *cwen* in Old English to reflect how they were pronounced; their modern spellings reflect changes made by French scribes. Loan words from Dutch, Latin, and other languages were added to English during this period, too.

The invention of the printing press marks the transition from Middle English to the Modern English period (1500–present). William Caxton brought the first printing press to England in 1476, and soon books and pamphlets were being mass-produced. Spelling became standardized as Samuel Johnson and other lexicographers compiled dictionaries, even though English pronunciation of words continues to evolve. Loan words continued to flow into English from almost every language in the world. Exploration and colonization in North America and around the world accounted for many of the loan words. Other words, such as *electric, democracy,* and *astronaut,* were created using Greek word parts. Figure 5-10 presents a list of loan words from languages around the world. New words are added to English every year, and the new words reflect new inventions and cultural practices. Many new words today,

Figure 5-10   Loan Words From Around the World

Language	Sample Words
African (many languages)	aardvark, banjo, cola, gumbo, mumbo jumbo, safari, trek, voodoo, zombie
American English	America, cafeteria, commuter, cowboy, frontier, hijack, jackknife, maverick, mustang, O.K., patio, pioneer, prairie, sierra, teenager, turkey, underground railroad, yankee
Arabic	alcohol, apricot, assassin, magazine, zenith, zero
Australian/New Zealand (aboriginal)	boomerang, kangaroo, kiwi
Celtic	walnut
Chinese	chop suey, tea, typhoon, wok
Czech	pistol, robot
Dutch	caboose, easel, frolic, pickle, waffle, yacht
Eskimo	igloo, kayak, mukluk, parka
Finnish	sauna
French	a la carte, ballet, beef, beige, chauffeur, chic, hors d'oeuvres, restaurant, sabotage
German	dollar, kindergarten, noodle, poodle, pretzel, vampire, waltz
Greek	atom, biology, chaos, cycle, epidemic, giant, helicopter, hero, pentagon, rhapsody, siren, thermometer
Hawaiian	aloha, hula, lei, luau, ukulele
Hebrew	cherub, hallelujah, jubilee, kosher, rabbi
Hindi	bangle, dungaree, juggernaut, jungle, pajamas, shampoo, thug
Hungarian	goulash, paprika
Icelandic	geyser
Irish	bog, leprechaun, shamrock
Italian	carnival, extravaganza, motto, piano, pizza, solo, spaghetti, umbrella, violin
Japanese	hibachi, honcho, judo, kimono, origami
Malaysian	bamboo
Mexican Spanish	adobe, bonanza, bronco, chocolate, coyote, marijuana, ranch, tacos, tamales, tomato
Native American (many languages)	barbecue, canoe, hammock, moccasin, papoose, raccoon, skunk, tepee, tomahawk
Persian	bazaar, divan, khaki, orange, peach, shawl, sherbet, turban
Polish	mazurka, polka
Polynesian	taboo, tattoo
Portuguese	albino, cobra, coconut, molasses, piranha
Russian	czar, sputnik, steppe, tundra, vodka
Scandinavian	cozy, egg, fjord, husband, knife, outlaw, rug, skate, ski, skin, sky, ugly, window
Scottish	clan, gold, slogan
South American Spanish/Portuguese	jaguar, llama
Spanish	alligator, guitar, hurricane, lasso, mosquito, potato, vanilla
Turkish	caviar, horde, khan, kiosk, yogurt
Welsh	penguin
Yiddish	bagel, chutzpah, klutz, pastrami

such as *e-mail* and *netiquette,* relate to the Internet. The word *Internet* is a recent word, too; it is less than 20 years old!

Students use etymological information in dictionaries and other books about word histories to learn how particular words developed and what the words mean. Etymological information is given in brackets at the beginning or end of dictionary entries. Here is the etymological information for three words:

democracy [1576, < MF < LL , Gr demokratia, demos (people) + kratia (cracy = strength, power)]

The word *democracy* entered English in 1576 through French, and the French word came from Latin and the Latin word from Greek. In Greek, the word *demokratia* means "power to the people."

house [bef. 900, ME hous, OE hus]

House is an Old English word that entered English before 900. It was spelled *hus* in Old English and *hous* in Middle English.

moose [1603, Algonquin, "he who strips bark"]

The word *moose* is Native American—from an Algonquin tribe in the northeastern part of the United States—and entered English in 1603. It comes from the Algonquin word for "he who strips bark."

Even though words have entered English from around the world, the three main sources of words are English, Latin, and Greek. Upper-grade students can learn to identify the languages that these words came from, and knowing the language backgrounds helps them to predict the spellings and meanings (Venezky, 1999).

English words are usually one- or two-syllable common, familiar words that may or may not be phonetically regular, such as *fox, arm, Monday, house, match, eleven, of, come, week, horse, brother,* and *dumb.* Words with *ch* (pronounced as /ch/), *sh, th,* and *wh* digraphs are usually English, as in *church, shell, bath,* and *what.* Many English words are compound words or use comparative and superlative forms, such as *starfish, toothache, fireplace, happier,* and *fastest.*

Many words from Latin are similar to comparable words in French, Spanish, or Italian, such as *ancient, judicial, impossible,* and *officer.* Latin words have related words or derivatives, such as *courage, courageous, encourage, discourage,* and *encouragement.* Also, many Latin words have *-tion/-sion* suffixes: *imitation, corruption, attention, extension,* and *possession.*

Greek words are the most unusual. Many are long words, and their spellings seem unfamiliar. The letters *ph* are pronounced /f/, and the letters *ch* are pronounced /k/ in Greek loan words, as in *autograph, chaos,* and *architect.* Longer words with *th,* such as *thermometer* and *arithmetic,* are Greek. The suffix *-ology* is Greek, as in the words *biology, psychology,* and *geology.* The letter *y* is used in place of *i* in the middle of some words, such as *bicycle* and *myth.* Many Greek words are composed of two parts: *bibliotherapy, microscope, biosphere, hypodermic,* and *telephone.* Figure 5-11 presents lists of English, Latin, and Greek words that teachers can use for word sorts and other vocabulary activities.

Related words have developed from English, Latin, and Greek sources. Consider the words *tooth, dentist,* and *orthodontist. Tooth* is an English word, which explains its irregular plural form, *teeth. Dentist* is a Latin word; *dent* means "tooth" in Latin, and the suffix *-ist* means "one who does." The word *orthodontist* is Greek; *ortho* means

Figure 5-11   English, Latin, and Greek Words

English	Latin	Greek
apple	addiction	ache
begin	administer	apology
between	advantage	arithmetic
bumblebee	beautiful	astronomy
child	capital	atmosphere
comb	confession	atomic
cry	continent	biology
cuff	couple	chaos
duckling	definition	chemical
earth	delicate	democracy
fireplace	discourage	disaster
fourteen	education	dynamic
freedom	erupt	elephant
Friday	explosion	geography
get	express	gymnastics
handsome	fraction	helicopter
have	fragile	hemisphere
horse	frequently	hieroglyphics
house	heir	kaleidoscope
kind	honest	metamorphosis
knight	honor	method
know	identify	myth
ladybug	interesting	octopus
lamb	January	phenomenal
lip	journal	photosynthesis
lock	junior	pneumonia
most	justice	pseudonym
mouth	nation	rhinoceros
nose	occupy	rhythm
out	organize	sympathy
quickly	primitive	synonym
ride	principal	telephone
silly	private	telescope
thank	procession	theater
this	salute	thermometer
twin	special	thermos
weather	uniform	trophy
whisper	vacation	type
why	valley	zodiac
wild	vegetable	zoo

"straighten" and *dont* means "tooth," so *orthodontist* means "one who straightens teeth." Other related triplets include:

book: bookstore (E), bibliography (Gr), library (L)
eye: eyelash (E), optical (Gr), binoculars (L)
foot: foot-dragging (E), tripod (Gr), pedestrian (L)
great: greatest (E), megaphone (Gr), magnificent (L)
see: foresee (E), microscope (Gr), invisible (L)
star: starry (E), astronaut (Gr), constellation (L)
time: time-tested (E), chronological (Gr), contemporary (L)
water: watermelon (E), hydrate (Gr), aquarium (L)

When students understand English, Latin, and Greek root words, they appreciate the relationships among words and their meanings.

Figurative Meanings of Words. Many words have both literal and figurative meanings. Literal meanings are the explicit, dictionary meanings, and figurative meanings are metaphorical or use figures of speech. For example, to describe winter as the coldest season of the year is literal, but to say that winter has icy breath is figurative. Two types of figurative language are idioms and comparisons. Idioms are groups of words, such as "in hot water," that have a special meaning. Idioms can be confusing to students because they must be interpreted figuratively rather than literally. "In hot water" is an old expression meaning to be in trouble. Cox (1980) explains that hundreds of years ago, there were no police officers, and people had to protect themselves from robbers. When a robber tried to break into a house, the homeowner might pour boiling water from a second-floor window onto the head of the robber, who would then be "in hot water." There are hundreds of idioms in English, and we use them every day to create word pictures that make language more colorful. Some examples are "out in left field," "a skeleton in the closet," "raining cats and dogs," "stick your neck out," "a chip off the old block," and "don't cry over spilled milk."

ELL

Figurative meanings are especially confusing to students learning English. Have your ELL students compare literal and figurative meanings of phrases and idioms so that they will understand the figurative meanings and how to use them orally and in writing.

Four excellent books of idioms for students are *Put Your Foot in Your Mouth and Other Silly Sayings* (Cox, 1980), *Scholastic Dictionary of Idioms: More than 600 Phrases, Sayings, and Expressions* (Terban, 1996), *Punching the Clock: Funny Action Idioms* (Terban, 1990), and *In a Pickle and Other Funny Idioms* (Terban, 1983). Because idioms are figurative sayings, many students—and especially those who are learning English as a second language—have difficulty learning them. It is crucial that students move beyond the literal meanings and become flexible in using language. One way for students to learn flexibility is to create idiom posters showing both literal and figurative meanings, as illustrated in Figure 5-12.

Metaphors and similes are comparisons that liken something to something else. A simile is a comparison signaled by the use of *like* or *as*. "The crowd was as rowdy as a bunch of marauding monkeys" and "My apartment was like an oven after the air-conditioning broke last summer" are two examples. In contrast, a metaphor compares two things by implying that one is something else, without using *like* or *as*. "The children were frisky puppies playing in the yard" is an example. Metaphors are stronger comparisons, as these examples show:

She's as cool as a cucumber.
She's a cool cucumber.
In the moonlight, the dead tree looked like a skeleton.
In the moonlight, the dead tree was a skeleton.

Differentiating between the terms *simile* and *metaphor* is less important than understanding the meaning of comparisons in books students read and having students use comparisons to make their writing more vivid. For example, a sixth-grade student compared anger to a thunderstorm using a simile. She wrote, "Anger is like a thunderstorm, screaming with thunder-feelings and lightning-words." Another student compared anger to a volcano. Using a metaphor, he wrote, "Anger is a volcano, erupting with poisonous words and hot-lava actions."

Students begin by learning traditional comparisons such as "happy as a clam" and "high as a kite," and then they learn to notice and invent fresh, unexpected comparisons. To introduce traditional comparisons to primary-grade students, teachers can use Audrey Wood's *Quick as a Cricket* (1982). Middle-grade students can invent new comparisons for stale comparisons such as "butterflies in your stomach." In *Anastasia*

Figure 5-12 A Sixth Grader's Idiom Poster for "In Hot Water"

Krupnik, for example, Lois Lowry (1979) substituted "ginger ale in her knees" for the trite "butterflies in her stomach" comparison to describe how nervous Anastasia was when she had to stand up to read her poem.

Choosing Words to Study

Teachers choose the most important words from books to teach. Important words include words that are essential to understanding the text, words that may confuse students, and general utility words students will use as they read other books (Allen, 1999). Teachers should avoid words that are unrelated to the central concept of the book or unit or words that are too conceptually difficult for students. As teachers choose words to highlight and for word-study activities, they consider their students, the book being read, and the instructional context.

Students do not have to know all of the words in a book to read and comprehend it or listen to it read aloud. Researchers estimate that students can tolerate books with as many as 15% unfamiliar words (Freebody & Anderson, 1983). Of course, students vary in the percentage of unfamiliar words they can tolerate, depending on the topic of the book, the role of the unfamiliar words, and their purpose for reading. It is unrealistic for teachers to expect students to learn every word in a book or expect to have to teach every word.

Spotlighting Words on Word Walls

Teachers post word walls in the classroom, made from large sheets of butcher paper and divided into sections for each letter of the alphabet. Students and the teacher write interesting, confusing, and important words on the word wall. Usually students choose the words to write on the word wall and may even do the writing themselves. Teachers add other important words that students have not chosen. Words are added to the word wall as they come up in books students are reading or during a thematic unit, not in advance. Students use the word wall to locate a word they want to use during a grand conversation or to check the spelling of a word they are writing, and teachers use the words listed on the word wall for word-study activities.

Some teachers use pocket charts and word cards instead of butcher paper for their word walls. This way the word cards can easily be used for word-study activities, and they can be sorted and rearranged on the pocket chart. After the book or unit is completed, teachers punch holes in one end of the cards and hang them on a ring. Then the collection of word cards can be placed in the writing center for students to use in writing activities.

Word walls play an important role in vocabulary learning. The words are posted in the classroom so that they are visible to all students, and because they are so visible, students will read them more often and refer to the chart when writing. Their availability will also remind teachers to use the words for word-study activities.

Students also make individual word walls by dividing a sheet of paper into 24 boxes, labeling the boxes with the letters of the alphabet; they put P and Q together in one box and X and Y in another box. Then students write important words and phrases in the boxes as they read and discuss the book. Figure 5-13 shows a sixth grader's word wall for *Hatchet* (1987), a wilderness survival story by Gary Paulsen.

Sometimes teachers categorize words in other ways. Middle- and upper-grade teachers often integrate grammar instruction with vocabulary and organize the words according to part of speech. Because many words can represent more than one part of speech depending on how they are used in sentences, students often need to carefully analyze how a word is used. For example, consider how the word *glowing* is used in *The crew watched the glowing stone for hours,* and *The stone was glowing brighter each day:* In the first sentence, *glowing* is an adjective, but in the second sentence, it is a verb. Figure 5-14 shows a fifth-grade class word wall organized by parts of speech using words from Chris Van Allsburg's *The Wretched Stone* (1991), a story about a strange glowing stone picked up on a sea voyage that captivates a ship's crew and has a terrible transforming effect on them. After students read and discussed the book, they reread it to locate and classify the words. They organized the word wall with nouns and adjectives side by side because adjectives modify nouns, and verbs and adverbs side by side because adverbs modify verbs.

Even though 25, 50, or more words may be added to the word wall, not all of them will be directly taught to students. As they plan, teachers create lists of words that will probably be written on word walls during the lesson. From this list, teachers choose the key words—the ones that are critical to understanding the book or the unit—and these are the words that they incorporate in minilessons.

Activities for Exploring Words

Word-study activities provide opportunities for students to explore the meaning of words listed on word walls, other words related to books they are reading, and words they are learning during social studies and science units. Through these activities, students develop concepts, learn the meanings of words, and make associations among words. None of these activities require students to simply write words and their definitions or to use the words in sentences or a contrived story.

Figure 5-13   A Sixth Grader's Alphabetized Word Wall for *Hatchet*

A	B	C	D
alone	bush plane	Canadian wilderness	divorce
absolutely terrified	Brian Robeson	controls	desperation
arrows	bruised	cockpit	destroyed
aluminum cookset	bow & arrow	crash	disappointment
		careless	devastating
		campsite	
E	**F**	**G**	**H**
engine	fire	gut cherries	hatchet
emergency	fuselage	get food	heart attack
emptiness	fish		hunger
exhaustion	foolbirds		hope
	foodshelf		
	54 days		
I	**J**	**K**	**L**
instruments			lake
insane			
incredible wealth			
M	**N**	**O**	**PQ**
memory			pilot
mosquitoes			panic
mistakes			painful
matches			porcupine quills
mental journal			patience
moose			
R	**S**	**T**	**U**
rudder pedals	stranded		unbelievable riches
rescue	secret		
radio	survival pack		
relative comfort	search		
raspberries	sleeping bag		
roaring bonfire	shelter		
raft	starved		
V	**W**	**XY**	**Z**
visitation rights	wilderness		
viciously thirsty	windbreaker		
valuable asset	wreck		
vicious whine	woodpile		
	wolf		

Nouns	Adjectives	Verbs	Adverbs
crew	wretched	abandon	approximately
voyage	grave	scuttle	roughly
danger	horrifying	save	unbelievably
entry	glowing	report	well
island	alert	lock	slowly
stone	dull	believe	rarely
adventure	unnatural	read	apparently
sailors	peculiar	play	steadily
shrieks	clumsy	fascinate	away
omen	stooped-over	sail	completely
rescue	feverish	sink	unfortunately
rescuers	hairy	write	quickly
vessel	upright	glowing	slightly
cargo	clever	sing	too
glow	strange	swing	quite
boredom	lush	fade	perfectly
quarters	overpowering	depend	soon
apes	terrible	grinning	surely
rock	powerful	staring	finally
storm	starboard	understand	so

Struggling Readers & Writers

GUIDELINE 6

Struggling Students Need to Know a Lot of Words. One of the biggest problems that struggling readers and writers face is limited background knowledge and vocabulary, and when students don't know the meanings of many words, they have more difficulty reading and writing. In particular, comprehension is affected because students don't understand what they are reading. The most important thing that teachers can do to help these students is to post words on classroom word walls because this activity will draw students' attention to the words. But word walls aren't enough. Teachers need to involve students in a variety of word activities so that they develop more complete word knowledge. The word wall helps students move from the unknown word stage to the initial recognition stage, but for students to move to partial or full word knowledge, they need to learn more about words through word-study activities and instruction.

Teachers help students use print skills and context clues to identify content area vocabulary.

1. *Word posters.* Students choose a word from the word wall and write it on a small poster. Then they draw and color a picture to illustrate the word. They also use the word in a sentence on the poster. This is one way that students can visualize the meaning of a word.

2. *Word maps.* Word maps are another way to visualize a word's meaning (Duffelmeyer & Banwart, 1992–1993; Schwartz & Raphael, 1985). Students draw a cluster[C] on a small card or a sheet of paper and write a word from the word wall in the center circle. Then they draw rays from the center and write important information about the word to make connections between the word and what they are reading or studying.

Figure 5-15 shows two word maps. A fourth grader drew the first word map to illustrate three meanings of the word *wet,* and a fifth grader who was reading *Bunnicula: A Rabbit-Tale of Mystery* (Howe & Howe, 1979) made the second word map, on *glistened,* a word from the first chapter.

3. *Word sorts.* Students sort a collection of words taken from the word wall into two or more categories in a word sort (Bear, Invernizzi, Templeton, & Johnston, 2000). Usually students choose the categories they will use for the sort, but sometimes the teacher chooses them. For example, words from a story might be sorted by character, or words from a thematic unit on machines might be sorted according to type of machine. The words can be written on cards, and then students sort a pack of word cards into piles. Or, students can cut apart a list of words, sort them into categories, and then paste the grouped words together.

4. *Word chains.* Students choose a word from the word wall and then identify three or four words to sequence before or after the word to make a chain. For example, the word *aggravate* can be chained like this: *irritate, bother, aggravate, annoy.* Students

Figure 5-15   Two Word Maps

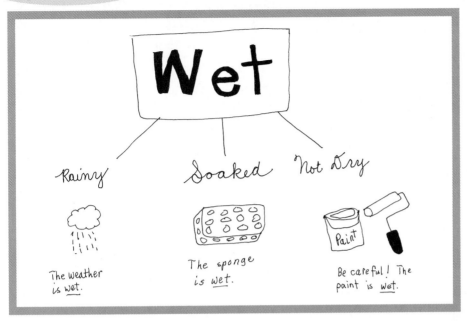

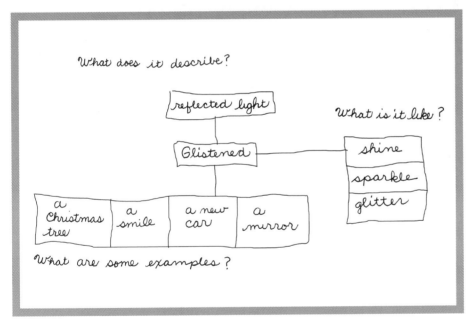

can draw and write their chains on a sheet of paper, or they can make a chain out of construction paper and write a word on each link.

5. *Semantic feature analysis.* Students select a group of related words, such as different kinds of birds, and then make a chart to classify them according to distinguishing characteristics (Heimlich & Pittelman, 1986). A semantic feature analysis on the solar system is presented in Figure 5-16. Students completed the semantic feature analysis by placing a check mark, a circle, or a question mark under the characteristics.

Figure 5-16 — A Semantic Feature Analysis on the Solar System

	is an inner planet	is an outer planet	has an atmosphere	supports life	made of rock and metal	made of gas	has moons	has rings
Mercury	✓	O	O	O	✓	O	O	O
Venus	✓	O	✓	O	✓	O	O	O
Earth	?	?	✓	✓	✓	O	✓	O
Mars	O	✓	✓	O	✓	O	✓	O
Jupiter	O	✓	O	O	O	✓	✓	✓
Saturn	O	✓	O	O	✓	O	✓	✓
Uranus	O	✓	O	O	✓	O	✓	✓
Neptune	O	✓	✓	O	✓	O	✓	O
Pluto	O	✓	O	O	✓	O	✓	O

Code: ✓ = yes
O = no
? = don't know

Review

Students add approximately 3,000 words to their vocabularies every year. They learn some of the words through instruction that teachers provide, but they learn far more words incidentally through reading, writing, watching television, and other activities outside of school. Teachers have an important role in providing opportunities for incidental word learning through reading and teaching students how to unlock word meanings. Words should always be studied as part of meaningful reading and writing activities or content-area study. Teachers post vocabulary word walls in the classroom, teach minilessons using word wall words, and involve students in a variety of word-study activities, including word maps and word sorts. The feature that follows presents a list of recommended practices that effective teachers use in teaching vocabulary.

- Complete a self-assessment to demonstrate your understanding of the concepts presented in this chapter
- Complete field activities that will help you expand your understanding of the middle-grade classroom and learning about the meanings of words
- Visit important web links related to teaching vocabulary to middle-grade students
- Look into your state's standards as they relate to word-learning strategies and the middle-grade student
- Communicate with other preservice teachers via the message board and discuss the issues of teaching vocabulary to students in grades 4 to 8

How Effective Teachers . . .
Teach Students About Vocabulary

1. Teachers provide daily opportunities for students to read stories and informational books because students learn many new words through reading.
2. Teachers read aloud every day because students learn many new words as they listen to books read aloud.
3. Teachers support students as they develop full word knowledge and learn to use words flexibly in a variety of contexts.
4. Teachers help students to develop a repertoire of word-learning strategies in order to learn words incidentally.
5. Teachers demonstrate how to use context clues to figure out the meaning of unknown words when reading independently.
6. Teachers choose the most useful words from the word wall for vocabulary activities.
7. Teachers teach minilessons on individual words, vocabulary concepts, and word-learning strategies.
8. Teachers provide support for students when they look up definitions in the dictionary.
9. Teachers teach many concepts about words, including multiple meanings, morphemic analysis, synonyms, antonyms, homonyms, etymologies, and figurative meanings.
10. Teachers involve students in meaningful word-study activities, such as word maps, word sorts, and semantic feature analysis, that are related to books students are reading and units they are studying.

Professional References

Allen, J. (1999). *Words, words, words*. Portsmouth, NH: Heinemann.

Anderson, R. C., Wilson, P. T., & Fielding, L. G. (1986). *Growth in reading and how children spend their time outside of school* (Technical Report No. 389). Urbana: University of Illinois, Center for the Study of Reading.

Baumann, J. F., & Kameenui, E. J. (1991). Research on vocabulary instruction: Ode to Voltaire. In J. Flood, J. M. Jensen, D. Lapp, & J. R. Squire (Eds.), *Handbook on teaching the English language arts* (pp. 604–632). New York: Macmillan.

Bear, D. R., Invernizzi, M., Templeton, S., & Johnston, F. (2000). *Words their way: Word study for phonics, vocabulary, and spelling instruction*. Upper Saddle River, NJ: Merrill/Prentice Hall.

Beck, I., & McKeown, M. (1991). Conditions of vocabulary acquisition. In R. Barr, M. Kamil, P. Mosenthal, & P. D. Pearson (Eds.), *Handbook of reading research* (Vol. 2, pp. 789–814). White Plains, NY: Longman.

Blachowicz, C. L. Z. (1993). C(2)QU: Modeling context use in the classroom. *The Reading Teacher, 47*, 268–269.

Blachowicz, C. L. Z., & Lee, J. J. (1991). Vocabulary development in the whole literacy classroom. *The Reading Teacher, 45*, 188–195.

Carr, E., & Wixon, K. K. (1986). Guidelines for evaluating vocabulary instruction. *Journal of Reading, 29*, 588–595.

Dale, E., & O'Rourke, J. (1986). *Vocabulary building*. Columbus, OH: Zaner-Bloser.

Duffelmeyer, F. A., & Banwart, B. H. (1992–1993). Word maps for adjectives and verbs. *The Reading Teacher, 46*, 351–353.

Freebody, P., & Anderson, R. C. (1983). Effects of vocabulary difficulty, text cohesion, and schema availability on reading comprehension. *Reading Research Quarterly, 18*, 277–294.

Graves, M. (1985). *A word is a word . . . or is it?* Portsmouth, NH: Heinemann.

Heimlich, J. E., & Pittelman, S. D. (1986). *Semantic mapping: Classroom applications*. Newark, DE: International Reading Association.

McKeown, M. G. (1985). The acquisition of word meaning from context by children of high and low ability. *Reading Research Quarterly, 20*, 482–496.

Nagy, W. E. (1988). *Teaching vocabulary to improve reading comprehension*. Urbana, IL: ERIC Clearinghouse on Reading and Communication Skills and the National Council of Teachers of English and the International Reading Association.

Nagy, W. E., Anderson, R. C., & Herman, P. A. (1987). Learning word meanings from context during normal reading. *American Educational Research Journal, 24*, 237–270.

Nagy, W. E., & Herman, P. (1985). Incidental vs. instructional approaches to increasing reading vocabulary. *Educational Perspectives, 23*, 16–21.

Nagy, W. E., Herman, P. A., & Anderson, R. C. (1985). Learning words from context. *Reading Research Quarterly, 20*, 172–193.

Rupley, W. H., Logan, J. W., & Nichols, W. D. (1998/1999). Vocabulary instruction in balanced reading programs. *The Reading Teacher, 52*, 336–346.

Schwartz, R., & Raphael, T. (1985). Concept of definition: A key to improving students' vocabulary. *The Reading Teacher, 39*, 198–205.

Stahl, S. A. (1999). *Vocabulary development*. Cambridge, MA: Brookline Books.

Stahl, S. A., Richek, M. G., & Vandevier, R. (1991). Learning word meanings through listening: A sixth grade replication. In J. Zutell & S. McCormick (Eds.), *Learning factors/teacher factors: Issues in literacy research. Fortieth yearbook of the National Reading Conference* (pp. 185–192). Chicago: National Reading Conference.

Stanovich, K. E. (1986). Matthew effects in reading: Some consequences of individual differences in the acquisition of literacy. *Reading Research Quarterly, 21*, 360–406.

Tompkins, G. E. (2004). Word clusters: Exploring the multiple meanings of words. In G. E. Tompkins & C. Blanchfield (Eds.), *50 vocabulary strategies* (pp. 156–160). Upper Saddle River, NJ: Merrill/Prentice Hall.

Tompkins, G. E., & Yaden, D. B., Jr. (1986). *Answering students' questions about words*. Urbana, IL: ERIC Clearinghouse on Reading and Communication Skills and National Council of Teachers of English.

Venezky, R. L. (1999). *The American way of spelling: The structure and origins of American English orthography*. New York: Guilford Press.

Children's Book References

Bollard, J. K. (1998). *Scholastic children's thesaurus*. New York: Scholastic.

Brewster, H. (1997). *Inside the Titanic*. Boston: Little, Brown.

Cheney, L. (2002). *America: A patriotic primer*. New York: Simon & Schuster.

Cole, J. (1997). *The magic school bus and the electric field trip*. New York: Scholastic.

Cox, J. A. (1980). *Put your foot in your mouth and other silly sayings*. New York: Random House.

Frazier, D. (2000). *Miss Alaineus: A vocabulary disaster*. San Diego, CA: Harcourt Brace.

Gwynne, F. (1970). *The king who rained*. New York: Windmill Books.

Gwynne, F. (1976). *A chocolate moose for dinner*. New York: Windmill Books.

Gwynne, F. (1980). *The sixteen hand horse*. New York: Prentice Hall.

Gwynne, F. (1988). *A little pigeon toad*. New York: Simon & Schuster.

Hellweg, P. (1997). *The American Heritage children's thesaurus*. Boston: Houghton Mifflin.

Howe, D., & Howe, J. (1979). *Bunnicula: A rabbit-tale of mystery*. New York: Atheneum.

Kentley, E. (2001). *Story of the Titanic*. London: Dorling Kindersley.

Lowry, L. (1979). *Anastasia Krupnik*. Boston: Houghton Mifflin.

Maestro, G. (1984). *What's a frank Frank? Tasty homograph riddles*. New York: Clarion Books.

Osborne, W., & Osborne, M. P. (1995). *Tonight on the Titanic*. New York: Random House.

Osborne, W., & Osborne, M. P. (2002). *Titanic: A nonfiction companion to Tonight on the Titanic*. New York: Random House.

Paulsen, G. (1987). *Hatchet*. New York: Simon & Schuster.

Presson, L. (1996). *What in the world is a homophone?* New York: Barron's.

Scillian, D. (2001). *A is for America*. Chelsea, MI: Sleeping Bear Press.

Spedden, D. C. S. (1994). *Polar, the Titanic bear*. Boston: Little, Brown.

Tanaka, S. (1996). *On board the Titanic: What it was like when the great liner sank*. New York: Hyperion.

Terban, M. (1982). *Eight ate: A feast of homonym riddles*. New York: Clarion Books.

Terban, M. (1983). *In a pickle and other funny idioms*. New York: Clarion Books.

Terban, M. (1990). *Punching the clock: Funny action idioms*. New York: Clarion Books.

Terban, M. (1992). *The dove dove: Funny homograph riddles*. New York: Clarion.

Terban, M. (1996). *Scholastic dictionary of idioms: More than 600 phrases, sayings, and expressions*. New York: Scholastic.

Van Allsburg, C. (1991). *The wretched stone*. Boston: Houghton Mifflin.

White, E. E. (1998). *Voyage on the great Titanic: The diary of Margaret Ann Brady*. New York: Scholastic.

Wittels, H., & Greisman, J. (1985). *A first thesaurus*. New York: Golden Books.

Wood, A. (1982). *Quick as a cricket*. London: Child's Play.

chapter 6

Facilitating Students' Comprehension

chapter
QUESTIONS

- How do capable and less capable readers differ?

- What is comprehension?

- How do teachers teach and monitor students' comprehension?

- Which strategies and skills do readers and writers learn?

- How do teachers teach strategies and skills?

Mr. Wyatt Teaches Inference

The 18 seventh graders in Mr. Wyatt's reading class listen intently as he reads aloud Chris Van Allsburg's fantasy picture-book story *The Wretched Stone* (1991). The story, told in diary format, is about a ship's crew that picks up a strange glowing stone on a sea voyage. The stone captivates the sailors and has a terrible transforming effect on them.

The students start to talk about the book as soon as the teacher finishes reading. Molly asks, "Where's the white dog?" "I don't think he's in this book," Jason responds. Mr. Wyatt reassures them that the white dog that Chris Van Allsburg includes in all his stories is there—at least part of him. They look through the book page by page for the dog and finally notice a white tail sticking up at the bottom of the page where monkey sailors are staring at the glowing stone. Then they shift their focus to the story itself. Because they don't understand it, they have many questions. Robert asks, "What's with that rock? I know it's important because it's the name of the story." "Did the stone really turn the sailors into monkeys? And did it turn them back into men?" Felicia asks, "What about the island?" Christopher offers, "The story said that it wasn't on any maps and it was weird and all." Mr. Wyatt is teaching his students to make inferences, and the questions they are asking show that they are thinking about the book, not just dismissing it as "dumb" or "boring."

"We'll figure the story out, and you'll have answers to your questions," Mr. Wyatt assures the students. "*The Wretched Stone* is a story where you need to make inferences to figure it out, and we know how to do that."

Mr. Wyatt continues, "Let's make sure that everyone understands the events in the story. Who can summarize the beginning?" Christopher briefly tells the first part of the story:

These sailors are on a ship and they stop at a weird island and pick up a glowing stone.

Jason continues with the middle of the story:

The sailors stare at the stone day after day after day. Then they turn into monkeys. There is a terrible storm, and the ship is broken into pieces, but the crew survives.

Felicia finishes the retelling:

Then the captain locks up the stone and the sailors become normal again. Finally they are rescued and they promise the Captain that they will never talk about what happened. One thing is funny—they still liked to eat bananas!

"Now, let's dig deeper into the book and figure it out—we're going to make inferences," Mr. Wyatt tells the class. He divides a sheet of chart paper into four columns, and labels the columns "background knowledge," "clues in the story," "questions," and "inferences." The first three categories prompt students' thinking so that they are able

Background Knowledge	Clues in the Story	Questions	Inferences
• The word *wretched* means "causing misery." • The people who work on a ship are called sailors or the crew. Usually they are hard workers but not readers and musicians. • Chris Van Allsburg writes and illustrates fantasy picture books. He has brown hair and a beard. He wears glasses. • In fantasies, magic and other impossible things can happen.	• The captain's last name is Hope. • The crew is clever. They can read, play music, and tell stories. • It is odd that the island is not on any maps. • The odor on the island seems sweet at first, but then it stinks. • The crew sit and stare at the glowing stone. They lose interest in reading, playing music, and telling stories. They stop working, too. • The crew change into monkeys because they keep watching the stone. • Capt. Hope looks just like Chris Van Allsburg. • The sailors who could read recovered the quickest.	• Why did Chris Van Allsburg make himself the captain? • Was it a real island or was it magic? • What is the wretched stone? • Why did the sailors turn into monkeys? • Why did the sailors who could read get well faster?	• Chris Van Allsburg wrote this book with hope for kids. • The wretched stone is television. • This book is a warning that watching too much TV is bad for you. • He wants kids to spend more time reading books because reading is good for you. • He wants kids to spend less time watching television. • Watching television is like the odor on the island. It is sweet and you like it at first, but too much of it stinks and is not good for you.

to make inferences. The completed inference chart is shown in Figure 6-1. The students are familiar with the chart because they've made one like this several times before. Mr. Wyatt begins with the "background knowledge" column. "What do we need to know about in order to understand this story?" Together, they decide that they need to know what the word *wretched* means, about sailing ships and crews, about author/illustrator Chris Van Allsburg, and about the fantasy genre.

"What does *wretched* mean?" Mr. Wyatt asks. Cassie guesses that it means "bad" or "terrible," and Latisha guesses that it means "poisoned." Jason checks the definition in the dictionary and finds three meanings:

1. unhappy or unfortunate
2. causing misery
3. poor quality

The class decides that the second meaning, causing misery, is the most appropriate because the glowing stone caused misery for the captain and his sailors.

Next, they talk about sailing ships and their crews. They think of Christopher Columbus and the other explorers who came to America. Mr. Wyatt directs the conversation and asks them about the sailors: "Are sailors typically readers, storytellers, and musicians?" The class decides that although some sailors may have liked to read, play music, and tell stories, most probably didn't because Chris Van Allsburg pointed out that this crew was special—they were clever.

Then Mr. Wyatt reviews information about Chris Van Allsburg from the "All About the Author and Illustrator" center in the classroom, and he shows the students a photograph of the author/illustrator. Immediately, Cassie notices the similarity between the photograph and the illustrations of the sea captain in the story, and she makes an inference: "It's really Chris Van Allsburg who is Captain Hope, and he has hope for us—I mean, for everyone who reads the book."

Finally, they talk briefly about fantasies. Mr. Wyatt reminds the students that things that are not possible in real life can happen in fantasies. The students point out the impossible things that have happened in the other Chris Van Allsburg stories they have read. Then Mr. Wyatt asks them what fantastic (or impossible) things happened in *The Wretched Stone,* and Christopher exclaims, "It's the stone! That is the impossible part."

The next day, the seventh graders watch and listen for clues as Mr. Wyatt rereads *The Wretched Stone.* They notice clues, including that the ship captain's name is Hope, the island is uncharted, and the sailors who could read recovered faster, and Mr. Wyatt writes them in the second column of the inference chart. Next, he asks them to think of questions they have about the story, and he writes these in the third column of the chart. They ask why the author made himself the ship's captain, what the stone symbolized, and why the sailors were turned into monkeys. The final step is for the students to make inferences by answering the questions they posed. With Mr. Wyatt's guidance, the students realize that Chris Van Allsburg wrote the story to warn students about the dangers of watching too much television. The students make several inferences that the teacher records in the fourth column.

This lesson continues for a third day as Mr. Wyatt rereads the book, and the students listen more confidently this time, recognizing the clues and understanding the inferences that they had missed earlier. Afterward, the students talk more about the story and conclude that it is "an awesome book," according to Latisha.

Mr. Wyatt teaches a 90-minute reading class for seventh-grade students who scored below the 40th percentile on the state's standardized achievement test. The students take this class in addition to the regular seventh-grade language arts course that focuses on literature, grammar, and writing. Mr. Wyatt divides the class time into three 30-minute blocks:

1. **Independent reading.** The students read self-selected books at their reading levels during this block that they call DEAR Time. DEAR stands for Drop Everything and Read, another name for Sustained Silent Reading[C]. Mr. Wyatt reads books during this time, too.

2. **Guided reading lessons.** The students work in four groups, based on their reading levels, and Mr. Wyatt meets with one group each day. He focuses on teaching students to apply reading strategies and to think aloud about their reading. The students not meeting with Mr. Wyatt are involved in other activities, usually vocabulary or writing activities related to the literature focus unit.

3. **Literature focus unit.** Mr. Wyatt reads aloud picture books and novels and uses the stories to teach comprehension. The stories also provide opportunities for vocabulary instruction and writing activities.

[C] See the Compendium of Instructional Procedures, which follows Chapter 12, for more information on terms marked with the symbol [C].

Currently, the students are involved in an author/illustrator study of Chris Van Allsburg, and Mr. Wyatt is using his picture books to teach inference. He found that his students were pretty good literal comprehenders, but they didn't know how to use their background knowledge and the clues in the text to ask questions and make inferences.

Mr. Wyatt reads aloud all of Chris Van Allsburg's books during the 3-week author/illustrator study, but he focuses on four of the books to teach inferencing: *Jumanji* (1981), *The Garden of Abdul Gasazi* (1979), *The Stranger* (1986), and *The Wretched Stone* (1991). The students are familiar with *Jumanji* and several of the others, but they describe them as "boring"—which means "confusing" in their vernacular. Mr. Wyatt agrees that some of Chris Van Allsburg's stories are hard to understand, but he promises that he will teach them how to figure them out.

To introduce inferencing, Mr. Wyatt uses *Miss Nelson Is Missing!* (Allard, 1977), the story of a class of elementary students who take advantage of their teacher's good nature until she disappears and they are faced with a vile substitute. All students are familiar with the story, but they admit that they don't understand it. At a literal level, the story suggests that Miss Nelson, a kind and understanding teacher, and Miss Viola Swamp, a mean substitute teacher, are different people, but actually Miss Nelson dresses up as the substitute teacher to teach her students a lesson.

Mr. Wyatt explains that to figure out a story, readers have to do four things:

1. Think about what you already know about the topic of the book, the vocabulary, the author, and the genre. This is called background knowledge.
2. Look for clues in the story. Sometimes the clues are in the text and sometimes they are in the illustrations, if there are any.
3. Ask questions about things that don't make sense.
4. Make inferences by answering the questions.

After Mr. Wyatt explains the four steps, the students work with him to make a chart with the steps to post in the classroom. They use interactive writing^C so that everyone will have the opportunity to participate in making the chart.

Next Mr. Wyatt and the students follow these four steps to make an inference chart similar to the one shown in Figure 6-1. After considering background knowledge, looking for clues in the story, and asking questions, the students infer that Miss Nelson and Miss Viola Swamp are the same person and that Miss Nelson pretended to be Miss Viola Swamp to teach her students to behave.

After this introduction to inferencing, Mr. Wyatt reads Chris Van Allsburg's books. They begin with *Jumanji* (Van Allsburg, 1981), a story of two bored children who play a jungle adventure board game; the animals and events described in the game come to life, threatening the children's safety. The children follow the directions to finish the game, and their home returns to normal. The students infer that they should follow directions to avoid dire consequences.

Several days later, Mr. Wyatt reads aloud *The Garden of Abdul Gasazi* (Van Allsburg, 1979), the story of a magician who turns a misbehaving dog into a duck. Instead of discussing the story as a class, he divides the students into pairs and asks them to discuss the story among themselves. Then he passes out a four-part inference chart for the students to use in analyzing the story and finding the answer to the question: What happened to the dog? A completed chart is shown in Figure 6-2. By thinking about their background knowledge, looking for clues in the story, and asking questions, all of the pairs figured out that the magician changed the dog into a duck but the spell didn't last a long time, and by the time the duck flew home, it changed back into a dog.

Next, Mr. Wyatt reads aloud *The Stranger* (Van Allsburg, 1986), the story of an unusual stranger that Farmer Bailey hits with his truck and brings home to recu-

Title **The Garden of Abdul Gasazi** Author **Chris Van Allsburg**

BACKGROUND KNOWLEDGE	QUESTIONS
Magicians do tricks. This story is a fantasy so magic can happen. Sometimes dogs don't behave.	Did the magician do it? How did Fritz get home? Why was Alan's hat in Miss Hester's yard?
CLUES FROM THE STORY	INFERENCES
Only time can change Fritz back into a dog. The duck was like Fritz because he took Alan's hat. Fritz the dog has Alan's hat at the end.	The magician did cast a spell and make the dog into a duck. The spell didn't last very long.

perate. The stranger seems to have a mysterious relationship to autumn; in fact, the students conclude that he is Jack Frost. Again the students divide into pairs to analyze the story and answer the question: Who is the stranger? The students complete an inference chart similar to the one shown in Figure 6-2.

During the author/illustrator study, the seventh graders are involved in other activities, too. They use the Internet to learn more about Chris Van Allsburg, they make a word wall[C] and study vocabulary words selected from the stories, and they also write fantasy stories based on the illustrations in *The Mysteries of Harris Burdick* (Van Allsburg, 1984). Each full-page black-and-white fantasy illustration is accompanied by a title and a sentence or two that the students work into their compositions. Mr. Wyatt has several copies of the book as well as a set of posters enlarged from the book so students can carefully study the illustration as they write. They work on the stories while their classmates are meeting in guided reading[C] groups.

Mr. Wyatt is pleased to see his students becoming more actively involved in the reading process. That they are actually asking questions and working to figure out what stories mean are big steps for his students. They will continue to work on inferencing during the next literature focus unit as they read *Maniac Magee* (Spinelli, 1990).

Comprehension is the goal of reading instruction in a balanced literacy program, no matter whether students are reading stories, poems, informational books, or content-area textbooks. Students must comprehend what they are reading in order to learn from the experience; they must make sense of their reading in order to maintain interest; and they must derive pleasure from the reading experience to become lifelong readers. Struggling students who are frustrated and who don't understand what they are reading don't find reading pleasurable and won't become lifelong readers. That's why Mr. Wyatt was teaching his students about making inferences in the vignette at the beginning of the chapter.

Even though you might think of comprehension as reading comprehension, it is crucial for writers, too. As they write, students use the same comprehension strategies to create compositions with clearly stated main ideas, relevant supporting details, effective transitions between ideas, and precise word choice. The reason why writers write is to share their ideas with readers, but compositions are unsuccessful when readers don't understand what writers have written.

Because of the importance of comprehension to both reading and writing, you might say that comprehension permeates almost everything teachers do, from building background knowledge about a topic to teaching minilessons[C] on the revision strategies to providing opportunities for students to make personal connections. The feature on page 179 shows the role of comprehension in a balanced literacy program.

COMPARING CAPABLE AND LESS CAPABLE READERS

Researchers have compared students who are capable readers and writers with other students who are less successful and have found some striking differences (Baker & Brown, 1984; Faigley, Cherry, Jolliffe, & Skinner, 1985; Paris, Wasik, & Turner, 1991). The researchers have found that more capable readers

- are fluent oral and silent readers
- view reading as a process of creating meaning
- decode rapidly
- have large vocabularies
- understand the organization of stories, plays, informational books, poems, and other texts
- use a variety of strategies
- monitor their understanding as they read

Similarly, capable writers

- vary how they write depending on the purpose for writing and the audience that will read the composition
- use the writing process flexibly
- focus on developing ideas and communicating effectively
- turn to classmates for feedback on how they are communicating
- monitor how well they are communicating in the piece of writing
- use formats and structures for stories, poems, letters, and other texts

The Role of Comprehension in a Balanced Literacy Program

Component	Description
Reading	No matter whether students are reading independently, reading in guided reading groups, doing shared reading, or listening to the teacher read aloud, the goal is comprehension.
Phonics and Other Skills	Comprehension skills include sequencing, categorizing, separating facts and opinions, and recognizing literary genres.
Strategies	Capable readers are metacognitive: They think about the strategies they use to activate background knowledge, direct their reading, monitor their understanding, deal with problems, and reflect on their reading experience.
Vocabulary	Understanding the meaning of words that students are reading is a prerequisite for comprehension.
Comprehension	Comprehension is the reader's process of using prior experiences and the author's text to construct meaning that is useful to that reader for a specific purpose.
Literature	As students read stories, they are involved in comprehension activities throughout the reading process.
Content-Area Study	As they read informational books and content-area textbooks, students are involved in comprehension activities throughout the reading process. Some activities are the same as for stories, but others are unique to informational books and content-area textbooks.
Oral Language	It is often more effective to teach comprehension skills and strategies through books read aloud so that students can focus on meaning rather than on word identification.
Writing	Students use the same processes and strategies when writing because the goal of writing is the readers' comprehension.
Spelling	Spelling is not an important component of comprehension

- use a variety of strategies
- postpone attention to mechanical correctness until the end of the writing process

Teachers often notice that the more capable readers and writers in their own classes exemplify many of these characteristics. A comparison of characteristics of capable and less capable readers and writers is presented in Figure 6-3. Young students who are

Figure 6-3   Capable and Less Capable Readers and Writers

Categories	Reader Characteristics	Writer Characteristics
Belief Systems	Capable readers view reading as a comprehending process, but less capable readers view reading as a decoding process.	Capable writers view writing as communicating ideas, whereas less capable writers see writing as putting words on paper.
Purpose	Capable readers adjust their reading according to purpose, whereas less capable readers approach all reading tasks the same way.	Capable writers adapt their writing to meet audience, purpose, and form demands, but less capable writers do not.
Fluency	Capable readers read fluently, whereas less capable readers read word by word, do not chunk words into phrases, and sometimes point at words as they read.	Capable writers sustain their writing for longer periods of time and pause as they draft to think and reread what they have written, whereas less capable writers write less and without pausing.
Background Knowledge	Capable readers relate what they are reading to their background knowledge, whereas less capable readers do not make this connection.	Capable writers gather and organize ideas before writing, but less capable writers do not plan before beginning to write.
Decoding/ Spelling	Capable readers identify unfamiliar words efficiently, whereas less capable readers make nonsensical guesses or skip over unfamiliar words and invent what they think is a reasonable text when they are reading.	Capable writers spell many words conventionally and use the dictionary to spell unfamiliar words, but less capable writers cannot spell many high-frequency words and depend on phonics to spell unfamiliar words.
Vocabulary	Capable readers have larger vocabularies than less capable readers do.	Capable writers use more sophisticated words and figurative language than less capable writers do.
Strategies	Capable readers use a variety of strategies as they read, whereas less capable readers use fewer strategies.	Capable writers use many strategies effectively, but less capable writers use fewer strategies.
Monitoring	Capable readers monitor their comprehension, but less capable readers do not realize or take action when they don't understand.	Capable writers monitor that their writing makes sense, and they turn to classmates for revising suggestions, but less capable writers do not.

Adapted from Faigley, Cherry, Jolliffe, & Skinner, 1985; Paris, Wasik, & Turner, 1991.

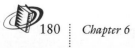

learning to read and write often exemplify many of the characteristics of less capable readers and writers, as do older students who are less successful readers and writers.

Less successful readers exemplify fewer of these characteristics or behave differently when they are reading and writing. Perhaps the most remarkable difference is that more capable readers view reading as a process of comprehending or creating meaning, whereas less capable readers focus on decoding. In writing, less capable writers make cosmetic changes when they revise, rather than changes to communicate meaning more effectively. These important differences indicate that capable students focus on comprehension and the strategies readers and writers use to understand what they read and to make sure that what they write will be comprehensible to others.

Another important difference between capable and less capable readers and writers is that those who are less successful are not strategic. They are naive. They seem reluctant to use unfamiliar strategies or those that require much effort. They do not seem to be motivated or to expect that they will be successful. Less capable readers and writers don't understand or use all stages of the reading and writing processes effectively. They do not monitor their reading and writing (Garner, 1987; Keene & Zimmermann, 1997). Or, if they do use strategies, they remain dependent on primitive ones. For example, as they read, less successful readers seldom look ahead or back into the text to clarify misunderstandings or make plans. Or, when they come to an unfamiliar word, they often stop reading, unsure of what to do. They may try to sound the word out, but if that is unsuccessful, they give up. In contrast, capable readers know several strategies, and if one strategy isn't successful, they try another.

Less capable writers move through the writing process in a lockstep, linear approach. They use a limited number of strategies, most often a "knowledge-telling" strategy in which they list everything they know about a topic with little thought to choosing information to meet the needs of their readers or to organizing the information to put related ideas together (Faigley et al., 1985). In contrast, capable writers understand the recursive nature of the writing process and turn to classmates for feedback about how well they are communicating. They are more responsive to the needs of the audience that will read their writing, and they work to organize their writing in a cohesive manner.

This research on capable and less capable readers and writers has focused on differences in comprehension and students' use of strategies. It is noteworthy that all research comparing readers and writers focuses on how students use reading and writing strategies, not on differences in their use of skills.

Too often, English language learners are less capable readers and read passively, applying few, if any, reading strategies.

THE COMPREHENSION PROCESS

Comprehension is a creative, multifaceted process in which students engage with the text (Tierney, 1990). Teachers often view comprehension as a mysterious process of making meaning or understanding what students read. It often seems mysterious because it is invisible; some students read and understand what they read, and others seem to read just as well but don't understand what they read. Sometimes comprehension problems relate to students' lack of fluency or limited vocabulary knowledge, but more often than not, students who don't comprehend seem no different from their classmates.

Three factors influence comprehension: the reader, the text, and the purpose (Irwin, 1991). The background knowledge that readers bring to the reading process influences how they understand the text as well as the strategies they know to use while reading. The text that is being read is the second factor: The author's ideas, the words the author uses to express those ideas, and how the ideas are organized and presented also affect comprehension. The purpose is the third factor: Readers vary the way they read according to their purpose. They read differently to cook a recipe, enjoy a letter from an old friend, understand the opinion expressed in an editorial, or read a novel.

Readers' comprehension varies because of these three factors. If you are a student learning how to teach reading, it seems obvious that your understanding will vary from your professor's. You and your professor have different levels of background knowledge and experience in teaching reading, and you and your professor are probably reading this chapter for different purposes. Perhaps you are reading the chapter to learn the main ideas or to prepare for a test; in contrast, your professor may be reading to prepare to give a presentation for the next class meeting or to identify questions for a quiz. But even though comprehension varies from reader to reader, comprehension can always be supported with ideas from the text.

Judith Irwin (1991) defines comprehension as the reader's process of using prior experiences and the author's text to construct meaning that is useful to that reader for a specific purpose. For a writer, comprehension is similarly described as a process of using prior experiences to create a text that will be meaningful to that writer for a specific purpose.

Readers do many things as they read in order to comprehend what they are reading, and writers do similar things to create meaningful texts. Irwin (1991) has identified five subprocesses of comprehension:

1. Microprocesses
2. Integrative processes
3. Macroprocesses
4. Elaborative processes
5. Metacognitive processes

Figure 6-4 presents an overview of these subprocesses, and instructional and assessment techniques are suggested.

Microprocesses

The microprocesses focus on fluency, the ability to read quickly, smoothly, and with expression. The three components of fluency are reading rate, word recognition, and prosody (Rasinski, 2000; Richards, 2000). Reading rate refers to the speed at which students read; to read fluently, students need to read at least 100 words per minute. Most students reach this rate by third grade, but older, struggling readers may still not read quickly enough to comprehend successfully. Word recognition is the second component of fluency. Students need to instantly and automatically recognize most of the words they read in order to read fluently, including high-frequency words and content-area vocabulary. Readers often encounter a few words that they do not know, but they use word-identification skills to quickly identify those words and continue reading. When students have to stop and decode words in every sentence, their reading will not be fluent because it will be too slow and lack smoothness. The third component, prosody, is the ability to read expressively with appropriate phrasing and intonation (Dowhower, 1991). Fluent readers' oral reading approximates talking, whereas less fluent readers read word-by-word and without expression.

Older students who are not reading fluently are reading texts that are too difficult for them. It is essential that teachers make sure that students have books and other texts at their instructional and independent levels to read. Finding appropriate books for stu-

Figure 6-4 · The Five Comprehension Subprocesses

Process	Instruction	Assessment
Microprocesses Readers chunk ideas into phrases within a sentence to read fluently. Students who read word by word have difficulty understanding what they are reading. Similarly, writers must write fluently, chunking ideas into sentences.	Choral reading[C] is a good way to help students chunk text because classmates and the teacher model appropriate chunking. Interactive writing and quickwrites are effective ways to develop writing fluency.	Teachers listen to students read aloud and check for appropriate chunking. For writing, they observe students as they write, checking for fluency.
Integrative processes Readers infer connections and relationships between clauses and sentences by noticing pronoun substitutions, recognizing synonym substitutions, inferring cause and effect, and recognizing connectives such as *also, however,* and *unless.* In writing, students use these substitutions to clarify relationships.	Teachers ask questions to help students understand these connections by directing their attention to these relationships; for writing, teachers use sentence-combining activities.	Teachers ask questions to check students' ability to use connectives and understand relationships among words in a paragraph, and they examine the paragraphs students write for these connections.
Macroprocesses Readers organize and summarize ideas as they read; that is, they look at the big picture of the entire text as well as the smaller units in the text. For writing, they use their knowledge of story structure, expository text structures, or poetic formulas to organize their compositions.	Students learn about structural patterns of different genres and draw graphic organizers to visually represent the main ideas. Students also do oral and written retellings and write summaries.	Teachers assess students' knowledge of macrostructures by examining students' graphic organizers, their retellings, and their compositions.
Elaborative processes Readers elaborate on the author's message and use their background knowledge to make connections to their own lives and other literature. Students make predictions as they read and identify with characters. In writing, students use classmates' feedback when they revise and provide enough details so readers can make connections.	Students learn to make text-to-self, text-to-world, and text-to-text connections as they talk about stories in grand conversations[C] and information books in instructional conversations[C] and write in reading logs[C].	Teachers observe students as they participate in discussions and read their reading log entries to check that they are making corrections. And teachers monitor students' compositions, checking that they provide enough detail so readers can make connections.
Metacognitive processes. Readers monitor their comprehension and use problem-solving strategies to read and write effectively.	Teachers model reading strategies by "thinking aloud" as they read aloud and model writing strategies during writing lessons. They provide information about literacy strategies in minilessons. Then students apply the strategies when they read and write.	Teachers observe students as they read and write and ask them to "think aloud" about the strategies they are using. Teachers also ask students to reflect on their use of strategies during a reading or writing conference.

Figure 6-5

Ways to Address Less Fluent Readers' Problems

Problem	Instructional Procedure
Students read slowly.	Have students use the repeated readings procedure[C] to build reading speed.
Students cannot decode individual words.	Check students' knowledge of phonics and teach concepts that they don't know.
Students try to sound out phonetically irregular words.	Explain that many common words in English cannot be completely sounded out.
Students cannot read high-frequency words.	Post a high-frequency word wall in the classroom and teach students to read the words.
Students guess at words based on the beginning sound.	Insist that students sound out the beginning, middle, and ending sound and then check the word to see that it makes sense in the context of the text.
Students do not remember a word the second or third time it is used in a passage.	Activate and build students' background knowledge and introduce key vocabulary before reading.
Students do not break multisyllabic words into syllables to decode them.	Teach students to break multisyllabic words into syllables and decode them syllable by syllable.
Students do not break multisyllabic words into root words and affixes to decode them.	Teach students about affixes and root words and how to use this knowledge to decode multisyllabic words.
Students point at words as they read.	Encourage students to use bookmarks instead of pointing.
Students repeat words and phrases.	Have students practice reading familiar text into a tape reorder without making any repetitions.
Students read without expression.	Do choral reading and readers theatre[C] activities to emphasize reading with expression.
Students read word by word.	Demonstrate how to chunk words in a sentence and have students practice chunking familiar text.
Students ignore punctuation marks.	Have students use a highlighter pen to mark punctuation marks before reading.

dents is the first step in solving fluency problems. Figure 6-5 lists some characteristics of less fluent readers and offers additional suggestions for addressing the problems.

As fluent readers read, they chunk the words in a sentence into phrases and select what is important from the sentence to keep in short-term memory. Chunking is important to comprehension because trying to remember every word they read is too heavy a load for readers' short-term memories. It is especially important that English language learners learn the ebb and flow of English phrases and sentences.

When all students are expected to read the same text during a literature focus unit or content-area unit, it is likely to be difficult for some students. To ensure that all students can read or listen to the text read fluently, teachers should:

- interest students in reading the text
- build background knowledge
- introduce key vocabulary
- read the first page or first chapter aloud to the class or with the class before students continue reading independently
- organize students to read with buddies when the text is a little too difficult
- use shared reading[C] with the teacher and more proficient readers taking turns to read aloud the text to the class when it is very difficult
- read aloud the text to students when it is very difficult

In contrast, students choose the books they read for literature circles and reading workshop, and they should choose books that interest them and that are at their own reading levels. This practice ensures that the texts can be read fluently.

Fluency and chunking are important for writers, too. Students develop writing fluency—usually by third grade—so that they can write quickly, without having to stop again and again to think about the conventions of print or how to spell high-frequency words. They chunk the words in their sentences into phrases to help them remember what they are writing because as they become proficient writers, ideas and the sentences to express those ideas come quickly. In fact, many middle-grade students complain that their minds work faster than their hands.

Teachers support students' writing development by:

- providing daily opportunities for writing
- having students write quickwrites

GUIDELINE 7

Struggling Readers Need to Read and Write Fluently. Many struggling readers do not read fluently. Some read slowly, word by word, and without expression, and others have to stop to decode words in almost every sentence. Sometimes they are trying to read a book that is too difficult for them. It is essential that students have books to read at their instructional and independent reading levels and that they become fluent readers as quickly as possible so that they can focus their reading energy on understanding what they're reading. If students are unable to decode phonetically regular words, such as *clip* or *shade,* they need more phonics instruction, and if they cannot read phonetically irregular high-frequency words, such as *would,* they need to practice these words, but they may benefit more from practice rereading familiar texts using repeated readings and choral reading to develop their reading speed and expression.

- posting key literature and content-area words on word walls
- teaching students the list of high-frequency words for older students (see Figure 4-12)

Integrative Processes

The integrative processes deal with the semantic and syntactic connections and relationships among sentences. Readers infer these connections and relationships by noticing pronoun substitutions, recognizing synonym substitutions, inferring cause and effect, and recognizing connectives such as *also, however, because,* and *unless.* Writers include these connections and relationships in paragraphs by using pronoun and synonym substitutions, providing inferential clues, and using connectives.

Teachers facilitate students' understanding of integrative processes when they are reading aloud or along with students and they stop reading to ask clarifying questions. This brief discussion can be done during reading, or teachers can reread the sentences after reading and then ask the questions.

These clarifying questions are also useful for assessing students' ability to use integrative processes. If students have difficulty answering the questions, teachers need to ask clarifying questions like these more often and model how they make connections and relationships among sentences.

Teachers can also examine students' compositions to see if they make these connections and relationships in their writing. If students don't demonstrate knowledge of integrative processes, they can practice combining sentences. When students combine sentences, they realize the inferred connections and relationships among sentences.

Students use macroprocessing as they create graphic organizers.

Macroprocesses

Macroprocesses relate to the big picture—the entire text. The two components of the macroprocesses are recognizing the structure of text and selecting the most important information to remember (Irwin, 1991). Readers organize and summarize ideas as they read, and writers organize their ideas in order to write coherently. Both readers and writers use their knowledge of the overall structure of texts for macroprocessing. Students learn about the elements of story structure, expository text structures, and poetic formulas, and they use this knowledge about the structure of text in order to comprehend what they read. (You will learn more about the structure of text in Chapter 7.)

Teachers teach students about the elements of story structure, expository text structures, and poetic formulas so that they can apply this knowledge in both reading and writing. They also teach students how to use graphic organizers that emphasize the structure of a text as a comprehension aid when reading and writing. They also do word sorts[C] that emphasize characters or events in a story or the main ideas in an informational book (Hoyt, 1999). Learning to differentiate between the more important and less important ideas is a part of macroprocessing, and this knowledge is crucial for both reading and writing. As students read, they choose the more important ideas to remember; when students write, they organize their compositions to focus on the more important ideas. If they are writing a story, they focus on the beginning, middle, and end; if they are writing a cause-and-effect essay, they explain the causes that produce an effect.

Teachers assess students' knowledge of macroprocesses through their oral and written retellings, their graphic organizers, and the summaries they write. Teachers can also examine the overall structure of the compositions students write.

Elaborative Processes

Students use elaborative processes to activate their background knowledge and make connections with the book they are reading or listening to as it is read aloud. They make three types of connections: text-to-self, text-to-world, and text-to-text connections (Fountas & Pinnell, 2001). In text-to-self connections, students link the ideas they are reading about to their own life experiences; they are personal connections. A story event or character may remind them of something or someone in their own lives, and information in a nonfiction book may remind them of an experience they have had. If students are reading a book about snakes, for example, they might connect the information they are reading about how a snake sheds its skin to a time when they found a snakeskin or a classmate brought one to school.

In text-to-world connections, students move beyond personal experience to relate what they are reading to the "world" knowledge they have learned both in and out of school. If they are reading about the Underground Railroad, for example, readers make connections to their knowledge about slavery, the Big Dipper constellation, or Harriet Tubman, who helped many slaves to escape. In addition, they make connections with what they know about railroad trains in order to compare them with the Underground Railroad.

When students make text-to-text connections, they link the text itself or an element of the text to another text they have read or to a familiar film, video, or television program. Text-to-text connections are also called "intertextuality" (de Beaugrande, 1980). Cairney (1990, 1992) identified these five characteristics of intertextuality:

1. *Individual and unique.* Students' literary experiences and the connections they make among them are different.

2. ***Dependent on literary experiences.*** Intertextuality is dependent on the types of books students have read, their purpose for and interest in reading, and the literary communities to which students belong.
3. ***Metacognitive awareness.*** Most students are aware of intertextuality and consciously make connections among texts.
4. ***Links to concept of story.*** Students' connections among stories are linked to their knowledge about literature.
5. ***Reading-writing connections.*** Students make connections between stories they read and stories they write.

Text-to-text connections are difficult for some students; however, Cairney's research indicates that students are aware of their past experiences with literature, and they use this literary knowledge as they read and write. Those students who have done more reading and who know more about literature are more likely to make text-to-text connections. Teachers can encourage students to make these connections and share them with classmates. Through modeling, more students will think about connections between books. Students also make literary connections as they incorporate ideas, structures, and language from stories and other books they have read into compositions they are writing.

Teachers encourage students to make personal, world, and literary connections to books throughout the reading process. During prereading, teachers often ask students to brainstorm or cluster "world" information related to a book they are going to read or to quickwrite about a personal experience related to a book.

Teachers often model how to make the three types of connections during the reading stage, or they stop reading periodically and ask students to tell about the connections they are thinking about. Teachers often make a chart with three columns labeled *text-to-self*, *text-to-world*, and *text-to-text*. Then the teacher or students write about their connections on small sticky notes that they place in the correct column of the chart. Figure 6-6 shows a sixth-grade class's connections chart that was made as they read *So Far From the Sea* (Bunting, 1998), a picture-book story of a Japanese-American family's recent visit to their grandfather's grave at the Manzanar War Relocation Center. Students also make three-column charts in their reading logs and write about the connections they are making while they are reading books.

During the responding stage, students make all three types of connections as they participate in grand conversations and write in reading logs. Teachers often ask students to make text-to-text connections at this stage, after students have had the opportunity to talk about and reflect on the story or other books they have read. During the exploring and applying stages, students continue to make connections as they assume the role of a character and make open-mind portraits[C], reenact the story, write simulated journals from the viewpoint of a character, make quilts[C], and develop other projects.

Students also use elaborative processes to go beyond literal comprehension and make inferences—conclusions that are not explicitly stated in the text (Keene & Zimmermann, 1997). Students have to activate background knowledge, recognize clues in the text, and ask questions in order to draw conclusions. In addition to the picture-book fantasies by Chris Van Allsburg, many other books require students to use inference to comprehend the story. Some of Eve Bunting's picture books, including *Smoky Night* (Bunting, 1994), are designed for older students, and many novels also require inferencing, including *Molly's Pilgrim* (Cohen, 1983), *Bunnicula: A Rabbit-Tale of Mystery* (Howe & Howe, 1979), *Tuck Everlasting* (Babbitt, 1975), and *Witness* (Hesse, 2001).

Text-to-Self	Text-to-World	Text-to-Text
My grandmother takes flowers when she goes to the cemetery because one of her husbands died.	I know that in World War II, Americans were fighting the Japanese because of Pearl Harbor, and they were fighting Hitler and the Germans, too.	This story is like <u>The Bracelet</u>. That girl and her family were taken to a camp in the desert. It was miserable there and she didn't deserve to have to go.
When my family is eating dinner, we look out the window at the mountains, too. I wonder if they are the same mountains that Laura's Dad's family saw from the relocation center?	In the book it's World War II, but I'm thinking about our war in Afghanistan.	Another book I know is <u>Journey to Topaz</u>. Topaz was another war relocation center and it was a terrible prison, too.
My Dad told me about this. My great-granddad had to go too, and it wasn't fair because he was a loyal American, but his parents were from Japan.		
I know how to make origami birds. My cousin and I learned last summer.		I've heard about a book called <u>Anne Frank</u>. She was Jewish and this sorta happened to her in Germany and she died, too.
We have an American flag on our car so everyone knows we love America.		

To help students reflect on their reading, Hoyt (1999) suggests the Two Words activity. Students choose two words to represent the book they have read. After they choose the words, they share their words, explain why they chose them, and say how they relate to the book or their own lives.

Teachers monitor students' use of the elaborative processes by checking to see that their predictions are reasonable, by listening to the comments students make during grand conversations, and by reading their entries in reading logs. In particular, teachers should notice when students make inferences and intertextual comments during grand conversations and in their reading log entries.

Metacognitive Processes

Metacognition is students' conscious awareness of their thinking (Baker & Brown, 1984). Both readers and writers use metacognitive strategies to monitor and evaluate their comprehension. Strategies such as predicting, visualizing, organizing, tapping prior knowledge, and self-questioning are conscious problem-solving behaviors that students use in order to read and write effectively. The strategies are metacognitive because students think about them as they read and write, applying and regulating their use.

During fourth through eighth grades, students' metacognitive knowledge grows as they learn about the reading and writing processes and the strategies that readers and writers use. Students' attention has moved from decoding to comprehension. In writing, their focus has shifted from forming letters and spelling to communicating ideas. As novice readers and writers, students apply strategies when teachers guide and direct them to, but as they become more effective readers and writers, students regulate their use of strategies independently.

Teachers introduce and review the strategies in minilessons. They model how to use the strategies and provide opportunities during guided reading and in other reading activities for students to practice using them. They also teach students to reflect on their use of strategies during think-alouds, in which students talk or write about thinking about reading and writing. Teachers can also assess students' use of strategies through think-alouds.

The five comprehension subprocesses operate simultaneously during the reading and writing processes. It would be wrong to conclude that first students comprehend phrases in sentences, then sentences in paragraphs, and then the entire text. Instead, all five subprocesses work together throughout a variety of activities so that students refine their understanding. Figure 6-7 lists some comprehension activities that students use when reading stories and informational books or content-area textbooks during the five stages of the reading process.

Levels of Comprehension

Researchers have identified three levels of comprehension—literal, inferential, and evaluative—and all three are necessary for students to understand what they read.

Even though literal comprehension is the foundation, students don't move sequentially from literal to inferential to evaluative levels. Teachers can use questions to help students move beyond literal comprehension. During grand conversations, for example, teachers may ask a few literal level questions, but most of the questions should require students to use inferential and evaluative thinking. These high-level questions encourage students to add layers and deepen their comprehension. Teachers also make sure that students move beyond literal-level responses in their reading log entries. One way to encourage deeper thinking is to ask questions or give quotes for students to react to in their entries.

Literal Comprehension.   Students focus on identifying main ideas and details, sequencing events, and noticing cause-and-effect relationships that are explicitly stated in the text at this most basic level.

Without understanding the main ideas, it is unlikely that students will infer and evaluate more complex ideas in the text. Teachers help students understand the basic ideas when they have students write summaries, retell stories, sequence story events using story boards[C], and complete clusters[C] and other graphic organizers with main ideas and details. Students and the teacher also focus on main

Stage	Stories	Informational Books and Content-Area Textbooks
Prereading	Develop background knowledge with books and discussions. Activate background knowledge with quickwrites and discussions. Make predictions. Use anticipation guides[C]. Provide information about the author. Read the first chapter together as a class.	Develop background knowledge with books, videos, and hands-on materials. Activate background knowledge with K-W-L charts[C], quickwrites, and discussions. Use anticipation guides. Do a text walk to overview the book and read headings, figures, and tables. Read the introduction and conclusion together as a class. Prepare graphic organizers.
Reading	Use shared reading or read aloud to students if the text is too difficult for them to read. Have students read with buddies. Model reading strategies. Use guided reading and monitor students' use of strategies. Use "close reading" of short passages. Use the "say something[C]" activity. Make additional predictions.	Use shared reading or read aloud to students if the text is too difficult for them to read. Have students read with buddies. Divide reading assignment into sections and have small groups read each section and then report back to the class. Take notes. Use "close reading" of short passages.
Responding	Discuss the text in a grand conversation. Write in reading logs or do a quickwrite.	Discuss the text in an instructional conversation. Write in learning logs[C] or do a quickwrite.
Exploring	Add words to the word wall. Reread the text or part of it. Examine literary opposites. Teach lessons on reading strategies and skills. Teach lessons on the elements of story structure. Teach lessons about the author or genre. Complete the anticipation guide. Make open-mind portraits. Examine selected sentences and paragraphs in the text.	Add words to the word wall. Reread the text or part of it. Teach lessons on reading strategies and skills. Teach lessons on expository text structures. Complete the anticipation guide or graphic organizer. Examine selected sentences and paragraphs in the text.
Applying	Make projects to deepen understanding. Read other books on the same topic. Compare related books or the book and film versions. Create multigenre projects.	Complete the K-W-L chart. Make projects to deepen understanding. Read other books on the same topic. Write reports and other books on the same topic. Create multigenre projects.

ideas and details during grand conversations, as students share ideas and clarify misconceptions.

Inferential Comprehension.   Students read between the lines to make inferences or draw conclusions. They often have to reread a story or a chapter of a novel to be able to synthesize their background knowledge with the author's clues and ask questions that point toward inferences or conclusions. Teachers begin by explaining what inferences are, how they differ from literal thinking, and why this kind of comprehension is important. Then they develop inference charts as Mr. Wyatt did in the vignette at the beginning of this chapter to help students move through these four steps:

1. Think of background knowledge about topics related to the story.
2. Look for clues in the story.
3. Ask questions about confusions.
4. Make inferences.

Through these four steps, students think more deeply about their reading and become more actively involved in the reading process.

Evaluative Comprehension.   Students go beyond the text and think more deeply about the ideas presented in the text at this level. They recognize instances of bias and unsupported inferences, detect propaganda and faulty reasoning, distinguish between facts and opinions, make personal connections, and react to the context of the text, the characters, and the language of the text.

When students have difficulty understanding what they read, the levels become more important. Teachers need to find out whether students have literal comprehension by asking them to retell or summarize the text. If students have this foundation, then teachers check students' inferential and evaluative comprehension by asking more in-depth questions about the text.

LITERACY STRATEGIES AND SKILLS

We all have skills we use automatically and self-regulated strategies we use thoughtfully for things we do well, such as driving defensively, playing volleyball, training a new pet, and maintaining classroom discipline. We apply skills that we have learned unconsciously and choose among skills as we think strategically. The strategies we use in these activities are problem-solving mechanisms that involve complex thinking processes.

When we are just learning how to drive a car, for example, we learn both skills and strategies. Some of the first skills we learn are how to start the engine, make left turns, and parallel park. With practice, these skills become automatic. Some of the first strategies we learn are how to pass another car and stay a safe distance behind other cars. At first, we have only a small repertoire of strategies, and we don't always use them effectively. That's one reason why we take driving lessons from a driving instructor and have a learner's permit that requires a more experienced driver to ride along with us. These more experienced drivers teach us defensive driving strategies. We learn strategies for driving on interstate highways, on slippery roads, and at night. With practice and guidance, we become more successful drivers, able to anticipate driving problems and take defensive actions.

The same is true for literacy. Strategic readers and writers control their own reading and writing and apply skills and strategies as they need them. They set purposes before reading, revise their plans as they read, and deal with the difficulties they encounter while reading and writing. Strategies allow students to monitor understanding and solve problems as they read. Students use strategies deliberately with some understanding of their usefulness or effectiveness. To become expert readers and writers, children must become strategic.

Reading and Writing Strategies

Capable readers and writers are actively involved in creating meaning. They select and use appropriate strategies, monitor their understanding as they read, and refine their

Figure 6-8   Twelve Strategies That Readers and Writers Use

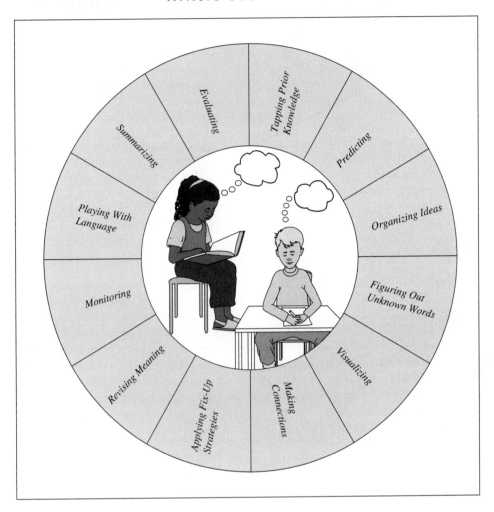

meaning as they write (Paris & Jacobs, 1984; Schmitt, 1990). This section focuses on 12 strategies that elementary students use for both reading and writing. These strategies are listed in Figure 6-8.

Tapping Prior Knowledge.   Students think about what they already know concerning the topic about which they will read or write. This knowledge includes information and vocabulary about topics such as dinosaurs, as well as information about authors and literary genres such as fantasies, alphabet books, and biographies. Students' knowledge is stored in schemata (or categories) and linked to other knowledge through a complex network of interrelationships. As students learn during the reading or writing task, they add the new information to their schemata.

Predicting.   Students make predictions or thoughtful "guesses" about what will happen in the books they are reading. These guesses are based on what students already know about the topic and the literary genre, or on what they have read thus far. Students often make one prediction before beginning to read and several others at key points in the story or at the beginning of each chapter when reading chapter books using the Directed Reading-Thinking Activity[C] (DRTA) (Stauffer, 1975). As they read, students either confirm or revise their predictions. When they are preparing to read informational books or content-area textbooks, students often preview the text in order to make predictions. They also ask questions for which they would like to find answers as they read or set purposes for reading. When they are writing, students make plans and set purposes for the pieces they are writing. They make predictions about which ideas are important and which ones will interest their readers. They revise their plans as their writing moves in new or unexpected directions. Young children also make predictions about how long their writing will be when they count out the number of pages for their books.

Organizing Ideas. Students organize ideas and sequence story events as they read, and they organize their ideas for writing using clusters and other graphic organizers. The way students organize ideas varies depending on whether they are reading and writing stories, informational books, or poetry. Each type of text has unique organizational patterns. When students read and write stories, they often organize the events into the beginning, middle, and end. When they read and write informational books, they often use description, sequence, comparison, or cause-and-effect structures. When they read and write poetry, students use various poetic forms, including haiku, free verse, and acrostics.

Figuring Out Unknown Words. Students need to decide whether to use phonic analysis, syllabic analysis, or morphemic analysis to identify an unfamiliar word or to skip over a word and continue reading. Sometimes they ask the teacher or a classmate about the word. When students are writing, they often need to write words that they don't know how to spell. They may write several letters to serve temporarily as a placeholder, and then check the spelling later by consulting a dictionary, a classmate, or the teacher. At other times, they sound out the word or "think it out." When thinking out the spelling, they have to consider root words, affixes, spelling patterns, and whether the word "looks right."

Visualizing. Students create mental pictures of what they are reading or writing. They often place themselves in the images they create, becoming a character in the story they are reading, traveling to that setting, or facing the conflict situations that the characters themselves face. Teachers sometimes ask students to close their eyes to help visualize the story or to draw pictures of the scenes and characters they visualize. How well students use visualization often becomes clear when students view film versions of books they have read. Students who use the visualization strategy are often disappointed with the film version and the actors who perform as the characters, whereas students who don't visualize are often amazed by the film and prefer it to the book version.

When they are writing, students use description and sensory detail to make their writing more vivid and bring it to life for the people who will read their books. Sometimes teachers have students brainstorm lists of words related to each of the five senses and then incorporate some of the words in pieces they are writing. They also encourage students to use comparisons—metaphors and similes—to make their writing more vivid.

Making Connections. Students personalize what they are reading by relating it to their own lives. They recall similar experiences or compare the characters to themselves or people they know. They connect the book they are reading to other literature they have read. Readers often make connections among several books written by one author or between two versions of the same story. Similarly, when they are writing, students make connections between what they are writing and books they have read or experiences they have had.

Applying Fix-up Strategies.   When students are reading, they sometimes realize that something is not making sense or that they are not understanding what they are reading; then they apply fix-up strategies. They may assume that things will make sense soon and continue reading, or they may reread, look at pictures, skip ahead, talk to a classmate about the book, or ask for help. Choosing an appropriate fix-up strategy is important so students can continue reading productively.

When writing, students apply fix-up strategies when they realize that their writing isn't working the way they want it to. They might reread what they have written to get a jump start on their writing, do more prewriting to gather and organize ideas, read a book on the topic, talk about their ideas with a classmate, or ask a classmate or the teacher to read the piece and give some feedback. Sometimes they draw a picture.

Revising Meaning.   Reading and writing are processes of making meaning, and as students read and write, they are continually revising their understanding and the meaning they are creating. Students often reread for more information or because something doesn't make sense. They also study a book's illustrations, learn through the process of sharing, and get ideas from classmates during discussions. As they write in reading logs, students often gain new insights about a book.

Students meet in writing groups[C] for classmates to read and react to their rough drafts so that they can revise their writing and make it stronger. Writers revise on the basis of the feedback they get from classmates. As they revise, students add words and sentences, make substitutions and deletions, and move their text around to communicate more effectively. They also add titles and illustrations to clarify meaning.

Monitoring.   Students monitor their understanding as they read, though they may be aware of this monitoring only when comprehension breaks down. Students also monitor their writing to see how well they are communicating. When they are reading and writing, students ask themselves questions to monitor their understanding, and they use fix-up strategies when they realize that understanding has broken down.

Playing With Language.   Students notice figurative and novel uses of language when they read, and they incorporate interesting language when they write. Some examples of playing with language are idioms, jokes, riddles, metaphors, similes, personification, sensory language, rhyme, alliteration, and invented words.

Summarizing.   Readers choose important ideas to remember. Summarizing is important because big ideas are easier to remember than lots of details. As students write, they often state their big ideas at the beginning of a paragraph and then support them with facts. They want their readers to be able to pick out the important ideas. During revising, writers ask for feedback about how well their readers remember the important ideas.

Evaluating.   Students make judgments about, reflect on, and value the books they are reading and writing. Readers think about what they have read, review the text, and evaluate their reading. They also value the books they read and what they do as readers. Writers do similar things: They ask themselves whether their own writing says what they want it to say—in other words, whether it is effective. They think about what they have experimented with in a particular piece of writing and reflect on the writing processes that they use. As a strategy, evaluation is not the teacher's judgment handed down to students, but rather students' own thinking about their goals and accomplishments.

Students don't use every one of these strategies every time they read or write, but effective readers and writers use most of them most of the time.

GUIDELINE 8

Struggling Students Need to Become Strategic Readers and Writers. One of the biggest differences between struggling students and their more capable classmates is that good readers and writers are strategic: They predict, monitor, organize, revise, and use other strategies to direct their reading and writing activities and solve problems as they arise. Without learning to actively and thoughtfully engage in the reading and writing processes, it is unlikely that students who struggle with comprehension will improve very much.

Teachers introduce strategies and explain their use in minilessons, model how to use them using think-alouds, and provide supervised and independent practice opportunities. Then teachers monitor students' strategy use by checking that they activate prior knowledge, recognize text structures, generate questions as they read, summarize, and make personal connections and connections between the text and the world around them. In addition, they notice when something doesn't make sense and apply an appropriate fix-up strategy.

Why Is It Important That Students Become Strategic Readers and Writers? Being strategic is an important characteristic of learning. Readers and writers use strategies to generate, organize, and elaborate meaning more expertly than they could otherwise. During the elementary grades, children learn all sorts of cognitive strategies, and the acquisition of reading and writing strategies coincides with this cognitive development. As students learn to reflect on their learning, for example, they learn to reflect on themselves as readers and writers; and as they learn to monitor their learning, they learn to monitor their reading and writing. Many of the cognitive strategies that students learn have direct application to reading and writing. In this way, students' growing awarenesses about thinking, reading, and writing are mutually supportive.

Strategies are cognitive tools that students can use selectively and flexibly as they become independent readers and writers. For students to become independent readers and writers, they need these thinking tools. These strategies are tools for learning across the curriculum; strategic reading and writing enhance learning in math, social studies, science, and other content areas. Children's competence in reading and writing affects all areas of the curriculum. Also, teachers can teach students how to apply reading and writing strategies (Paris et al., 1991). Just as driving instructors and more experienced drivers can teach novice drivers about defensive driving, teachers can demonstrate and explain strategic reading and writing and provide students with opportunities for guided practice.

Even though these strategies are called reading and writing strategies, they are the same strategies students use when they listen and talk and view and visually represent (Brent & Anderson, 1993; Tompkins, 2002).

Reading and Writing Skills

Skills are information-processing techniques that readers and writers use automatically and unconsciously as they construct meaning. Many skills focus at the word level, but some require readers and writers to attend to larger chunks of text. For example, readers use skills such as decoding unfamiliar multisyllabic words, noting details, and sequencing events; and writers employ skills such as forming possessives, using punctuation marks, and capitalizing people's names. Skills and strategies are not the same thing, because strategies are problem-solving tactics selected deliberately to achieve particular goals (Paris et al., 1991). The important difference between skills and strategies is how they are used. During fourth through eighth grades, students learn to use five types of reading and writing skills.

1. *Comprehension skills.* Students use comprehension skills in conjunction with reading and writing strategies. For example, they recognize literary genres and organizational patterns. Other comprehension skills include separating facts and opinions, comparing and contrasting, and recognizing literary genres and structures.

2. *Print skills.* Students use print skills as they decode or spell multisyllabic words. They focus on spelling skills during the editing stage of the writing process. Examples of print skills include breaking words into syllables, using root words and affixes to decode and spell words, capitalizing proper nouns and adjectives, and using abbreviations.

To read more about print skills, turn back to Chapter 4, "Refining Students' Print Skills."

3. *Language skills.* Students use language skills to analyze words they are reading and to choose more precise words and phrases when they are writing. These skills include locating the meanings of words, noticing idioms, using figurative language, and choosing synonyms.

4. *Reference skills.* Students use reference skills to read newspaper articles, locate information in dictionaries and other informational books, and use library references. These skills include alphabetizing a list of words, comparing word meanings in a dictionary, using a table of contents and an index, and reading and making graphs.

5. *Study skills.* Students use study skills to remember what they read during content-area units and when studying for tests. Skimming and scanning, taking notes, making clusters, and previewing a book before reading are examples of study skills.

Examples of the five types of skills are presented in Figure 6-9.

Teachers often wonder when they should teach these skills. School districts often prepare curriculum guides or frameworks that list the skills to be taught at each grade level, and they are usually listed on scope-and-sequence charts that accompany basal reader programs. On scope-and-sequence charts, textbook makers identify the grade level at which a skill should be introduced and the grade levels at which it is practiced. These resources provide guidelines, but teachers must decide which skills to teach based on their students' level of literacy development and the reading and writing activities in which their students are involved. During literature focus units and literature circles, students use many skills, and teachers often go beyond the grade-level list of skills as students use reading and writing for a variety of purposes.

Why Distinguish Between Skills and Strategies? Skills are more commonly associated with reading and writing instruction than strategies are, and for many years, teachers and parents equated teaching skills with teaching reading. They believed that the best way to help children learn to read was to teach them a set of discrete skills, using drill-and-practice worksheets and workbooks (Smith, 1965). But research during the last 35 or more years has shown that reading is a constructive process in which readers construct meaning by interacting with texts (Pearson, Roehler, Dole, & Duffy, 1990). Writing is also a constructive process, and writers construct meaning as they compose texts. Readers and writers use strategies differently than skills: They use strategies to orchestrate higher-order thinking skills when reading and writing, whereas they use skills automatically and unconsciously when reading and writing. Although it continues to be important that students learn to use reading and writing skills automatically, of far greater importance is children's ability to use reading and

Figure 6-9   Five Types of Skills That Readers and Writers Use

Type	Sample Skills	
Comprehension Skills Students use comprehension skills when they are reading in order to understand and summarize, and they use these skills when they are writing in order to make their writing easier to understand.	Sequence Categorize Classify Note details Recognize literary genres	Identify cause and effect Compare and contrast Use context clues Notice organizational patterns of poetry, plays, business and friendly letters, stories, essays, and reports
Decoding and Spelling Skills Students use decoding skills to identify words when reading and many of the same skills to spell words when they are writing.	Sound out words using phonics Use classroom resources Consult a dictionary or glossary Use abbreviations	Apply spelling rules Recognize high-frequency words Divide words into syllables Capitalize proper nouns and adjectives
Language Skills Students use language skills when they focus on particular words during word study activities, and their knowledge of these types of words influences their reading and writing.	Use contractions Use possessives Use similes and metaphors Notice idioms and slang Choose synonyms Recognize antonyms Recognize parts of speech	Differentiate among homonyms Use root words and affixes Appreciate rhyme and other poetic devices Use punctuation marks Use simple, compound, and complex sentences
Reference Skills Students use reference skills when they read informational books, do research, and write reports and other types of expository writing.	Sort in alphabetical order Use a glossary or dictionary Locate etymologies in the dictionary Use the pronunciation guide in the dictionary Locate information in books and on the Internet	Use a table of contents Use an index Use a card catalogue Read and make graphs, tables, and diagrams Use bibliographic forms Locate synonyms in a thesaurus
Study Skills Students use study skills when they review and prepare for tests.	Make outlines and clusters Take notes Paraphrase Follow directions	Skim Scan Preview

writing strategies. When skills and strategies are lumped together, teachers tend to neglect reading and writing strategies because they are more familiar with skills.

Teaching Strategies and Skills

In balanced literacy classrooms, teachers use two approaches—direct instruction and teachable moments—to teach strategies and skills (Spiegel, 1992). Teachers plan and teach minilessons on skills and strategies on a regular basis. These direct-instruction lessons are systematic and planned in conjunction with books or other selections students are reading or books that teachers are reading aloud. Students

Figure 6-10 Guidelines for Skill and Strategy Instruction

---

1. Teach Minilessons
Teachers present minilessons to teach skills and strategies. During the lesson, teachers explain and model the procedure. Then students practice the skill or strategy and later apply it in reading and writing activities.

2. Differentiate Between Skills and Strategies
Teachers understand that skills are automatic behaviors that readers and writers use, whereas strategies are problem-solving tactics, and they differentiate between skills and strategies as they teach minilessons and model how they use strategies. They are also careful to use the terms "skills" and "strategies" correctly when they talk to students.

3. Provide Step-by-Step Explanations
Teachers describe the skill or strategy step by step so that it is sensible and meaningful to students. For strategies, they can use think-aloud procedures to demonstrate how the strategy is used. Teachers also explain to students why they should learn the skill or strategy, how it will make reading and writing easier, and when to use it.

4. Use Modeling
Teachers model using strategies for students in the context of authentic reading and writing activities, rather than in isolation. Students are also encouraged to model using strategies for classmates.

5. Provide Practice Opportunities
Students have opportunities to practice the skill or strategy in meaningful reading and writing activities. Teachers need to ensure that all students are successful using the skill or strategy so that they will be motivated to use it independently.

6. Apply in Content Areas
Teachers provide opportunities for students to use the skill or strategy in reading and writing activities related to social studies, science, and other content areas. The more opportunities students have to use the skill or strategy, the more likely they are to learn it.

7. Use Reflection
Teachers ask students to reflect on their use of the skill or strategy after they have had the opportunity to practice it and apply it in meaningful reading and writing activities.

8. Hang Charts of Skills and Strategies
Teachers often hang lists of skills and strategies students are learning in the classroom and encourage students to refer to them when reading and writing. Separate charts should be used for skills and strategies so that students can remember which are which.

Adapted from Winograd & Hare, 1988; Pressley & Harris, 1990.

learn other strategies and skills incidentally through teachable moments as they observe and work collaboratively with teachers and classmates. In both kinds of instruction, teachers support students' learning, and students apply what they are learning in authentic literacy activities. Guidelines for skill and strategy instruction are presented in Figure 6-10.

Teachers explain and model strategies in minilessons.

Minilessons.   Minilessons (Atwell, 1998) are 15- to 30-minute direct-instruction lessons designed to help students learn literacy skills and become more strategic readers and writers. Sometimes these lessons continue for several days. In these lessons, students and the teacher are focused on a single goal; students are aware of why it is important to learn the skill or strategy, and they are explicitly taught how to use a particular skill or strategy through modeling, explanation, and practice. Then independent application takes place using authentic literacy materials. Through minilessons, responsibility is transferred from teacher to student (Bergman, 1992; Duffy & Roehler, 1987; Pearson & Gallagher, 1983).

Many researchers recommend using a whole-part-whole organization for teaching skills and strategies (Flood & Lapp, 1994; Trachtenburg, 1990). Students read and respond to a text—this is the whole; then teachers focus on a skill or strategy and teach a minilesson using examples from the text whenever possible—this is the part. Finally, students return to the text or another text to apply what they have learned by doing more reading or writing or doing a project—this is the whole again. The skills approach to reading is described as part-to-whole, and the holistic approach is described as whole-to-part. The whole-part-whole approach takes both into account. Instead of isolated drill-and-practice activities that are often meaningless to students, this approach encourages teachers to clearly connect what students are learning in minilessons to authentic literacy activities.

The minilesson feature on page 201 shows how a fourth-grade teacher taught her students about literary opposites (Temple, 1992) during a literature focus unit on *Amos and Boris* (Steig, 1971). In the story, a whale named Amos rescues a shipwrecked mouse named Boris, and later Boris saves Amos when he becomes beached near Boris's home. Literary opposites are any opposites in a story—two very different settings, characters, events, and emotions in the story, for example—and most stories have more than one pair of opposites. One of the opposites in *Amos and Boris* is that the two animals, who are so different, become friends. Not only are they different in size, but one is a land animal and the other lives in the ocean.

Minilesson

Topic: Literary Opposites
Grade: Fourth Grade
Time: One 45-minute period

During a literature focus unit on *Amos and Boris* (Steig, 1971), a story of an unlikely friendship between a mouse and a whale, Mrs. Donnelly teaches this minilesson on literary opposites. Her goal is to help her fourth-grade students think more deeply about the theme of the story. Mrs. Donnelly describes her students as good literal comprehenders; they can identify the characters and retell the story, but they have difficulty with inferential comprehension.

1. Introduce the Topic

"Let's talk about opposites," Mrs. Donnelly explains to her fourth graders. "One way to understand a story better is to think of opposites. There are many different kinds of opposites in stories—sometimes there are kind and mean characters, stories that take place in different settings, and events happen in stories that are happy and sad. If you think about the opposites, it will often help you identify a theme."

2. Share Examples

Mrs. Donnelly reviews Jan Brett's *Town Mouse, Country Mouse* (1994), a story the students have read before, and uses the think-aloud technique to point out these opposites:

town-country	mouse-cat	mouse-owl
plain-fancy	dark-light	quiet-noisy

She writes the list on the chalkboard and stands back to reflect on it.

3. Provide Information

Then Mrs. Donnelly circles *plain-fancy* and thinks aloud:

Yes, I think *plain* and *fancy* are important opposites. I can think about lots of examples of *plain* and *fancy:* Plain and fancy clothes, plain and fancy food, and plain and fancy houses. These two mice are really different. The country mouse likes plain things and the city mouse likes fancy things. So, I think that one of the author's messages was that it is good to be different or unique.

"You can talk to a friend the way I talked to you or write a quickwrite to figure out a theme," Mrs. Donnelly points out. She also explains that some opposites may not be so useful; *mouse-owl* or *dark-light,* for example.

4. Guide Practice

Mrs. Donnelly asks students to reread *Amos and Boris* with partners and look for opposites. After reading, Mrs. Donnelly's students list these opposites:

big-little	helping-being helped	life-death
hope-hopeless	forgetting-remembering	in the water-on land

Then Mrs. Donnelly asks the fourth graders to each choose one of the pairs of opposites and quickwrite about it in order to discover a theme of the story. One student writes:

I think *big-little* is the most important opposite. The mouse is the little animal and of course the big animal is the whale. A theme is a little animal can help a big animal. This story is like "The Lion and the Mouse." I think the same for people. Kids can help their parents.

Students share their quickwrites with partners and then some students read aloud to the class.

5. Assess Learning

Mrs. Donnelly reviews students' quickwrites to gauge their understanding of literary opposites. She also encourages students to think about opposites in the stories they are reading during reading workshop and asks them about the opposites as she conferences with them.

Teachable Moments.   Teachers often use informal techniques called "teachable moments" to share their knowledge as expert readers and writers. These give students opportunities to apply what they are learning in authentic reading and writing activities (Staab, 1990). Sometimes teachers take advantage of teachable moments to explain or demonstrate something with the whole class, and at other times they use them with small groups of students.

Modeling is an instructional technique that teachers use to demonstrate to students how to perform an unfamiliar reading or writing skill or strategy (Bergman, 1992). Teachers are expert readers and writers, and through modeling, they show students—novice readers and writers—how to perform a strategy, skill, or other task so that students can build their own understanding of the activity. And classmates also serve as models for each other.

Teachers informally model reading and writing strategies for students whenever they participate in literacy activities. Middle-grade students learn about revising text as they work with the teacher to revise the rough draft of a collaborative report[C] that has been written on chart paper. As students work with teachers and observe them, they develop the understanding that readers and writers do some things automatically but at other times have to take risks, think out solutions to problems, and deal with ambiguities.

Teachers use think-alouds to model for students the thought processes they go through as they use reading and writing skills and strategies (Baumann & Schmitt, 1986; Davey, 1983; Wade, 1990). Through this modeling, students become more aware of the metacognitive processes capable readers and writers use and learn to think aloud about their own use of strategies. Teachers who work with older students think aloud about their use of strategies during reading and writing activities.

Teachers also take advantage of teachable moments to share information about strategies and skills with students. They introduce, review, or extend a skill or strategy in these very brief lessons. As teachers listen to students read aloud or talk about the processes they use during reading, they often have an opportunity to teach a particular strategy or skill (Atwell, 1998). Similarly, as teachers conference with students about their writing or work with students to revise or edit their writing, they share information about writing skills and strategies with their students. Students also ask questions about skills and strategies or volunteer information about how they handled a reading or writing problem. Teachers who are careful observers and who listen closely to their students don't miss these teachable moments.

Why Teach Skills and Strategies?   Some teachers argue about whether to teach strategies and skills directly or implicitly. The position in this book is that teachers have the responsibility to teach students how to read and write, and part of that responsibility is teaching students the skills and strategies that capable readers and writers use. Although it is true that students learn many things inductively through meaningful literacy experiences, direct instruction is important, too. Effective teachers do teach skills and strategies.

Researchers have compared classrooms in which teachers focused on teaching skills directly with other programs in which skills and strategies were taught inductively, and they concluded that the traditional skills programs were no more effective according to students' performance on standardized reading texts. Moreover, researchers suggest that traditional skills programs may be less effective when we take into account that students in the balanced reading programs also think of themselves as readers and writers and have more knowledge about written language.

Freppon (1991) compared the reading achievement of first graders in traditional and balanced reading classrooms and found that the balanced group was more successful. Similarly, Reutzel and Hollingsworth (1991) compared students who were taught skills with students who spent an equal amount of time reading books, and they found that neither group did better on skill tests. This research suggests that students who do not already know skills and strategies do benefit from instruction, but the instruction must stress application to authentic reading and writing activities.

Carefully planned instruction, however, may be especially important for minority students. Lisa Delpit (1987) cautions that many students who grow up outside the dominant culture are disadvantaged when certain knowledge, strategies, and skills expected by teachers are not made explicit in their classrooms. Explicitness is crucial because people from different cultures have different sets of understanding. When they teach children from other cultures, teachers often find it difficult to get their meaning across unless they are very explicit (Delpit, 1991). Delpit's writing has created a stir because she claims that African American children and other nonmainstream children frequently are not given access to the codes of power unless literacy instruction is explicit. Too often, teachers assume that children make the connection between the strategies and skills they are teaching and the future use of those strategies and skills in reading and writing, but Delpit claims that many do not.

On the other hand, several studies suggest that both mainstream and nonmainstream students learn best with balanced reading instruction. Morrow (1992) and Dahl and Freppon (1995) found that minority students in balanced reading classrooms do as well as students in skill-based classrooms, plus they develop a greater sense of the purposes of literacy and see themselves as readers and writers.

 VISIT CHAPTER 6 ON THE COMPANION WEBSITE AT
www.prenhall.com/tompkins

- Complete a self-assessment to demonstrate your understanding of the concepts presented in this chapter
- Complete field activities that will help you expand your understanding of the middle-grade classroom and facilitating students' comprehension
- Visit important web links related to middle-grade reading and writing comprehension
- Look into your state's standards as they relate to reading and writing skills and strategies and the middle-grade student
- Communicate with other preservice teachers via the message board and discuss the issues involved in helping students in grades 4 to 8 become capable readers and writers

Review

Comprehension is a creative, multifaceted process that students use for reading and writing. For reading, it is the reader's process of using prior experiences and the author's text to construct meaning that is useful to that reader for a specific purpose. The five subprocesses are microprocesses, integrative processes, macroprocesses, elaborative processes, and metacognitive processes. Students use both strategies and skills for reading and writing. Strategies are problem-solving behaviors, and skills are information-processing techniques that students use automatically and unconsciously. Teachers use both direct instruction and teachable moments to teach strategies and skills in balanced reading classrooms. Ways that effective teachers facilitate students' comprehension are reviewed in the following feature.

1. Teachers understand the differences between capable and less capable readers and writers.
2. Teachers use modeling and explanation to help students become more capable readers and writers.
3. Teachers incorporate choice and authenticity into their instructional programs to influence students' motivation.
4. Teachers view comprehension as a multifaceted process involving five subprocesses.
5. Teachers incorporate comprehension activities representing all five subprocesses into the reading process.
6. Teachers monitor and assess students' ability to use all five subprocesses.
7. Teachers teach 12 strategies: tapping prior knowledge, predicting, organizing ideas, figuring out unknown words, visualizing, making connections, applying fix-up strategies, revising meaning, monitoring, playing with language, summarizing, and evaluating.
8. Teachers teach five types of skills: comprehension skills, print skills, language skills, reference skills, and study skills.
9. Teachers teach minilessons on skills and strategies to the whole class or to small groups, depending on students' needs.
10. Teachers take advantage of teachable moments to answer students' questions and clarify misconceptions.

Professional References

Atwell, N. (1998). *In the middle: New understandings about writing, reading, and learning* (2nd ed.). Portsmouth, NH: Heinemann.

Baker, L., & Brown, A. L. (1984). Metacognitive skills and reading. In P. D. Pearson, M. Kamil, R. Barr, & P. Mosenthal (Eds.), *Handbook of reading research* (Vol. 1, pp. 353–394). New York: Longman.

Baumann, J. F., & Schmitt, M. C. (1986). The what, why, how, and when of comprehension instruction. *The Reading Teacher, 39,* 640–647.

Bergman, J. L. (1992). SAIL—A way to success and independence for low-achieving readers. *The Reading Teacher, 45,* 598–602.

Brent, R., & Anderson, P. (1993). Developing children's classroom listening strategies. *The Reading Teacher, 47,* 122–126.

Cairney, T. (1990). Intertextuality: Infectious echoes from the past. *The Reading Teacher, 43,* 478–484.

Cairney, T. (1992). Fostering and building students' intertextual histories. *Language Arts, 69,* 502–507.

Dahl, K. L., & Freppon, P. A. (1995). A comparison of inner-city children's interpretations of reading and writing instruc-tion in the early grades in skills-based and whole language classrooms. *Reading Research Quarterly, 30,* 50–74.

Davey, B. (1983). Think-aloud—Modelling the cognitive processes of reading comprehension. *Journal of Reading, 27,* 44–47.

de Beaugrande, R. (1980). *Text, discourse, and process.* Norwood, NJ: Ablex.

Delpit, L. (1987). The silenced dialogue: Power and pedagogy in educating other people's children. *Harvard Educational Review, 58,* 280–298.

Delpit, L. (1991). A conversation with Lisa Delpit. *Language Arts, 68,* 541–547.

Dowhower, S. L. (1991). Speaking of prosody: Fluency's unattended bedfellow. *Theory into Practice, 30,* 165–173.

Duffy, G. G., & Roehler, L. R. (1987). Improving reading instruction through the use of responsible elaboration. *The Reading Teacher, 20,* 548–554.

Dweck, C. S. (1986). Motivational processes affecting learning. *American Psychologist, 41,* 1040–1048.

Faigley, L., Cherry, R. D., Jolliffe, D. A., & Skinner, A. M. (1985). *Assessing writers' knowledge and processes of composing.* Norwood, NJ: Ablex.

Flood, J., & Lapp, D. (1994). Developing literary appreciation and literacy skills: A blueprint for success. *The Reading Teacher, 48,* 76–79.

Fountas, I. C., & Pinnell, G. S. (2001). *Guiding readers and writers, grades 3–6.* Portsmouth, NH: Heinemann.

Freppon, P. A. (1991). Children's concepts of the nature and purpose of reading in different instructional settings. *Journal of Reading Behavior, 23,* 139–163.

Garner, R. (1987). *Metacognition and reading comprehension.* Norwood, NJ: Ablex.

Hoyt, L. (1999). *Revisit, reflect, retell: Strategies for improving reading comprehension.* Portsmouth, NH: Heinemann.

Irwin, J. W. (1991). *Teaching reading comprehension processes* (2nd ed). Boston: Allyn & Bacon.

Johnston, P., & Winograd, P. (1985). Passive failure in reading. *Journal of Reading Behavior, 17,* 279–301.

Keene, E. O., & Zimmermann, S. (1997). *Mosaic of thought: Teaching comprehension in a reader's workshop.* Portsmouth, NH: Heinemann.

Morrow, L. M. (1992). The impact of a literature-based program on literacy achievement, use of literature, and attitudes of children from minority backgrounds. *Reading Research Quarterly, 27,* 251–275.

Oldfather, P. (1995). Commentary: What's needed to maintain and extend motivation for literacy in the middle grades. *Journal of Reading, 38,* 420–422.

Paris, S. G., & Jacobs, J. E. (1984). The benefits of informed instruction for children's reading awareness and comprehension skills. *Child Development, 55,* 2083–2093.

Paris, S. G., Wasik, B. A., & Turner, J. C. (1991). The development of strategic readers. In R. Barr, M. L. Kamil, P. B. Mosenthal, & P. D. Pearson (Eds.), *Handbook of reading research* (Vol. 2, pp. 609–640). New York: Longman.

Pearson, P. D., & Gallagher, M. C. (1983). The instruction of reading comprehension. *Contemporary Educational Psychology, 8,* 317–344.

Pearson, P. D., Roehler, L. R., Dole, J. A., & Duffy, G. G. (1990). *Developing expertise in reading comprehension: What should be taught? How should it be taught?* (Technical Report No. 512). Champaign, IL: University of Illinois, Center for the Study of Reading.

Pressley, M., & Harris, K. R. (1990). What we really know about strategy instruction. *Educational Leadership, 48,* 31–34.

Rasinski, T. V. (2000). Speed does matter in reading. *The Reading Teacher, 54,* 146–151.

Reutzel, D. R., & Hollingsworth, P. M. (1991). Reading comprehension skills: Testing the skills distinctiveness hypothesis. *Reading Research and Instruction, 30,* 32–46.

Richards, M. (2000). Be a good detective: Solve the case of oral reading fluency. *The Reading Teacher, 53,* 534–539.

Schmitt, M. C. (1990). A questionnaire to measure children's awareness of strategic reading processes. *The Reading Teacher, 43,* 454–461.

Smith, N. B. (1965). *American reading instruction.* Newark, DE: International Reading Association.

Spiegel, D. L. (1992). Blending whole language and systematic direct instruction. *The Reading Teacher, 46,* 38–46.

Staab, C. F. (1990). Teacher mediation in one whole literacy classroom. *The Reading Teacher, 43,* 548–552.

Stauffer, R. G. (1975). *Directing the reading-thinking process.* New York: Harper & Row.

Temple, C. (1992). Lots of plots: Patterns, meanings, and children's literature. In C. Temple & P. Collings (Eds.), *Stories and readers: New perspectives on literature in the elementary classroom* (pp. 3–13). Norwood, MA: Christopher-Gordon.

Tierney, R. J. (1990). Redefining reading comprehension. *Educational Leadership, 47,* 37–42.

Tompkins, G. E. (2002). *Language arts: Content and teaching strategies* (5th ed.). Upper Saddle River, NJ: Merrill/Prentice Hall.

Trachtenburg, P. (1990). Using children's literature to enhance phonics instruction. *The Reading Teacher, 43,* 648–654.

Wade, S. E. (1990). Using think alouds to assess comprehension. *The Reading Teacher, 43,* 442–453.

Winograd, P., & Hare, V. C. (1988). Direct instruction of reading comprehension strategies: The nature of teacher explanation. In C. Weinstein, E. Goetz, & P. Alexander (Eds.), *Learning and study strategies: Issues in assessment, instruction, and evaluation* (pp. 121–139). San Diego, CA: Academic Press.

Children's Book References

Allard, H. (1977). *Miss Nelson is missing!* Boston: Houghton Mifflin.

Babbitt, N. (1975). *Tuck everlasting.* New York: Farrar, Straus & Giroux.

Brett, J. (1994). *Town mouse, country mouse.* New York: Putnam.

Bunting, E. (1994). *Smoky night.* San Diego, CA: Harcourt Brace.

Bunting, E. (1998). *So far from the sea.* New York: Clarion Books.

Cohen, B. (1983). *Molly's pilgrim.* New York: Lothrop, Lee & Shepard.

Hesse, K. (2001). *Witness.* New York: Scholastic.

Howe, D., & Howe, J. (1979). *Bunnicula: A rabbit-tale of mystery.* New York: Aladdin.

Spinelli, J. (1990). *Maniac Magee.* New York: Scholastic.

Steig, W. (1971). *Amos and Boris.* New York: Farrar, Straus & Giroux.

Van Allsburg, C. (1979). *The garden of Abdul Gasazi.* Boston: Houghton Mifflin.

Van Allsburg, C. (1981). *Jumanji.* Boston: Houghton Mifflin.

Van Allsburg, C. (1984). *The mysteries of Harris Burdick.* Boston: Houghton Mifflin.

Van Allsburg, C. (1986). *The stranger.* Boston: Houghton Mifflin.

Van Allsburg, C. (1991). *The wretched stone.* Boston: Houghton Mifflin.

7

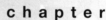

Becoming Familiar With the Structure of Text

- How are narrative texts organized?
- How are expository texts organized?
- How are poetic texts structured?
- How does the structure of text affect students' reading and writing?

Mr. Abrams's Fourth Graders Learn About Frogs

The fourth graders in Mr. Abrams's class are studying frogs. They began by talking about frogs and making a class K-W-L chart[C] (Ogle, 1986), listing what they already know about frogs in the "K: What We Know" column and things they want to learn in the "W: What We Wonder About" column. At the end of the unit, students will finish the chart by listing what they have learned in the "L: What We Have Learned" column. The fourth graders want to know how frogs and toads are different and if it is true that you get warts from frogs. Mr. Abrams assures them that they will learn the answers to many of their questions and makes a mental note to find the answer to their question about warts.

Aquariums with frogs and frog spawn are arranged in one area in the classroom. Mr. Abrams has brought in five aquariums and filled them with frogs he collected in his backyard and others he "rented" from a local pet store, and he has also brought in frog spawn from a nearby pond. The fourth graders are observing the frogs and frog spawn daily and drawing diagrams and making notes in their learning logs[C].

A word wall[C] is posted on one side of the classroom, and students are writing important words related to the unit in alphabetical order on the chart. They add small pictures to illustrate more difficult words. The words that the students are adding include *amphibian, camouflage, cold blooded, endangered, froglet, gills, hibernation, lungs, metamorphosis, predators, skin, spawn, tadpoles, tongue,* and *tympanum.* The students refer to the word wall and use the words as they make notes in their learning logs and participate in other writing activities related to the unit. Mr. Abrams also uses these words for language arts minilessons[C] on syllables, parts of speech, and other skills.

Mr. Abrams sets out a text set with three types of books about frogs—stories, informational books, and poetry books—on a special shelf in the classroom library. Mr. Abrams reads many of the books aloud to the class. When he begins, he reads the title and shows students several pages and asks them whether the book is a story, an informational book, or a poem. After they determine the genre, they talk about their purpose for listening. If it is an informational book, he writes a question or two on the chalkboard to give students a purpose for listening. During their instructional conversation[C] after reading, the students answer the questions. Students also read and reread many of these books during an independent reading time that Mr. Abrams calls DEAR time.

Mr. Abrams has also gotten a class set of *Amazing Frogs and Toads* (Clarke, 1990), an informational book with striking photograph illustrations and well-organized presentations of information. From the vast amount of information in *Amazing Frogs and Toads,* Mr. Abrams chooses nine questions, and he designs them to address some of the questions on the "W: What We Wonder" section of the K-W-L chart, to highlight important information in the text, and to focus on the five expository text structures, the patterns used for nonfiction texts that students read and write. Mr. Abrams is teaching the fourth graders that informational books, like stories, have special organizational elements. Here are his nine questions organized according to the expository structures:

1. What are amphibians? (Description)
2. What do frogs look like? (Description)
3. What is the life cycle of a frog? (Sequence)

4. How do frogs eat? (Sequence)
5. How are frogs and toads alike and different? (Comparison)
6. Why do frogs hibernate? (Cause and Effect)
7. How do frogs croak? (Cause and Effect)
8. How do frogs use their eyes and eyelids? (Problem and Solution)
9. How do frogs escape from their enemies? (Problem and Solution)

[C] See the Compendium of Instructional Procedures, which follows Chapter 12, for more information on terms marked with the symbol [C].

Mr. Abrams reads the book once with the whole class using shared reading[C] and they discuss the interesting information in the book in an instructional conversation. He divides the class into nine small groups and has each group choose a question about frogs to research in the book. Students reread the book, hunting for the answer to their question. Mr. Abrams has already taught the students to use the table of contents and the index to locate facts in an informational book. After they locate and reread the information, they use the writing process to develop a poster to answer the question and share what they have learned. He meets with each group to help them design their posters, to revise and edit their writing, and to help them present their information in the best way possible.

After the students complete their posters, they share them with the class through brief presentations, and the posters are displayed in the classroom. Two of the students' posters are shown in Figure 7-1; the life cycle poster emphasizes the sequence structure, and the "Frogs Have Big Eyes" poster explains that the frog's eyes help it solve problems—finding food, hiding from enemies, and seeing underwater.

Mr. Abrams's students use the information in the posters to write books about frogs. Students choose three posters and write one- to three-paragraph chapters to report the information from the poster. Students meet in writing groups[C] to revise their rough drafts and then edit with a classmate and with Mr. Abrams. Finally, students word process their final copies and add illustrations, a title page, and a table of contents. Then they compile their books and "publish" them by sharing them with classmates from the author's chair.

Armin wrote this chapter on "Hibernation" in his book:

Hibernation means that an animal sleeps all winter long. Frogs hibernate because they are cold blooded and they might freeze to death if they didn't. They find a good place to sleep like a hole in the ground, or in a log, or under some leaves. They go to sleep and they do not eat, or drink, or go to the bathroom. They sleep all winter and when they wake up it is spring. They are very, very hungry and they want to eat a lot of food. Their blood warms up when it is spring because the temperature warms up and when they are warm they want to be awake and eat. They are awake in the spring and in the summer, and then in the fall they start to think about hibernating again.

Jessica wrote this chapter on "The Differences Between Frogs and Toads" in her book:

You might think that frogs and toads are the same but you would be wrong. They are really different but they are both amphibians. I am going to tell you three ways they are different.

First of all, frogs really love water so they stay in the water or pretty close to it. Toads don't love water. They usually live where it is dry. This is a big difference between frogs and toads.

Figure 7-1   **Two Posters About Frogs**

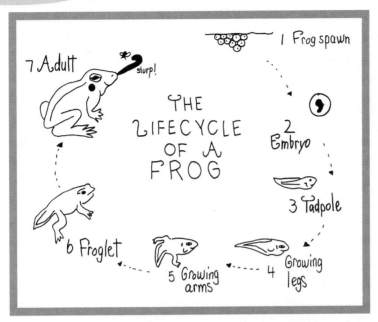

THE LIFECYCLE OF A FROG

1 Frog spawn
2 Embryo
3 Tadpole
4 Growing legs
5 Growing arms
6 Froglet
7 Adult — slurp!

FROGS HAVE BIG EYES

1. Big Eyes
Frogs have big eyes to see their food and their enemies.

2. On Top
Their eyes are on top so they can peek out of the water.

3. Two Eyelids
They have regular and clear eyelids so they can see underwater.

Second, you should look at frogs and toads. They look different. Frogs are slender and thin but toads are fat. Their skin is different, too. Frogs have smooth skin and toads have bumpy skin. I would say that toads are not pretty to look at.

Third, frogs have long legs but toads have short legs. That probably is the reason why frogs are wonderful jumpers and toads can't. They move slowly. They just hop. When you watch them move, you can tell that they are very different.

Frogs and toads are different kinds of amphibians. They live in different places, they look different, and they move in different ways. You can see these differences when you look at them and it is very interesting to study them.

Mr. Abrams and his students develop a rubric to assess their books. The rubric addresses the following points about the chapters:

- The chapter title describes the chapter.
- The information in each chapter is presented clearly.
- Vocabulary from the word wall is used in each chapter.
- The information in each chapter is written in one or more indented paragraphs.
- The information in each chapter has very few spelling, capitalization, and punctuation errors.
- There is a useful illustration in each chapter.

Other points on the rubric consider the book as a whole:

- The title page lists the title and the author's name.
- All pages in the book are numbered.
- The table of contents lists the chapters and the pages for each chapter.
- The title is written on the cover of the book.
- The illustrations on the cover of the book relate to frogs.

The students evaluate their books using a 4-point scale, and Mr. Abrams also uses the rubric to assess students' writing. He conferences with students and shares his scoring with them. Also, he helps the students set goals for their next writing project.

To end the unit, Mr. Abrams asks his students to finish the K-W-L chart. In the third column, "L: What We Have Learned," students list some of the information they have learned, including:

Frogs are amphibians that hibernate in the winter.
There are 3,000 kinds of frogs.
Leopard frogs are the most common kind of frog.
Tadpoles breathe through gills but frogs breathe through lungs.
Tadpoles are vegetarians but frogs eat worms and insects.
Snakes, rats, birds, and foxes are the frogs' enemies.
Some frogs in the rainforest are brightly colored and poisonous, too.
Some frogs are hard to see because they have camouflage coloring.
Male frogs puff up their air sacs to croak and make sounds.
Frogs have teeth but they swallow their food whole.
The largest American frog is the bullfrog.
Frogs have two sets of eyelids and one set is clear so frogs can see when they are underwater.
Frogs can jump ten times their body length but toads can't—they're hoppers.
Frogs live near water and toads live on land.

Middle-grade students read all three types of literature—stories, informational books, and poems—just as the students in Mr. Abrams's classroom do. These "real" books are called trade books. Many students also use reading textbooks (often called basal readers) and social studies, science, and other content-area textbooks. Reading textbooks contain stories, informational articles, and poetry, too. In recent years, there has been a great deal of controversy about whether trade books or textbooks should be used to teach reading. Lapp, Flood, and Farnan (1992) believe that textbooks and trade books are compatible and that students should read both types.

Stories, informational books, and poems have unique structures or organizational patterns. Stories are organized differently from poems and informational books. For example, *The Very Hungry Caterpillar* (Carle, 1969) is a repetitive story that chronicles the life cycle of a butterfly, and *The Icky Bug Counting Book* (Pallotta, 1992) is an informational book highlighting 26 species of insects, one on each page. Sometimes teachers call all literature that students read and write "stories," but stories are unique: They have specific structural elements, including characters and plot. Teachers need to introduce the three types of literature and use the labels for each type correctly.

The stories students write reflect the stories they have read. Dressel (1990) found that the quality of fifth graders' writing was dependent on the quality of the stories they read and listened to read aloud, regardless of students' reading levels. Similarly, when students learn about the structure of informational books and content-area textbooks, both their reading comprehension and their nonfiction writing improve (Flood, Lapp, & Farnan, 1986; McGee & Richgels, 1985; Piccolo, 1987).

The feature on page 212 explains the role of text structure in a balanced literacy program. As you continue reading this chapter, you will learn more about the ideas presented in the feature.

ELEMENTS OF NARRATIVE STRUCTURE

Stories give meaning to the human experience, and they are a powerful way of knowing and learning. When preschoolers listen to family members tell stories and read them aloud, they develop an understanding or concept about stories by the time they come to school. Students use and refine this knowledge as they read and write more sophisticated stories during fourth through eighth grades.

Stories are available in picture-book and chapter-book formats. Picture books have brief texts, usually spread over 32 pages, in which text and illustrations combine to tell a story. The text is minimal, and the illustrations supplement the sparse text. The illustrations in many picture books are striking. Some picture books, such as *Rosie's Walk* (Hutchins, 1968), about a clever hen who outwits a fox, are for primary-grade students, but others, such as *Pink and Say* (Polacco, 1994), about a black and a white Civil War soldier, were written with middle-grade students in mind. Fairy tales have also been retold as picture books; Trina Schart Hyman's *The Sleeping Beauty* (1977) is an especially beautiful picture book. Another type of picture book is wordless picture books, such as *Tuesday* (Wiesner, 1991) and *Good Dog, Carl* (Day, 1985), in which the story is told entirely through the illustrations.

Novels are longer stories written in a chapter format. Novels for middle-grade students include *Charlotte's Web* (White, 1952) and *Bunnicula: A Rabbit-Tale of Mystery* (Howe & Howe, 1979). Complex stories such as *The Giver* (Lowry, 1993) are more suitable for seventh- and eighth-grade students. Novels have few illustrations,

ELL

English language learners are better able to use macroprocesses to comprehend stories when they know about the elements of narrative structure because these elements serve as a skeleton for the story.

The Role of Text Structure in a Balanced Literacy Program

Component	Description
Reading	No matter whether students are doing the reading themselves or listening to teachers read aloud, students learn about text structure through reading.
Phonics and Other Skills	One of the most important comprehension skills is recognizing text structures.
Strategies	Students apply their knowledge of text structures when they make predictions, organize ideas, visualize, monitor their understanding, summarize, and evaluate their reading.
Vocabulary	Vocabulary is not an important component of text structure.
Comprehension	Students learn about text structures to improve their comprehension, specifically macroprocessing.
Literature	All three types of literature—stories, informational books, and poems—embody specialized text structures that students can learn to recognize and apply in their own writing.
Content-Area Study	Students learn about expository text structures as they read informational books and content-area textbooks, and they apply their knowledge of narrative, expository, and poetic structures as they read text sets of books as part of content-area units.
Oral Language	Students explore the structure of text as they talk about stories and poems in grand conversations[C] and informational texts and content-area texts in instructional conversations.
Writing	Students apply their knowledge of text structure when they write stories, reports, poems, and other types of compositions.
Spelling	Spelling is not an important component of text structure.

if any, and the illustrations usually do not play an integral role in the book, as they do in picture books.

Stories have unique structural elements that distinguish them from other forms of literature. Five story elements are plot, characters, setting, point of view, and theme. These elements work together to structure a story, and authors manipulate them to make their stories hold readers' attention.

Plot

Plot is the sequence of events involving characters in conflict situations. A story's plot is based on the goals of one or more characters and the processes they go through to attain these goals (Lukens, 1999). The main characters want to achieve a goal, and other characters are introduced to oppose the main characters or prevent them from being successful. The story events are set in motion by characters as they attempt to overcome conflict, reach their goals, and solve their problems. The most basic aspect of plot is the division of the main events of a story into three parts: beginning, middle, and end.

Specific types of information are included in each of the three story parts. In the beginning, the author introduces the characters, describes the setting, and presents a problem. Together, the characters, setting, and events develop the plot and sustain the theme through the story. In the middle, the plot unfolds, with each event preparing readers for what will follow. Conflict heightens as the characters face roadblocks that keep them from solving their problems. How the characters tackle these problems adds suspense to keep readers interested. In the end, all is reconciled and readers learn whether the characters' struggles are successful.

Conflict is the tension or opposition between forces in the plot, and it is what interests readers enough to continue reading the story. Conflict usually occurs

- between a character and nature
- between a character and society
- between characters
- within a character (Lukens, 1999)

Figure 7-2 lists stories representing the four conflict situations.

Conflict between a character and nature occurs in stories in which severe weather plays an important role, as in *Julie of the Wolves* (George, 1972), and in stories set in isolated geographic locations, such as *Island of the Blue Dolphins* (O'Dell, 1960), in which the Indian girl Karana struggles to survive alone on a Pacific island.

In some stories, a character's activities and beliefs differ from those of other members of the society, and the differences cause conflict between that character and the local society. One example of this type of conflict is *The Witch of Blackbird Pond* (Speare, 1958), in which Kit Tyler is accused of being a witch because she continues activities in a New England Puritan community that were acceptable in the Caribbean community where she grew up but that are not acceptable in her new home.

Conflict between characters is common in children's literature. In *Tales of a Fourth Grade Nothing* (Blume, 1972), for instance, the never-ending conflict between Peter and his little brother, Fudge, is what makes the story interesting.

The fourth type of conflict is conflict within a character. In *Shiloh* (Naylor, 1991), 11-year-old Marty Preston must find the courage to stand up to mean Mr. Travers and save a mistreated dog.

Attempts to solve the problem introduced at the beginning of a story are what drive the plot. Conflict situations develop in the middle of the story as characters meet roadblocks or other obstacles to solving the problem. Finally the problem is resolved at the end. Plot development involves four components:

1. *A problem.* A problem that introduces conflict is presented at the beginning of the story.
2. *Roadblocks.* Characters face roadblocks in attempting to solve the problem in the middle of the story.
3. *The high point.* The high point in the action occurs when the problem is about to be solved. This high point separates the middle and the end of the story.
4. *The solution.* The problem is solved and the roadblocks are overcome at the end of the story.

Figure 7-2   Stories That Illustrate the Four Types of Conflict

Conflict Between a Character and Nature

George, J. C. (1972). *Julie of the wolves.* New York: Harper & Row.

George, J. C. (1988). *My side of the mountain.* New York: Puffin.

O'Dell, S. (1960). *Island of the blue dolphins.* Boston: Houghton Mifflin.

Paulsen, G. (1987). *Hatchet.* New York: Bradbury Press.

Sperry, A. (1968). *Call it courage.* New York: Macmillan.

Steig, W. (1987). *Brave Irene.* New York: Farrar, Straus & Giroux.

Conflict Between a Character and Society

Bunting, E. (1994). *Smoky night.* San Diego: Harcourt Brace.

Haddix, M. P. (1998). *Among the hidden.* New York: Simon & Schuster.

Lowry, L. (1989). *Number the stars.* New York: Atheneum.

Lowry, L. (1993). *The giver.* Boston: Houghton Mifflin.

Nixon, J. L. (1987). *A family apart.* New York: Bantam.

Philbrick, R. (2000). *The last book in the universe.* New York: Scholastic.

Speare, E. G. (1958). *The witch of Blackbird Pond.* Boston: Houghton Mifflin.

Spinelli, J. (1997). *Wringer.* New York: HarperCollins.

Uchida, Y. (1971). *Journey to Topaz.* Berkeley, CA: Creative Arts.

Conflict Between Characters

Blume, J. *Tales of a fourth grade nothing.* New York: Dutton.

Brittain, B. (1991). *Wings.* New York: HarperCollins.

Cohen, B. (1983). *Molly's pilgrim.* New York: Lothrop, Lee & Shepard.

Cushman, K. (1994). *Catherine, called Birdy.* New York: HarperCollins.

Hesse, K. (2001). *Witness.* New York: Scholastic.

Hobbs, W. (1989). *Bearstone.* New York: Atheneum.

Smith, R. K. (1984). *The war with grandpa.* New York: Yearling.

Steig, W. (1982). *Doctor De Soto.* New York: Farrar, Straus & Giroux.

Conflict Within a Character

Bauer, M. D. (1986). *On my honor.* Boston: Houghton Mifflin.

Bunting, E. (1999). *Blackwater.* New York: HarperCollins.

Byars, B. (1970). *The summer of the swans.* New York: Viking.

Gantos, J. (1998). *Joey Pigza swallowed the key.* New York: Farrar, Straus & Giroux.

Naylor, P. R. (1991). *Shiloh.* New York: Atheneun.

Pinkney, A. D. (1995). *Hold fast to dreams.* New York: Morrow.

Ryan, P. M. (2000). *Esperanza rising.* New York: Scholastic.

Staples, S. F. (1989). *Shabanu: Daughter of the wind.* New York: Knopf.

Taylor, T. (1969). *The cay.* New York: Doubleday.

Figure 7-3 presents a plot diagram shaped like a mountain that incorporates these four components. Fifth graders completed the diagram after reading *Esperanza Rising* (Ryan, 2000), the story of a privileged Mexican girl who has to begin a new life as a farm laborer in California after her father dies.

The problem is introduced at the beginning of the story, and the characters are faced with trying to solve it; the problem determines the conflict. The problem in *Hatchet* (Paulsen, 1987), for example, is that 13-year-old Brian is alone in the Canadian wilderness after the plane in which he is flying to visit his divorced father crashes. Conflict develops as Brian tries to survive in the wilderness. The story seems to embody conflict between a character and nature.

After introducing the problem, authors use conflict to throw roadblocks in the way of an easy solution. As characters remove one roadblock, the author devises another to further thwart the characters. Postponing the solution by introducing roadblocks is the core of plot development. Stories may contain any number of roadblocks, but many children's stories contain three, four, or five.

Brian faces many conflicts as he tries to find food to eat in the wilderness. He has to figure out how to make a fire to cook the birds, fish, and other animals he catches. He is attacked by bees, a porcupine, and a moose. And a storm that destroys his shelter adds to the conflict.

Figure 7-3   A Plot Diagram for *Esperanza Rising*

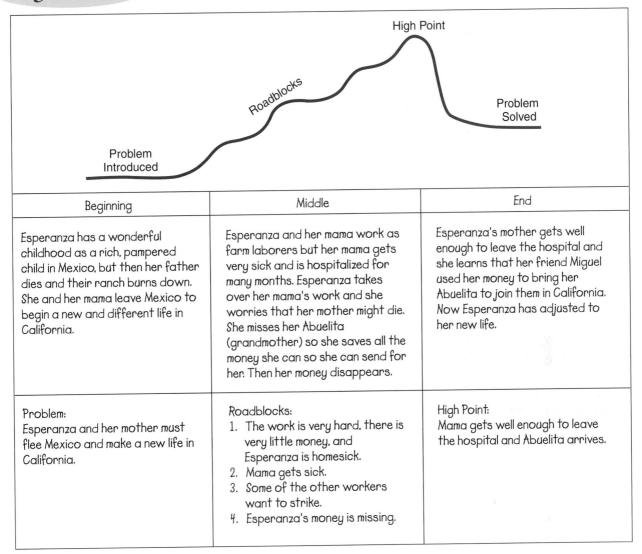

Beginning	Middle	End
Esperanza has a wonderful childhood as a rich, pampered child in Mexico, but then her father dies and their ranch burns down. She and her mama leave Mexico to begin a new and different life in California.	Esperanza and her mama work as farm laborers but her mama gets very sick and is hospitalized for many months. Esperanza takes over her mama's work and she worries that her mother might die. She misses her Abuelita (grandmother) so she saves all the money she can so she can send for her. Then her money disappears.	Esperanza's mother gets well enough to leave the hospital and she learns that her friend Miguel used her money to bring her Abuelita to join them in California. Now Esperanza has adjusted to her new life.
Problem: Esperanza and her mother must flee Mexico and make a new life in California.	Roadblocks: 1. The work is very hard, there is very little money, and Esperanza is homesick. 2. Mama gets sick. 3. Some of the other workers want to strike. 4. Esperanza's money is missing.	High Point: Mama gets well enough to leave the hospital and Abuelita arrives.

The high point of the action occurs when the solution of the problem hangs in the balance. Tension is high, and readers continue reading to learn whether the main characters solve the problem. In *Hatchet*, readers cheer when Brian finally gets the survival pack out of the downed plane. One of the items in the pack is an emergency transmitter, and even though Brian doesn't think it is still emitting signals, readers realize that his rescue is close at hand.

As the story ends, the problem is solved and the goal is achieved: A pilot hears the emergency signal and rescues Brian 54 days after the plane crash, long after searchers had given up hope of finding him alive. As Brian greets the pilot, readers realize that they have witnessed Brian's passage into manhood: He has survived in the wilderness, and he has survived his parents' divorce. Author Gary Paulsen has used conflict within a character, many readers conclude, to drive a riveting adventure story.

Students can chart the plot of a story using a plot profile to track the tension or excitement in a story (Johnson & Louis, 1987). Figure 7-4 presents a plot profile for

Figure 7-4   A Plot Profile for *Stone Fox*

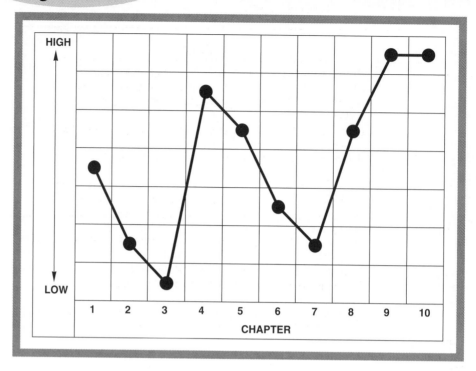

Stone Fox (Gardiner, 1980), a story about a boy who wins a dogsled race to save his grandfather's farm. A class of fourth graders met in small groups to talk about each chapter, and after these discussions, the whole class came together to decide how to mark the chart. At the end of the story, students analyzed the chart and rationalized the tension dips in chapters 3 and 7. They decided that the story would be too stressful without these dips.

Characters

Characters are the people or personified animals who are involved in the story. Characters are often the most important structural element because the story is centered on a character or group of characters. Usually, one or two fully rounded characters and several supporting characters are involved in a story. Fully developed main characters have many character traits, both good and bad; that is to say, they have all the characteristics of real people. Inferring a character's traits is an important part of reading. Through character traits, we get to know a character well and the character seems to come to life. A list of stories with fully developed main characters is presented in Figure 7-5.

Characters are developed in four ways: through appearance, action, dialogue, and monologue. Some description of the characters' physical appearance is usually included when they are introduced. Readers learn about characters by the description of their facial features, body shapes, habits of dress, mannerisms, and gestures. In *The Giver* (1993), Lois Lowry describes the main character, Jonas, as having light eyes rather than dark eyes like most of the people in his community. This physical feature introduces the idea that Jonas is different, and as the story continues, Jonas's life takes a very different direction.

Figure 7-5

Stories With Fully Developed Main Characters

Character	Story
Leigh	Cleary, B. (1983). *Dear Mr. Henshaw.* New York: Morrow.
Nick	Clements, A. (1996). *Frindle.* New York: Simon & Schuster.
Emily	Cooper, S. (1993). *The boggart.* New York: Margaret McElderry Books.
Kenny	Curtis, C. P. (1995). *The Watsons go to Birmingham—1963.* New York: Delacorte.
Birdy	Cushman, K. (1994). *Catherine, called Birdy.* New York: HarperCollins.
Johnny	Forbes, E. (1974). *Johnny Tremain.* Boston: Houghton Mifflin.
Little Willy	Gardiner, J. R. (1980). *Stone Fox.* New York: Harper & Row.
Sam	George, J. C. (1959). *My side of the mountain.* New York: Dutton.
Jonas	Lowry, L. (1993). *The giver.* Boston: Houghton Mifflin.
Sarah	MacLachlan, P. (1985). *Sarah, plain and tall.* New York: Harper & Row.
Marty	Naylor, P. R. (1991). *Shiloh.* New York: Atheneum.
Karana	O'Dell, S. (1960). *Island of the blue dolphins.* Boston: Houghton Mifflin.
Gilly	Paterson, K. (1978). *The great Gilly Hopkins.* New York: Crowell.
Charley	Ryan, P. M. (1998). *Riding Freedom.* New York: Scholastic.
Esperanza	Ryan, P. M. (2000). *Esperanza rising.* New York: Scholastic.
Stanley	Sachar, L. (1998). *Holes.* New York: Farrar, Straus & Giroux.
Matt	Speare, E. (1983). *The sign of the beaver.* Boston: Houghton Mifflin.
Mafatu	Sperry, A. (1968). *Call it courage.* New York: Macmillan.
Shabanu	Staples, S. F. (1989). *Shabanu: Daughter of the wind.* New York: Knopf.
Irene	Steig, W. (1986). *Brave Irene.* New York: Farrar, Straus & Giroux.
Cassie	Taylor, M. (1976). *Roll of thunder, hear my cry.* New York: Dial.
Moon Shadow	Yep, L. (1975). *Dragonwings.* New York: Harper & Row.

The second way—and often the best way—to learn about characters is through their actions. In Van Allsburg's *The Stranger* (1986), readers deduce that the stranger is Jack Frost because of what he does: He watches geese flying south for the winter, blows a cold wind, labors long hours without becoming tired, has an unusual rapport with wild animals, and is unfamiliar with modern conveniences.

Dialogue is the third way characters are developed. What characters say is important, but so is how they speak. The register of a character's language is determined by the social situation. A character might speak less formally with friends than with respected elders or characters in positions of authority. The geographic location of the story and the characters' socioeconomic status also determine how characters speak. In *Roll of Thunder, Hear My Cry* (Taylor, 1976), for example, Cassie and her family speak Black English, a dialect.

Authors also provide insight into characters by revealing their thoughts, or internal monologue. In *Sylvester and the Magic Pebble* (Steig, 1969), thoughts and wishes are central to the story. Sylvester, a donkey, foolishly wishes to become a rock, and he spends a miserable winter that way. Steig shares the donkey's thinking with us. He thinks about his parents, who are frantic with worry, and we learn how Sylvester feels in the spring when his parents picnic on the rock he has become.

Setting

In some stories, the setting is barely sketched, and these are called backdrop settings. The setting in many folktales, for example, is relatively unimportant, and the convention "Once upon a time . . . " is enough to set the stage. In other stories, the setting is elaborate and is essential to the story's effectiveness; these settings are called integral settings (Lukens, 1999). A list of stories with integral settings is shown in Figure 7-6. The setting in these stories is specific, and authors take care to ensure the authenticity of the historical period or geographic location in which the story is set.

Four dimensions of setting are location, weather, time period, and time. Location is an important dimension in many stories. The Alaskan North Slope in *Julie of the Wolves* (George, 1972) is integral to this story's effectiveness. The setting is artfully described and adds something unique to the story. In contrast, many stories take place in predictable settings that do not contribute to the stories' effectiveness.

Weather is a second dimension of setting and, like location, is crucial in some stories. A rainstorm is essential to the plot development in *Bridge to Terabithia* (Paterson, 1977), but in other books, weather is not mentioned because it does not affect the outcome of the story. Many stories take place on warm, sunny days.

The third dimension of setting is the time period, an important element in stories set in the past or in the future. If *The Witch of Blackbird Pond* (Speare, 1958) and *Number the Stars* (Lowry, 1989) were set in different eras, for example, they would lose much of their impact. Today, few people would believe that Kit Tyler is a witch or that Jewish people are the focus of government persecution. In stories that take

---

Figure 7-6   Stories With Integral Settings

Babbit, N. (1975). *Tuck everlasting.* New York: Farrar, Straus & Giroux.

Bunting, E. (1994). *Smoky night.* San Diego: Harcourt Brace.

Choi, S. N. (1991). *Year of impossible goodbyes.* Boston: Houghton Mifflin.

Conrad, P. (1985). *Prairie songs.* New York: HarperCollins.

Cooper, S. (1999). *King of shadows.* New York: Simon & Schuster.

Curtis, C. P. (1995). *The Watsons go to Birmingham—1963.* New York: Delacorte.

Cushman, K. (1994). *Catherine, called Birdy.* New York: HarperCollins.

Cushman, K. (1996). *The ballad of Lucy Whipple.* New York: Clarion.

Fleischman, P. (1993). *Bull Run.* New York: HarperCollins.

Fleischman, S. (1963). *By the great horn spoon!* Boston: Little, Brown.

George, J. C. (1972). *Julie of the wolves.* New York: Harper & Row.

Hesse, K. (1997). *Out of the dust.* New York: Scholastic.

L'Engle, M. (1962). *A wrinkle in time.* New York: Farrar, Straus & Giroux.

Lowry, L. (1989). *Number the stars.* Boston: Houghton Mifflin.

Lowry, L. (1993). *The giver.* Boston: Houghton Mifflin.

Mead, A. (1995). *Junebug.* Nerw York: Farrar, Straus & Giroux.

Myers, W. D. (1988). *Scorpions.* New York: Harper & Row.

Paterson, K. (1977). *Bridge to Terabithia.* New York: Crowell.

Paulsen, G. (1987). *Hatchet.* New York: Simon & Schuster.

Polacco, P. (1988). *The keeping quilt.* New York: Simon & Schuster.

Polacco, P. (1988). *Rechenka's eggs.* New York: Philomel.

Ryan, P. M. (2000). *Esperanza rising.* New York: Scholastic.

Sachar, L. (1998). *Holes.* New York: Farrar, Straus & Giroux.

Say, A. (1990). *El Chino.* Boston: Houghton Mifflin.

Speare, E. G. (1958). *The witch of Blackbird Pond.* Boston: Houghton Mifflin.

Speare, E. G. (1983). *The sign of the beaver.* Boston: Houghton Mifflin.

Staples, S. F. (1989). *Shabanu: Daughter of the wind.* New York: Knopf.

Uchida, Y. (1993). *The bracelet.* New York: Philomel.

Whelan, G. (2000). *Homeless bird.* New York: HarperCollins.

Wilder, L. I. (1971). *The lost winter.* New York: Harper & Row.

Yep, L. (1975). *Dragonwings.* New York: Harper & Row.

---

place in the future, such as *A Wrinkle in Time* (L'Engle, 1962), things are possible that are not possible today.

The fourth dimension, time, involves both time of day and the passage of time. Most stories ignore time of day, except for scary stories that take place after dark. Many short stories span a brief period of time—often less than a day, and sometimes less than an hour. In *Jumanji* (Van Allsburg, 1981), Peter and Judy's bizarre adventure, during which their house is overtaken by exotic jungle creatures, lasts only several hours. *Hatchet* (Paulsen, 1987) takes place in less than 2 months. Other stories, such as *Charlotte's Web* (White, 1952), span a year or longer while the main character grows to maturity.

Students can draw story maps to depict the setting of a story. These maps might show the path a character traveled or the passage of time in a story. Figure 7-7 shows a map for *Number the Stars* (Lowry, 1989). In this chapter book set in Denmark during

Figure 7-7   A Story Map for *Number the Stars*

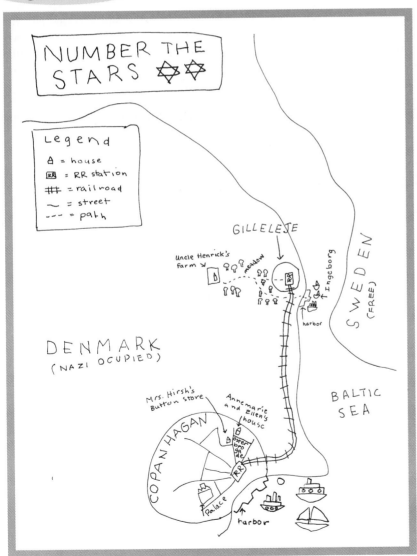

World War II, a Christian girl and her family help a Jewish family flee to safety in Sweden. The map shows the families' homes in Copenhagen, their trip to a fishing village, and the ship they hid away on to escape to Sweden.

Point of View

Stories are written from a particular viewpoint, and this perspective determines to a great extent readers' understanding of the characters and events of the story. The four points of view are first-person viewpoint, omniscient viewpoint, limited omniscient viewpoint, and objective viewpoint (Lukens, 1999). A list of stories written from each point of view is presented in Figure 7-8.

The first-person viewpoint is used to tell a story through the eyes of one character using the first-person pronoun "I." In this point of view, the reader experiences the story as the narrator tells it. The narrator, usually the main character, speaks as an eyewitness and a participant in the events. For example, in *Alexander and the Terrible, Horrible, No Good, Very Bad Day* (Viorst, 1977), Alexander tells about a day everything seemed to go wrong for him. One limitation of this viewpoint is that the narrator must remain an eyewitness.

In the omniscient viewpoint, the author is godlike, seeing and knowing all. The author tells readers about the thought processes of each character without worrying about how the information is obtained. *Doctor De Soto* (Steig, 1982), a story about a mouse dentist who outwits a fox with a toothache, is told from the omniscient view-

Figure 7-8   Stories That Illustrate the Four Points of View

First-Person Viewpoint

Bunting, E. (1994). *Smoky night.* San Diego: Harcourt Brace.

Cohen, B. (1983). *Molly's pilgrim.* New York: Morrow.

Cushman, K. (1994). *Catherine, called Birdy.* New York: HarperCollins.

Gantos, J. (1998). *Joey Pigza swallowed the key.* New York: Farrar, Straus & Giroux.

Howe, D., & Howe, J. (1979). *Bunnicula: A rabbit-tale of mystery.* New York: Atheneum.

MacLachlan, P. (1985). *Sarah, plain and tall.* New York: Harper & Row.

Omniscient Viewpoint

Babbit, N. (1975). *Tuck everlasting.* New York: Farrar, Straus & Giroux.

Lewis, C. S. (1981). *The lion, the witch and the wardrobe.* New York: Macmillan.

Myers, W. D. (1988). *Scorpions.* New York: Harper & Row.

Steig, W. (1982). *Doctor De Soto.* New York: Farrar, Straus & Giroux.

Limited Omniscient Viewpoint

Gardiner, J. R. (1980). *Stone Fox.* New York: Harper & Row.

Lowry, L. (1989). *Number the stars.* Boston: Houghton Mifflin.

Lowry, L. *The giver.* Boston: Houghton Mifflin.

Sachar, L. (1998). *Holes.* New York: Farrar, Straus & Giroux.

Spinelli, J. (1997). *Wringer.* New York: HarperCollins.

Steig, W. (1969). *Sylvester and the magic pebble.* New York: Simon & Schuster.

Whelan, G. (2000). *Homeless bird.* New York: HarperCollins.

Objective Viewpoint

Bodkin, O. (1998). *The crane wife.* San Diego, CA: Harcourt Brace.

Louie, A. (1982). *Yeh Shen: A Cinderella story from China.* New York: Philomel.

Napoli, D. J., & Chen, R. (1999). *Spinners.* New York: Dutton.

Steptoe, J. (1987). *Mufaro's beautiful daughters: An African tale.* New York: Lothrop, Lee & Shepard.

Zelinsky, P. O. (1994). *Swamp Angel.* New York: Dutton.

Multiple Viewpoints

Creech, S. (2000). *The wanderer.* New York: HarperCollins.

Fleischman, P. (1993). *Bull Run.* New York: HarperCollins.

Hesse, K. (2001). *Witness.* New York: Scholastic.

Wolff, V. E. (1998). *Bat 6.* New York: Scholastic.

point. Steig lets readers know that the fox wants to eat the dentist as soon as his toothache is cured and that the mouse dentist is aware of the fox's thoughts and plans a clever trick.

The limited omniscient viewpoint is used so that readers know the thoughts of one character. The story is told in third person, and the author concentrates on the thoughts, feelings, and experiences of the main character or another important character. Gary Paulsen used this viewpoint for *Hatchet* (1987) in order to be able to explore Brian's thoughts as he struggled to survive in the wilderness as well as his coming to terms with his parents' divorce. And Lois Lowry used the limited omniscient viewpoint in *Number the Stars* (1989), so that Annemarie, the Christian girl, can reveal her thoughts about the lies she tells to the Nazi soldiers in this World War II story.

In the objective viewpoint, readers are eyewitnesses to the story and confined to the immediate scene. They learn only what is visible and audible and are not aware of what any characters think. Most fairy tales, such as *The Little Red Hen* (Zemach, 1983), are told from the objective viewpoint. The focus is on recounting events, not on developing the personalities of the characters.

Some stories are written from more than one point of view, too. In *Witness* (Hesse, 2001), for example, the people of a small Vermont town take turns telling how in 1924 they turned against their African American and Jewish neighbors when the Ku Klux Klan moved in. Stories written from multiple viewpoints illustrate the importance of point of view and help students to understand that people's viewpoints differ.

Most teachers introduce the four viewpoints in sixth, seventh, or eighth grade, but all students should experiment with point of view to understand how the author's viewpoint affects a story. One way to demonstrate point of view is to contrast *The Three Little Pigs* (Galdone, 1970), the traditional version of the story told from an objective viewpoint, with *The True Story of the 3 Little Pigs!* (Scieszka, 1989), a self-serving narrative told from a first-person viewpoint by Mr. A. Wolf. In this satirical retelling, the wolf tries to explain away his bad image. Students are struck by how different the two versions are and how the narrator filters the information.

Theme

Theme is the underlying meaning of a story, and it embodies general truths about human nature (Lehr, 1991; Lukens, 1999). Theme usually deals with the characters' emotions and values. Themes can be stated either explicitly or implicitly; explicit themes are stated openly and clearly in the story, whereas implicit themes must be inferred. Themes are developed as the characters attempt to overcome the obstacles that interfere with their reaching their goals. In a fable, the theme is often stated explicitly at the end, but in most stories, the theme emerges through the thoughts, speech, and actions of the characters as they seek to resolve their conflicts.

Stories usually have more than one theme, and the themes generally cannot be articulated with a single word. *Charlotte's Web* (White, 1952) has several "friendship" themes, one explicitly stated and others inferred from the text. Friendship is a multidimensional theme—qualities of a good friend, unlikely friends, and sacrificing for a friend, for instance. Teachers can probe students' thinking as they work to construct a theme and move beyond one-word labels (Au, 1992).

The minilesson featured on page 223 demonstrates how Mrs. Miller, a seventh-grade teacher, reviewed the concept of theme. Then her students applied what they learned during the minilesson as they read a book and analyzed its themes in literature circles.

Minilesson

Topic: Theme
Grade: Seventh Grade
Time: 20 minutes

Mrs. Miller's seventh graders are studying the Middle Ages and are reading novels set in that period, such as *Catherine, Called Birdy* (Cushman, 1994), in literature circles. Mrs. Miller brings the class together to teach a mini-lesson on theme before asking the students in each literature circle to analyze the theme of the book they are reading.

1. Introduce Topic

"It's time to talk about theme because most of you are getting toward the end of the book you're reading," Mrs. Miller begins. "Before, I asked you to focus on the setting to learn more about medieval life as you were reading and discussing the book. Now, I want you to think about your book in a different way: I want you to think about the theme. Let's review: Theme is the universal message in the book. It might be about friendship, courage, acceptance, determination, or some other important quality."

2. Share Examples

Mrs. Miller uses *Hatchet* (Paulsen, 1987), a survival story that students read in September, as an example. "Did Brian save himself?" the teacher asks. Everyone agrees that he did. "So what is the theme of the story?" Mrs. Miller asks. Students identify survival as the theme, and Mrs. Miller asks them to explain it in a sentence. Jared suggests, "Sometimes you have to do a lot of disgusting things if you want to survive." Mrs. Miller agrees. Carole offers, "I think the theme is that you may not think that you have the guts and the brains to survive, but if you get trapped in the wilderness, you will find that you do." Again she agrees. Jo-Jo expresses the theme another way: "It's like in the movie *Castaway.* Brian has to get mad—really mad and a little crazy, too, but he gets mad enough to survive. You have to stand up and prove to yourself that you can survive." Again she agrees. Mrs. Miller draws a cluster[C] on the chalkboard and writes *survival* in the center circle. Then she draws out rays and writes on them the sentences that the students offered.

3. Provide Information

"Theme isn't obvious the way plot, characters, and setting are," Mrs. Miller explains. She tells the class that to uncover the theme, they need to think about the conflicts facing the character and the way the character goes about solving the problem. "Then you have to answer the question: 'What is the author trying to tell me about life?'" she concludes.

4. Guide Practice

The minilesson ends as the students return to their literature circles to talk about the theme of their book. Mrs. Miller asks them to think of one or more one-word qualities and then to draw out at least three possible sentence-long themes. As they analyze the theme, they draw clusters on chart paper.

5. Assess Learning

Mrs. Miller moves from group to group, talking with students about theme. She checks their clusters and helps them draw out additional themes to add to them.

Students apply their knowledge of story structure as they discuss novels they are reading.

Literary Devices

In addition to the five elements of story structure, authors use literary devices to make their writing more vivid and memorable. Without these literary devices, writing can be dull (Lukens, 1999). A list of six literary devices that fourth- through eighth-grade students learn to recognize is presented in Figure 7-9. Imagery is probably the most commonly used literary device; many authors use imagery as they paint rich word pictures that bring their characters and settings to life. Authors use metaphors and similes to compare one thing to another, personification to endow animals and objects with human qualities, and hyperbole to exaggerate or to stretch the truth. They also create symbols as they use one thing to represent something else. In Chris Van Allsburg's *The Wretched Stone* (1991), for example, the glowing stone that distracts the crew from reading, from spending time with their friends, and from doing their jobs, symbolizes television or, perhaps, computers. For students to understand the theme of the story, they need to recognize symbols. The author's style conveys the tone or overall feeling in a story; some stories are humorous, some are uplifting celebrations of life, and others are sobering commentaries on society.

Young children focus on the events and characters in a story as they read, but as students become more sophisticated readers, they learn to notice both what the author says and how he or she says it. Teachers facilitate students' growth in reading and responding to stories by directing their attention to literary devices and the author's style during the responding and exploring stages of the reading process.

Why Do Teachers Need to Know About Narrative Structure?

Most teachers are familiar with story terms such as *character, plot,* and *setting,* but to plan for reading instruction, teachers need to understand how authors combine the story elements to craft stories. Teachers cannot assume that teacher's manuals or other guides will be available for every story they read with their students, or that these

Figure 7-9 Literary Devices

Comparison	Authors compare one thing to another or view something in terms of something else. When the comparison uses the word *like* or *as,* it is a simile; when the comparison is stated directly, it is a metaphor. For example, "the ocean is like a playground for whales" is a simile; "the ocean is a playground for whales" is a metaphor. Metaphors are stronger comparisons because they are more direct.
Hyperbole	Authors use hyperbole when they overstate or stretch the truth to make obvious and intentional exaggerations for a special effect. "It's raining cats and dogs" and "my feet are killing me" are two examples of hyperbole. American tall tales also have rich examples of hyperbole.
Imagery	Authors use descriptive or sensory words and phrases to create imagery or a picture in the reader's mind. Sensory language stirs the reader's imagination. Instead of saying "the kitchen smelled good as grandmother cooked Thanksgiving dinner," authors create imagery when they write "the aroma of a turkey roasting in the oven filled grandmother's kitchen on Thanksgiving."
Personification	Authors use personification when they attribute human characteristics to animals or objects. For example, "the moss crept across the sidewalk" is personification.
Symbolism	Authors often use a person, place, or thing as a symbol to represent something else. For example, a dove symbolizes peace, the Statue of Liberty symbolizes freedom, and books symbolize knowledge.
Tone	Authors create an overall feeling or effect in the story through their choice of words and use of other literary devices. For example, *Bunnicula: A Rabbit-Tale of Mystery* (Howe & Howe, 1979) and *Catherine, Called Birdy* (Cushman, 1994) are humorous stories, and *Babe: The Gallant Pig* (King-Smith, 1995) and *Sarah, Plain and Tall* (MacLachlan, 1985) are uplifting, feel-good stories.

guides provide the necessary information about story structure. Teachers must be prepared to think about the structure of stories they will use in their classrooms.

For example, after reading *Sarah, Plain and Tall* (MacLachlan, 1985), teachers might think about how the story would be different if Sarah, not Anna, were telling the story. They might wonder if the author meant to send a message of promise of future happiness for the family by setting the story in the springtime. They also might speculate that the storm was the turning point in the story or wonder about the role of colors. This kind of thoughtful reflection allows teachers to know the story better, prepare themselves to guide their students through the story, and plan activities to help students explore the story's meaning.

Teachers teach minilessons about story elements so that students can use this knowledge to enhance their comprehension. According to Irwin (1991), when students recognize the author's organization pattern, they are better able to comprehend what they are reading or listening to being read aloud. During grand conversations, teachers often direct students' attention to how a particular conflict situation or viewpoint has influenced a story. Similarly, when teachers conference with students about stories they are writing, knowledge about story structure and related terminology, such as *rising action, dialogue,* and *theme,* enriches the conversation.

EXPOSITORY TEXT STRUCTURES

Stories have been the primary genre for reading and writing instruction in the middle grades because it has been assumed that constructing stories in the mind is a fundamental way of learning (Wells, 1986). Recent research suggests, however, that children may prefer to read informational books and are able to understand them as well as they do stories (Pappas, 1993). Certainly, children are interested in learning about their world—about life in castles during the Middle Ages, threats to the environment of Antarctica, or Amelia Earhart's ill-fated flight around the world—and informational books provide this knowledge.

Students often assume an efferent stance as they read informational books to locate facts, but they do not always use efferent reading (Rosenblatt, 1978). Many times, students pick up an informational book to check a fact and then continue reading—aesthetically—because they are fascinated by what they are reading. They get carried away in the presentation of information, just as they do when reading stories. At other times, students read books about topics they are interested in, and they read aesthetically, engaging in the lived-through experience of reading and connecting what they are reading to their own lives and prior reading experiences.

Russell Freedman, who won the 1988 Newbery Award for *Lincoln: A Photobiography* (1987), talks about the purpose of informational books and explains that it is not enough for an informational book to provide information: "[An informational book] must create a vivid and believable world that the reader will enter willingly and leave only with reluctance. . . . It should be just as compelling as a good story" (1992, p. 3). High-quality informational books like Freedman's encourage students to read aesthetically because they engage readers and tap their curiosity. There is a new wave of engaging and artistic informational books being published today, and these books show increased respect for children. Peter Roop (1992) explains that for years, informational books were the "ugly duckling" of children's literature, but now they have grown into a beautiful swan.

Four qualities of informational books are accuracy, organization, design, and style (Vardell, 1991). First and foremost, the facts must be current and complete. They must be well researched, and, when appropriate, varying points of view should be presented. Stereotypes are to be avoided, and details in both the text and the illustrations must be authentic. Second, information should be presented clearly and logically, using organizational patterns to increase the book's readability. Third, the book's design should be eye-catching and enhance its usability. Illustrations should complement the text, and explanations should accompany each illustration. Last, the style should be lively and stimulating so as to engage readers' curiosity and wonder.

Informational books are available today on topics ranging from biological sciences, physical sciences, and social sciences to arts and biographies. *Cactus Hotel* (Guiberson, 1991) is a fine informational book about the desert ecosystem; the author discusses the life cycle of a giant saguaro cactus and describes its role as a home for desert creatures. Other books, such as *Whales* (Simon, 1989), illustrated with striking full-page color photos, and *Antarctica* (Cowcher, 1990), illustrated with dramatic double-page paintings, are socially responsible and emphasize the threats people pose to animals and the earth. Other books present historical and geographic concepts. *A Street*

Through Time (Millard, 1998), for instance, traces the evolution of one street from the Stone Age to the present day, and *Knights* (Steele, 1998) tells about the lives of knights during medieval times. These books have lavish illustrations and detailed text that provide an enriching reading experience and enhanced concept development.

Some informational books focus on letters and numbers. Although many alphabet and counting books with pictures of familiar objects are designed for young children, others provide a wealth of information on various topics. In his alphabet book *Illuminations* (1989), Jonathan Hunt presents detailed information about medieval life, and in *The Underwater Alphabet Book* (1991), Jerry Pallotta provides information about 26 types of fish and other sea creatures. Africa is the topic of *Moja Means One: Swahili Counting Book,* by Muriel and Tom Feelings (1971), and Ann Herbert Scott presents information about cowboys in *One Good Horse: A Cowpuncher's Counting Book* (1990). In some of these books, new terms are introduced and illustrated, and in others, the term is explained in a sentence or a paragraph. Other informational books focus on mathematical concepts (Whitin & Wilde, 1992). Tana Hoban's *26 Letters and 99 Cents* (1987) presents concepts about money, *What Comes in 2's, 3's and 4's?* (Aker, 1990) introduces multiplication, and *If You Made a Million* (Schwartz, 1989) focuses on big numbers.

Biographies are also informational books, and the biographies being written today are more realistic than in the past, presenting well-known personalities, warts and all. Jean Fritz's portraits of Revolutionary War figures, such as *Will You Sign Here, John Hancock?* (1976), are among the best known, but she has also written comprehensive biographies, including *The Great Little Madison* (1989). Fritz and other authors often include notes in the back of books to explain how the details were researched and to provide additional information. Only a few autobiographies are available to students, but more are being published each year. Autobiographies about authors and illustrators, such as Cynthia Rylant's *Best Wishes* (1992) and Lois Lowry's *Looking Back: A Book of Memories* (1998), are also popular with students.

Other books present information within a story context. Some combination informational/story books are imaginative fantasies; the Magic School Bus series is perhaps the best known. In *The Magic School Bus Inside a Beehive* (Cole, 1996), for example, Ms. Frizzle and her class study bees and take a field trip on the magic school bus into a beehive to learn about the life cycle of honeybees, how honey is made, and bee society. The page layout is innovative, with charts and reports containing factual information presented at the outside edges of most pages.

Informational books are organized in particular ways called expository text structures. Five of the most common organizational patterns are description, sequence, comparison, cause and effect, and problem and solution (Meyer & Freedle, 1984; Niles, 1974). Figure 7-10 describes these patterns, presents sample passages and cue words that signal use of each pattern, and suggests an appropriate graphic organizer for each structure. When readers are aware of these patterns, they understand what they are reading better, and when writers use these structures to organize their writing, it is more easily understood by readers. Sometimes the pattern is signaled clearly by means of titles, topic sentences, and cue words, and sometimes it is not.

Description

In this organizational pattern, a topic is described by listing characteristics, features, and examples. Phrases such as *for example* and *characteristics are* cue this structure. Examples of books using description include *Spiders* (Gibbons, 1992) and *Mercury* (Simon, 1993), in which the authors describe many facets of their topic. When students delineate any topic, such as the Mississippi River, eagles, or Alaska, they use description.

ELL

When ELL students are aware of the expository text structures, they organize, summarize, and recall what they have read more effectively because the structure provides a focus for their reading.

Figure 7-10   The Five Expository Text Structures

Pattern	Description	Graphic Organizer	Sample Passage
Description	The author describes a topic by listing characteristics, features, and examples. Cue words include *for example* and *characteristics are.*		The Olympic symbol consists of five interlocking rings. The rings represent the five continents from which athletes come to compete in the games. The rings are colored black, blue, green, red, and yellow. At least one of these colors is found in the flag of every country sending athletes to compete in the Olympic games.
Sequence	The author lists items or events in numerical or chronological order. Cue words include *first, second, third, next, then,* and *finally.*	1. _____ 2. _____ 3. _____ 4. _____ 5. _____	The Olympic games began as athletic festivals to honor the Greek gods. The most important festival was held in the valley of Olympia to honor Zeus, the king of the gods. This festival became the Olympic games in 776 B.C. They were ended in A.D. 394. No Olympic games were held for more than 1,500 years. Then the modern Olympics began in 1896. Almost 300 male athletes competed in the first modern Olympics. In the 1900 games, female athletes were allowed to compete. The games have continued every four years since 1896 except during World War II.
Comparison	The author explains how two or more things are alike and/or how they are different. Cue words include *different, in contrast, alike, same as,* and *on the other hand.*	Alike Different	The modern Olympics is very unlike the ancient Olympic games. While there were no swimming races in the ancient games, for example, there were chariot races. There were no female contestants, and all athletes competed in the nude. Of course, the ancient and modern Olympics are also alike in many ways. Some events, such as the javelin and discus throws, are the same. Some people say that cheating, professionalism, and nationalism in the modern games are a disgrace to the Olympic tradition. But according to the ancient Greek writers, there were many cases of cheating, nationalism, and professionalism in their Olympics, too.

(continues)

Sequence

In this pattern, items or events are listed or explained in numerical or chronological order. Cue words for sequence include *first, second, third, next, then,* and *finally.* Caroline Arnold describes the steps in creating a museum display in *Dinosaurs All Around: An Artist's View of the Prehistoric World* (1993), and David Macaulay describes how a castle is built in *Castle* (1977). Students use the sequence pattern to write directions for completing a math problem or for the stages in an animal's life cycle. The events in a biography are often written in the sequence pattern.

Comparison

In the comparison structure, two or more things are compared. *Different, in contrast, alike,* and *on the other hand* are cue words and phrases that signal this structure. In

Figure 7-10 (continued)

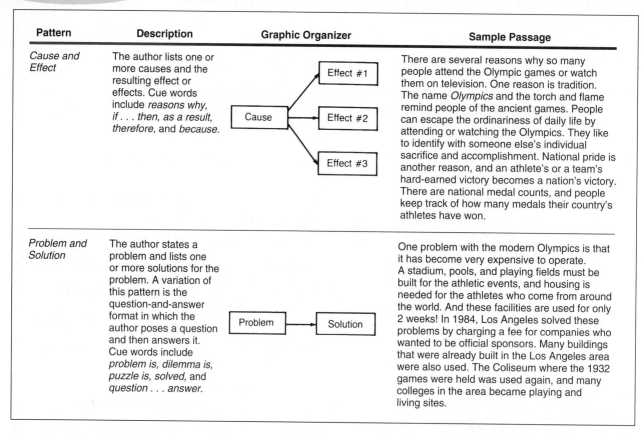

Pattern	Description	Graphic Organizer	Sample Passage
Cause and Effect	The author lists one or more causes and the resulting effect or effects. Cue words include *reasons why, if . . . then, as a result, therefore,* and *because.*	Cause → Effect #1, Effect #2, Effect #3	There are several reasons why so many people attend the Olympic games or watch them on television. One reason is tradition. The name *Olympics* and the torch and flame remind people of the ancient games. People can escape the ordinariness of daily life by attending or watching the Olympics. They like to identify with someone else's individual sacrifice and accomplishment. National pride is another reason, and an athlete's or a team's hard-earned victory becomes a nation's victory. There are national medal counts, and people keep track of how many medals their country's athletes have won.
Problem and Solution	The author states a problem and lists one or more solutions for the problem. A variation of this pattern is the question-and-answer format in which the author poses a question and then answers it. Cue words include *problem is, dilemma is, puzzle is, solved,* and *question . . . answer.*	Problem → Solution	One problem with the modern Olympics is that it has become very expensive to operate. A stadium, pools, and playing fields must be built for the athletic events, and housing is needed for the athletes who come from around the world. And these facilities are used for only 2 weeks! In 1984, Los Angeles solved these problems by charging a fee for companies who wanted to be official sponsors. Many buildings that were already built in the Los Angeles area were also used. The Coliseum where the 1932 games were held was used again, and many colleges in the area became playing and living sites.

Horns, Antlers, Fangs, and Tusks (Rauzon, 1993), for example, the author compares animals having distinctive types of headgear. When students compare and contrast book and movie versions of a story, reptiles and amphibians, or life in ancient Greece with life in ancient Egypt, they use this organizational pattern.

Cause and Effect

The writer explains one or more causes and the resulting effect or effects. *Reasons why, if . . . then, as a result, therefore,* and *because* are words and phrases that cue this structure. Explanations of why dinosaurs became extinct, the effects of pollution on the environment, or the causes of the Civil War are written using this pattern. *How Do Apples Grow?* (Maestro, 1992) and *What Happens to a Hamburger?* (Showers, 1985) are two books that exemplify this structure.

Problem and Solution

In this structure, the writer states a problem and offers one or more solutions. For example, in *Man and Mustang* (Ancona, 1992), the author describes the problem of wild mustangs and explains how they are rescued. A variation is the question-and-answer format, in which the writer poses a question and then answers it. One question-and-answer book is . . . *If You Traveled West in a Covered Wagon* (Levine, 1986). Cue words and phrases include *the problem is, the puzzle is, solve,* and *question . . . answer.* Students use this structure when they write about why money was invented, why endangered animals should be saved, or why dams are needed to ensure a permanent water supply. They often use the problem-solution pattern in writing advertisements and other persuasive writing as well. Figure 7-11 lists other books that illustrate each of the five expository text structures.

Why Do Teachers Need to Know About Expository Text Structures?

When teachers use informational books and content-area textbooks as instructional materials, they should consider how the books are organized as they prepare for

Figure 7-11 Informational Books Representing the Expository Text Structures

Description

Branley, F. M. (1986). *What the moon is like.* New York: Harper & Row.

Horvatic, A. (1989). *Simple machines.* New York: Dutton.

Lauber, P. (1998). *Painters of the caves.* Washington, DC: National Geographic Society.

McPherson, J. M. (2002). *Field of fury: The American Civil War.* New York: Simon & Schuster.

Patent, D. H. (1992). *Feathers.* New York: Cobblehill.

Simon, S. (1989). *Storms.* New York: Morrow.

Simon, S. (2000). *Gorillas.* New York: HarperCollins.

Sequence

Aliki. (1992). *Milk from cow to carton.* New York: HarperCollins.

Haskins, J. (1987). *Count your way through China.* Minneapolis: Lerner.

Jaspersohn, W. (1998). *Ice cream.* New York: Macmillan.

Melmed, L. K. (2003). *Capital! Washington, DC from A to Z.* New York: HarperCollins.

Provensen, A. (1990). *The buck stops here.* New York: HarperCollins.

Schanzer, R. (1997). *How we crossed the west: The adventures of Lewis and Clark.* Washington, DC: National Geographic Society.

Thomas, V. M. (1997). *Lest we forget: The passage from Africa to slavery and emancipation.* New York: Crown.

Comparison

Gibbons, G. (1984). *Fire! Fire!* New York: Harper & Row.

Lasker, J. (1976). *Merry ever after: The story of two medieval weddings.* New York: Viking.

Markle, S. (1993). *Outside and inside trees.* New York: Bradbury Press.

Munro, R. (1987). *The inside-outside book of Washington, D.C.* New York: Dutton.

Rauzon, M. J. (1993). *Horns, antlers, fangs, and tusks.* New York: Lothrop, Lee & Shepard.

Spier, P. (1987). *We the people.* New York: Doubleday.

Cause and Effect

Branley, F. M. (1985). *Volcanoes.* New York: Harper & Row.

Branley, F. M. (1986). *What makes day and night?* New York: Harper & Row.

Heller, R. (1983). *The reason for a flower.* New York: Grosset & Dunlap.

Schmandt-Besserat, D. (1999). *The history of counting.* New York: Morrow.

Showers, P. (1985). *What happens to a hamburger?* New York: Harper & Row.

Problem and Solution

George, J. C. (2000). *How to talk to your dog.* New York: HarperCollins.

Heller, R. (1986). *How to hide a whippoorwill and other birds.* New York: Grosset & Dunlap.

Lauber, P. (1990). *How we learned the earth is round.* New York: Crowell.

Levine, E. (1988). *If you traveled on the Underground Railroad.* New York: Scholastic.

Springer, J. (1997). *Listen to us, the world's working children.* Toronto: Groundwood Books.

Tanaka, S. (1999). *Secrets of the mummies: Uncovering the bodies of ancient Egyptians.* New York: Hyperion.

Wollard, K. (1999). *How come? Planet Earth.* New York: Workman.

Combination

Aliki. (1981). *Digging up dinosaurs.* New York: Harper & Row.

Armstrong, J. (1998). *Shipwreck at the bottom of the world: The extraordinary true story of Shackleton and the Endurance.* New York: Crown.

Guiberson, B. Z. (1991). *Cactus hotel.* New York: Henry Holt.

Hoyt-Goldsmith, D. (1992). *Hoang Anh: A Vietnamese-American boy.* New York: Holiday House.

Tanaka, S. (2002). *New dinos.* New York: Atheneum.

Struggling Readers and Writers Need to Use Graphic Organizers.

Struggling readers usually need assistance in learning how to use graphic organizers to improve their comprehension of informational books and content-area textbooks. Teachers introduce a graphic organizer before reading to help students activate background knowledge, and then students use the organizer to take notes during reading and review main ideas and write summaries after reading. Teachers model how to use graphic organizers before, during, and after reading, and then they provide numerous opportunities for supervised practice until students can use graphic organizers independently.

When students are preparing to write reports and other informational texts, they create graphic organizers to gather and organize ideas. The choice of an organizer is crucial; it needs to fit the writing topic and purpose. If students are going to write a comparison essay, for example, they need a different graphic organizer than if they are preparing to write instructions in sequential order.

instruction. Often teachers do what Mr. Abrams did in the vignette at the beginning of this chapter: They give students a purpose for reading and develop graphic organizers to record information after reading. Researchers have confirmed that when students use the five expository text structures to organize their reading and writing, they are more effective readers and writers. Most of the research on expository text structures has focused on older students' use of these patterns in reading; however, elementary students also use the patterns and cue words in their writing (Langer, 1986; Raphael, Englert, & Kirschner, 1989; Tompkins, 2004).

Students also use expository text structures when they write informational books, essays, and other nonfiction forms, as Mr. Abrams's students did in the vignette. When students don't use expository text structures, they have more difficulty organizing their writing into sections and into paragraphs. They are more likely to jump from topic to topic and to include unrelated information in paragraphs.

POETIC FORMS

Poetry "brings sound and sense together in words and lines," according to Donald Graves, "ordering them on the page in such a way that both the writer and reader get a different view of life" (1992, p. 3). Poetry surrounds us; children chant jump-rope rhymes on the playground and dance in response to songs and their lyrics. Larrick (1991) believes that we enjoy poetry because of the physical involvement the words evoke. Also, people play with language as they invent rhymes and ditties, create new words, and craft powerful comparisons.

Today, more poets are writing for children, and more books of poems for children are being published than ever before. No longer is poetry confined to rhyming verse about daffodils, clouds, and love; recently published poems about dinosaurs, Halloween, chocolate, baseball, and insects are very popular. Children choose to read poetry and share favorite poems with classmates. They read and respond to poems containing beautiful language and written on topics that are meaningful to them.

Three types of poetry books are published for children. A number of picture-book versions of single poems in which each line or stanza is illustrated on a page are available, such as *Paul Revere's Ride* (Longfellow, 2001). Other books are specialized collections of poems, either written by a single poet or related to a single theme, such as dinosaurs. Comprehensive anthologies are the third type of poetry books for children, and they feature 50 to 500 or more poems arranged by category. One of the best anthologies is Jack Prelutsky's *The Random House Book of Poetry for Children* (2000). A list of poetry books with examples of each of the three types is presented in Figure 7-12.

Poems for children assume many different forms, including rhymed verse, narrative poems, haiku, and free verse. Additional poetic forms are useful for students to be familiar with and use when they write poems.

Figure 7-12   Collections of Poetry Written for Middle-Grade Students

Picture Book Versions of Single Poems

Bates, K. L. (2003). *America the beautiful* (W. Minor, Illus.). New York: Putnam.

Carroll, L. (2003). *Jabberwocky* (J. Stewart, Illus.). Cambridge, MA: Candlewick.

Frost, R. (2001). *Stopping by woods on a snowy evening* (S. Jeffers, Illus.). New York: Dutton.

Longfellow, H. W. (2001). *The midnight ride of Paul Revere* (C. Bing, Illus.). Brooklyn, NY: Handprint Books.

Sandburg, C. (1993). *Arithmetic*. New York: Harcourt Brace.

Spier, P. (1973). *The star-spangled banner*. New York: Random House.

Thayer, E. L. (2000). *Casey at the bat: A ballad of the republic sung in the year 1888* (C. Bing, Illus.). New York: Putnam.

Specialized Collections

Bagert, B. (Ed.). (1995). *Edgar Allan Poe*. New York: Sterling.

Fleischman, P. (1985). *I am phoenix: Poems for two voices*. New York: Harper & Row.

Fleischman, P. (1988). *Joyful noise: Poems for two voices*. New York: Harper & Row.

Florian, D. (1998). *Insectlopedia*. San Diego, CA: Harcourt Brace.

Frost, R. (1982). *A swinger of birches: Poems of Robert Frost for young people*. Owings Mill, MD: Stemmer House.

George, K. O. (1998). *Old elm speaks: Tree poems*. New York: Clarion Books.

Glenn, M. (1997). *Jump ball: A basketball season in poems*. New York: Lodestar Books.

Greenfield, E. (1988). *Under the Sunday tree*. New York: Harper & Row.

Hopkins, L. B. (Sel.). (1999). *Spectacular science: A book of poems*. New York: Aladdin.

Hughes, L. (1994). *The dream keeper and other poems*. New York: Knopf.

Janeczko, P. B. (Sel.). (1993). *Looking for your name: A collection of contemporary poems*. New York: Orchard Books.

Jones, H. (Ed.). (1993). *The trees stand shining: Poetry of the North American Indians*. New York: Dial.

Koontz, D. (2001). *The paper doorway: Funny verse and nothing worse*. New York: HarperCollins.

Kuskin, K. (2003). *Moon, have you met my mother? The collected poems of Karla Kuskin*. New York: HarperCollins.

Lansky, B. (2002). *My dog ate my homework: A collection of funny poems*. New York: Meadowbrooke Press.

McCord, D. (1974). *One at a time*. Boston: Little, Brown.

Prelutsky, J. (1984). *The new kid on the block*. New York: Greenwillow.

Prelutsky, J. (1996). *A pizza the size of the sun*. New York: Greenwillow.

Prelutsky, J. (2000). *It's raining pigs and noodles*. New York: Greenwillow.

Siebert, D. (1989). *Heartland*. New York: Crowell.

Silverstein, S. (1974). *Where the sidewalk ends*. New York: Harper & Row.

Swados, E. (2002). *Hey you! C'mere: A poetry slam*. New York: Scholastic.

Wong, J. S. (1994). *Good luck gold and other poems*. New York: McElderry Books.

Comprehensive Anthologies

de Regniers, B. S., Moore, E., White, M. M., & Carr, J. (Compilers). (1988). *Sing a song of popcorn: Every child's book of poems*. New York: Scholastic.

Kennedy, X. J., & Kennedy, D. M. (Compilers). (1982). *Knock at a star: A child's introduction to poetry*. Boston: Little, Brown.

Prelutsky, J. (Sel.). (1999). *The 20th century children's poetry treasury*. New York: Knopf.

Prelutsky, J. (Compiler). (2000). *The Random House book of poetry for children*. New York: Random House.

Rhymed Verse

The most common type of poetry is rhymed verse, as in *Hailstones and Halibut Bones* (O'Neill, 1989), *My Parents Think I'm Sleeping* (Prelutsky, 1985), and *Sierra* (Siebert, 1991). Poets use various rhyme schemes, and the effect of the rhyming words is a poem that is pleasurable to read and listen to when it is read aloud. Students should savor the rhyming words but not be expected to pick out the rhyme scheme.

Rhyme is the sticking point for many would-be poets. In searching for a rhyming word, students often create inane verse; for example:

> *I see a funny little goat*
> *Wearing a blue sailor's coat*
> *Sitting in an old motorboat.*

Certainly students should not be forbidden to write rhyming poetry, but rhyme should never be imposed as a criterion for acceptable poetry. Students should be encouraged to use rhyme when it fits naturally into their writing. When students write poetry, they are searching for their own voices, and they need freedom to do that. Freed from the pressure to create rhyming poetry and from other constraints, students create sensitive word pictures, vivid images, and unique comparisons.

One type of rhymed verse—limericks—can be used effectively with older students. A limerick is a short verse form popularized by Edward Lear that incorporates both rhyme and rhythm. The poem consists of five lines; the first, second, and fifth lines rhyme, and the third and fourth lines rhyme with each other and are shorter than the other three. The rhyme scheme is a-a-b-b-a. The last line often contains a funny or surprise ending, as in this limerick written by an eighth grader.

> *There once was a frog named Pete*
> *Who did nothing but sit and eat.*
> *He examined each fly*
> *With so careful an eye*
> *And then said, "You're dead meat."*

Poet X. J. Kennedy (1982) suggests introducing students to limericks by reading aloud some of Lear's verses so that students can appreciate their rhythm; one collection of Lear's limericks is *There Was an Old Man: A Gallery of Nonsense Rhymes* (Lear, 1994). Writing limericks is a challenging assignment, but students can be successful if they write class collaboration poems. Arnold Lobel has also written a book of unique pig limericks, *Pigericks* (1983); After reading Lobel's pigericks, students will want to write "fishericks" or "buggericks."

Narrative Poems

Poems that tell a story are narrative poems. Perhaps our best-known narrative poem is Clement Moore's classic, "The Night Before Christmas." Other narrative poems include Longfellow's *Paul Revere's Ride* (2001), illustrated by Christopher Bing; Alfred Noyes's *The Highwayman* (1983), illustrated by Charles Mikolaycak; and Jeanette Winter's *Follow the Drinking Gourd* (1988), which is about the Underground Railroad.

Haiku and Related Forms

Haiku is a Japanese poetic form that contains just 17 syllables arranged in three lines of 5, 7, and 5 syllables. Haiku poems deal with nature and present a single clear image. Haiku is a concise form, much like a telegram. Because of its brevity, it has been

Students read books of poetry written by Jack Prelutsky during an author study.

considered an appropriate form of poetry for children to read and write. A fourth grader wrote this haiku about a spider web she saw one morning:

> *Spider web shining*
> *Tangled on the grass with dew*
> *Waiting quietly.*

Books of haiku to share with students include *Shadow Play: Night Haiku* (Harter, 1994) and *Cool Melons—Turn to Frogs! The Life and Poems of Issa* (Gollub, 1998). The artwork in these picture books may give students ideas for illustrating their haiku poems.

A poetic form similar to haiku is the cinquain, a five-line poem containing 22 syllables in a 2-4-6-8-2 syllable pattern. Cinquains often describe something, but they may also tell a story. Have students ask themselves what their subject looks like, smells like, sounds like, and tastes like, and record their ideas using a five-senses cluster. The formula is as follows:

Line 1: a one-word subject with two syllables
Line 2: four syllables describing the subject
Line 3: six syllables showing action
Line 4: eight syllables expressing a feeling or observation about the subject
Line 5: two syllables describing or renaming the subject

Students in a fourth-grade class wrote cinquains as part of a thematic unit on westward movement. One student wrote this cinquain about the transcontinental railroad:

> *Railroads*
> *One crazy guy's*
> *Transcontinental dream . . .*
> *With a golden spike it came true.*
> *Iron horse*

Another student wrote about the gold rush:

> *Gold rush*
> *Forty-niners*
> *were sure to strike it rich*
> *Homesickness, pork and beans, so tired.*
> *Panning*

Another related form is the diamante (Tiedt, 2002), a seven-line contrast poem written in the shape of a diamond. This poetic form helps students apply their knowledge of opposites and parts of speech. The formula is:

Line 1: one noun as the subject
Line 2: two adjectives describing the subject
Line 3: three participles (ending in -*ing*) telling about the subject
Line 4: four nouns (the first two related to the subject and the last two related to the opposite)
Line 5: three participles telling about the opposite
Line 6: two adjectives describing the opposite
Line 7: one noun that is the opposite of the subject

Free Verse

Free verse is unrhymed poetry, and rhythm is less important in free verse than in other types of poetry. Word choice and visual images take on greater importance in free verse. One popular collection of free verse is *Neighborhood Odes* (Soto, 1992), and in these poems, Gary Soto writes about his childhood as a Mexican American child living in Fresno, California. Soto adds a few Spanish words to his poems to sharpen the pictures they paint of life in his neighborhood.

In free verse, students choose words to describe something and put them together to express a thought or tell a story, without concern for rhyme or other arrangements. The number of words per line and use of punctuation vary. In the following poem, an eighth grader poignantly describes "Loneliness" using only 15 well-chosen words.

> *A lifetime*
> *Of broken dreams*
> *And promises*
> *Lost love*
> *Hurt*
> *My heart*
> *Cries*
> *In silence*

Students can use several methods for writing free verse. They can select words and phrases from brainstormed lists and clusters to create the poem, or they can write a paragraph and then "unwrite" it to create the poem by deleting unnecessary words. They arrange the remaining words to look like a poem.

Other Poetic Forms

Students use a variety of other forms when they write poems, even though few adults use them. These forms provide a scaffold or skeleton for students' poems. After collecting words, images, and comparisons, students craft their poems, choosing words and arranging them to create a message. Meaning is always most important, and form follows the search for meaning. Poet Kenneth Koch (2000), working with students in the elementary grades, developed some simple formulas that make it easy for nearly every child to become a successful poet. These formulas call for students to begin every line the same way or to insert a particular kind of word in every line. The formulas use repetition, a stylistic device that is more effective for young poets than rhyme. Some forms may seem more like sentences than poems, but the dividing line between poetry and prose is a blurry one, and these poetry experiences help children move toward poetic expression.

Color Poems.   Students begin each line of their poems with a color. They can repeat the color in each line or choose a different color (Koch, 2000). In this example, a class of seventh graders writes about yellow:

> *Yellow is shiny galoshes*
> *splashing through mud puddles.*
> *Yellow is a street lamp*
> *beaming through a dark, black night.*
> *Yellow is the egg yolk*
> *bubbling in a frying pan.*
> *Yellow is the lemon cake*
> *that makes you pucker your lips.*
> *Yellow is the sunset*
> *and the warm summer breeze.*
> *Yellow is the tingling in your mouth*
> *after a lemon drop melts.*

Students can also write more complex poems by expanding each idea into a stanza, as this poem about black illustrates.

> *Black is a deep hole*
> *sitting in the ground*
> *waiting for animals*
> *that live inside.*
>
> *Black is a beautiful horse*
> *standing on a high hill*
> *with the wind*
> *swirling its mane.*
>
> *Black is a winter night sky*
> *without stars*
> *to keep it*
> *company.*
>
> *Black is a panther*
> *creeping around a jungle*
> *searching for*
> *its prey.*

Hailstones and Halibut Bones (O'Neill, 1989) is another source of color poems; however, O'Neill uses rhyme as a poetic device, and it is important to emphasize that students' poems need not rhyme.

Acrostic Poems.   Students begin an acrostic poem by writing a word vertically. They then write a word or phrase beginning with each letter to complete the poem. As part of literature focus units, for example, students can write about a book title or a character's name. This acrostic poem about *Jumanji* (Van Allsburg, 1981) was written by a fourth grader:

> *Jungle adventure game and*
> *Un for a while.*
> *Monkeys ransacking kitchens*
> *And boa constrictors slithering past.*
> *No way out until the game is done—*
> *Just reach the city of Jumanji.*
> *I don't want to play!*

Five-Senses Poems.   Students write about a topic using each of the five senses. Sense poems are usually five lines long, with one line for each sense, but sometimes an extra line is added, as this poem written by a sixth grader demonstrates:

> *Being Heartbroken*
> *Sounds like thunder and lightning*
> *Looks like a carrot going through a blender*
> *Tastes like sour milk*
> *Feels like a splinter in your finger*
> *Smells like a dead fish*
> *It must be horrible!*

It is often helpful to have students develop a five-senses cluster and collect ideas for each sense. Students select from the cluster the most vivid or strongest idea for each sense to use in a line of the poem.

Preposition Poems.   Students begin each line of a preposition poem with a preposition, and a delightful poetic rewording of lines often results from the attempt. Seventh grader Mike wrote this preposition poem about a movie superhero:

> *Superman*
> *Within the city*
> *In a phone booth*
> *Into his clothes*
> *Like a bird*
> *In the sky*
> *Through the walls*
> *Until the crime*
> *Among us*
> *Is defeated!*

It is helpful for children to brainstorm a list of prepositions to refer to when they write preposition poems. Students may find that they need to ignore the formula for a line or two to give the content of their poems top priority, or they may mistakenly begin a line with an infinitive (e.g., "to say") rather than a preposition. These forms provide a structure or skeleton for students' writing that should be adapted as necessary.

Why Do Teachers Need to Know About Poetic Forms?

When students read and recite poetry, the emphasis is on introducing them to poetry so that they have a pleasurable experience. Students need to have fun as they do choral readings of poems, pick out favorite lines, and respond to poems. Teachers should be aware of poetic forms so that they can point out the form when it is appropriate or provide information about a poetic form when students ask. For example, sometimes when students read free verse, they say it isn't poetry because it doesn't rhyme. At this time, it's appropriate to point out that poetry doesn't have to rhyme and that this poem *is* a poem—that this type of poetry is called free verse. Teachers might also explain that in free verse, creating an image or projecting a voice is more important than the rhyme scheme. It is not appropriate for students to analyze the rhyme scheme or search out the meaning of the poem. Instead, children should focus on what the poem means to them. Teachers introduce poetic forms when students are writing poetry. When students use poetic formulas such as color poems, acrostics, and haiku, they are often more successful than when they attempt to create rhyming verse, because the formulas provide a framework for students' writing.

VISIT CHAPTER 7 ON THE COMPANION WEBSITE AT
www.prenhall.com/tompkins

- Complete a self-assessment to demonstrate your understanding of the concepts presented in this chapter
- Complete field activities that will help you expand your understanding of the middle-grade classroom and teaching the structure of text
- Visit important web links related to teaching expository text structures, story elements, and poetic forms to middle-grade students
- Look into your state's standards as they relate to teaching the structure of text to middle-grade students
- Communicate with other preservice teachers via the message board and discuss the issues of teaching the structure of text to students in grades 4 to 8

Review

Three broad types of literature are stories, informational books, and poetry, and they are included in basal readers and published as trade books. Each type of text has a unique structure or organization. Story elements are plot, characters, setting, point of view, and theme. Informational books and content-area textbooks are organized into expository text structures, of which the five most common patterns are description, sequence, comparison, cause and effect, and problem and solution. The most common poetic forms for students are rhymed verse, narrative poems, haiku, and free verse. Teachers need to be aware of the structure of text so that they can help students become more successful readers and writers. Guidelines for effectively teaching students about the structure of text are summarized in the following feature.

1. Teachers point out differences among narrative, expository, and poetic texts.
2. Teachers help students set aesthetic or efferent purposes for reading.
3. Teachers include all three types of literature—stories, informational books, and poems—in text sets.
4. Teachers choose high-quality literature because they understand that students' writing reflects what they are reading.
5. Teachers teach minilessons about story elements, expository structures, and poetic forms.
6. Teachers have students examine story elements in stories they are reading as part of literature focus units and literature circles.
7. Teachers have students examine expository text structure in informational books and content-area textbooks they are reading as part of thematic units.
8. Teachers have students make graphic organizers and other charts to emphasize the structure of texts while taking notes.
9. Teachers have students examine poetic structures and then write poems using the same patterns.
10. Teachers have students use their knowledge of text structure when writing stories, informational books, and poems.

Professional References

Au, K. H. (1992). Constructing the theme of a story. *Language Arts, 69,* 106–111.

Dressel, J. H. (1990). The effects of listening to and discussing different qualities of children's literature on the narrative writing of fifth graders. *Research in the Teaching of English, 24,* 397–414.

Flood, J., Lapp, D., & Farnan, N. (1986). A reading-writing procedure that teaches expository paragraph structure. *The Reading Teacher, 39,* 556–562.

Freedman, R. (1992). Fact or fiction? In E. B. Freeman & D. G. Person (Eds.), *Using nonfiction tradebooks in the elementary classroom: From ants to zeppelins* (pp. 2–10). Urbana, IL: National Council of Teachers of English.

Graves, D. H. (1992). *Explore poetry.* Portsmouth, NH: Heinemann.

Irwin, J. W. (1991). *Teaching reading comprehension processes* (2nd ed.). Boston: Allyn & Bacon.

Johnson, T. D., & Louis, D. R. (1987). *Literacy through literature.* Portsmouth, NH: Heinemann.

Koch, K. (2000). *Wishes, lies, and dreams: Teaching children to write poetry.* New York: HarperPerennial.

Langer, J. A. (1986). *Children reading and writing: Structures and strategies.* Norwood, NJ: Ablex.

Lapp, D., Flood, J., & Farnan, N. (1992). Basal readers and literature: A tight fit or a mismatch? In K. D. Wood & A. Moss (Eds.), *Exploring literature in the classroom: Contents and methods* (pp. 35–57). Norwood, MA: Christopher-Gordon.

Larrick, N. (1991). *Let's do a poem! Introducing poetry to children.* New York: Delacorte.

Lehr, S. S. (1991). *The child's developing sense of theme: Responses to literature.* New York: Teachers College Press.

Lukens, R. J. (1999). *A critical handbook of children's literature* (6th ed.). New York: Longman.

McGee, L. M., & Richgels, D. J. (1985). Teaching expository text structures to elementary students. *The Reading Teacher, 38,* 739–745.

Meyer, B. J., & Freedle, R. O. (1984). Effects of discourse type on recall. *American Educational Research Journal, 21,* 121–143.

Niles, O. S. (1974). Organization perceived. In H. L. Herber (Ed.), *Perspectives in reading: Developing study skills in secondary schools.* Newark, DE: International Reading Association.

Ogle, D. M. (1986). K-W-L: A teaching model that develops active reading of expository text. *The Reading Teacher, 39,* 564–570.

Pappas, C. (1993). Is narrative "primary"? Some insights from kindergartners' pretend readings of stories and information books. *Journal of Reading Behavior, 25,* 97–129.

Piccolo, J. A. (1987). Expository text structures: Teaching and learning strategies. *The Reading Teacher, 40,* 838–847.

Raphael, T. E., Englert, C. S., & Kirschner, B. W. (1989). Acquisition of expository writing skills. In J. M. Mason (Ed.), *Reading and writing connections* (pp. 261–290). Boston: Allyn & Bacon.

Roop, P. (1992). Nonfiction books in the primary classroom: Soaring with the swans. In E. B. Freeman & D. G. Person (Eds.), *Using nonfiction tradebooks in the elementary classroom: From ants to zeppelins* (pp. 106–112). Urbana, IL: National Council of Teachers of English.

Rosenblatt, L. (1978). *The reader, the text, the poem: The transactional theory of the literary work.* Carbondale: Southern Illinois University Press.

Tiedt, I. (2002). *Tiger lilies, toadstools, and thunderbolts: Engaging K–8 students with poetry.* Newark, DE: International Reading Association.

Tompkins, G. E. (2004). *Teaching writing: Balancing process and product* (4th ed.). Upper Saddle River, NJ: Merrill/Prentice Hall.

Vardell, S. (1991). A new "picture of the world": The NCTE Orbis Pictus Award for outstanding nonfiction for children. *Language Arts, 68,* 474–479.

Wells, G. (1986). *The meaning makers: Children learning language and using language to learn.* Portsmouth, NH: Heinemann.

Whitin, D. J., & Wilde, S. (1992). *Read any good math lately? Children's books for mathematical learning, K–6.* Portsmouth, NH: Heinemann.

Children's Book References

Aker, S. (1990). *What comes in 2's, 3's, and 4's?* New York: Simon & Schuster.

Ancona, G. (1992). *Man and mustang.* New York: Macmillan.

Arnold, C. (1993). *Dinosaurs all around: An artist's view of the prehistoric world.* New York: Clarion.

Blume, J. (1972). *Tales of a fourth grade nothing.* New York: Dutton.

Carle, E. (1969). *The very hungry caterpillar.* New York: Philomel.

Clarke, B. (1990). *Amazing frogs and toads.* New York: Knopf.

Cole, J. (1996). *The magic school bus inside a beehive.* New York: Scholastic.

Cowcher, H. (1990). *Antarctica.* New York: Farrar, Straus & Giroux.

Cushman, K. (1994). *Catherine, called Birdy.* New York: HarperCollins.

Day, A. (1985). *Good dog, Carl.* New York: Green Tiger Press.

Feelings, M., & Feelings, T. (1971). *Moja means one: Swahili counting book.* New York: Dial.

Fleischman, P. (1985). *I am phoenix: Poems for two voices.* New York: Harper & Row.

Fleischman, P. (1988). *Joyful noise: Poems for two voices.* New York: Harper & Row.

Freedman, R. (1987). *Lincoln: A photobiography.* New York: Clarion.

Fritz, J. (1976). *Will you sign here, John Hancock?* New York: Coward-McCann.

Fritz, J. (1989). *The great little Madison.* New York: Putnam.

Galdone, P. (1970). *The three little pigs.* New York: Seabury.

Gardiner, J. R. (1980). *Stone Fox.* New York: Harper & Row.

George, J. C. (1972). *Julie of the wolves.* New York: Harper & Row.

Gibbons, G. (1992). *Spiders.* New York: Holiday House.

Gollub, M. (1998). *Cool melons—turn to frogs! The life and poems of Issa.* New York: Lee & Low.

Guiberson, B. Z. (1991). *Cactus hotel.* New York: Henry Holt.

Harter, P. (1994). *Shadow play: Night haiku.* New York: Simon & Schuster.

Hesse, K. (2001). *Witness.* New York: Scholastic.

Hoban, T. (1987). *26 letters and 99 cents.* New York: Greenwillow.

Howe, D., & Howe, J. (1979). *Bunnicula: A rabbit-tale of mystery.* New York: Atheneum.

Hunt, J. (1989). *Illuminations.* New York: Bradbury.

Hutchins, P. (1968). *Rosie's walk.* New York: Macmillan.

Hyman, T. S. (1977). *The sleeping beauty.* New York: Holiday House.

Kennedy, X. J. (1982). *Knock at a star: A child's introduction to poetry.* Boston: Little, Brown.

King-Smith, D. (1995). *Babe: The gallant pig.* New York: Random House.

Lear, E. (1994). *There was an old man: A gallery of nonsense rhymes.* New York: Morrow.

L'Engle, M. (1962). *A wrinkle in time.* New York: Farrar, Straus & Giroux.

Levine, E. (1986). *. . . If you traveled west in a covered wagon.* New York: Scholastic.

Lobel, A. (1983). *Pigericks: A book of pig limericks.* New York: Harper & Row.

Longfellow, H. W. (2001). *The midnight ride of Paul Revere.* Brooklyn, NY: Handprint Books.

Lowry, L. (1989). *Number the stars.* Boston: Houghton Mifflin.

Lowry, L. (1993). *The giver.* Boston: Houghton Mifflin.

Lowry, L. (1998). *Looking back: A book of memories.* New York: Delacorte.

Macaulay, D. (1977). *Castle.* Boston: Houghton Mifflin.

MacLachlan, P. (1985). *Sarah, plain and tall.* New York: Harper & Row.

Maestro, B. (1992). *How do apples grow?* New York: HarperCollins.

McCloskey, R. (1969). *Make way for ducklings*. New York: Viking.

Millard, A. (1998). *A street through time*. New York: DK Publishing.

Naylor, P. R. (1991). *Shiloh*. New York: Atheneum.

Noyes, A. (1983). *The highwayman*. New York: Lothrop, Lee & Shepard.

O'Dell, S. (1960). *Island of the blue dolphins*. Boston: Houghton Mifflin.

O'Neill, M. (1989). *Hailstones and halibut bones*. New York: Doubleday.

Pallotta, J. (1991). *The underwater alphabet book*. Watertown, MA: Charlesbridge.

Pallotta, J. (1992). *The icky bug counting book*. Watertown, MA: Charlesbridge.

Paterson, K. (1977). *Bridge to Terabithia*. New York: Crowell.

Paulsen, G. (1987). *Hatchet*. New York: Simon & Schuster.

Polacco, P. (1994). *Pink and Say*. New York: Putnam.

Prelutsky, J. (1985). *My parents think I'm sleeping*. New York: Greenwillow.

Prelutsky, J. (2000). *The Random House book of poetry for children*. New York: Random House.

Rauzon, M. J. (1993). *Horns, antlers, fangs, and tusks*. New York: Lothrop, Lee & Shepard.

Ryan, P. M. (2000). *Esperanza rising*. New York: Scholastic.

Rylant, C. (1992). *Best wishes*. Katonah, NY: Richard C. Owen.

Schwartz, D. (1989). *If you made a million*. New York: Lothrop, Lee & Shepard.

Scieszka, J. (1989). *The true story of the 3 little pigs!* New York: Viking.

Scott, A. H. (1990). *One good horse: A cowpuncher's counting book*. New York: Greenwillow.

Showers, P. (1985). *What happens to a hamburger?* New York: Harper & Row.

Siebert, D. (1991). *Sierra*. New York: HarperCollins.

Simon, S. (1989). *Whales*. New York: Crowell.

Simon, S. (1993). *Mercury*. New York: Morrow.

Soto, G. (1992). *Neighborhood odes*. San Diego: Harcourt Brace Jovanovich.

Speare, E. G. (1958). *The witch of Blackbird Pond*. Boston: Houghton Mifflin.

Steele, P. (1998). *Knights*. New York: Kingfisher.

Steig, W. (1969). *Sylvester and the magic pebble*. New York: Simon & Schuster.

Steig, W. (1982). *Doctor De Soto*. New York: Farrar, Straus & Giroux.

Taylor, M. D. (1976). *Roll of thunder, hear my cry*. New York: Dial.

Van Allsburg, C. (1981). *Jumanji*. Boston: Houghton Mifflin.

Van Allsburg, C. (1986). *The stranger*. Boston: Houghton Mifflin.

Van Allsburg, C. (1991). *The wretched stone*. Boston: Houghton Mifflin.

Viorst, J. (1977). *Alexander and the terrible, horrible, no good, very bad day*. New York: Atheneum.

White, E. B. (1952). *Charlotte's web*. New York: Harper & Row.

Wiesner, D. (1991). *Tuesday*. New York: Clarion.

Winter, J. (1988). *Follow the drinking gourd*. New York: Knopf.

Zemach, M. (1983). *The little red hen*. New York: Farrar, Straus & Giroux.

chapter *8*

Teaching With Narrative Texts

chapter
QUESTIONS

- Which books should students read?

- What is a literature focus unit?

- What are literature circles?

- What are the benefits of using literature focus units and literature circles?

Mrs. Bradshaw's Students Read in Book Clubs

The students in Mrs. Bradshaw's fourth- and fifth-grade classroom have divided into six small-group literature circles that they call "book clubs" to read and respond to these chapter books:

- *On My Honor* (Bauer, 1986), a story about a boy who breaks a promise to his father, with disastrous results.
- *Freckle Juice* (Blume, 1971), a humorous story about a boy who tries to rid himself of his freckles.
- *Shiloh* (Naylor, 1991), a heartwarming boy-and-dog story that has been made into a movie.
- *Bunnicula: A Rabbit-Tale of Mystery* (Howe & Howe, 1979), a fantasy about a bunny who just might be a vampire.
- *How to Eat Fried Worms* (Rockwell, 1973), a humorously revolting story about a boy who makes a bet that he can eat 15 worms in 15 days.
- *Bridge to Terabithia* (Paterson, 1977), a touching story of friendship between two lonely children.

All six of these books are good stories and are popular with fifth graders. Two have won the Newbery Medal for excellence, and one is a Newbery Honor Book (runner-up for the Newbery Medal). Mrs. Bradshaw chose these books after reflecting on the interests and needs of the students in the classroom, and based on requests and recommendations from her students. The reading levels of the books range from second to fifth grade.

Mrs. Bradshaw has a set of six of each of these books, and she introduced the books using a book talk[C]. Students had a day to preview the books and sign up for one of the groups. After students get into groups, Mrs. Bradshaw holds a class meeting to set the guidelines for this unit. Students will have 75 minutes each day for 5 days to read and respond to the books. Students in each group set their own schedules for reading, discussing the book, and writing in reading logs[C]. They decide how they will read the book, plan for at least three grand conversations[C], write at least three entries in their reading logs, and develop a presentation to share their book with the class at the end of the unit. Mrs. Bradshaw distributes a "Book Club Notes" sheet for students to use to keep track of their schedules and the assignments. A copy of this sheet is shown in Figure 8-1. Students keep this sheet and their reading logs in their book club folders.

The students in each book club talk about their books and make plans. Four of the groups decide to write their first reading log entry before beginning to read, and the other two groups begin reading right away. As the students read, write, and talk about their books, Mrs. Bradshaw moves from group to group and writes anecdotal notes to monitor students' progress.

Mrs. Bradshaw joins the *Bridge to Terabithia* group as they finish reading the first chapter, and one student asks about the dedication. Mrs. Bradshaw shares that she read that Katherine Paterson wrote this book after the child of a friend of hers died, and she guesses that the Lisa mentioned in the dedication is that child. Another student asks about the setting of the story, and from the information in the first chapter, the group deduces that the story is set in a rural area outside Washington, DC. Several students comment on how

Figure 8-1   Mrs. Bradshaw's Assignment Sheet

Book Club Notes

Name _____ Date _____

Book _____

Schedule

1	2	3	4	5

Requirements

☐ Read the book

☐ Discuss the book 1 _____ 2 _____ 3 _____

☐ Write in a reading log 1 _____ 2 _____ 3 _____

☐ Make a project

Assessment Tools

C See the Compendium of Instructional Procedures, which follows Chapter 12, for more information on terms marked with the symbol^C.

vividly Paterson describes Jess and his family. After speculating on who might be moving into the old Perkins place, they continue reading.

Next, Mrs. Bradshaw moves to the book club reading *Freckle Juice* and helps them set up their group schedule. The students in this group decide to read together. They will take turns reading aloud as the other group members follow along and help with unfamiliar words. Mrs. Bradshaw stays with this group as they read the first three pages. Then she encourages them to continue reading and moves on to another group.

The next day, the book club reading *Bunnicula: A Rabbit-Tale of Mystery* asks Mrs. Bradshaw to meet with them. They have a lot of questions and confusions about vampires and Dracula. Mrs. Bradshaw is prepared for their requests, and she brings with her the "V" and "D" volumes of an encyclopedia and several other books about vampires. She spends 20 minutes with the group, helping them find information and clarify confusions. She also joins with the *How to Eat Fried Worms* book club as they read chapter 3. The students ask Mrs. Bradshaw what *monshure* is, and she explains that Alan is pretending to speak French. As they continue reading chapters 4 and 5, she points out similar instances. Once they finish reading, the group discusses the chapters they have read and talks about whether they would have made a similar bet. They compare themselves to Billy, the boy who eats the worms, and talk about how real the story seems and how they feel themselves tasting the worm as Billy eats it. Mrs. Bradshaw seizes the moment for an impromptu lesson on reading strategies, and she explains that good readers often seem to connect with or become a character in a story and can see, hear, smell, and even taste the same things the character does.

A few days later, Mrs. Bradshaw meets with the *Shiloh* book club as they are writing in their reading logs. Students in this group decided to write double-entry journals[C]; they write interesting quotes from the book in one column and their reactions to the quotes in another column. Students are writing quotes and reactions from the last three chapters of the book. Todd chooses "I begin to see now I'm no better than Judd Travers—willing to look the other way to get something I want" (p. 124), and writes:

> *Marty IS better than Judd Travers. This book makes you realize that things are not just right and wrong and most of the time right and wrong and good and bad and fair and not fair get a little mixed up. Marty is keeping quiet about the doe for a real important reason. The deer is dead and that can't be helped but Marty can save Shiloh. He must save the dog. He's a much better person than he thinks even though he did do some wrong. Part of the reason you know he is a good person is that he knows he did the wrong things. He has a conscience. Judd don't have a conscience, none at all.*

Next, Mrs. Bradshaw meets with the *On My Honor* book club as they discuss the end of the book. Kara comments, "I don't think Joel should feel so guilty about Tony dying. It wasn't his fault." Mrs. Bradshaw asks, "Whose fault was it?" Several children say it was Tony's fault. Will explains, "He knew he couldn't swim and he went swimming anyway. That was just plain dumb." "What about Joel's dad?" Mrs. Bradshaw asks, "Was it his fault, too?" Brooke says, "His dad seems like he thinks he's guilty and he tells Joel he's sorry." Jared offers another opinion, "It was just an accident. I don't think it was anyone's fault. No one killed Tony on purpose. He just died." The group continues to talk about the effect of Tony's death on his own family and on Josh and his family.

Mrs. Bradshaw and the students in this multiage classroom have created a community of learners. They have learned to work together in small groups. They are responsible for assignments and are supportive of their classmates. They know the literacy routines and procedures to use during the book club unit. The classroom is arranged to facilitate their learning; they know where supplies are kept and how to use them. Mrs. Bradshaw assumes a number of roles during the unit: She chooses books, organizes the unit, provides information and encouragement, teaches lessons, monitors students' progress, and assesses their work.

On the fifth day, students in each book club share their projects with the class. The purpose of these projects is to celebrate the reading experience and bring closure to it. An added benefit is that students "advertise" the books during these sharing sessions, and then other students want to read them. Each group takes approximately 5 to 10 minutes to share their projects. The *How to Eat Fried Worms* group goes first; they present a book commercial. Group members tell a little about the story and dare students to eat the worms—big earthworms or night crawlers—that they have brought to school. One student, Nathan, explains that it is perfectly safe to eat the worms and extols their nutritional benefits. Even so, no one volunteers.

Next, the group reading *Freckle Juice* shares two projects. Two students share a graph they have made showing how many children in the class have freckles, and the other students present a commercial to sell a bottle of guaranteed "freckle juice."

The group reading *Bunnicula: A Rabbit-Tale of Mystery* explains that they've read a mystery about vegetables turning white, and they show some vegetables they have made out of light-colored clay as evidence. They point out two tiny marks on each vegetable. One student, Bill, pretends to be Harold, the family dog who wrote the book, and he explains that their pet rabbit—Bunnicula—who seemed to be harmless at first, may be responsible for sucking the vegetable juices out of the vegetables. Dolores displays a stuffed animal bunny dressed in a black cape to look like a vampire. The group recommends that classmates read this book if they want to find out what happens to Bunnicula.

The *Shiloh* group shares information from the local ASPCA, and Angelica reads an "I Am" poem about Marty that the group has written:

> *I am a boy who knows right from wrong*
> *but I will do anything to save that dog.*
> *I know how to treat a dog.*
> *I say, "Please don't kick him like that."*
> *I am afraid of Judd Travers.*
> *But I will do anything to save Shiloh.*
> *I dream of Shiloh being mine.*
> *I have a secret hiding place for him.*
> *I catch Judd Travers killing a doe out of season.*
> *I will make mean Mr. Travers sell Shiloh to me.*
> *I work hard for 20 hours to earn $40 to buy him.*
> *I learn that nothing is as simple as it seems.*
> *I am a boy who knows right from wrong*
> *but I will do anything to save my dog.*

The group reading *Bridge to Terabithia* presents a tabletop diorama they have made of the setting for the story. The students include Jess's and Leslie's homes, their school, and the magical kingdom of Terabithia in their diorama. They use a variety of craft materials for the project. They make the foundation out of papier mache and the buildings from boxes covered with construction paper. They use toy farm animals, pets, and cars to add details to the homes. They cut tree boughs for the wooded magical kingdom and include a piece of twine tied to one branch for the rope swing, and Laura, one of the group members, brings two dolls to complete the scene—one is Jess and the other is Leslie.

Last, Hector and Carlos from the group reading *On My Honor* role-play Joel and Tony, the two boys in the story. They reenact the scene where the boys decide to go swimming. They explain that Tony drowns, and then the boy playing Joel describes what it was like to search for Tony and then pretend that he didn't know what had happened to him. Then the other group members ask their classmates what they would have done after Tony died if they had been Joel.

After all the projects have been presented, many students trade books with classmates, and students spend the next 2 days independently reading any book they choose. Many students read one of the other books read during the book clubs, but some students bring other books from home to read or choose a different book from the class library.

M rs. Bradshaw's students are likely to become lifelong readers because they love books and enjoy reading and discussing them. Many of them choose to read as a leisure-time activity. Books of children's and adolescent literature carry readers to far-off lands and times, stretch their imaginations, expand their knowledge of people and the world, and transform them by giving life new meaning. Charlotte Huck (1998) explains: "I believe in the transforming power of literature to take you out of yourself and return you to yourself—a changed self" (p. 4). Powerful experiences with literature, like those that Mrs. Bradshaw's students experienced, heighten children's interest in reading and at the same time expand their reading abilities.

In this chapter, you will read about two ways—literature focus units and literature circles—to provide opportunities for students in grades 4 through 8 to read and respond to literature. The feature on page 248 shows how literature focus units and literature circles fit into a balanced literacy program. As you continue reading this chapter, you will learn more about the ideas presented in the feature.

CHOOSING LITERATURE

Teachers choose high-quality trade books for literature focus units and literature circles. Sometimes the books have been identified as *core* books that must be taught at their grade level, or teachers choose other high-quality books that are appropriate for students at their grade level. Teachers like Mrs. Bradshaw in the vignette consider both the interest level and the reading level of the books they choose; the books must be interesting to students, and they must be at the appropriate reading level.

Narrative Genres

Stories can be categorized in different ways, and one way is according to genres or types of stories (Buss & Karnowski, 2000). Three broad genres are folklore, fantasies, and realistic fiction. Traditional stories, including fables, fairy tales, and myths, are folklore. Many of these stories were told and retold for centuries before they were written down. Fantasies are make-believe stories. They may be set in imaginary worlds or in a future world where characters do impossible things. In some fantasies, such as *Charlotte's Web* (White, 1952), animals can talk. Realistic fiction, in contrast, is believable stories. Some stories take place in the past and others in the modern world. Figure 8-2 presents an overview of the story genres and lists sample stories illustrating each one.

The minilesson feature presented on page 250 shows how Mrs. Mills teaches her seventh graders about narrative genres. She conducts these lessons in connection with reading workshop, a 35-minute period when her students read self-selected books independently. Mrs. Mills regularly asks the students to classify the books they are reading according to genre and to explain how genre affects the story. For example, in historical fiction, the students note that the characters get involved in events that are important because of the historical time period of the story. If the story were taking place today, the events might not be important.

Teachers need to consider the types of books they choose for students to read and the impact of their choices on students' literacy development. Researchers who have examined teachers' choices have found that they often suggest an unconscious gender or racial bias because few books that are chosen feature the experiences of females or of ethnic minorities, and even fewer were written by people from these groups (Jipson & Paley, 1991; Shannon, 1986; Traxel, 1983). These researchers call this pattern the "selective tradition," and they worry about this practice because books reflect and

Even though the books chosen for literature focus units and literature circles can be very challenging for English language learners, these books enrich students' understanding of American culture and history as well as their language development.

The Role of Literature Focus Units and Literature Circles in a Balanced Literacy Program

Component	Description
Reading	Students read and respond to high-quality literature in these two approaches. They usually read the books independently, but teachers can read aloud featured books in literature focus units when they are too difficult for students to read themselves.
Phonics and Other Skills	Teachers teach skills during minilessons[C]—this is part of the exploring stage of the reading process.
Strategies	Teachers teach minilessons about strategies during literature focus units, and students apply strategies as they read books independently and assume roles to discuss books during literature circles.
Vocabulary	Students learn new words as they read and respond to books they are reading. During literature focus units, teachers post words on word walls[C] and during literature circles, students examine words during group discussions.
Comprehension	Students move beyond literal comprehension as they think, talk, and write about novels they are reading during literature focus units and literature circles.
Literature	Students read high-quality literature, including multicultural literature, during literature focus units and literature circles.
Content-Area Study	Books used for literature focus units and literature circles can connect to social studies or other content-area units.
Oral Language	Students participate in grand conversations to talk about featured books in literature focus units, and they assume roles and participate in discussions during literature circles.
Writing	Students use writing in both literature focus units and literature circles. They write in reading logs and use the writing process as they write reports, stories, poems, and other projects.
Spelling	Spelling is not an important component in literature focus units or literature circles.

Figure 8-2   Narrative Genres

Category	Genre	Description and Examples
Folklore	Fables	Brief tales told to point out a moral. For example: *Town Mouse, Country Mouse* (Brett, 1994) and *The Tortoise and the Hare: An Aesop Fable* (Stevens, 1984).
	Folktales	Stories in which heroes and heroines demonstrate virtues to triumph over adversity. For example: *Rumpelstiltskin* (Zelinsky, 1986) and *The Three Billy Goats Gruff* (Stevens, 1987).
	Myths	Stories created by ancient peoples to explain natural phenomena. For example: *Ingri and Edgar Parin d'Aulaire's Book of Greek Myths* (d'Aulaire & d'Aulaire, 1980).
	Legends	Stories, including hero tales and tall tales, that recount the courageous deeds of people as they struggled against each other or against gods and monsters. For example: *The Sword and the Circle: King Arthur and the Knights of the Round Table* (Sutcliff, 1994) and *Paul Bunyan, a Tall Tale* (Kellogg, 1984).
Fantasy	Modern Literary Tales	Stories written by modern authors that exemplify the characteristics of folktales. For example: *The Ugly Duckling* (Andersen, 1981) and *Sylvester and the Magic Pebble* (Steig, 1988).
	Fantastic Stories	Imaginative stories that explore alternate realities and contain one or more elements not found in the natural world. For example: *Jeremy Thatcher, Dragon Hatcher* (Coville, 1991) and *Charlotte's Web* (White, 1952).
	Science Fiction	Stories explore scientific possibilities. For example: *The Giver* (Lowry, 1993), and *Stinker From Space* (Service, 1988).
	High Fantasy	These stories focus on the conflict between good and evil and often involve quests. For example: *The Lion, the Witch and the Wardrobe* (Lewis, 1994) and *A Wrinkle in Time* (L'Engle, 1962).
Realistic Fiction	Contemporary Stories	Stories that portray the real world and contemporary society. For example: *Hatchet* (Paulsen, 1987) and *Tales of a Fourth Grade Nothing* (Blume, 1972).
	Historical Stories	Realistic stories set in the past. For example: *The Watsons Go to Birmingham—1963* (Curtis, 1995) and *Sarah, Plain and Tall* (MacLachlan, 1985).

Minilesson

Topic: Fantasy Genres
Grade: Seventh Grade
Time: 30 minutes

Mrs. Mills's seventh-grade students have examined folklore, fantasy, and realism genres, and in today's mini-lesson, they are going to examine and compare fantastic stories, high fantasy, and science fiction. The teacher asks eight students who are reading these three types of stories to be prepared to do book talks about their books during the minilesson.

1. Introduce the Topic
Mrs. Mills reviews the charts the students have made about genres that are posted on the classroom wall. She explains that today they are going to learn more about the fantasy genre.

2. Share Examples
Eight students do 1-minute book talks about these fantasies they are reading or have read recently:

A Wrinkle in Time (L'Engle, 1962)
Harry Potter and the Sorcerer's Stone (Rowling, 1998)
Skellig (Almond, 1999)
The Black Cauldron (Alexander, 1965)

The Ear, the Eye, and the Arm (Farmer, 1994)
The Hobbit (Tolkien, 1938)
The Lion, the Witch and the Wardrobe (Lewis, 1950)
The Root Cellar (Lunn, 1983)

The students listen carefully to the book talks and agree that these books are fantasies, but they notice some differences, too: Some books involve time warps, and others involve alternate worlds or characters with magical powers.

3. Provide Information
Mrs. Mills explains three types of fantasies that her students often read, listing the characteristics of each on a chart. In fantastic stories, authors alter one or more characteristics of everyday reality, create strange and curious worlds, or use time warps to move characters into the past or future. In science fiction, authors use technology to create future societies, and the theme often deals with the future of humanity. In high fantasies, characters who possess supernatural powers embark on quests to overcome evil in new worlds created by the author. Students consider each of the books introduced earlier and classify them according to genre.

4. Guide Practice
Next, the teacher does brief book talks on other fantasy books selected from the classroom library and encourages students to read these books. As she talks about each one, she mentions the characteristics that make it a fantastic story, science fiction, or high fantasy and asks students to identify the genre. The books Mrs. Mills shares are:

Dr. Dredd's Wagon of Wonders (Brittain, 1987)
Graven Images (Fleischman, 1982)
Interstellar Pig (Sleator, 1984)
The Golden Compass (Pullman, 1996)

The Last Book in the Universe (Philbrick, 2000)
The Sword and the Circle: King Arthur and the Knights of the Round Table (Sutcliff, 1981)
The Wolves of Willoughby Chase (Aiken, 1963)

Students eagerly ask to borrow each book after it is discussed.

5. Assess Learning
Mrs. Mills continues to informally assess students' learning as she conferences with them during reading workshop. She asks, "Can you classify your book?" "What genre is your book?" and "How do you know that it represents this genre?"

convey sociocultural values, beliefs, and attitudes to readers. It is important that teachers be aware of the ideas conveyed by their selection patterns and become more reflective about the books they choose for classroom use.

The Best of the Best

Teachers who use literature as the basis for their reading programs must be knowledgeable about children's and adolescent literature. The first step in becoming knowledgeable is to read many of the books available for children today. Many of the stories in basal readers are also available as trade books or are excerpted from novels. Teachers need to locate the complete versions of basal reader selections to share with their students. Children's librarians and the salespeople in children's bookstores are very helpful and willing to suggest books for teachers.

As they read and make selections for classroom use, teachers should keep in mind guidelines for selecting literature. The most important guideline is that teachers should choose books that they like themselves. Teachers are rarely, if ever, successful in teaching books they don't like. The message that they don't like the book comes across loud and clear, even when teachers try to hide their feelings. Teachers should consider these questions when they select stories for their students to read:

Is the book a good story?
Is the plot original and believable?
Are the characters real and believable?
Do the characters grow and change in the story?
Does the author avoid stereotyping?
Does the story move beyond the setting and have universal implications?
Is the theme worthwhile?
Are the style of writing and use of language appropriate?
Does the book exemplify the characteristics of a genre?
How does the book compare with others on the same subject or in the same genre? (Huck, Hepler, & Hickman, 1987; Norton, 2003)

The literature selections that teachers use as featured selections for literature focus units and literature circles should embody these qualities.

Each year, a number of books written for children are recognized for excellence and receive awards. The two best-known awards are the Caldecott Medal for excellence in illustration and the Newbery Medal for excellence in writing. Examples of Caldecott award and honor books for upper-grade students include *Sylvester and the Magic Pebble* (Steig, 1969), *Smoky Night* (Bunting, 1994), and *The Garden of Abdul Gasazi* (Van Allsburg, 1979), and examples of Newbery award and honor books include *Holes* (Sachar, 1998), *A Single Shard* (Park, 2001), and *The Watsons Go to Birmingham—1963* (Curtis, 1993). Teachers should be familiar with many of these award-winning books and consider selecting one or more of them to use in their classrooms as featured selections in literature focus units.

Multicultural Literature

Multicultural literature is "literature that represents any distinct cultural group through accurate portrayal and rich detail" (Yokota, 1993, p. 157); it has generally been described as stories and books by and about people of color. Stories such as Sharon Flake's *The Skin I'm in* (1998), about how 13-year-old Maleeka, uncomfortable because her skin is very dark, learns to love who she is and what she looks like, and Gary Soto's *Too Many Tamales* (1993), about a Mexican American child who loses her mother's diamond ring in a batch of tamales she is making, provide glimpses of contemporary life in two cultural groups. Other books tell the history of various cultural and ethnic groups. *So Far From the Sea* (Bunting, 1998), for instance, tells how Japanese Americans were interned in desolate camps during World War II, and *Anthony Burns: The Defeat and Triumph of a Fugitive Slave* (Hamilton, 1988) describes how slaves risked their lives to be free.

Figure 8-3 presents information on books about four cultural groups: African Americans, Asian Americans, Hispanic Americans, and Native Americans. These umbrella labels can be deceiving, however, because substantial differences exist among the cultures within a category. For example, there are no composite Native Americans; instead, Eskimos and the more than 100 Native American tribes in North America are grouped together under the Native American umbrella label. For an annotated listing of more than 300 multicultural books, see *Kaleidoscope: A Multicultural Booklist for Grades K–8* (Bishop, 1994).

Educators recommend selecting multicultural literature that is "culturally conscious" (Sims, 1982)—that is to say, literature that accurately reflects a group's culture, language, history, and values without perpetuating stereotypes. Such literature often deals with issues of prejudice, discrimination, and human dignity. According to Yokota (1993), these books should be rich in cultural details, use authentic dialogue, and present cultural issues in enough depth that readers can think and talk about them. Inclusion of cultural group members should be purposeful. They should be distinct individuals whose lives are rooted in the culture; they should never be included simply to fulfill a quota.

Multicultural literature must meet the criteria for good literature as well as for cultural consciousness. One example is *The Watsons Go to Birmingham—1963* (Curtis, 1995), an award-winning story about an African American family living in Flint, Michigan, and the harsh realities of racial discrimination that the family encounters on a trip to Birmingham, Alabama, during the hate-filled summer of 1963. This well-written story is both historically and culturally accurate.

Why Use Multicultural Literature?

Whether your students represent diverse cultures or not, there are many reasons to use multicultural literature in fourth- through eighth-grade classrooms. First of all, multicultural literature is good literature. Students enjoy reading stories, and through reading, they learn more about what it means to be human and that people of all cultural groups have similar emotions, needs, and dreams (Bishop, 1992). Allen Say's *El Chino* (1990), for example, tells about a Chinese American who achieves his dream of becoming a great athlete, and the book provides a model for children and adults of all ethnic groups.

Second, through multicultural books, students learn about the wealth of diversity in the United States and develop sensitivity to and appreciation for people of other cultural groups (Walker-Dalhouse, 1992). *Teammates* (Golenbock, 1990), for example, tells about the friendship of baseball greats Jackie Robinson and Pee Wee Reese, and it teaches a valuable lesson in tolerance and respect. Multicultural literature also challenges racial and ethnic stereotypes by providing an inside view of a culture.

Third, students broaden their knowledge of geography and learn different views of history through multicultural literature. They read about the countries that minority groups left as they immigrated to America, and often students gain nonmainstream perspectives about historical events. For example, in *Journey to Topaz* (1971), Yoshiko Uchida tells of her experiences in Japanese American internment camps in the United States during World War II. As they read and respond to multicultural books, students

Figure 8-3 Multicultural Literature

Cultural Group	Description	Books
African Americans	More books are available today about African Americans than about the other cultural groups. Some books deal with the harsh realities of life during slavery and afterwards, and others focus on contemporary life in the United States.	Armstrong, W. H. (1969). *Sounder.* New York: HarperCollins. Curtis, C. P. (1999). *Bud, not Buddy.* New York: Delacorte. Flake, S. G. (1998). *The skin I'm in.* New York: Hyperion. Mead, A. (1995). *Junebug.* New York: Farrar, Straus & Giroux. Myers, W. D. (1998). *Scorpions.* New York: HarperCollins. Slote, A. (1991). *Finding Buck McHenry.* New York: HarperCollins. Taylor, M. D. (1976). *Roll of thunder, hear my cry.* New York: Dial. Winter, J. (1988). *Follow the drinking gourd.* New York: Knopf.
Asian Americans	Books about Asian Americans deal with specific Asian American groups, not generalities. The characters go beyond common stereotypes and correct historical errors and omissions. Many books are about the authors' own experiences of growing up in the United States.	Bunting, E. (1994). *Smoky night.* San Diego: Harcourt Brace. Bunting, E. (1998). *So far from the sea.* New York: Clarion. Denenberg, B. (1999). *The journal of Ben Uchida.* New York: Scholastic. Lord, B. B. (1984). *In the year of the boar and Jackie Robinson.* New York: HarperCollins. Marsden, C. (2002). *The gold-threaded dress.* Cambridge, MA: Candlewick. Mochizuki, K. (1993). *Baseball saved us.* New York: Lee & Low. Whelan, G. (1992). *Goodbye, Vietnam.* New York: Knopf. Yep, L. (1975). *Dragonwings.* New York: HarperCollins.
Hispanic Americans	Few Hispanic American writers write for children and adolescents, even though Hispanic Americans are one of the largest cultural groups in the United States. Two major authors are Nicholasa Mohr, who writes about Puerto Rican Americans, and Gary Soto, who writes about Mexican Americans.	Cisneros, S. (1983). *The house on Mango Street.* New York: Vintage Books. Jimenez, F. (1999). *The circuit: Stories from the life of a migrant child.* Boston: Houghton Mifflin. Mohr, N. (1979). *Felita.* New York: Dial. Mohr, N. (1988). *In Nueva York.* Houston: Arte Publico. Rice, D. (2001). *Crazy loco.* New York: Dial. Ryan, P. M. (2000). *Esperanza rising.* New York: Scholastic. Soto, G. (1992). *The skirt.* New York: Delacorte. Soto, G. (2000). *Baseball in April and other stories.* San Diego: Harcourt Brace.
Native Americans	Books are available about Native Americans, but few have been written by Native American authors. Most books are retellings of myths and legends. Books about the tribes and biographies about Native American chiefs are also available.	Erdrich, L. (1999). *The birchbark house.* New York: Hyperion. George, J. C. (1972). *Julie of the wolves.* New York: HarperCollins. Hobbs, W. (1996). *Far north.* New York: Morrow. Osborne, M. P. (2000). *Adaline's falling star.* New York: Scholastic. Smith, C. L. (2001). *Rain is not my Indian name.* New York: HarperCollins. Smith, C. L. (2002). *Indian shoes.* New York: HarperCollins. Speare, E. G. (1983). *The sign of the beaver.* Boston: Houghton Mifflin. Speare, E. G. (2001). *Calico captive.* Boston: Houghton Mifflin.

challenge traditional assumptions and gain a more balanced view of historical events and the contributions of people from various cultural groups. They learn that traditional historical accounts have emphasized the contributions of European Americans, particularly those made by men.

Fourth, multicultural literature raises issues of social injustice—prejudice, racism, discrimination, segregation, colonization, anti-Semitism, and genocide. Almost every book listed in Figure 8-3 can be used to stimulate discussion about the injustice that minority groups in the United States have encountered.

Using multicultural literature has additional benefits for nonmainstream students. When students read books about their own cultural group, they develop pride in their cultural heritage and learn that their culture has made important contributions to the United States and to the world (Harris, 1992a, 1992b). In addition, these students often become more interested in reading because they are able to better identify with the characters and with the events in those characters' lives.

Teachers' choices of books for instruction and for inclusion in the classroom library influence students in other ways, too. Students tend to choose familiar books and those that reflect their own cultures for reading workshop and other independent reading activities (Rudman, 1976). If teachers read aloud culturally conscious books, include them in literature focus units, and display them in the classroom library, these books become familiar and are more likely to be picked up and read independently by students.

LITERATURE FOCUS UNITS

Literature focus units are one way that teachers organize for literacy instruction. Teachers choose a trade book or basal reader selection and build a literature focus unit around the featured selection. Literature focus units include these components:

- a featured selection
- a text set of related reading materials
- opportunities to read the featured book as well as the text set
- ways to comprehend and respond to the featured book
- vocabulary activities
- minilessons on strategies, skills, and procedures
- projects in which students apply what they have learned

These units include activities incorporating all five stages of the reading process. Teachers involve students in prereading activities as they build background experiences and activate students' prior knowledge. Next, students read the featured book and respond to it in grand conversations and in entries in reading logs. Students participate in exploring activities as they learn vocabulary and participate in minilessons. Last, students apply their learning as they create projects and share them with their classmates at the end of the unit. Through these activities, students become a community of readers.

Framework for a Literature Focus Unit

Teachers plan literature focus units featuring popular and award-winning stories for children and adolescents. Some literature focus units feature a single book, either a picture book or a novel, whereas others feature a text set of books for a genre unit or an author study unit. Figure 8-4 presents a list of trade books, genres, and authors recommended for literature focus units for fourth through eighth grades. During these units, students move through the five stages of the reading process as they read and respond to stories and learn more about reading and writing.

Steps in Developing a Unit

Teachers develop a literature focus unit through a six-step series of activities, beginning with choosing the literature for the unit and setting goals, then identifying and scheduling activities, and finally deciding how to assess students' learning. An overview of the six steps in developing a literature focus unit is presented in Figure 8-5 on p. 258. Although there are literature focus unit planning guides available for purchase in school supply stores, teachers need to make the plans themselves because they are the ones most knowledgeable about their students, the books they have available, the time available for the unit, the skills and strategies they want to teach, and the activities they want to develop.

Literature focus units featuring a picture book are usually completed in 1 week, and units featuring a novel are completed in 2, 3, or 4 weeks. Genre and author units may last 2, 3, or 4 weeks. Rarely, if ever, do literature focus units continue for more than a month. When teachers drag out a unit for 6 weeks or longer, they risk killing students' interest in that particular book or, worse yet, their love of literature or reading.

Step 1: Select the Literature.   Teachers begin by selecting the reading material for the literature focus unit. The featured selection may be a story in a picture book format, a novel, or a story selected from a basal reading textbook. Teachers collect multiple copies of the book or books for the literature focus unit. When teachers use trade books, they have to collect class sets of the books for the unit. Many school districts have class sets of selected books available for loan to teachers; however, in other school districts, teachers have to request that administrators purchase multiple copies of books or buy them themselves through book clubs.

Once the book (or books) is selected, teachers collect additional related books for the text set. Books for the text set include:

- other versions of the same story
- other books written by the same author
- books with the same theme
- books with similar geographic or historical settings
- books in the same genre
- informational books on a related topic
- books of poetry on a related topic

Teachers collect one or two copies of 10, 20, 30, or more books for the text set and add these to the classroom library during the focus unit. Books for the text set are placed on a special shelf or in a crate in the library center. Early in the unit, teachers do a book talk to introduce the books, and then students read them during independent reading time.

Teachers also identify and collect supplemental materials related to the featured selection, including charts, diagrams, models, book boxes[C] of materials to use in introducing the book, and information about the author and illustrator. Teachers also locate multimedia resources, including CD-ROMs and videotapes of the featured

Category	Grade 4	Grade 5
Books	Avi. (1996). *Poppy.* New York: Orchard. Blume, J. (1972). *Tales of a fourth grade nothing.* New York: Dutton. Cohen, B. (1983). *Molly's pilgrim.* New York: Morrow. Dahl, R. (1964). *Charlie and the chocolate factory.* New York: Knopf. Gardiner, J. R. (1980). *Stone Fox.* New York: HarperCollins. King-Smith, D. (1983). *Babe: The gallant pig.* New York: Crown. Steig, W. (1969). *Sylvester and the magic pebble.* New York: Simon & Schuster. White, E. B. (1952). *Charlotte's web.* New York: HarperCollins.	Avi. (1984). *The fighting ground.* New York: HarperCollins. Coville, B. (1991). *Jeremy Thatcher, dragon hatcher.* San Diego, CA: Harcourt Brace. Lowry, L. (1989). *Number the stars.* Boston: Houghton Mifflin. MacLachlan, P. (1985). *Sarah, plain and tall.* New York: HarperCollins. Naylor, P. R. (1991). *Shiloh.* New York: Macmillan. Paterson, K. (1977). *Bridge to Terabithia.* New York: HarperCollins. Ryan, P. M. (2000). *Esperanza rising.* New York: Scholastic. Speare, E. G. (1983). *The sign of the beaver.* Boston: Houghton Mifflin.
Genres	Realistic stories Fantastic stories	Historical stories Tall tales
Authors	William Steig Patricia MacLachlan Beverly Cleary	Jean Fritz Steven Kellogg Chris Van Allsburg

selection, multimedia materials to provide background knowledge on the topic, and videotapes about the author.

Step 2: Set Goals.   Teachers set goals for the literature focus unit. They decide what they want their students to learn during the unit, the skills and strategies they plan to teach, and the types of activities they want students to do. Teachers identify three or four broad goals for the unit and then refine these goals as they develop the unit.

Step 3: Develop a Unit Plan.   Teachers read or reread the selected book or books and then think about the focus they will use for the unit. Sometimes teachers focus on an element of story structure, the historical setting, the author or genre, or a topic related to the book, such as desert life.

   After determining the focus, teachers think about which activities they will use at each of the five stages of the reading process. For each stage, teachers ask themselves these questions:

1.   *Prereading*
   • What background knowledge do students need before reading?
   • What key concepts and vocabulary should I teach before reading?
   • How will I introduce the story and stimulate students' interest for reading?

Figure 8-4 (continued)

Grade 6	Grade 7	Grade 8
Babbitt, N. (1975). *Tuck everlasting.* New York: Farrar, Straus & Giroux.	Fleischman, P. (1993). *Bull Run.* New York: HarperCollins.	Avi. (1991). *Nothing but the truth.* New York: Orchard.
Howe, D., & Howe, J. (1979). *Bunnicula: A rabbit-tale of mystery.* New York: Atheneum.	George, J. C. (1972). *Julie of the wolves.* New York: HarperCollins.	Cushman, K. (1994). *Catherine, called Birdy.* New York: HarperCollins.
Konigsburg, E. L. (1967). *From the mixed-up files of Mrs. Basil E. Frankwiler.* New York: Macmillan.	Hesse, K. (1997). *Out of the dust.* New York: Scholastic.	Hesse, K. (2001). *Witness.* New York: Scholastic.
Paterson, K. (1978). *The great Gilly Hopkins.* New York: HarperCollins.	Hinton, S. E. (1967). *The outsiders.* New York: Viking.	Lee, H. (1982). *To kill a mockingbird.* New York: Warner.
Paulsen, G. (1987). *Hatchet.* New York: Viking.	L'Engle, M. (1962). *A wrinkle in time.* New York: Farrar, Straus & Giroux.	Lowry, L. (1993). *The giver.* Boston: Houghton Mifflin.
Sachar, L. (1998). *Holes.* New York: Farrar, Straus & Giroux.	Philbrick, R. (1993). *Freak the mighty.* New York: Scholastic.	O'Dell, S. (1996). *The black pearl.* New York: Yearling.
Spinelli, J. (1997). *Wringer.* New York: HarperCollins.	Uchida, Y. (1971). *Journey to Topaz.* Berkeley, CA: Creative Arts.	Peck, R. N. (1972). *A day no pigs would die.* New York: Random House.
Taylor, M. (1976). *Roll of thunder, hear my cry.* New York: Dial.	Whelan, G. (2000). *Homeless bird.* New York: Scholastic.	Yep, L. (1987). *Dragonwings.* New York: HarperCollins.
Fantastic stories Myths	Science fiction Historical stories	High fantasy Hero tales
Gary Paulsen Christopher Paul Curtis Jack Gantos	Virginia Hamilton Lois Lowry Richard Peck	Karen Cushman Scott O'Dell Laurence Yep

2. *Reading*
   - How will students read this story?
   - What reading strategies will I model or ask students to use?
   - How can I make the story more accessible for less able readers?

3. *Responding*
   - Will students write in reading logs? How often?
   - Will students participate in grand conversations? How often?

4. *Exploring*
   - Which words will be added to the word wall?
   - Which vocabulary activities will be used?
   - Will students reread the story?
   - What skill and strategy minilessons will I teach?
   - What word-study or wordplay activities will be used?
   - How will books from the text set be used?
   - What writing, drama, and other reading activities will be used?
   - What can I share about the author, illustrator, or genre?

5. *Applying*
   - What projects might students choose to pursue?
   - How will books from the text set be used?
   - How will students share projects?

Figure 8-5   Steps in Developing a Literature Focus Unit

---

1. Select the Literature

- Identify the featured selection for the unit.
- Collect multiple copies of the featured selection for students to read individually, with partners, or in small groups.
- Collect related books for the text set, including stories, informational books, and poems.
- Identify supplemental materials, including information about the author and multimedia resources.

2. Set Goals

- Identify four or five broad goals or learning outcomes for the unit.
- Choose skills and strategies to teach.
- Expect to refine these goals as the unit is developed.

3. Develop a Unit Plan

- Read or reread the featured selection.
- Think about the focus for the unit and the goals or learning outcomes.
- Plan activities for each of the five stages of the reading process.

4. Coordinate Grouping Patterns With Activities

- Decide how to incorporate whole-class, small-group, partner, and individual activities.
- Double-check that all four types of grouping are used during the unit.

5. Create a Time Schedule

- Include activities representing all five stages of the reading process in the schedule for the literature focus unit.
- Incorporate minilessons to teach reading and writing procedures, concepts, skills, and strategies.
- Write weekly lesson plans.

6. Manage Record Keeping and Assessment

- Use unit folders in which students keep all assignments.
- Develop assignment checklists for students to use to keep track of their work during the unit.
- Monitor students' learning using observations, anecdotal notes, conferences, and work samples.

Teachers often jot notes on a chart divided into sections for each stage. Then they use the ideas they have brainstormed as they plan the unit. Usually, not all of the brainstormed activities will be used in the literature focus unit, but teachers select the most important ones according to their focus and the time available. Teachers do not omit any of the reading process stages, however, in an attempt to make more time available for activities during any one stage.

Step 4: Coordinate Grouping Patterns With Activities.   Teachers think about how to incorporate whole-class, small-group, partner, and individual activities into their unit plans. It is important that students have opportunities to read and write independently as well as to work with small groups and to come together as a class. If the

Teachers determine a focus for the literature focus unit and then plan activities to accomplish their goals.

featured selection that students are reading will be read together as a class, then students need opportunities to reread it with a buddy or independently or to read related books independently. These grouping patterns should be alternated during various activities in the unit. Teachers often go back to their planning sheet and highlight activities with colored markers according to grouping patterns.

Step 5: Create a Time Schedule.   Teachers create a time schedule that provides sufficient time for students to move through the five stages of the reading process and to complete the activities planned for the literature focus unit. Balanced literacy programs require large blocks of time—at least 2 hours—in which students read, listen, talk, and write about the literature they are reading.

Teachers also plan minilessons to teach reading and writing procedures, concepts, skills, and strategies identified in their goals and those needed for students to complete the activities that teachers plan. Of course, teachers also present impromptu minilessons when students ask questions or need to know how to use a procedure, skill, or strategy, but many minilessons are planned. Sometimes teachers have a set time for minilessons in their weekly schedule, and sometimes they arrange their schedules so that they teach minilessons just before they introduce related activities or assignments.

Using this block of time, teachers write weekly lesson plans. The stages are not clearly separated and they do overlap, but prereading, reading, responding, exploring, and applying activities are included in the lesson plan.

Step 6: Manage Record Keeping and Assessment.   Teachers often distribute unit folders for students to use. They keep all work, reading logs, reading materials, and related materials in the folder. Then at the end of the unit, students turn in their completed folders for teachers to evaluate. Keeping all the materials together makes the unit easier for both students and teachers to manage.

Teachers also plan ways to document students' learning and assign grades. One type of record keeping is an assignment checklist. This sheet is developed with students and distributed at the beginning of the literature focus unit. Students keep track of their

GUIDELINE 10

Struggling Readers Need to Listen to Grade-Level Appropriate Literature. Even if struggling readers cannot read the featured novels used in literature focus units, they still benefit by participating in these units. They usually can understand the story if it is read aloud to them, and through the read-aloud experience, students acquire new word knowledge, examine story structure and genres, and learn about literature. Students also develop their comprehension abilities as much through read-alouds as when they are doing the reading themselves. Teachers do need to be alert, however, to the possibility that the story may be beyond a struggling reader's listening capacity level and be prepared to provide more assistance, if needed. Teachers can build more background knowledge about the historical period, geographic location, or culture featured in the book, show a film of the story, or give a summary of each chapter before reading it aloud, if students need additional scaffolding.

work during the unit and sometimes negotiate to change the sheet as the unit evolves. Students keep the lists in their unit folders and mark off each item as it is completed. At the end of the unit, students turn in their completed checklist and other work.

Teachers also monitor students' learning as they observe students reading, writing, and working in small groups. Students and teachers also meet in brief conferences during literature focus units to talk about the featured selection and other books in the text set students are reading, projects students do during the extending stage of the reading process, and other assignments. Often these conferences are brief, but they give teachers insight into students' learning. Teachers make anecdotal notes of their observations and conferences, and they also examine students' work samples to monitor learning.

Units Featuring a Novel

Teachers develop literature focus units using novels, such as *Holes* (Sachar, 1998), *The Sign of the Beaver* (Speare, 1983), and *Number the Stars* (Lowry, 1989). Teachers need to decide how to schedule the reading of the book. Will students read one or two chapters each day? How often will they respond in reading logs or grand conversations? It is important that teachers reread the book to note the length of chapters and to identify key points in the book where students will want time to explore and respond to the ideas presented there.

Figure 8-6 presents a 4-week lesson plan for Lois Lowry's *Number the Stars,* a story of friendship and courage set in Nazi-occupied Denmark during World War II. The daily routine during the first 2 weeks is:

1. **Reading.** Students and the teacher read two chapters using shared reading[C].
2. **Responding to the reading.** Students participate in a grand conversation about the chapters they have read, write in reading logs, and add important words from the chapters to the class word wall.
3. **Minilesson.** The teacher teaches a minilesson on a reading strategy or presents information about World War II or about the author.
4. **More reading.** Students read related books from the text set independently.

Figure 8-6 A 4-Week Lesson Plan for *Number the Stars*

	Monday	Tuesday	Wednesday	Thursday	Friday
Week 1	Build background on World War II The Resistance movement ML: Reading maps of Nazi-occupied Europe Read aloud *The Lily Cupboard*	Introduce NTS Begin word wall Read Ch. 1 & 2 Grand conversation Reading log Add to word wall Book talk on text set	Read Ch. 3 & 4 Grand conversation Reading log Word wall ML: Connecting with a character Read text set books	Read Ch. 5 Grand conversation Reading log Word wall ML: Visualizing Nazis in apartment (use drama)	Read Ch. 6 & 7 Grand conversation Reading log Word wall ML: Information about the author and why she wrote the book
Week 2	Read Ch. 8 & 9 Grand conversation Reading log Word wall ML: Compare home front and war front Read text set books	Read Ch. 10 & 11 Grand conversation Reading log Word wall ML: Visualizing the wake (use drama) →	Read Ch. 12 & 13 Grand conversation Reading log Word wall ML: Compare characters—make Venn diagram →	Read Ch. 14 & 15 Grand conversation Reading log Word wall ML: Make word maps of key words →	Finish book Grand conversation Reading log Word wall ML: Theme of book →
Week 3	Plan class interview project Choose individual projects Independent reading/projects	Activities at Centers: 1. Story map 2. Word sort 3. Plot profile 4. Quilt → →	→	→	→
Week 4	Revise interviews Independent reading/projects	→ →	Edit interviews Share projects	Make final copies	Compile interview book

The schedule for the last 2 weeks is different. During the third week, students choose a class project (interviewing people who were alive during World War II) and individual projects. They work in teams on activities related to the book and continue to read other books about the war. During the final week, students finish the class interview project and share their completed individual projects.

Units Focusing on a Genre

During a genre unit, students learn about a particular genre or category of literature, such as tall tales or science fiction. Students read stories illustrating the genre and then participate in a variety of activities to deepen their knowledge about the genre. In these units, students participate in the following activities:

- reading several stories illustrating a genre
- learning the characteristics of the genre
- reading other stories illustrating the genre
- responding to and exploring the genre stories
- writing or rewriting stories exemplifying the genre

Recommended genre units are also included in Figure 8-4.

Units Featuring an Author

Students learn about authors who write the books they read as part of literature focus units. They need to develop concepts of author so that they think of authors as real people—real people who eat breakfast, ride bikes, and take out the garbage, just as they do. When students think of authors as real people, they view reading and literature in a different, more personal way. The concept of author also carries over to writing. As they learn about authors, students realize that they too can write books. They can learn about the writing process from these authors.

One of the best ways to interest students in learning about authors is to teach a unit focusing on a favorite author. In these units, students learn about the author's life and read many of his or her books. Studying authors is easier than ever today, because many authors have written autobiographies, have appeared in videos, and have websites on the Internet. Recommended authors for author units are also included in Figure 8-4.

To plan for a unit on an author, teachers collect books written by a particular author, as well as related materials about the author's life. Six types of materials are:

1. a collection of books written by the author
2. audiotape or videotape versions of the books
3. posters about the books or the author provided by publishers or made by students
4. autobiographies, biographical brochures and pamphlets, and other information about the author
5. letters written by the author to the teacher or former students
6. audiotapes, videotapes, and filmstrips featuring the author

Teachers can locate a variety of materials about authors, if they are willing to do a little extra work. They can check publishers' and authors' websites for photographs and information. Also, most publishers have pamphlets, bookmarks, and posters available for newly published books by successful authors. The Children's Book Council (568 Broadway, New York, NY 10012) regularly publishes a newsletter with information about the promotional materials available from publishers. Teachers can subscribe, or their school library or local public library may have copies available. Librarians can be very helpful in locating information about authors. Many librarians keep files of information about authors that they will share with teachers.

Authors are profiled in a variety of professional resources, such as Roginsky's (1985, 1989) two-volume resource *Behind the Covers: Interviews With Authors and Illustrators of Books for Children and Young Adults*. Authors have also written autobiographical books for children, such as Patricia Polacco's *Firetalking* (1994) and James Howe's *Playing With Words* (1994). Each year, more and more of these books are published, and these personal glimpses into authors' lives are very popular with students. Teachers can also check professional journals and magazines, including *Book Links, Language Arts, Horn Book,* and *The Reading Teacher,* for articles about authors.

For an author study of Chris Van Allsburg, for example, teachers collect copies of all of Van Allsburg's picture books and read them:

- *The Garden of Abdul Gasazi* (1979), the story of a mean magician who turns a dog into a duck
- *Jumanji* (1981), the story of two children who play a fantastic jungle adventure game
- *Ben's Dream* (1982), the story of Ben's trip to famous landmarks in his dreams
- *The Wreck of the Zephyr* (1983), the story of how a boy's ambition to be the greatest sailor in the world turns to ruin
- *The Mysteries of Harris Burdick* (1984), a collection of black-and-white drawings with titles and captions
- *The Polar Express* (1985), the story of a young child who travels to the North Pole on Christmas Eve and learns to believe in the magic of Christmas
- *The Stranger* (1986), the story of Jack Frost's recuperation at the Baileys' farm after he is hit by Farmer Bailey's car
- *The Z Was Zapped* (1987), an alliterative alphabet book
- *Two Bad Ants* (1988), the tale of two ants venturing far from their home, told from the ants' viewpoint
- *Just a Dream* (1990), the story of how Walter learns to value the environment through a series of dreams
- *The Wretched Stone* (1991), a story told as a ship captain's log of how the crew turned into monkeys after staring mindlessly at a glowing stone
- *The Widow's Broom* (1992), the story of a magical broom and how the villagers feared the broom because it was different
- *The Sweetest Fig* (1993), the story of Monsieur Bibot, a coldhearted dentist who gets what he deserves when his long-suffering dog eats a fig with magical powers
- *Bad Day at Riverbend* (1995), the story of Riverbend, a colorless, sleepy western town, and what happens when it is covered with a greasy slime of color
- *Zathura* (2002), a sequel to *Jumanji* in which the Budwing brothers have a space adventure as they play the game

Next, teachers decide which books to focus on and read together as a class, which books students will read in small groups, and which books students will read independently. They also choose activities based on the books and plan minilesson topics. Then they develop a lesson plan according to the time and resources they have available for the unit.

A plan for a 3-week author unit is presented in Figure 8-7. In this plan, the teacher spends the first 2 days on *Jumanji* and the next day on *The Polar Express*. Then students spend 4 days in book clubs. Students divide into small groups, and each day, they read one of Van Allsburg's books. Students rotate through groups so that in 4 days they read four books. Next, students read *The Z Was Zapped* and write a class alliterative alphabet book[C]. For the next 2 days, students read and respond as a class to *The Wretched Stone* and *Bad Day at Riverbend*, and the teacher teaches minilessons on theme using these two books as examples. During the third week, students write descriptions and stories for the illustrations in *The Mysteries of Harris Burdick* and write letters to Chris Van Allsburg. They also read and reread Van Allsburg's books independently and with buddies. To end the unit, students vote on their favorite Van Allsburg book and have a read-around[C] in which they read aloud their favorite quotes from various books. They also do a cubing[C] about the author and his books.

Benefits of Using Literature Focus Units

Literature focus units are successful because students read and respond to award-winning stories and other high-quality books. They connect what they are reading to their own lives, and think about themes such as bravery, friendship, cleverness, and loyalty. The featured selection also provides an authentic context for instruction. Students learn vocabulary words and expressions from the selection through reading, responding, and exploring activities, and they have many opportunities to examine the sentence structure that the author used. Instruction is authentic and meaningful because teachers tie strategy and skills instruction to the selection. In this way, students are able to apply what they are learning to their reading and writing.

Literature focus units are teacher-directed, and teachers play several important roles. They share their love of literature, direct students' attention to structural features and literary devices, and help students analyze a story. They model the strategies that capable readers use and guide students to read more strategically. They also scaffold students, providing support and guidance so that students can be successful. Through this instruction and support, students learn about reading and literature, and they apply what they have learned as they participate in literature circles, a more student-directed approach.

LITERATURE CIRCLES

One of the best ways to nurture children's love of reading is through literature circles—small, student-led book discussion groups that meet regularly in the classroom. In the vignette, Mrs. Bradshaw called her literature circles "book clubs" (Raphael & McMahon, 1994), and some teachers call them "literature study groups" (Peterson & Eeds, 1990; Smith, 1998).

In literature circles, children meet in small groups to read and discuss self-selected books. Harvey Daniels (1994) calls literature circles "a new kind of reading group" (p. 6). The reading materials are quality books of children's and adolescent literature, including stories, poems, biographies, and informational books. What matters most is that students are reading something that interests them and that the reading level is manageable. In these groups, students choose the books they want to read and form temporary groups to read and respond to the books. Next, they set a reading and discussion schedule. Then they read independently or with buddies and come together to talk about their reading in discussions that are like grand conversations. Sometimes

Figure 8-7 A 3-Week Author Unit on Chris Van Allsburg

	Monday	Tuesday	Wednesday	Thursday	Friday
Week 1	Introduce unit Read *Jumanji* Grand conversation Word wall Reading logs Write sequels	Continue sequels Watch videotape of book Make Venn diagram to compare book and video	Continue sequels Read *The Polar Express* Grand conversation Word wall Reading logs	Introduce book clubs (small groups read a CVA book each day and write in reading logs)	Book clubs (continued) ML: Fantasy
Week 2	Book clubs (continued) 1. *The Sweetest Fig* 2. *The Garden of Abdul Gasazi* ML: Chris Van Allsburg	Book clubs (continued) 3. *Just a Dream* 4. *The Witch's Broom* 5. *Two Bad Ants* ML: Writing letters to authors	Read *The Z Was Zapped* Grand conversation Word wall Create class alphabet book ML: Alliteration	Read *The Wretched Stone* Grand conversation Word wall Reading log ML: Theme	Read *Bad Day at Riverbend* Grand conversation Word wall Reading log ML: Theme (continued)
Week 3	Share *The Mysteries of Harris Burdick* Begin writing stories for pictures Read and reread CVA books	Continue writing stories Write letters to author	→ →	→ Share stories → Mail letters →	Vote on favorite CVA book Make a cube about CVA Read-around

the teacher meets with the group, and at other times, the group meets independently. After finishing the book, students also prepare projects in order to share the book with classmates. A literature circle on one book may last from a day or two to a week or two, depending on the length of the book and the age of the students.

The characteristics of literature circles are:

1. Students choose their own reading materials from books assembled by the teacher.
2. Students form small, temporary groups, based on book choice.
3. The small groups read different books.
4. Groups meet regularly according to schedules that students set up to discuss their reading.
5. Students make notes to guide their reading and their discussions.
6. Students choose topics for the grand conversations and ask open-ended questions during the discussions.
7. Teachers are facilitators, not group members or instructors.
8. Teachers evaluate literature circles by observing students during group meetings and with information learned through student self-evaluations.
9. The classroom is a community of learners, and students are actively engaged in reading and discussing the books they are reading.
10. After reading a book, students share with their classmates, and then choose new books to read (Daniels, 1994).

These characteristics exemplify the three key features of literature circles—choice, literature, and response.

Key Features of Literature Circles

As teachers organize for literature circles, they make decisions about choice, literature, and response. They structure the program so that students can make choices about the literature they read, and they develop a plan for response so that students can think deeply about books they are reading and respond to them.

Choice. Students make many choices in literature circles. They choose the books they will read and the groups in which they participate. They share in setting the schedule for reading and discussing the book, and they choose the roles they assume in the discussions. They also choose how they will share the book with classmates. Teachers structure literature circles so that students have these opportunities, but even more important, they prepare students for making choices. Teachers prepare students by creating a community of learners in their classrooms in which students assume responsibility for their learning and can work collaboratively with classmates. In traditional classrooms, children often work competitively with classmates, but in literature circles, students collaborate in order to set schedules, discuss their reading, and develop responses.

Literature. The books chosen for literature circles should be interesting to students and at their reading level. Books that are likely to lead to good discussions have interesting plots, richly developed characters, powerful or poetic language, and thought-provoking themes (Samway & Whang, 1996). The books must seem manageable to the students, especially during their first literature circles. Samway and Whang recommend choosing shorter books or picture books at first so that students don't become bogged down. It's also important that teachers have read and liked the books they choose or they won't be able to do convincing book talks about them. In addition, they won't be able to contribute to the book discussions. A list of recommended novels for literature circles is presented in Figure 8-8.

ELL

For English learners to be successful in literature circles, consider using contemporary realistic fiction set in the students' culture, or provide picture books as choices.

Grade	Books
4	Ada, A. F. (1993). *My name is Maria Isabel.* New York: Atheneum.
	Bauer, M. D. (1986). *On my honor.* Boston: Houghton Mifflin.
	Catling, P. S. (1952). *The chocolate touch.* New York: Morrow.
	Cleary, B. (1983). *Dear Mr. Henshaw.* New York: Morrow.
	Coerr, E. (1988). *Chang's paper pony.* New York: HarperCollins.
	Creech, S. (1990). *Absolutely normal chaos.* New York: HarperCollins.
	Dahl, R. (1964). *The magic finger.* New York: Puffin.
	Danzinger, P. (1994). *Amber Brown is not a crayon.* New York: Putnam.
	Erickson, J. R. (1983). *The original adventures of Hank the cowdog.* New York: Puffin.
	Fleischman, S. (1986). *The whipping boy.* New York: Greenwillow.
	Park, B. (1997). *Skinny-bones.* New York: Random House.
	Smith, R. K. (1984). *The war with grandpa.* New York: Delacorte.
	Spinelli, J. (1991). *Fourth grade rats.* New York: Scholastic.
	Van Leeuwen, J. (1969). *The great cheese conspiracy.* New York: Random House.
	Taylor, M. D. (1987). *The friendship.* New York: Puffin.
5	Bauer, M. D. (1986). *On my honor.* Boston: Houghton Mifflin.
	Byars, B. C. (1996). *Tornado.* New York: HarperCollins.
	Clearly, B. (1965). *The mouse and the motorcycle.* New York: Morrow.
	Clements, A. (1996). *Frindle.* New York: Aladdin.
	Creech, S. (2000). *The wanderer.* New York: Scholastic.
	Cushman, K. (1996). *The ballad of Lucy Whipple.* New York: Clarion.
	Dahl, R. (1970). *Fantastic Mr. Fox.* New York: Puffin.
	Ellis, D. (2000). *The Breadwinner.* Toronto: Groundwood.
	Fox, L. (1984). *One-eyed cat.* New York: Bradbury Press.
	Ruckman, I. (1984). *Night of the twisters.* New York: HarperCollins.
	Sachar, L. (1987). *There's a boy in the girls' bathroom.* New York: Knopf.
	Smith, R. K. (1972). *Chocolate fever.* New York: Coward, McCann & Geoghegan.
	Soto, G. (1990). *Baseball in April and other stories.* San Diego, CA: Harcourt Brace.
	Taylor, M. D. (1990). *Mississippi bridge.* New York: Puffin.
	Wilder, L. I. (1991). *Little house on the prairie.* New York: HarperCollins.
6	Cooper, S. (1999). *King of shadows.* New York: Simon & Schuster.
	Creech, S. (1994). *Walk two moons.* New York: HarperCollins.
	Curtis, C. P. (1995). *The Watsons go to Birmingham—1963.* New York: Delacorte.
	DiCamillo, K. (2000). *Because of Winn-Dixie.* Cambridge, MA: Candlewick.
	Fleischman, P. (1998). *Whirligig.* New York: Holt.
	Fletcher, R. (1998). *Flying solo.* New York: Random House.
	Gantos, J. (2000). *Joey Pigza loses control.* New York: Farrar, Straus & Giroux.
	Hesse, K. (1997). *Out of the dust.* New York: Scholastic.
	O'Dell, S. (1960). *Island of the blue dolphins.* Boston: Houghton Mifflin.
	O'Dell, S. (1970). *Sing down the moon.* Boston: Houghton Mifflin.
	Paterson, K. (1977). *Bridge to Terabithia.* New York: HarperCollins.
	Pullman, P. (1999). *The firework-maker's daughter.* New York: Scholastic.
	Rowling, J. K. (1999). *Harry Potter and the chamber of secrets.* New York: Scholastic.
	Spinelli, J. (1990). *Maniac Magee.* New York: Little, Brown.
	Taylor, M. (1976). *Roll of thunder, hear my cry.* New York: Dial.

(continues)

Figure 8-8 *(continued)*

Grade	Books
7	Almond, D. (1999). *Skellig.* New York: Delacorte.
	Coman, C. (1988). *What Jamie saw.* New York: Penguin.
	Crew, L. (1989). *Children of the river.* New York: Dell.
	Curtis, C. P. (1999). *Bud, not Buddy.* New York: Delacorte.
	Filipovis, Z. (1997). *Zlata's diary: A child's life in Sarajevo.* New York: Viking.
	Flake, S. G. (1998). *The skin I'm in.* New York: Hyperion.
	Haddix, M. P. (1998). *Among the hidden.* New York: Aladdin.
	Hamilton, V. (1974). *M. C. Higgins, the great.* New York: Macmillan.
	Lawrence, I. (1998). *The wreckers.* New York: Delacorte.
	Myers, W. D. (1988). *Scorpions.* New York: HarperCollins.
	O'Brien, R. C. (1974). *Mrs. Frisby and the rats of NIMH.* New York: Simon & Schuster.
	Wolff, V. E. (1998). *Bat 6.* New York: Scholastic.
8	Adams, R. (2001). *Watership down.* New York: Perennial.
	Beatty, P. (1987). *Charley Skedaddle.* New York: Morrow.
	Conrad, P. (1985). *Prairie songs.* New York: HarperCollins.
	Cooper, S. (1973). *The dark is rising.* New York: Simon & Schuster.
	Cormier, R. (1977). *I am the cheese.* New York: Pantheon.
	Cushman, K. (2000). *Matilda Bone.* Boston: Houghton Mifflin.
	Hiaasen, C. (2002). *Hoot.* New York: Knopf.
	Lally, S. (1999). *A hive for the honeybee.* New York: Scholastic.
	London, J. (1994). *White Fang.* New York: Puffin.
	Park, L. S. (2001). *A single shard.* New York: Clarion.
	Paulsen, G. (1998). *Soldier's heart: A novel of the Civil War.* New York: Delacorte.
	Staples, S. F. (1989). *Shabanu: Daughter of the wind.* New York: Knopf.
	Westall, R. (1978). *Blitzcat.* New York: Scholastic.
	Zindel, P. (1968). *The pigman.* New York: HarperCollins.

Response. Students meet several times during a literature circle to discuss the book and extend their comprehension of it. Through these discussions, students summarize their reading, make personal and literary connections, learn vocabulary, explore the author's use of story structure, and note literary language. Students learn that comprehension develops in layers. From an initial comprehension gained through reading, students deepen and expand their understanding through the discussions. They learn to return to the text to reread sentences and paragraphs in order to clarify a point or state an opinion. They also refine their ability to respond to books through these discussions.

How often students meet to discuss a book varies according to the book and the students. When students are reading a picture book, they usually read the entire book before meeting to discuss it. But when they are reading chapter books, students usually meet for an initial discussion after reading the first few chapters and then several more times as they continue reading the book, as Mrs. Bradshaw's students did in the vignette at the beginning of this chapter.

Karen Smith (1998) describes the discussions her students have after they finish reading a book as "intensive study." They often involve several group meetings. At the first session, students share personal responses; they talk about the characters and events of the story, share favorite parts, and ask questions to clarify confusions. At the end of the first session, students and the teacher decide what they want to study at the next session. They may choose to focus on an element of story structure—character development or foreshadowing, for example. Students prepare for the second discus-

Students in a literature circle share their reading log entries.

sion by rereading excerpts from the book related to the focus they have chosen. Then, during the second session, students talk about how the author used that element of story structure in the book, and they often make charts and diagrams, such as a plot profile or an open-mind portrait^C, to organize their thoughts.

The reason why students examine the structural elements of stories is to help them develop literary insights. Teachers assist by providing information, offering comments, asking insightful questions, and guiding students to make comments. Many teachers ask questions to probe students' thinking; a list of possible questions is presented in Figure 8-9. However, Smith (1998) cautions that simply asking a list of questions is rarely productive. Teachers should adapt questions and use them judiciously to help students think more deeply about the stories. Eeds and Peterson (1991) advise teachers to listen carefully to what students say as they talk about a book and to introduce literary terminology such as *conflict, foreshadowing,* and *theme* when appropriate.

Instead of asking, for example, "What are the conflicts in the story?" teachers ask themselves that question and then comment about one conflict in the story that they found interesting. Then teachers invite students to talk about other conflicts they noticed, and finally, students reflect on the importance of the various conflict situations. Or, teachers can take advantage of a comment that a student makes about a conflict and then guide the discussion toward conflict situations.

Students need many opportunities to respond to literature before they will be successful in literature circles. One of the best ways to prepare students for literature circle discussions is by reading aloud to them every day and involving them in grand conversations (Smith, 1998). Teachers create a community of learners through these read-aloud experiences, and they can demonstrate ways to respond to literature that are reflective and thoughtful. Teachers also encourage students to respond to the

Figure 8-9   Questions to Help Students Focus on Literary Elements

Element	Questions
Plot	What are the conflicts in the story? How does the author develop the conflicts? What events lead to the high point in the story? What devices did the author use to develop the plot?
Character	Which characters are fully developed and which are flat? How does the author tell us about the characters? By what they do? By how they look? By what they say? By what they think? How does the story show the development of the characters? If you were a character in the story, which one would you be? Why?
Setting	How does the setting influence the story? Is the setting important to the story? How is time marked in the story? Does the author use flashbacks or foreshadowing? How much time passes in the story?
Point of View	Is the story written from first person or third person? Are the characters' feelings and thoughts presented? How does the author describe the characters?
Theme	What symbols does the author use? What universal truths does the story present?

Adapted from Eeds & Peterson, 1991; Peterson & Eeds, 1990.

books, and they reinforce students' comments when they share their thoughts and feelings, examine the structure of texts, and talk about their use of literacy strategies as they listened to the teacher read aloud.

Gilles (1998) examined students' talk during literature circle discussions and identified four types of talk:

1. *Talk about the book.* Students summarize their reading and talk about the book by applying what they have learned about the structure of stories and other texts as they:
   - retell events
   - identify main ideas
   - summarize the plot
   - discuss characters
   - examine the setting
   - explore themes and symbols

2. *Talk about the reading process.* Students think metacognitively and reflect on the process they used to read the book as they:
   - reflect on how they used strategies
   - explain their reading problems and how they solved them
   - identify sections that they reread and why they reread them
   - talk about their thinking as they were reading
   - identify parts they understood or misunderstood

Virtual Field Experience

How to Use the Accompanying CD-ROM

*F*ollowing examples of good teaching is one means of becoming an effective teacher. Simply reading and researching, however, is not enough. Witnessing meaningful teaching firsthand; observing master teachers; and reflecting on actions, decisions, and artistry behind good teaching can take you further along on your journey toward becoming a better teacher. The CD-ROM included in this edition allows you to observe, reflect on, and learn from a master teacher.

Introducing the CD

This CD contains video clips, grouped by theme, that will lead you through a full day of classroom decisions in a middle grades classroom engaged in literature circles.

Margin notes throughout the text lead you to connections between chapter content and the CD. Take this time to look closely at what you'll find as you open the CD.

Study Buttons
This CD illustrates a teacher and students engaged in various aspects of literacy learning. Each teaching topic has its own button on the navigation bar on the left of the screen. By clicking on the topic of your choice, you move into the specific video clips and discussions of that topic.

Video Clips
Each topic includes nine video clips. Individual clips are labeled according to the topics illustrated. Simply click on the thumbnail of one clip to watch the video segment. Across the bottom of the video screen you'll find buttons that allow you to pause, fast forward, and rewind the clip.

Text Button
The commentators' text for the CD is provided in this area and is available for copying and pasting to your own study.

Internet Button
Clicking on the Internet button will allow you to select and launch an Internet browser such as Netscape Communicator or Microsoft Explorer. Once an Internet browser is running, you can visit the links provided or insert an Internet address and go to literature sources, discussion groups, e-mail, or other relevant sites.

Reflection Comments
As soon as a specific video clip is highlighted, comments concerning that clip also become available.

The Purpose of the CD

This CD provides immediate access to living classroom examples of teaching and learning principles. The examples provide context and anchor thinking in the realities of an authentic classroom.

The *Reflection Comments* allow you to understand a variety of reasons why selected video clips are interpreted as being examples of certain teaching or learning principles. The perspectives reveal the richness of meaning embedded in the living classroom when seen from the viewpoint of various stakeholders, including Gail Tompkins, Laurie Goodman, students involved, and the professional literature that provides the research base behind the teacher's decisions. Be sure to click on the arrow at the bottom that begins the audio.

Click on a topic in the Help Topics menu to find a textual explanation of that item.

Help Topics
The ? button provides a wealth of clear, step-by-step information. Clicking on the ? button opens the help file, where you will find explanations and directions for every button and a guided walk-through using the CD and building your own study.

Click on the Navigation Tutorial button for a 5-minute guide through the navigation, purpose, and uses for the CD.

The two-minute Custom Studies Tutorial is a clear guide through perhaps the most innovative and meaningful piece on the CD, the opportunity to build your own video case — perfect for an electronic teaching portfolio. We will cover that more fully over the next two pages.

Study Builder

To create your own study, begin by clicking the *Study Builder* button on the left-hand navigation bar. Begin with your own question, then look for answers in the numerous video clips provided. For example, consider how you would teach struggling readers or how you would manage the rest of the class during small-group instruction. Compare and contrast teaching and learning principles as they are applied with students at different levels of intellectual, emotional, and physical development. Focus on these or any other question by isolating clips in which Laurie Goodman's teaching supplies answers.

A total of 8 clips can be used in each of your personal ethnographies. *Isolate* and *sequence clips* from the 24 archived clips provided. Drag and drop your selected clips onto an open slot in the grid, then save and name your study. Now you're ready to finish by customizing your study under the *Custom Studies* button.

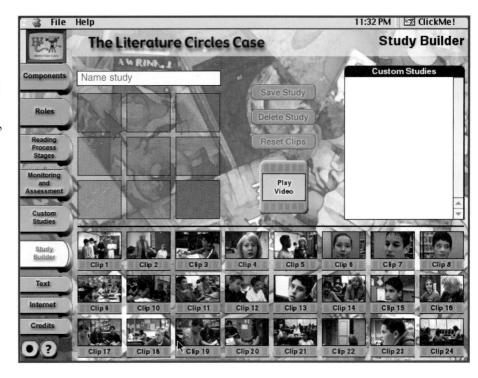

Step by Step

1. Decide on a question.
2. Select clips that focus on that query.
3. Drag and drop the clips into the 8 open slots.
4. Name the study.
5. Save the study.
6. Move on to the *Custom Studies* step.

For a more complete walk-through of this module, click on the *Help* button, then on *Study Builder* under *Help Topics*.

Custom Study

Next, click on *Custom Studies*. Click on the name of your saved study in the Custom Studies field and add your own comments concerning each clip and the way it fits into your study in the Custom Studies commentary. Or add selected commentary from the researchers and participants by clicking on *Text* on the navigation bar, choosing a category, and scrolling through the categorized transcripts. When you find the appropriate comments, simply highlight the section, use the *Edit* button to copy the selection, and paste it into the commentary field on your custom study.

The Custom Studies Tutorial found on the Help screen provides a helpful reminder, should you need a bit of assistance creating your study.

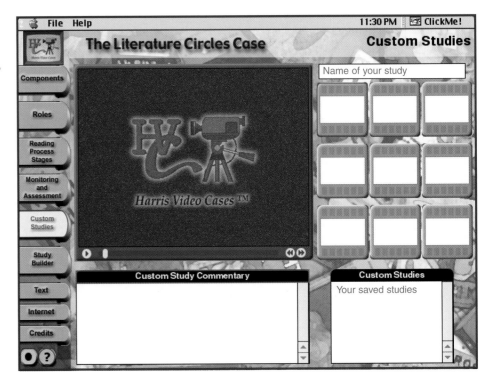

Step by Step

1. Open saved study.
2. Click on chosen clip.
3. Add comments of your own, or pull comments from the text button.
4. When you've added all your elements, save your study to your own hard drive or floppy disk.

Each custom study you create can be used to fulfill an assignment or become part of your electronic teaching portfolio. Create as many custom studies as you like and examine your own understanding of any number of teaching strategies, techniques, and concerns.

3. **Talk about connections.** Students make connections between the book and their own lives as well as to other literature they have read as they:
   - explain connections to their lives
   - compare this book to another book
   - make connections to a film or television show they have viewed
4. **Talk about group process and social issues.** Children use talk to organize the literature circle and sustain the discussion. They also use talk to examine social issues and current events related to the book, such as homelessness and divorce, as they:
   - decide who will be group leader
   - determine the schedule, roles, and responsibilities
   - draw in nonparticipating students
   - bring the conversation back to the topic
   - extend the discussion to social issues and current events

Some teachers have students assume roles and complete assignments in preparation for discussion group meetings (Daniels, 1994; Daniels & Bizar, 1998). One student is the discussion director, and this student assumes the leadership role and directs the discussion. To prepare, the discussion director chooses topics and formulates questions to guide the discussion. Other students prepare by selecting a passage to read aloud, identifying vocabulary words for study, making personal and literary connections, summarizing the reading or identifying main ideas for a nonfiction text, drawing a picture or making a graphic related to the book, and investigating a topic related to the book. These seven roles are detailed in Figure 8-10. Having students assume specific roles may seem artificial, but it teaches them about the types of responses they can make in literature circles.

Teachers often prepare assignment sheets for each of the roles their students assume during a literature circle and then pass out copies before students begin reading. Students complete one of the assignment sheets before each discussion. Figure 8-11 shows a "word wizard" assignment sheet that an eighth grader completed as he read *Holes* (Sachar, 1998), the story of a boy named Stanley Yelnats who is sent to a hellish correctional camp where he finds a real friend, a treasure, and a new sense of himself. As word wizard, this student chooses important words from the story to study. In the first column on the assignment sheet, the student writes the word and the number of the page on which it was found. Then, in the second column, the student checks the dictionary for the word's meaning, lists several meanings when possible, and places check marks next to the meanings that are appropriate for how the word is used in the book. Students also check the etymology of the word in the dictionary, and in the third column, they list the language the word came from and when it entered English.

During the discussion about the second section of *Holes,* the word *callused* became important. The student explained that *callused* means "toughened" and "hardened," and that in the story, Stanley and the other boys' hands became callused. He continued to say that the third meaning, "unsympathetic," didn't make sense. This comment provided an opportunity for the teacher to explain how *callused* could mean "unsympathetic," and students decided to make a chart to categorize characters in the story who had callused hands and those who were unsympathetic. The group concluded that the boys with callused hands were sympathetic to each other, but the adults at the correctional camp who didn't have callused hands were often unsympathetic and had callused hearts. Talking about the meaning of a single word—*callused*—led to a new and different way of looking at the characters in the story.

Figure 8-10 Roles Students Play in Literature Circles

Role	Responsibilities
Discussion Director	The discussion director guides the group's discussion and keeps the group on task. To get the discussion started or to redirect the discussion, the discussion director may ask: • What did the reading make you think of? • What questions do you have about the reading? • What do you predict will happen next?
Passage Master	The passage master focuses on the literary merits of the book. This student chooses several memorable passages to share with the group and tells why he or she chose each one.
Word Wizard	The word wizard is responsible for vocabulary. This student identifies four to six important, unfamiliar words from the reading and looks them up in the dictionary. The word wizard selects the most appropriate meaning and other interesting information about the word to share with the group.
Connector	The connector makes connections between the book and the students' lives. These connections might include happenings at school or in the community, current events or historical events from around the world, or something from the connector's own life. Or the connector can make comparisons with other books by the same author or on the same topic.
Summarizer	The summarizer prepares a brief summary of the reading to convey the main ideas to share with the group. This student often begins the discussion by reading the summary aloud to the group.
Illustrator	The illustrator draws a picture or diagram related to the reading. The illustration might relate to a character, an exciting event, or a prediction. The student shares the illustration with the group, and the group talks about it before the illustrator explains it.
Investigator	The investigator locates some information about the book, the author, or a related topic to share with the group. This student may search the Internet, check an encyclopedia or library book, or interview a person with special expertise on the topic.

Adapted from Daniels, 1994; Daniels & Bizar, 1998.

Figure 8-11 An Eighth Grader's Literature Circle Role Sheet

Word Wizard

Name *Ray*   Date *Dec. 7*   Book *Holes*

You are the Word Wizard in this literature circle. Your job is to look for important words in the book and learn about them. Complete this chart before your literature circle meets.

Word and Page Number	Meanings	Etymology
callused p. 80 "his callused hands"	✓ to toughen ✓ to make hard ? unsympathetic	Latin 1565
penetrating p. 82 "a penetrating stare"	? to enter ✓ sharp or piercing	Latin 1520
condemned p. 88 "a condemned man"	✓ found guilty	Latin 1300
writhed p. 91 "his body writhed with pain"	✓ to twist the body in pain	English 900

Implementing Literature Circles

Students begin by selecting books, and then as a group, they establish a schedule for reading and discussing the book. Students meet with or without the teacher for these discussions. After reading, students create projects to share their books with the class. These literature circle activities involve all five stages of the reading process.

1. **Prereading.** Teachers prepare text sets with five to seven related titles and collect six or seven copies of each book. They give a brief book talk to introduce the new books, and then students sign up for the book they want to read. One way to do this is to set each book on the chalk tray and have students sign their names on the chalkboard above the book they want to read. Or, teachers can set the books on a table and place a sign-up sheet beside each one. Students need time to preview the books, and then they choose the one they want to read after considering the topic and the difficulty of the text. Once in a while, students don't get to read their first choice, but they can always read it another time, perhaps during another literature circle or during reading workshop.

The books in the text set vary in length and difficulty, but students are not placed in groups according to reading level. Students choose the books they want to read, and as they preview the books, they consider how good a "fit" a book is, but that is not their only consideration. They often choose to read the book they find most interesting or the book their best friend has chosen. Students can usually manage whatever book they choose because of support and assistance from their group or through

To see literature circles in action, view the CD-ROM titled *Literature Circles: Responding to Literature in an 8th Grade Classroom* that accompanies this text.

sheer determination. Once in a while, however, teachers counsel students to choose another book or they provide an additional copy of the book so the students can practice at home or with a tutor at school.

Then students form literature circles to read each book; usually no more than six or seven students participate in a literature circle. The group begins by setting a schedule for reading and discussing the book within the time limits that the teacher has set. Sometimes students also choose discussion roles so that they can prepare for the discussion after reading.

2. *Reading.* Students read the book independently or with a partner, depending on the difficulty level of the book. It is also possible for students to listen to a book at a listening center if they cannot read the book themselves. Students consult the schedule they developed so that they know when they have to complete each reading assignment and be ready to participate in the discussion. After reading, students sometimes prepare for the discussion by noting in their reading logs unfamiliar words, favorite quotes, or questions to ask during the discussion. Or, if they have assumed discussion roles, they complete their assignments to prepare for the discussion.

3. *Responding.* After reading the first section of the book (or the entire book if it is a picture book), students meet to talk about their reading. They participate in a grand conversation. The teacher or group discussion director begins this open-ended conversation by asking, "What did you think?" Often the teacher participates in the discussion, but sometimes students meet on their own if several groups are meeting at the same time.

Students also write in reading logs during this stage. They might write reactions, use a double-entry journal format to write and respond to favorite quotes, or assume the role of a character and write a simulated journal.

4. *Exploring.* Literature discussions extend into the exploring stage of the reading process. After students share their responses, teachers often teach minilessons. They may focus on an element of story structure, provide information about the author or the genre, or teach a literacy skill or strategy.

5. *Applying.* Students create a project after they finish reading. Sometimes they simply plan a way to share the book with the class, and in other classrooms, they develop more extensive projects. They may examine an element of story structure in detail, research a topic related to the book, create an art or drama project, read other books by the same author, or write poems, a book, or another text related to the book. They also meet with the teacher to evaluate the literature circle, the book, and their participation in the group. Finally, the group shares the book and their projects with the rest of the class.

The steps in implementing literature circles are reviewed in Figure 8-12.

Monitoring and Assessing Students' Learning

Teachers have a variety of options for monitoring students' work and assessing their learning during literature circles: They can observe students as they participate in literature circles, monitor their work and progress using checklists and assignment sheets, assess students' written work, and examine their self-assessments. Specifically, teachers can participate in these four types of activities:

1. **Observing students**
   - Observe students collaborating with classmates.
   - Observe students reading independently.

Figure 8-12 Steps in Implementing Literature Circles

1. **Prereading**
   - Give a book talk to introduce new books.
   - Have students sign up for the book they want to read.
   - Form literature circles to read each book.
   - Have the group set a schedule for reading and responding to the book.

2. **Reading**
   - Have students read the book independently or with a partner.
   - Use a listening center if the book is difficult for some students.
   - Have students prepare for the discussion by taking notes as they read, identifying favorite quotes, or brainstorming questions to ask during the discussion.

3. **Responding**
   - Have students talk about the book in a grand conversation. Begin by asking, "What did you think?"
   - Have students share their reactions, ask questions to clarify misunderstandings, and make connections to their lives and other literature.
   - Have students write in reading logs.

4. **Exploring**
   - Teach a lesson on an element of story structure.
   - Provide information about the author or the genre.
   - Teach a literacy skill or strategy.

5. **Applying**
   - Have students create a project.
   - Have students meet with you to evaluate the literature circle, the book, and their participation in the group.
   - Have the group share the book and their projects with the class.

- Observe students participating in discussions.
- Observe students' sharing of books and projects.

2. *Monitoring students' progress*
   - Monitor students' schedules and assignment sheets.
   - Monitor the sheets students complete for their roles in literature circles.

3. *Assessing students' work*
   - Assess students' reading log entries.
   - Assess students' projects.

4. *Examining students' reflections*
   - Read students' self-assessment letters.
   - Examine students' responses on a self-assessment checklist.
   - Conference with students about their assessment.

Students can write self-reflections in which they discuss their participation in their group, their reactions to the book they read and discussed, and their reading process. They can also complete assessment forms and checklists in which they assess their own work. An eighth-grade evaluation form is shown in Figure 8-13. Students complete this form at the end of a literature circle and then meet with the teacher to discuss their learning.

Figure 8-13 An Eighth-Grade Evaluation Form
for Literature Circles

Literature Circles Evaluation

Name _____   Beginning Date _____

Book _____   Ending Date _____

Who were the members of your group?

_____

Which roles did you play? What did you do in each role?

☐ Director

☐ Word Wizard

☐ Summarizer

☐ Passage Master

☐ Investigator

_____

How did your group work? Reflect on your experience.

_____

How did the group enhance your understanding of the book?

Assessment Tools

Benefits of Using Literature Circles

Literature circles are an important component of a balanced reading program because students have opportunities to read and discuss stories and other books with their classmates in a supportive community of learners. Some of the benefits of using literature circles are:

1. Students view themselves as readers.
2. Students have opportunities to read high-quality books that they might not have chosen on their own.
3. Students read widely.
4. Students are inspired to write.
5. Students develop reading preferences.
6. Students have many opportunities to develop critical and creative thinking.
7. Students learn responsibility for completing assignments.
8. Students learn to self-assess their learning and work habits (Hill, Johnson, & Noe, 1995; Samway & Whang, 1996).

Other teacher-researchers echo these benefits and also conclude that literature circles are very effective in their classrooms (Short & Pierce, 1998).

VISIT CHAPTER 8 ON THE COMPANION WEBSITE AT
www.prenhall.com/tompkins

- Complete a self-assessment to demonstrate your understanding of the concepts presented in this chapter
- Complete field activities that will help you expand your understanding of teaching with narrative text in the middle-grade classroom
- Visit important web links related to choosing high-quality literature and incorporating it in literature circles and literature focus units in the middle-grade classroom
- Look into your state's standards as they relate to teaching middle-grade students to read and respond to high-quality literature
- Communicate with other preservice teachers via the message board and discuss the issues of using literature focus units and literature circles with students in grades 4 to 8
- Complete CD-ROM activities that will help you make virtual field experience connections to teaching with narrative text

Review

Two ways that teachers organize literacy instruction are literature focus units and literature circles, and through these two approaches, students read and respond to high-quality literature. Three types of literature focus units are novel units, genre units, and author units. Literature circles are small, student-led discussion groups.

Students choose books to read that interest them, and they form temporary reading and discussion groups to read a particular book. The key features of literature circles are choice, literature, and response. The feature that follows reviews how effective teachers use literature focus units and literature circles in their classrooms.

How Effective Teachers . . .
Teach With Narrative Text

1. Teachers choose high-quality literature, including multicultural literature, for literature focus units.
2. Teachers carefully develop literature focus units using the six-step approach described in this chapter.
3. Teachers incorporate activities from all five stages of the reading process in literature focus units.
4. Teachers focus on providing opportunities for students to respond to literature and learn about authors and elements of story structure during literature focus units.
5. Teachers choose quality books, including multicultural literature, for literature circles that interest students and vary in reading level.
7. Teachers allow literature circle groups to set their own reading and discussion schedules.
8. Teachers encourage students to assume roles for literature circle discussions so that they think more deeply about the books they are reading.
9. Teachers and students participate in discussions to talk about the book and share their responses.
10. Teachers use assessment checklists to monitor and assess students' learning during literature focus units and literature circles.

Professional References

Bishop, R. S. (1992). Multicultural literature for children: Making informed choices. In V. J. Harris (Ed.), *Teaching multicultural literature in grades K–8* (pp. 37–54). Norwood, MA: Christopher-Gordon.

Bishop, R. S. (Ed.). (1994). *Kaleidoscope: A multicultural booklist for grades K–8.* Urbana, IL: National Council of Teachers of English.

Buss, K., & Karnowski, L. (2000). *Reading and writing literary genres.* Newark, DE: International Reading Association.

Daniels, H. (1994). *Literature circles: Voice and choice in the student-centered classroom.* York, ME: Stenhouse.

Daniels, H., & Bizar, M. (1998). *Methods that matter: Six structures for best practice classrooms.* York, ME: Stenhouse.

Eeds, M., & Peterson, R. (1991). Teacher as curator: Learning to talk about literature. *The Reading Teacher, 45,* 118–126.

Gilles, C. (1998). Collaborative literacy strategies: "We don't need a circle to have a group." In K. G. Short & K. M. Pierce (Eds.), *Talking about books: Literature discussion groups in K–8 classrooms* (pp. 55–68). Portsmouth, NH: Heinemann.

Harris, V. J. (1992a). Multiethnic children's literature. In K. D. Wood & A. Moss (Eds.), *Exploring literature in the classroom: Content and methods* (pp. 169–201). Norwood, MA: Christopher-Gordon.

Harris, V. J. (Ed.). (1992b). *Teaching multicultural literature in grades K–8.* Norwood, MA: Christopher-Gordon.

Hill, B. C., Johnson, N. J., & Noe, K. L. S. (Eds.). (1995). *Literature circles and response.* Norwood, MA: Christopher-Gordon.

Huck, C. S. (1998). The power of children's literature in the classroom. In K. G. Short & K. M. Pierce (Eds.), *Talking about books: Literature discussion groups in K–8 classrooms* (pp. 3–15). Portsmouth, NH: Heinemann.

Huck, C. S., Hepler, S., & Hickman, J. (1987). *Children's literature in the elementary school* (4th ed.). New York: Holt, Rinehart and Winston.

Jipson, J., & Paley, N. (1991). The selective tradition in teachers' choice of children's literature: Does it exist in the elementary classroom? *English Education, 23,* 148–159.

Norton, D. E. (2003). *Through the eyes of a child: An introduction to children's literature* (6th ed.). Upper Saddle River, NJ: Merrill/Prentice Hall.

Peterson, R., & Eeds, M. (1990). *Grand conversations: Literature groups in action.* New York: Scholastic.

Raphael, T. E., & McMahon, S. I. (1994). Book club: An alternative framework for reading instruction. *The Reading Teacher, 48,* 102–117.

Roginsky, J. (1985, 1989). *Behind the covers: Interviews with authors and illustrators of books for children and young adults* (Vols. 1–2). Englewood, CO: Libraries Unlimited.

Rudman, M. (1976). *Children's literature: An issues approach* (2nd ed.). New York: Longman.

Samway, K. D., & Whang, G. (1996). *Literature study circles in a multicultural classroom.* York, ME: Stenhouse.

Shannon, P. (1986). Hidden within the pages: A study of social perspective in young children's favorite books. *The Reading Teacher, 39,* 656–661.

Short, K., & Pierce, K. M. (Eds.). (1998). *Talking about books: Literature discussion groups in K–8 classrooms.* Portsmouth, NH: Heinemann.

Sims, R. B. (1982). *Shadow and substance.* Urbana, IL: National Council of Teachers of English.

Smith, K. (1998). Entertaining a text: A reciprocal process. In K. G. Short & K. M. Pierce (Eds.), *Talking about books: Literature discussion groups in K–8 classrooms* (pp. 17–31). Portsmouth, NH: Heinemann.

Traxel, J. (1983). The American Revolution in children's fiction. *Research in the Teaching of English, 17,* 61–83.

Walker-Dalhouse, D. (1992). Using African-American literature to increase ethnic understanding. *The Reading Teacher, 45,* 416–422.

Yokota, J. (1993). Issues in selecting multicultural children's literature. *Language Arts, 70,* 156–167.

Children's Book References

Aiken, J. (1963). *The wolves of Willoughby Chase.* New York: Doubleday.

Alexander, L. (1965). *The black cauldron.* New York: Holt, Rinehart and Winston.

Almond, D. (1999). *Skellig.* New York: Delacorte.

Andersen, H. C. (1981). *The ugly duckling.* New York: Macmillan.

Bauer, M. D. (1986). *On my honor.* Boston: Houghton Mifflin.

Blume, J. (1971). *Freckle juice.* New York: Bradbury Press.

Blume, J. (1972). *Tales of a fourth grade nothing.* New York: Dutton.

Brett, J. (1994). *Town mouse, country mouse.* New York: Putnam.

Brittain, B. (1987). *Dr. Dredd's wagon of wonders.* New York: HarperCollins.

Bunting, E. (1994). *Smoky night.* San Diego, CA: Harcourt Brace.

Bunting, E. (1998). *So far from the sea.* New York: Clarion.

Coerr, E. (1988). *Chang's paper pony.* New York: Harper & Row.

Coville, B. (1991). *Jeremy Thatcher, dragon hatcher.* San Diego: Harcourt Brace.

Curtis, C. P. (1995). *The Watsons go to Birmingham—1963.* New York: Delacorte.

d'Aulaire, I., & d'Aulaire, E. P. (1980). *Ingri and Edgar Parin d'Aulaire's book of Greek myths.* New York: Doubleday.

dePaola, T. (1988). *The legend of the Indian paintbrush.* New York: Putnam.

Farmer, N. (1994). *The ear, the eye, and the arm.* New York: Orchard.

Flake, S. G. (1998). *The skin I'm in.* New York: Hyperion.

Fleischman, P. (1982). *Graven images.* New York: Harper-Collins.

Fraser, M. A. (1993). *Ten mile day and the building of the transcontinental railroad.* New York: Henry Holt.

Goble, P. (1982). *Star boy.* New York: Bradbury.

Golenbock, P. (1990). *Teammates.* San Diego: Harcourt Brace Jovanovich.

Hamilton, V. (1988). *Anthony Burns: The defeat and triumph of a fugitive slave.* New York: Knopf.

Howe, D., & Howe, J. (1979). *Bunnicula: A rabbit-tale of mystery.* New York: Atheneum.

Howe, J. (1994). *Playing with words.* Katonah, NY: Richard C. Owen.

Kellogg, S. (1984). *Paul Bunyan, a tall tale.* New York: Morrow.

L'Engle, M. (1962). *A wrinkle in time.* New York: Farrar, Straus & Giroux.

Lewis, C. S. (1950). *The lion, the witch and the wardrobe.* New York: Macmillan.

Lowry, L. (1989). *Number the stars.* Boston: Houghton Mifflin.

Lowry, L. (1993). *The giver.* Boston: Houghton Mifflin.

Lunn, J. (1983). *The root cellar.* New York: Scribner.

MacLachlan, P. (1985). *Sarah, plain and tall.* New York: Harper & Row.

Naylor, P. R. (1991). *Shiloh.* New York: Atheneum.

Park, L. S. (2001). *A single shard.* New York: Clarion.

Paterson, K. (1977). *Bridge to Terabithia.* New York: Harper & Row.

Paulsen, G. (1987). *Hatchet.* New York: Bradbury.

Philbrick, R. (2000). *The last book in the universe.* New York: Scholastic.

Polacco, P. (1994). *Firetalking.* Katonah, NY: Richard C. Owen.

Pullman, P. (1996). *The golden compass.* New York: Knopf.

Rockwell, T. (1973). *How to eat fried worms.* New York: Franklin Watts.

Rowling, J. K. (1998). *Harry Potter and the sorcerer's stone.* New York: Scholastic.

Sachar, L. (1998). *Holes.* New York: Farrar, Straus & Giroux.

Say, A. (1990). *El Chino.* Boston: Houghton Mifflin.

Service, P. (1988). *Stinker from space*. New York: Scribner.

Sleator, W. (1984). *Interstellar pig*. New York: Dutton.

Soto, G. (1993). *Too many tamales*. New York: Putnam.

Speare, E. G. (1983). *The sign of the beaver*. Boston: Houghton Mifflin.

Steig, W. (1969). *Sylvester and the magic pebble*. New York: Simon & Schuster.

Stevens, J. (1984). *The tortoise and the hare: An Aesop fable*. New York: Holiday House.

Stevens, J. (1987). *The three billy goats Gruff*. San Diego, CA: Harcourt Brace.

Sutcliff, R. (1981). *The sword and the circle: King Arthur and the knights of the round table*. New York: Penguin.

Sutcliff, R. (1994). *The sword and the circle: King Arthur and the knights of the round table*. New York: Puffin.

Tolkien, J. R. R. (1938). *The hobbit*. Boston: Houghton Mifflin.

Uchida, Y. (1971). *Journey to Topaz*. Berkeley, CA: Creative Arts.

Van Allsburg, C. (1979). *The garden of Abdul Gasazi*. Boston: Houghton Mifflin.

Van Allsburg, C. (1981). *Jumanji*. Boston: Houghton Mifflin.

Van Allsburg, C. (1982). *Ben's dream*. Boston: Houghton Mifflin.

Van Allsburg, C. (1983). *The wreck of the Zephyr*. Boston: Houghton Mifflin.

Van Allsburg, C. (1984). *The mysteries of Harris Burdick*. Boston: Houghton Mifflin.

Van Allsburg, C. (1985). *The polar express*. Boston: Houghton Mifflin.

Van Allsburg, C. (1986). *The stranger*. Boston: Houghton Mifflin.

Van Allsburg, C. (1987). *The Z was zapped*. Boston: Houghton Mifflin.

Van Allsburg, C. (1988). *Two bad ants*. Boston: Houghton Mifflin.

Van Allsburg, C. (1990). *Just a dream*. Boston: Houghton Mifflin.

Van Allsburg, C. (1991). *The wretched stone*. Boston: Houghton Mifflin.

Van Allsburg, C. (1992). *The widow's broom*. Boston: Houghton Mifflin.

Van Allsburg, C. (1993). *The sweetest fig*. Boston: Houghton Mifflin.

Van Allsburg, C. (1995). *Bad day at Riverbend*. Boston: Houghton Mifflin.

Van Allsburg, C. (2002). *Zathura*. Boston: Houghton Mifflin.

White, E. B. (1952). *Charlotte's web*. New York: HarperCollins.

Zelinsky, P. O. (1986). *Rumpelstiltskin*. New York: Dutton.

chapter 9

Teaching With Content-Area Textbooks

- How can teachers make content-area textbooks more reader friendly or "considerate"?

- Why aren't content-area textbooks a complete program?

- Why should students use informational books, stories, and poems as well as textbooks to learn across the curriculum?

- How do teachers develop thematic units?

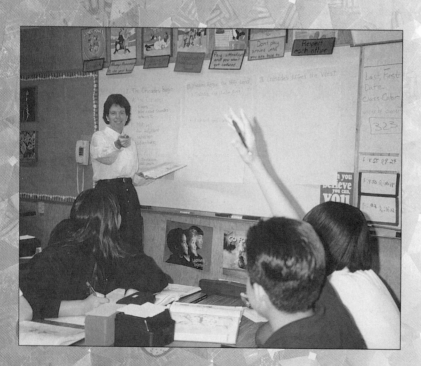

Ms. Boland's Students Study Medieval Life

Ms. Boland's eighth graders are learning about medieval life in their integrated English/social studies block class. This class has been designated a "laptop" class, and students use laptop computers to take notes, write learning log[C] entries, research on the Internet, and develop PowerPoint presentations. They also send e-mail messages to Ms. Boland.

Ms. Boland begins the unit by having her students read Karen Cushman's *Catherine, Called Birdy* (1994), a novel written in diary form. Catherine, the main character and author of the diary, is a young noblewoman in 1290, and she provides a fascinating glimpse into medieval life. The book's humorous tone makes it very popular.

Every few days, students meet in small groups called literature circles to discuss the book, and Ms. Boland sits in on many of the discussions to help students focus on both the events in the story and the historical information they are learning about medieval life. They also write reading log[C] entries using their laptops. They use a three-column chart for each chapter, writing a summary in one column, historical notes in the second column, and a personal, historical, or literary connection in the third column.

After building students' background knowledge and engendering interest by reading *Catherine, Called Birdy,* reading several informational picture books about medieval life, including *Knights* (Steele, 1998), and viewing the video version of David Macaulay's *Castle* (1977), produced by Unicorn Projects (1983), Ms. Boland is confident that her students are ready to begin reading the chapter in their social studies textbook on the Middle Ages.

Ms. Boland previews the chapter with students. They do a text walk together, reading the chapter title, the five main headings in the chapter, the subheadings, and the questions at the end of the chapter. They notice boldfaced words in the text, such as *chivalry,* which they've already learned, and others that are unfamiliar, such as *Saracen.* Ms. Boland reads aloud the sentences with the words, and the students use context clues whenever possible to figure out the meaning of the words. Ms. Boland explains the other words that can't be figured out. They also examine the illustrations, maps, and diagrams in the chapter.

Ms. Boland divides the students into five groups, and each group will be responsible for reading and reporting back on one section of the chapter. Ms. Boland passes out copies of a study sheet to each group to direct their focus to main ideas in each section as they read and prepare to report back. During their presentations, she will distribute additional copies of the study sheet to all students in the class so that they can complete them as they listen to the presentation. The study sheet for the group reading the section on becoming a knight is presented in Figure 9-1.

Each group also adds important vocabulary words from their section of the textbook chapter to "Ye Olde Word Wall," which is posted in the classroom, and students also make their own personal word walls[C] on their laptop computers or using file folders that they have divided into sections for each letter of the alphabet. The class's word wall is shown in Figure 9-2. Ms. Boland's students wrote the words on this word wall in

BECOMING A KNIGHT

Knights were the most important _fighting_ men in the Middle Ages. With the invention of the _stirrups_, the mounted soldiers in the cavalry became the most important part of the army, and knights became more and more powerful off the battlefield, too.

LEARNING TO BE A KNIGHT

Step 1: A Page	Step 2: A Knight's Esquire	Step 3: A Knight
Age 7	Age 14	Age 21
Live with a noble family. Serve meals and learn manners. Learn to ride horses and fight.	Dress a knight for battle. Serve a knight in battle.	Pray all night in a vigil. Dubbed in a ceremony. Receive a sword and spurs.

CODE OF BEHAVIOR

There was more to knighthood than fighting. Knights were expected to follow a code of behavior called _Chivalry_. At first the word just meant _horsemanship_, but it came to mean a way of life. The knights' four duties were:

1. Be honorable.
2. Be brave.
3. Protect the weak.
4. Respect women.

Unfortunately, many knights failed to live up to these high standards.

THE MAID OF ORLEANS

Although women could not become knights, a French woman named _Joan of Arc_ dressed in armor and led the knights in an attack against the English in 1429. What happened to her? _She was burned at the stake._

Figure 9-2 "Ye Olde Word Wall" on the Middle Ages

A	B	C	D
allegiance	bard	castle	dungeon
armor	Black Death	chivalry	destrier
apprentice	bailey	Christendom	dub
archer	battlements	coat-of-arms	dukedom
	battering ram	constable	drawbridge
	belfry	cathedral	
	blacksmith	curfew	
	banquet	crossbow	
	bloodletting	crusade	
	baron	Charlemagne	
		chain mail	
		court	
		charger	

EF	G	H	IJ
falconry	great hall	hauberk	jousting
feudal system	garderobe	herald	jester
	Gawain	heraldry	Jerusalem
	Genghis Khan	heathen	illuminated manuscript
	guilds	humors	
		Holy Land	

K	L	M	N
knight	lance	Middle Ages	nobles
knight-errant	longbow	Medieval	nun
King Arthur	lady-in-waiting	melee	
keep		minstrel	
King John		moat	
knave		mace	
		monk	
		mead	
		mail	
		mortally	
		mercenary	
		manor	
		Magna Carta	

O	P	QR	S
order	page	quintain	serf
	pilgrim	ransom	steed
	pilgrimage	retainer	sword
	peasants	Robin Hood	Saracen
	pope		scabbard
	plague		siege
	pillory		solar
	portcullis		squire
			Samurai
			sally port
			steward
			stockman

T	UV	W	XYZ
tournament	vassal	well	yew
twelvemonth	vigil	watchtower	
tax	unicorn		
tapestry	vanquish		
troubadours	villein		
	visor		

three colors to apply what they recently learned about words entering English from languages around the world. The English words (e.g., *knight, sword*) were written in black, the words from French and Latin (e.g., *plague, medieval*) in blue, and the words from Greek (e.g., *pope, Saracen*) in red. The students were surprised that most of the words were from French and Latin, such as *archer, castle, chivalry, feudal, moat, melee, pilgrimage, serf, siege, squire, troubadours, vassal,* and *villein,* so Ms. Boland taught a minilesson C about the Norman conquest and explained that the lords and ladies in England spoke French (a Latin-based language) during the 12th and 13th centuries.

Ms. Boland and her students develop centers for each literature or social studies unit. They meet to discuss possible center ideas and identify six to eight centers that they will develop for the unit. Students work in small groups to design the centers, collect the needed materials, and write directions. Directions for the centers are displayed on cardboard project boards, and other materials or manipulative materials are put in a tub. Then the centers are set up on counters and tables around the edge of the classroom. Students introduce the centers to their classmates and clarify the activities. For this unit, students develop six centers and they are required to complete at least four of them. The students' centers are described in Figure 9-3. As students complete work at the centers, they usually put their work in their learning logs, which are 3-ring binders divided into sections.

To showcase their learning, Ms. Boland's students create an interactive museum about medieval life. Students working in groups of five create displays on cathedrals, the life of a knight, castles, food, fun and fashion, and other topics. Their displays include posters, artifacts, and PowerPoint presentations. Students work together to research their topics using classroom resources and the Internet. As they work, students assume roles in the group, including:

- Facilitator, who keeps the group on task and solves problems.
- Research coordinator, who makes sure group members know their research topics.
- Internet troubleshooter, who assists group members using the Internet.
- Harmonizer, who helps the group work together smoothly.
- Supply person, who gets needed materials from Ms. Boland.

The students receive grades on the research for their displays and PowerPoint presentations, on their oral presentations, and for their ability to work cooperatively in small groups. Ms. Boland and her students develop a 5-point rubric to assess their research for the museum display. They develop the rubric before beginning to research so that they understand what is expected of them. Figure 9-4 shows the rubric.

Earlier in the school year, Ms. Boland taught students how to do research using books and the Internet, take notes in their own words, and develop a PowerPoint presentation. In this unit, her focus is on the students' oral presentation skills. In a series of minilessons after students begin assembling their displays, she models how to talk about their displays, present a demonstration, and share information with the audience.

Each group creates a display on a topic related to medieval life for a 6-foot table using posters or display boards, PowerPoint presentations, and artifacts. In addition, students prepare costumes to wear on museum day. Once

Figure 9-3   Centers for a Unit on the Middle Ages

Center	What the Students Do	How Ms. Boland Monitors Students' Work
Reading	Students read three books or articles from the text set on the Middle Ages.	Students document their reading through entries in their learning logs.
Art	Students make a rubbing of a knight, lady, or castle on black paper using gold or silver crayons.	Students add their completed rubbing to their learning logs.
Poetry	Students write "I am" poems from the viewpoint of a medieval person. They also write color poems, found poems, or other types of poems about the Middle Ages.	Students choose one or more of their poems to revise and edit, and they print out a copy to add to their learning logs.
Vocabulary	Students do a word sort^C of words from the word wall using small word cards. They also choose three words from the word wall and make word maps for each word using index cards that are available in the center.	Students glue the word sort cards on construction paper in the categories that they develop, and add the finished word sort to their learning logs. They post their word maps at the center, and at the end of the unit, they will collect them and add them to their learning logs.
Internet	Students visit at least three Internet sites to learn more about the Middle Ages.	Students print out information that they find most interesting and add it to their learning logs.
Documents	Students make a map of the Crusades or a diagram showing the parts of a castle using materials at the center.	Students add the document to their learning logs.

they have their materials completed, students rehearse their oral presentations, working hard to employ the techniques that Ms. Boland modeled for them.

On museum day, the students' displays are set up in the library, and the costumed students stand beside their displays as other students at the school, parents, school board members, and other community members visit the museum. The students talk with the visitors, sharing information, explaining artifacts, and playing the PowerPoint presentations. The Middle Ages seem to come to life as the students describe a knight's clothing and armor, trace the route of the Crusaders, explain the designs and colors on a coat of arms, and demonstrate jousting using toy knights on horseback while medieval music plays in the background.

Middle Ages Research Rubric

5 Excellent
- More than four sources of information, including the Internet
- Notes are written in your own words
- Time and effort are clearly demonstrated in note taking
- PowerPoint presentation is well designed, very interesting and effective, with many facts, and has no mechanical errors.
- Bibliography is correct
- Three or more artifacts with clear labels or explanations

4 Very Good
- Four sources of information, including the Internet
- Notes mostly written in your own words
- Above average time and effort used in note taking
- PowerPoint presentation is well organized, interesting, factual, and has few mechanical errors
- Bibliography has very few errors
- Two artifacts with clear labels or explanations

3 Good
- Three sources of information, including the Internet
- Notes are mostly written in your own words
- Average amount of time and effort used in note taking
- PowerPoint presentation is clearly organized and factual but has some mechanical errors
- Bibliography has some errors
- One artifact with clear labels or explanations

2 Poor
- Two sources of information, including the Internet
- Notes are mostly copied from sources
- Little time and effort used in note taking
- PowerPoint presentation is difficult to follow, provides limited information, and the mechanical errors make it hard to read
- Bibliography has many errors
- One or more artifacts without clear labels

1 Failing
- One source of information
- Notes are copied from sources
- Little or no effort used in note taking
- PowerPoint presentation lacks organization, provides little useful information, and is very difficult to read because of mechanical errors
- No bibliography, or only part of a bibliography
- No artifacts

Assessment Tools

ontent-area textbooks are important resources that students use to learn about social studies, science, and other content areas, but they should never be considered a complete program. Teachers organize content-area learning into thematic units so that their students can be actively involved in reading. Thematic units offer an enriched learning experience. Stories, poems, and informational books are used both before reading content-area textbooks to build students' concept and vocabulary base and after reading to provide more in-depth information.

The Role of Content-Area Textbooks in a Balanced Literacy Program

Component	Description
Reading	Reading content-area textbooks is a special kind of reading, and students need to know how to read efferently and use comprehension aids to read more effectively.
Phonics and Other Skills	Students apply phonics knowledge as they decode multisyllabic technical terms, and they identify main ideas to remember as they read and study.
Strategies	Students activate background knowledge, notice text structures, organize information, summarize, and use other strategies as they read content-area textbooks.
Vocabulary	Teachers present key vocabulary before reading, develop word walls to spotlight important technical terms, and involve students in a variety of vocabulary activities.
Comprehension	Teachers use a variety of activities to make inconsiderate content-area textbooks easier for students to read and understand.
Literature	Students read stories, informational books, and poems from text sets to support and extend what they are learning through content-area textbooks.
Content-Area Study	Content-area textbooks are designed for content-area study, but textbooks are not a complete program. Instead, textbooks should be part of thematic units.
Oral Language	Students work in small groups and talk as they complete graphic organizers, brainstorm ideas, make posters to share their learning, and create projects.
Writing	Students complete graphic organizers, write in learning logs, and do other compositions to demonstrate their learning.
Spelling	Students learn to spell content-related vocabulary as they make word walls, participate in vocabulary activities, and write reports and other compositions.

Students need to know how to read content-area textbooks because these books differ from other reading materials. Content-area textbooks have unique conventions and structures that students can learn to use as aids in reading and remembering what they have read. They also need to be able to identify and remember main ideas and connect them with their background knowledge. Because many students find textbooks more challenging to read than other books, teachers need to know how to support their students' reading so that they will be successful.

As you read this chapter, you'll learn about the role of content-area textbooks in a balanced approach to literacy instruction. As the balanced literacy feature on this page shows, students apply what they are learning about reading, writing, and oral language as they learn social studies, science, and other content areas.

CONTENT-AREA TEXTBOOKS

Textbooks have traditionally been the centerpiece of social studies, science, and other content-area classes, but these textbooks have shortcomings that limit their effectiveness. Too often, content-area textbooks are unappealing to students, too difficult for students to read and understand, and cover too many topics superficially. It is up to teachers to plan instruction to make content-area textbooks more comprehensible and supplement students' learning with other reading and writing activities during thematic units. Figure 9-5 offers a list of guidelines for using content-area textbooks.

Unique Conventions of Content-Area Textbooks

Content-area textbooks look different than other types of books, and have unique conventions, including:

1. Headings and subheadings to direct readers' attention to the main ideas.
2. Photographs and drawings to illustrate the main ideas.
3. Figures, maps, and tables to provide diagrams and detailed information visually.
4. Margin notes to provide supplemental information or to direct readers to additional information on a topic.
5. Highlighted vocabulary words to identify key vocabulary.
6. An index to assist readers in locating specific information.
7. A glossary to assist readers in pronouncing and defining key vocabulary words.
8. Study questions at the end of the chapter for readers to use to check their comprehension.

The purpose of these conventions is to make the textbook easier to read. It is important that students understand these conventions because they can use them to make reading content-area textbooks more effective and improve their comprehension (Harvey & Goudvis, 2000). Teachers teach minilessons about these conventions and how to use them to read more effectively.

Characteristics of "Considerate" Textbooks

Some content-area textbooks are easier to read than others. Certain textbooks, for example, have a clear organization or structure, whereas others seem to jump from topic to topic. Some textbooks develop topics in depth, but others briefly mention many, many topics. Textbooks are said to be *reader friendly* or *considerate* of readers (Anderson & Armbruster, 1986) when they include these characteristics:

- The objectives, purposes, or main ideas are clearly stated at the beginning of each chapter.
- Adequate background information is included.
- Technical terms are defined.
- Each chapter has an overall structure that links the main ideas.

When textbooks are not considerate, teachers must adjust their instruction to make the text more comprehensible.

Figure 9-5   Guidelines for Using Content-Area Textbooks

1. Teach Students About the Unique Conventions of Textbooks
Teachers introduce students to the unique conventions in content-area textbooks, including headings that outline the chapter, helpful graphics, and technical words defined in the text, and show how to use them as comprehension aids.

2. Create Questions Before Reading
Before reading each section of a chapter, students turn the section heading into a question and read to find the answer to the question. As they read, students take notes, and then they answer the question they created after reading.

3. Introduce Key Terms
Teachers introduce only the key terms as part of a prereading activity before students read the textbook assignment. After reading, the teacher and students develop a word wall with the important words.

4. Focus on Big Ideas
Students focus on the big ideas instead of trying to remember all the facts or other information.

5. Use Graphic Organizers
Teachers have students complete graphic organizers as they read because these visual representations emphasize the big ideas and the connections among them.

6. Include Activities to Make Textbooks More Comprehensible
Students' understanding is enhanced through activities such as exclusion brainstorming[C], anticipation guides[C], and instructional conversations[C].

7. Teach Students to Take Notes
Rather than just advising students to take notes, teachers teach them a procedure to use. Teachers begin by modeling the procedure, next they read and take notes along with students, and finally, after many practice opportunities, students take notes with partners and individually.

8. Ask Self-Questions
Teachers encourage students to be active readers, to ask themselves questions as they read, and to monitor their reading.

9. Use Listen-Read-Discuss Format
Teachers use a listen-read-discuss format. To begin, the teacher presents the key concepts orally, and then students read and discuss the chapter. Or, the students read the chapter as a review activity rather than as the introductory activity.

10. Create Text Sets
Teachers supplement content-area textbook assignments with a text set of informational books and articles, stories, poems, and Internet resources.

Making Content-Area Textbooks More Comprehensible

Teachers use a variety of activities during each stage of the reading process to make content-area textbooks more considerate and to improve students' comprehension of what they have read. Figure 9-6 lists ways teachers can make content-area textbooks more comprehensible at each stage of the reading process. Teachers choose one or

Struggling Readers Need to Learn How to Read Content-Area Textbooks.

Struggling readers generally approach all reading assignments the same way—they open to the first page and read it straight through. That's a mistake, however, because content-area textbooks are different from novels, and students need to take advantage of a textbook's special features to make reading easier. Students need to learn how to activate prior knowledge by previewing a textbook chapter. They read the introduction, the headings, conclusion, and the end-of-chapter questions and examine photos and illustrations. They locate highlighted vocabulary words, use context clues to figure out the meaning, and check unfamiliar words in the glossary. As they read, students think about the main ideas and make connections. They stop after reading each section to summarize. After reading the entire chapter, they make sure they can answer the end-of-chapter questions. Struggling students learn to read content-area textbooks as teachers explain the special features and model how to take advantage of them.

Content-area textbooks are especially difficult for English language learners to read. Teachers can support these students by building background knowledge, introducing key vocabulary, and teaching the main ideas in advance, before they introduce the reading assignment to the rest of the class, so that ELL students will become more familiar with the topic through two presentations before reading the textbook assignment.

more activities at each stage to support their students' reading, but they never try to do all of the activities listed in the figure during a single reading assignment.

Stage 1: Prereading. Teachers play an important role during the prereading stage; teachers often feel that what they do during this stage determines whether students' reading experience will be successful. There are six purposes:

1. Activate students' background knowledge
2. Build new background knowledge about the topic
3. Develop students' interest and motivation for reading
4. Introduce key concepts and vocabulary related to the reading assignment
5. Preview the text
6. Set purposes for reading

Teachers use a variety of activities to prepare students to read a textbook chapter, and the activities often serve more than one purpose. K-W-L charts (Ogle, 1986, 1989) are a good example. In this activity, students and the teacher make a chart of the things they already know about a topic and the things they want to learn as they read about the topic. As students participate in this activity, their background knowledge is activated and developed, and as they share their knowledge and develop questions about things they want to learn, they become more motivated and set their own purposes for reading.

Other ways to activate and build students' background knowledge about the topic include showing films and videos, taking students on field trips, having students write quickwrites, and reading aloud stories and informational books. Teachers use the gamelike formats of anticipation guides (Head & Readence, 1986) and exclusion brainstorming (Johns, Van Leirsburg, & Davis, 1994) to develop students' interest and motivation. In anticipation guides, teachers introduce a set of statements on the topic of the chapter; students agree or disagree with each statement and then read the assignment to see if they are right. In exclusion brainstorming, students examine a list of words and decide which ones are related to the reading assignment. As students

Figure 9-6 Ways to Make Content-Area Textbooks More Comprehensible

Stage	Purposes	Activities
Prereading	Activate background knowledge Build background knowledge Develop interest and motivation Introduce key concepts and vocabulary Preview the text Set purposes	K-W-L charts[C] Field trips Films and videos Quickwriting[C] Trade books Anticipation guides Exclusion brainstorming Concept maps Word wall Prereading plan[C] Graphic organizers Possible sentences[C] Text walk
Reading	Ensure fluent reading Identify main ideas Organize ideas and details	Listen before reading Read with a buddy Small group read and share Reciprocal teaching Highlighting Graphic organizers Say something[C]
Responding	Clarify understanding Reflect on main ideas Summarize Make connections	Instructional conversations Think-pair-share Learning logs Double-entry journals[C] Write summaries
Exploring	Study vocabulary words Review main ideas Connect main ideas and details	Word walls Word maps and posters Word sorts Read-arounds[C] Data charts[C] Semantic feature analysis[C] Graphic organizers Skim and scan Question-answer-relationships (QAR)
Applying	Draw conclusions Expand knowledge Personalize learning Share knowledge	Read other books Conduct research Write stories, reports, and poems Cubings[C] Create PowerPoint presentations Present oral reports

complete these activities, they become more interested in the topic and want to read the textbook chapter to check their answers.

Teachers introduce key concepts and vocabulary through all prereading activities, but they emphasize key concepts when they create a prereading plan in which teachers introduce a key concept discussed in the chapter and students brainstorm words and

Students view a video program to activate and build background knowledge before reading a chapter in their content-area textbooks.

ideas related to the concept (Langer, 1981). They also begin a word wall and introduce graphic organizers that students complete during reading and discuss afterward. Another activity is possible sentences (Moore & Moore, 1992; Stahl & Kapinus, 1991), in which students compose sentences that might be in the textbook chapter using two or more vocabulary words from the chapter. Later, as they read the chapter, students check to see if their sentences are included or are accurate enough so that they could be used in the chapter.

To preview the chapter before reading, teachers take students on a "text walk" through the chapter. They look through the chapter, noting main headings, looking at illustrations, and reading diagrams and charts. Sometimes students turn the main headings into questions and prepare to read to find the answers to the questions.

Students need to have a purpose when they read content-area textbooks so that they can be purposefully involved in finding an answer. Teachers set purposes through a variety of prereading activities, including K-W-L charts, anticipation guides, exclusion brainstorming, and graphic organizers. Teachers can also have students read the questions at the end of the chapter, have students assume responsibility for finding the answer to a specific question, and then read to find the answer. After reading, students share their answers with the class.

Stage 2: Reading.   Students read the assigned textbook chapter in this stage, and teachers make sure that students can read it and are prepared to identify the main ideas. There are three purposes:

1.   Ensure that students can read the assignment fluently.
2.   Assist students in identifying the main ideas.
3.   Help students organize ideas and details.

Students won't be successful if they can't read the textbook assignment. Sometimes activating and building background knowledge and introducing key vocabulary is all that teachers need to do to ensure that students can read the assignment fluently, but sometimes students need more support than that. When students can't read the chapter, teachers have several options. They can read the chapter aloud to students before students read it independently. In this way, students will be familiar with the main ideas and vocabulary when they begin reading. Or, students can read with a buddy or partner and stop at the end of each paragraph to say something to help them identify main ideas and remember what they just read. Or teachers can divide the reading assignment into sections and assign groups of students to read each section and report back to the class. In this way, the reading assignment is shorter and classmates can read aloud to classmates or read along with them. Students learn the material from the entire chapter as they listen to classmates share their sections. After this sharing experience, students may then be able to go back and read the chapter.

Teachers help students identify main ideas and organize main ideas and details as they highlight parts of the text using marking pens or small sticky notes or by completing graphic organizers as they read. Students can also turn the headings into questions and then take notes to answer the questions after they read each section.

Stage 3: Responding.   Teachers help students develop and refine their comprehension in this stage as they think, talk, and write about the information they have read. There are four purposes:

1. Clarify students' misunderstandings.
2. Encourage students to reflect on main ideas from the reading assignment.
3. Help students summarize the main ideas.
4. Make connections to students' lives and the world.

Students react to the chapter, ask questions to clarify confusions, and make connections to their own lives as they participate in instructional conversations, which are similar to grand conversations[C] (Goldenberg, 1992/1993). In these discussions, the main ideas are discussed and students make comments, ask questions, and connect the information they are learning to background knowledge and their own lives. Teachers are the discussion leaders, and they ask questions to stimulate thinking, provide information, expand students' language using vocabulary from the chapter, and coax students to participate in the conversation.

Students also talk about their reading in small groups and with partners. One popular strategy is think-pair-square-share, in which students begin by thinking about a topic individually for several minutes. Next, they pair up with classmates to share their thoughts and hear other points of view. Then each pair of students gets together with another pair, forming a square, a group of four students, to share their thinking. Finally, students come back together as a class to discuss the topic.

Writing is another way for students to deepen their understanding. They reflect on their reading by writing in learning logs about important ideas and interesting details. Or, students can use double-entry journals to record quotes or important information and then write to reflect on information from the chapter.

Students also write summaries in which they concisely synthesize the main ideas and describe the relationships among them. They also make generalizations or draw conclusions. Summary writing requires students to use complex cognitive strategies as they analyze what they read to determine which parts are important and which are unnecessary and to figure out the relationships among the ideas. Students use what they have learned about the structure of narrative, expository, and poetic texts when they summarize because the structure points to the main ideas and the relationships among them. Researchers indicate that students summarize events in their lives every day, but because the thinking is unconscious, they often have trouble when asked to summarize an oral presentation or a reading assignment in school (Brozo & Simpson, 2003; Marzano, Norford, Paynter, Pickering, & Gaddy, 2001). The minilesson feature on page 297 shows how Mr. Surabian teaches his fourth graders to write summaries.

Stage 4: Exploring.   Teachers ask students to dig into the text during the exploring stage to focus on vocabulary, examine the text, and analyze the main ideas. There are three purposes:

1.   Have students study vocabulary words.
2.   Review the main ideas in the chapter.
3.   Help students to connect main ideas and details.

As they study the important vocabulary words in the chapter, students post words on word walls, make word maps and posters to study the meaning of words, or do word sorts according to main ideas. To focus on main ideas and details, students make data charts and list information according to main ideas. Figure 9-7 shows a data chart that fourth graders made as they studied the regions of their state. Students often hold onto these charts and use them to write reports or for other projects. They can also complete a semantic feature analysis to chart important information.

Students share their completed graphic organizers to review the main ideas in the chapter, or they can work in small groups to make posters to highlight main ideas and details from sections of the chapter. Then each group presents the information to the class and displays the poster on the wall.

Students learn to use two special types of reading—skimming and scanning—in content-area textbook activities. In skimming, students read quickly and superficially to get the general idea; in scanning, they reread quickly to locate specific information. Students skim as they preview or to locate a word for the word wall. In contrast, students use scanning to locate details for data charts and to find specific sentences for a read-around.

Stage 5: Applying.   Teachers support students as they extend their learning and apply what they have learned in a variety of projects and other activities. There are four purposes:

1.   Expand students' knowledge about the topic.
2.   Encourage students to draw conclusions.
3.   Have students personalize their learning.
4.   Expect students to share their knowledge.

Students read other books, consult the Internet, interview people, and conduct research to extend their knowledge about the topic. As they write and develop presentations and use the information they have learned, they often draw conclusions. Cubing (Neeld, 1986) is a good way to encourage students to think about a topic and consider it from different viewpoints. To make a cube, students describe a topic, compare it to something else, associate the topic with something else, analyze the topic, apply the topic, and argue for or against it. The "apply" side from a sixth-grade class's

Minilesson

Topic: Writing Summaries
Grade: Fourth Grade
Time: Five 30-minute sessions

Mr. Surabian plans to teach his students how to write a summary; only a few of his students seem familiar with the term *summary writing,* and none of the fourth graders know how to write one. Writing a summary is one of the state's fourth-grade standards, and the prompt for the state's fourth-grade writing assessment often requires summary writing. The teacher recognizes that his students need both instruction in how to write a summary and many opportunities to practice summary writing if they are to be successful on the state's achievement tests.

1. Introduce the Topic

Mr. Surabian explains that a summary is a brief statement of the main points of an article. He presents a poster with these characteristics of a summary:

- A summary tells the main ideas.
- A summary is organized to show connections between the main ideas.
- A summary has a generalization or a conclusion.
- A summary is written in a student's own words.
- A summary is brief.

2. Share Examples

Mr. Surabian shares a one-page article about Wilbur and Orville Wright and the summary he has written about it. The students check that the summary meets all of the characteristics on the poster. Then he shares a second article about mummification, and the students pick out the main ideas and highlight them. Next, Mr. Surabian draws a diagram to show the relationships among the ideas, and they develop a generalization or conclusion statement. Then he shares his summary, and the fourth graders check that he included the main ideas and that the summary meets all of the characteristics on the poster.

3. Provide Information

The next day, Mr. Surabian reviews the characteristics of a summary and shares an article about motorcycles. Together the students read it, identify and highlight the main ideas, draw a diagram to illustrate the relationships among the ideas, and create a generalization or conclusion statement. After this preparation, they write a summary of the article. They check that their summary meets the characteristics listed on the classroom poster. On the third day, Mr. Surabian and his students repeat the process with another article about rain forests.

4. Guide Practice

On the fourth day, Mr. Surabian shares an article about the Mississippi River. The students read and discuss it, identifying the main ideas, relationships among the ideas, and possible conclusions. Then the teacher divides the students into small groups, and each group writes a summary. Afterward, they share their summaries and check them against the poster. The class repeats this activity the next day; this time, they read about porpoises. Mr. Surabian shortens the time spent discussing the article and identifying main ideas and conclusions so that students must assume more responsibility for developing and writing the summary.

5. Assess Learning

Mr. Surabian assesses students' learning by monitoring them as they work in small groups. He identifies several students who need additional practice, and he plans additional minilessons with them.

Figure 9-7   A Fourth Grader's Data Chart on California

REGION	VEGETATION	ANIMALS	PLACES	HISTORY	ECONOMY
North	Redwood tres	Grizzly Bears Salmon	Eureka Napa Valley	Sutter's Fort GOLD!	Logging Wine
North Coast	Redwood trees Giant Sequoia tres	Seals Sea Otters Monarch Butterflies	San Francisco	Chinatown Cable Cars Earthquake	Computers Ghirardelli chocolate Levis
South Coast	Palm tres Orange tres	Gray whales Condors	Los Angeles Hollywood	El Camino Real missions O.J. Simpson Earthquake	Disneyland TV + movies airplanes
Central Valley	Poppies	Quail	Fresno Sacramento	capital Pony Express Railroad	grapes Peaches Cotton Almond
Sierra Nevada	Giant Sequoia Lupine	Mule Deer Golden eagles Black Baers	Yosemite	John Muir	Skiing

cubing on ancient Greece is shown in Figure 9-8. To make this cube, the students painted a large square box. Then they worked in six groups to write each viewpoint. Then they attached their final copies to the box and added decorations.

Students often write reports, create PowerPoint presentations, or present oral reports to share what they have learned, but many other projects are possible. Students can write poems, present dramatic presentations, or create paper or cloth quilts[C] with information recorded on each square.

In the vignette at the beginning of the chapter, Ms. Boland used many of these activities in each stage of the reading process. She used trade books (stories and informational books) to activate and build background knowledge and did a text walk to preview the chapter during the prereading stage. In the reading stage, the students completed graphic organizers as they read, and during the responding stage, they shared their completed graphic organizers and discussed the main ideas in an instructional conversation. They studied vocabulary words and participated in centers during the exploring stage, and as a culminating activity, students created museum displays to extend and share their knowledge.

Learning How to Study

Students in fourth through eighth grades are often asked to remember content-area material that they've read for an instructional conversation or other discussion, to take

Figure 9-8   One Side of a Sixth-Grade Class's
Cubing on Ancient Greece

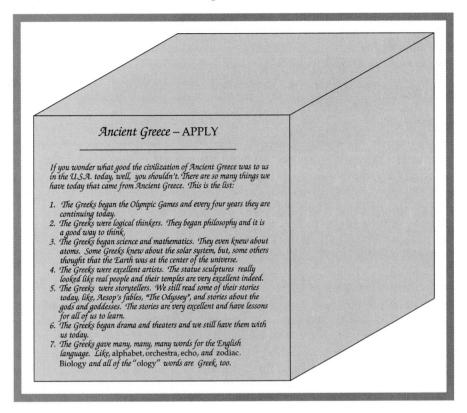

Ancient Greece – APPLY

If you wonder what good the civilization of Ancient Greece was to us in the U.S.A. today, well, you shouldn't. There are so many things we have today that came from Ancient Greece. This is the list:

1. *The Greeks began the Olympic Games and every four years they are continuing today.*
2. *The Greeks were logical thinkers. They began philosophy and it is a good way to think.*
3. *The Greeks began science and mathematics. They even knew about atoms. Some Greeks knew about the solar system, but, some others thought that the Earth was at the center of the universe.*
4. *The Greeks were excellent artists. The statue sculptures really looked like real people and their temples are very excellent indeed.*
5. *The Greeks were storytellers. We still read some of their stories today, like, Aesop's fables, "The Odyssey", and stories about the gods and goddesses. The stories are very excellent and have lessons for all of us to learn.*
6. *The Greeks began drama and theaters and we still have them with us today.*
7. *The Greeks gave many, many, many words for the English language. Like, alphabet, orchestra, echo, and zodiac. Biology and all of the "ology" words are Greek, too.*

a test, or for an oral or written project. The traditional way to study is to try to memorize a list of facts, but researchers have found that other strategies—those that require students to think critically and elaborate ideas—are the most effective (Brozo & Simpson, 2003). As they study, students need to:

- restate main ideas in their own words
- make connections among main ideas
- add details to each of the main ideas
- ask questions about the importance of the ideas
- monitor whether they understand the ideas

Students use these five strategies as they study class notes and complete graphic organizers, draw clusters^C or other diagrams and add main ideas and details, or orally rehearse by explaining main ideas to themselves.

Taking Notes.   When students take notes, they identify what is most important and then restate it in their own words. They select and organize main ideas, identify organizational patterns, paraphrase and summarize information, and use abbreviations and symbols to take notes more quickly. Copying information verbatim is less effective than restating information because students are less actively involved in understanding what they are reading.

Students take notes in different ways. They can make outlines or bulleted lists, draw flow charts, clusters, and other diagrams, or make double-entry journals with notes in one column and their interpretations in the other column. Or, if students can mark on the text they are reading, they underline or highlight main ideas and write notes in the margin.

Too often, teachers encourage students to take notes without teaching them how to do it. It is important that teachers share copies of notes they've taken so students see different styles of note taking, and that they demonstrate note taking—identifying main ideas, organizing them, and restating information in their own words—as students read an article or excerpt from a content-area textbook. Once students understand how to identify main ideas and to state the ideas in their own words, they need opportunities to practice note taking. First, they work in small groups to take notes collaboratively, and then they work with a partner.

Teachers often use study guides, as Ms. Boland did in the vignette at the beginning of the chapter, to direct students toward the main ideas when they read content-area textbooks. Teachers create the study guides using diagrams, charts, lists, and sentences, and students complete them as they read using information and vocabulary from the chapter. Afterward, they review their completed study guides with partners, small groups, or the whole class and check that their work is correct.

It's also important that teachers teach students how to review notes to study for quizzes and tests. Too often, students think they're done with notes once they've written them because they don't understand that the notes are a study tool.

Question-Answer-Relationships (QAR). Students use Taffy Raphael's question-answer-relationships (QAR) technique (Raphael & McKinney, 1983; Raphael & Wonnacott, 1985) to understand how to answer questions written at the end of content-area textbook chapters. The technique teaches students to be consciously aware of whether they are likely to find the answer to a question "right there" on the page, between the lines, or beyond the information provided in the text. By being aware of the requirements posed by a question, students are in a better position to be able to answer it correctly and to use the activity as a study strategy.

GUIDELINE 12

Struggling Students Need to Learn How to Study. It rarely works to simply tell struggling students to study because they often don't know how to study. Studying is a process that involves three parts. First, students activate background knowledge and prepare to read a content-area textbook chapter. They preview the chapter, noting the organization and main ideas. Second, as they read each section, students stop to take notes or complete study guides. They also make personal connections and connections to the world around them; these connections are important because people rarely remember information without connections. Teachers ensure that students understand the main ideas and key vocabulary words as they participate in instructional conversations and they check students' notes and study guides. Finally, students learn how to review their notes: They reread their notes, draw diagrams to show the organization among the ideas, and orally rehearse answers to questions the teacher has supplied or to questions they have generated.

QAR differentiates among four types of questions and the kinds of thinking required to answer them. Some questions require only literal thinking, whereas others demand higher inferential or evaluative levels of thinking. The four types of questions are:

1. *Right There Questions.* Readers find the answer "right there" in the text, usually in the same sentence as the words from the question. These are literal-level questions.
2. *Think and Search Questions.* The answer is in the text, but readers must search for it in different parts of the text and put the ideas together. Students use inferential thinking to answer these questions.
3. *Author and Me Questions.* Readers use a combination of the author's ideas and their own ideas to answer the question. Students use both inferential thinking and personal connections to answer these questions.
4. *On My Own Questions.* Readers use their own ideas to answer the question; sometimes it is not even necessary to read the text to answer it. These are evaluative level questions.

The first two types of questions are known as "in the book" questions because the answers to the questions can be found in the book, and the last two types of questions are "in the head" (Raphael, 1986) questions because they require information and ideas not presented in the book.

Teachers introduce the four types of questions and explain that the goal of this technique is for students to become more aware of the strategic nature of comprehension. Figure 9-9 presents a QAR chart developed by an eighth grader. Students

Figure 9-9 An Eighth Grader's QAR Chart

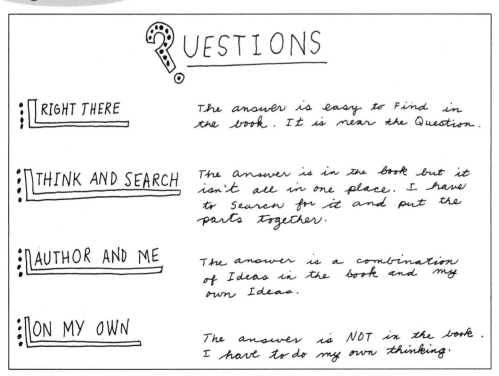

QUESTIONS

RIGHT THERE — The answer is easy to find in the book. It is near the Question.

THINK AND SEARCH — The answer is in the book but it isn't all in one place. I have to Search for it and put the parts together.

AUTHOR AND ME — The answer is a combination of Ideas in the book and my own Ideas.

ON MY OWN — The answer is NOT in the book. I have to do my own thinking.

need plenty of practice identifying the types of questions and deciding how they will answer questions before they actually write answers.

The SQ3R Study Strategy. Students in the seventh and eighth grade also need to learn how to use the SQ3R study strategy[C], a five-step technique in which students survey, question, read, recite, and review as they study a content-area reading assignment. The SQ3R study strategy incorporates before-, during-, and after-reading components. This study strategy was devised in the 1930s and has been researched and thoroughly documented as a very effective technique (Anderson & Armbruster, 1984; Caverly & Orlando, 1991; Topping & McManus, 2002).

Teachers introduce the SQ3R study strategy and provide opportunities for students to practice each step. At first, students can work together as a class as they use the strategy with a text the teacher is reading to them. Then students can work with partners and in small groups before using the strategy individually. Teachers need to emphasize that if students simply begin reading the first page of the assignment without doing the first two steps, they won't be able to remember as much of what they read. When students are in a hurry and skip some of the steps, the strategy will not be as successful.

Why Aren't Content-Area Textbooks Enough?

Sometimes content-area textbooks are used as the entire instructional program in social studies or science, but that's not a good idea. Textbooks typically only survey topics; other instructional materials are needed to provide depth and understanding. Students need to read, write, and discuss topics. It is most effective to use the reading process and then extend students' learning with projects. Developing thematic units with content-area textbooks as one resource is a much better idea than using content-area textbooks as the only reading material.

Teachers supervise as students identify main ideas and take notes from content-area textbooks.

THEMATIC UNITS

Thematic units are interdisciplinary units that integrate reading and writing with social studies, science, and other curricular areas. Students are often involved in planning the thematic units and identifying some of the questions they want to explore and the activities that interest them. Students are involved in authentic and meaningful learning activities, not reading chapters in content-area textbooks in order to answer the questions at the end of the chapter. Textbooks are often used as a resource, but only one of many available resources. Students explore topics that interest them and research answers to questions they have posed and are genuinely interested in answering. Students share their learning at the end of the unit, as Ms. Boland's students did in the vignette at the beginning of the chapter, and are assessed on what they have learned as well as the processes they used in learning and working in the classroom.

English language learners develop in-depth knowledge through thematic units because they study concepts in authentic and meaningful ways.

Teachers organize content-area study into thematic units, and together with students, they identify big ideas to investigate. Units are time-consuming because student-constructed learning takes time. Teachers can't try to cover every topic; if they do, their students will probably learn very little. Teachers must make careful choices as they plan units, because only a relatively few topics can be presented in depth during a school year. During thematic units, students need opportunities to question, discuss, explore, and apply what they are learning (Harvey, 1998). It takes time for students to become deeply involved in learning so that they can apply what they are learning in their own lives. The only way students acquire a depth of knowledge is by focusing on key concepts.

How to Develop a Thematic Unit

To begin planning a thematic unit, teachers choose the general topic and then identify three or four key concepts that they want to develop through the unit. The goal of a unit is not to teach a collection of facts but to help students grapple with several big understandings (Tunnell & Ammon, 1993). Next, teachers identify the resources that they have available for the unit and develop their teaching plan. An overview of nine important considerations in developing a thematic unit is presented in Figure 9-10 and discussed in the following sections.

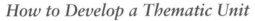

1. ***Collect a text set of stories, informational books, magazine and Internet articles, and poems.*** Teachers collect books, magazine and Internet articles, and reference books for the text set related to the unit. The text set is placed in the special area in the classroom library for materials related to the unit. Teachers plan to read some books aloud to students, and others will be read independently or in small groups. These materials can also be used for minilessons—to teach students, for example, about expository text structures or how to take notes. Other books can be used as models or patterns for writing projects. Teachers also write poems on charts to share with students or arrange a bulletin board display of the poems.

2. ***Coordinate content-area textbook readings.*** Teachers review the content-area textbook chapter related to the unit and decide how to use it most effectively in the unit. They might decide to use the textbook to introduce the unit, have students read it along with other activities, or use it to review main ideas at the end of the unit. They also think about how they can make the textbook more comprehensible and decide on activities for each stage of the reading process.

Figure 9-10   The Steps in Developing a Thematic Unit

1. Collect a text set of reading materials
- Include books, magazine and Internet articles, and reference books in the text set
- Place the text set in a special area in the classroom library
- Identify some books to read aloud to students
- Identify other books for literature circles, minilessons, or other special projects

2. Coordinate content-area textbook readings
- Review textbook chapter(s) related to the unit
- Decide how and when to use the textbook
- Identify ways to make the textbook more comprehensible
- Prepare anticipation guides, graphic organizers, and other materials to support textbook use

3. Locate Internet and other multimedia materials
- Collect multimedia materials related to the unit
- Review the multimedia materials
- Decide which materials to use to develop students' background knowledge
- Decide which materials to use to teach key concepts
- Decide which materials to use in centers and for students' projects

4. Identify potential words for the word wall
- Preview the content-area textbook and books in the text set to identify potential words for the word wall
- Plan vocabulary activities using these words

5. Plan how students will use learning logs
- Decide how to use learning logs
- Make a sample learning log

6. Identify literacy skills and strategies to teach
- Choose skills and strategies to introduce or review
- Plan minilessons to teach these literacy skills and strategies using content area materials

7. Design centers to support content-area and literacy learning
- Plan centers to practice literacy skills and strategies
- Design other centers to examine content-area concepts and vocabulary

8. Brainstorm possible projects
- Identify a list of possible culminating projects
- Collect needed materials and supplies

9. Plan for the unit assessment
- Decide how to assess students' learning
- Create checklists, rubrics, and other forms

3. *Locate Internet and other multimedia materials.* Teachers locate videos, CD-ROMs, Internet websites, computer programs, maps, models, and other materials to be used in connection with the unit. Some materials are used to develop students' background knowledge about the unit, and others are used in teaching the key concepts. Teachers use some multimedia materials for lessons and set up other materials in centers. Also, students create multimedia materials during the unit to display in the

classroom. For more information about using the Internet, check the Technology Link on pages 306–307.

4. ***Identify potential words for the word wall.*** Teachers preview books in the text set and identify potential words for the word wall. This list is useful in planning vocabulary activities, but teachers do not simply use their word lists for the classroom word wall. Students and the teacher develop the classroom word wall as they read and discuss the key concepts and other information related to the unit.

5. ***Plan how students will use learning logs.*** Teachers plan for students to keep learning logs in which they can take notes, write questions, make observations, clarify their thinking, and write reactions to what they read during thematic units (Tompkins, 2004).

6. ***Identify literacy skills and strategies to teach during the unit.*** Teachers plan minilessons to teach literacy skills and strategies, such as using an index, skimming and scanning a text, researching on the Internet, writing an alphabet book[C], and conducting an interview. Students have opportunities to apply what they are learning in minilessons in reading and writing activities.

7. ***Design centers to support content-area and literacy learning.*** Teachers plan centers for students to work at independently or in small groups to practice strategies and skills that were first presented to the whole class and to explore topics and materials related to the unit. Possible centers include a computer research center, a reading center with text set books and other reading materials, a listening center, a writing center, a word work center, a map- and chart-making center, a learning log center, and a project center.

8. ***Brainstorm possible projects students may create to extend their learning.*** Teachers think about projects students may choose to develop to extend and personalize their learning during the unit. This planning makes it possible for teachers to collect needed supplies and to have suggestions ready to offer to students who need assistance in choosing a project. Students work on the project independently or in small groups and then share it with the class at the end of the theme. Projects involve reading, writing, talk, art, music, or drama. Some suggestions are:

- Read a biography related to the unit.
- Create a poster to illustrate a key concept.
- Do a cubing to examine the topic from different viewpoints.
- Make a quilt about the unit.
- Create and present a PowerPoint presentation.
- Write a story related to the unit.
- Perform a readers theatre[C] production, puppet show, or other dramatization related to the unit.
- Write a poem, song, or rap related to the unit.
- Write a report about one of the key concepts.
- Create a commercial or advertisement related to the unit.
- Create a tabletop display or diorama about the unit.

9. ***Plan for the assessment of the unit.*** Teachers consider how they will assess students' learning as they make plans for activities and assignments. In this way, teachers

Technology Link

Researching on the Internet

Students can use the vast information resources available on the World Wide Web as they prepare to write reports and present oral reports (Harvey, 1998). Displays at websites include text information, pictures, sound, video, and animated graphics, and they also provide connections to related information using hypertext links. Although most websites have been developed by adults, some have been created by elementary students as part of thematic units, and students especially enjoy visiting these sites. Students can keep abreast of current news events and weather reports at some websites, investigate scientific discoveries and delve into history at other sites, or visit on-line museums and art galleries (Heide & Stilborne, 1999).

The World Wide Web is easy to navigate. Students locate websites with information related to their topics using search engine software. One of the best search engines for students is Yahoo for Kids: www.yahooligans.com. On the search engine's homepage, students type in the topic for the search, and the software program searches for websites related to the topic. A list of websites with their URL addresses and brief annotations then appears on the homepage.

Students review the list and then click on an address to connect to that website. Students look over the site, and if it seems useful, they "bookmark" it or add it to their list of "favorites" so that they can return to it easily. Then students connect to other websites and read the information available there, take notes, and bookmark them if they want to return to them. Students can print out copies of all of the information available in the websites, but they are usually most interested in printing photographs, diagrams, maps, and other graphics to incorporate into their reports. Using the World Wide Web not only enhances students' content-area learning, it also increases their computer literacy at the same time (Leu & Leu, 1998).

can explain to students at the beginning of the unit how they will be assessed and check to see that their assessment will emphasize students' learning of the main ideas.

Teachers consider the resources they have available, brainstorm possible activities, and then develop clusters to guide their planning. The goal in developing plans for a thematic unit is to consider a wide variety of resources that integrate listening, talking, reading, and writing with the content of the theme (Pappas, Kiefer, & Levstik, 1990).

A Fourth-Grade Unit on Desert Life

During this 3-week unit, students investigate the plants, animals, and people that live in the desert. They learn about desert ecosystems, how deserts form, and how they change. They keep learning logs in which they take notes and write reactions to books they are reading. Students divide into book clubs during the first week to read books about the desert. During the second week of the unit, students participate in an author study of Byrd Baylor, a woman who lives in the desert and writes about desert life, and they read many of her books. During the third week, students participate in a reading workshop to read other desert books and reread favorite books. To apply their learning, students participate in projects, including writing desert riddles, making a chart of a desert ecosystem, and drawing a desert mural. Together as a class, stu-

Possible Pitfalls

The World Wide Web is unregulated, and some websites are not appropriate for children because of pornographic, racist, and other offensive content. All schools should use Internet filtering software to block children's access to inappropriate websites. Although some students may be actively searching for these sites, many others stumble into them accidentally when they mistype a URL address.

There is always a possibility that information presented in websites is inaccurate or misleading because there is no editorial review or other regulation of sites as there is in publishing books, magazines, and newspapers. Students should be aware that some information may be incorrect, and teachers should preview websites if possible, or at least review sites whenever students raise questions.

In addition, when students freely browse the Internet, they may waste valuable instructional time as they explore websites and hypertext links. Also, some students become frustrated as they end up at sites that are "under construction" or not available.

The Teacher's Role

Because of the possible problems with websites and Internet access, teachers should preview sites before students use the Internet to conduct research. Many teachers prefer to prepare a list for students of appropriate websites related to the topic rather than giving them free access to the World Wide Web. They can mark these sites with bookmarks or develop a handout for students listing the URL addresses. Teachers can also create their own web pages that incorporate the appropriate hypertext links. Many teachers compile a list of on-line resources in a card file or computer database for each thematic unit to simplify their previewing.

The World Wide Web is an important complement to books, and it links students to the world of information technology. For more information, check *The Teacher's Complete and Easy Guide to the Internet* (Heide & Stilborne, 1999) and *Teaching With the Internet: Lessons From the Classroom* (Leu & Leu, 1998).

dents can write a desert alphabet book or a collaborative report[C] about deserts. A planning cluster for a unit on desert life is presented in Figure 9-11.

A Sixth-Grade Unit on Ancient Egypt

Students learn about this great ancient civilization during a monthlong unit. Key concepts include the influence of the Nile River on Egyptian life, the contributions of this civilization to contemporary America, a comparison of ancient to modern Egypt, and the techniques Egyptologists use to locate tombs of the ancient rulers and to decipher Egyptian hieroglyphics. Students will read books in literature circles and choose other books from the text set to read during reading workshop. Students and the teacher will add vocabulary to the word wall, and students will use the words in a variety of activities.

Teachers will teach minilessons on writing simulated journals, map-reading skills, Egyptian gods, mummification, and writing poems for two voices. Students will also work in writing workshop as they write reports, biographies, or collections of poetry related to the thematic unit. As a culminating activity, students will create individual projects and share them on Egypt day, when they assume the roles of ancient Egyptians, dress as ancient people did, and eat foods of the period. Figure 9-12 presents a planning cluster for a sixth-grade unit on ancient Egypt.

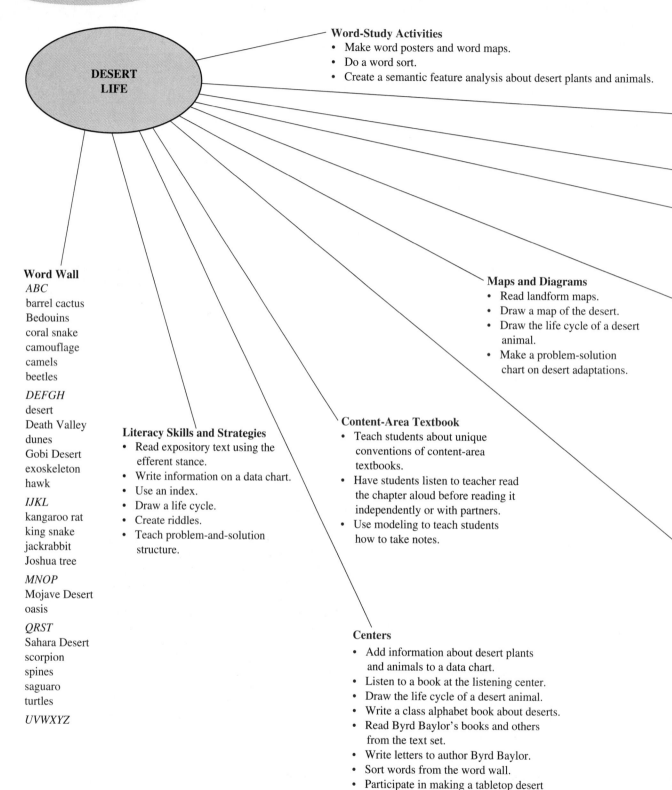

Figure 9-11 A Planning Cluster for a Fourth-Grade Unit on Desert Life

DESERT LIFE

Word-Study Activities
• Make word posters and word maps.
• Do a word sort.
• Create a semantic feature analysis about desert plants and animals.

Word Wall
ABC
barrel cactus
Bedouins
coral snake
camouflage
camels
beetles

DEFGH
desert
Death Valley
dunes
Gobi Desert
exoskeleton
hawk

IJKL
kangaroo rat
king snake
jackrabbit
Joshua tree

MNOP
Mojave Desert
oasis

QRST
Sahara Desert
scorpion
spines
saguaro
turtles

UVWXYZ

Literacy Skills and Strategies
• Read expository text using the efferent stance.
• Write information on a data chart.
• Use an index.
• Draw a life cycle.
• Create riddles.
• Teach problem-and-solution structure.

Content-Area Textbook
• Teach students about unique conventions of content-area textbooks.
• Have students listen to teacher read the chapter aloud before reading it independently or with partners.
• Use modeling to teach students how to take notes.

Maps and Diagrams
• Read landform maps.
• Draw a map of the desert.
• Draw the life cycle of a desert animal.
• Make a problem-solution chart on desert adaptations.

Centers
• Add information about desert plants and animals to a data chart.
• Listen to a book at the listening center.
• Draw the life cycle of a desert animal.
• Write a class alphabet book about deserts.
• Read Byrd Baylor's books and others from the text set.
• Write letters to author Byrd Baylor.
• Sort words from the word wall.
• Participate in making a tabletop desert diorama.

Learning Log
- Take notes.
- Write quickwrites.
- Draw diagrams.
- List vocabulary words.

Author Study
- Share information about Byrd Baylor.
- Read her books set in the desert.
- Write letters to the author.

Projects
- Identify deserts on world map.
- Write desert riddles.
- Draw a chart of the desert ecosystem.
- Make a tabletop desert scene.
- Write an "All About the Desert" book.
- Write an "I am" poem patterned on *Desert Voices*.
- Research a question about the desert.
- Draw a desert mural.

K-W-L Chart
- Use to introduce the theme.
- Identify research questions.
- Use to conclude unit.

Books

Bash, B. (1989).
  Desert giant.
  Boston: Little, Brown.
Baylor, B. (1976).
  Hawk, I'm your brother.
  New York: Scribner.
Baylor, B. (1981).
  Desert voices.
  New York: Scribner.
Fowler, A. (1997).
  It could still be a desert.
  Chicago: Childrens Press.
Guiberson, B. Z. (1991).
  Cactus hotel. New York:
  Holt.

Hirschi, R. (1992).
  Discover my world: Desert.
  New York: Bantam.
Mora, P. (1994).
  The desert is my mother.
  Houston: Piñata Books.
Siebert, D. (1988).
  Mojave. New York:
  Harper & Row.
Simon, S. (1990).
  Deserts. New York:
  Morrow.
Taylor, B. (1992).
  Desert life. New York:
  Dorling Kindersley.

Technology
- View Internet sites about the desert, including www.desertusa.com and www.inthedesertchildrensproject.org.
- Work in small groups to play the simulation game at www.projects.edtech. sandi.net/kimbrough/desert.
- Develop Powerpoint or CD-ROM presentations about the desert.

Figure 9-12   A Planning Cluster for a Sixth-Grade Unit on Ancient Egypt

ANCIENT EGYPT

Maps and Diagrams
- Make a time line of ancient Egypt.
- Create a Venn diagram comparing ancient and modern Egypt.
- Read maps of ancient and modern Egypt.
- Draw maps of Egypt.

Learning Logs
Keep a learning log with quickwrites, notes, maps, charts, and diagrams.

Technology
- View Internet sites about ancient Egypt, including the British Museum's website, www.ancientegypt.co.uk.
- Work in small groups to play missions game at www.webquest.com/egypt/ancientegypt.
- Create a multigenre project on ancient Egypt that includes a PowerPoint or CD-Rom component.

Word-Study Activities
- Make word maps.
- Do a word sort.
- Create a semantic feature analysis.
- Make a word chain.
- Write an alphabet book on Egypt.

K-W-L Chart
- Introduce K-W-L chart at the beginning of the unit.
- Identify research questions for collaborative or individual reports.
- Use to conclude the unit.

Literacy Skills and Strategies
- Use anticipation guides.
- Use the SQ3R study strategy.
- Read expository text using efferent stance.
- Make a time line.
- Analyze root words and affixes.
- Use syllabication to identify words.

Word Wall

ABCD
canopic jars
Africa
Champollion
Amun-Ra
dynasty

EFGH
Egypt
Hatshepsut
embalming
hieroglyphs
Egyptologist

IJKLM
irrigation
lotus
Imhotep
Luxor
Memphis
mummification
Middle Kingdom

NOPQ
pharaohs
Nile River
Nefertiti
natron
pyramid

Old Kingdom
New Kingdom
obelisk
papyrus

RST
Ramses the Great
Tutankhamun
senet
scribes
Rosetta stone

UVWXYZ
Valley of the Kings
vizier

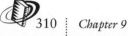

Cubing

Make a cube exploring the ancient Egyptian civilization.

Content-Area Textbook

- Preview chapter with students before reading.
- Divide chapter into sections and have a small group read each section and report to the class.
- Have students complete study guides.
- Use QAR procedure to answer end-of-chapter questions.

Centers

- Draw a map of Egypt.
- Make a mummy.
- Write hieroglyphics.
- Make a god poster.
- Sort words from the word wall.
- Collect parts of speech from text set books.
- Read text set books.
- Research ancient Egypt on the Internet.

Projects

- Keep a simulated journal as an ancient Egyptian.
- Make a time line of the ancient civilization.
- Make a poster about a god or goddess.
- Present an oral report about how to mummify someone.
- Make a salt map of Egypt and mark ancient landmarks.
- Write a collection of poems about ancient Egypt.
- Make paper.
- Present an "interview" of several ancient Egyptians.
- Write a book about the ways the Egyptian civilization has influenced ours.
- Research the Rosetta stone.
- Read two books about ancient Egypt.
- Make a chart comparing ancient and modern Egypt.

Books

Aliki. (1979). *Mummies made in Egypt*. New York: HarperCollins.

Carter, D. S. (1987). *His majesty, Queen Hatshepsut*. New York: HarperCollins.

Der Manueliàn, P. (1991). *Hieroglyphs from A to Z*. New York: Scholastic.

Giblin, J. C. (1990). *The riddle of the Rosetta stone*. New York: HarperCollins.

Gregory, K. (1999). *Cleopatra VII, daughter of the Nile*. New York: Scholastic.

Harris, G. (1992). *Gods and pharaohs from Egyptian mythology*. New York: Peter Bedrick.

Katan, N. J., & Mintz, B. (1981). *Hieroglyphs: The writing of ancient Egypt*. New York: McElderry.

Lattimore, D. N. (1992). *The winged cat: A tale of ancient Egypt*. New York: HarperCollins.

Macaulay, D. (1975). *Pyramid*. Boston: Houghton Mifflin.

McMullen, K. (1992). *Under the mummy's spell*. New York: Farrar, Straus & Giroux.

Perl, L. (1987). *Mummies, tombs, and treasure: secrets of ancient Egypt*. New York: Clarion.

Stanley, D., & Vennema, P. (1994). *Cleopatra*. New York: Morrow.

Stolz, M. (1988). *Zekmet the stone carver: A tale of ancient Egypt*. San Diego: Harcourt Brace.

Ventura, P., & Ceserani, G. P. (1985). *In search of Tutankhamun*. Morristown, NJ: Silver Burdett.

- Complete a self-assessment to demonstrate your understanding of the concepts presented in this chapter
- Complete field activities that will help you expand your understanding of the middle-grade classroom and teaching with content-area textbooks
- Visit important web links related to the role of content-area textbooks in a balanced middle-grade literacy program
- Look into your state's standards as they relate to use of content-area textbooks with middle-grade students
- Communicate with other preservice teachers via the message board and discuss the issues of incorporating content-area textbooks in thematic units and in each stage of the reading process with students in grades 4 to 8

Review

Content-area textbooks are an important component in thematic units, but they are not a complete program. These textbooks have unique conventions and are often difficult for students to read. Teachers can make them more comprehensible by incorporating a variety of activities during each stage of the reading process. Teachers use text sets of books as well as textbooks and multimedia materials as they develop thematic units. The ways that effective teachers use content-area textbooks in thematic units are reviewed in the feature that follows.

How Effective Teachers . . .
Teach With Content-Area Textbooks

1. Teachers teach students about the unique conventions of content-area textbooks.
2. Teachers use content-area textbooks as one resource in thematic units.
3. Teachers recognize the characteristics of considerate texts.
4. Teachers use a variety of activities during each stage of the reading process to make content-area textbooks more comprehensible.
5. Teachers provide students with opportunities to talk and write about what they are reading in content-area textbooks.
6. Teachers teach students how to take notes and study effectively.
7. Teachers develop text sets of books, magazines, and Internet resources to supplement content-area textbooks.
8. Teachers focus on big ideas in content-area units.
9. Teachers list important words on word walls and use a variety of activities to teach vocabulary.
10. Teachers have students create projects to apply and share their learning.

Professional References

Anderson, T. H., & Armbruster, B. B. (1984). Studying. In P. D. Pearson, R. Barr, M. L. Kamil, & P. Mosenthal (Eds.), *Handbook of reading research* (pp. 657–679). New York: Longman.

Anderson, T. H., & Armbruster, B. B. (1986). Readable textbooks, or, selecting a textbook is not like buying a pair of shoes. In J. Orasanu (Ed.), *Reading comprehension: From research to practice.* Hillsdale, NJ: Erlbaum.

Brozo, W. G., & Simpson, M. L. (2003). *Readers, teachers, learners: Expanding literacy across the content areas* (4th ed.). Upper Saddle River, NJ: Merrill/Prentice Hall.

Caverly, D. C., & Orlando, V. P. (1991). Textbook study strategies. In D. C. Caverly & V. P. Orlando (Eds.), *Teaching reading and study strategies at the college level* (pp. 86–165). Newark, DE: International Reading Association.

Goldenberg, C. (1992/1993). Instructional conversations: Promoting comprehension through discussion. *The Reading Teacher, 46,* 316–326.

Harvey, S. (1998). *Nonfiction matters: Reading, writing, and research in grades 3–8.* York, ME: Stenhouse.

Harvey, S., & Goudvis, A. (2000). *Strategies that work: Teaching comprehension to enhance understanding.* York, ME: Stenhouse.

Head, M. H., & Readence, J. E. (1986). Anticipation guides: Meaning through prediction. In E. K. Dishner, T. W. Bean, J. E. Readence, & D. W. Moore (Eds.), *Reading in the content areas* (2nd ed., pp. 229–234). Dubuque, IA: Kendall/Hunt.

Heide, A., & Stilborne, L. (1999). *The teacher's complete and easy guide to the Internet.* New York: Teachers College Press.

Johns, J. L., Van Leirsburg, P., & Davis, S. J. (1994). *Improving reading: A handbook of strategies.* Dubuque, IA: Kendall/Hunt.

Langer, J. A. (1981). From theory to practice: A prereading plan. *Journal of Reading, 25,* 152–157.

Leu, D. J., & Leu, D. D. (1998). *Teaching with the Internet: Lessons from the classroom* (2nd ed.). Norwood, MA: Christopher-Gordon.

Marzano, R. J., Norford, J. S., Paynter, D. E., Pickering, D. J., & Gaddy, B. B. (2001). *A handbook for classroom instruction that works.* Alexandria, VA: Association for Supervision and Curriculum Development.

Moore, D. W., & Moore, S. A. (1992). Possible sentences: An update. In E. K. Dishner, T. W. Bean, J. E. Readence, & D. W. Moore (Eds.), *Reading in the content areas* (3rd ed., pp. 303–310). Dubuque, IA: Kendall/Hunt.

Neeld, E. C. (1986). *Writing* (2nd ed.). Glenview, IL: Scott Foresman.

Ogle, D. M. (1986). K-W-L: A teaching model that develops active reading of expository text. *The Reading Teacher, 39,* 564–570.

Ogle, D. M. (1989). The know, want to know, learn strategy. In K. D. Muth (Ed.), *Children's comprehension of text: Research into practice* (pp. 205–223). Newark, DE: International Reading Association.

Pappas, C. C., Kiefer, B. Z., & Levstik, L. S. (1990). *An integrated language perspective in the elementary school: Theory into action.* New York: Longman.

Raphael, T., & McKinney, J. (1983). Examination of fifth- and eighth-grade children's question-answering behavior: An instructional study in metacognition. *Journal of Reading Behavior, 15,* 67–86.

Raphael, T., & Wonnacott, C. (1985). Heightening fourth grade students' sensitivity to sources of information for answering comprehension questions. *Reading Research Quarterly, 20,* 282–296.

Raphael, T. E. (1986). Teaching question-answer-relationships, revisited. *The Reading Teacher, 39,* 516–523.

Stahl, S. A., & Kapinus, B. (1991). Possible sentences: Predicting word meanings to teach content area vocabulary. *The Reading Teacher, 45,* 36–43.

Tompkins, G. E. (2004). *Teaching writing: Balancing process and product* (4th ed.). Upper Saddle River, NJ: Merrill/Prentice Hall.

Topping, D., & McManus, R. (2002). *Real reading, real writing: Content-area strategies.* Portsmouth, NH: Heinemann.

Tunnell, M. O., & Ammon, R. (Eds.). (1993). *The story of ourselves: Teaching history through children's literature.* Portsmouth, NH: Heinemann.

Children's Book References

Cushman, K. (1994). *Catherine, called Birdy.* New York: HarperCollins.

Macaulay, D. (1977). *Castle.* Boston: Houghton Mifflin.

Macaulay, D. (1983). *Castle* (video). Washington, DC: Unicorn Projects Inc.

Steele, P. (1998). *Knights.* New York: Kingfisher.

chapter 10

Connecting Reading and Writing

- Why should teachers connect reading and writing?

- What types of journals do students use when reading novels and during content-area units?

- What types of compositions can students create as projects?

Fourth-Grade English Learners Read and Write About Pilgrims

The 21 English learners in Mrs. Lee's fourth-grade classroom are studying pilgrims—the Pilgrims who came to America in 1620 in search of religious freedom, the immigrants who arrived at Ellis Island in the late 1800s and early 1900s, and modern-day pilgrims, like the students in this class, whose families recently immigrated to America for peace, freedom, and opportunity. Mrs. Lee's students are English language learners; approximately half have come from Central America, and others are from Southeast Asia, the Middle East, Africa, and Russia.

Mrs. Lee begins the thematic unit focusing on the Pilgrims of 1620. She reads aloud *Giving Thanks: The 1621 Harvest Feast* (Waters, 2001), *The Pilgrims' First Thanksgiving* (McGovern, 1992), *The Pilgrims and Me* (Donnelly, 2002), and other informational books to learn about the Pilgrims, and the students read other easy-to-read books, including *The First Thanksgiving* (Hayward, 1990), themselves. They collect important words for the word wall[C], including *courage, feast, Massasoit, Mayflower, New World, Plymouth, Puritans, slave,* and *Squanto,* and they draw small pictures to illustrate each word that they post on the wall.

The fourth graders make learning logs[C] by stapling together booklets of lined and unlined paper and use them to write and draw about what they are learning. They include these types of entries in their logs:

- drawings and quickwrites[C] about pilgrims
- a list of words related to the theme
- paragraphs about pilgrims
- Venn diagrams comparing Pilgrims and Indians
- quotes from books they are reading
- a data chart[C] comparing the Pilgrims of 1620 to pilgrims in 1900 and modern-day pilgrims
- a time line showing when groups of immigrants came to America
- a picture of the Statue of Liberty with labels for the various parts
- information about persuasive writing

Through these activities, students explore concepts they are learning and record information they want to remember about pilgrims.

As they learn about the Pilgrims of 1620, the students write paragraphs about the Pilgrims' difficult life in the New World, how Squanto helped them, and the reasons why the Pilgrims came to America. Mrs. Lee uses interactive writing[C] to create the paragraphs on chart paper to hang in the classroom, and the students also make their own copies of the paragraphs in their learning logs. The class writes this paragraph about Squanto:

Squanto was a friendly Wampanoag Indian who helped the Pilgrims. He taught them how to catch fish, how to hunt, and how to grow crops. He helped them plant corn, beans, pumpkins, and squash. Squanto probably saved the Pilgrims' lives. They were very thankful for Squanto's help.

Mrs. Lee uses interactive writing differently than her kindergarten and first-grade colleagues do. Her students already understand that text is written from left to right across a page, and they know how to form the letters and spell many high-frequency words, but as they write this paragraph together, Mrs. Lee takes advantage of many teaching opportunities. She reviews commas and possessives, demonstrates how to combine sentences, explains pronoun referents, reminds students to check the word wall to spell theme words correctly, and brainstorms ways to create a closing sentence.

Another day, Mrs. Lee shares *The Very First Thanksgiving Day* (Greene, 2003), a book designed for young children and written in language-rich cumulative verses. The students beg Mrs. Lee to reread the book, and they eagerly join in the reading whenever they can. They notice the chronology—from the Thanksgiving feast in 1621 back to the Pilgrims' setting sail from England in 1620 and then forward again to the feast. Because the students enjoy the book so much, Mrs. Lee adapts it for choral reading[C]. She types the text, marking it for five individual or group voices and adding refrains for the whole class to read. Then she makes copies for each student and they read it together, with individual students, small groups, and the whole class reading the different parts. The students read it again and again, sometimes several times during the day at their request, and in the process, they develop more fluency, acquire new vocabulary, and celebrate what they are learning about pilgrims.

Several days later, Mrs. Lee reads aloud three books by Kate Waters about the children living in Massachusetts in the 1620s: *Sarah Morton's Day: A Day in the Life of a Pilgrim Girl* (1989), *Samuel Eaton's Day: A Day in the Life of a Pilgrim Boy* (1993), and *Tapenum's Day: A Wampanoag Indian Boy in Pilgrim Times* (1996). The full-color photos in these books help to clarify the text for Mrs. Lee's students. After reading the books, the class makes a Venn diagram to compare and contrast the Pilgrims and the Indians. As they finish the chart, Mohammed astutely observes that the Indians had easier lives because they knew how to live in Massachusetts, whereas the Pilgrims struggled more as they tried to live as they had in England, and Angelina makes a connection between coming to America in 1620 and nowadays, pointing out that it's always hard when people first come to America because life is different here.

After developing this background knowledge about the Pilgrims, Mrs. Lee and the students create a dramatic center in one corner of the classroom that looks like a Pilgrim's home, and Mrs. Lee stocks the center with Pilgrim and Indian costumes and artifacts. The students take turns dressing up in the costumes and role-playing in the center to learn what it feels like to be a Pilgrim in Massachusetts in 1620. For a few minutes each afternoon, students dress up in the costumes and participate in role-play activities while Mrs. Lee tells a story about the Pilgrims. She makes it up as she goes along. Here is the beginning of one role-play story:

> *It is a December evening, and the weather is very cold. The Pilgrims are in their dark home, and they stay close to the fireplace to stay warm. The only light comes from the fireplace and one candle on the table. Father is reading the Bible aloud to the family. Everyone listens to him. Then they hear a knock at the door. Father goes to open the door and asks, "Who's there?" before he opens the door. It is their friend Squanto and two other Indians who have come for a visit. Father invites the Indians to come inside and get warm by the*

[C] See the Compendium of Instructional Procedures, which follows Chapter 12, for more information on terms marked with the symbol [C].

fireplace. Squanto has a bag with him, and he gives it to Mother. She opens it and finds a turkey and some Indian corn. She is so happy to have some fresh food to cook for dinner because she is tired of the dried food that they usually eat. She smiles and thanks him. Father invites the Indians to stay and eat dinner with them. Daughter sets the table for dinner while Mother cooks. Father, the Indians, and Son sit by the fire and talk . . .

After spending a week and a half studying the Pilgrims of 1620, Mrs. Lee shifts their study to the immigrants (or pilgrims) who came to America in the late 19th and early 20th centuries. She arbitrarily chooses the year 1900 to represent this period. She teaches the students about the Statue of Liberty, Ellis Island, and the immigrants from Europe who entered America in New York. She shows the students an 18-inch replica of the Statue of Liberty that she bought while visiting New York City and photos from her visit to Ellis Island. Next, she reads aloud the Maestros' *The Story of the Statue of Liberty* (1986). Then she reads picture-book stories about immigrants coming to America and entering the country through Ellis Island, including *Coming to America: The Story of Immigration* (Maestro, 1996), *Watch the Stars Come Out* (Levinson, 1985), and *Journey to Ellis Island: How My Father Came to America* (Bierman, 1998).

After developing the students' background knowledge about immigrants coming to America from Europe in this period, she introduces *Molly's Pilgrim* (Cohen, 1983), the story of Molly and her mother who come to America from Russia for religious freedom. This book is formatted in two ways: It is available as a picture book and as an easy-to-read book. Mrs. Lee's students are reading the easy-to-read version, which is written at the third-grade (3.0) reading level. This is an appropriate book for these students because most of them are reading at second- and third-grade reading levels.

Mrs. Lee's students often have difficulty comprehending what they read—especially making inferences—and *Molly's Pilgrim* is a good book to use to teach comprehension because it is not obvious until the end of the story that Molly and her mother are pilgrims. As they read, she asks the students to summarize the plot and then make connections between their background knowledge and the clues in the book. Here are the questions that she asks to encourage inferential thinking:

Why do the other kids think Molly is different? (p. 9)
How long has Molly's family been in America? (p. 12)
How long does it take to become "American" like the other kids? (p. 12)
Why did Molly's family come to America? (p. 13)
Why did Molly's mother say, "Like us"? (p. 23)
Why did Molly's mother make the pilgrim doll look like herself? (p. 25)
Is Molly's mother right that she's a pilgrim? (p. 26)
Is Molly a pilgrim too? (p. 26)
Is Elizabeth right that Molly's doll is not a pilgrim? (p. 31)
Is Miss Stickley right that Molly's doll is not a pilgrim? (p. 35)
Why did Miss Stickley change her mind? (p. 37)
Are Molly and her mother pilgrims? (p. 38)
What is Barbara Cohen, the author of this book, telling us about pilgrims?
    (p. 40)

Students talk about these questions as they read the story the first time and again in grand conversations[C] and as they write quickwrites afterward. Through these activities, the students grasp the idea that Molly and her mother are pilgrims because they came to America for religious freedom, just as the Pilgrims of 1620 did.

Mrs. Lee uses the question of whether Molly and her mother are pilgrims as the impetus to introduce persuasive writing. Fourth-grade teachers in Mrs. Lee's district are expected to teach students to write persuasive paragraphs and essays. Mrs. Lee begins by introducing the concept of persuasive writing and explaining that students use persuasive writing when they have strong opinions and want to convince someone of something. She introduces the question: Were Molly and her mother pilgrims? The students quickly agree that they were, but Mrs. Lee counters that some people might not agree. "How could we convince them?" Mrs. Lee asks. The students brainstorm a list of reasons to support their position. They choose the three strongest ideas to use in their persuasive paragraph—Molly and her mother came to America on a boat like the Pilgrims of 1620 did; Molly and her mother came for religious freedom; and the Pilgrims of 1620 got the idea for Thanksgiving from a Jewish holiday, and because Molly and her mother are Jewish, Thanksgiving is their holiday, too.

Mrs. Lee explains that persuasive paragraphs have three parts: a position statement, three reasons, and a conclusion. Next, she introduces a graphic organizer with boxes for the three parts, and together Mrs. Lee and her students complete the organizer with their ideas. Then Mrs. Lee guides the students as they create a paragraph, using the sentences from the graphic organizer. Mrs. Lee uses the language experience approach[C] and takes the students' dictation so that they can focus on developing ideas and forming sentences to express those ideas. They take two days to develop and refine their composition using the writing process, and Mrs. Lee makes copies of the completed paragraph for each student. Figure 10-1 shows the graphic organizer and the paragraph that the students developed collaboratively.

For the last week of the unit, Mrs. Lee turns the focus to the students in her class and their families' experiences coming to America. The class develops a list of questions and the students take the list home to use in interviewing their parents and grandparents. Then the students return and share their stories. After they share their stories orally, they draw pictures and write about their families' immigration experiences. Some students write individually, and others need Mrs. Lee's assistance. For some students, she takes their dictation using the language experience approach, and she conferences with others to help them develop and express their ideas. The students word process their final copies and read them from the author's chair. Finally, Mrs. Lee puts them together to make a class book, which is placed in the classroom library. Not only do the students enjoy reading and rereading their classmates' stories, but they also take turns sharing them with their families.

As a culminating activity, the students develop a data chart to compare the pilgrims of 1620, 1900, and their families. Figure 10-2 shows the data chart that they create. The chart that the class makes is posted in the classroom, and the students complete individual copies for their learning logs. Enrico summarizes the class's sentiments when he announces, "I'm proud to be a pilgrim. I didn't know I was, but now I do. It's a good thing, and there will be more pilgrims coming to America forever."

Figure 10-1
Fourth Graders' Graphic Organizer and Persuasive Paragraph About *Molly's Pilgrim*

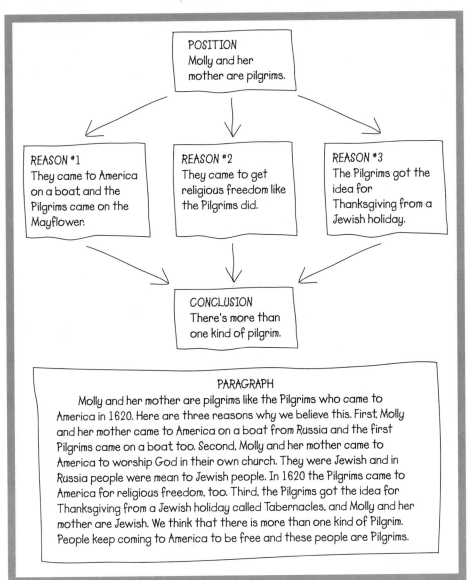

POSITION
Molly and her mother are pilgrims.

REASON #1
They came to America on a boat, and the Pilgrims came on the Mayflower.

REASON #2
They came to get religious freedom like the Pilgrims did.

REASON #3
The Pilgrims got the idea for Thanksgiving from a Jewish holiday.

CONCLUSION
There's more than one kind of pilgrim.

PARAGRAPH
Molly and her mother are pilgrims like the Pilgrims who came to America in 1620. Here are three reasons why we believe this. First, Molly and her mother came to America on a boat from Russia and the first Pilgrims came on a boat, too. Second, Molly and her mother came to America to worship God in their own church. They were Jewish and in Russia people were mean to Jewish people. In 1620 the Pilgrims came to America for religious freedom, too. Third, the Pilgrims got the idea for Thanksgiving from a Jewish holiday called Tabernacles, and Molly and her mother are Jewish. We think that there is more than one kind of Pilgrim. People keep coming to America to be free and these people are Pilgrims.

Figure 10-2   A Data Chart About Pilgrims

Questions	Pilgrims in 1620	Pilgrims in 1900	Pilgrims in 2000
Where did they come from?	The Pilgrims came from England.	The pilgrims came from Russia, Italy, Ireland, and other places in Europe. Some people came from China, too.	Today, pilgrims come from all over the world. They come from El Salvador, Thailand, Russia, Pakistan, Mexico, Nigeria, Afghanistan, and South Africa.
Where did they arrive?	They sailed to Plymouth Rock in Massachusetts.	Many pilgrims sailed to Ellis Island in New York. The Chinese came to San Francisco.	Some come by car, and some come by airplane. They fly to Miami, New York, and Los Angeles.
What did they look like?	They wore black-and-white clothes. Girls and women wore hats and aprons. Boys and men wore short pants, long socks, and hats.	They wore the same clothes they wore in their old countries, but the Americans thought their clothes looked funny.	They wear regular clothes like other people, but if they travel a long time, their clothes get dirty.
Why did they come?	They wanted to have their own church.	They came for religious freedom and to have a better life.	People come to America today to live in peace and to have a better life. Some come for religious freedom, too.
What was hard for them?	Everything was hard for them. They had to build their houses, plant crops, and learn to hunt.	Pilgrims didn't have much money, so it was hard to live, and some Americans were mean to them.	People don't have much money, so it is very hard to live. People have to get a Green Card so they can work.
Who helped them?	Squanto and some Indians helped them.	Only their families and neighbors from the old country helped them.	Their families and friends from their church help them.

Researchers agree that reading and writing should be connected because reading has a powerful impact on writing, and vice versa (Tierney & Shanahan, 1996). When students read about a topic before writing, their writing is enhanced because of what they learn about the topic and the genre, and when students

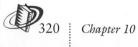

write about a book they are reading, their comprehension is deepened because they are exploring ideas and relationships. Because of this strong relationship, Mrs. Lee has her students write to explore, summarize, and reinforce their learning even though they are still learning English. The vocabulary for reading and writing is the same, and when students both read and write, they have twice as many opportunities to learn new words and how to use them in sentences. As her students wrote persuasive paragraphs, for example, they expanded their comprehension of the book they had read and what they had learned about pilgrims during the content-area unit. Mrs. Lee makes a conscious effort to include writing activities because she understands that when they connect reading and writing, students learn more and their literacy abilities develop more quickly.

There are other reasons for connecting reading and writing, too. Students use the same strategies for both reading and writing. Students make predictions, revise, monitor, and use fix-up strategies for both reading and writing. Because the strategies are the same, students gain valuable practice through both reading and writing.

In addition, the reading and writing processes are virtually the same. Through both reading and writing, students learn a multistep process for developing and expanding meaning. The process begins with activating and building background knowledge, moves through reading and writing, and ends with the application of new knowledge.

The focus in this chapter is writing—keeping journals and writing reports, poems, persuasive essays, and letters—and you will learn ways to connect reading and writing to enhance students' literacy learning. Writing is an essential component in a balanced literacy program. The feature on page 322 shows how writing supports reading.

KEEPING JOURNALS

Students keep journals as they read novels and study during thematic units because writing is a tool for thinking and learning. As they write in journals, students do quickwrites, make clusters^C, and make other types of entries. They use writing for these purposes:

Record experiences
Stimulate interest in a topic
Take note of important information
Draw diagrams to understand organization
Explore thinking
Develop comprehension
Wonder, predict, and hypothesize
Engage the imagination
Generate lists of words
Ask questions
Activate prior knowledge
Assume the role of another person
Reflect on learning

Mrs. Lee had her students keep journals for many of these purposes in the vignette at the beginning of the chapter. Figure 10-3 lists the four types of journals that students in grades 4 through 8 write as they read novels and participate in thematic units.

The Role of Writing in a Balanced Literacy Program

Component	Description
Reading	Students use very similar processes for reading and writing.
Phonics and Other Skills	Students apply many of the same skills for both reading and writing.
Strategies	Students apply the same strategies for both reading and writing.
Vocabulary	Students learn vocabulary through reading and content-area study, and they use these newly learned words when they write.
Comprehension	The negotiation of meaning is virtually the same when students are reading and writing.
Literature	Students' writing is a reflection of the books they have read. Through reading, students learn about genres, narrative, expository, and poetic structures, and sentence structure.
Content-Area Study	Students use both reading and writing to learn during a content area unit.
Oral Language	Talk plays an essential role in both reading and writing. As students talk, they develop ideas and clarify meaning.
Writing	Students keep journals, and they use the writing process for more formal, polished stories, reports, poems, and other compositions.
Spelling	As students spell words, they apply and refine their knowledge of phonics.

Reading Logs

Students write in reading logs about the stories and other books they are reading during literature focus units, literature circles, and reading workshop (Barone, 1990; Hancock, 1992, 1993). As students read or listen to books read aloud, they respond to the book, make predictions, clarify misunderstandings, connect the book to events in their own lives, and analyze story structure. Students can also list unfamiliar words, jot down quotable quotes, and take notes about the characters, plot, or other elements of the story, but the primary purpose of these journals is for students to think about the book, connect literature to their own lives, and develop their own interpretation. Reading logs go by a variety of names, including literature response journals (Hancock, 1992), literature journals (Five, 1986), and reading journals (Wollman-Bonilla, 1989), but no matter what they are called, their purpose remains the same.

Researchers have examined students' responses and noticed patterns in their reading log entries. Hancock (1992, 1993) identified eight response patterns, which are shown in Figure 10-4. The first four patterns are personal meaning-making options, in which students make inferences about chapters, offer predictions, ask questions, or

Figure 10-3   Four Types of Journals

Journal	What Students Do in the Journal	How It Is Used With Novels	How It Is Used With Informational Books and Content-Area Textbooks
Reading Logs	Students do quickwrites; some entries are in response to prompts and others are free choice.	Students use reading logs to write reflections and summaries while reading stories.	(not generally used with these books)
Learning Logs	Students do quickwrites, make clusters and diagrams, brainstorm lists of words, and include other charts, maps, and drawings.	(not generally used with these books)	Students use to take notes about main ideas, list key vocabulary, and draw graphic organizers and other diagrams.
Double-entry Journals[C]	Students divide journal pages into two columns and make lists in the left column and quickwrite answers or reflections in the right column.	Students write quotes, questions, or predictions in the left column and write reflections in the right column.	Students write important information, questions, or quotes in the left column and make connections or write answers in the right column.
Simulated Journals	Students write journal entries and sometimes draw pictures to accompany them.	Students assume the role of a book character and write journal entries from that person's viewpoint.	Students assume the role of the subject of a biography or a historical person and write journal entries from that person's viewpoint.

discuss confusions. The next three patterns focus on chapter and plot development; students are more involved with the novel, and they offer reactions to the characters and events of the story. The last category of response is literary evaluation, in which students evaluate books and reflect on their own literary tastes.

These patterns can extend the possibilities of response by introducing teachers and students to a wide variety of response options. Hancock (1992, 1993) recommends that teachers begin by assessing the kinds of responses students are currently making: They can read students' reading logs, categorize the types of responses, tally the patterns, and make an assessment. Often students use only a few patterns, not the wide range that is available. Teachers can teach minilessons[C] and model patterns of

Figure 10-4   Patterns of Response in Students' Reading Log Entries

Categories	Response Patterns	Description
Personal Meaning Making	Monitoring Understanding	Students get to know the characters and explain how the story is making sense to them. These responses usually occur at the beginning of a book.
	Making Inferences	Students share their insights into the feelings and motives of a character. They often begin their comments with "I think."
	Making, Validating, or Invalidating Predictions	Students speculate about what will happen later in the story and also confirm or refute predictions they made previously.
	Expressing Wonder or Confusion	Students reflect on the way the story is developing. They ask "I wonder why" questions and write about confusions.
Character and Plot Development	Character Interaction	Students show that they are personally involved with a character, sometimes writing "If I were ____ , I would . . ." They express empathy and share related experiences from their own lives. Also, they may give advice to the character.
	Character Assessment	Students judge a character's actions and often use evaluative terms such as *nice* and *dumb*.
	Story Involvement	Students reveal their involvement in the story as they express satisfaction with how the story is developing. They may comment on their desire to continue reading or may use terms such as *disgusting, weird,* and *awesome* to react to sensory aspects of the story.
Literary Evaluation	Literary Criticism	Students offer "I liked/I didn't like" opinions and praise or condemn an author's style. Sometimes students compare the book with others they have read or compare the author with other authors with whom they are familiar.

Adapted from Hancock, 1992, 1993.

responses that students aren't using, and they can ask questions when they read journals to prompt students to think in new ways about the story they are reading.

For example, a sixth grader wrote this entry after reading the third chapter of *The Summer of the Swans* (Byars, 1970); the focus is on character interaction:

> *I think looks are not the most important thing because the way you act is. When some people look good and still act good—that's when people are really lucky, but I just think you should go ahead and appreciate the way you look.*

These two entries were written by seventh graders after reading *The Giver* (Lowry, 1993). Even though they reach different conclusions about the book, their focus is story involvement:

> *I can't believe it ended this way. They froze to death. I think they died but I wish they found freedom and happiness. It is very sad.*

The end is cool. Jonas and Gabe come back to the community but now it is changed. There are colors and the people have feelings. They believe in God and it is Christmas.

Learning Logs

Students use learning logs to record and react to what they are learning in social studies, science, or other content areas. Laura Robb (2003) explains that learning logs are "a place to think on paper" (p. 60). Students write in these journals to discover gaps in their knowledge and to explore relationships between what they are learning and their past experiences. Through these activities, students practice taking notes, writing descriptions and directions, and other writing skills. They also learn how to reflect on and evaluate their own learning (Stanford, 1988).

Students often keep learning logs as part of thematic units in social studies. In their logs, students write in response to informational books and content-area textbooks, list vocabulary related to the theme, create time lines, and draw diagrams and maps. For example, as part of a study of the Civil War, eighth graders might include the following in their learning logs:

- informal quickwrites about the causes of the war and other topics related to the war
- a list of words related to the theme
- a chart of major battles in the war
- a Venn diagram comparing the viewpoints of the North and the South
- a time line showing events related to the war
- a map of the United States at the time of the war, with battle locations marked
- notes after viewing several films about the Civil War era
- a list of favorite quotes from Lincoln's "Gettysburg Address"
- a response to a chapter book such as *Charley Skedaddle* (Beatty, 1987), *Brady* (Fritz, 1987), or *Across Five Aprils* (Hunt, 1987)

Through these learning log activities, students explore concepts they are learning and record information they want to remember about the Civil War.

Science-related learning logs can take several forms. In the first type, students make daily entries during a unit of study. They may take notes during a presentation by the teacher or a classmate, after viewing a film, or at the end of each class period. Sometimes students make entries in list form, sometimes in clusters or charts, and at other times in paragraphs. A second type is an observation log in which students make a series of entries as seedlings grow or baby animals hatch. A lab report is a third type of learning log. In these logs, students list the materials and procedures used in the experiment, present data on an observation chart, and then discuss the results.

Double-Entry Journals

Double-entry journals are just what their name suggests: Students divide their journal pages into two parts and write different types of information in each part (Barone, 1990; Berthoff, 1981). Students use double-entry journals for reading logs or for learning logs. When they make double-entry reading logs, students often write quotes from the story they are reading in the left column and relate each quote to their own life or

Students write lab reports in learning logs.

to literature they have read in the right column. Through this type of journal, students become more actively involved in what they are reading, note sentences that have personal, world, or literary connections, and become more sensitive to the author's language.

Fifth graders drew and wrote in double-entry journals as they read *Bunnicula: A Rabbit-Tale of Mystery,* a hilarious Halloween story by Deborah and James Howe (1979). Before reading each chapter, students wrote predictions about what would happen in the chapter in one column, and after reading, they drew and wrote about what actually did happen. An excerpt from a fifth grader's journal is presented in Figure 10-5. This student's responses indicate that she is engaged in the story and is connecting the story to her own life as well as to another story she has read.

Double-entry journals can be used in other ways, too. Instead of recording quotes from the book, students can write "Reading Notes" in the left column and then add "Reactions" in the right column. In the left column, students write about events they read about in the chapter; then they make personal connections to the events in the right column. As an alternative, students can use the heading "Reading Notes" for one column and "Discussion Notes" for the other. Students write reading notes as they read or immediately after reading. Later, after they discuss the story or chapter of a longer book in a grand conversation, students add discussion notes.

Students also use double-entry format in learning logs. They can write important facts in one column and their reactions to the facts in the other column, or questions about the topic in the left column and answers in the right column. As with other types of double-entry journals, it is the second column where students make more interpretive comments. Figure 10-6 shows a sixth grader's double-entry journal written during a unit on drug prevention. In the left column, the student wrote information she was learning, and in the right column, she made personal connections to the information.

Simulated Journals

In some stories, such as *Catherine, Called Birdy* (Cushman, 1994), the author assumes the role of a character and writes a series of diary entries from the character's point of view. Here is an excerpt from one of Birdy's entries, which describes life in the Middle Ages:

Figure 10-5

An Excerpt From a Fifth Grader's
Double-Entry Journal on *Bunnicula: A
Rabbit-Tale of Mystery*

Chapter	Prediction	What Really Happened
3	I think that Chester will have night mares becose of the story.	They found a WHITE tomato.
4	I think that Chester will want to learn about vampires and he might even turn into one. ALL ABOUT VAMPIRES	He fond a Zuckini. It was white and it had 2 little holes in it.
5	I think they will find a white squash or some other vegatables.	Toby doont no that the rabbit is a VAMPIRE.

12th Day of October
No more sewing and spinning and goose fat for me!
Today my life is changed. How it came about is this:
We arrived at the abbey soon after dinner, stopping just outside the entry gate at the guesthouse next to the mill. The jouncing cart did my stomach no kindness after jellied eel and potted lamb, so I was most relieved to alight. (Cushman, 1994, p. 25)

These books can be called simulated journals. They are rich with historical details and feature examples of both the vocabulary and sentence structure of the period. At the end of the book, authors often include information about how they researched the period and explanations about the liberties they took with the characters or events that are recorded.

Figure 10-6 A Page From a Sixth Grader's Double-Entry Journal

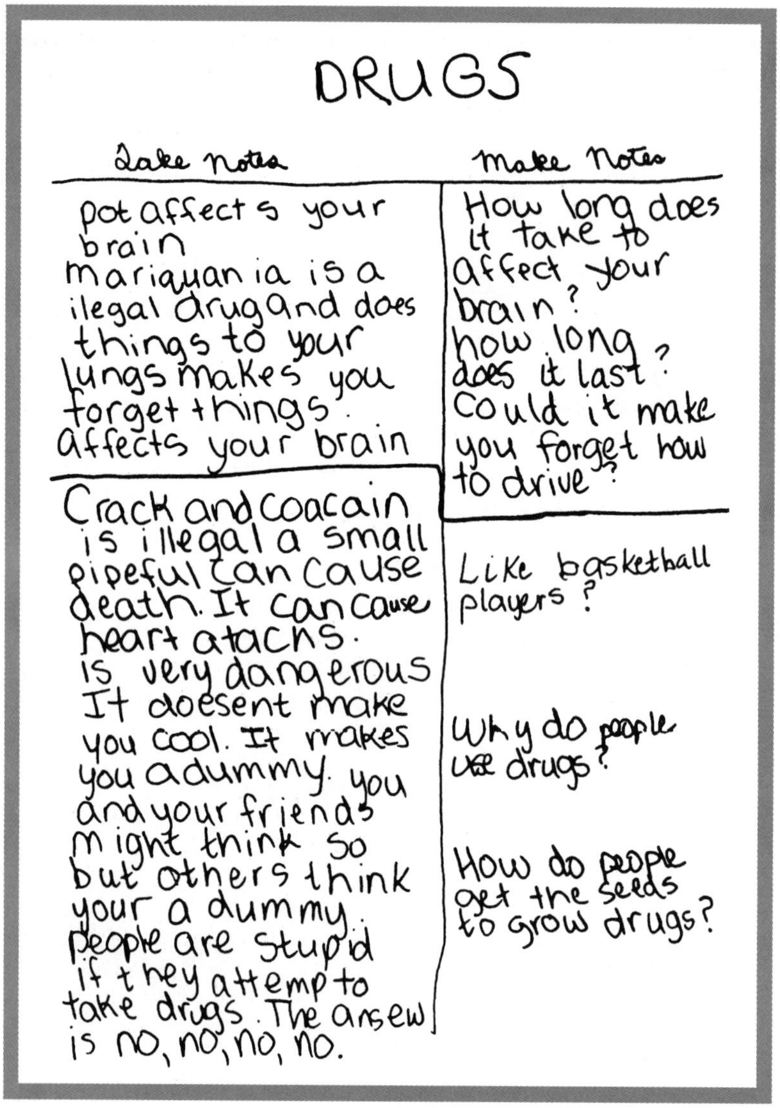

DRUGS

Take notes	Make Notes
pot affects your brain mariquania is a ilegal drug and does things to your lungs makes you forget things. affects your brain	How long does it take to affect your brain? how long does it last? Could it make you forget how to drive?
Crack and coacain is illegal a small pipeful can cause death. It can cause heart atacns. is very dangerous It doesent make you cool. It makes you a dummy. you and your friends might think so but others think your a dummy. people are stupid if they attemp to take drugs. The ansew is no, no, no, no.	Like basketball players? Why do people use drugs? How do people get the seeds to grow drugs?

Scholastic Books has created two series of historical journals appropriate for fourth-through eighth-grade students; one series is for girls, and one is for boys. *A Journey to the New World: The Diary of Remember Patience Whipple* (Lasky, 1996), *A Picture of Freedom: The Diary of Clotee, a Slave Girl* (McKissack, 1997), and *Across the Wide and Lonesome Prairie: The Oregon Trail Diary of Hattie Campbell* (Gregory, 1997) are from the Dear America series; each book provides a glimpse into American history from a young girl's perspective. The My Name Is America series features books written from a boy's point of view. Three examples are *The Journal of Patrick Seamus Flaherty: United States Marine Corps* (White, 2002), *The Journal of Ben Uchida: Citizen 13559, Mirror Lake Internment Camp* (Denenberg, 1999), and *The Journal of William Thomas Emerson: A Revolutionary War Patriot* (Denenberg, 1998). These books are handsomely bound to look like old journals with heavy paper rough cut around the edges.

Students, too, can write simulated journals by assuming the role of another person and writing from that person's viewpoint. They assume the role of a historical figure when they read biographies or as part of social studies units. As they read stories, students assume the role of a character in the story. In this way, students gain insight into other people's lives and into historical events. When students write from the viewpoint of a famous person, they begin by making a "life line," a time line of the person's life. Then they pick key dates in the person's life and write entries about those dates. A look at a series of diary entries written by a fifth grader who has assumed the role of Benjamin Franklin shows how the student chose the important dates for each entry and wove in factual information:

December 10, 1719
Dear Diary,
My brother James is so mad at me. He just figured out that I'm the one who wrote the articles for his newspaper and signed them Mistress Silence Dogood. He says I can't do any more of them. I don't understand why. My articles are funny. Everyone reads them. I bet he won't sell as many newspapers anymore. Now I have to just do the printing.

February 15, 1735
Dear Diary,
I have printed my third "Poor Richard's Almanack." It is the most popular book in America and now I am famous. Everyone reads it. I pretend that somebody named Richard Saunders writes it, but it's really me. I also put my wise sayings in it. My favorite wise saying is "Early to bed, early to rise, makes a man healthy, wealthy, and wise."

April 19, 1752
Dear Diary,
I did a very dangerous experiment today. I wanted to learn about electricity so I flew a kite in a thunderstorm. I put a key on the string and lightning hit the kite, and there were sparks on the key. That proves lightning is electricity. But I don't want anyone else to do that experiment. It is too dangerous.

June 22, 1763
Dear Diary,
I've been an inventor for many years now. There are a lot of things I have invented like the Franklin stove (named after me) and bifocal glasses, and the lightning rod, and a long arm to get books off of the high shelves. That's how I work. I see something that we don't have and if it is needed, I figure out how to do it. I guess I just have the knack for inventing.

May 25, 1776
Dear Diary,
Tom Jefferson and I are working on the Declaration of Independence. The patriots at the Continental Congress chose us to do it but it is dangerous business. The Red Coats will call us traitors and kill us if they can. I like young Tom from Virginia. He'll make a good king of America some day.

April 10, 1785
Dear Diary,
I returned home to Philadelphia today from England. What a day it was. When my ship came to the dock, there was a crowd of people waiting to see ME. Then I heard bells ringing and cannons fired to welcome me home. I read the newspaper and it said I was a hero! What an honor.

April 16, 1790
Dear Diary,
I am dying. I only have a day or two to live. But it's OK because I am 84 years old. Not very many people live as long as I have or do so many things in a life. I was a printer by trade but I have also been a scientist, an inventor, a writer, and a statesman. I have lived to see the Philadelphia that I love so very much become part of a new country. Good-bye to my family and everyone who loves me.

Students can use simulated journals in two ways: as a journal or as a refined and polished composition—a demonstration of learning project. When students use simulated journals as a tool for learning, they write the entries as they are reading a book in order to get to know the character better, or during a thematic unit as they are learning about the historical period. In these entries, students are exploring concepts and making connections between what they are learning and what they already know. These journal entries are less polished than when students write a simulated journal as a culminating project for a unit. For a project, students plan out their journals carefully, choose important dates, and use the writing process to draft, revise, edit, and publish their journals. They often add covers typical of the historical period. For example, a simulated journal written as part of a unit on ancient Greece might be written on a long sheet of butcher paper and rolled like a scroll, or a pioneer journal might be backed with paper cut from a brown grocery bag to resemble an animal hide.

Teaching Students to Keep Journals

Students usually write in journals that they make by stapling small booklets of paper together, and they often decorate the covers of their journals to complement the novel they are reading or their content-area unit. Rather than using one spiral-bound notebook for the entire school year, students usually make new journals for each novel or thematic unit.

Teachers introduce students to journal writing using minilessons in which they explain the purpose of the journal-writing activity and the procedures for gathering ideas, writing in a journal, and sharing with classmates. Teachers often model the procedure by writing a sample entry on the chalkboard or on chart paper as students observe. Then students make their own first entries, and several read their entries aloud. Through this sharing, students who are still unclear about the writing activity have additional models on which to base their own writing.

Students use a variety of strategies as they write in journals. Four of the most common ones are brainstorming, quickwriting, clustering, and charting data. Students also draw maps and diagrams, write key words, and draw pictures. They choose the strategy that is most appropriate for the writing activity and the most useful for supporting their thinking and learning.

Teachers monitor students' writing by checking their journals and reading at least some of the entries on a regular basis. They read to be sure that students are relating

Struggling Students Need to Connect Reading and Writing. The benefits of connecting reading and writing are numerous, but struggling students often resist writing. They complain that they don't know what to write, and when pressured to write, they write very little. So, it's important for teachers to find effective ways to work with struggling writers to help them write about their reading, write informally as a learning tool, and use writing in culminating projects to share knowledge. There are no easy solutions, but students' writing improves when teachers teach them how to write using the writing process, share sample compositions when assigning writing so students know what's expected of them, and write collaborative compositions for practice. Teachers also use the language experience approach when they want to focus on generating, organizing, and revising ideas and interactive writing to review mechanical skills. In addition, students' first writing experiences should be brief to build their confidence and feelings of success.

what they are reading or studying with their journal entries and that they are incorporating vocabulary from the word wall. Teachers often assign points for each entry. The entries can be graded as "done" or "not done," or teachers can award points for the quality of students' entries, but because the writing is usually informal, teachers do not base their grades on mechanical correctness. However, it is not unreasonable for teachers to expect students to spell high-frequency and word wall words correctly and to write legibly in their journal entries.

WRITING PROJECTS

Students also use writing to demonstrate their learning. This type of writing is more formal, and students use the writing process to revise and edit their writing before making a final copy.

Reports

Reports are the best-known type of writing to demonstrate learning, and students write many types of reports, ranging from posters and alphabet books[C] to collaborative reports[C] and individual reports[C]. Too often, students are not exposed to report writing until they are faced with writing a term paper in high school, and then they are overwhelmed with learning how to take notes on note cards, how to organize and write the paper, and how to compile a bibliography. There is no reason to postpone report writing until students reach high school; early, successful experiences with informative writing teach students about content-area topics as well as how to write reports (Harvey, 1998; Krogness, 1987; Tompkins, 2004).

Posters.   Students combine visual and verbal elements when they make posters (Moline, 1995). They draw pictures and diagrams and write labels and commentary. Students can also list the resources they consulted in a bibliography. For example, students might:

Students share a poster project that they developed in a thematic unit.

- draw detailed diagrams of the inner and outer planets in the solar system
- chart the life cycle of frogs or the steps in mummification
- identify the parts of a complex machine
- label the clothing a Revolutionary War soldier wore and the supplies he carried
- create time lines of a historical period
- identify important events of a person's life on a life line
- chart the explorers' voyages to America and around the world on a world map

As part of a reading and writing workshop on informational books, a fifth grader read *The Magic School Bus Inside a Beehive* (Cole, 1996) and created a poster to share what he had learned. The poster is shown in Figure 10-7.

Students use a process approach to create posters such as the one shown in Figure 10-7. They plan the information they want to include in the poster and consider how to devise attention-getting displays using headings, illustrations and diagrams, captions, boxes, and rules. Students prepare a rough draft of the sections of their posters and revise and edit the sections as they go through the writing process. Then they make a final copy of each section, glue the sections onto a sheet of posterboard, and share their posters with classmates as they would share finished pieces of writing.

Alphabet Books. Students use the letters of the alphabet to organize the information they want to share in an alphabet book. These collaborative report books incorporate the sequence structure, because the pages are arranged in alphabetical order. Alphabet books such as *Ashanti to Zulu: African Traditions* (Musgrove, 1976), about African cultures, *Z Is for Zamboni: A Hockey Alphabet* (Napier, 2002), *The Queen's Progress: An Elizabethan Alphabet* (Mannis, 2003), and *Illuminations* (Hunt, 1989), about medieval life, can be used as models. Students begin by brainstorming information related to the topic being studied and identify a word or fact for each letter of the alphabet. Then students work individually, in pairs, or in small groups to compose

Figure 10-7   A Fifth Grader's Poster About Bees

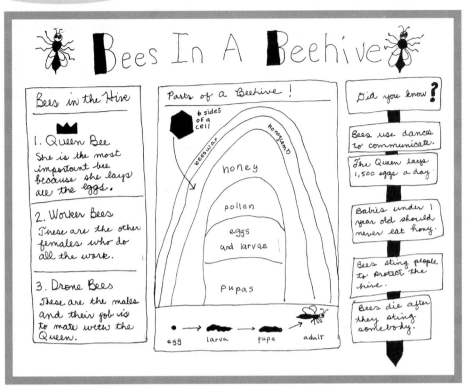

Bees In A Beehive

Bees in the Hive

1. Queen Bee
She is the most important bee because she lays all the eggs.

2. Worker Bees
These are the other females who do all the work.

3. Drone Bees
These are the males and their job is to mate with the Queen.

Parts of a Beehive!

6 sides of a cell

beeswax   honeycomb

honey

pollen

eggs and larvae

pupas

egg   larva   pupa   adult

Did you know?

Bees use dances to communicate.

The Queen lays 1,500 eggs a day.

Babies under 1 year old should never eat honey.

Bees sting people to protect the hive.

Bees die after they sting somebody.

---

pages for the book. The format for the pages is similar to the one used in alphabet books written by professional authors. Students write the letter in one corner of the page, draw an illustration, and write a sentence or paragraph to describe the word or fact. The text usually begins "_____ is for _____," and then a sentence or paragraph description follows. The H page from a sixth grade class's alphabet book on ancient Egypt is presented in Figure 10-8.

Collaborative Reports.   Students work together to write collaborative reports. Sometimes students each write one page for the report, or they can work together in small groups to write chapters for the report. Students create collaborative reports on almost any science or social studies topic.

Students might write collaborative biographies; each student or small group writes about one event or accomplishment in the person's life, and then the pages are assembled in chronological order. Or, students work in small groups to write chapters for a collaborative report on the planets in the solar system, ancient Egypt, or the Oregon Trail.

As part of a unit on the American Revolution, a fifth-grade class developed a collaborative report. Students brainstormed a variety of topics, including the battles of Lexington and Concord, the Declaration of Independence, Betsy Ross, "No taxation without representation," and King George III. Students each chose a topic and created a page for the class book on that topic using both art and writing. Students used the writing process to revise and edit their chapters, and then they were compiled into

Figure 10-8 A Page From a Sixth-Grade ABC Book on Ancient Egypt

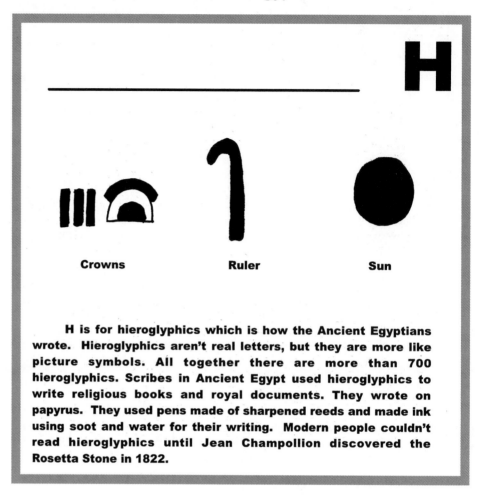

Crowns   **Ruler**   **Sun**

H is for hieroglyphics which is how the Ancient Egyptians wrote. Hieroglyphics aren't real letters, but they are more like picture symbols. All together there are more than 700 hieroglyphics. Scribes in Ancient Egypt used hieroglyphics to write religious books and royal documents. They wrote on papyrus. They used pens made of sharpened reeds and made ink using soot and water for their writing. Modern people couldn't read hieroglyphics until Jean Champollion discovered the Rosetta Stone in 1822.

a book. Figure 10-9 shows the page about King George III. Students benefit from writing a collaborative report before writing individual reports because they learn how to write a report, with the group as a scaffold or support system, before tackling individual reports. Also, working in groups lets them share the laborious parts of the work.

Individual Reports.   Students also write individual reports as projects during thematic units. Toby Fulwiler (1985) recommends that students do "authentic" research, in which they explore topics that interest them or hunt for answers to questions that puzzle them. When students become immersed in content-area study, questions arise that they want to explore, and increasingly students are turning to the Internet to research topics.

Teaching Students to Write Reports.   Students learn how to write reports through a series of minilessons and experiences writing class collaboration reports. Through the minilessons, teachers explain how to choose a topic, collect information and format information, and write the report. Then students practice what they are learning as they work with partners or in small groups to write collaborative reports. Through

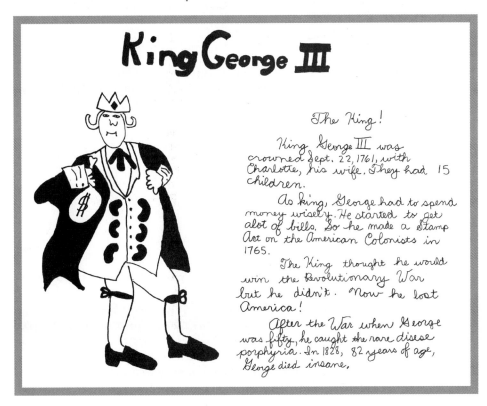

King George III

The King!

King George III was crowned Sept. 22, 1761, with Charlotte, his wife. They had 15 children.

As king, George had to spend money wisely. He started to get alot of bills. So he made a Stamp Act on the American Colonists in 1765.

The King thought he would win the Revolutionary War but he didn't. Now he lost America!

After the War when George was fifty, he caught the rare disease porphyria. In 1828, 82 years of age, George died insane.

these experiences, students gain both the expertise and the confidence to write individual reports. The steps in writing a report are:

1. *Explain the form for the report.* Teachers introduce the form—posters, alphabet books, or reports—for the project. They point out the special requirements and share samples done by students in previous classes.

2. *Choose a topic.* Students choose a topic for their report from the content-area unit they are studying. If the topic is too broad, teachers help students to narrow the topic to something more specific.

3. *Collect information and organize the report.* Students read, take notes, and use clusters, data charts, or other graphics to gather and organize information for the report.

4. *Use the writing process to write the report.* Students write a rough draft using the information they gathered in the previous step. Then they meet in writing groups[C] to share their drafts and make revisions based on the feedback they receive from their classmates. Next, students proofread and edit their reports, and last, they prepare their final copies.

Teachers use the same steps when students are writing collaborative and individual reports.

Students need to know what the requirements are for the report and how they will be assessed. Many teachers develop a checklist or grading sheet with the requirements for the project and distribute it to students before they begin working. In this way, students know what is expected of them and assume responsibility for completing each step of the assignment.

Students keep all their papers in a folder along with the checklist or grading sheet, and as each requirement is completed, they check it off. In this way, students monitor their own work and learn that writing is a process, not just a final product. When the project is completed, students submit their entire folder to the teacher to be assessed.

Poetry

Students in grades 4 through 8 often write poems as projects after reading books and as part of thematic units. They write formula poems by beginning each line or stanza with a word or line, they create free-form poems, and they follow the structure of model poems as they create their own poems.

"I Am" Poems.   Students assume the role of a person and write a poem from that person's viewpoint. They begin and end the poem (or each stanza) with "I am _____" and begin all the other lines with "I." In this poem, an eighth grader writes from the viewpoint of John F. Kennedy after reading a biography about the 35th president:

> I am John Fitzgerald Kennedy.
> I commanded a PT boat in World War II.
> I saved my crew after a Japanese ship hit us.
> I became a politician because that's what my dad wanted me
> to do.
> I was elected the 35th president of the United States.
> I said, "Ask not what your country can do for you—ask what you
> can do for your country."
> I believed in equal rights for blacks and whites.
> I began the Peace Corps to help the world live free.
> I cried the tears of assassination because
> Lee Harvey Oswald shot me dead.
> I left my young family in America's love.
> I am John Fitzgerald Kennedy.

Students can also assume the role of a concept or event and write an "I Am" Poem from that viewpoint. For example, students can become the Statue of Liberty or a pyramid in ancient Egypt. In this poem written collaboratively by a fifth-grade class, the students assume the viewpoint of the Revolutionary War:

> I am the Revolutionary War.
> I cause many deaths.
> I hear the screams in the night
> From the memories of the dead.
> I tar and feather the captured loyalists.
> I say, "Give me liberty or give me death."
> I am FREEDOM.
>
> I am the Revolutionary War.
> I hear gun shots ring out.
> I make some brothers into enemies.
> I give liberty.
> I cause painful tears to fall.
> I am FREEDOM.

"If I Were in Charge of the World."   Students use Judith Viorst's poem "If I Were in Charge of the World" (1981) as a model for poems that they write. They assume the

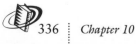

role of a book character, the person featured in a biography they are reading, or a historical personality and write a poem from that person's viewpoint. They begin each stanza with the line, "If I were in charge of the world." An eighth grader wrote this poem from Birdy's viewpoint after reading *Catherine, Called Birdy* (Cushman, 1994):

> *If I were in charge of the world,*
> *fathers would be different.*
> *A father would think of a daughter*
> *As someone to love, not someone to sell.*
> *He would want his daughter to be happy*
> *And have herself decide who she wanted to marry.*
> *He would want to protect his daughter*
> *And want to know his daughter loved him.*
> *If fathers were different,*
> *daughters would be different, too.*
> *A daughter would want to please her father,*
> *not to embarrass and humiliate him.*

Poems for Two Voices. In this unique type of free verse, poems are written in two columns, side by side. The columns are read together by two readers or two groups of readers. One reader reads the left column, and the other reader reads the right column. When both readers have words—either the same words or different words—written on the same line, they read them simultaneously so that the poem sounds like a musical duet.

The two best-known books of poems for two readers are Paul Fleischman's *I Am Phoenix: Poems for Two Voices* (1985), which is about birds, and his Newbery Award–winning *Joyful Noise: Poems for Two Voices* (1988), which is about insects. Students, too, can write poems for two voices; Loraine Wilson (1994) suggests that topics with contrasting viewpoints are the most effective.

A small group of fifth graders wrote this poem for two voices as a project after reading *Number the Stars* (Lowry, 1989), the story of the friendship of two girls, a Christian and a Jew, set in Denmark during World War II.

I am Annemarie, a Christian.	*I am Ellen, a Jew.*
I hate this war.	*I hate this war.*
	The Nazis want to kill me.
The Nazis want to kill my friend.	
Why?	*Why?*
I want to help my friend.	
	Can you help me?
My mother will take you	
to her brother, my uncle.	
He is a fisherman.	
	Your uncle is a fisherman?
He will hide you on his ship.	
	He will hide me on his ship?
He will take you to Sweden.	
To freedom.	*To freedom.*
I am Annemarie, a Christian.	
	I am Ellen, a Jew.
I want to help my friend.	
	I need the help of my friends
	or I will die.
I hate this war.	*I hate this war.*

Found Poems.   Students create poems by culling words and phrases from a story they are reading or from an informational book or content-area textbook and arranging the words and phrases to create a free-form poem. This found poem was written by a sixth grader about *Hatchet* (Paulsen, 1987), the story of a boy who spends 54 days in the wilderness learning to survive initially with only the aid of a hatchet given to him by his mother, but who learns in the end to survive his parents' divorce.

> *He was 13.*
> *Always started with a single word:*
> *Divorce.*
> *An ugly word.*
> *A breaking word, an ugly breaking word.*
> *A rearing ugly word that meant fights and yelling.*
> *Secrets.*
> *Visitation rights.*
> *A hatchet on his belt.*
> *His plane.*
> *The pilot had been sighted.*
> *He rubbed his shoulder.*
> *Aches and pains.*
> *A heart attack.*
> *The engine droned.*
> *A survival pack which had emergency supplies.*
> *Brian Robeson.*
> *Alone.*
> *Help, p-l-e-a-s-e.*

Teaching Students to Write Poems.   Students learn to write poems through mini-lessons about poetic forms, through reading poems, and through writing poems. It is not enough simply to invite students to read or write poetry; they need instruction and structured reading and writing experiences in order to develop a concept of poetry.

As students learn about poetry and read and write poems, they learn these concepts:

- Poems create word pictures and word plays
- Poems can be about any topic
- There are many formats or patterns for poems
- Poems don't have to rhyme
- Poems can involve alliteration, metaphors and similes, onomatopoeia, repetition, or rhyme
- Poems can be arranged in different ways on a page
- Capital letters and punctuation marks are optional

Developing a concept of poetry is important because many students have misconceptions about what poetry is and how to write poetry. Probably the most common misconception is that poems must rhyme.

Once students have developed a basic understanding of poetry, they are ready to begin writing. The steps in teaching students to write poems are:

1.   **Introduce the poetic form.** Teachers present the poetic form and explain what is incorporated in each line or stanza. They often develop a chart that describes the form to help students remember the information.

2. *Share sample poems.* Teachers share poems that follow the poetic form. Poems included in this book can be shared, as well as poems published in books of poetry and poems written by students in a previous class. Teachers also point out how each poem adheres to the poetic form.

3. *Review the poetic form.* Teachers review the pattern or formula and share another poem that follows the form. Then teachers ask students to explain how the poem adheres to the form.

4. *Write a class collaboration poem.* Teachers have students work together to write a class collaboration poem before writing individual poems, or students can work together in small groups to write collaborative poems. After they write their poems, they share them with classmates and explain how the poem follows the form. Through this step, students gain practice using the form before writing poems individually.

5. *Writing individual poems using the writing process.* Now students write their own poems related to the novel they are reading or the thematic unit they are studying. They prewrite to gather and organize ideas, write rough drafts, meet in writing groups to receive feedback, make revisions based on their feedback, and then edit their poems with a classmate and with the teacher. Then students share their poems with the class.

Through this procedure, students learn how to write a poem rather than simply being assigned to write a poem. This step-by-step approach assures that students understand how to write a poem, and they are more likely to be successful when they write poems individually.

Persuasion

People can be persuaded in three basic ways. The first appeal a writer can make is based on reason. People seek to make logical generalizations and draw cause-and-effect conclusions, whether from absolute facts or from strong possibilities. For example, people can be persuaded to practice more healthful living if told about the results of medical research. It is necessary, of course, to distinguish between reasonable and unreasonable appeals. For example, urging people to stand on their head every day for 30 minutes based on the claim that it will increase their intelligence is an unreasonable appeal.

A second way to persuade is through an appeal to character. Other people are important to us, and we can be persuaded by what another person recommends if we trust that person. Trust comes from personal knowledge of the person or from the reputation of someone who is trying to persuade. Does the persuader have the expertise or experience necessary to endorse a product or a cause? For example, can we believe what scientists say about the dangers of nuclear energy? Can we believe what a sports personality says about the effectiveness of a particular sports shoe?

The third way people can be persuaded is by an appeal to their emotions. Emotional appeals can be as strong as intellectual appeals because people have a strong concern for their well-being and the rights of others. We support or reject arguments according to our strong feelings about what is ethical and socially responsible. At the same time, fear and the need for peer acceptance are strong feelings that also influence our opinions and beliefs.

Any of the three appeals can be used to try to persuade another person. For example, when a child tries to persuade her parents that her bedtime should be delayed by 30 minutes, she might argue that neighbors allow their children to stay up later; this is an appeal to character. If the argument focuses on the amount of sleep that an

11-year-old needs, it is an appeal to reason. When the child finally announces that she has the earliest bedtime of anyone in her fourth-grade class and it makes her feel like a baby, the appeal is to the emotions.

These same three types of appeal are used for in-school persuasion. When trying to persuade classmates to read a particular book in a "book-selling" poster project, for example, students might argue that the book should be read because it is short and interesting (reason), because it is hilarious and you'll laugh (emotion), or because it is the most popular book in the fifth grade and everyone else is reading it (character).

Much like a story, an argument has a beginning, a middle, and an end. In the beginning, writers state their position, argument, or opinion clearly. In the middle, the opinion is developed as writers select and present three or more reasons or pieces of evidence to support their position. These reasons may appeal to logic, character, or emotions. Writers sequence the evidence in a logical order and use concrete examples whenever possible. They often use cue words such as *first, second,* and *third* to alert readers to the organization. Seventh and eighth graders also refute counterarguments in the middle. In the end, writers lead their readers to draw the conclusion that they intend through giving a personal statement, making a prediction, or summarizing the major points. The organization of an argument is illustrated in Figure 10-10.

Marion Crowhurst (1991) has identified several problems in students' persuasive writing that their organizational scheme can help to ameliorate. First, students' persuasive compositions are typically shorter than the stories and reports that they write. In these shorter compositions, students neither develop their arguments nor provide reasons to support their claims. Second, their persuasive essays show poor organization because students are unfamiliar with how an argument should be structured. Third, students' writing style is often inappropriate. Their language is informal, and they use words such as *also* to tie arguments together rather than the more sophisticated stylistic devices, such as *if . . . then* statements, typically used in persuasive writing. When students talk their way through the organizational scheme as a prewriting activity and listen to classmates discuss their plans, they develop more sophisticated writing styles and tighter arguments.

Although the organization of an argument typically involves a statement, the development of three (or more) reasons, and a conclusion, this scheme is not equivalent to a traditional five-paragraph theme. Persuasive writing requires a more elaborate scheme than the simplistic, formulaic five-paragraph theme (Crowhurst, 1991). In persuasive writing, students devise ways to introduce an argument, present supporting reasons, draw conclusions, and persuade the reader to accept the writer's viewpoint.

Posters. Students use a combination of drawing and writing to state a position on a persuasive poster. Children are surrounded by persuasive posters, ranging from "Keep America Beautiful" billboard signs and "Don't Drink and Drive" bumper stickers to the motivational posters typically displayed in school hallways and cafeterias. Students make similar projects during literature focus units and thematic units. As part of a unit on drugs, a class of sixth graders designed posters to display in their community to warn people about the dangers of drugs. In the poster presented in Figure 10-11, the student used a logical cause-and-effect appeal to warn of the dangers of driving under the influence of alcohol or drugs.

Essays. Students write persuasive essays in which they argue on topics they have strong beliefs and opinions about. They articulate the reasons in support of their po-

ELL

Even though persuasive writing is often considered the most difficult genre, don't assume that children who are learning English as a second language don't know how to use persuasion and can't be successful in making persuasive posters. They will surprise you!

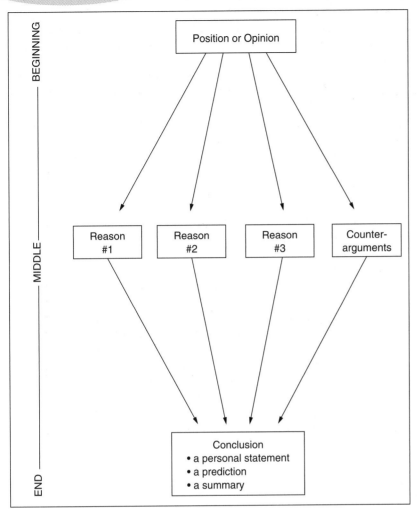

Figure 10-10   Graphic Organizer for an Argument

BEGINNING

Position or Opinion

MIDDLE

| Reason #1 | Reason #2 | Reason #3 | Counter-arguments |

END

Conclusion
• a personal statement
• a prediction
• a summary

sitions and refute possible counterarguments. In this paragraph-long essay, a fifth grader argues why Martin Luther King Jr. deserves a national holiday.

Martin Luther King Jr. deserves a national holiday because he was a great American. Dr. King spent his whole life helping African Americans achieve equality. At that time, there was segregation and sometimes African Americans had to sit at the back of the bus and eat in separate parts of restaurants. That wasn't fair! Dr. King believed the best way to get equal treatment was through peaceful protests. He said that riots were bad. Dr. King was a brave man who sacrificed his family's safety and even his own life for his beliefs. He is still a role model for Americans who continue to work for freedom and equality for all people. The national holiday for Martin Luther King Jr. on January 20th each year reminds everyone of his dream.

Figure 10-11 A Sixth Grader's Advertisement About Drugs

Gamble with drugs & the odds are, you'll lose

Beer

Letters. Students also write letters to persuade family members, friends, and community people. As with other types of letters, these persuasive letters are written to real audiences and are mailed, such as this letter written by a student to the principal of her school.

Dear Mr. Lucas,

 Mrs. Williams has been reading a wonderful book to us. It is called Holes and it was written by Louis Sachar. It is such a good book that it won the Newbery Medal. That means it was the best book of the year. Now the book has been made into a movie, and our class wants to go to see it.

 I think that you should let us go for three very good reasons. First of all, it is educational. After we go to see the movie, we will come back and make a circle diagram and compare the book with the movie. Then we will write an essay to explain which one we liked better. That sounds educational, don't you think?

 The second reason is that would be a fun trip. We would have fun on the bus and at the movie. Our class has worked hard this year, and this trip is something that we will remember after we leave Ericson School and go to the middle school. I think we deserve the trip.

 The third reason is that everyone in the class wants to go. Mrs. Williams wants to, too. I know you might say that there isn't any money for field trips, but I have an answer for you. We will ask our parents to pay some money so that we can go. I asked my dad and he said he would pay for me. So I think that I have taken care of the problem.

*I hope you will let us go on a field trip to see the movie.
Mr. Lucas, maybe you would like to come with us? I think you
would have a fun time.*

Sincerely,
Crystal

In her letter, this student has followed the design of an argument: She begins by stating her position; next she offers three reasons to support her position; and then she refutes a counterargument. She concludes with an emotional appeal—inviting the principal to come to the movies and have fun with them.

As part of literature focus units, students assume the role of a character and write simulated letters to another character. As part of a unit on *The Giver* (Lowry, 1993), for example, seventh graders wrote persuasive letters from one character to another offering advice about how to make the community better. In this letter, a student writes from Jonas's viewpoint.

Dear Giver,
   *Gabe and I are here in Elsewhere. It is a loving community.
We are safe and happy. Now it is up to you to help the community. I think you should let them deal with the memories themselves and let them make choices. You have to teach them how
to make choices and try to make them use them wisely.*
   *Let them use the memories for good. The memories of war
would teach them that war is bad. The memories of color would let
them enjoy life more, if they could see color. The feelings of love
would make them very happy. They could learn from these memories. They could learn of the past, good or bad, sad or happy. If
they have memories, they could have feelings. They could have
wisdom. They could have happiness. They could be free.*
   *I know what you think. You think there would be chaos if the
community had the memories. Bad and evil things could happen,
but Giver, life is like that. You have the memories and you know
what could happen. That's why you are there to help them.*

Your son,
Jonas

This student's letter is persuasive. He argues that when people have memories, they can become wise, happy, and free. In the final paragraph, Josh refutes a counterargument, that giving people memories will lead to chaos, by suggesting that the Giver can help the community through the difficult adjustment.

Teaching Students to Write Persuasively.   Teachers introduce students to persuasive writing by examining how persuasion is used in everyday life. Teachers talk with students about the points of view and positions that people take on various issues. Students might brainstorm a list of examples of persuasion they notice in the family, school, and community. They collect advertisements from magazines and newspapers or make a display of photos of billboards and posters with persuasive arguments that they notice in the community.

Teachers also share examples of trade books in which persuasion is used. Mrs. Lee used *Molly's Pilgrim* (Cohen, 1983) for a minilesson on persuasive writing in the vignette at the beginning of this chapter; other books with persuasive appeals include *The True Story of the 3 Little Pigs!* (Scieszka, 1989), *Nettie's Trip South* (Turner, 1987), *Encounter* (Yolen, 1992), and *The Wretched Stone* (Van Allsburg, 1991).

Topics for persuasive writing come from stories students are reading as well as from content-area study. Students argue about whether the book or movie version of a story is better, about whether a character made the right choice, or about a favorite book. As part of thematic units, students use writing to persuade others to stop smoking, avoid drugs, ban nuclear weapons, stop polluting the environment, endorse political candidates, or support community, state, or national issues.

Teachers introduce students to persuasive writing through a series of minilessons in which students investigate persuasive techniques. Then students apply what they have learned to write persuasive essays and letters as part of literature focus units and thematic units. The minilessons are important because research has shown that students benefit from direct instruction on persuasive writing (Crowhurst, 1991). Possible topics for minilessons include: the three ways to persuade people, how to organize an argument, and how to refute counterarguments. Through these lessons, students increase their awareness of the power of persuasion and its pervasiveness today. They also learn how arguments are organized so that they will be prepared to design persuasive posters and write persuasive letters and essays. Mrs. Ohashi's minilesson on writing persuasive essays is presented in the minilesson feature on page 345.

Multigenre Projects

In a multigenre project (Allen, 2001; Romano, 1995, 2000), students explore a science or social studies topic through several genres. They combine content-area study with writing in significant and meaningful ways. Tom Romano (2000) explains that the benefit of this approach is that each genre offers ways of learning and understanding that the others do not; students gain different understandings, for example, by writing a simulated journal entry, an alphabet book, and a cubing[C]. Teachers or students identify a *repetend*, a common thread or unifying feature for the project, which helps students move beyond the level of remembering facts to a deeper, more analytical level of understanding.

Students use a variety of genres for their projects, depending on the information they want to present and their repetend. Figure 10-12 presents a list of 25 genres, including clusters, reports, poems, maps, letters, and data charts, that students can use in their multigenre projects. Students generally use three or more genres in a multigenre project and include both textual and visual genres. What matters most is that the genres amplify and extend the repetend.

Not only can students create multigenre projects, but some authors/illustrators use the technique in children's trade books. *The Magic School Bus on the Ocean Floor* (Cole, 1992) and other books in the Magic School Bus series are examples of multigenre books. Each book features a story about Ms. Frizzle and her students on a fantastic science adventure, and on the side panels of pages, a variety of explanations, charts, diagrams, and essays are presented. Together the story and informational side panels present a more complete, multigenre presentation or project. Other multigenre books for older students are *To Be a Slave* (Lester, 1968), *Nothing But the Truth* (Avi, 1991), *Tears of a Tiger* (Draper, 1994), and *Ernest L. Thayer's Casey at the Bat: A Ballad of the Republic Sung in the Year 1888* (Bing, 2000).

Minilesson

Topic: Persuasive Essays
Grade: Fourth Grade
Time: 30 minutes

Mrs. Ohashi's fourth graders have studied persuasion, collected examples of persuasion in their community, and examined television commercials to determine the advertiser's purpose. Today the teacher is going to reread *The True Story of the 3 Little Pigs!* (Scieszka, 1989) and ask students to decide if they believe the wolf's version.

1. Introduce the topic
Mrs. Ohashi quickly retells "The Three Little Pigs" to familiarize students with the traditional folktale and then introduces Scieszka's version of the story, told from the wolf's viewpoint.

2. Share examples
Mrs. Ohashi reads *The True Story of the 3 Little Pigs!* aloud to students and asks them to think about the wolf's use of persuasion in the story.

3. Provide information
The students talk about the wolf's version, noting the wolf's persuasive techniques, including his friendly attitude and repeated use of the word *true*. Next, they make a chart with three columns. In the left column, students list the wolf's bad deeds as described in the folktale, in the middle column, they list the wolf's arguments and excuses, and in the right column, they decide whether they believe the wolf. For example, the pigs said that the wolf huffed and puffed and blew two houses down, and the wolf argued that he went to the pigs' houses to borrow a cup of sugar and sneezed. The children decide that they don't believe the wolf. After they finish the chart, it becomes clear that although they enjoyed the wolf's story, they believe the traditional version of the story.

4. Guide practice
"You don't believe the wolf's story, and you can explain your thinking in a persuasive essay," Mrs. Ohashi explains. She quickly reviews how to complete a graphic organizer and write a persuasive essay. The children begin by identifying lines of reasoning for their arguments from the chart they developed in the previous step. They complete graphic organizers by listing three reasons for their decisions and their conclusions. Mrs. Ohashi circulates around the classroom, providing assistance as needed and checking their completed graphic organizers. Then students write the first drafts of their essays independently.

5. Assess learning
Mrs. Ohashi checks the students' graphic organizers as they complete them, and she will read their completed essays to assess their learning.

Figure 10-12 Genres for Multigenre Projects

acrostics	Students spell a key word vertically and then write a phrase or sentence beginning with each letter to create a poem or other composition.
biographical sketch	Students write a biographical sketch of a person related to the topic being studied.
cartoons	Students draw a cartoon or copy a published cartoon from a book or Internet article.
charts	Students organize and display textual and visual information on a chart.
clusters	Students draw clusters or other diagrams to display information concisely.
cubes	Students examine a topic from six perspectives.
data charts	Students create a data chart to list and compare information.
found poems	Students collect words and phrases from a book or article and arrange the words and phrases to make a poem.
"I am" poems	Students create an "I am" poem about a person or a topic.
letters	Students write simulated letters or make copies of real letters related to the topic.
life lines	Students draw life lines and mark important dates related to a person's life.
maps	Students make copies of actual maps or draw maps related to the topic.
newspaper articles	Students make copies of actual newspaper articles or write simulated articles related to the topic.
open-mind portraits	Students draw open-mind portraits of people related to the topic.
photos	Students download photos from the Internet or make copies of photos in books.
postcards	Students create postcards with a picture on one side and a message on the other.
questions-answers	Students write a series of questions and answers related to the topic.
quotes	Students collect quotes about the topic from materials they are reading.
riddles	Students write riddles with information related to the topic.
simulated journals	Students write simulated-journal entries from the viewpoint of a person related to the topic.
songs	Students write lyrics about the topic that are sung to familiar tunes.
stories	Students write stories related to the topic.
time lines	Students draw time lines to sequence events related to the topic.
Venn diagrams	Students draw Venn diagrams to compare the topic with something else.
word wall	Students make an alphabetized word wall or word cards of key words related to the topic.

- Complete a self-assessment to demonstrate your understanding of the concepts presented in this chapter
- Complete field activities that will help you expand your understanding of the middle-grade classroom and use of reading and writing activities to enhance learning
- Visit important web links related to connecting reading and writing with middle-grade students
- Look into your state's standards as they relate to connecting reading and writing and the middle-grade student
- Communicate with other preservice teachers via the message board and discuss the issues of teaching students in grades 4 to 8 to keep journals and reading and learning logs, write reports, write persuasive pieces, and other types of writing projects

Review

Teachers connect reading and writing because reading and writing are similar processes of meaning making and because making connections enhances students' learning. Students keep journals as they read novels and participate in thematic units, and they share their learning through a variety of writing projects, including reports, poems, and persuasive writing. The key concepts presented in this chapter are reviewed in the feature that follows.

How Effective Teachers . . .
Connect Reading and Writing

1. Teachers understand that the reading and writing processes are related.
2. Teachers have students write in reading logs as they read novels and other stories.
3. Teachers have students write in learning logs as part of thematic units.
4. Teachers have students use double-entry journals to think more deeply about books they are reading and topics they are studying as part of thematic units.
5. Teachers have students write simulated journals from the role of a character or a historical personality.
6. Teachers have students share what they learn in thematic units through various types of reports.
7. Teachers introduce report writing by having students write collaborative compositions.
8. Teachers have students write a variety of poems as projects.
9. Teachers involve students in persuasive writing projects as part of literature focus units and thematic units.
10. Teachers have students create multigenre projects to showcase their learning.

Professional References

Allen, C. A. (2001). *The multigenre research paper: Voice, passion, and discovery in grades 4–6*. Portsmouth, NH: Heinemann.

Barone, G. (1990). The written responses of young children: Beyond comprehension to story understanding. *The New Advocate, 3*, 49–56.

Berthoff, A. (1981). *The making of meaning*. Upper Montclair, NJ: Boynton/Cook.

Crowhurst, M. (1991). Interrelationships between reading and writing persuasive discourse. *Research in the Teaching of English, 25*, 314–338.

Five, C. L. (1986). Fifth graders respond to a changed reading program. *Harvard Educational Review, 56*, 395–405.

Fulwiler, T. (1985). Research writing. In M. Schartz (Ed.), *Writing for many roles* (pp. 207–230). Upper Montclair, NJ: Boynton/Cook.

Fulwiler, T. (1987). *The journal book*. Portsmouth, NH: Boynton/Cook.

Hancock, M. R. (1992). Literature response journals: Insights beyond the printed page. *Language Arts, 69*, 36–42.

Hancock, M. R. (1993). Exploring and extending personal response through literature journals. *The Reading Teacher, 46*, 466–474.

Harvey, S. (1998). *Nonfiction matters: Reading, writing, and research in grades 3–8*. York, ME: Stenhouse.

Krogness, M. E. (1987). Folklore: A matter of the heart and the heart of the matter. *Language Arts, 64*, 808–818.

Moline, S. (1995). *I see what you mean: Children at work with visual information*. York, ME: Stenhouse.

Robb, L. (2003). *Teaching reading in social studies, science, and math*. New York: Scholastic.

Romano, T. (1995). *Writing with passion: Life stories, multiple genres*. Portsmouth, NH: Heinemann/Boynton/Cook.

Romano, T. (2000). *Blending genre, alternating style: Writing multiple genre papers*. Portsmouth, NH: Heinemann/Boynton/Cook.

Stanford, B. (1988). Writing reflectively. *Language Arts, 65*, 652–658.

Tierney, R. J., & Shanahan, T. (1996). Research on the reading-writing relationship: Interactions, transactions, and outcomes. In R. Barr, M. L. Kamil, P. Mosenthal, & P. D. Pearson (Eds.), *Handbook of reading research* (vol. 2, pp. 246–280). Mahwah, NJ: Lawrence Erlbaum.

Tompkins, G. E. (2004). *Teaching writing: Balancing process and product* (5th ed.). Upper Saddle River, NJ: Merrill/Prentice Hall.

Wilson, L. (1994). *Write me a poem: Reading, writing, and performing poetry*. Portsmouth, NH: Heinemann.

Wollman-Bonilla, J. E. (1989). Reading journals: Invitations to participate in literature. *The Reading Teacher, 43*, 112–120.

Children's Book References

Avi. (1991). *Nothing but the truth*. New York: Orchard.

Beatty, P. (1987). *Charley Skedaddle*. New York: Morrow.

Bierman, C. (1998). *Journey to Ellis Island: How my father came to America*. New York: Hyperion.

Bing, C. (2000). *Ernest L. Thayer's Casey at the bat: A ballad of the republic sung in the year 1888*. Brooklyn, NY: Handprint Books.

Byars, B. (1970). *The summer of the swans*. New York: Viking.

Cohen, B. (1983). *Molly's pilgrim*. New York: Lothrop, Lee & Shepard.

Cole, J. (1992). *The magic school bus on the ocean floor*. New York: Scholastic.

Cole, J. (1996). *The magic school bus inside a beehive*. New York: Scholastic.

Cushman, K. (1994). *Catherine, called Birdy*. New York: HarperCollins.

Denenberg, B. (1998). *The journal of William Thomas Emerson: A Revolutionary War patriot*. New York: Scholastic.

Denenberg, B. (1999). *The journal of Ben Uchida: Citizen 13559, Mirror Lake Internment Camp*. New York: Scholastic.

Donnelly, J. (2002). *The pilgrims and me*. New York: Grosset & Dunlap.

Draper, S. M. (1994). *Tears of a tiger*. New York: Atheneum.

Fleischman, P. (1985). *I am phoenix: Poems for two voices*. New York: HarperCollins.

Fleischman, P. (1988). *Joyful noise: Poems for two voices*. New York: HarperCollins.

Fritz, J. (1987). *Brady*. New York: Viking.

George, J. C. (1993). *The first Thanksgiving*. New York: Philomel.

Greene, R. G. (2002). *The very first Thanksgiving day*. New York: Atheneum.

Gregory, K. (1997). *Across the wide and lonesome prairie: The Oregon Trail diary of Hattie Campbell*. New York: Scholastic.

Hayward, L. (1990). *The first Thanksgiving*. New York: Random House.

Howe, D., & Howe, J. (1979). *Bunnicula: A rabbit-tale of mystery*. New York: Atheneum.

Hunt, I. (1987). *Across five Aprils*. New York: Follett.

Hunt, J. (1989). *Illuminations*. New York: Bradbury Press.

Lasky, K. (1996). *A journey to the new world: The diary of Remember Patience Whipple*. New York: Scholastic.

Lester, J. (1968). *To be a slave*. New York: Dial.

Levinson, R. (1985). *Watch the stars come out*. New York: Dutton.

Maestro, B. (1996). *Coming to America: The story of immigration*. New York: Scholastic.

Maestro, B., & Maestro, G. (1986). *The story of the Statue of Liberty*. New York: Lothrop, Lee & Shepard.

Mannis, C. D. (2003). *The queen's progress: An Elizabethan alphabet*. New York: Viking.

McGovern, A. (1993). *The pilgrims' first Thanksgiving*. New York: Scholastic.

McKissack, P. C. (1997). *A picture of freedom: The diary of Clotee, a slave girl*. New York: Scholastic.

Musgrove, M. (1976). *Ashanti to Zulu: African traditions*. New York: Dial.

Napier, M. (2002). *Z is for Zamboni: A hockey alphabet*. Chelsea, MI: Sleeping Bear Press.

Paulsen, G. (1987). *Hatchet*. New York: Simon & Schuster.

San Souci, R. (1991). *N. C. Wyeth's pilgrims*. San Francisco: Chronicle Books.

Scieszka, J. (1989). *The true story of the 3 little pigs!* New York: Viking.

Turner, A. (1987). *Nettie's trip south*. New York: Macmillan.

Van Allsburg, C. (1991). *The wretched stone*. Boston: Houghton Mifflin.

Viorst, J. (1981). *If I were in charge of the world and other worries*. New York: Atheneum.

Waters, K. (1989). *Sarah Morton's day: A day in the life of a pilgrim girl*. New York: Scholastic.

Waters, K. (1993). *Samuel Eaton's day: A day in the life of a pilgrim boy*. New York: Scholastic.

Waters, K. (1996). *Tapenum's day: A Wampanoag Indian boy in pilgrim times*. New York: Scholastic.

Waters, K. (2001). *Giving thanks: The 1621 harvest feast*. New York: Scholastic.

White, E. E. (2002). *The journal of Patrick Seamus Flaherty: United States Marine Corps*. New York: Scholastic.

Yolen, J. (1992). *Encounter*. Orlando, FL: Harcourt Brace.

chapter 11

Working With Struggling Readers and Writers

- What kind of instruction do struggling readers and writers need?

- What is differentiated instruction?

- How do teachers use guided reading in the middle grades?

- How do teachers match students and books?

Mrs. Shasky Differentiates Instruction

The 31 students in Mrs. Shasky's sixth-grade class are reading *The Breadwinner* (Ellis, 2001), the story of a girl who seeks work disguised as a boy so that she can support her family during the Taliban era in Afghanistan. Some of the students are sitting on a sofa or lounging on floor pillows in the reading area in the back of the classroom; they are reading independently. Others are clustered around Mrs. Shasky, listening as she reads the same book aloud. She reads softly so that she won't distract the students reading in the back of the classroom. Some of the students close to Mrs. Shasky follow along in their copies, but others look at Mrs. Shasky, listening intently.

Mrs. Shasky provides two ways to read the novel because her students have a broad range of reading levels, from third through sixth grade. Her students who read at the fifth- and sixth-grade levels can read the book independently, but her 12 struggling readers who read at the third- and fourth-grade levels need extra support. That's why she reads the book aloud to them.

After she finishes reading the chapter, the class comes together for a grand conversation[C]. The students have many questions about Afghanistan and life under Taliban rule, and Mrs. Shasky often takes more of the discussion time than she would like to answer their questions, but gradually the students are developing the background knowledge they need to understand the story. This is the time when Mrs. Shasky teaches comprehension, so she asks inferential questions that require students to go beyond literal information. For example, she asks, "Why did the Taliban arrest Parvana's father?" Hector quickly answers with what he remembers reading in the novel: "Because he went to college in another country, and they don't want teachers to do that." Mrs. Shasky persists, "Why doesn't the Taliban want teachers or other people to study in another country?" No one has an idea, so Mrs. Shasky asks the question another way: "Lots of teachers in America go to other countries to study. You know that I went to visit schools in China last summer. Why is that a good idea?" The students offer several reasons—to learn about other people, to learn new things, and to learn new ways of teaching. "Wouldn't the Taliban want teachers to do these things, too?" Mrs. Shasky asks. Marisela replies, "No, the Taliban closed the schools because they want to control everyone. They don't like teachers who have new ideas because they could make trouble." "How could they make trouble?" Mrs. Shasky continues. Jared suggests, "Parvana's father and the other teachers could tell people that there is a better way to live, and then everyone could get together and fight the Taliban and kill them and have a free country like ours."

As they talk, several students add new words to the word wall[C] posted on a nearby wall. The words they add include: *burqa, hospitable, turban, chador, nan, exhaustion,* and *toshak.* Mrs. Shasky refers students to the word wall, and they use some of these words later in the morning during their Word Study period.

Literature study is only one part of Mrs. Shasky's literacy block. Here is her morning schedule:

| 8:30–9:00 | Independent Reading |
| 9:00–10:00 | Literature Study |

10:00–10:15	Minilesson[C]	
10:15–11:15	Projects/Guided Reading	
11:15–11:45	Word Study	

[C] See the Compendium of Instructional Procedures, which follows Chapter 12, for more information on terms marked with the symbol [C].

During each of these activities, Mrs. Shasky differentiates instruction so the wide range of students in her classroom can be successful. Figure 11-1 explains some of the ways she supports her struggling readers and writers.

Mrs. Shasky begins the literacy block each morning with independent reading. All students read independently in leveled books for 30 minutes using a commercial program called Accelerated Reader. Students read books at their reading level and complete comprehension checks on the computer after each book. Mrs. Shasky supervises students as they read, moving from desk to desk and listening to individual students read. She also monitors their progress on the comprehension checks. A chart is posted in the classroom so students can track their reading growth.

Figure 11-1 — Ways Mrs. Shasky Differentiates Instruction

Schedule	Grade-Level Students	Struggling Students
8:30–9:00 Independent Reading	Students read self-selected books at their reading level and check their comprehension using a computer program.	Students read self-selected books at their reading level and check their comprehension using a computer program.
9:00–10:00 Literature Study	Students read the featured novel independently and then participate in grand conversations.	Students listen to the teacher read the featured novel aloud. Then they participate in grand conversations.
10:00–10:15 Minilesson	Mrs. Shasky presents whole-class minilessons on grade-level literacy topics.	Mrs. Shasky presents whole-class minilessons on grade-level literacy topics and other minilessons for small groups according to need. She uses the language experience approach[C] and interactive writing[C] to make charts.
10:15–11:15 Projects/Guided Reading	Students are involved in literacy projects related to the featured novel.	Students participate in guided reading groups and work in small groups to do projects related to the featured novel.
11:15–11:45 Word Study	Students participate in whole-class and small-group word study activities and lessons. They use an individualized approach to study spelling words and take tests.	Students participate in whole-class and small-group word study activities and lessons. They use an individualized approach to study spelling words and take tests.

Next students participate in a literature study of a novel. Books are usually chosen from the district's recommended reading list for sixth grade, and Mrs. Shasky supplements with other books like *The Breadwinner* that are timely or that she thinks would appeal to her students. The novel becomes a vehicle for teaching reading strategies and literary analysis.

The third activity is a minilesson. Mrs. Shasky teaches minilessons on strategies, genres, story structure, literary devices, and other grade-level standards. Sometimes the whole class participates in the minilesson, and at other times, the lesson is designed for a specific group of students. She tries to tie all lessons into the novel they are currently reading. Today, she teaches a minilesson to the whole class on character development and explains that authors develop characters in four ways: appearance, actions, talking, and thinking. She asks students to think about Parvana, the main character in *The Breadwinner,* and how the author, Deborah Ellis, developed her. As the students share ideas, Mrs. Shasky draws a clusterlike diagram on chart paper and writes Parvana's name in the center circle. She divides the diagram into four sections and writes *appearance, actions, talking,* and *thinking* in each section. Next, she writes a sentence or two that students have made in each section. Mrs. Shasky steps back and rereads the chart, and then she asks, "Which of the four ways of character development is most important in *The Breadwinner*? What is Deborah Ellis trying to tell us?" The students are torn between "appearance" and "actions." Nita says, "It's her clothes. She has to dress like a boy." Javier disagrees, "No, it's what she is doing. She is pretending to be a boy to help her family. That's what matters." With more discussion, most students agree with Javier. A student's copy of the character development diagram is shown in Figure 11-2.

Most of the students return to their desks to write in their reading logs[C] or work on projects, but Mrs. Shasky keeps a group of struggling readers who need more practice writing summaries with her to write a summary statement about character development. She uses the language experience approach to quickly take the students' dictation as they develop this summary statement about character development, which they will later share with the whole class.

Deborah Ellis tells us about Parvana in four ways: appearance, actions, talking, and thinking. The most important way we learn about Parvana is by her actions. She pretends she is a boy to make money so her family doesn't starve.

Next, the students move on to projects related to *The Breadwinner.* For this book, they write entries in reading logs, collect favorite sentences and write them on sentence strips, use the Internet to research Afghanistan, make maps of the Middle East, and create an open-mind portrait[C] of a character from the novel or develop another project. The list of activities is posted in the classroom so that students know what they are expected to do.

While students are working, Mrs. Shasky meets with small groups of struggling readers for guided reading lessons. One group is reading at early third-grade level (Reading Recovery Level M), the second group is reading at late third-grade/early fourth-grade level (Reading Recovery Level P), and the third group is reading at fourth-grade level (Reading Recovery Level R). She usually meets with two groups each day for 25 to 30 minutes each and they read short chapter books at their reading levels. They read and discuss one or two chapters each day, and then they are to reread the chapters independently or with a buddy before they meet again.

Figure 11-2 A Character Diagram About Parvana

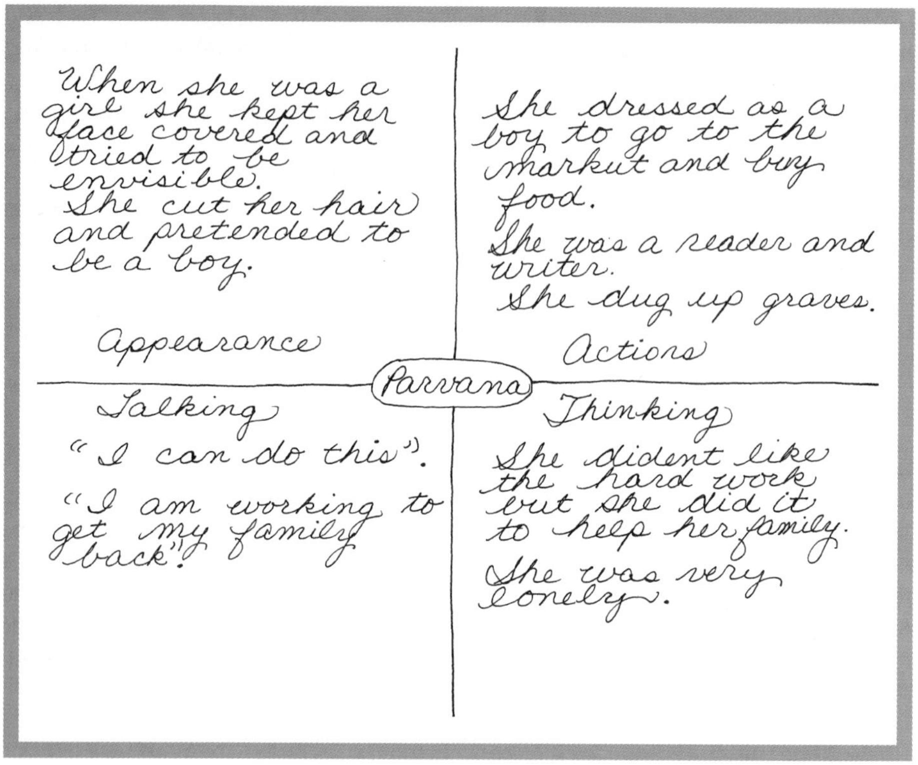

When she was a girl she kept her face covered and tried to be invisible.
She cut her hair and pretended to be a boy.

Appearance

She dressed as a boy to go to the market and buy food.
She was a reader and writer.
She dug up graves.

Actions

Parvana

Talking

"I can do this".

"I am working to get my family back".

Thinking

She dident like the hard work but she did it to help her family.
She was very lonely.

The group reading at the early third-grade level is reading Dan Greenburg's wacky series, The Zack Files, about a fifth grader named Zack who has amazing things happen to him, such as becoming invisible. In the book they've just finished reading, *How I Went From Bad to Verse* (Greenburg, 2000), Zack is bitten by an insect and catches Rhyme Disease. He speaks only in rhyme, and worse yet, he floats above the ground and turns blue. Finally, his science teacher, Mrs. Coleman-Levin, cures him and his life returns to normal—at least until the next book. The students silently reread the last two chapters in the book, and they talk again about Zack's unusual symptoms and Mrs. Coleman-Levin's unusual cures.

Mrs. Shasky makes a chart about symptoms and cures on a white board beside her and passes out copies of the chart for the students to complete after they fill out the chart on the white board. First, the students list the three symptoms that Zack exhibited (rhyming, floating, and blue skin) on the class chart using interactive writing techniques to phrase and write their answers. Next, they complete the chart by explaining how Mrs. Coleman-Levin cured each symptom. The students return to Chapter 8 to reread and check that they remember the cures (wearing a re-versible jacket, reciting a poem backwards, and thinking happy thoughts). They complete the class chart and their own copies of the chart. Mrs. Shasky monitors their writing and requires that they write legibly and spell words correctly. She encourages them to check the spelling of words on the white board or in their books.

Then the students go through a ceremonial process and list the book on a chart of the books they have read as a group. *How I Went From Bad to Verse* is number 28 on the list, and the students are amazed! "I've never read so many books before in my life," Ana comments, and the group agrees. "I told my Tio Roberto that I am a good reader now," Mark says. The students will take the book home tonight to read to their parents, a sibling, a grandparent, or a neighbor.

Mrs. Shasky asks if they would like to read another book from The Zack Files series, and they eagerly agree. She reaches for another set of books from the bookcase behind her and passes out copies of *Don't Count on Dracula* (Greenburg, 2000) for students to get a first look at. They'll start reading the book tomorrow, but several students can't resist looking through the book now.

After conducting another guided reading[C] group, Mrs. Shasky moves the class to the last segment of the literacy block: word study. Students do a combination of vocabulary and individualized spelling activities during word study. On Monday, Mrs. Shasky takes the entire 30 minutes for spelling. She administers the pretest, and students check it themselves. Then they choose the words they will study during the week and make two copies of the word list, one for themselves and one for Mrs. Shasky to keep. Because she has implemented an individualized spelling program, students study different words, depending on their abilities. The students practice their spelling words each day, and on Friday, they take the final spelling test.

To read more about individualized spelling, turn back to Chapter 4, "Refining Students' Print Skills."

On Tuesday, Wednesday, and Thursday, students participate in vocabulary lessons to study the meanings of specific words, to examine root words and affixes, and to learn to use a dictionary and thesaurus. They use words from the word wall for most activities.

Over the past 5 weeks, Mrs. Shasky has taught a series of lessons on these root words:

ann/enn *(year): annual, anniversary, millennium*
graph *(write): paragraph, autobiography, photograph*
mar/mer *(sea): mermaid, submarine, marsh*
tele *(far): telecast, telephone, telethon*
volv *(roll): revolution, evolution, revolver*

The students have made clusters with these root words and brainstormed lists of words that come from them on chart paper, and these charts are posted around the classroom. Today, students are examining words from the word wall to identify other root words.

Because Mrs. Shasky wants to do more to help her struggling readers, she developed a twice-a-week after-school tutoring session that she calls Shasky's Reading Club. She invited the 12 students reading at third- and fourth-grade levels to stay after school each Tuesday and Thursday to participate in the club. She began the club after parent conferences in early October. She explained the importance of providing these struggling readers with additional instruction and time for reading. The parents of all 12 students committed to picking up their students twice a week after the reading club.

During the 45-minute reading club meeting, students do two types of reading: They read self-selected books independently and they participate in guided reading groups. Mrs. Shasky is pleased to see these students' growth over the 4 months the club has been operating. During the club meetings, she has noticed that her struggling students behave like her grade-level readers do during the school day. Instead of being reticent and unsure of themselves as they sometimes are during the school day, they participate willingly in discussions and confidently assume leadership roles.

As the club meeting begins, the 12 students have picked up books they are reading and have settled on the sofa and on floor pillows in the back of the classroom. Mrs. Shasky checks that everyone has an appropriate leveled book to read, and then she calls a group of 4 students reading at Reading Recovery level P (late third-/early fourth-grade level). They're reading Jon Scieszka's The Time Warp Trio series of easy-reading chapter books. In these stories, three modern-day friends warp back into history and find themselves in adventures. They've already read *Your Mother Was a Neanderthal* (1993) and *Tut Tut* (1996).

Now they're reading *Knights of the Kitchen Table* (1991), in which the boys travel back to the days of the Knights of the Round Table. A giant and a dragon threaten Camelot, and the boys are ready to help King Arthur and the knights. The first few chapters were difficult because the students didn't know the King Arthur stories, but Mrs. Shasky told the stories to build their background knowledge. The vocabulary was unfamiliar, too—*vile knaves, lance, visor, methinks,* and *foul-mouthed enchanters,* for example—but now the group is into the story. They read about the boys reaching Camelot and meeting King Arthur, Queen Guenevere, and Merlin when they read Chapter 5 today in class. They begin by rereading the chapter and doing a read-around[C], where they take turns randomly reading aloud their favorite sentences from the chapter. Then Mrs. Shasky takes them on a text walk of Chapter 6, and they examine a full-page illustration of the giant. Hector predicts, "I think Sir Joe the Magnificent will kill both the giant and the dragon." "You should say he will *slay* them. *Slay* means to kill," explains Jesus. Mrs. Shasky asks how the students might slay the giant and the dragon, and the boys quickly suggest using swords or guns, but the illustrations in Chapter 6 don't provide any clues.

Mrs. Shasky explains that this riddle is going to be important in the chapter: Why did the giant wear red suspenders? The students aren't familiar with suspenders, so Mrs. Shasky shows them a pair of her husband's suspenders. She models wearing them and explains that sometimes her husband wears suspenders instead of a belt to hold his pants up.

Marisela, who has been listening quietly while the boys in the group eagerly talked about slaying dragons and giants, asks, "Why did the giant wear suspenders? Mrs. Shasky, what is the answer?" The teacher explains that they'll learn the answer as they read the chapter, and then Marisela predicts, "You have to be smart to know the answer to a riddle, so I think those boys will use their brains to save Camelot." Mrs. Shasky smiles in agreement and says, "Let's read Chapter 6 to see if Marisela's prediction is right."

The students read the five pages in the chapter in less than 10 minutes, and while they are reading, Mrs. Shasky helps students decode several unfamiliar words and explains a confusing section when two boys ask about it. The group now knows the answer to the riddle: Why did the giant wear red suspenders? To hold his pants up. They like the riddle and show interest in reading more riddles. Mrs. Shasky says that she'll get some riddle books for them tomorrow. They continue to discuss the chapter, and Jesus sums up the group's feelings by saying, "Bleob [the giant] should be dead and gone by now. I just want to keep reading and find out what happens." Because the giant and the dragon do destroy themselves in the next chapter, Mrs. Shasky lets the students take the books back to the reading corner and read the next chapter to find out what happens.

Then Mrs. Shasky calls a second group for a guided reading lesson while the other two groups continue reading on their own. The second group finishes reading with Mrs. Shasky when only several minutes remain before the reading club ends, so Mrs. Shasky joins the group in the back of the classroom and asks each student to briefly tell what he or she has been reading. Then the students put their books back in their desks or take them home to continue reading, and they are excused.

Mrs. Shasky provides three kinds of support for her struggling readers and writers. First, she provides support for struggling students during regular classroom reading and writing activities. During literature study, for example, Mrs. Shasky read aloud to students who could not read the featured novel independently. Second, she adapts lessons so that her struggling students get additional instruction. During the projects period, Mrs. Shasky includes guided reading lessons for her struggling students. Third, she provides tutoring for her struggling students. Mrs. Shasky meets with her struggling readers after school twice a week for Shasky's Reading Club.

It is crucial that struggling readers and writers in fourth through eighth grades get help. Juel (1988) found that there is a 90% chance that students who are struggling readers at the end of first grade will continue to be struggling readers in fourth grade.

Early-intervention programs have been very successful and can provide insight about how to work with older struggling readers and writers. Five guidelines are:

1. Teachers need to provide more time for reading and writing instruction during the school day. During second reading lessons, teachers can follow up and review after whole-class instruction.
2. Teachers need to group students flexibly so that instruction can match student needs.
3. Teachers need to have a variety of literacy materials available for students that match their reading levels and interests.
4. Teachers need to provide both direct and informal instruction together with opportunities for application.
5. Teachers need to establish home support networks. (Strickland, Ganske, & Monroe, 2002)

The feature on page 358 shows how teachers involve struggling readers and writers in a balanced literacy program. As you continue reading, you will learn how to use differentiated instruction to provide extra support so that all students can be successful.

DIFFERENTIATED INSTRUCTION

Teachers know that their students vary—their interests and motivation, their background knowledge and prior experiences, and their culture and language proficiency as well as their reading and writing capabilities—so it's important to allow for these differences as they plan for instruction. According to Carol Ann Tomlinson (2001), differentiated instruction "means 'shaking up' what goes on in the classroom so that students have multiple options for taking information, making sense of ideas, and expressing what they learn" (p. 1). Differentiating instruction is especially important for struggling readers and writers who haven't been successful and who cannot

Ways That Teachers Assist Struggling Readers and Writers in a Balanced Literacy Program

Component	Description
Reading	Teachers provide additional reading instruction, opportunities for students to have more reading practice, and books at students' reading levels.
Phonics and Other Skills	Teachers teach phonics and other skills through guided reading lessons.
Strategies	Teachers teach strategies during guided reading lessons, and students apply the strategies they have learned during independent reading.
Vocabulary	Teachers teach vocabulary through literature focus units, content-area units, and guided reading lessons.
Comprehension	Teachers help struggling readers to develop comprehension during each stage of the reading process.
Literature	Teachers read aloud novels that are too difficult for students to read themselves, and students read leveled books that interest them.
Content-Area Study	Teachers support struggling students' reading and writing in content-area units.
Oral Language	Struggling students often listen to the teacher read books aloud, and they participate in a variety of talk activities during the reading and writing processes.
Writing	Teachers support students' writing in a variety of ways and use the language experience approach and interactive writing as teaching tools.
Spelling	Teachers individualize spelling instruction so that all students are learning words at their level.

Differentiating instruction is as important for English learners as it is for other struggling readers and writers. Teachers provide opportunities for students to work together and structure learning activities so they can be successful.

read grade-level textbooks. In the vignette, for example, Mrs. Shasky adapted her instruction to meet her students' needs and provided options for students so that they could be successful.

Working With Struggling Readers

Probably the most effective way to work with struggling readers in the middle grades is guided reading. Teachers use guided reading to work with small groups of students who are reading books at their instructional level, with approximately 90–94% accuracy (Clay, 1991). During guided reading, teachers use the reading process and support students' reading and their use of reading strategies (Fountas & Pinnell, 2001). Students do the actual reading themselves, although the teacher may read aloud with students to get them started on the first page or two. Beginning readers often mumble the words softly as they read, and this practice helps the teacher keep track of students' reading and the strategies they are using. Older students who are more fluent readers usually read silently during guided reading. Guided reading is not round-robin reading, in which students take turns reading pages aloud to the group.

Teachers choose the books that students read during guided reading, and the books are carefully chosen to reflect the students' reading levels and their knowledge of and ability to use reading strategies. Teachers have many books available for students who are reading on grade level, but finding appropriate books for struggling readers can be difficult. Figure 11-3 presents a list of easy-to-read series written at second, third, fourth, and fifth grade levels that teachers can use with struggling middle-grade students. Like Mrs. Shasky's students in the vignette, struggling readers usually enjoy reading series books because the books in a series are predictable and students enjoy reading about familiar characters and events.

Teachers read the book in preparation for the lesson and plan how they will teach it. They consider how to develop students' background knowledge and which main ideas to develop before reading. They choose a strategy to teach, prepare for word work activities, and plan other after-reading activities. Many teachers use little sticky notes to mark teaching points in the book.

Guided reading lessons usually last approximately 30 minutes. When middle-grade students are reading chapter books, the reading process takes longer, often a week or more to complete a book. As with other types of reading lessons, teachers follow the five stages of the reading process for guided reading.

1. *Prereading.* Teachers introduce the new book and prepare students to read. Teachers often begin by activating or building background knowledge on a topic related to the book. They introduce the book by showing the cover, reading the title and the author's name, and talking about the problem in the story or one or two main ideas in an informational book or article. They set the purpose for reading, and students often make predictions. Teachers continue with a book walk to present an overview of the selection, but they do not read it aloud to students. During the book walk, teachers point out format considerations or diagrams and other special features. They introduce vocabulary words that are essential to the meaning of the text and teach or review a strategy that students should use while reading.

2. *Reading.* Teachers guide students through one or more readings of the selection. Sometimes students and the teacher read the first page or two of the book together to get off to a successful start. Then students read the rest of the selection independently, reading aloud softly to themselves or silently, depending on their reading level. Teachers monitor students as they read, prompting for strategies and word identification as needed. They move from student to student, listening in as the student reads aloud. Many teachers take a running record[C] as students read aloud. Students often have a brief writing assignment to do after they finish reading and while they wait for classmates to finish.

3. *Responding.* Students discuss with the teacher the book they have just finished reading. Teachers move from literal questions to higher-level inferential and critical questions to lead students to think more deeply about the selection. Higher-level questions include:

What would happen if . . . ?
Why did . . . ?
If . . . , what might have happened next?
If you were . . . , what would you . . . ?

Figure 11-3 Easy-to-Read Series for Struggling Readers

Reading Level	Series	Genre
2	A to Z Mysteries by Ron Roy (Random House)	Mystery
	Andrew Lost by J. C. Greenburg (Random House)	Informational
	Cam Jansen by David A. Adler (Puffin)	Adventure
	Jackie Chan Adventures by Eliza Willard (Grosset & Dunlap)	Adventure
	Jigsaw Jones Mysteries by James Preller (Scholastic)	Mystery
	Magic Tree House by Mary Pope Osborne (Random House)	Adventure
	Marvin Redpost by Louis Sachar (Random House)	Adventure
	Ricky Ricotta's Mighty Robots by Dav Pilkey (Scholastic)	Science Fiction
	Scooby-Do Mysteries by James Gelsey (Scholastic)	Mystery
	The Zack Files (some are third-grade level) by Dan Greenburg (Grosset & Dunlap)	Fantasy
3	Abracadabra! by Peter Lerangis (Scholastic)	Mystery
	The Adventures of the Bailey School Kids by Debbie Dadley and Marcia Thornton Jones (Scholastic)	Adventure
	The Boxcar Children by Gertrude Chandler Warner (Albert Whitman)	Mystery
	Captain Underpants by Dav Pilkey (Scholastic)	Humor
	Hank the Cowdog by John R. Erickson (Puffin)	Fantasy
	The Magic School Bus Chapter Books by Joanna Cole (Scholastic)	Informational
	My America by Mary Pope Osborne (Scholastic)	Historical Fiction
	The Secrets of Droon by Tony Abbott (Scholastic)	Fantasy
	Sports by Matt Christopher (Little, Brown)	Sports
	The Zack Files (some are second-grade level) by Dan Greenburg (Grosset & Dunlap)	Fantasy
4	Animal Ark by Ben M. Baglio (Scholastic)	Animals
	The Babysitters Club by Ann M. Martin (Scholastic)	Adventure
	Deltora Quest by Emily Rodda (Scholastic)	Fantasy
	Dolphin Diaries by Ben M. Baglio (Scholastic)	Animals
	Encyclopedia Brown by Donald J. Sobol (Dutton)	Mystery
	Goosebumps by R. L. Stine (Scholastic)	Horror
	Guardians of Ga'hoole by Kathryn Lasky (Scholastic)	Fantasy
	Island/Everest/Dive Series by Gordon Korman (Scholastic)	Adventure
	Pyrates by Chris Archer (Scholastic)	Adventure
	The Time Warp Trio by Jon Scieszka (Puffin)	Fantasy
5	The Amazing Days of Abby Hayes by Anne Mazer (Scholastic)	Contemporary
	Animorphs by K. A. Applegate (Scholastic)	Science Fiction
	The Black Stallion by Walter Farley (Random House)	Animals
	Dinotopia by Peter David (Random House)	Science Fiction
	From the Files of Madison Finn by Laura Dower (Hyperion)	Contemporary
	Heartland by Lauren Brooke (Scholastic)	Animals
	Remnants by K. A. Applegate (Scholastic)	Science Fiction
	The Saddle Club by Bonnie Bryant (Random House)	Animals
	Thoroughbred by Joanna Campbell (HarperCollins)	Animals
	Unicorns of Balinor by Mary Stanton (Scholastic)	Fantasy

Teachers teach students to read strategically during guided reading lessons.

What did . . . make you think of?

What did you like best about this book?

Through the discussion, students make text-to-self, text-to-world, and text-to-text connections with the book. Afterward, teachers often have students write in reading logs or share what they wrote earlier.

4. *Exploring.* Teachers involve students in three types of instruction: First, teachers review and reinforce the reading strategy that students used as they read the book. Sometimes teachers model how they used the strategy or ask students to reread a page from the book and think aloud about their strategy use. The second type of instruction is literary analysis: Teachers explain genres, present information about story elements or other text structures, and locate examples of literary devices in the selection. Sometimes students create story maps^C or other graphic organizers. Third, through word work activities, teachers focus students' attention on words from the selection. Teachers review vocabulary words from the selection and teach students word-identification skills, such as breaking words into syllables and identifying root words and affixes.

5. *Applying.* Students apply the strategies they are learning in independent reading activities. Students often read independently during reading workshop or in preparation for literature circle discussions. The activities in a guided reading lesson for middle-grade students are summarized in Figure 11-4.

Teachers observe students as they read during guided reading lessons. They spend a few minutes observing each student, sitting either in front of or right beside the student. Teachers observe the student's behaviors for evidence of strategy use and confirm the student's attempts to identify words and solve reading problems. Some of the strategies and problem-solving behaviors that teachers look for are:

- self-monitoring
- checking predictions
- sounding out unfamiliar words

Guided reading lessons are strongly recommended for English language learners who are struggling readers because during these lessons, teachers match students to books, provide strategy lessons, and closely monitor students' learning.

Figure 11-4   Steps in a Guided Reading Lesson

Stage	Activities
1. *Prereading*	• Activate or build background knowledge about a topic related to the book. • Show the cover of the book and read the title and author's name. • Talk about the genre and special structural elements in the book. • Introduce main ideas and key vocabulary. • Do a book walk as an overview of the book, but do not read the book. • Set a purpose for reading and have students make predictions. • Teach a strategy for students to use during reading.
2. *Reading*	• Read the first page aloud to students. • Have students read the book independently, reading silently. • Prompt for strategies and word identification, as needed. • Move from student to student to listen in as they read. • Have students do an informal writing assignment while they wait for classmates to finish reading.
3. *Responding*	• Have a grand conversation to discuss the book. • Encourage students to make text-to-self, text-to-world, and text-to-text connections. • Ask inferential and evaluative-level questions, such as "What would happen if . . . ?" • Ask students to find evidence in the book to support their answers. • Have students write in reading logs or share what they wrote earlier.
4. *Exploring*	• Review a reading strategy. • Teach about genre, text structure, or literary devices. • Review vocabulary words from the book. • Teach word-identification skills, including syllabication and root words and affixes.
5. *Applying*	• Apply strategies in independent reading during reading workshop or Sustained Silent Reading[C].

- checking to see if the word makes sense
- checking to see that a word is appropriate in the syntax of the sentence
- using all sources of information
- attempting to read an unfamiliar word
- self-correcting
- chunking phrases to read more fluently

Teachers take notes about their observations and use the information in deciding what minilessons to teach and what books to choose for children to read.

Teachers also take running records of one or two children during each guided reading lesson and use this information as part of their assessment. Teachers check to see that the books children are reading are at their instructional level and that they are continuing to progress as expected to increasingly difficult levels of books.

OVERVIEW OF GUIDELINES

Guidelines for Working With Struggling Readers and Writers. In each chapter of this text, you've read one or two guidelines for working with struggling students. Here is the complete list of the 14 guidelines:

1. **Struggling students need to spend more time reading and writing.**
   Struggling students often spend little time reading and writing, but daily practice opportunities are essential for students' literacy development.

2. **Struggling writers need to revise their writing.**
   Too often, struggling writers think they are finished once they've written a draft of their composition, but they need to learn to use the writing process to clarify, expand, and refine their writing.

3. **Struggling readers need books at their reading levels.**
   Students are more successful when they read books at their instructional level, but struggling readers are often assigned books to read according to their grade level, whether they are reading at that level or not.

4. **Struggling readers and writers need to be phonemically aware.**
   The ability to blend and segment sounds is essential so that students can use phonics skills to decode unfamiliar words when reading and spell words when writing.

5. **Struggling readers and writers need to know high-frequency words.**
   Because more than half the words that students read and write are high-frequency words, students are more successful when they can read and write these words automatically.

6. **Struggling students need to know a lot of words.**
   Word knowledge is essential in both reading and writing, but struggling students generally have small vocabularies. Students need to know the meaning of the words they're reading and use sophisticated and technical words in their writing.

7. **Struggling students need to read and write fluently.**
   Being able to read and write fluently—quickly and smoothly—is an essential prerequisite if students are to become successful readers and writers. Without adequate fluency, students have difficulty with comprehension.

8. **Struggling students need to become strategic readers and writers.**
   Because the biggest difference between capable and struggling students is that capable readers and writers are strategic, it is essential that all students learn to use strategies to direct, monitor, and evaluate their reading and writing.

9. **Struggling readers and writers need to use graphic organizers.**
   Students use graphic organizers to examine the structure of stories, informational books, and poems, and then they apply this knowledge to enhance comprehension.

10. **Struggling readers need to listen to grade-level-appropriate literature.**
    Even though struggling readers cannot read grade-level-appropriate literature independently, it is important that they listen to stories, informational books, and poetry read aloud and participate in related response activities.

(continues)

11. Struggling readers need to learn how to read content-area textbooks.

Many students mistakenly read content-area textbooks the same way they read novels, without taking advantage of their unique conventions. When students know how to use these conventions, they are more successful.

12. Struggling students need to learn how to study.

Many struggling students don't study because they don't know how to go about it. It's important that students learn to take notes and to review them so that they can be successful.

13. Struggling students need to connect reading and writing.

Reading and writing are similar processes, and students enhance their learning when they write about what they're reading and apply what they've read when they write.

14. Struggling students need to become engaged readers and writers.

Too often, struggling readers aren't motivated, and active involvement in reading and writing activities is essential because students who aren't engaged are less likely to be successful.

For struggling students in grades 4 through 8 to become successful, teachers need to address all 14 of these guidelines.

What About Basal Readers?

Publishers of basal reading textbooks tout their programs as complete literacy programs containing all the materials needed for students to become successful readers. The accessibility of reading materials is clearly one advantage of textbooks: Teachers have copies of grade-level textbooks for every student.

The teacher's edition provides detailed information on how to teach the basal reading program and use the variety of supplemental materials provided with the textbook. The skills and strategies to be taught are specified in the program, and directions are provided for how to teach them and how to assess students' learning. This information is especially useful for inexperienced and struggling teachers.

It is unrealistic, however, to assume that a commercial reading program could be a complete literacy program for all students. Teachers who have students reading below grade level need reading materials at these students' level. The same is true for teachers working with students who read above grade level. Teachers have to supplement their program with appropriate reading materials. In some schools, teachers share basal reading textbooks with teachers in other grades; at other schools, teachers locate sets of leveled books to use with below-grade-level readers. In addition, students need many more opportunities to read and reread books than are provided in a basal reading program, so teachers stock their classroom libraries with books and provide daily time for independent reading.

At the center of a basal reading program is the student textbook or anthology. In fourth through sixth grades, there is usually one book. Most basal reader programs end in sixth grade because seventh and eighth graders read trade books or literature textbooks. Basal readers are colorful and inviting books, often featuring pictures of exciting adventures and fanciful locations on the covers of books for grades 4 through 6. The selections in each textbook are grouped into units, and each unit includes stories, poems, and informational articles. Many multicultural selections have been added, and usually illustrations feature ethnically diverse people. Information about authors and illustrators is given for many selections. The textbooks contain a table of contents and a glossary.

Commercial reading programs provide a wide variety of materials to support student learning; consumable workbooks are probably the best-known support material. Students write letters, words, and sentences in these books to practice phonics, comprehension, and vocabulary skills. In addition, transparencies and blackline masters of additional worksheets are available for teachers to use in teaching skills and strategies. Blackline masters of parent letters are also available.

Some multimedia materials, including audiocassettes, CD-ROMs, and videos, are included with the programs. Teachers can use these materials at listening centers and computer centers. Collections of trade books are available for each grade level to provide supplemental reading materials.

Basal reader programs also offer a variety of assessment tools. Teachers use placement evaluations or informal reading inventories to determine students' reading levels and for placement in reading groups. They use running records to informally monitor students' reading. There are also selection and unit tests to determine students' phonics, vocabulary, and comprehension achievement. Information is also provided on how to administer the assessments and analyze the results.

A teacher's instructional guidebook is provided at each grade level. This oversize handbook provides comprehensive information about how to plan lessons, teach the selections, and assess students' progress. The selections are shown in reduced size in the guidebook, and each page includes background information about the selection, instructions for reading the selections, and coordinating skill and strategy instruction. In addition, information is presented about which supplemental books to use with each selection and how to assess students' learning. Figure 11-5 summarizes the materials provided in most basal reading programs.

Using Literacy Centers

Literacy centers contain meaningful, purposeful literacy activities that students can work at in small groups. Students practice phonics skills at the phonics center, sort word cards at the vocabulary center, or listen to books related to a book they are reading at the listening center. Figure 11-6 describes 13 literacy centers used in middle-grade classrooms. Centers are usually organized in special places in the classroom or at groups of tables (Fountas & Pinnell, 1996).

Literacy centers are usually associated with primary classrooms, but they can be used effectively at all grade levels, even in seventh and eighth grades. In some classrooms, all students work at centers at the same time; in other classrooms, most students work at centers while the teacher works with a small group of students.

The activities in these literacy centers relate to stories students are reading and skills and strategies recently presented in minilessons. Students often manipulate objects, sort word cards, reread books, write responses to stories, and practice skills in centers. Some literacy centers, such as reading and writing centers, are permanent, but others change according to the books students are reading and the activities planned.

In some classrooms, students flow freely from center to center according to their interests; in other classrooms, students are assigned to centers or are required to work at some "assigned" centers and choose among other "choice" centers. Students can sign attendance sheets when they work at each literacy center or mark off their names on a class list tacked to each center. Rarely do students move from center to center in

Figure 11-5 — Materials in Basal Reading Programs

Materials	Description
Textbook or Anthology	The student's book of reading selections. The selections are organized thematically and include literature from trade books. Often the textbook is available in a series of softcover books or a single hardcover book.
Supplemental Books	Collections of trade books for each grade level. In grades 4 to 6, books are often related to unit themes.
Workbooks	Consumable books of phonics, comprehension, and vocabulary worksheets.
Transparencies	Color transparencies to use in teaching skills and strategies.
Blackline Masters	Worksheets that teachers duplicate and use to teach skills and provide additional practice.
Teacher's Guide	An oversize book that presents comprehensive information about how to teach reading using the basal reading program. The selections are shown in reduced size, and background information about the selection, instructions for teaching the selections, and instructions on coordinating skill and strategy instruction are given on each page. In addition, information is presented about which supplemental books to use with each selection and how to assess students' learning.
Parent Materials	Blackline masters that teachers can duplicate and send home to parents. Information about the reading program and lists of ways parents can work with their children at home are included. Often these materials are available in both English and Spanish.
Assessment Materials	A variety of assessments, including selection assessments, running records, placement evaluations, and phonics inventories, are available along with teacher's guides.
Multimedia	Audiocassettes of some selections, CD-ROMs of some selections that include interactive components, related videos, and website connections are provided.

a lockstep approach every 15 to 30 minutes; instead, they move from one center to another when they finish what they are doing.

Figure 11-7 shows the checklist eighth-grade students used as they worked at centers as part of a unit on the Constitution. Some centers are required; they are marked with an asterisk. Students are expected to complete the "required" centers and two others of their choice. They put a check mark in the "Student's Check" column when they finish work there. Students keep their checklists in their unit folders, and they add any worksheets or papers they do at a center. Having a checklist or another approach to monitor students' progress helps them develop responsibility for completing their assignments.

Figure 11-6   Literacy Centers

Center	Description
Author	Information about an author that students are studying is displayed in this center. Often posters, books, and videotapes about the author are available for students to examine, and students may also write letters to the author at this center.
Class Collaborations[C]	Students write pages to be added to a class book at this center. Each student contributes a page according to guidelines established before students visit the center. Afterward, the teacher compiles and binds the book.
Computers	A bank of computers with word processing and drawing programs and other computer programs are available at the center.
Data Charts[C]	As part of social studies and science units, students compile information for data charts. Students consult informational books and reference books at the center and add information to a large class data chart or to individual data charts.
Library	A wide variety of books and other reading materials, organized according to topic or reading level, are available in classroom libraries. Students choose books at their reading level to read and reread.
Listening	Students use a tape player and headphones to listen to stories and other texts read aloud. Often copies of the texts are available so that students can read along as they listen.
Making Words[C]	Letter cards, magnetic letters, and white boards that students use to spell and write words are available in this center. Students often create specific words that follow a spelling pattern or sort letters to spell a variety of two-, three-, four-, and five-letter words.
Poetry	Charts describing various poetic forms are available in this center, and students write formula poems here. They often use poetic forms that teachers have already introduced to the class.
Proofreading	Students use spellcheckers, word walls of high-frequency words, and dictionaries at this center to proofread compositions they have written. Students often work with partners.
Skills	Students practice skills teachers have taught in minilessons at this center. Teachers place the materials they used in the minilesson in the center for students to use. Students sort word cards, write additional examples on charts, and manipulate other materials.
Spelling	Students use white boards and magnetic letters to practice spelling words.
Word Sorts[C]	Students sort word cards into categories according to meaning or structural forms. Sometimes, students paste the sorted words on sheets of poster board, and at other times, they sort the words as a practice activity and do not paste them into categories.
Writing	This center is stocked with writing materials, including pens, papers, blank books, postcards, dictionaries, and word walls, that students use for a variety of writing activities. Bookmaking supplies such as cardboard, wallpaper, cloth, paper, wide-arm staplers, yarn, brads, and marking pens are also available in this center.

Working With Struggling Writers

Many students in grades 4 through 8 struggle with writing. Some have problems developing and organizing ideas for a composition, some have problems with spelling, capitalization, punctuation, and grammar skills, and others struggle with the writing process and using writing strategies. There are some students, too, who complain that their hands and arms hurt when they write, some who show little interest and do the bare minimum, and others who are so frustrated with writing that they refuse to write

Figure 11-7   An Eighth-Grade Centers Checklist

US Constitution Centers Checklist

Name _____   Period _____

Center	Activity	Student's Check	Teacher's Check
Word Wall	Choose three words from the word wall and make word study cards for each word.		
Puzzle Center	Complete the "Branches of Government" puzzle.		
Library Center	Use the informational books at the center to complete the Constitution time line.		
Internet Center	Research the Constitution on the Internet and complete the study guide.		
Writing Center	Study Howard Christy's painting "The Signing of the Constitution" and write a poem or descriptive essay about it.		
*Legislative Branch Center	Complete activities at this student-developed center.		
*Executive Branch Center	Complete activities at this student-developed center.		
*Judicial Branch Center	Complete activities at this student-developed center.		
*The Bill of Rights Center	Complete activities at this student-developed center.		
*Alphabet Book Center	Choose a letter and create a page for the Class Constitution Alphabet Book.		

Assessment Tools

at all. These struggling writers need both instruction about writing and more opportunities to practice writing in order to become more successful. Figure 11-8 lists 20 problems that struggling writers face and suggests ways to address each problem.

Instruction takes several forms. Teachers present minilessons on paragraphing, brainstorming ideas, revising and editing techniques, and other topics to the whole class and to small groups of struggling writers, and through these lessons, students learn about writing strategies and skills. Teachers often have students examine anonymous student samples saved from previous years as part of their lessons. Students can use rubrics to score these samples and revise and edit weaker papers to apply what they are learning in the lesson. As part of some minilessons, teachers also model how they write and think aloud about how to use writing strategies.

Two instructional strategies that teachers use with older struggling writers are the language experience approach and interactive writing. Even though these procedures

Figure 11-8   Ways to Address Struggling Writers' Problems

Category	Problem	Solutions
Ideas	Student complains, "I don't know what to write."	Have student • brainstorm a list of ideas and pick the most promising one. • talk with classmates to get ideas. • draw a picture to develop an idea. Suggest to student several specific situations related to the assigned topic.
	Composition lacks focus.	After writing a draft, have student highlight sentences that pertain to the focus, cut the other parts, and elaborate the highlighted ideas. Give student a very focused assignment. In a minilesson, share samples of unfocused writing for student to revise.
	Composition lacks interesting details.	Have student • brainstorm words related to each of the five senses and then add some of the words to the composition. • draw a picture related to the topic of the composition and then add details reflected in the picture. In minilessons, • teach vivid verbs and adjectives. • teach the visualization strategy.
Organization	Composition lacks organization.	Help student decide on paragraph organization before beginning to write. In minilessons, • teach concept of main idea using many types of texts. • have student examine the structure of sample compositions.
	Composition is divided into paragraphs, but some sentences in the paragraph do not belong.	Have student • reread each paragraph, checking that each sentence belongs. • work with partner to check sentences in each paragraph. In minilessons, • teach paragraph structure. • have student examine the structure of paragraphs and locate sentences that don't belong.
	Composition lacks an exciting lead.	Have student • try several leads with a personal experience, a question, a quotation, humor, or a comparison. • get feedback about the effectiveness of the lead in a writing group[C]. In a minilesson, have student examine the leads in stories and informational books.
	Ideas in the composition aren't sequenced.	Write the sentences on sentence strips for student to sequence. In a minilesson, teach sequence words, such as *first, next, last,* and *finally*.
	Composition follows a circular pattern.	Have student create a graphic organizer before beginning to write. Assist student in identifying the main idea for each paragraph before beginning to write. In a minilesson, teach sequence of ideas.
Word Choice	Composition lacks interesting vocabulary.	Have student • refer to word walls posted in the classroom for vocabulary. • focus on adding more interesting vocabulary words during revising. In a minilesson, have student revise sample compositions to add interesting vocabulary.
Writing Process	Student doesn't reread or revise composition.	In minilessons, • model revision with sample compositions. • compare the quality of unrevised and revised compositions. Include revision as a requirement in the assessment rubric.

(continues)

Figure 11-8   (continued)

Category	Problem	Solutions
Writing Process (continued)	Student doesn't make constructive revisions.	Use writing groups. Conference with student to examine the revisions during the revising stage. Include substantive revision as a requirement on the assessment rubric. In minilessons, teach and model the types of revision.
	Student plagiarizes.	Use the writing process. Make student accountable for clusters, data charts, or note cards. Have student do the research and writing in class, not at home. In a minilesson, teach student how to take notes and develop a composition from the notes.
Mechanics	Composition is difficult to read because of misspelled words.	Have student • refer to high-frequency and content-area word walls when writing. • edit with a partner. Conference with student to correct remaining errors in the editing stage. Set high expectations. In minilessons, • teach student to proofread. • have student examine and correct errors in sample compositions. Encourage student to do more reading.
	Composition is difficult to read because of capitalization and punctuation errors.	Have editing partners identify and correct capitalization and punctuation errors during the editing stage. Conference with the student to identify and correct remaining errors during editing. In minilessons, • teach capitalization and punctuation concepts. • have student examine sample compositions for errors and correct them.
	Composition is difficult to read because of grammatical errors.	Have editing partners identify and correct grammatical errors during the editing stage. Conference with student to correct remaining errors during editing. In minilessons, • teach grammatical concepts. • have student examine and correct errors in sample compositions.
	Composition has weak sentence structure.	Have editing partners address sentence structure during the editing stage. In minilessons, • teach sentence structure. • teach sentence combining and then have student practice it.
	Composition is difficult to read because of poor handwriting or messiness.	Have student • use word processing. • use manuscript rather than cursive handwriting. • try various types of paper and writing instruments. Take student's dictation, if necessary.
Attitude and Motivation	Student does the bare minimum.	Conference with student to determine why he/she is hesitant. Brainstorm ideas with student during prewriting. In minilessons, • model how to expand a sentence into a paragraph. • have student practice expanding a brief composition into a better-developed one.
	Student is too dependent on teacher approval.	Have student • check with a classmate before coming to the teacher. • sign up for conferences with the teacher. Make sure student understands expectations and procedures.
	Student refuses to write.	Conference with student to determine and address the problem. Try language experience approach and interactive writing. Have student write a collaborative composition with a small group or a partner. Keep first writing assignments very short to ensure success.

were developed for use in primary classrooms, they are very effective with students in the middle grades who are not fluent writers. Teachers often use the language experience approach to take students' dictation when the focus of the lesson or activity is on developing and organizing ideas. They focus on having the students use talk to generate ideas and the sentences and paragraphs to express those ideas and, then they take students' dictation and write the composition because it would take too long for the students to do their own writing or because the students don't have enough writing fluency to sustain the writing themselves.

In interactive writing, teachers and students share the pen and do the writing together. Teachers support students and correct the mechanical errors they make. Teachers use interactive writing when they want students to do the writing themselves and when the focus is on mechanical skills—spelling, capitalization, punctuation, and grammar. As the students take turns doing the writing on chart paper, the teacher reviews skills and monitors each student's knowledge. At the same time, students write their own copies of the composition being written on chart paper, which gives them the opportunity to apply what they are learning. Because of the support the teacher provides, the piece that students write will be well developed and mechanically correct. It's a positive writing experience, and the struggling students' confidence grows.

Students also need opportunities to write independently every day. They use writing as a tool for learning as they write informally in reading logs, learning logs, clusters, and quickwrites[C]. They also need to use the writing process to create more polished compositions, including stories, poems, reports, letters, and other genres. Through these extended writing activities, students experience the writing process, learn to use writing strategies, and develop the stamina to see a composition from beginning to end.

Involving struggling writers in daily reading opportunities is another essential component of writing instruction because through reading experiences, students develop background knowledge, examine genres, apply reading and writing strategies, and acquire vocabulary words. Students need time to read books at their own reading level, and they also need daily opportunities to listen to the teacher read aloud high-quality novels and informational books that they can't read independently.

DETERMINING THE DIFFICULTY LEVEL OF BOOKS

Thousands and thousands of trade books are available for students in grades 4 through 8, and effective teachers match students with books written at appropriate difficulty levels. Even though many books seem to be of similar difficulty because of the size of print, length of book, or number of illustrations, they are not necessarily at the same reading level. Students need interesting books written at an appropriate level of difficulty because they are more likely to read books that are neither too hard nor too easy, and research has shown that students who do the most reading make the greatest gains in reading (Gunning, 1998).

Traditional Readability Formulas

For the past 40 years or more, teachers have used readability formulas to estimate the difficulty level of trade books and textbooks. Readability levels can serve as rough gauges of text difficulty and are reported as grade-level scores. If a book has a readability score of fifth grade, for example, teachers can assume that many average fifth-grade

Struggling readers need to learn how to choose interesting books at their reading level.

readers will be able to read it. Sometimes readability scores are marked with *RL* and a grade level, such as *RL 5*, on the back covers of paperback trade books.

Traditional readability scores are usually determined using vocabulary difficulty and sentence complexity, as measured by word and sentence length. However, the formulas don't take into account the experience and knowledge that readers bring to their reading, their cognitive and linguistic backgrounds, or their motivation or purpose for reading.

One fairly quick and simple readability formula is the Fry Readability Graph, developed by Edward Fry (1968). Figure 11-9 presents the Fry Readability Graph and lists the steps in using the formula to predict the reading-level score for a text, ranging from first grade through college level. Teachers should always consider using a readability formula as an aid in evaluating textbook and trade book selections for classroom use, but they cannot assume that materials rated as appropriate for a particular grade level will be appropriate for all students at that grade level. Teachers need to recognize the effectiveness of readability formulas as a tool but remember that these formulas have limitations.

Many reading selections that might seem very different actually score at the same level. For example, *Sarah, Plain and Tall* (MacLachlan, 1985), *Tales of a Fourth Grade Nothing* (Blume, 1972), *Bunnicula: A Rabbit-Tale of Mystery* (Howe & Howe, 1979),

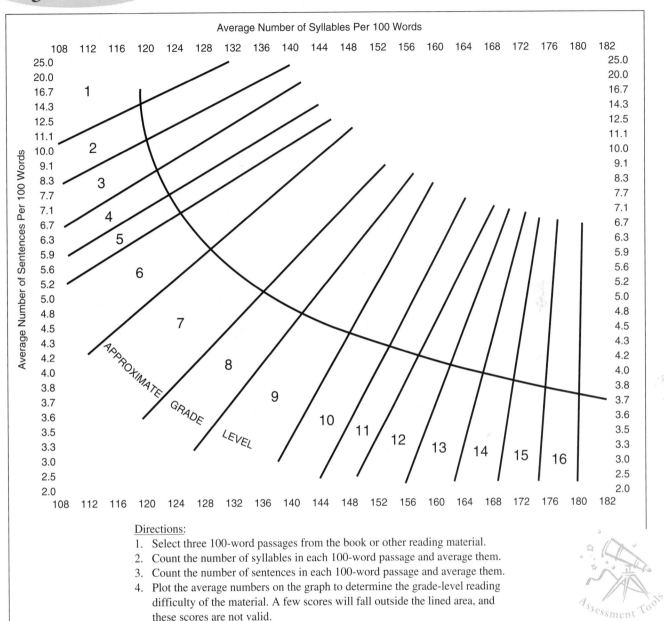

Figure 11-9   The Fry Readability Graph

Average Number of Syllables Per 100 Words

Average Number of Sentences Per 100 Words

1 2 3 4 5 6 7 8 9 10 11 12 13 14 15 16

APPROXIMATE GRADE LEVEL

Directions:
1. Select three 100-word passages from the book or other reading material.
2. Count the number of syllables in each 100-word passage and average them.
3. Count the number of sentences in each 100-word passage and average them.
4. Plot the average numbers on the graph to determine the grade-level reading difficulty of the material. A few scores will fall outside the lined area, and these scores are not valid.

From "A Readibility Formula That Saves Time," by E. Fry, 1968, *Journal of Reading, 11,* p. 587.

and *The Hundred Penny Box* (Mathis, 1975) all score at the third-grade reading level according to Fry's Readability Graph, even though their lengths, illustrations, topics, and type sizes differ significantly.

The Reading Recovery Approach to Leveling Books

Basal readers and other texts have traditionally been leveled according to grade levels, but grade-level designations, especially for struggling readers, are too broad. Reading Recovery teachers have developed a text gradient to match students to books that are

Because the reading levels of English learners in the middle grades are often affected by their knowledge of technical vocabulary and their ability to understand longer, more complex sentences, teachers must consider their students' level of English proficiency when selecting leveled books.

neither too hard nor too easy for them (Fountas & Pinnell, 1996, 1999, 2001). They have identified seven factors that are related to the difficulty level of texts.

1. ***Book and print features.*** The length of the book, the size of print, the amount of print on a page, and the layout of print on the page affect the difficulty level. Illustrations, diagrams, and other graphic features that extend the meaning also influence whether readers will be successful.

2. ***Content.*** The degree of familiarity with the topic influences the difficulty level: Books about familiar topics are easier for students to read than books with more sophisticated content because students are more likely to be successful when they have background knowledge to use during reading. Students' interest in the topic also influences text difficulty.

3. ***Vocabulary.*** The range and variety of words used in a book affect the difficulty level. Books for beginning readers typically use a limited number of high-frequency words, phonetically regular words, and other words often used in conversation; in contrast, books for advanced readers have more sophisticated, specialized, and technical words, and these multisyllabic words are often of Latin and Greek origin.

4. ***Language and literary features.*** The complexity and sophistication of the language used in a book influence the difficulty level. When the language is similar to children's oral language patterns, the book is easier to read. Books with longer, more sophisticated sentences, figurative language, and literary devices such as hyperbole and symbolism are more difficult to read and understand.

5. ***Sentence complexity.*** The length of sentences in the book affects the difficulty level. Books for beginning readers use primarily simple sentences, but books for advanced readers often have longer sentences with embedded clauses and more sophisticated use of punctuation marks.

6. ***Text structure.*** The complexity of the text structure and genre influences the difficulty level. Students learn to read stories and informational books. Beginning readers are successful with books with simple plots and straightforward presentations of information, but advanced readers can handle more complex books. They read novels with complicated plots and episodic structures. They also read informational books on more abstract topics that incorporate more sophisticated organizational structures and detailed charts and other graphics.

7. ***Themes and ideas.*** The sophistication of the theme and the complexity of the ideas presented in the book influence the difficulty level. Even though students may be able to decode the words, the book still may not be appropriate if the themes and ideas are too mature for them.

Using these criteria, Reading Recovery teachers identified 26 levels for kindergarten through sixth grade. A sample trade book for each level is shown in Figure 11-10; 8,500 other leveled books are listed in *Matching Books to Readers: Using Leveled Books in Guided Reading, K–3* (Fountas & Pinnell, 1999) and *Guiding Readers and Writers Grades 3–6* (Fountas & Pinnell, 2001). Teachers are applying the same criteria to level books for use in their classrooms. After they level the books, teachers code them with letters written on colored circles and place all books at the same level together in baskets or boxes.

Teachers use running records to identify each student's instructional level. Then teachers group students into homogeneous groups, but the groups remain flexible and students move from group to group according to their reading level. Teachers use lev-

Figure 11-10 Trade Books Leveled According to Reading Recovery Criteria

Level	Grade	Sample Book
A	K	Burningham, J. (1985). *Colors.* New York: Crown.
B	K–1	Carle, E. (1987). *Have you seen my cat?* New York: Scholastic.
C	K–1	Williams, S. (1989). *I went walking.* Orlando, FL: Harcourt Brace.
D	1	Peek, M. (1985). *Mary wore her red dress.* New York: Clarion.
E	1	Hill, E. (1980). *Where's Spot?* New York: Putnam.
F	1	Hutchins, P. (1968). *Rosie's walk.* New York: Macmillan.
G	1	Shaw, N. (1986). *Sheep in a jeep.* Boston: Houghton Mifflin.
H	1–2	Kraus, R. (1970). *Whose mouse are you?* New York: Macmillan.
I	1–2	Wood, A. (1984). *The napping house.* San Diego, CA: Harcourt Brace Jovanovich.
J	2	Rylant, C. (1991). *Henry and Mudge and the bedtime thumps.* New York: Simon & Schuster.
K	2	Stevens, J. (1992). *The three billy goats Gruff.* New York: Holiday House.
L	2–3	Allard, H. (1985). *Miss Nelson is missing!* Boston: Houghton Mifflin.
M	2–3	Park, B. (1992). *Junie B. Jones and the stupid smelly bus.* New York: Random House.
N	3	Danziger, P. (1994). *Amber Brown is not a crayon.* New York: Scholastic.
O	3–4	Cleary, B. (1981). *Ramona Quimby, age 8.* New York: HarperCollins.
P	3–4	Mathis, S. B. (1975). *The hundred penny box.* New York: Scholastic.
Q	4	Howe, D., & Howe, J. (1979). *Bunnicula: A rabbit-tale of mystery.* New York: Atheneum.
R	4	Paulsen, G. (1987). *Hatchet.* New York: Viking.
S	4–5	Paterson, K. (1984). *The great Gilly Hopkins.* New York: Crowell.
T	4–5	Curtis, C. P. (1999). *Bud, not Buddy.* New York: Delacorte.
U	5	Lowry, L. (1989). *Number the stars.* Boston: Houghton Mifflin.
V	5–6	Sachar, L. (1998). *Holes.* New York: Farrar, Straus & Giroux.
W	5–6	Choi, S. N. (1991). *Year of impossible goodbyes.* Boston: Houghton Mifflin.
X	6	Hesse, K. (1997). *Out of the dust.* New York: Scholastic.
Y	6	Lowry, L. (1993). *The giver.* Boston: Houghton Mifflin.
Z	6	Hinton, S. E. (1967). *The outsiders.* New York: Puffin/Penguin.

Fountas & Pinnell, 1999, 2001.

eling to organize small groups for guided reading or whenever they want to match children to books at the appropriate level of difficulty.

The Lexile Framework

The newest approach to matching books to readers is the Lexile Framework, developed by MetaMetrics and available through Scholastic, Inc. Lexile levels range from 100 to 1300, representing kindergarten through 12th grade. Several standardized achievement tests are linked to the Lexile Framework, and students' scores are now reported in lexile levels. Or, students can determine their independent, instructional, and frustration scores according to lexile levels by completing the Scholastic Reading Inventory, a computerized reading test in which they silently read text passages and answer comprehension questions.

Many trade books are designated by lexile levels so that teachers can help students choose appropriate books according to their lexile levels. The sixth-grade level, for example, ranges from lexile levels 850 to 1000; trade books that have been leveled in the sixth-grade range according to the Lexile Framework include *Shiloh* (Naylor, 1991), *The Lion, the Witch and the Wardrobe* (Lewis, 1994), and *The Black Pearl* (O'Dell, 1967). Whether these particular books are appropriate for students reading

Figure *11-11* Trade Books Leveled According to the Lexile Framework

Level	Grade	Book
100–149	K	Carle, E. (1989). *The very busy spider.* New York: Philomel. Ehlert, L. (1987). *Growing vegetable soup.* San Diego, CA: Harcourt Brace. Parrish, P. (1999). *Amelia Bedelia.* New York: HarperCollins.
150–199	K–1	Marshall, J. (1993). *Fox on wheels.* New York: Dial. Shaw, N. (1988). *Sheep in a shop.* Boston: Houghton Mifflin. Ziefert, H. (1999). *Turnip.* New York: HarperCollins.
200–249	1	Bridwell, N. (1985). *Clifford the big red dog.* New York: Scholastic. Hoff, S. (1993). *Danny and the dinosaur.* New York: HarperCollins. Lobel, A. (1983). *Mouse soup.* New York: HarperCollins.
250–299	1	Bonsall, C. N. (1982). *Case of the dumb bells.* New York: HarperCollins. Guarino, D. (1989). *Is your mama a llama?* New York: Scholastic. McDermott, G. (1987). *Anansi the spider.* New York: Holt.
300–349	1–2	Allard, H. (1977). *Miss Nelson is missing!* Boston: Houghton Mifflin. Hutchins, P. (1986). *The doorbell rang.* New York: Greenwillow. Pinkwater, D. (1999). *Second-grade ape.* New York: Scholastic.
350–399	2	Brenner, B. (1993). *Wagon wheels.* New York: HarperCollins. Polacco, P. (1994). *Babushka's doll.* New York: Aladdin. Thaler, M. (1989). *The teacher from the black lagoon.* New York: Scholastic.
400–449	2	Benchley, N. (1987). *Sam the minuteman.* New York: HarperCollins. Coerr, E. (1986). *The Josefina story quilt.* New York: HarperCollins. Rey, H. A. (1941). *Curious George.* Boston: Houghton Mifflin.
450–499	2–3	Carle, E. (1988). *A house for hermit crab.* New York: Simon & Schuster. Henkes, K. (1991). *Chrysanthemum.* New York: Morrow. Sharmat, M. (1989). *Gregory the terrible eater.* New York: Scholastic.
500–549	3	Fowler, A. (1991). *It's a good thing there are insects.* Chicago: Childrens Press. Noble, T. H. (1980). *The day Jimmy's boa ate the wash.* New York: Dial. Rathmann, P. (1995). *Officer Buckle and Gloria.* New York: Putnam.
550–599	3–4	Carle, E. (1977). *The grouchy lady bug.* New York: HarperCollins. McCully, E. A. (1992). *Mirette on the highwire.* New York: Putnam. Sobol, D. (1982). *Encyclopedia Brown saves the day.* New York: Dell.
600–649	3–4	Cole, J. (1992). *The magic school bus on the ocean floor.* New York: Scholastic. McKissack, P. (1986). *Flossie and the fox.* New York: Dial. Polacco, P. (1990). *Thunder cake.* New York: Philomel.
650–699	4	Brett, J. (1995). *Armadillo rodeo.* New York: Putnam. Lowry, L. (1989). *Number the stars.* Boston: Houghton Mifflin. White, E. B. (1952). *Charlotte's web.* New York: Harper & Row.

at the sixth-grade level depends on the topics of the books, authors' writing styles, and students' interests. However, the lexile levels provide assistance in matching students to books. Figure 11-11 presents a list of trade books ranging from 100–1300.

The Lexile Framework appears to be a promising program, because the wide range of possible scores allows teachers at all grade levels to more closely match stu-

Figure **11-11** *(continued)*

Level	Grade	Book
700–749	4	Coville, B. (1991). *Jeremy Thatcher, dragon hatcher.* San Diego, CA: Harcourt Brace. Howe, D., & Howe, J. (1979). *Bunnicula: A rabbit-tale of mystery.* New York: Atheneum. Waters, K. (1989). *Sarah Morton's day.* New York: Scholastic.
750–799	4–5	Cleary, B. (1955). *Beezus and Ramona.* New York: Morrow. Creech, S. (1994). *Walk two moons.* New York: HarperCollins. Westall, R. (1994). *Blitzcat.* New York: Scholastic.
800–849	5	Dahl, R. (1964). *Charlie and the chocolate factory.* New York: Knopf. Levine, E. (1995). *If you lived at the time of Martin Luther King.* New York: Scholastic. Spinelli, J. (1990). *Maniac Magee.* New York: Scholastic.
850–899	5–6	Cleary, B. (1977). *Ramona and her father.* New York: Morrow. Naylor, P. (1991). *Shiloh.* New York: Simon & Schuster. Wells, R. E. (1993). *Is a blue whale the biggest thing there is?* New York: Whitman.
900–949	6–7	Armstrong, W. H. (2001). *Sounder.* New York: HarperCollins. Cleary, B. (1983). *Dear Mr. Henshaw.* New York: Morrow. Lewis, C. S. (1994). *The lion, the witch and the wardrobe.* New York: HarperCollins.
950–999	7	Fritz, J. (1987). *Shh! We're writing the Constitution.* New York: Putnam. O'Dell, S. (1967). *The black pearl.* Boston: Houghton Mifflin. Rylant, C. (1992). *Missing May.* New York: Orchard.
1000–1049	8	Freedman, R. (1987). *Indian chiefs.* New York: Holiday House. O'Dell, S. (1990). *Island of the blue dolphins.* Boston: Houghton Mifflin. Philbrick, R. (1993). *Freak the mighty.* New York: Scholastic.
1050–1099	9–10	Lester, J. (1968). *To be a slave.* New York: Dial. McGovern, A. (1991). *Robin Hood of Sherwood Forest.* New York: Scholastic. Tolkien, J. R. R. (1973). *The hobbit.* Boston: Houghton Mifflin.
1100–1149	10–11	Macaulay, D. (1975). *Pyramid.* Boston: Houghton Mifflin. McKinley, R. (1984). *The hero and the crown.* New York: Greenwillow. Pinkney, A. D. (1994). *Dear Benjamin Banneker.* San Diego, CA: Harcourt Brace.
1150–1199	11–12	Aaseng, N. (2000). *Navajo code talkers.* New York: Walker. Brooks, B. (1984). *The moves make the man.* New York: HarperCollins. Stanley, J. (1994). *I am an American: A true story of Japanese internment.* New York: Scholastic.
1200–1300	12	Alcott, L. M. (1968). *Little women.* Boston: Little, Brown. Burroughs, E. R. (1978). *Tarzan of the apes.* New York: HarperCollins. Haskins, J. (1980). *The march on Washington.* New York: Scholastic.

dents and books. As more and more books are leveled using the Lexile Framework, it seems likely that lexile levels will become increasingly important in reading instruction; however, matching students to books is often more complicated because students' background knowledge, motivation, and other individual factors influence reading success.

- Complete a self-assessment to demonstrate your understanding of the concepts presented in this chapter
- Complete field activities that will help you expand your understanding of the middle-grade classroom and struggling readers and writers
- Visit important web links related to using differentiated instruction to meet the needs of all middle-grade students
- Look into your state's standards as they relate to teaching struggling middle-grade readers and writers
- Communicate with other preservice teachers via the message board and discuss the issues of determining the difficulty level of books, using basal readers, and adapting instruction for students in grades 4 to 8

How Effective Teachers . . .
Work With Struggling Readers and Writers

1. Teachers understand that struggling readers need additional instruction, more time to read, and books at their reading levels.
2. Teachers use differentiated instruction to meet the needs of all students.
3. Teachers involve students in whole-class, small-group, and individual literacy activities.
4. Teachers use guided reading to teach reading to struggling readers.
5. Teachers recognize that basal readers are effective for struggling readers only when the textbooks are written at the appropriate grade level.
6. Teachers use the language experience approach and interactive writing to support their struggling writers.
7. Teachers teach struggling writers to use the writing process to develop and refine their compositions.
8. Teachers set up centers for small groups of students to practice skills they are learning.
9. Teachers use traditional readability formulas, the Reading Recovery approach to leveling books, or the Lexile Framework to determine the difficulty level of books.
10. Teachers match students to books according to interest and difficulty level.

Review

Most teachers have some struggling readers and writers in their fourth- through eighth-grade classrooms, and teachers need to adapt their instructional programs to meet their students' needs. Researchers suggest that struggling readers need more reading instruction, more opportunities for reading, and books written at their reading levels. Similarly, struggling writers need to see writing modeled for them, require help with the actual writing, and need more opportunities to express their thoughts in writing. The best way to meet the needs of all students is through differentiated instruction, in which teachers use a variety of whole-class, small-class, and individualized literacy activities. Teachers work to match students with books that they read during guided reading lessons and for other types of reading activities using traditional readability formulas, the Reading Recovery approach to leveling books, and the Lexile Framework. Guidelines for working with struggling readers and writers are summarized in the feature on pages 378–379.

Professional References

Clay, M. M. (1991). *Becoming literate: The construction of inner control.* Portsmouth, NH: Heinemann.

Fountas, I. C., & Pinnell, G. S. (1996). *Guided reading: Good first teaching for all children.* Portsmouth, NH: Heinemann.

Fountas, I. C., & Pinnell, G. S. (1999). *Matching books to readers: Using leveled books in guided reading, K–3.* Portsmouth, NH: Heinemann.

Fountas, I. C., & Pinnell, G. S. (2001). *Guiding readers and writers grades 3–6: Teaching comprehension, genre, and content literacy.* Portsmouth, NH: Heinemann.

Fry, E. (1968). A readability formula that saves time. *Journal of Reading, 11,* 587.

Gunning, T. G. (1998). *Best books for beginning readers.* Boston: Allyn & Bacon.

Juel, C. (1988). Learning to read and write: A longitudinal study of 54 children from first through fourth grade. Paper presented at the annual meeting of the American Educational Research Association, New Orleans, LA.

Ohlhausen, M. M., & Jepsen, M. (1992). Lessons from Goldilocks: "Somebody's been choosing my books but I can make my own choices now!" *The New Advocate, 5,* 31–46.

Strickland, D. S., Ganske, K., & Monroe, J. K. (2002). *Supporting struggling readers and writers: Strategies for classroom interventions 3–6.* York, ME: Stenhouse.

Tomlinson, C. A. (2001). *How to differentiate instruction in mixed-ability classrooms* (2nd ed.). Alexandria, VA: Association for Supervision and Curriculum Development.

Children's Book References

Blume, J. (1972). *Tales of a fourth grade nothing.* New York: Dutton.

Ellis, D. (2001). *The breadwinner.* Berkeley, CA: Publishers Group West.

Greenburg, D. (2000a). *Don't count on Dracula.* New York: Grosset & Dunlap.

Greenburg, D. (2000b). *How I went from bad to verse.* New York: Grosset & Dunlap.

Howe, D., & Howe, J. (1979). *Bunnicula: A rabbit-tale of mystery.* New York: Atheneum.

Lewis, C. S. (1994). *The lion, the witch and the wardrobe.* New York: HarperCollins.

MacLachlan, P. (1985). *Sarah, plain and tall.* New York: Harper & Row.

Mathis, S. B. (1975). *The hundred penny box.* New York: Viking.

Naylor, P. (1991). *Shiloh.* New York: Simon & Schuster.

O'Dell, S. (1967). *The black pearl.* Boston: Houghton Mifflin.

Scieszka, J. (1991). *Knights of the kitchen table.* New York: Penguin.

Scieszka, J. (1993). *Your mother was a Neanderthal.* New York: Viking.

Scieszka, J. (1996). *Tut tut.* New York: Penguin.

chapter 12

Becoming Lifelong Readers and Writers

- Why is it important that students become lifelong readers and writers?

- What are the components of reading workshop?

- What are the components of writing workshop?

- How do teachers manage a workshop classroom?

Ms. Torres's Students Love to Read

During the first 2 weeks of school, Ms. Torres asks her eighth graders to complete three interest inventories because she wants to learn about her students so she can plan instruction and literacy activities that will be meaningful to them. One interest inventory is personal; it's about their hobbies, computer access, study habits, and the languages they and their parents speak and read. She wants to know whether her students' parents speak and read English so that she will know if a translator is needed for telephone calls, conferences, and notes sent home. The second interest inventory focuses on reading, and the third on writing. Ms. Torres wants to know about the books her students like and how they view themselves as readers, and she wants to know about their previous writing experiences, the kinds of writing they like best, and how she can help them become better writers. Figure 12-1 shows Ms. Torres's three interest inventories.

Ms. Torres reads the interest inventories and reflects on what her students tell her. She is especially concerned about students who don't like to read and write, and she does a great many things in her classroom to try to engage these students. She also studies the standardized test score data that her district provides as well as comments from the students' seventh-grade language arts teachers. She makes a file with the information she receives about each student, and if she still needs more information, she conducts an informal reading inventory with that student to determine reading level and examines writing samples from that student's portfolio to learn more.

Before the school year began, Ms. Torres set up her language arts classroom with a sofa tucked in the back corner, work tables along another wall, student desks arranged into five small groups, and her desk squeezed into another corner. She wants it to be welcoming and comfortable for the students. A bank of four computers networked to a printer are set up on another side of the classroom, and a moveable cart stocked with markers, scissors, glue, and a variety of papers sits in the front of the classroom. One wall is decorated with colorful posters of athletes and television/film stars advising students to read, a blank word wall[C] made from construction paper and laminated is posted on another wall, the posters that her students made last year about the writing process remain above the windows on the third wall (to be replaced by new posters that the students will make this year), and space is left beside a white board in the front of the classroom for charts that the students will make about reading strategies. Class sets of novels, textbooks, reference books, dictionaries, and thesauri are shelved under the windows.

A library center with two bookshelves and a revolving rack sit empty, and Ms. Torres's extensive collection of books is packed away in a storage closet. The library center has no books on the first day of school because Ms. Torres waits until she reads the interest inventories before deciding which books to set out and how to organize them.

After she reads the students' interest inventories, Ms. Torres makes a chart with the categories of books that her students identified, and she chooses books from her collection to fit each category, making sure that the books cover the range of reading levels in the class. She puts the books in the classroom library, arranging them in categories. To make it easier for her students to find the books they want, she color-codes

Figure 12-1   Ms. Torres's Three Interest Inventories

<table>
<tr><td>

Personal Interest Inventory

1. What are your favorite hobbies, activities, and sports?
2. What do you know a lot about?
3. What are your favorite television shows, movies, or music?
4. Where do you study at home?
5. Do you have a computer to use outside of school? How do you use it?
6. Do you have Internet access?
7. Do you have a dictionary to use outside of school?
8. About how many books do you have at home?
9. What languages do you speak? How well?
10. What languages do your parents speak? How well?

</td><td>

Reading Interest Inventory

1. What kinds of books do you like to read?
2. Who are your favorite authors? Why do you enjoy their books?
3. What are your favorite genres?
4. What do you read besides books (for example, newspapers, comics, magazines)?
5. Where do you usually get your reading materials?
6. When and where do you like to read?
7. What do you do well as a reader?
8. What is hardest for you as a reader?
9. What are you doing to improve your reading?
10. How can I help you improve your reading?
11. How often do you read at home?
12. Do you like to read? Why or why not?

</td><td>

Writing Interest Inventory

1. What is your favorite kind of writing assignment in school?
2. What is your favorite topic and genre?
3. What are your strengths as a writer?
4. What is hardest for you as a writer?
5. What are you doing to improve your writing?
6. How can I help you improve your writing?
7. What do you write at home? How often?
8. Do you like to write? Why or why not?

</td></tr>
</table>

the categories on the chart and the labels for the categories on the bookshelves. The library center begins with these categories:

Mystery books	Harry Potter stories
Science fiction	Stories by Lemony Snicket
Adventure stories	Stories by Avi
Scary books	Stories by Louis Sachar
Humorous books	Biographies of athletes
Animal stories	Biographies of TV and movie stars
Time warp stories	Biographies of musicians
Sports stories	Books about World War II

C See the Compendium of Instructional Procedures, which follows this chapter, for more information on terms marked with the symbol C.

During the school year, the categories evolve and change as students do more reading and learn new things. At the semester break, Ms. Torres surveys the students again and reorganizes the library to reflect their new interests.

Ms. Torres introduces the library center and explains its organization using the color-coded chart. As she talks about each category, she shares a book or two and invites a student to borrow the book and read it. She continues until every student has a book. Her check-out system is simple: Students pick up a book they'd like to read and return it when they're done. She doesn't ask them to sign out books.

A brightly colored scarf is draped across the top of one bookcase and a sign reads "Ms. Torres Recommends . . . "; Gary Paulsen's *Canyons* (1990), Suzanne Fisher Staples's *Dangerous Skies* (1996), Karen Cushman's *Matilda Bone* (2000), and Jane Yolen's *The Devil's Arithmetic* (1988) are arranged on the scarf so that the inviting pictures on the front of their dust jackets are visible to the class. Ms. Torres's enthusiasm is clear as she explains that these are some of her favorite books. She gives a quick book talk^C to introduce each one. She continues to explain that each week, she will give a book talk introducing several new books and invite the students to read them.

A large basket containing newspapers and magazines rests on the floor of the library center. Ms. Torres brings the local newspaper that is delivered to her home each morning and puts it in the basket for students to read. She also has copies of *Sports Illustrated for Kids, National Geographic Kids, Kids Discover,* and *Scope* in the basket. Her school provides *Scope,* Ms. Torres purchases subscriptions to two magazines, and this year they have a third subscription thanks to an appreciative parent.

Ms. Torres spends a great deal of time and effort creating her library center because she says, "It's the heart of my classroom." She feels that one of the most important things she does is connect students and books; it's her goal to have every one of her students love books and become a lifelong reader.

Once the students have access to books, Ms. Torres is ready to begin reading workshop. She uses the first 30 minutes of the students' 105-minute language arts period for this independent reading time. Students come into class, get out their books, and begin reading. Ms. Torres takes attendance as students settle into their books, then she checks that everyone has a book and is reading. Next, she briefly conferences with two or three students about their reading, and then spends the last few minutes of reading workshop reading herself. Sometimes she reads the newspaper, magazines, or new books that the librarian has lent to her.

After the independent reading time, there is a 10-minute sharing time. Ms. Torres and her students do different things during the sharing period. On Mondays and Tuesdays, students share books they've read and hand them off to other students to read; on Wednesdays, Ms. Torres introduces the new books that she's adding to the library center; and on Thursdays and Fridays, students take turns reading aloud short inspirational stories from one of Jack Canfield's "Chicken Soup for the Soul" books. Ms. Torres has four books in the series— *Chicken Soup for the Teenage Soul* (Canfield, Hansen, & Kirberger, 1997), *Chicken Soup for the Preteen Soul* (Canfield, 2000), *Chicken Soup for the Sports Fan's Soul* (Canfield, Hansen, Tunney, Donnelly, & Donnelly, 2000), and *Chicken Soup for the Cat and Dog Lover's Soul* (Canfield, 1999)—in the library center, and students bring other volumes from home to share. They select a short piece and practice reading it aloud before their day to share, and then they read it to the class. The stories inevitably lead to discussion, and students gauge the effectiveness of their selection and their reading by the discussion that follows. Ms. Torres began having students read short stories aloud after several students asked her if they could share a story with the class, and it has evolved into a very special community-building time as well as a worthwhile oral language activity where students demonstrate their ability to stand up in front of their peers with poise and model literate behavior.

Some days, Ms. Torres teaches a minilesson^C to introduce or review a reading strategy, and on other days, she moves directly into other language arts activities. She alternates literature focus units featuring the core literature books that her district has selected for eighth grade with writing workshop. During literature focus units, Ms. Torres reads a novel with her students, teaches literary elements and vocabulary, and involves students in response activities. She also reads aloud picture books, informational books, and other novels that support the core book.

During writing workshop, students have 45 minutes to write independently, and Ms. Torres uses 15 to 20 minutes to teach minilessons on writing strategies, favorite authors, and genres. Students use the writing process to write compositions on self-selected topics. They share their writing with classmates in writing groups[C], work with classmates to edit their rough drafts, and finally share their finished compositions with the class. Ms. Torres also teaches four genres, one during each quarter: cause-and-effect essays, response to literature essays, persuasive essays, and poetry, and students also do these types of writing during writing workshop.

Ms. Torres loves to read and write, and she wants her students to become lifelong readers and writers. Everything she does in her language arts classroom furthers her goal: her classroom environment, the classroom library, reading and writing workshop activities, literature focus units, her confidence in her students, and her enthusiasm.

Teachers have two broad goals for their students: They want their students to become capable readers and writers, and they want them to choose to read and write for a variety of purposes throughout their lives. That is, they want them to become lifelong readers and writers. Teachers' attitudes and their instructional approaches are crucial in determining whether students engage in reading and writing. *Engagement* is a key term; it means that students are interested and actively involved.

As students move through the middle grades, their interest in reading and writing often diminishes, so it is important that teachers understand the factors that affect motivation and the literacy activities that engage students most effectively. Reading and writing workshop are strongly recommended because students become actively engaged with texts. The activities are authentic, and students make choices about the books they read and the writing projects they pursue. The feature on page 385 shows how reading and writing workshop fit into a balanced approach to literacy development.

ENGAGING STUDENTS WITH READING AND WRITING

Motivation is intrinsic, the innate curiosity within each of us that makes us want to figure things out. It is social, too: We want to socialize, share ideas, and participate in group activities. Motivation is more than one characteristic; however, it is a network of interacting factors (Alderman, 1999). Often students' motivation to become better readers and writers diminishes as they reach the middle grades, and struggling students demonstrate less enthusiasm for reading and writing than other students do.

The Role of Reading and Writing Workshop in a Balanced Literacy Program

Component	Description
Reading	Students gain necessary reading practice during reading workshop and are more likely to become lifelong readers.
Phonics and Other Skills	Students practice reading and writing skills through workshop activities.
Strategies	Students apply the strategies they have learned through reading and writing activities.
Vocabulary	The most important way that students learn vocabulary is through reading, and reading workshop provides an extended opportunity for students to read.
Comprehension	Students' focus is on comprehension as they read during reading workshop and write during writing workshop.
Literature	Students choose the books they read during reading workshop from classroom libraries. It is important that teachers have a wide selection of books and other reading materials available for students to choose from.
Content-Area Study	Students can read books related to thematic units during reading workshop and write reports and other compositions on content-area topics during writing workshop.
Oral Language	Students listen to books read aloud during reading workshop and give book talks to share the books they've read. During writing workshop, classmates discuss their compositions.
Writing	Writing is at the heart of a writing workshop. Students use the writing process to draft, refine, and polish their compositions.
Spelling	Students apply their knowledge of spelling as they participate in writing workshop.

Factors That Affect Motivation

Many factors contribute to students' engagement in reading and writing. Some focus on teachers—what they believe and do—and others focus on students (Unrau, 2004). Figure 12-2 summarizes the factors affecting students' engagement in literacy activities and what teachers can do to nurture students' interest.

	Factors	What Teachers Should Do
Teacher Factors	Attitude	• Show students that you care about them. • Show excitement and enthusiasm about what you're teaching. • Stimulate students' curiosity and desire to learn.
	Community	• Create a nurturing and inclusive classroom community. • Insist that students treat classmates with respect.
	Instruction	• Focus on students' long-term learning. • Teach students to be strategic readers and writers. • Engage students in authentic activities. • Offer students choices of activities and reading materials.
	Rewards	• Use specific praise and positive feedback. • Use external rewards only when students' interest is very low.
Student Factors	Expectations	• Expect students to be successful. • Teach students to set realistic goals.
	Collaboration	• Encourage students to work collaboratively. • Minimize competition. • Allow students to participate in making plans and choices.
	Reading and Writing Competence	• Teach students to use reading and writing strategies. • Provide guided reading[C] lessons for struggling readers. • Use interactive writing[C] to teach writing skills to struggling writers. • Provide daily reading and writing opportunities.
	Choices	• Use interest inventories to identify students' interests. • Teach students to choose interesting books at their reading levels. • Encourage students to write about topics that interest them.

Teacher Factors.   Everything that teachers do affects their students' interest and engagement with literacy, but four of the most important factors are teachers' attitude or excitement, the community that teachers create in their classrooms, the instructional approaches teachers use, and the reward systems they use.

1. ***Attitude.*** It seems obvious that when teachers show that they care about their students and exhibit excitement and enthusiasm for learning, students are more likely to become engaged. Effective teachers also stimulate students' curiosity and encourage them to explore ideas. They emphasize intrinsic over extrinsic motivation because they understand that students' intrinsic desire to learn is more powerful than grades and other extrinsic motivators.

2. ***Community.*** Students are more likely to engage in reading and writing when their classroom is a learning community that respects and nurtures all students. Students and the teacher show respect for each other, and students learn how to work well with classmates in small groups. In a community of learners, students enjoy social interaction and feel connected to their classmates and their teacher.

3. ***Instruction.*** The types of literacy activities in which students are involved affect their interest and motivation. Turner and Paris (1995) compared authentic literacy activities such as reading and writing workshop with skills-based reading programs and concluded that students' motivation was determined by the daily classroom activities.

They found that open-ended activities and projects in which students were in control of the processes they used and the products they created were the most successful.

4. *Rewards.* Many teachers consider using rewards to encourage students to do more reading and writing, but Alfie Kohn (1993) and others believe that extrinsic incentives are harmful because they undermine students' intrinsic motivation. Incentives such as pizzas, free time, or "money" to spend in a classroom "store" are most effective when students' interest is very low and they are reluctant to participate in literacy activities. Once students become more interested, teachers withdraw these incentives and use less tangible incentives, including positive feedback and praise (Stipek, 1993).

Student Factors. Intrinsic motivation is not something that teachers or parents can force on students; rather, it is an innate desire that students must develop themselves. They are more likely to become engaged with reading and writing when they expect to be successful, when they work collaboratively with classmates, when they are capable readers and writers, and when they have opportunities to make choices and develop ownership of their work.

1. *Expectations.* Students with little hope of success are unlikely to become engaged in literacy activities. Teachers play a big role in shaping students' expectations, and teacher expectations are often self-fulfilling (Good & Brophy, 2000): If teachers believe that their students can be successful, it is more likely that they will be. Stipek (1993) found that in classrooms where teachers take a personal interest in their students and expect that all of them can learn, the students are more successful.

2. *Collaboration.* When students work with classmates in pairs and in small groups, they are often more interested and engaged in activities than when they read and write alone. Collaborative groups support students because they have opportunities to share ideas, learn from each other, and enjoy the collegiality of their classmates. Competition, in contrast, does not develop intrinsic motivation; instead, it decreases many students' interest in learning.

3. *Reading and writing competence.* Not surprisingly, students' competence in reading and writing affects their motivation. Students who read well are more likely to be motivated to read than those who read less well, and the same is true for writers. Teaching students how to read and write is an essential factor in developing students' motivation. Teachers find that once struggling readers and writers improve their reading and writing abilities, they become more interested.

4. *Choices.* Students in the middle grades want to have a say in which books they read and which topics they write about. By making choices, students develop more responsibility for their work and ownership of their accomplishments. Reading and writing workshop are instructional approaches that honor students' choices. In reading workshop, students choose books they are interested in reading and that are written at their reading level, and in writing workshop, students write about topics that interest them.

Oldfather (1995) conducted a 4-year study to examine the factors influencing students' motivation. She found that students were more highly motivated when they had opportunities for authentic self-expression as part of literacy activities. The students she interviewed reported that they were more highly motivated when they had ownership of the learning activities. Specific activities they mentioned included opportunities to:

- express their own ideas and opinions
- choose topics for writing and books for reading

Students who read every day are more likely to become lifelong readers.

- talk about books they are reading
- share their writing with classmates
- pursue authentic activities—not worksheets—using reading, writing, listening, and talking

Ivey and Broaddus (2001) reported similar conclusions from their study of the factors that influence sixth graders' desire to read. Three of their conclusions are noteworthy. First, students are more interested in reading when their teachers make them feel confident and successful. A nurturing classroom community is an important factor. Second, students are more intrinsically motivated when they have ownership of their literacy learning. Students place great value on being allowed to choose interesting books and other reading materials. Third, students become more engaged with books when they have time for independent reading and opportunities to listen to the teacher read aloud. Students reported that they enjoy listening to teachers read aloud because teachers make books more comprehensible and more interesting because of the background knowledge that they provide. In the vignette at the beginning of the chapter, Ms. Torres incorporated many of these researchers' recommendations in her classroom.

Characteristics of Exceptional Teachers

Most of us remember an exceptional teacher or two who made a difference in our lives. Researchers have examined the characteristics of some of these special teachers to determine what makes them exceptional. The results of these studies suggest ways that all of us can nurture and encourage our students to become more engaged in reading and writing.

Struggling Students Need to Become Engaged Readers and Writers. Nothing builds confidence and motivation like success! The single most important thing that teachers can do to help students become engaged readers and writers is to teach them how to read and write, making sure that they have a range of strategies to use to guide and monitor their reading and writing and to solve problems as they arise. As students become more successful readers and writers, they will naturally become more interested in reading and writing. Teachers need to match students to books that they find interesting and can read and involve students with writing activities that are authentic. The teacher's attitude is another important consideration: When teachers are positive and confident that students can learn, they are much more likely to be successful. In addition, when students' interest is very low, teachers should consider implementing an extrinsic rewards system but then gradually substitute intrinsic rewards as students become more successful.

Ruddell (1995) researched influential reading and writing teachers—those who had a profound effect on students' lives—and found that these teachers stimulated students' internal motivation through the classroom community they created and through the literacy activities in which students were involved. Ruddell found that these influential teachers encouraged students to assume an aesthetic stance as they read and responded to books. In contrast, noninfluential teachers tried to motivate students externally, through peer pressure, competition, and grades. They encouraged students to assume an efferent stance when reading stories. Rather than exploring students' relationships with characters in discussions, they asked factual questions and judged students' responses against predetermined "correct" answers.

Students Who Adopt Avoidance Strategies

By the time some students reach the middle grades, they have lost confidence in their ability to learn to read and write because of past failures and other negative experiences. These students often adopt strategies for avoiding failure rather than strategies for making meaning; these strategies are defensive tactics (Dweck, 1986; Paris, Wasik, & Turner, 1991). Unmotivated readers give up or remain passive, uninvolved in reading (Johnson & Winograd, 1985). They are not likely to read voluntarily; however, some students do feign interest or pretend to be involved even though they are not. Others don't think reading is important, and they choose to focus on other curricular areas—math or sports, for instance. Some students complain about feeling ill or that other students are bothering them. They place blame on anything but themselves.

Struggling readers and writers get caught in a cycle of failure (Strickland, Ganske, & Monroe, 2002). They have difficulty reading and writing, so they avoid literacy activities whenever they can. By avoiding these activities, they don't get the practice they need to become better readers and writers, and they fall farther and farther behind their classmates.

There are other students who avoid reading and writing entirely. They just don't do it. Still other students read books that are too easy for them or write short pieces so that they don't have to exert much effort. Even though these strategies are self-serving, students use them because they lead to short-term success. The long-term result, however, is devastating because these students fail to learn to read and write well. Because it takes quite a bit of effort to read and write strategically, it is especially important that students experience personal ownership of the literacy activities going on in their classrooms and know how to manage their own reading and writing behaviors.

THE WORKSHOP APPROACH

The workshop approach involves three key characteristics: time, choice, and response. First, in a workshop, students have large chunks of time and the opportunity to read and write. Instead of being add-ons for when students finish schoolwork, reading and writing become the core of the literacy curriculum.

Second, students have ownership of their learning through self-selection of books they read and their topics for writing. Instead of reading books selected by the teacher or reading the same book together as a class, students select the books they want to read, books that are suitable for their interests and reading levels. During writing workshop, students plan their writing projects. They choose topics related to hobbies, content-area units, and other interests, and they also select the format for their writing.

The third characteristic is response. In reading workshop, students respond to books they are reading in reading logs[C] that they share during conversations with the teacher and with classmates. Similarly, in writing workshop, students share with classmates rough drafts of books and other compositions they are writing, and they share their completed and published compositions with genuine audiences.

Reading workshop and writing workshop are different types of workshops. Reading workshop fosters real reading of self-selected books. Students usually read 25, 50, or more books during the school year. Cora Lee Five, a fifth-grade teacher, reported that her students read between 25 and 144 books during the year (Five, 1988).

Similarly, writing workshop fosters real writing (and the use of the writing process) for genuine purposes and for authentic audiences. Each student writes and publishes 25, 50, or more books during the year. As they write, students come to see themselves as authors and become interested in learning about the authors of the books they read.

Teachers often use both workshops, or if their schedule does not allow, they may alternate the two. Schedules for reading and writing workshop at the fourth-, sixth-, and eighth-grade levels are presented in Figure 12-3.

Reading Workshop

Nancie Atwell introduced reading workshop in 1987 as an alternative to traditional reading instruction. In reading workshop, students read books that they choose themselves and respond to books through writing in reading logs and conferences with teachers and classmates (Atwell, 1998). This approach represents a change in what we believe about how children learn and how literature should be used in the classroom: Whereas traditional reading programs emphasized dependence on a teacher's guide to determine how and when particular strategies and skills should be taught, reading workshop is an individualized reading program. Atwell developed reading workshop with her middle-school students, but it has been adapted and used successfully at every grade level, first through eighth (Hornsby, Parry, & Sukarna, 1992; Hornsby, Sukarna, & Parry, 1986; McWhirter, 1990). There are several different versions of

Reading workshop is especially valuable for English language learners who often do not read as much as their classmates and who need additional reading practice with books at their reading levels.

Figure 12-3 **Schedules for Reading and Writing Workshop**

Fourth Grade

10:30–11:00	Students read self-selected books and respond to the books in reading logs.
11:00–11:15	Students share with classmates books they have finished reading and do informal book talks about them. Students often pass the "good" books to classmates who want to read them next.
11:15–11:30	The teacher teaches a reading/writing minilesson.
11:30–11:55	The teacher reads a novel aloud, one or two chapters each day. After reading, students talk about the book in a grand conversation[C].
	—Continued after lunch—
12:45–1:15	Students write books independently.
1:15–1:30	Students share their published books with classmates.

Sixth Grade

8:20–8:45	The teacher reads a novel aloud to students, and students talk about their reactions in a grand conversation.
8:45–9:30	Students write independently using the writing process. They also conference with the teacher.
9:30–9:40	The teacher teaches a reading/writing minilesson.
9:40–10:25	Students read self-selected books independently.
10:25–10:40	Students share published writings and give book talks to classmates about books they have read.

Eighth Grade

During alternating months, students participate in reading workshop or writing workshop.

1:00–1:45	Students read or write independently.
1:45–2:05	The teacher presents a minilesson on a reading or writing procedure, concept, strategy, or skill.
2:05–2:15	Students share with their classmates books they have read or compositions they have published.

reading workshop, but they usually contain five components: reading, responding, sharing, teaching minilessons, and reading aloud to students.

Component 1: Reading. Students spend 30 to 60 minutes each day independently reading books and other written materials. Frank Smith (1984) claims that to learn to read, students need to read every day, and several times each day for varied purposes. Teachers need to provide plenty of reading time in class, and not simply assume that students will practice at home what they are learning at school. In a report entitled *Becoming a Nation of Readers,* researchers reported that in classrooms without a reading workshop component, middle-grade students spend only about 15 minutes each day reading independently (Anderson, Hiebert, Scott, & Wilkinson, 1985). Similarly, McWhirter (1990) surveyed her eighth graders and found that 97% reported that they do not read on their own for pleasure. Moreover, research suggests that higher achievement is associated with more time allocated to academic activities (Brophy & Good, 1986).

Students choose the books that they read during reading workshop. Often they depend on recommendations from classmates. They also read books on particular topics—horses, science fiction, dirt bikes—or by favorite authors, such as Gary Paulsen, Chris Van Allsburg, and Louis Sachar. Ohlhausen and Jepsen (1992) developed a strategy for choosing books that they called the "Goldilocks Strategy." These teachers created three categories of books—"Too Easy" books, "Too Hard" books, and "Just Right" books—using "The Three Bears" folktale as their model. The books in the "Too Easy" category were books students had read before or could read fluently, "Too Hard" books were unfamiliar and confusing, and books in the "Just Right" category were interesting and had just a few unfamiliar words. The books in each category vary according to a student's reading level. This approach works at any grade level. Figure 12-4 presents a chart about choosing books using the Goldilocks Strategy.

When students choose their own books, they take ownership of the reading. Students' reading fluency and enjoyment of reading are related to sustained encounters with interesting texts (Smith, 1984). Reading and responding to literature are at the heart of reading workshop.

Students read all sorts of books during reading workshop, including stories, informational books, biographies, and books of poetry. They also read magazines. Most of their reading materials are selected from the classroom library, but students also bring other books from home and borrow books from classmates, from the public library, and from the school library. Students read many award-winning books during reading

Figure 12-4   A Class Chart Applying the Goldilocks Strategy

How to Choose the Best Books for YOU

"Too Easy" Books

1. The book is short.
2. The print is big.
3. You have read the book before.
4. You know all the words in the book.
5. The book has a lot of pictures.
6. You are an expert on this topic.

"Just Right" Books

1. The book looks interesting.
2. You can decode most of the words in the book.
3. Mrs. Reeves has read this book aloud to you.
4. You have read other books by this author.
5. There's someone to give you help if you need it.
6. You know something about this topic.

"Too Hard" Books

1. The book is long.
2. The print is small.
3. There aren't many pictures in the book.
4. There are a lot of words that you can't decode.
5. There's no one to help you read this book.
6. You don't know much about this topic.

workshop, but they also read series of popular books and technical books related to their hobbies and special interests. These books are not necessarily the same books that teachers use for literature focus units and literature circles, but students often choose to reread books they have read earlier in the school year or the previous year in literature studies.

Teachers need to have literally hundreds of books in their class libraries, including books written at a range of reading levels, in order to have enough books so that every student can read during reading workshop. Figure 12-5 lists many trade books that might be placed in classroom libraries and used for reading workshop in fourth through eighth grades. Of course, many of the books listed are suitable for other grade levels, too.

Teachers need to introduce students—especially reluctant readers—to the books in the classroom library so that they can more effectively choose books to read during reading workshop. The best way to preview books is by using a very brief book talk to interest students in the book. In a book talk, teachers tell students a little about the book, show the cover, and perhaps read the first paragraph or two (Prill, 1994–1995). Teachers also give book talks to introduce text sets of books, and students give book talks as they share books they have read with the class during the sharing part of reading workshop.

Teachers often read their own books and magazines or read a book of children's literature during reading workshop. Through their example, they are modeling and communicating the importance of reading. Teachers also conference with students about the books they are reading. As they conference, they talk briefly and quietly with students about their reading. Students may also read aloud favorite quotes or an interesting passage to the teacher.

Component 2: Responding. Students usually keep reading logs in which they write their initial responses to the books they are reading. Sometimes students dialogue with the teacher about the book they are reading. A journal allows for ongoing written conversation between the teacher and individual students (Atwell, 1998; Staton, 1988). Responses often demonstrate students' reading strategies and offer insights into their thinking about literature. Seeing how students think about their reading helps teachers guide their learning.

Teachers play an important role in helping students expand and enrich their responses to literature (Hancock, 1993). They help students move beyond writing summaries and toward reflecting and making connections between literature and their own lives (Barone, 1990; Kelly, 1990). In addition, they collect students' journals periodically to monitor their responses. Wollman-Bonilla (1989) recommends writing back and forth with students, with the idea that students write more if the teacher responds. Also, teachers can model and support students' responses in their own responses. However, because responding to students' journals is very time-consuming, teachers should keep their responses brief and not respond to every entry.

Some students write minimal or very limited responses in journals. It is important that students read books they find personally interesting and that they feel free to share their thoughts, feelings, and questions with a trusted audience—usually the teacher. Sometimes writing entries on a computer and using e-mail to share the entries with students in another class or with other interested readers increase students' interest in writing more elaborate responses, as the Technology Link on page 396 shows.

Responding in reading logs replaces doing workbook pages or worksheets. Teachers traditionally use worksheets as a management tool or because they think their use will increase students' reading levels. In *Becoming a Nation of Readers* (Anderson et al., 1985), the authors reported that students spend up to 70% of reading instructional

Figure 12-5   Books for Reading Workshop Collections

Fourth Grade

Ayres, K. (1996). *Family tree.* New York: Delacorte.

Creech, S. (2001). *Love that dog.* New York: HarperCollins.

Dahl, R. (1992). *Esio trot.* New York: Viking.

Fritz, J. (1976). *What's the big idea, Ben Franklin?* New York: Coward-McCann.

Giff, P. R. (1997). *Lily's crossing.* New York: Delacorte.

Goble, P. (1988). *Her seven brothers.* New York: Bradbury. (And other books by this author.)

Haskins, J. (1989). *Count your way through Mexico.* Minneapolis: Carolrhoda.

Jennings, P. (2001). *The beastly arms.* New York: Scholastic.

King-Smith, D. (1995). *The school mouse.* New York: Scholastic.

Le Guin, U. K. (1988). *Catwings.* New York: Orchard.

Levine, E. (1986). *. . . If you traveled west in a covered wagon.* New York: Scholastic.

MacLachlan, P. (1985). *Sarah, plain and tall.* New York: Harper & Row.

Monjo, F. N. (1970). *The drinking gourd.* New York: Harper & Row.

Pilkey, D. (1997). *The adventures of Captain Underpants.* New York: Scholastic.

Prelutsky, J. (1996). *A pizza the size of the sun.* New York: Greenwillow.

Rockwell, T. (1973). *How to eat fried worms.* New York: Franklin Watts.

Sachar, L. (1991). *Dogs don't tell jokes.* New York: Knopf.

Scieszka, J. (1989). *The true story of the 3 little pigs!* New York: Viking.

Smith, R. K. (1972). *Chocolate fever.* New York: Coward.

Spinelli, J. (1993). *Fourth grade rats.* New York: Scholastic.

Van Allsburg, C. (1981). *Jumanji.* Boston: Houghton Mifflin.

Fifth Grade

Avi. (1984). *The fighting ground.* New York: Harper & Row.

Cleary, B. (1983). *Dear Mr. Henshaw.* New York: Morrow.

Cleary, B. (1991). *Strider.* New York: Morrow.

Clements, A. (1996). *Frindle.* New York: Aladdin.

Coerr, E. (1977). *Sadako and the thousand paper cranes.* New York: Putnam.

Cole, J. (1989). *Anna Banana: 101 jump-rope rhymes.* New York: Morrow.

Creech, S. (1990). *Absolutely normal chaos.* New York: HarperCollins.

Dahl, R. (1964). *Charlie and the chocolate factory.* New York: Knopf.

Hurwitz, J. (1994). *School spirit.* New York: Morrow.

King-Smith, D. (1988). *Martin's mice.* New York: Crown.

Kline, S. (1990). *Horrible Harry in room 2B.* New York: Viking.

Maguire, G. (1995). *The good liar.* New York: HarperCollins.

McGovern, A. (1992). *. . . If you lived in colonial times.* New York: Scholastic.

Pinkwater, D. M. (1977). *Fat men from space.* New York: Dell.

Schwartz, D. M. (1985). *How much is a million?* New York: Scholastic.

Taylor, M. D. (1990). *Mississippi bridge.* New York: Dial.

Van Allsburg, C. (1985). *The polar express.* Boston: Houghton Mifflin. (And other books by this author.)

Wiesner, D. (1991). *Tuesday.* New York: Clarion.

Wilder, L. I. (1953). *Little house in the big woods.* New York: Harper & Row. (And other books in the series.)

Sixth Grade

Byars, B. (1968). *The midnight fox.* New York: Viking.

Clements, A. (2001). *The school story.* New York: Aladdin.

Creech, S. (2000). *The wanderer.* New York: Scholastic.

Filipovic, Z. (1993). *Zlata's diary: A child's life in Sarajevo.* New York: Viking.

Fleischman, S. (1990). *The midnight horse.* New York: Greenwillow.

Fletcher, R. (1998). *Flying solo.* New York: Clarion

Gilson, J. (1985). *Thirteen ways to sink a sub.* New York: Lothrop, Lee & Shepard.

Howe, D., & Howe, J. (1979). *Bunnicula: A rabbit-tale of mystery.* New York: Atheneum. (And other books in the series.)

Karr, K. (1998). *The great turkey walk.* New York: Farrar, Straus & Giroux.

Kehret, P. (1993). *Terror at the zoo.* New York: Cobblehill.

Klise, K. (1998). *Regarding the fountain: A tale, in letters, of liars and leaks.* New York: Avon Books.

L'Engle, M. (1962). *A wrinkle in time.* New York: Farrar, Straus & Giroux.

Lewis, C. S. (1950). *The lion, the witch and the wardrobe.* New York: Macmillan.

Macaulay, D. (1975). *Pyramid.* Boston: Houghton Mifflin.

Mazer, A. (Ed.). (1993). *America street: A multicultural anthology of stories.* New York: Persea.

Naylor, P. R. (1991). *Shiloh.* New York: Atheneum.

Paterson, K. (1977). *Bridge to Terabithia.* New York: Harper & Row.

Figure 12-5 *(continued)*

Sixth Grade, *continued*

Ride, S., & O'Shaughnessy, T. (1994). *The third planet: Exploring the earth from space.* New York: Crown.

Scieszka, J. (1999). *It's all Greek to me.* New York: Viking.

Slote, A. (1991). *Finding Buck McHenry.* New York: HarperCollins.

Soto, G. (1990). *Baseball in April and other stories.* Orlando: Harcourt Brace.

Seventh Grade

Aaseng, N. (1992). *Navajo code talkers.* New York: Walker.

Avi. (1991). *Nothing but the truth.* New York: Orchard.

Cameron, E. (1973). *The court of the stone children.* New York: Puffin.

Conrad, P. (1985). *Prairie songs.* New York: HarperCollins.

Danzinger, P. (1979). *Can you sue your parents for malpractice?* New York: Delacorte.

Flake, S. G. (1998). *The skin I'm in.* New York: Hyperion.

Fleischman, P. (1998). *Whirligig.* New York: Henry Holt.

Fox, P. (1984). *One-eyed cat.* New York: Bradbury.

Jukes, M. (1988). *Getting even.* New York: Knopf.

Krementz, J. (1989). *How it feels to fight for your life.* Boston: Little, Brown.

McKinley, R. (1984). *The hero and the crown.* New York: Greenwillow. (And other books by this author.)

O'Dell, S. (1960). *Island of the blue dolphins.* Boston: Houghton Mifflin.

Paterson, K. (1991). *Lyddie.* New York: Dutton.

Paulson, G. (1987). *Hatchet.* New York: Delacorte. (And other books by this author.)

Rawls, W. (1961). *Where the red fern grows.* New York: Doubleday.

Salisbury, G. (1994). *Under the blood-red sun.* New York: Delacorte.

Service, P. F. (1988). *Stinker from space.* New York: Fawcett.

Siebert, D. (1991). *Sierra.* New York: Harper & Row.

Wallace, B. (1992). *Buffalo gal.* New York: Holiday House.

Yolen, J. (1998). *The devil's arithmetic.* New York: Puffin.

Eighth Grade

Brooks, B. (1984). *The moves make the man.* New York: HarperCollins.

Cooper, S. (1999). *King of shadows.* New York: Aladdin.

Duncan, L. (1981). *Stranger with my face.* Boston: Little, Brown.

Freedman, R. (1987). *Lincoln: A photobiography.* New York: Clarion.

Gallo, D. R. (Ed.). (1993). *Join in: Multiethnic short stories.* New York: Delacorte.

George, J. C. (1989). *Shark beneath the reef.* New York: Harper & Row.

Hermes, P. (1991). *Mama, let's dance.* Boston: Little, Brown.

Janeczko, P. (Ed.). (1991). *Preposterous: Poems of youth.* New York: Orchard.

Lunn, J. (1991). *The root cellar.* New York: Puffin.

Macaulay, D. (1988). *The way things work: From levers to lasers, cars to computers—A visual guide to the world of machines.* Boston: Houghton Mifflin.

Moore, K. (1994). *. . . If you lived at the time of the Civil War.* New York: Scholastic.

Murphy, C. R. (1992). *To the summit.* New York: Lodestar.

Myers, W. D. (1990). *The mouse rap.* New York: HarperCollins.

Naylor, P. R. (1992). *All but Alice.* New York: Atheneum

Paterson, K. (1980). *Jacob have I loved.* New York: HarperCollins.

Paulsen, G. (1990). *Canyons.* New York: Delacorte.

Reaver, C. (1994). *A little bit dead.* New York: Delacorte.

Sleator, W. (1986). *Interstellar pig.* New York: Dutton.

Sperry, A. (1968). *Call it courage.* New York: Collier.

Zindel, P. (1968). *The pigman.* New York: HarperCollins.

time engaged in completing worksheets and workbook pages, even though these provide only perfunctory levels of reading practice in traditional classrooms.

During reading and responding time, there is little or no talking; students are engrossed in reading and writing independently. Rarely do students interrupt classmates, go to the rest room, or get drinks of water, except in case of emergency. They do not use reading workshop time to do homework or other schoolwork.

Component 3: Sharing. For the last 15 minutes of reading workshop, the class gathers together to discuss books they have finished reading. Students talk about the book and why they liked it. Sometimes they read a brief excerpt aloud or formally pass the

Technology Link

Electronic Dialoguing About Reading, Literature, and Books

Students can use e-mail to share responses about books they are reading. Students write responses to books they are reading independently and send them to students in another classroom, older students, or preservice teachers at a university. Moore (1991) described a program set up between Eastern Michigan University and a fifth-grade class in the Ypsilanti School District in which teachers in a graduate course dialogued with students in the class. Students wrote about books they were reading, and the teachers responded. The teachers encouraged students to expand their entries, make personal connections, and reflect on their reading. One fifth grader, Chih Ping, wrote these responses about Judy Blume's *Superfudge* (1980):

11/7: I am enjoying *Superfudge*. My favorite character is Fudge. I like him because he is so funny.

11/21: I think Peter's new house is real good because in Pine Grove the apartments aren't as good. I have moved before. I just moved here and lived here like about two years. This is my second year at Chapelle. It also seemed hard for me at school. After I met Robert (one of my best friends) it became easy at school. He plays in band and I play in orchestra. I am good at playing in orchestra. I play a violin. Sometimes the teacher tells me to teach the violinist how to play a song (Violinist = people who want to play violin) while she taught other people how to play the guitar and a person how to play the viola. (p. 283)

These two entries show how this student's responses became more elaborate through dialoguing by e-mail. For more information about electronic dialoguing, see Moore (1991).

book to a classmate who wants to read it. Sharing is important because it helps students form a community to value and celebrate each other's accomplishments (Hansen, 1987).

Component 4: Teaching Minilessons. The teacher spends 5 to 15 minutes teaching minilessons, brief lessons on reading workshop procedures and reading strategies and skills. Topics for minilessons are usually drawn from students' observed needs, comments students make during conferences, and procedures that students need to know how to do for reading workshop. Minilessons are sometimes taught to the whole class, and at other times, they are taught to small groups. Figure 12-6 lists possible minilesson topics.

Component 5: Reading Aloud to Students. Teachers often read novels and other books aloud to the class as part of reading workshop. They choose high-quality literature that students might not be able to read themselves, award-winning books that they feel every student should be exposed to, or books that relate to a social studies or science theme. After reading, students participate in a grand conversation to talk about the book and share the reading experience. This activity is important because students listen to a story read aloud and respond to it together as a community of learners, not as individuals.

Figure 12-6 Minilesson Topics for Reading and
Writing Workshop

Activity	Procedures	Concepts	Strategies/Skills
Reading Workshop	Choose a book Abandon a book Listen to book read aloud Read independently Decode unfamiliar words Respond in reading logs Use double-entry journals[C] Give a book talk Conference	Aesthetic reading Efferent reading Comprehension Story genre Story elements Intertextuality Literary devices Sequels Author information	Identify unfamiliar words Visualize Predict and confirm Engage with text Identify with characters Elaborate on the plot Notice opposites Monitor understanding Connect to one's own life Connect to previously read stories Value the story Evaluate the story
Writing Workshop	Choose a topic Cluster[C] ideas Make a table of contents Participate in writing groups Proofread Use the dictionary Conference with the teacher Write an "All About the Author" page Make hardcover books Share published writing Use author's chair Use rubrics	The writing process Audience Purposes for writing Writing forms Proofreaders' marks Authors Illustration techniques Wordplay	Gather ideas Organize ideas Draft Revise Use metaphors and similes Use imagery Sentence combining Edit Identify and correct spelling errors Use capital letters correctly Use punctuation marks correctly Use dialogue Value the composition

Is Sustained Silent Reading the Same as Reading Workshop?

Sustained Silent Reading (SSR)[C] is an independent reading time set aside during the school day for students in one class or the entire school to silently read self-selected books. In some schools, everyone—students, teachers, principals, secretaries, and custodians—stops to read, usually for 15 to 30 minutes. SSR is a popular reading activity in schools that is known by a variety of names, including Drop Everything and Read (DEAR), Sustained Quiet Reading Time (SQUIRT), and Our Time to Enjoy Reading (OTTER).

Teachers use SSR to increase the amount of reading students do every day and to develop their ability to read silently and without interruption (Hunt, 1967; McCracken & McCracken, 1978). A number of studies have shown that SSR is beneficial in developing students' reading ability (Krashen, 1993; Pilgreen, 2000). In addition, SSR promotes a positive attitude toward reading and encourages students to develop the habit of daily reading. It is based on these guidelines:

1. Students choose the books they read.
2. Students read silently.
3. The teacher serves as a model by reading during SSR.
4. Students choose one book or other reading material for the entire reading time.
5. The teacher sets a timer for a predetermined, uninterrupted time period, usually between 15 and 30 minutes.
6. All students in the class or school participate.
7. Students do not write book reports or participate in other after-reading activities.
8. The teacher does not keep records or evaluate students on their performance. (Pilgreen, 2000)

Even though SSR was specifically developed without follow-up activities, teachers often use a few carefully selected, brief follow-up activities to sustain students' interest in books. Sometimes students discuss their reading with a partner, or volunteers give book talks to tell the whole class about their books. As students listen to one another, they get ideas about books that they might like to read in the future. In some classrooms, students develop a ritual of passing on the books they have finished reading to interested classmates, much like students do during reading workshop.

Reading workshop and SSR are similar. The goal of both programs is to provide opportunities for students to read self-selected books independently, and the reading component of reading workshop is similar to SSR. Both programs work best in classrooms where the teacher and students have created a community of learners. It seems obvious that students need to feel relaxed and comfortable in order to read for pleasure, and a community of learners is a place where students do feel comfortable because they are respected and valued by classmates and the teacher.

Important differences exist, however. Reading workshop has five components—reading, responding, sharing, teaching minilessons, and reading aloud to students—whereas SSR has only one—reading. Reading workshop is recognized as an instructional approach because it incorporates both independent reading and instruction through minilessons. In contrast, SSR is a supplemental program. Students read books and sometimes do book talks to share their favorite books with classmates, but there is not an instructional component to SSR. Both reading workshop and SSR have been found to be effective, but teachers need to determine what their instructional goals are before choosing to implement reading workshop or SSR in their classrooms.

Writing Workshop

Writing workshop is an excellent way to implement the writing process (Atwell, 1998; Calkins, 1994; Fletcher & Portalupi, 2001; Gillet & Beverly, 2001; Graves, 1994). Students write on topics that they choose themselves, and they assume ownership of their writing and learning. At the same time, the teacher's role changes from being a provider of knowledge to serving as a facilitator and guide. The classroom becomes a community of writers who write and who share their writing. There is a spirit of pride and acceptance in the classroom.

In a writing workshop classroom, students have writing folders in which they keep all papers related to the writing project they are working on. They also keep writing notebooks in which they jot down images, impressions, dialogue, and experiences that they can build upon for writing projects (Calkins, 1991). Students have access to different kinds of paper, some lined and some unlined, as well as writing instruments such as pencils and red and blue pens. They also have access to the classroom library; many times, students' writing grows out of favorite books they have read. They may write a sequel to a book or retell a story from a different viewpoint.

As they write, students sit at desks or tables arranged in small groups. The teacher circulates around the classroom, conferencing briefly with students, and the classroom atmosphere is free enough that students converse quietly with classmates and move around the classroom to assist others or share ideas. There is space for students to meet for writing groups, and often a sign-up sheet for writing groups is posted in the classroom. A table is available for the teacher to meet with individual students or small groups for conferences, writing groups, proofreading, and minilessons.

Writing workshop is a 60- to 90-minute period scheduled each day. During this time, students are involved in three components: writing, sharing, and minilessons. Sometimes a fourth activity, reading aloud to students, is added to writing workshop when it is not used in conjunction with reading workshop.

Component 1: Writing. Students spend 30 to 45 minutes or longer working independently on writing projects. Just as students in reading workshop choose books and read at their own pace, in writing workshop, students work at their own pace on writing projects they have chosen themselves. Most students move at their own pace through all five stages of the writing process—prewriting, drafting, revising, editing, and publishing. Teachers often begin writing workshop by reviewing the five stages of the writing process, setting guidelines for writing workshop, and taking the class through one writing activity. A set of guidelines for writing workshop that one seventh-grade class developed is presented in Figure 12-7.

Teachers conference with students as they write. Many teachers prefer moving around the classroom to meet with students rather than having the students come to a table to meet with them—too often, a line forms as students wait to meet with the teacher, and students lose precious writing time. Some teachers move around the classroom in a regular pattern, meeting with one fifth of the students each day. In this way, they can conference with every student during the week.

Other teachers spend the first 15 to 20 minutes of writing workshop stopping briefly to check on 10 or more students each day. Many use a zigzag pattern to get to all parts of the classroom each day. These teachers often kneel down beside each student, sit on the edge of the student's seat, or carry their own stool to each student's desk. During the 1- or 2-minute conferences, teachers ask students what they are writing, listen to them read a paragraph or two, and then ask what they plan to do next. Then these teachers use the remaining time during writing workshop to conference more formally with students who are revising and editing their compositions. Students often sign up for these conferences. The teachers find strengths in students' writing, ask questions, and discover possibilities during these revising conferences. Some teachers like to read the pieces themselves, and others like to listen to students read their papers aloud. As they interact with students, teachers model the kinds of responses that students are learning to give to each other.

As students meet to share their writing during revising and editing, they continue to develop their sense of community. They share their rough drafts with classmates in writing groups composed of four or five students. In some classrooms, teachers join the writing groups whenever they can, but students normally run the groups themselves. They take turns reading their rough drafts to each other and listen as their

It is just as important for English language learners to participate in writing workshop as it is for other students. Through writing authentic and meaningful texts, English learners develop writing fluency and learn English written language conventions; fluency will precede conventions.

Teachers focus on improving the content of the writing during revision—not on grammatical errors—whether the student is an English language learner or a native English speaker.

Figure 12-7 A Seventh-Grade Class's Guidelines for Writing Workshop

Ten Writing Workshop Rules

1. Keep everything in your writing folder.
2. Write rough drafts in pencil.
3. Double-space all rough drafts so you will have space to revise, and write on only one side of a page.
4. Revise in blue ink.
5. Edit in red ink.
6. Show your thinking, and never erase except on the final copy.
7. Don't throw anything away—keep everything.
8. Date every piece of writing.
9. Keep a record of the compositions you write in your writing folder.
10. Work hard!

classmates offer compliments and suggestions for revision. In contrast, students usually work with one partner to edit their writing, and they often use red pens.

After proofreading their drafts with a classmate and then meeting with the teacher for final editing, students make the final copy of their writings. Students often want to print out their writings using the computer so that their final copies will appear professional. Many times, students compile their final copies to make books during writing workshop, but sometimes they attach their writing to artwork, make posters, or write letters that will be mailed. Not every piece is necessarily published, however; sometimes students decide not to continue with a piece of writing. They file the piece in their writing folders and start something new.

Component 2: Sharing.   For the last 10 to 15 minutes of writing workshop, the class gathers together to share their new publications and make other related announcements. Students sit in a special author's chair to read their compositions aloud. After each reading, classmates offer compliments. They may also make other comments and suggestions, but the focus is on celebrating completed writing projects, not on revising the composition to make it better.

Component 3: Teaching Minilessons.   During this 5- to 15-minute period, teachers provide short, focused lessons on writing workshop procedures, qualities of good writing, and writing strategies and skills, such as organizing ideas, proofreading, and using quotation marks for dialogue. Teachers often make a transparency of an anonymous student's piece of writing (often a student in another class or from a pre-

Students learn to think of themselves as writers as they share their compositions with classmates.

vious year) and then display it using an overhead projector. Students read the writing, and the teacher uses it to teach the lesson, which may focus on giving suggestions for revision, combining sentences, proofreading, or writing a stronger lead sentence. Teachers also use excerpts from books students are reading for minilessons to show students how published authors use writing skills and strategies. Refer to Figure 12-6 for a list of minilessons for writing workshop. These minilessons are similar to those taught in reading workshop. And for other ideas for minilessons, check *Craft Lessons: Teaching Writing K–8* (Fletcher & Portalupi, 1998), *Writing Rules! Teaching Kids to Write for Life, Grades 4–8* (Brusko, 1999), and *Reviser's Toolbox* (Lane, 1999).

Many minilessons occur during writing workshop when students ask questions or when the teacher notices that students misunderstand or misapply a procedure, concept, strategy, or skill. A sample minilesson is featured on page 402. Ms. Hodas reviews paragraphing skills with her fifth-grade class after she notices that students are not dividing their text into paragraphs or crafting well-developed paragraphs.

Teachers also share information during minilessons about authors and how they write. For students to think of themselves as writers, they need to know what writers do. Each year, there are more and more autobiographies written by authors. James Howe, author of *Bunnicula: A Rabbit-Tale of Mystery* (Howe & Howe, 1979), has written an autobiography, *Playing With Words* (1994), in which he reflects on his desire since childhood to make people laugh and describes his writing routine and how he makes time to read and write every day. Some of the other books in the Meet the Author series are *Lois Lowry* (Markham, 1995), *Avi* (Markham, 1996), and *Gary Paulsen* (Peters, 1999).

Managing a Workshop Classroom

It takes time to establish a workshop approach in the classroom, especially if students are used to reading from basal readers. Students need to learn how to become responsible for their own learning. They need to develop new ways of working and learning, and they have to form a community of readers and writers in the classroom

Minilesson

Topic: Paragraphs
Grade: Fifth Grade
Time: 15 minutes

Ms. Hodas's fifth graders are writing reports about inventions during writing workshop. Together as a class, students developed clusters with information about the inventions they had studied, and then students worked independently to write rough drafts using the information from their clusters. More than half of the students have finished their rough drafts and are participating in revising groups. As Ms. Hodas conferences with students about their writing, she notices that many of them are not breaking their writing into paragraphs or writing well-developed paragraphs. She decides to bring the class together for a brief minilesson on paragraphing.

1. Introduce Topic
"Let's stop for a minute and talk about paragraphs," Ms. Hodas says. "What do you know about paragraphs?" Students talk about organizing ideas into paragraphs, keeping to one topic in a paragraph, using a topic sentence and a concluding sentence, and indenting paragraphs. Ms. Hodas is pleased that students remember what she has taught them about paragraphing and refers them to the chart on paragraphs posted in the classroom that they created earlier in the school year.

2. Share Examples
Ms. Hodas asks students to reread their rough drafts to themselves. Afterward, she asks them to check that they have organized their writing into paragraphs. The students who have not written in paragraphs add the paragraph indent symbol to indicate where new paragraphs should begin.

3. Provide Information
"Now let's look at your first paragraph," Ms. Hodas says. She asks each student to reread his or her first paragraph, checking for a topic sentence, detail sentences that stick to the topic, and a final sentence that sums up the paragraph. Students who find that their paragraphs are not well developed start revising or writing notes in the margin of their papers about how they want to revise the paragraph. They continue rereading their rough drafts, checking that all paragraphs are well crafted.

4. Guide Practice
Ms. Hodas asks for a volunteer to read a paragraph aloud for the class to examine. Jonas reads his first paragraph—a well-crafted paragraph—aloud to the class, and the students pick out the topic sentence, the detail sentences, and the concluding sentence. They agree that all sentences stick to the topic. Next, William reads another strong paragraph aloud and students pick out all of the components. Then Ms. Hodas asks for other students to volunteer to read aloud paragraphs that they need to revise so that classmates can give some suggestions. Because Ms. Hodas has created a community of learners in the classroom, students are willing to share their paragraphs even when the writing is not their best work. Three students each read a paragraph aloud, and classmates identify the missing pieces and offer suggestions.

5. Assess Learning
The minilesson ends with Ms. Hodas inviting students who want more assistance to meet with her at the conferencing table. The other students return to working independently or with partners at their desks.

(Gillet & Beverly, 2001). For reading workshop, students need to know how to select books, how to read aesthetically, and other reading workshop procedures. For writing workshop, students need to know how to develop and refine a piece of writing, how to make books and booklets for their compositions, and other writing workshop procedures. Sometimes students complain that they don't know what to write about, but in time they learn how to brainstorm possible topics and to keep a list of topics in their writing workshop notebooks.

Teachers begin to establish the workshop environment in their classroom from the first day of the school year by allowing students to choose the books they read and the topics for writing. Teachers provide time for students to read and write and teach them how to respond to books and to their classmates' writing. Through their interactions with students, the respect they show to students, and the way they model reading and writing, teachers establish the classroom as a community of learners.

Teachers develop a schedule for reading and writing workshop with time allocated for each component, as shown in Figure 12-3. In their schedules, teachers allot as much time as possible for students to read and write. After developing the schedule, teachers post it in the classroom and talk with students about the activities and discuss their expectations with them. Teachers teach the workshop procedures and continue to model them as students become comfortable with the routines. As students share what they are reading and writing at the end of workshop sessions, their enthusiasm grows and the workshop approaches are successful.

Students keep two folders—one for reading workshop and one for writing workshop. In the reading workshop folder, students keep a list of books they have read, notes from minilessons, reading logs, and other materials. In the writing workshop folder, they keep all rough drafts and other compositions, a list of all compositions, topics for future pieces, and notes from minilessons.

Many teachers use a classroom chart to monitor students' work on a daily basis. At the beginning of reading workshop, students (or the teacher) record what book they are reading or if they are writing in a reading log, waiting to conference with the teacher, or browsing in the classroom library. For writing workshop, students identify the writing project they are involved in or the stage of the writing process they are in. A sample writing workshop chart is shown in Figure 12-8. Teachers can also use the chart to award weekly "effort" grades, to have students indicate their need to conference with the teacher, or to have students announce that they are ready to share the book they have read or to publish their writing. Nancie Atwell (1998) calls this chart "the state of the class." Teachers can review students' progress and note which students need to meet with the teacher or receive additional attention. When students fill in the chart themselves, they develop responsibility for their actions and a stronger desire to accomplish tasks they set for themselves.

Teachers should take time during reading and writing workshop to observe students as they interact and work together in small groups. Researchers who have observed in reading and writing workshop classrooms report that some students, even as young as first graders, are excluded from group activities because of sex, ethnicity, and socioeconomic status (Henkin, 1995; Lensmire, 1992); the socialization patterns in elementary and middle school classrooms seem to reflect society's. Henkin recommends that teachers be alert to the possibility that boys might share books only with other boys or that some students won't find anyone willing to be their editing partner. If teachers see instances of discrimination in their classrooms, they should confront it directly and work to foster a classroom environment where students treat each other equitably.

Figure 12-8 "State of the Class" Chart

	Writing Workshop Chart							
Names	Dates 3/18	3/19	3/20	3/21	3/22	3/25	3/26	3/27
Antonio	4	5	5	5	5	1	1	1 2
Bella	2	2	2 3	2	2	4	5	5
Charles	3	3 1	1	2	2 3	4	5	5
Dina	4 5	5	5	1	1	1	1	2 3
Dustin	3	3	4	4	4	5	5 1	1
Eddie	2 3	2	2 4	5	5	1	1 2	2 3
Elizabeth	2	3	3	4	4	4 5	5	1 2
Elsa	1 2	3 4	4 5	5	5	1	2	2

Code:
1 = Prewriting   2 = Drafting   3 = Revising   4 = Editing   5 = Publishing

Benefits of Using Reading and Writing Workshop

There are many reasons to recommend the workshop approach. In reading workshop, students select and read genuine literature that is interesting and is written at their reading level. The literature has complex sentence patterns and presents challenging concepts and vocabulary. Through reading workshop, students become more fluent readers and learn to deepen their appreciation of books and reading. As students read, they are developing lifelong reading habits. They are introduced to different genres and choose favorite authors. Most important, they come to think of themselves as readers, and this realization makes them more likely to become lifelong readers.

In writing workshop, students create their own compositions and come to see themselves as writers. They practice writing strategies and skills and learn to choose words carefully to articulate their ideas. Perhaps most important, as they see firsthand the power of writing to entertain, inform, and persuade; students are more likely to become lifelong writers.

Samway, Whang, and their students (1991) reported that the two most important benefits of reading workshop are that students become a community of learners and that they view themselves as readers. As students read and respond to books, they understand themselves and their classmates better and gain confidence in themselves as readers. In addition, their ability to choose reading materials becomes more sophisticated during the school year. Students are much more enthusiastic about reading workshop than traditional reading approaches. The authors offer advice to teachers about the necessary components of reading workshop: Students want to read complete books, not excerpts; they want to choose the books they read; and they need plenty of time to read and talk about books.

Many teachers fear that their students' scores on standardized achievement tests will decline if they implement a workshop approach in their classrooms, even though many teachers have reported either an increase in test scores or no change at all (Five, 1988; Swift, 1993). Kathleen Swift (1993) reported the results of a yearlong study comparing two groups of her students; one group read basal reader stories, and the other participated in reading workshop. The reading workshop group showed significantly greater improvement, and Swift also reported that students participating in reading workshop showed more positive attitudes toward reading.

VISIT CHAPTER 12 ON THE COMPANION WEBSITE AT
www.prenhall.com/tompkins

- Complete a self-assessment to demonstrate your understanding of the concepts presented in this chapter
- Complete field activities that will help you expand your understanding of implementing reading and writing workshop in the middle-grade classroom
- Visit important web links related to reading and writing workshop
- Look into your state's standards as they relate to encouraging middle-grade students to read and respond to books and to develop and refine compositions
- Communicate with other preservice teachers via the message board and discuss the issues of helping students in grades 4 to 8 become lifelong readers and writers

How Effective Teachers . . .
Conduct Reading and Writing Workshop

1. Teachers allow students to choose the books they want to read.
2. Teachers teach students how to select books using the Goldilocks Strategy.
3. Teachers recognize reading workshop as an instructional approach and provide plenty of time for students to read and respond to books.
4. Teachers use conferences and the responses students write in reading logs to monitor their reading progress.
5. Teachers build students' enthusiasm for reading and books through book talks and sharing.
6. Teachers teach minilessons and have students apply what they have learned through reading and writing.
7. Teachers allow students to choose their own topics and forms for writing.
8. Teachers have students use the writing process to develop and refine their compositions.
9. Teachers encourage students to publish their writing in books.
10. Teachers have students celebrate their completed writings and share them using an author's chair.

Review

The workshop approach involves students in meaningful reading and writing experiences. Students read and respond to books in reading workshop, and they write and publish books in writing workshop. Effective teachers incorporate the three key characteristics of the workshop approach—time, choice, and response—in their workshops. The five components of reading workshop are reading, responding, sharing, teaching minilessons, and reading aloud to students. The components of writing workshop are similar: writing, sharing, and teaching minilessons. Sometimes teachers combine reading and writing workshop, alternate them, or use writing workshop as students complete projects related to literature focus units or content-area thematic units. A list of effective practices for the workshop approach is presented in the feature on pages 405–406.

Professional References

Alderman, M. K. (1999). *Motivation for achievement: Possibilities for teaching and learning.* Mahwah, NJ: Erlbaum.

Anderson, R. C., Hiebert, E. H., Scott, J. A., & Wilkinson, I. A. G. (1985). *Becoming a nation of readers.* Washington, DC: National Institute of Education.

Atwell, N. (1998). *In the middle: New understandings about reading and writing with adolescents* (2nd ed.). Upper Montclair, NJ: Boynton/Cook.

Barone, D. (1990). The written responses of young children: Beyond comprehension to story understanding. *The New Advocate, 3,* 49–56.

Baumann, J. F., & Duffy, A. M. (1997). *Engaged reading for pleasure and learning: A report from the National Reading Research Center.* Athens, GA: National Reading Research Center.

Brophy, J. E., & Good, T. L. (1986). Teacher behavior and student achievement. In M. C. Wittrock (Ed.), *Handbook of research on teaching* (3rd ed., pp. 328–375). New York: Macmillan.

Brusko, M. (1999). *Writing rules! Teaching kids to write for life, grades 4–8.* Portsmouth, NH: Heinemann.

Calkins, L. M. (1991). *Living between the lines.* Portsmouth, NH: Heinemann.

Calkins, L. M. (1994). *The art of teaching writing* (Rev. ed.). Portsmouth, NH: Heinemann.

Dweck, C. S. (1986). Motivational processes affecting learning. *American Psychologist, 41,* 1040–1048.

Five, C. L. (1988). From workbook to workshop: Increasing children's involvement in the reading process. *The New Advocate, 1,* 103–113.

Fletcher, R., & Portalupi, J. (1998). *Craft lessons: Teaching writing K–8.* York, ME: Stenhouse.

Fletcher, R., & Portalupi, J. (2001). *Writing workshop: The essential guide.* Portsmouth, NH: Heinemann.

Gillet, J. W., & Beverly, L. (2001). *Directing the writing workshop: An elementary teacher's handbook.* New York: Guilford Press.

Good, T., & Brophy, J. E. (2000). *Looking in classrooms* (2nd ed.). New York: Longman.

Graves, D. H. (1994). *A fresh look at writing.* Portsmouth, NH: Heinemann.

Hancock, M. R. (1993). Exploring and extending personal response through literature journals. *The Reading Teacher, 46,* 466–474.

Hansen, J. (1987). *When writers read.* Portsmouth, NH: Heinemann.

Henkin, R. (1995). Insiders and outsiders in first-grade writing workshops: Gender and equity issues. *Language Arts, 72,* 429–434.

Hornsby, D., Parry, J., & Sukarna, D. (1992). *Teach on: Teaching strategies for reading and writing workshops.* Portsmouth, NH: Heinemann.

Hornsby, D., Sukarna, D., & Parry, J. (1986). *Read on: A conference approach to reading.* Portsmouth, NH: Heinemann.

Hunt, L. (1967). Evaluation through teacher-pupil conferences. In T. C. Barrett (Ed.), *The evaluation of children's reading achievement* (pp. 111–126). Newark, DE: International Reading Association.

Ivey, G., & Broaddus, K. (2001). "Just plain reading": A survey of what makes students want to read in middle school classrooms. *Reading Research Quarterly, 36,* 350–377.

Johnston, P., & Winograd, P. (1985). Passive failure in reading. *Journal of Reading Behavior, 17,* 279–301.

Kelly, P. R. (1990). Guiding young students' response to literature. *The Reading Teacher, 43,* 464–470.

Kohn, A. (1993). *Punished by rewards: The trouble with gold stars, incentive plans, A's, praise, and other bribes.* Boston: Houghton Mifflin.

Krashen, S. (1993). *The power of reading.* Englewood, CO: Libraries Unlimited.

Lane, B. (1999). *Reviser's toolbox.* Shoreham, VT: Discover Writing Press.

Lensmire, T. (1992). *When children write*. New York: Teachers College Press.

McCracken, R., & McCracken, M. (1978). Modeling is the key to sustained silent reading. *The Reading Teacher, 31,* 406–408.

McWhirter, A. M. (1990). Whole language in the middle school. *The Reading Teacher, 43,* 562–565.

Moore, M. A. (1991). Electronic dialoguing: An avenue to literacy. *The Reading Teacher, 45,* 280–286.

Ohlhausen, M. M., & Jepsen, M. (1992). Lessons from Goldilocks: "Somebody's been choosing my books but I can make my own choices now!" *The New Advocate, 5,* 31–46.

Oldfather, P. (1995). Commentary: What's needed to maintain and extend motivation for literacy in the middle grades. *Journal of Reading, 38,* 420–422.

Paris, S. G., Wasik, B. A., & Turner, J. C. (1991). The development of strategic readers. In R. Barr, M. L. Kamil, P. B. Mosenthal, & P. D. Pearson (Eds.), *Handbook of reading research* (vol. 2, pp. 609–640). New York: Longman.

Pilgreen, J. L. (2000). *The SSR handbook: How to organize and manage a sustained silent reading program.* Portsmouth, NH: Boynton/Cook/Heinemann.

Prill, P. (1994–1995). Helping children use the classroom library. *The Reading Teacher, 48,* 363–364.

Robb, L. (1993). A cause for celebration: Reading and writing with at-risk students. *The New Advocate, 6,* 25–40.

Robb, L. (2000). *Teaching reading in middle school: A strategic approach to teaching reading that improves comprehension and thinking.* New York: Scholastic.

Ruddell, R. B. (1995). Those influential literacy teachers: Meaning negotiators and motivation builders. *The Reading Teacher, 48,* 454–463.

Samway, K. D., Whang, G., Cade, C., Gamil, M., Lubandina, M. A., & Phommachanh, K. (1991). Reading the skeleton, the heart, and the brain of a book: Students' perspectives on literature study circles. *The Reading Teacher, 45,* 196–205.

Smith, F. (1984). *Reading without nonsense*. New York: Teachers College Press.

Staton, J. (1988). ERIC/RCS report: Dialogue journals. *Language Arts, 65,* 198–201.

Stipek, D. J. (1993). *Motivation to learn: From theory to practice* (2nd ed.). Boston: Allyn & Bacon.

Strickland, D. S., Ganske, K., & Monroe, J. K. (2002). *Supporting struggling readers and writers: Strategies for classroom intervention 3–6.* Portland, ME: Stenhouse.

Swift, K. (1993). Try reading workshop in your classroom. *The Reading Teacher, 46,* 366–371.

Turner, J., & Paris, S. G. (1995). How literacy tasks influence children's motivation for literacy. *The Reading Teacher, 48,* 662–673.

Unrau, N. (2004). *Content area reading and writing: Fostering literacies in middle and high school cultures.* Upper Saddle River, NJ: Merrill/Prentice Hall.

Wollman-Bonilla, J. E. (1989). Reading to participate in literature. *The Reading Teacher, 43,* 112–120.

Children's Book References

Blume, J. (1980). *Superfudge*. New York: Dutton.

Canfield, J. (1999). *Chicken soup for the cat and dog lover's soul*. Deerfield Beach, FL: Health Communications.

Canfield, J. (2000). *Chicken soup for the preteen soul*. Deerfield Beach, FL: Health Communications.

Canfield, J., Hansen, M. V., & Kirberger, K. (1997). *Chicken soup for the teenage soul*. Deerfield Beach, FL: Health Communications.

Canfield, J., Hansen, M. V., Tunney, J., Donnelly, M., & Donnelly, C. (2000). *Chicken soup for the sports fan's soul*. Deerfield Beach, FL: Health Communications.

Cushman, K. (2000). *Matilda Bone*. New York: Clarion.

Howe, D., & Howe, J. (1979). *Bunnicula: A rabbit-tale of mystery*. New York: Atheneum.

Howe, J. (1994). *Playing with words*. Katonah, NY: Richard C. Owen.

Markham, L. (1995). *Lois Lowry*. Huntington Beach, CA: Learning Works/Creative Teaching Press.

Markham, L. (1996). *Avi*. Huntington Beach, CA: Learning Works/Creative Teaching Press.

Paulsen, G. (1990). *Canyons*. New York: Delacorte.

Peters, S. T. (1999). *Gary Paulsen*. Huntington Beach, CA: Learning Works/Creative Teaching Press.

Staples, S. F. (1996). *Dangerous skies*. New York: Farrar, Straus & Giroux.

Yolen, J. (1988). *The devil's arithmetic*. New York: Viking.

Compendium of
Instructional Procedures

In this *Compendium of Instructional Procedures*, forty-four instructional procedures used in balanced reading classrooms are presented, with step-by-step directions and student samples. You have read about story maps, grand conversations, word sorts, minilessons, word walls, reading logs, and other procedures in the 12 chapters of the text; they were marked with a ᶜ to cue you to consult the Compendium for more detailed information. The Compendium is a handy resource to consult as you develop lesson plans and teach in middle-grade classrooms. A list of the procedures follows.

Alphabet books

Anticipation guides

Book boxes

Book talks

Choral reading

Cloze procedure

Clusters, maps, and webs

Collaborative books and reports

Cubing

Data charts

Directed reading-thinking activity

Double-entry journals

Exclusion brainstorming

Grand conversations

Guided reading

Individual books and reports

Instructional conversations

Interactive writing

K-W-L charts

Language experience approach

Learning logs

Making words

Minilessons

Open-mind portraits

Possible sentences

Prereading plan

Quickwrites

Quilts

Read-arounds

Readers theatre

Reading logs

Repeated readings

Running records

Say something

Semantic feature analysis

Shared reading

SQ3R study strategy

Story boards

Story maps

Sustained silent reading

Tea party

Word sorts

Word walls

Writing groups

ALPHABET BOOKS

Students construct alphabet books much like the alphabet trade books published for children (Tompkins, 2004). They often make alphabet books as projects during literature focus units and content-area units. Students can make alphabet books collaboratively as a class or in a small group. Interested students can make individual alphabet books, but with 26 pages to complete, it is an arduous task. The steps in constructing an alphabet book with a group of students are:

1. *Examine alphabet trade books.* Students examine alphabet trade books published for children to learn how the books are designed and how the authors use titles, text, and illustrations to lay out their pages. Good examples include *America: A Patriotic Primer* (Cheney, 2002) and *Illuminations* (Hunt, 1989). Or, students can examine student-made alphabet books made by other classes.

2. *Make an alphabet list.* Students write the letters of the alphabet in a column on a long sheet of butcher paper for the group to use for brainstorming words for the book.

3. *Have students brainstorm words.* Students identify words beginning with each letter of the alphabet related to the literature focus unit or content-area unit, and they write these words on the sheet of butcher paper. Students often consult the word wall[C] and books in the text set as they think of related words.

4. *Have students choose letters.* Students each choose the letter for the page they will create.

5. *Design the format of the page.* As a class or small group, students decide where the letter, the illustration, and the text will be placed.

6. *Write the pages.* Students use the writing process to draft, revise, and edit their pages. Then students make final copies of their pages, and one student makes the cover.

7. *Compile the pages.* Students and the teacher compile the pages in alphabetical order and bind the book.

Alphabet books are often used as projects at the end of a unit of study, such as pioneers, oceans, World War II, or California missions. The 'U' page from a fourth-grade class's alphabet book on the California missions is shown in Figure 1.

ANTICIPATION GUIDES

Anticipation guides (Head & Readence, 1986) are lists of statements about a topic that students discuss before reading content-area textbooks and informational books. Teachers prepare a list of statements about the topic; some of the statements should be true and accurate, and others incorrect or based on misconceptions. Before reading, students discuss each statement and agree or disagree with it. Then they discuss the statements again after reading. The purpose of this activity is to stimulate students' interest in the topic and to activate prior knowledge. A fifth-grade anticipation guide about Canada is shown in Figure 2.

The steps in developing an anticipation guide are:

1. *Identify several major concepts.* Teachers consider their students' knowledge about the topic and any misconceptions they might have as they identify concepts related to the reading assignment or unit.

2. *Develop a list of three to six statements.* Teachers write a statement about each major concept they identified. These statements should be general enough to stimulate discussion and useful for clarifying misconceptions. The list can be written on a chart, or individual copies can be duplicated for each student.

Figure 1

The "U" Page From a Fourth-Grade Class's Alphabet Book

Some of the Indians thought life was UNBEARABLE at the missions. They thought this because they couldn't hunt or do the things they were used to. Once they were at the missions they couldn't leave. They were sometimes beaten if they did.

3. *Discuss the statements on the anticipation guide.* Teachers introduce the anticipation guide and have students respond to the statements. Students think about the statements and decide whether they agree or disagree with each one.

4. *Read the text.* Students read the text and compare their responses to what the reading material states.

5. *Discuss the statements again.* After reading, students reconsider their earlier responses to each statement and locate information in the text that supports or refutes the statement.

Students can also try their hand at writing anticipation guides. When students are reading informational books in literature circles, they can create an anticipation guide after reading and then share the guide with classmates when they present the book during a sharing time.

Figure 2   Anticipation Guide on Canada

Before Reading		Statements	After Reading	
Yes	No		Yes	No
		Canada is the second largest country in the world.		
		The official language of Canada is English.		
		Canada is very much like the United States.		
		Canada's economy is based on its wealth of natural resources.		
		Canada has always fought on the American side during wars.		
		Today, most Canadians live within 200 miles of the American border.		

BOOK BOXES

Teachers and students collect three or more objects or pictures related to a story, informational book, or poem and put them in a box along with the book or other reading material. For example, a book box for *Sarah, Plain and Tall* (MacLachlan, 1983) might include seashells, a train ticket, a yellow bonnet, colored pencils, a map of Sarah's trip from Maine to the prairie, and letters. Or, for *Tuck Everlasting* (Babbitt, 1975), teachers can collect a small vial of water, a man's yellow hat, a toy frog, a sign saying "Welcome to Treegap," and a music box. The steps in preparing a book box are:

1. *Read the book.* While reading the book, teachers notice important objects that are mentioned and think about how they might collect these objects or replicas of them.

2. *Choose a book box.* Teachers choose a box, basket, or plastic tub to hold the objects, and decorate it with the name of the book, pictures, and words.

3. *Fill the book box.* Teachers place three or more objects and pictures in the box to represent the book. When students are making book boxes, they may place an inventory sheet in the box with all the items listed and an explanation of why the items were selected.

4. *Share the completed book box.* When teachers make book boxes, they use them to introduce the book and provide background information before reading. In contrast, students often make book boxes as a project during the extending stage of the reading process and share them with classmates at the end of a unit.

Book boxes are especially useful for students learning English as a second language and for nonverbal students who have small vocabularies and difficulty developing sentences to express ideas.

Book talks are brief teasers that teachers present to interest students in particular books. Teachers use book talks to introduce students to books in the classroom library, books for literature circles, or a text set of books for a unit or books written by a particular author. Students also give book talks to share books they have read during reading workshop. The steps are:

1. *Select one or more books to share.* When teachers share more than one book, the books are usually related in some way; they may be part of a text set, written by the same author, or on a related topic.

2. *Plan a brief presentation for each book.* During the 1- or 2-minute presentation, teachers tell the title and author of the book and give a brief summary. They also explain why they liked it and why students might be interested in it. The teacher may also read a short excerpt and show an illustration.

3. *Display the books.* Teachers show the book during the book talk and then display it on a chalk tray or shelf to encourage students' interest.

The same steps are used when students give book talks. If students have prepared a project related to the book, they also share it during the book talk.

A good way to develop students' reading fluency is through choral reading. Poems are usually the texts chosen for choral reading, but other texts can also be used. As students read aloud, they practice chunking words together, varying their reading speed, and reading more expressively. Students take turns reading lines or sentences of the text as they read together as a class or in small groups. Four possible arrangements for choral reading are:

- *Echo reading.*   The leader reads each line, and the group repeats it.
- *Leader and chorus reading.*   The leader reads the main part of the poem, and the group reads the refrain or chorus in unison.
- *Small-group reading.*   The class divides into two or more groups, and each group reads one part of the poem.
- *Cumulative reading.*   One student or one group reads the first line or stanza, and another student or group joins in as each line or stanza is read so that a cumulative effect is created.

The steps in choral reading are:

1. *Select a poem for choral reading.* Teachers select a poem or other text to use for choral reading and copy it onto a chart or make multiple copies for students to read.

2. *Arrange the text for choral reading.* Teachers work with students to decide how to arrange the text for reading. They add marks to the chart or have students mark individual copies so that they can follow the arrangement.

3. *Do the choral reading.* Students read the poem or other text together several times, and teachers emphasize that students should pronounce words clearly and read with expression. Teachers may want to tape-record students' reading so that they can hear themselves.

Choral reading makes students active participants in the poetry experience, and it helps them learn to appreciate the sounds, feelings, and magic of poetry. It is recommended for ESL students because it is an enjoyable, low-anxiety activity that helps children learn English intonation patterns and improve their reading fluency. Many poems can be used for choral reading; begin with humorous poems such as "Eyeballs for Sale!" "I'm Practically Covered With Needles and Pins," and "Rat for Lunch!" from Jack Prelutsky's *A Pizza the Size of the Sun* (1996). Three other recommended books of poetry are *Knock at a Star: A Child's Introduction to Poetry* (Kennedy & Kennedy, 1999), *Kids Pick the Funniest Poems: Poems That Make Kids Laugh* (Lansky, 1991), and *Neighborhood Odes* (Soto, 1992).

CLOZE PROCEDURE

The cloze procedure is an informal tool for assessing students' comprehension. Teachers use the cloze procedure to gather information about readers' abilities to deal with the content and the structure of texts they are reading. They construct a cloze passage by choosing an excerpt from a book—a story, an informational book, or a content-area textbook—that students have read and deleting roughly every fifth word in the passage; the deleted words are replaced with blanks. Then students read the passage and add the missing words. Students use their knowledge of syntax (the order of words in English) and semantics (the meaning of words within sentences) to predict the missing words in the text passage. Only the exact word is considered the correct answer. The following cloze activity was devised by a fourth-grade teacher to assess students' understanding during a unit on astronomy. The three paragraphs were taken from a class book, and each was written by a different student:

> The nine planets travel around the sun. The _____ is a planet that travels around the sun once a year. The planets between the sun and the Earth are called the _____ planets and the others are the _____ planets. The planets are Mercury, _____, Earth, Mars, Jupiter, _____, Uranus, _____, and Pluto. The sun, the planets, and their _____ make up the _____ system.
>
> Stars are giant shining balls of hot _____. The _____ are dark, and we can only _____ them because they reflect the _____ of the sun. Planets and stars look almost the same at night, but planets do not _____. Stars stay in the same place in the _____, but planets _____ around.
>
> Jupiter is the _____ planet in the solar system. It is the _____ planet from the _____. Jupiter is covered with thick _____ so we can't see it from Earth. Astronomers can see a giant _____ spot on the clouds. Maybe it is sort of like a hurricane. Believe it or not, Jupiter has both _____ and _____. It is very _____ on Jupiter, but there could be life there.

The steps in the cloze procedure are:

1. ***Select a passage and retype it.*** Teachers select an excerpt from a story, content-area textbook, or informational book for the cloze activity. Then they retype the text. The first sentence is typed exactly as it appears in the original text. Beginning with the second sentence, one of the first five words is deleted and replaced with a blank, then every fifth word in the remainder of the passage is deleted and replaced with a blank. Teachers often vary the cloze procedure and delete specific content words rather than every fifth word. Character names and words related to key events in the story might be omitted. For passages from informational books, teachers often delete key terms.

2. *Complete the cloze activity.* Students read the entire text silently, and then they reread the text and predict or "guess" the word that goes in each blank. Students write the words in the blanks.

3. *Score students' work.* Teachers award one point each time the missing word is identified. The percentage of correct answers is determined by dividing the number of points by the number of blanks. Compare the percentage of correct word replacements with this scale:

61% or more correct:	independent level
41–60% correct:	instructional level
40% or less correct:	frustration level

The cloze procedure can also be used to determine whether an unfamiliar trade book or textbook is appropriate to use for classroom instruction. Teachers prepare a cloze passage and have all students or a random sample of students follow the procedure identified here. Then teachers score students' responses and use a one-third to one-half formula to determine the text's appropriateness for their students: If students correctly predict more than 50% of the deleted words, the passage is easy reading, but if they predict less than 30% of the missing words, the passage is too difficult for classroom instruction. The instructional range is 30–50% correct predictions (Reutzel & Cooter, 2000). The percentages are different from those in the scale because students are reading an unfamiliar passage instead of a familiar one.

CLUSTERS, MAPS, AND WEBS

Clusters are weblike diagrams with the topic written in a circle centered on a sheet of paper. Main ideas are written on rays drawn out from the circle, and branches with details and examples are added to complete each main idea (Rico, 1983). Clusters are used to organize information students are learning and to organize ideas before beginning to write a composition. A fourth-grade class's cluster about the four layers of the rain forest is shown in Figure 3. Teachers and students can work together to make a cluster, or students can work in small groups or make clusters individually. The steps are:

1. *Draw the center of the cluster.* Teachers or students select a topic and write the word in the center of a circle drawn on a chart or sheet of paper.

2. *Brainstorm a list of words.* Students brainstorm as many words and phrases as they can that are related to the topic, and then they organize the words into categories. The teacher may prompt students for additional words or suggest categories.

3. *Add main ideas and details.* Students determine the main ideas and details from the brainstormed list of words. The main ideas are written on rays drawn out from the circled topic and circled, and details are written on rays drawn out from the main idea circles.

Clusters are sometimes called maps and webs, and they are similar to story maps[C]. In this book, the diagrams are called clusters when used for writing, and they are called maps when used for reading.

COLLABORATIVE BOOKS AND REPORTS

Students divide the work of writing an informational book or report when they work collaboratively. They each contribute one page for a class book or work with partners or in small groups to research and write sections of the report. Then the students' work is compiled, and the book or report is complete (Tompkins, 2004). Students use

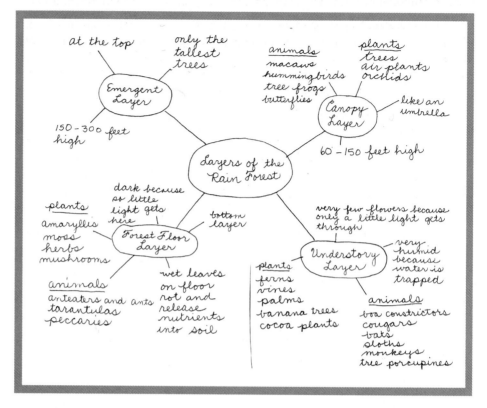

a process approach as they research their topics and compose their sections of the report or book. The steps are:

1. **Choose the topic.** Students choose specific topics related to the general topic of the unit for their pages or sections. Students work in small groups, with partners, or individually to research and write their sections of the informational book or report.

2. **Plan the organization.** If students are each contributing one page for a class informational book, they might draw a picture and add a fact or other piece of information. Students working on chapters for a longer report will need to design research questions. These questions emerge as students study a topic and brainstorm a list of questions on a chart posted in the classroom. If they are planning a report on the human body, for example, the small groups that are studying each organ may decide to research the same three questions: "What does the organ look like?" "What job does the organ do?" and "Where is the organ located in the human body?"

3. **Rehearse the procedure.** Teachers and students write one section of the report or book together as a class before students begin working on their section of the report.

4. **Gather and organize ideas.** Students gather and organize information for their sections. Those working in small groups or with partners search for answers to the research questions. Students can use clusters[C] or data charts[C] to record the information they gather. The research questions are the same for each data-collection instrument.

On a cluster, students add information as details to each main-idea ray; if they are working with data charts, they record information from the first source in the first row under the appropriate question, from the second source in the second row, and so on.

5. *Draft the sections of the report.* Students write rough drafts of their sections. When students are working in small groups, one student is the scribe and writes the draft while the other students dictate sentences, using information from a cluster or data chart. Next, they share their drafts with the class and make revisions on the basis of feedback they receive. Last, students proofread and correct mechanical errors.

6. *Compile the pages or sections.* Students compile their completed pages or sections, and then the entire book or report is read aloud so students can catch inconsistencies or redundant passages. Students also add front and back pages. For an informational book, students add a title page and covers. For reports, students also write a table of contents, an introduction, and a conclusion and add a bibliography at the end.

7. *Publish the informational book or report.* Students make a final copy with all the parts of the book or report in the correct sequence. For longer reports, it is much easier to print out the final copy if the sections have been drafted and revised on a computer. To make the book sturdier, teachers often laminate the covers (or all pages in the book) and bind everything together using yarn, brads, or metal rings.

8. *Make copies for students.* Teachers often make copies of the informational book or report for each student, whereas the special bound copy is often placed in the class or school library.

CUBING

Students use cubing to explore a topic from six dimensions or viewpoints (Neeld, 1986). Cubes have six sides, and there are six dimensions in this instructional procedure:

- *Describe the topic.* Students represent the topic in words, including its colors, shapes, and sizes, in order to create a mental image.
- *Compare the topic to something else.* Students consider how it is similar to or different from this other thing.
- *Associate the topic with something else.* Students explain why the topic makes them think of this other thing.
- *Analyze the topic.* Students tell how it is made or what it is composed of.
- *Apply the topic.* Students explain how it can be used or what can be done with it.
- *Argue for or against the topic.* Students take a stand and list reasons to support their argument.

Cubing involves the following steps:

1. *Construct a cube.* Students use cardboard to construct a cube, or they can use a cardboard box, such as a square department store gift box. Next they cut six squares of paper to fit onto the sides of the cube. Later they will write and draw their responses on these square pieces of paper and attach them to the cube.

2. *Divide students into groups.* Students divide into six small groups to do the cubing. Each group examines the topic from one of the six dimensions.

Figure 4 A Seventh Grader's Circle for a Cube About *The Giver*

3. ***Examine the topic from the six dimensions.*** Students in each group consider the topic from the dimension they have been assigned. They brainstorm ideas and decide on a response. Then they write and draw their response on a square sheet of paper that has been cut to fit the cube.

4. ***Complete the cube.*** Students attach their completed responses to each side of the cube and share their work with classmates.

Cubing is a useful procedure for helping students to think more deeply about the main ideas presented in content-area units. Middle-grade students can cube topics such as Antarctica, the U.S. Constitution, endangered animals, the Underground Railroad, and ancient Greece.

A cube can also be made by stapling together six construction paper or tagboard circles to form the three-dimensional shape. Students draw a square inside the circle and draw a picture in it. Then they add words, sentences, or symbols in the rounded sections. Figure 4 shows a circle from a cube that a small group of seventh graders made after reading *The Giver* (Lowry, 1993). The student drew a picture of the Giver talking to Jonas in the center square and wrote four phrases describing the Giver in the outside sections.

Figure 5   A Data Chart for a Report on the Human Body

Human Body Report Data Chart

Organ _____   Researchers _____

_____

Source of information	What does it look like?	Where is it located?	What job does it do?	Other important information

DATA CHARTS

Data charts are grids that students make and use as a tool for organizing information about a topic (McKenzie, 1979). In literature focus units, students use data charts to record information about versions of folktales and fairy tales, such as "Cinderella" stories, or a collection of books by an author, such as Gary Paulsen, Eve Bunting, or Chris Van Allsburg. In content-area units, data charts are used to record information about the solar system, Native American tribes, or ancient civilizations. Students also use data charts to gather and organize information before writing reports. A data chart for a report on the human body is shown in Figure 5. The steps in making a data chart are:

1. *Design the data chart.* Teachers or students choose a topic and decide how to set up the data chart: Characteristics of the topic are listed across the top of the chart, and space is left in the far left column for students to add examples or resources.

2. *Draw the chart.* Teachers or students create a skeleton chart on butcher paper for a class project or on a sheet of unlined paper for an individual project. Then they write the characteristics across the top of the chart and the examples or resources down the left column.

3. *Complete the chart.* Students complete the chart by adding words, pictures, sentences, or paragraphs in each cell.

Students use data charts in a variety of ways. They can make a chart in their reading logs,[C] contribute to a class chart during a content-area unit, make a data chart with a classmate as a project after reading a book, or make a data chart as part of a writing project.

DIRECTED READING-THINKING ACTIVITY

Students are actively involved in reading stories or listening to stories read aloud in the Directed Reading-Thinking Activity (DRTA) because they make predictions and read or listen to confirm their predictions (Stauffer, 1975). DRTA is a useful approach for teaching students how to use the predicting strategy. It helps students think about the structure of stories, and it can be used with both picture book and chapter book stories. However, DRTA should not be used with informational books and content-area textbooks, because with nonfiction texts, students do not predict what the book will be about, but rather read to locate main ideas and details. The steps in DRTA are:

1. ***Introduce the story.*** Before beginning to read, teachers might discuss the topic or show objects and pictures related to the story in order to draw on prior knowledge or create new experiences. They also show students the cover of the book and ask them to make a prediction about the story using one or more of these questions:

- What do you think a story with a title like this might be about?
- What do you think might happen in this story?
- Does this picture give you any ideas about what might happen in this story?

If necessary, the teacher reads the first paragraph or two to provide more information for students to use in making their predictions. After a brief discussion in which all students commit themselves to one or another of the alternatives presented, the teacher asks these questions:

- Which of these ideas do you think would be the likely one?
- Why do you think that idea is a good one?

2. ***Read the beginning of the story.*** Teachers have students read the beginning of the story or listen to the beginning of the story read aloud. Then the teacher asks students to confirm or reject their predictions by responding to questions such as:

- What do you think now?
- What do you think will happen next?
- What do you think would happen if . . . ?
- Why do you think that idea is a good one?

Students continue reading or the teacher continues reading aloud, stopping at several key points to repeat this step.

3. ***Have students reflect on their predictions.*** Students talk about the story, expressing their feelings and making connections to their own lives and experiences with literature. Then students reflect on the predictions they made as they read or listened to the story read aloud, and they provide reasons to support their predictions. Teachers ask these questions to help students think about their predictions:

- What predictions did you make?
- What in the story made you think of that prediction?
- What in the story supports that idea?

The Directed Reading-Thinking Activity is useful only when students are reading or listening to an unfamiliar story so that they can be actively involved in the prediction-confirmation cycle.

DOUBLE-ENTRY JOURNALS

A special type of reading log[C] is a double-entry journal (Barone, 1990; Berthoff, 1981). Students divide their journal pages into two columns. In the left column, students write quotes from the story or informational book they are reading, and in the right column, they reflect on each quote. They may relate a quote to their own lives, react to it, write a question, or make some other comment. Excerpts from a fifth grader's double-entry journal about *The Lion, the Witch and the Wardrobe* (Lewis, 1994) are shown in Figure 6. The steps are:

1. *Design journal pages.* Students divide the pages in their reading logs into two columns, labeling the left column "In the Text" or "Quotes" and the right column "My Responses," "Comments," or "Reflections."

2. *Write quotes in journals.* As students read, or immediately after reading, they copy one or more important or interesting quotes in the left column of the reading logs.

3. *Reflect on the quotes.* Students reread the quotes and make notes in the right column about their reasons for choosing the quote. Sometimes it is easier if students share the quotes with a reading buddy or in a grand conversation[C] before they write comments or reflections in the right column.

Double-entry journals can be used in several other ways, too. For example, instead of recording quotes from the story, students can write "Reading Notes" in the left column

Figure 6

Excerpts From a Fifth Grader's Double-Entry Journal About *The Lion, the Witch and the Wardrobe*

In the Text	My Response
Chapter 1 I tell you this is the sort of house where no one is going to mind what we do.	I remember the time that I went to Beaumont, Texas to stay with my aunt. My aunt's house was very large. She had a piano and she let us play it. She told us that we could do whatever we wanted to.
Chapter 5 "How do you know" he asked, "that your sister's story is not true?"	It reminds me of when I was little and I had an imaginary place. I would go there in my mind. I made up all kinds of make-believe stories about myself in this imaginary place. One time I told my big brother about my imaginary place. He laughed at me and told me I was silly. But it didn't bother me because nobody can stop me from thinking what I want.
Chapter 15 Still they could see the shape of the great lion lying dead in his bonds. They're nibbling at the cords.	When Aslan died I thought about when my Uncle Carl died. This reminds me of the story where the lion lets the mouse go and the mouse helps the lion.

and then add "Reactions" in the right column. In the left column, students can write about the events they read about in the chapter, and in the right column, make personal connections to the events.

EXCLUSION BRAINSTORMING

Exclusion brainstorming is a preparing activity that teachers use to activate students' prior knowledge and expand their understanding about a social studies or science topic before reading (Blachowicz, 1986). Teachers present students with a list of words, and students identify words on the list that they think relate to the topic as well as those that do not belong. As they talk about the words and try to decide which ones are related to the topic, students refine their knowledge of the topic, are introduced to some key vocabulary words, and set a purpose for reading. Then, after reading, students review the list of words again and decide whether they chose the correct words. The steps are:

1. *Choose a list of words.* Teachers choose words related to a book students will read or a content-area unit that students will study and include a few words that do not fit with the topic. Then teachers write the list on chart paper and make individual copies for students.

2. *Mark the list.* Students read the list of words and work in small groups or together as a class to decide which ones are related to the topic and which are not. Then students circle the words they think are not related.

3. *Learn about the topic.* Students read the book or study the unit, noticing whether the words in the exclusion brainstorming activity are mentioned.

4. *Check the list.* After reading or studying the unit, students check their exclusion brainstorming list and make corrections based on their new knowledge. They cross out unrelated words, whether or not they circled them earlier.

Exclusion brainstorming can also be used with literature when teachers want to focus on a historical setting or another social studies or science concept before reading the story. A fourth-grade teacher created the exclusion brainstorming list shown in Figure 7 before reading *The Ballad of Lucy Whipple* (Cushman, 1996), the story of a young girl who travels with her family to California during the gold rush. The teacher used this activity to introduce some of the vocabulary in the story and to help students develop an understanding of life during the California gold rush. Students circled seven words before reading, and after reading they crossed out three words, all different from the ones they had circled earlier.

GRAND CONVERSATIONS

A grand conversation is a book discussion in which students deepen their comprehension and reflect on their feelings during the responding stage of the reading process (Eeds & Wells, 1989; Peterson & Eeds, 1990). These discussions often last 10 to 30 minutes, and students sit in a circle so that they can see each other. The teacher serves as a facilitator, but the talk is primarily among the students. Traditionally, literature discussions have been "gentle inquisitions"; here the talk changes to dialoguing among students. The steps are:

1. *Read the book.* Students prepare for the grand conversation by reading the book or a part of the book, or by listening to the teacher read it aloud.

2. *Prepare for the grand conversation.* Students may respond to the book in a quick-write[C] or in a reading log[C] in order to begin reflecting on the story. This step is optional.

Figure 7   An Exclusion Brainstorming About *The Ballad of Lucy Whipple*

covered wagons	California	~~easy money~~
(lending library)	mud	gold
big dreams	(towns)	banks
miserable	~~houses~~	happiness
~~strike it rich~~	wild fires	clipper ships
(boarding houses)	(get married)	(Massachusetts)
writing letters	(Indians)	stage coaches
prospectors	Mama	(slaves)

3. ***Discuss the book.*** Students come together as a class or in a smaller group to discuss the book. The students take turns sharing their ideas about the events in the story, the literary language and favorite quotes, the author's craft, and the illustrations. To start the grand conversation, the teacher asks students to share their personal responses. Possible openers are "What did you think?" and "Who would like to share?" Students may read from their quickwrites or reading log entries. They all participate and may build on classmates' comments and ask for clarifications. So that everyone gets to participate, many teachers ask students to make no more than two or three comments until everyone has spoken once. Students may refer to the book or read a short piece to make a point, but there is no round-robin reading. Teachers can also participate in the discussion, offering comments and clarifying confusions.

4. ***Ask questions.*** After students have had a chance to share their reflections, teachers ask questions to focus students' attention on one or two aspects of the story that have been missed. Teachers might focus on illustrations, authors, or an element of story structure. Or, they may ask students to compare this book with a similar book, the film version of the story, or other books by the same author. Pauses may occur, and when students indicate that they have run out of things to say, the grand conversation ends. If students are reading a chapter book, teachers may ask students to make predictions before continuing to read the book.

5. ***Write in reading logs.*** Teachers may have students write (or write again) in a reading log. This step is optional, but students often have many ideas for reading log entries after participating in the discussion. Also, students may record their predictions before continuing to read chapter books.

Grand conversations are discussions about stories; discussions about informational books and content-area textbooks are called instructional conversations[C], and their focus is slightly different.

GUIDED READING

Teachers use guided reading to read a book with a small group of students who read at approximately the same reading level. This strategy is recommended for struggling readers who need direct instruction and opportunities for supervised reading. Teachers select a book that students can read at their instructional level, that is, with approximately 90–94% accuracy. Teachers use the reading process and support students' reading and their use of reading strategies during guided reading (Fountas & Pinnell, 2001). Students do the actual reading themselves, and they usually read silently at their own pace through the entire book. Guided reading is not round-robin reading, in which students take turns reading pages aloud to the group.

During guided reading, students read books that they have not read before. Students reading at the first- or second-grade level often read books that can be completed during one lesson, but older students who are reading chapter books take several days or longer to read them.

The steps in using guided reading with middle-grade students are:

1. *Choose an appropriate book for the small group of students.* The students should be able to read the book with 90–94% accuracy. Teachers collect copies of the book for each student in the group.

2. *Introduce the book to the group.* Teachers show the cover, reading the title and the author's name, and activating students' background knowledge on a topic related to the book. They often introduce key vocabulary as they talk about the book, but they don't use vocabulary flash cards to drill the students on new vocabulary. Students make predictions and do a text walk, looking at the illustrations and talking about them (if the book has illustrations).

3. *Have students read the book independently.* Teachers determine how much the students will read and then supervise as students read silently. They assist students with decoding unfamiliar words or using reading strategies as needed. Teachers observe students as they read and periodically take running records[C] to assess students' use of word-identification skills and comprehension strategies. Students who finish reading more quickly than their classmates either reread or do a quickwrite[C] about the book they are reading.

4. *Provide opportunities for students to respond to the book.* Students talk about the book, ask questions, and relate it to others they have read, such as in grand conversations[C]. Teachers ask questions to help students make inferences and think more deeply about the book.

5. *Involve students in exploring activities.* Teachers teach minilessons[C] and provide opportunities for students to look back at the text and study vocabulary words.

Three types of exploring activities are:

- *Strategy and skill instruction:* Teach a reading strategy or word-identification skill.
- *Literary analysis:* Examine an element of story structure or a genre using the book being read as an example.
- *Word work:* Review vocabulary words and teach students to use root words and affixes or context clues to identify unfamiliar words.

6. *Provide opportunities for independent reading.* Teachers provide opportunities for students to read the book they are reading or to read other books at the same level during reading workshop or Sustained Silent Reading[C].

Guided reading is a valuable instructional procedure because students have opportunities to read books at their instructional level and to receive explicit instruction on word-identification skills and comprehension strategies in a small-group setting.

INDIVIDUAL BOOKS AND REPORTS

Students write individual reports and informational books much like they write collaborative books and reports[C]: They design research questions, gather information to answer the questions, and compile what they have learned in a report. However, writing individual reports demands two significant changes: First, students narrow their topics, and second, they assume the entire responsibility for writing the report (Tompkins, 2004). The steps are:

1. *Choose and narrow topics.* Students choose topics for informational books and reports from a content area, hobbies, or other interests. After choosing a general topic, such as cats or the solar system, they need to narrow the topic so that it is manageable. The broad topic of cats might be narrowed to pet cats or tigers, and the solar system to one planet.

2. *Design research questions.* Students design research questions by brainstorming a list of questions in a learning log[C]. They review the list, combine some questions, delete others, and finally arrive at four to six questions that are worthy of answering. Once they begin their research, they may add new questions and delete others if they reach a dead end.

3. *Gather and organize information.* During the prewriting step, students use clusters[C] or data charts[C] to gather and organize information. Data charts, with their rectangular spaces for writing information, serve as a transition for middle-grade students between clusters and note cards.

4. *Write the reports.* Students use the writing process to write their reports. They write a rough draft from the information they have gathered. Each research question can provide the basis for a paragraph, a page, or a chapter in the report. Teachers work with students to revise and edit their books or reports. Students meet in writing groups[C] to share their rough drafts and make revisions based on the feedback they receive from their classmates. After they revise, students use an editing checklist to proofread their reports and identify and correct mechanical errors.

5. *Publish the books.* Students recopy their reports in book form and add covers, a title page, a table of contents, and bibliographic information. Research reports can also be published in several other ways; for example, as a video presentation, a series of illustrated charts or dioramas, or a dramatization.

Students often write informational books and reports as projects during literature focus units, writing workshop, and content-area units. Through these activities, students have opportunities to extend and personalize their learning and to use the writing process.

INSTRUCTIONAL CONVERSATIONS

Instructional conversations are like grand conversations[C] except that they are about nonfiction topics, not about literature. These conversations provide opportunities for students to talk about the main ideas they are learning in content-area units and enhance both students' conceptual learning and their linguistic abilities (Goldenberg, 1992/1993). Like grand conversations, these discussions are interesting and engaging, and students are active participants, building on classmates' ideas with their own comments. Teachers are participants in the conversation, making comments much like the students do, but they also assume the teacher role to clarify misconceptions, ask questions, and provide instruction. Goldenberg has identified these content and linguistic elements of an instructional conversation:

- The conversation focuses on a content-area topic.
- Students activate or build knowledge about the topic during the instructional conversation.
- Teachers provide information and directly teach concepts when necessary.
- Teachers promote students' use of more complex vocabulary and language to express the ideas being discussed.
- Teachers encourage students to provide support for the ideas they present using information found in content-area textbooks, text sets, and other unit-related resources in the classroom.
- Students and teachers ask higher-level questions, often questions with more than one answer, during the instructional conversation.
- Students participate actively in the instructional conversation and make comments that build upon and expand classmates' comments.
- The classroom is a community of learners where both students' and teachers' comments are respected and encouraged.

The steps in an instructional conversation are:

1. **Choose a focus.** Teachers choose a focus for the instructional conversation. It should be related to the goals of a content-area unit or main ideas presented in an informational book or in a content-area textbook.

2. **Prepare for the instructional conversation.** Teachers present background knowledge in preparation for the discussion, or students may read an informational book or selection from a content-area textbook to learn about the topic.

3. **Begin the conversation.** Students come together as a class or in a smaller group for the instructional conversation. Teachers begin with the focus they have identified. They make a statement or ask a question, and then students respond, sharing information they have learned, asking questions, and offering opinions. Teachers assist students as they make comments, helping them extend their ideas and use appropriate vocabulary. In addition, teachers write students' comments in a list or on a cluster[C] or other graphic organizer.

4. **Expand the conversation.** After students have discussed the teacher's focus, the conversation continues and moves in other directions. Students may share other interesting information, make personal connections to information they are learning, or ask questions. Teachers may also want to have students do a read-around[C] and share important ideas from their reading.

5. **Write in learning logs.** Students write and draw diagrams in learning logs[C] and record the important ideas discussed during the instructional conversation. Students may refer to the brainstormed list or cluster that the teacher made during the first part of the discussion.

Instructional conversations are useful for helping students grapple with important ideas they are learning in social studies, science, and other content areas. When students are discussing literature, they should use grand conversations.

In interactive writing, or "sharing the pen," as it is often called, students and the teacher write a sentence, paragraph, or longer text together as the teacher reviews capitalization, punctuation, spelling, and other writing skills. This procedure was developed for young emergent writers, but it is a useful strategy for older, struggling writers (Button, Johnson, & Furgerson, 1996; Tompkins & Collom, 2004). Teachers in the middle grades often work with small groups of students to orally compose a text and guide students as they take turns to share the job of writing it on chart paper. Depending on students' level of writing fluency, knowledge of spelling, capitalization, punctuation, and grammar skills, and handwriting ability, teachers have students write the text word by word, phrase by phrase, or sentence by sentence on chart paper so that everyone in the group can see the text.

Teachers expect students to spell words correctly, use appropriate capitalization and punctuation, phrase sentences in standard English, and use legible handwriting during interactive writing activities. They monitor students' writing and assist them in correcting errors. They cover the error with white correction tape and have students fix it by writing on the tape. If a student makes a mistake while correcting an error, another piece of correction tape is placed on top of the first piece, and the student tries again. When students make errors, teachers take advantage of the teachable moments that errors provide to clarify misunderstandings and briefly review writing skills.

At the same time students are taking turns to write the text on chart paper, they also write individual copies of the text on small white boards or on notebook paper or in journals. Teachers encourage students to check what is being written on the chart paper so that they are spelling words correctly and applying other writing skills appropriately in their individual writing. Through this supervised practice, students practice using writing skills, develop legible handwriting, and become more fluent writers.

Figure 8 presents a paragraph written interactively by a group of 7 eighth graders during a social studies unit on the Underground Railroad. These students were struggling English learners whose families had recently emigrated from Mexico, so their comparison of the Underground Railroad of the 1850s to how some Mexicans enter California illegally isn't too surprising and illustrates the sophisticated thinking that middle-grade students are capable of. The students spent 5 days reviewing what they had learned in the unit and clarifying misconceptions, crafting the paragraph, and writing the sentences. Their teacher helped them combine ideas and craft longer, more complex sentences in the paragraph than these students could speak or write on their own, but by the end of the school year, their oral and written sentences were longer and more sophisticated than was typical of English language learners at that school. The teacher credits interactive writing for the improvement.

Interactive writing can be used for both informal writing such as brainstorming lists of ideas, taking notes, and creating quickwrites[C], and it can also be used to write essays, reports, poems, and other more formal, process-oriented compositions. The steps are:

1. *Collect materials.* The teacher collects chart paper, colored marking pens, white correction tape, a dictionary and a thesaurus, and a pointer. Each student selects one color making pen, and the teacher uses a black pen to write difficult words and make corrections, if needed. Students write their names at the top or bottom of the chart paper with their colored pen so that teachers know which student used a particular color. When each student uses a different color, it is easy for the teacher to monitor the students' writing and the types of errors they are making. Small white boards, dry-erase pens, and erasers or paper and pens are also distributed to students who are participating in the activity.

The Underground Railroad that slaves traveled to freedom on is like the way Mexicans come to California today to find work. Both underground railroads are dangerous trips, and they go from south to north. People travel at night and there are hiding places and safe houses on both underground railroads. Just like the slave owners hunted for the escaped slaves, the INS agents try to catch the illegal aliens. When people are desperate they will travel on secret underground railroads that are not underground and are not railroads at all.

2. *Plan for the activity.* The teacher brings the students together and explains the interactive writing activity. Together the teacher and students brainstorm ideas to activate prior knowledge, and sometimes the teacher generates a list of key words or main ideas or rereads aloud a chapter from a novel or a section from a content-area textbook.

3. *Create a text.* The teacher and students orally create or negotiate a text—often a sentence or paragraph—together. Students repeat the text several times to keep it in mind as they write it. If the text will be longer than one paragraph, they create and write one paragraph and repeat steps 3 and 4 until the composition is completed.

4. *Write the text.* Students and the teacher write the text sentence by sentence. Students repeat the first sentence, and they take turns coming to the chart to write individual words or phrases, or one student may write the entire sentence. How much writing each student does depends on the students' level of writing fluency. As students are taking turns to write on the chart paper, they also make individual copies of the text on white boards or on notebook paper. After each sentence is written, students reread it on chart paper and check their individual copies to make sure they have written it correctly. Then they continue to take turns as they write the remaining sentences or paragraphs in the text.

5. *Make corrections.* The teacher monitors students as they write on chart paper and make individual copies. When a student makes an error, the teacher points out the error, covers it with white correction tape, and helps the student correct it. If students don't recognize the error or understand the correction, the teacher explains the concept or skill involved.

6. *Display the completed text.* After the writing is completed, students reread the entire text, and then it is displayed in the classroom.

Interactive writing is used with older students who aren't yet fluent writers. With teacher guidance and supervision, students learn to apply writing skills, and they also learn writing strategies. They learn how to create sentences and hold them in their minds while they write them. They learn to reread what they have written and make sure that one sentence flows into the next one. They also learn about the structure of paragraphs and how to write a topic sentence. After practicing these strategies during interactive writing, they are more likely to apply them in their independent writing.

K-W-L CHARTS

Teachers use K-W-L charts during content-area units (Ogle, 1986, 1989). The chart has three columns, labeled K, W, and L; the letters stand for What We Know, What We Want to Learn (What We Wonder), and What We Learned. Teachers introduce a K-W-L chart at the beginning of a content-area unit and use the chart to activate students' background knowledge and identify interesting questions. The questions often stimulate students' interest in the topic. At the end of the unit, students complete the last section of the chart, listing what they have learned. This instructional procedure helps students to combine new information with prior knowledge and develop their vocabularies. The steps are:

1. *Post a K-W-L chart.* Teachers post a large sheet of butcher paper on a classroom wall, dividing it into three columns and labeling the columns K (What We Know), W (What We Want to Learn or What We Wonder), and L (What We Learned).

2. *Complete the K column.* At the beginning of the unit, teachers ask students to brainstorm what they know about the topic. Teachers write this information in phrases or complete sentences in the K (What We Know) column. Students also suggest questions they would like to explore during the unit.

3. *Complete the W column.* Teachers write the questions that students suggest in the W (What We Want to Learn or What We Wonder) column. Teachers continue to add questions to the W column throughout the unit.

4. *Complete the L column.* At the end of the unit, students brainstorm a list of information they have learned to complete the L column of the chart. It is important to note that students do not try to answer each question listed in the W column, although the questions in that column may trigger some information that they have learned. Teachers write the information that students suggest in the L column.

Figure 9 shows a K-W-L chart made by a class of sixth graders as they learned about the *Titanic*. The students completed the K column before reading a story about the tragedy in their basal reading textbooks. After reading and discussing the story, they brainstormed questions for the W column and then read from a text set of books that the teacher had collected. Finally, they completed the L column with information they learned. Afterward, the students wrote reports to share their information.

Students can also make individual K-W-L charts to organize, document, and reflect on their learning during a social studies or science unit. Individual charts can be written in learning logs or flip books. To make flip books, students fold several long sheets of paper in half horizontally and make two cuts to create K, W, and L flip pages, as shown in Figure 10. The back page in the booklet is not cut to provide stability for the booklet. Students write the letters on the top flaps and lift each flap to write information and brainstorm questions. After they finish the unit, students can examine the information and questions they wrote and reflect on what they have learned and on their work during the unit.

Figure 9   A K-W-L Chart on the *Titanic*

K What We Know	W What We Wonder	L What We Learned
It sunk. It happened a long time ago. The Titanic sailed from England. The ship was supposed to be unsinkable. It hit an iceberg. There were not enough lifeboats for everyone. A lot of people died. The tragedy happened on its first voyage—its maiden voyage. There was a movie of it.	Why wasn't the crew watching for icebergs? Why did the ship sail so far north where there were icebergs? How many people died? How many people survived? Are any survivors alive today? Why weren't there enough lifeboats? Why didn't the radio operator pay attention to the warning? How long did it take to sink? Why did people think it was unsinkable? How long would it take to die in the ocean? How could the survivors live with the terrible memories? Could this happen today?	The Titanic sank on April 15, 1912. The ship sank 4 hours after hitting the iceberg. Only 868 people survived. Most of the survivors were women and children. A passenger named Molly Brown became the famous "Unsinkable Molly Brown." The Carpathia picked up most of the survivors. Name is from the Greek god Titan. It means "giant." People were treated differently if they were first, second, or third class. If the lifeboats didn't go far enough away from the ship before it sank, they could be sucked under with the ship. Today all ships have enough lifeboats for everyone on it. Tragedy brings out the best and worst of people.

Figure 10 An Individual K-W-L Flip Book

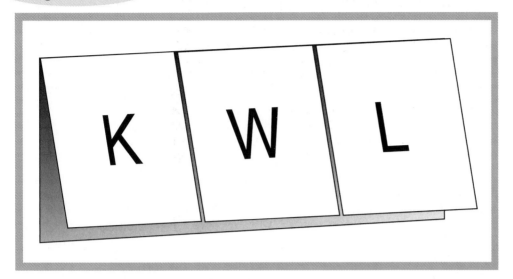

The language experience approach (LEA) is based on children's language and experiences (Ashton-Warner, 1965; Lee & Allen, 1963; Stauffer, 1970). It is designed for young children who are emerging into literacy and for older struggling readers. Even students who have not been successful with other types of reading activities can usually read what they have dictated. In this approach, students dictate words and sentences about their experiences, and the teacher writes the dictation for them. As they write, teachers model how written language works. The text they develop becomes the reading material because it has been written with conventional English spelling, capitalization, and punctuation. Because the language comes from the students themselves and because the content is based on their experiences, they are able to read the familiar text easily. Reading and writing are connected because students are actively involved in reading what they have written. The steps in the language experience approach are:

LANGUAGE EXPERIENCE APPROACH

1. ***Provide an experience.*** The experience serves as the stimulus for the writing. For group writing, it can be an experience shared in school, a book read aloud, a field trip, or some other experience that students are familiar with. For individual writing, the stimulus can be any experience that is important for the particular student.

2. ***Talk about the experience.*** The teacher and students talk about the experience to generate words and review the experience so that the students' dictation will be more interesting and complete. Teachers often begin with an open-ended question, such as "What are we going to write about?" As students talk about their experiences, they clarify and organize ideas, use more specific vocabulary, and extend their understanding.

3. ***Record the student's dictation.*** Texts for pairs or individual students are written on sheets of writing paper or in small booklets, and group texts are written on chart paper. Teachers print neatly and spell words correctly, but they preserve students' language as much as possible. It is a great temptation to change the student's language to the teacher's own, in either word choice or grammar, but editing should be kept to a minimum so that students do not get the impression that their language is inferior or inadequate.

For individual texts, teachers continue to take the student's dictation and write until the student finishes or hesitates. If the student hesitates, the teacher rereads what has been written and encourages the student to continue. For group texts, students take turns dictating sentences, and after writing each sentence, the teacher rereads it.

4. ***Read the text aloud, pointing to each word.*** This reading reminds students of the content of the text and demonstrates how to read it aloud with appropriate intonation. Then students join in the reading. After reading group texts together, individual students can take turns rereading. Group texts can also be copied so each student has a copy to read independently.

5. ***Extend the writing and reading experience.*** Students might draw illustrations to accompany the text, or they can add this text to a collection of their writings to read and reread. Teachers often put a sheet of plastic over class charts so students can circle key words or other familiar words in the text. When they write individual texts, students can also read their texts to classmates from the author's chair. Students can take their own individual texts and copies of the class text home to share with family members.

6. ***Make sentence strips.*** Teachers rewrite the text on sentence strips or on small strips of tagboard that students keep in envelopes. They read and sequence the sentence strips, and after they can read the sentence strips smoothly, students cut the strips into individual words. Students arrange the words into the familiar sentence and then create new sentences with the word cards. Later, the word cards are added to the student's word bank. Word banks can be made from small boxes, or holes can be punched in the word cards and they can be added to a word ring.

Teachers use the language experience approach to create interesting reading materials that English learners can read. The student cuts pictures out of magazines and glues them into a notebook. Then the teacher and the student identify and label several important words in the picture and create a sentence related to it. Next the teacher writes the sentence underneath the picture and the student rereads it. Each day, the teacher and the student create a new page, and soon the student has a book of sentences to practice reading.

LEARNING LOGS

Students write in learning logs as part of content-area units. Learning logs, like other types of journals, are booklets of paper in which students record information they are learning, write questions and reflections about their learning, and make charts, diagrams, and clusters[C] (Tompkins, 2004). The steps are:

1. ***Prepare learning logs.*** Students make learning logs at the beginning of a unit. They typically staple together sheets of lined writing paper and plain paper for drawing diagrams and add construction paper covers.

2. ***Write entries.*** Students make entries in their learning logs as part of content-area unit activities. They take notes, draw diagrams, do quickwrites[C], and make clusters.

3. ***Monitor students' entries.*** Teachers read students' entries, and in their responses they answer students' questions and clarify confusions.

Students' writing is impromptu in learning logs, and the emphasis is on using writing as a learning tool rather than creating polished products. Even so, students should work carefully and spell words found on the word wall[C] correctly.

Making words is an activity in which students arrange letter cards to spell words. As they make words using letter cards, they review and practice phonics and spelling concepts (Cunningham & Cunningham, 1992; Gunning, 1995). Teachers choose key words that exemplify particular phonics or spelling patterns for students to practice from books students are reading or from a content-area unit. Then they prepare a set of letter cards that small groups of students or individual students can use to spell words. The teacher leads students as they create many, progressively longer words using the letters. A making words activity that a sixth-grade class completed while studying ancient Egypt is shown in Figure 11. The steps in making words are:

1. **Make letter cards.** Teachers make a set of small letter cards (1- to 2-inch-square cards) for students to use in word-making activities. For high-frequency letters (vowels, *s, t,* and *r*), teachers make three or four times as many letter cards as there are students in the class. For less frequently used letters, they make one or two times as many letter cards as there are students in the class. They print the lowercase letter form on one side of the letter cards and the uppercase form on the other side. Teachers package cards with each letter separately in small boxes, plastic trays, or plastic bags. They may also want to make a set of large letter cards (3- to 6-inch-square cards) to display in a pocket chart or on the chalkboard during the activity.

2. **Choose a word for the activity.** Teachers choose a word to use in the word-making activity, but they do not tell students what the word is. The word is often taken from a word wall[C] in the classroom and relates to a book students are reading or to a content-area unit. The word should be long enough and have enough vowels that students can easily make at least 10 words using the letters.

Figure 11   **A Sixth-Grade Making Words Activity Using the Word *Hieroglyphics***

2	3	4	5	6	7
go	her	hope	cries	prices	crisply
he	she	high	horse	highly	spicier
or	yes	hero	chose	chores	hospice
so	ice	rose	girls	psycho	
is	pig	rice	chili	higher	
hi	hop	chip	Chile	crispy	
	cry	iris	crisp		
	shy	pigs	shore		
	lie	girl	spice		
	pie	core	spire		
	ore	rosy	choir		
		goes	price		
		pier			

3. *Distribute letter cards.* A student distributes the needed letter cards to individual students or to small groups of students, and students arrange the letter cards on one side of their desks. It is crucial that students have letter cards to manipulate; it is not sufficient to write the letters on the chalkboard, because students can spell more words using the cards and because some students need the tactile activity to be able to spell the words.

4. *Make words using the cards.* Students manipulate the letter cards to spell two-letter words. As students spell words, teachers make a chart and record the words that students spell correctly using the letter cards on the chart. Teachers can also use the large letter cards to spell words along with the students or to help students correctly spell a tricky word. After spelling all possible two-letter words, students spell three-letter words, four-letter words, and so forth, until they use all of the letter cards and figure out the chosen word.

5. *Repeat the activity at a center.* After completing the word-making activity, teachers put the chart the class created and several sets of letter cards in a literacy center so that students can repeat the activity. As students make words, they write them on a chart. First they list two-letter words, then three-letter words, and so forth. Students can refer to the chart, if needed.

Students can also use letter cards to practice spelling rimes. For example, to practice the *-ake* rime, students use the *b, c, f, h, l, m, r, s, t,* and *w* letter cards and the *-ake* rime card. Using the cards, students make these words: *bake, shake, cake, make, flake, rake, lake, take,* and *wake.* Teachers often add several other letter cards, such as *d, p,* and *v,* to make the activity more challenging.

MINILESSONS

Teachers teach minilessons on literacy procedures, concepts, strategies, and skills (Atwell, 1987). These lessons are brief, often lasting only 15 to 30 minutes. Minilessons are usually taught as part of the reading process during the exploring stage, or as part of the writing process during the editing stage. The steps in conducting a minilesson are:

1. *Introduce the topic.* Teachers begin the minilesson by introducing the procedure, concept, strategy, or skill. They name the topic and provide essential information about it.

2. *Share examples of the topic.* Teachers share examples taken from books students are reading or students' own writing projects.

3. *Provide information about the topic.* Teachers provide additional information about the procedure, concept, strategy, or skill and make connections to students' reading or writing.

4. *Provide opportunities for guided practice.* Teachers involve students in guided practice activities so that students can bring together the information and the examples introduced earlier.

5. *Assess students' learning.* Teachers check that students understand the procedure, concept, strategy, or skill well enough to apply it independently. They often monitor students during guided practice or review students' work, but sometimes teachers administer a quiz or other more formal assessment.

Teachers present minilessons to the whole class or to small groups to introduce or review a topic. The best time to teach a minilesson is when students will have immediate opportunities to apply what they are learning. Afterward, it is crucial that teachers provide additional opportunities for students to use the procedures, concepts, strategies, or skills they are learning in meaningful ways and in authentic literacy activities.

To help students think more deeply about a character and reflect on story events from the character's viewpoint, students draw an open-mind portrait of the character. These portraits have two parts: The face of the character is on one page, and the mind of the character is on the second page. A fourth grader's open-mind portrait of Sarah, the mail-order bride in *Sarah, Plain and Tall* (MacLachlan, 1983), is shown in Figure 12. The steps are:

1. ***Make a portrait of a character.*** Students draw and color a large portrait of the head and neck of a character in a book they are reading.

2. ***Cut out the portrait and open-mind pages.*** Students cut out the character's portrait and trace around the character's head on one or more sheets of paper. Students may make open-mind portraits with one "mind" page or with several pages in order to show what the character is thinking at important points in the story or in each chapter of a chapter book. Then they cut out the mind pages and attach the portrait and mind pages with a brad or staple to a sheet of heavy construction paper or cardboard. The portrait goes on top. It is important that students place the brad or staple at the top of the portrait so that there will be space to write and draw on the mind pages.

Figure 12   **An Open-Mind Portrait of Sarah of *Sarah, Plain and Tall***

3. *Design the mind pages.* Students lift the portrait and draw and write about the character, from the character's viewpoint, on the mind pages. They focus on what the character is thinking and doing at various points in the story.

4. *Share completed open-mind portraits.* Students share their portraits with classmates and talk about the words and pictures they chose to include in the mind of the character.

POSSIBLE SENTENCES

Teachers use the possible sentences activity to introduce vocabulary before students read a content-area textbook chapter or other informational article or book (Moore & Moore, 1992; Stahl & Kapinus, 1991). Students create sentences incorporating key vocabulary words before reading the selection, and then they read to see if they used the words correctly. This activity gives students a clearly defined purpose for reading and encourages them to use context clues to determine the meaning of words. The steps are:

1. *Identify key vocabulary words.* Students and the teacher identify key vocabulary words as they do a text walk through a content-area textbook chapter or other text. The teacher lists the words on the chalkboard or an overhead projector as they are identified.

2. *Create sentences using the words.* Students, working in pairs or individually, create sentences using at least two words from the list. The sentences should be related to the content of the selection. The teacher writes the sentences on the chalkboard or on an overhead, even if the words are used incorrectly, and underlines the key words.

3. *Read the selection.* Students read the selection to check the accuracy of their possible sentences. Teachers encourage students to use context clues in the text to determine the meaning of the words or check the meaning of the words in the textbook's glossary or a dictionary, if necessary.

4. *Evaluate the sentences.* Teachers reread each of the possible sentences with students and decide whether the words are used correctly based on the information provided in the text students have read. Then students decide how to revise the sentences that are inaccurate and make the revisions on the chalkboard or on the overhead projector.

Researchers have reported that possible sentences is an effective strategy for teaching vocabulary words (Stahl & Kapinus, 1991). This activity is worthwhile because the words students are learning are related and because students are making connections between background knowledge and information they are learning.

PREREADING PLAN

The prereading plan is a diagnostic and instructional procedure used when students are reading informational books and content-area textbooks (Tierney, Readence, & Dishner, 1995). Teachers use this strategy to diagnose students' prior knowledge and provide necessary background knowledge so that students will be prepared to understand what they will be reading. The steps are:

1. *Discuss a key concept.* Teachers introduce a key concept to students using a word, phrase, or picture to initiate a discussion. Then students brainstorm words about the topic and record their ideas on a chart. Teachers help students make con-

nections among the brainstormed ideas. Teachers present additional vocabulary and clarify any misconceptions.

2. *Quickwrite about the topic.* Students write a quickwrite[C] about the topic using words from the brainstormed list.

3. *Share the quickwrites.* Students share their quickwrites with classmates, and teachers ask questions to help students clarify and elaborate their quickwrites.

This activity is especially important when students have little technical vocabulary or background knowledge about a topic, and for students who are learning English as a second language.

QUICKWRITES

Students use quickwriting as they write in response to literature and for other types of impromptu writing. Quickwriting, originally called "freewriting" and popularized by Peter Elbow (1973), is a way to help students focus on content rather than mechanics. Students reflect on what they know about a topic, ramble on paper, generate words and ideas, and make connections among the ideas. Young children often do quickwrites in which they draw pictures and add labels. Some students do a mixture of writing and drawing. Figure 13 presents a fifth grader's quickwrites written while reading *The Breadwinner* (Ellis, 2000), the story of girl who pretended to be a boy to earn money to buy food for her family when the Taliban ruled Afghanistan. For each quickwrite, the teacher provided several words, such as *Taliban, breadwinner, Parvana,* and *burqa,* and students selected one word as the topic of their quickwrite. She also asked the students to include information from the story and make connections to their own lives. The steps are:

1. *Choose a topic.* Students identify a topic for their quickwrite and write it at the top of the paper.

2. *Write or draw about the topic.* Students write sentences or paragraphs and/or draw a picture related to the topic. Students should focus on interesting ideas, make connections between the topic and their own lives, and reflect on their reading or learning.

3. *Share quickwrites.* After students write, they usually share their quickwrites in small groups or during grand conversations[C], and then one student in each group shares with the class.

Students do quickwrites for a variety of purposes in several of the stages of the reading process, including:

- to activate background knowledge before reading
- as an entry for reading logs[C]
- to define or explain a word on the word wall[C]
- to analyze the theme of a story
- to describe a favorite character
- to compare book and film versions of a story
- to discuss a favorite book during an author study
- to discuss the project the student is creating

Students also do similar quickwrites during content-area units.

Figure *13* A Fifth Grader's Quickwrites About *The Breadwinner*

Parvana

I feel sorry for Parvana and no, I would not want to be her. I would hate to carry water all the time and have to stay inside with my Mom. I think I would like to go to work with my Dad but I would be very sad if a bomb blew his leg off and that happened to Parvana's Dad. If I lived over there in Afghanistan my life would be very bad. I would be very scared. I would be afraid my family would die and I would be all alone. There would be no one to take care of me. I think this book is about war and the theme is that war is bad. I'm not sure but that's what I think now.

A Breadwinner

A breadwinner is the person in your family who goes to work every day to make money to take care of your family. I have two breadwinners in my family. My Mom is a teacher and my Dad is a plumber. They both make money. They pay for our house and buy food and clothes and lots of other stuff. I would not want to be the breadwinner because I'm a kid and I would be scared. I don't think I could make enough money to pay for everything. I feel sorry for Parvana because she has to be the breadwinner because the soldiers came and took her Dad to prison.

Burqas

The Taliban made the women wear these ugly clothes called burqas if they went outside. There was just a little opening for their eyes and nothing else at all. I don't know why the Taliban did it. I guess they just hate women. I would try to stay close to my Mom so I wouldn't get lost because in the book it said that it was hard for kids to find their Moms because they all looked alike in the burqas. Women could never go outside without their burqas and if they did terrible things happened to them. That is very mean and I am glad it could not happen in the U.S.A.

QUILTS

Students make squares out of construction paper and arrange them to make a quilt to respond to a book they have read or to present information they have learned in a content-area unit. Quilts about stories are designed to highlight the theme, reinforce symbolism, and recall favorite sentences in a book students have read. A square from an eighth-grade class quilt about *The Giver* (Lowry, 1993) is shown in Figure 14. Students drew a picture of a pivotal moment in the story in the center square and then

Figure 14   An Eighth Grader's Square for a Quilt
About *The Giver*

wrote four key words and explained them in the outside sections. The steps in making a quilt are:

1. ***Design the quilt square.*** Teachers and students choose a design for the quilt square that is appropriate for the story—its theme, characters, or setting—or that reflects the topic of the content-area unit. Students can choose a quilt design or create their own design that captures an important dimension of the story or unit. They also choose colors for each shape in the quilt square.

2. ***Make the squares.*** Students each make a square and add an important piece of information from the unit or a favorite sentence from the story around the outside of the quilt square or in a designated section of the square.

3. ***Assemble the quilt.*** Teachers tape the squares together and back the quilt with butcher paper, or staple the squares side by side on a large bulletin board.

Quilts can be made of cloth, too. As an end-of-the-year project or to celebrate Book Week, teachers cut out squares of light-colored cloth and have students use fabric markers to draw pictures of their favorite stories and add the titles and authors. Then teachers or other adults sew the squares together, add a border, and complete the quilt.

READ-AROUNDS

Read-arounds are celebrations of stories and other books, usually performed at the end of literature focus units or literature circles. Students choose favorite passages from a book to read aloud. Read-arounds are sometimes called "Quaker readings" because of their "unprogrammed" format. The steps are:

1. *Choose a favorite passage.* Students skim a book they have already read to locate one or more favorite passages (a sentence or paragraph) and mark the passages with bookmarks.

2. *Practice reading the passage.* Students rehearse reading the passages so that they can read them fluently.

3. *Read the passages.* Teachers begin the read-around by asking a student to read a favorite passage aloud to the class. Then there is a pause and another student begins to read. Teachers don't call on students; any student may begin reading when no one else is reading. The passages can be read in any order, and more than one student can read the same passage. Teachers, too, read their favorite passages. The read-around continues until everyone who wants to has read.

Students like participating in read-arounds because the featured book is like a good friend. They enjoy listening to classmates read favorite passages and noticing literary language. They seem to move back and forth through the story, remembering events and reliving the story.

READERS THEATRE

Readers theatre is a dramatic production of a script by a group of readers (Martinez, Roser, & Strecker, 1998/1999). Each student assumes a role and reads the character's lines in the script. Readers interpret a story without using much action. They may stand or sit, but they must carry the whole communication of the plot, characterization, mood, and theme by using their voices, gestures, and facial expressions. Readers theatre avoids many of the restrictions inherent in theatrical productions: Students do not memorize their parts; elaborate props, costumes, and backdrops are not needed; and long, tedious hours are not spent rehearsing. For readers theatre presentations, students can read scripts in trade books and textbooks, or they can create their own scripts. The steps are:

1. *Select a script.* Students and the teacher select a script and then read and discuss it as they would any story.

2. *Choose parts.* Students volunteer to read each part and mark their lines on the script. They also decide how to use their voice, gestures, and facial expressions to interpret the character they are reading.

3. *Rehearse the production.* They read the script several times, striving for accurate pronunciation, voice projection, and appropriate inflections. Less rehearsal is needed for an informal, in-class presentation than for a more formal production; nevertheless, interpretations should always be developed as fully as possible.

4. *Stage the production.* Readers theatre can be presented on a stage or in a corner of the classroom. Students stand or sit in a row and read their lines in the script. They stay in position through the production or enter and leave according to the characters' appearances "onstage." If readers are sitting, they may stand to read their lines; if they are standing, they may step forward to read. The emphasis is not on production quality; rather, it is on the interpretive quality of the readers' voices and expressions. Costumes and props are unnecessary; however, adding a few small props enhances interest and enjoyment as long as they do not interfere with the interpretive quality of the reading.

Students keep reading logs to write their reactions and opinions about books they are reading or listening to the teacher read aloud. Students also add lists of words from the word wall[C], diagrams about story elements, and information about authors and genres (Tompkins, 2004). For a chapter book, students write after reading every chapter or two. The steps are:

1. *Prepare the reading logs.* Students make reading logs by stapling paper into booklets. They write the title of the book on the cover and add an appropriate illustration.

2. *Write entries.* Students write their reactions and reflections about the book or chapter they have read or listened to the teacher read aloud. Instead of summarizing the book, students relate the book to their own lives or to other literature they have read. Students may also list interesting or unfamiliar words, jot down quotable quotes, and take notes about characters, plot, or other story elements. The primary purpose of reading logs, though, is for students to think about the book, deepen their understanding of it, and connect literature to their lives.

3. *Read and respond to the entries.* Teachers read students' entries and write comments back to students about their interpretations and reflections. Some teachers read and respond to all entries, and other teachers, because of time limitations, read and respond selectively. Because students' writing in reading logs is informal, teachers do not expect them to spell every word correctly, but it is not unreasonable to expect students to spell characters' names and other words on the word wall correctly.

Teachers often encourage students to reread the featured book several times during literature focus units and to reread favorite books during reading workshop. Students become more fluent readers when they reread books, and each time they reread a book, their comprehension deepens. Jay Samuels (1979) has developed an instructional procedure to help students increase their reading fluency and accuracy through rereading. The steps in the individualized procedure are:

1. *Conduct a pretest.* The student chooses a textbook or trade book and reads a passage from it aloud while the teacher records the reading time and any miscues.

2. *Practice rereading the passage.* The student practices rereading the passage orally or silently several times.

3. *Conduct a posttest.* The student rereads the passage while the teacher again records the reading time and notes any miscues.

4. *Compare pre- and posttest results.* The student compares his or her reading time and accuracy between the first and last readings. Then the student prepares a graph to document his or her growth between the first and last readings.

This procedure is useful for students who are slow and inaccurate readers. When teachers monitor students' readings on a regular basis, students will become more careful readers. Making a graph to document growth is an important component of the procedure, because the graph provides concrete evidence of the student's growth.

Teachers observe individual students as they read aloud and take running records of students' reading to assess their reading fluency (Clay, 1985). Through a running record, teachers calculate the percentage of words the student reads correctly and then analyze the miscues or errors. Running records are easy to take, although teachers need some practice before they are comfortable with the procedure. Teachers make a check mark on a sheet of paper as the student reads each word correctly. They use other marks to indicate words that the student doesn't know or reads incorrectly. The steps in conducting a reading record are:

1. *Choose a book.* Teachers have the student choose an excerpt 100 to 200 words in length from a book he or she is reading. For beginning readers, the text may be shorter.

2. *Take the running record.* As the student reads the excerpt aloud, the teacher makes a record of the words read correctly as well as those read incorrectly. The teacher makes check marks on a sheet of blank paper for each word read correctly. Errors are marked in these ways:

- If the student reads a word incorrectly, the teacher writes the incorrect word and the correct word under it:

    gentle
    ⎯⎯⎯⎯⎯
    generally

- If the student self-corrects an error, the teacher writes *SC* (for self-correction) following the incorrect word:

    bath SC
    ⎯⎯⎯⎯⎯
    bathe

- If the student attempts to pronounce a word, the teacher records each attempt and adds the correct text underneath:

    com- com- company
    ⎯⎯⎯⎯⎯⎯⎯⎯⎯⎯
    companion

- If the student skips a word, the teacher marks the error with a dash:

    ⎯
    ⎯⎯⎯⎯
    own

- If the student says words that are not in the text, the teacher writes an insertion symbol (caret) and records the inserted words:

    where he
    ⎯⎯⎯⎯⎯
    ∧

- If the student can't identify a word and the teacher pronounces the word for the student, the teacher writes *T:*

    T
    ⎯⎯⎯⎯
    routine

- If the student repeats a word or phrase, the repetition is not scored as an error, but the teacher notes the repetition by drawing a line under the word or phrase (marked in the running record with check marks) that was repeated:

    ✓✓✓
    ⎯⎯⎯⎯⎯

A sample running record is shown in Figure 3-4.

3. *Calculate the percentage of miscues.* Teachers calculate the percentage of miscues or oral reading errors. When the student makes 5% or fewer errors, the book is

considered to be at the independent level for that student. When there are 6–10% errors, the book is at the instructional level, and when there are more than 10% errors, the book is too difficult—the frustration level.

4. *Analyze the miscues.* Teachers look for patterns in the miscues in order to determine how the student is growing as a reader and to determine what skills and strategies the student should be taught. A miscue analysis of a running record is shown in Figure 3-5.

Many teachers conduct running records with all their students at the beginning of the school year and at the end of grading periods. In addition, teachers do running records more often during guided reading groups and with students who are not making expected progress in reading in order to track their growth as readers and make instructional decisions.

SAY SOMETHING

When students are reading with a buddy, they can use the say something strategy to stop and talk about their reading. By sharing their responses, they will improve their comprehension (Harste, Woodward, & Burke, 1984). Students of all ages enjoy reading with a buddy and using the say something strategy to clarify misconceptions, make predictions, and share reactions. The steps are:

1. *Divide students into pairs for reading.* Teachers divide students into pairs for buddy reading. Students can read stories, informational books, basal reader selections, or content-area textbooks.

2. *Read one page.* Students read a page of text before stopping to talk. They can read silently or mumble-read, or one student can read to the other. The type of reading depends on the level of the book and the students participating in the activity.

3. *Briefly talk about the page.* After they finish reading the page, students stop to talk. They each make a comment or ask a question before continuing to read. Sometimes the discussion continues longer because of a special interest or a question, but after a brief discussion, students read the next page and then stop to talk again. For content-area textbooks, students often stop after reading a single paragraph to talk about their reading because the text is often densely written and clarification is needed.

Teachers often use a book they are reading aloud to the class to model the procedure. After they read a page, they make a comment to the class and one student is chosen to make a response. With this practice, students are better able to use the say something strategy independently.

SEMANTIC FEATURE ANALYSIS

Teachers use semantic feature analysis (SFA) to help students examine the characteristics of vocabulary words or content-area concepts (Pittelman, Heimlich, Berglund, & French, 1991). In SFA, teachers create a grid for the analysis with words or concepts listed on one axis and the characteristics or components listed on the other axis. Students reading a novel, for example, can do a semantic feature analysis with vocabulary words listed on one axis and the characters' names on the other. As students complete the SFA, they decide which words relate to which characters and use pluses and minuses to mark the relationships on the grid. Or, in a social studies unit, students can do a semantic feature analysis to review what they are learning about America as a culturally pluralistic society; the groups of people who immigrated to the United States are listed on one axis, and historical features on the other axis. Then students complete the SFA by marking each cell on the grid. A fifth-grade class's semantic feature analysis on

Figure 15 Fifth Graders' Semantic Feature Analysis on Immigration

	Arrived in the 1600s	Arrived in the 1700s	Arrived in the 1800s	Arrived in the 1900s	Came to to Ellis Island	Came for religious freedom	Came for safety	Came for opportunity	Were refugees	Experienced prejudice
English	+	+	−	−	−	+	−	+	−	−
Africans	+	+	+	−	−	−	−	−	−	+
Irish	−	−	+	−	−	−	+	+	+	+
Other Europeans	−	+	+	+	+	−	+	+	+	+
Jews	−	−	+	+	+	+	+	−	+	+
Chinese	−	−	+	−	−	−	−	−	−	+
Latinos	−	−	−	+	−	−	−	+	−	+
Southeast Asians	−	−	−	+	−	−	+	+	+	+

Code: + = yes
− = no
? = don't know

immigration is shown in Figure 15. After completing this grid, the students examined the grid for patterns and identified three important ideas:

1. Different peoples immigrated to America at different times.
2. The Africans who came as slaves were the only people who were brought to America against their will.
3. The English were the only immigrants who didn't suffer prejudice.

The steps in doing a semantic feature analysis are:

1. *Create a grid.* Teachers create a grid with vocabulary or concepts listed on the vertical axis and characteristics or categories on the horizontal axis.

2. *Complete the grid.* Students complete the grid cell by cell. They consider the relationship between the item in the vertical axis and the items in the horizontal axis. Then they mark the cell with a plus to indicate a relationship, a minus to indicate no relationship, and a question mark when they are unsure.

3. *Reflect on the grid.* Students and the teacher examine the grid for patterns and make insights or draw conclusions based on the patterns.

Teachers often do SFA with the whole class, but students can work in small groups or individually to complete the grid. The reflection should be done as a whole-class activity, however, so that students can share their insights.

This activity helps students to organize information and vocabulary they are learning into concepts and to develop networks of relationships among concepts (Stahl, 1999). Teachers sometimes find it difficult to develop the grid for an SFA activity, but it's worth the effort because this activity helps students to think more deeply about what they are learning. The insights students gain after completing the grid make the effort worthwhile.

SHARED READING

Teachers use shared reading to read books with students who could not read those books independently (Holdaway, 1979). Shared reading was developed to read big books with young emergent readers, but it can also be used with older students. It is a step between reading aloud to students and independent reading (Parkes, 2000). Students each have a copy of the text—a novel, content-area textbook, or other selection—and the teacher or another fluent reader reads aloud while students listen and follow along in the book. The steps in shared reading with middle-grade students are:

1. *Introduce the text.* Teachers talk about the book or other text by activating or building background knowledge on topics related to the book and by reading the title and the author's name aloud.

2. *Read the text aloud.* Teachers read the book aloud while students follow along in their own copies of the book. Sometimes teachers and students who are fluent readers take turns doing the reading, but shared reading is not the same as round robin reading, where each student takes a turn doing the reading, whether they are fluent readers or not.

3. *Have a grand conversation*[C]. Teachers invite students to talk about the text, ask questions, and share their responses.

4. *Continue the process.* When teachers are reading novels and other long texts, they repeat steps 2 and 3 as they read the entire book.

Shared reading is a useful strategy for reading featured books in literature focus units with struggling readers, English language learners, and other students who cannot read the book independently. If the text is more than 2 years above the students' reading level, however, it may be more productive to do a read-aloud instead because students can become very frustrated trying to follow along in a book that is much too difficult for them. Reading aloud is similar to shared reading, except that students do not have copies of the book being read.

SQ3R STUDY STRATEGY

In the SQ3R study strategy (Anderson & Armbruster, 1984), students use five steps—survey, question, read, recite, and review—to read and remember information in content-area reading assignments. This strategy is very effective when students know how to apply it correctly. The five steps are:

1. *Survey.* Students preview the reading assignment, noting headings and skimming (rapidly reading) the introduction and summary. They note the main ideas that are presented. This step helps students activate prior knowledge and organize what they will read.

2. *Question.* Students turn each heading into a question before reading the section. Reading to find the answer to the question gives students a purpose for reading.

3. *Read.* Students read the section to find the answer to the question they have formulated. They read each section separately.

4. *Recite.* Immediately after reading each section, students recite from memory the answer to the question they formulated and other important information they have read. Students can answer the questions orally or in writing.

5. *Review.* After finishing the entire reading assignment, students take a few minutes to review what they have read. They ask themselves the questions they developed from each heading and try to recall the answers they learned by reading. If students took notes or wrote answers to the questions in the fourth step, they should try to review without referring to the written notes.

STORY BOARDS

Story boards are cards to which the illustrations and text (or only the illustrations) from a picture book have been attached. Teachers make story boards by cutting apart two copies of a picture book. Students use story boards to sequence the events of a story, to examine a picture book's illustrations, and for other exploring activities. The steps in making story boards are:

1. *Collect two copies of a book.* It is preferable to use paperback copies of the books because they are less expensive to purchase. In a few picture books, all the illustrations are on either the right-hand or left-hand pages, so only one copy of these books is needed for illustration-only story boards. In Chris Van Allsburg's *The Mysteries of Harris Burdick* (1984), for example, all illustrations are on the right-hand pages.

2. *Cut the books apart.* Teachers remove the covers and separate the pages. Next, they trim the edges of the cut-apart sides.

3. *Attach the pages to pieces of cardboard.* Teachers glue each page or double-page spread to a piece of cardboard, making sure that each page in the story will be included.

4. *Laminate the cards.* Teachers laminate the cards so that they can withstand use by students.

5. *Use the cards in sequencing activities.* Teachers pass out the cards in random order to students. Students read their pages, think about the sequence of events in the story, and arrange themselves in a line around the classroom to sequence the story events.

Story boards can also be used when there are only a few copies of a picture book so that students can identify words for the word wall[C], notice literary language, and examine the illustrations.

For novels, students can create their own story boards, one for each chapter. Students can divide into small groups, and each group works on a different chapter. Students make a poster with a picture illustrating the chapter and a paragraph-length summary of the chapter. A group of eighth graders created the story board presented in Figure 16. It summarizes chapter 2 of *Dragonwings* (Yep, 1975), the story of Moon Shadow, a young boy who comes from China to San Francisco in 1903 to join the father he has never met.

STORY MAPS

Teachers and students make a variety of diagrams and charts to examine the structure of stories they are reading (Bromley, 1991; Claggett, 1992; Macon et al., 1991). Six types of story maps are:

- Beginning-middle-end diagrams to examine the plot of a story
- Character clusters[C] to examine the traits of a main character (Macon et al., 1991)

Figure 16 — An Eighth-Grade Story Board From Dragonwings

> **Chapter 2**
> "The Company"

Moon Shadow meets his Uncle Bright Star. He had worked in the California Gold Rush and building the railroad. Then Windrider, Moon Shadow's dad, shows Moon Shadow around, to make him feel safe at home. They go past the Barbary Coast where the white demons live to his new home in Chinatown, the town of the Tang People. It looks like his old home in China. Moon Shadow's dad gave him a kite to fly. It was like a blue and green butterfly. Moon Shadow loved his new kite. Moon Shadow hasn't flown his kite yet, but I bet that he can't wait! They all go into a big house called the Company of the Peach Order Vow and then Uncle Bright Star's son named Black Dog comes. He is in a gang and he takes drugs. He tells everyone that the demons hate them and want to kill them. Then they heard the sound of a window shattering. So they went downstairs and they saw that a window was broken and the white demons were yelling and shouting at them. Moon Shadow is scared but Windrider protects him.

- Venn diagrams to compare book and film versions of a story or for other comparisons
- Plot profiles to chart the tension in each chapter of a chapter book (Johnson & Louis, 1987)
- Sociograms to explore the interpersonal relationships among characters (Johnson & Louis, 1987)
- Clusters to probe the theme, setting, genre, author's style, or other dimensions of the story

"Skeleton" diagrams for these six types of story maps are presented in Figure 17. Students use information from the story they are reading and add words, sentences, and illustrations to complete the story maps.

The steps in using story maps are:

1. *Choose a story map.* Teachers choose the type of story map that is appropriate for the story and the purpose of the lesson.

2. *Draw the diagram.* Teachers make a "skeleton" diagram on the chalkboard or on a chart.

3. *Complete the diagram.* Teachers work with students to complete the diagram. Students usually work together as a class the first time they do a story map. The next few

Figure 17   Six Types of Story Maps

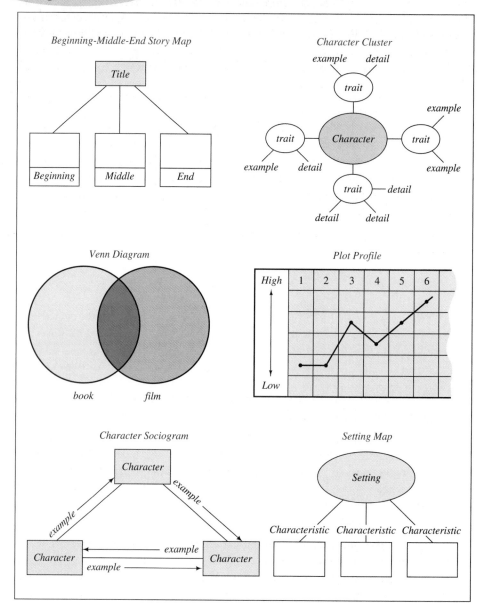

Beginning-Middle-End Story Map

Title

Beginning | Middle | End

Character Cluster

example   detail
trait
trait   Character   trait
example   detail
example
example
trait — detail
detail   detail

Venn Diagram

book   film

Plot Profile

High   1 2 3 4 5 6
Low

Character Sociogram

Character
example
example
example
Character   example   Character
example

Setting Map

Setting

Characteristic   Characteristic   Characteristic

times they do the story map, they work in small groups. After this experience, students make maps individually. For most story maps, students use a combination of words and pictures.

Students often make story maps as an exploring activity, but they can also choose to make a story map as a project. There are many other types of story maps students can make, and teachers can invent their own maps to help students visualize other structures and relationships in stories.

Sustained silent reading (SSR) is an independent reading time set aside during the school day for students in one class or the entire school to silently read self-selected books. In some schools, everyone—students, teachers, principals, secretaries, and custodians—stops to read, usually for a 15- to 30-minute period. SSR is a popular reading activity in schools that is known by a variety of names, including "drop everything and read" (DEAR), "sustained quiet reading time" (SQUIRT), and "our time to enjoy reading" (OTTER).

Teachers use SSR to increase the amount of reading students do every day and to develop their ability to read silently and without interruption (Hunt, 1967; McCracken & McCracken, 1978). Through numerous studies, SSR has been found to be beneficial in developing students' reading ability (Krashen, 1993; Pilgreen, 2000). In addition, it promotes a positive attitude toward reading and encourages students to develop the habit of daily reading. Because students choose the books they will read, they have the opportunity to develop their own tastes and preferences as readers. SSR is based on these guidelines:

1. Students choose the books they read.
2. Students read silently.
3. The teacher serves as a model by reading during SSR.
4. Students choose one book or other reading material for the entire reading time.
5. The teacher sets a timer for a predetermined, uninterrupted time period, usually from 15 to 30 minutes.
6. All students in the class or school participate.
7. Students do not write book reports or participate in other after-reading activities.
8. The teacher does not keep records or evaluate students on their performance. (Pilgreen, 2000)

To have a successful SSR program, students need to have access to lots of books in a classroom library or the school library and know how to use the Goldilocks Strategy (see p. 392) to choose books at their reading level. If students don't have books that interest them written at their reading level, they won't be able to read independently for extended periods of time.

The steps in sustained silent reading are:

1. *Set aside a time for SSR.* Teachers allow time every day for uninterrupted, independent reading. It may last for only 10 minutes in a first-grade classroom or 20 to 30 minutes or more in the upper grades. Teachers often begin with a 10-minute period and then extend the SSR period as students build endurance and ask for more time.

2. *Ensure that students have books to read.* For capable readers, SSR is a time for independent reading. Students keep a book at their desks to read during SSR and use a bookmark to mark their place in the book. Beginning readers may read new books or choose three or four leveled readers that they have already read to reread during SSR. For children who cannot read on their own, partner reading may be substituted for independent reading.

3. *Set a timer for a predetermined time.* Teachers keep a kitchen timer in the classroom, and after everyone gets out a book to read, set the timer for the SSR reading period. To ensure that students are not disturbed during SSR, some teachers place a "do not disturb" sign on the door.

4. *Read along with students.* Teachers read a book, magazine, or newspaper for pleasure while students read. This way, teachers model what capable readers do and that reading is a pleasurable activity.

Even though SSR was specifically developed without follow-up activities, many teachers use a few carefully selected and brief follow-up activities to sustain students' interest in reading books (Pilgreen, 2000). Students often discuss their reading with a partner, or volunteers give book talks[C] to tell the whole class about their books. As students listen to one another, they get ideas about books that they might like to read in the future. Sometimes students develop a ritual of passing on the books they have finished reading to interested classmates.

TEA PARTY

Students and the teacher participate in a tea party to read or reread excerpts from a story, informational book, or content-area textbook. Sometimes teachers have students reread favorite excerpts to celebrate a book they have finished reading, or they use tea party to introduce a new chapter in a content-area textbook. Teachers make several copies of selected excerpts, back them with tagboard, and laminate them. Then students move around the classroom, reading their cards to each other and talking about the excerpt they have read.

Tea party is similar to read-arounds[C] in that students read excerpts from books and other reading materials. However, these two literacy strategies often serve different instructional purposes: Teachers usually select the excerpts that students read for tea party to introduce or review important concepts, summarize the events in a story, or focus on an element of story structure, whereas for read-arounds, students choose the excerpts that are particularly meaningful to them. Also, students are more active, moving around the classroom and socializing with individual classmates during tea party, whereas students remain seated and share with the whole class during read-arounds.

The steps in tea party are:

1. *Make the cards.* Teachers make cards with excerpts from a story, informational book, or content-area textbook that students are reading. They laminate the cards, or use sentence strips or story boards[C] with younger students.

2. *Practice reading.* Students practice reading the excerpts to themselves several times until they can read them fluently.

3. *Share excerpts.* Students move around the classroom, stopping to read their excerpts to other students. When students pair up, they take turns reading their excerpts. After the first student reads, the students discuss the text; then the other student reads, and both students comment on the second student's text. Then students move apart and find other classmates to read their cards to.

4. *Share excerpts with the class.* Students return to their desks after 10 to 15 minutes, and teachers invite several students to read their excerpts to the class or talk about what they learned through the tea party activity.

Tea party is a good way to celebrate the conclusion of a literature focus unit or a thematic unit. Students can pick the excerpts they want to read, and the tea party activity reinforces the main ideas taught during the unit. Teachers also use tea party to introduce a thematic unit by taking excerpts from informational books or content-area textbooks that present the main ideas and key vocabulary to be taught during the unit. Figure 18 shows six tea party cards from a class set that a seventh-grade teacher used to introduce a unit on ecology. The teacher collected some of the sentences and para-

Figure *18* Tea Party Cards With Information About Ecology

Recycling means using materials over and over or making them into new things instead of throwing them away.	**Acid rain** happens when poisonous gases from factories and cars get into rain clouds. Then the gases mix with rain and fall back to earth. It is harmful to our environment and to the people and animals on earth.
Plastic bottles, plastic forks, and plastic bags last forever! A big problem with plastic is that it doesn't **biodegrade.** Instead of filling landfills with plastic, it should be recycled.	Many cities have air filled with pollution called **smog.** This pollution is so bad that the sky looks brown, not blue.
The **ozone layer** around the earth protects us from the harmful rays of the sun. This layer is being damaged by gases called chlorofluorocarbons or **CFCs.** These gases are used in air conditioners, fire extinguishers, and styrofoam.	Americans cut down 850 million trees last year to make **paper products.** Sound like a lot of trees? Consider this: One tree can be made into approximately 700 grocery bags, and a large grocery store uses about that many bags in an hour!

graphs from informational books and a textbook chapter that students would read, and she wrote other selections herself. One or two key words are highlighted on each card to help students focus their attention on key words. Students read and discussed the excerpts and began a word wall[C] with the key words. These two activities activated students' background knowledge about ecology and began to build new concepts.

WORD SORTS

Students examine words and their meanings, sound-symbol correspondences, or spelling patterns using word sorts (Morris, 1982; Schlagal & Schlagal, 1992). Students sort a group of words (or objects or pictures) according to one of these characteristics:

- Conceptual relationships, such as words related to one of several characters in a story or words related to the inner or outer planets in the solar system
- Sound-symbol relationships, such as words in which the final *y* sounds like long *i* (*cry*) and words in which the final *y* sounds like long *e* (*baby*)
- Spelling patterns and rules, such as long-*e* words with various spelling patterns (*sea, greet, be, Pete*)
- Number of syllables, such as *pig, happy, afternoon,* and *television*
- Syllable division rules, using words such as *mag-net, can-dle, ti-ger, stor-y,* and *po-et*

- Parts of speech
- English, Latin, and Greek etymologies of words, using words such as *teeth* (English), *nation* (Latin), and *thermometer* (Greek)

Sometimes teachers determine the categories for the sort, and at other times, students choose the categories. When teachers determine the categories, it is a closed word sort, and when students choose them, it is an open word sort (Bear, Invernizzi, Templeton, & Johnston, 2000). The steps in this instructional strategy are:

1. *Compile a list of words.* Teachers compile a list of 20 to 50 words that exemplify a particular pattern and write the words on small cards.

2. *Determine the categories for the sort.* Teachers determine the categories for the sort and tell students, or students read the words and determine the categories themselves. They may work individually or together in small groups or as a class.

3. *Sort the cards.* Students sort the words into two or more categories and write the sorted words on a chart or glue the sorted word cards onto a piece of chart paper.

4. *Share the completed sorts.* Students share their word sort with classmates, emphasizing the categories they used for their sort.

Many of the words chosen for word sorts should come from high-frequency word walls[C], books students are reading, or content-area units. Figure 19 shows three word sorts using words from *Holes* (Sachar, 1998). The first is an open concept sort; the students sorted words from the story and created their own categories. The second is a closed sort by syllables: the students counted the syllables in each word and organized them according to length. The third is another closed

Figure 19   Three Sorts Using Words From *Holes*

A Sort by Concept

Stanley	Zero	Camp Green Lake	Mr. Sir	The Warden	The Escape
unlucky	nobody	wasteland	grotesque	Ms. Walker	miracle
sneakers	Hector Zeroni	guards	cowboy hat	holes	sploosh
Caveman	confession	investigation	swollen	venom	thumbs-up sign
overweight	homeless	yellow-spotted lizard	tattoo	miserable	impossible
callused	Clyde Livingston's shoes	scorpions	sunflower seeds	fingernail polish	ledges
million dollars	digger	girl scout camp	guard	make-up kit	Big Thumb
suitcase	frail	temperature	tougher	freckles	happiness

Figure 19 Continued

A Sort by Syllables

1-Syllable Words	2-Syllable Words	3-Syllable Words	4-Syllable Words	5-Syllable Words
sir	tattoo	scorpion	violently	unfortunately
twitch	blisters	unlucky	astonishment	momentarily
loot	venom	juvenile	temperature	accelerated
gnats	murky	metallic	imprisonment	electricity
holes	canteen	wheelbarrows	concentrated	curiosity
thief	swollen	tomorrow	tarantula	extraordinary
weight	toxic	agony	unbearable	considerably
sack	shovel	sunflower	impossible	investigation

A Sort by Parts of Speech

Adjectives	Nouns	Verbs	Adverbs
half-opened	wasteland	chewing	surely
scratchy	curiosity	waits	previously
tougher	fossil	howled	quickly
dizzy	digger	swallowed	blankly
desolate	allergies	startled	well
throbbing	pitchfork	watches	intently
metallic	warden	gazes	supposedly
unlucky	scorpions	drank	almost
shriveled	sneakers	wiggled	always
callused	Caveman	scooped	angrily

sort; this time, the words are sorted by part of speech. The students identified the part of speech each word represents and used the dictionary to check the unfamiliar words. Then they sorted the words according to the four parts of speech their teacher specified.

WORD WALLS

Word walls are alphabetized collections of words posted in the classroom that students can refer to when they are reading and writing and for word-study activities. Words for the word wall can be written on large sheets of butcher paper or on cards displayed in pocket charts, and they are often written in alphabetical order so that students can locate the words more easily.

There are three types of word walls. One type is a high-frequency word wall, where teachers post high-frequency words. Although high-frequency word walls are a feature of primary classrooms, they are less common in middle-grade classrooms; nevertheless, teachers should post a word wall with words such as *because, friend, school, their,* and *would* if their students continue to misspell them. A second type of word

Figure 20 A Literature Word Wall for *Sarah, Plain and Tall*

AB	C	D	E
Anna	Caleb	dough	eagerly
biscuits	coarse	dunes	energetic
bonnet	carpenter		
ayuh	cruel		
	chores		
	collapsed		
FG	**H**	**IJ**	**KL**
gophers	hearthstones	Indian paintbrush	longing
feisty	homely		
fogbound	hollow		
	harshly		
	housekeeper		
M	**NO**	**P**	**QR**
mild mannered	nip	Papa	rascal
Maine	oyster	prairie	roamer
	offshore	paddock	
		pesky	
		preacher	
		pitchfork	
S	**T**	**UVW**	**XYZ**
sing	troublesome	widened	
Sarah	tumbleweed	woodchuck	
shovel	treaded (water)	wooly ragwort	
slippery		wild-eyed	
squall		windbreak	
suspenders		wretched	
shuffling			

wall is a content-area word wall, on which teachers and students write important words related to the unit. A third type of word wall is a literature word wall, where teachers and students write interesting, confusing, and important words from the story they are reading. A literature word wall for *Sarah, Plain and Tall* (MacLachlan, 1983) is shown in Figure 20. The three types of word walls should be posted separately in the classroom because if the words are mixed, students will have difficulty categorizing them.

The steps in using a literature word wall are:

1. *Prepare the word wall.* Teachers hang a long sheet of butcher paper on a blank wall in the classroom and divide it into alphabetical categories. Or, teachers can display a large pocket chart on a classroom wall and prepare a stack of cards on which to write the words. Then they add the title of the book students are reading at the top of the word wall.

2. *Introduce the word wall.* Teachers introduce the word wall and add character names and several other key words during preparing activities before reading.

3. *Add words to the word wall.* After reading a picture book or after reading each chapter of a chapter book, students suggest additional "important" words for the word wall. Students and the teacher write the words in alphabetical categories on the butcher paper or on word cards, making sure to write large enough so that most students can see the words. Or, if a pocket chart is being used, students arrange the word cards in alphabetical order.

4. *Use the word wall for exploring activities.* Students use the word wall words for a variety of vocabulary activities, such as word sorts[C] and story maps[C]. Students also refer to the word wall when they are writing in reading logs[C] or working on projects.

For other types of word walls, teachers follow a similar approach to post words on the word walls and highlight the words through various activities.

WRITING GROUPS

During the revising stage of the writing process, students meet in writing groups to share their rough drafts and get feedback on how well they are communicating (Tompkins, 2004). Revising is probably the most difficult part of the writing process because it is difficult for students to evaluate their writing objectively. Students need to learn how to work together in writing groups and provide useful feedback to classmates. The steps are:

1. *Read drafts aloud.* Students take turns reading their rough drafts aloud to the group. Everyone listens politely, thinking about compliments and suggestions they will make after the writer finishes reading. Only the writer looks at the composition, because when classmates and the teacher look at it, they quickly notice and comment on mechanical errors, even though the emphasis during revising is on content. Listening as the writing is read aloud keeps the focus on content.

2. *Offer compliments.* After listening to the rough draft read aloud, classmates in the writing group offer compliments, telling the writer what they liked about the composition. These positive comments should be specific, focusing on strengths, rather than the often-heard "I liked it" or "It was good"; even though these are positive comments, they do not provide effective feedback. When teachers introduce revision, they should model appropriate responses because students may not know how to offer specific and meaningful comments. Teachers and students can brainstorm a list of appropriate comments and post it in the classroom for students to refer to. Comments

may focus on organization, introductions, word choice, voice, sequence, dialogue, theme, and so on. Possible comments are:

I like the part where . . .

I'd like to know more about . . .

I like the way you described . . .

Your writing made me feel . . .

I like the order you used in your writing because . . .

3. *Ask clarifying questions.* After a round of positive comments, writers ask for assistance with trouble spots they identified earlier when rereading their writing, or they may ask questions that reflect more general concerns about how well they are communicating. Admitting the need for help from one's classmates is a major step in learning to revise. Possible questions to ask classmates are:

What do you want to know more about?

Is there a part I should throw out?

What details can I add?

What do you think the best part of my writing is?

Are there some words I need to change?

4. *Offer other revision suggestions.* Members of the writing group ask questions about things that were unclear to them and make suggestions about how to revise the composition. Almost any writer resists constructive criticism, and it is especially difficult for middle-grade students to appreciate suggestions. It is important to teach students what kinds of comments and suggestions are acceptable so that they will word what they say in helpful rather than hurtful ways. Possible comments and suggestions that students can offer are:

I got confused in the part about . . .

Do you need a closing?

Could you add more about . . . ?

I wonder if your paragraphs are in the right order because . . .

Could you combine some sentences?

5. *Repeat the process.* The writing group members repeat the process so that all students have an opportunity to share their rough drafts. The first four steps are repeated for each student's composition. This is the appropriate time for teachers to provide input as well.

6. *Make plans for revision.* At the end of the writing group session, each student makes a commitment to revise his or her writing based on the comments and suggestions of the group members. The final decision on what to revise always rests with the writers themselves, but with the understanding that their rough drafts are not perfect comes the realization that some revision will be necessary. When students verbalize their planned revisions, they are more likely to complete the revision stage. Some students also make notes for themselves about their revision plans. After the group disbands, students make the revisions.

Professional References

Anderson, T. H., & Armbruster, B. B. (1984). Studying. In P. D. Pearson, R. Barr, M. L. Kamil, & P. Mosenthal (Eds.), *Handbook of reading research* (pp. 657–679). New York: Longman.

Ashton-Warner, S. (1965). *Teacher.* New York: Simon & Schuster.

Atwell, N. (1987). *In the middle: Writing, reading, and learning with adolescents.* Portsmouth, NH: Heinemann.

Barone, D. (1990). The written responses of young children: Beyond comprehension to story understanding. *The New Advocate, 3,* 49–56.

Bear, D. R., Invernizzi, M., Templeton, S., & Johnston, F. (2000). *Words their way: Word study for phonics, vocabulary, and spelling instruction.* Upper Saddle River, NJ: Merrill/Prentice Hall.

Berthoff, A. E. (1981). *The making of meaning.* Montclair, NJ: Boynton/Cook.

Blachowicz, C. L. Z. (1986). Making connections: Alternatives to the vocabulary notebook. *Journal of Reading, 29,* 643–649.

Bromley, K. D. (1991). *Webbing with literature: Creating story maps with children's books.* Boston: Allyn & Bacon.

Button, K., Johnson, M. J., & Furgerson, P. (1996). Interactive writing in a primary classroom. *The Reading Teacher, 49,* 446–454.

Claggett, F. (1992). *Drawing your own conclusions: Graphic strategies for reading, writing, and thinking.* Portsmouth, NH: Heinemann.

Clay, M. M. (1985). *The early detection of reading difficulties* (3rd ed.). Portsmouth, NH: Heinemann.

Cunningham, P. M., & Cunningham, J. W. (1992). Making words: Enhancing the invented spelling-decoding connection. *The Reading Teacher, 46,* 106–115.

Eeds, M., & Wells, D. (1989). Grand conversations: An exploration of meaning construction in literature study groups. *Research in the Teaching of English, 23,* 4–29.

Elbow, P. (1973). *Writing without teachers.* London: Oxford University Press.

Fountas, I. C., & Pinnell, G. S. (1996). *Guided reading: Good first teaching for all children.* Portsmouth, NH: Heinemann.

Fountas, I. C., & Pinnell, G. S. (2001). *Guiding readers and writers, grades 3–6.* Portsmouth, NH: Heinemann.

Goldenberg, C. (1992/1993). Instructional conversations: Promoting comprehension through discussion. *The Reading Teacher, 46,* 316–326.

Gunning, T. G. (1995). Word building: A strategic approach to the teaching of phonics. *The Reading Teacher, 48,* 484–488.

Harste, J. C., Woodward, V. A., & Burke, C. L. (1984). *Language stories and literacy lessons.* Portsmouth, NH: Heinemann.

Head, M. H., & Readence, J. E. (1986). Anticipation guides: Meaning through prediction. In E. K. Dishner, T. W. Bean, J. E. Readence, & D. W. Moore (Eds.), *Reading in the content areas* (2nd ed., pp. 229–234). Dubuque, IA: Kendall/Hunt.

Holdaway, D. (1979). *Foundations of literacy.* Aukland, NZ: Ashton Scholastic.

Hunt, L. (1967). Evaluation through teacher-pupil conferences. In T. C. Barrett (Ed.), *The evaluation of children's reading achievement* (pp. 111–126). Newark, DE: International Reading Association.

Johnson, T. D., & Louis, D. R. (1987). *Literacy through literature.* Portsmouth, NH: Heinemann.

Krashen, S. (1993). *The power of reading.* Englewood, CO: Libraries Unlimited.

Lee, D. M., & Allen, R. V. (1963). *Learning to read through experience* (2nd ed.). New York: Meredith.

Macon, J. M., Bewell, D., & Vogt, M. E. (1991). *Responses to literature, grades K–8.* Newark, DE: International Reading Association.

Martinez, M., Roser, N. L., & Strecker, S. (1998/1999). "I never thought I could be a star": A readers theatre ticket to fluency. *The Reading Teacher, 52,* 326–334.

McCracken, R., & McCracken, M. (1978). Modeling is the key to sustained silent reading. *The Reading Teacher, 31,* 406–408.

McKenzie, G. R. (1979). Data charts: A crutch for helping pupils organize reports. *Language Arts, 56,* 784–788.

Moore, D. W., & Moore, S. A. (1992). Possible sentences: An update. In E. K. Dishner, T. W. Bean, J. E. Readence, & D. W. Moore (Eds.), *Reading in the content areas: Improving classroom instruction* (3rd ed., pp. 303–310). Dubuque, IA: Kendall/Hunt.

Morris, D. (1982). "Word sort": A categorization strategy for improving word recognition. *Reading Psychology, 3,* 247–259.

Neeld, E. C. (1986). *Writing* (2nd ed.). Glenview, IL: Scott Foresman.

Ogle, D. M. (1986). K-W-L: A teaching model that develops active reading of expository text. *The Reading Teacher, 39,* 564–570.

Ogle, D. M. (1989). The know, want to know, learn strategy. In K. D. Muth (Ed.), *Children's comprehension of text: Research into practice* (pp. 205–223). Newark, DE: International Reading Association.

Parkes, B. (2000). *Read it again! Revisiting shared reading.* York, ME: Stenhouse.

Peterson, R., & Eeds, M. (1990). *Grand conversations: Literature groups in action.* New York: Scholastic.

Pilgreen, J. L. (2000). *The SSR handbook: How to organize and manage a sustained silent reading program.* Portsmouth, NH: Boynton/Cook/Heinemann.

Pittelman, S. D., Heimlich, J. E., Berglund, R. L., & French, M. P. (1991). *Semantic feature analysis: Classroom applications.* Newark, DE: International Reading Association.

Reutzel, D. R., & Cooter, R. B., Jr. (2000). *Teaching children to read: From basals to books* (3rd ed.). Upper Saddle River, NJ: Merrill/Prentice Hall.

Rico, G. L. (1983). *Writing the natural way*. Los Angeles: Tarcher.

Samuels, S. J. (1979). The method of repeated readings. *The Reading Teacher, 32*, 403–408.

Schlagal, R. C., & Schlagal, J. H. (1992). The integral character of spelling: Teaching strategies for multiple purposes. *Language Arts, 69*, 418–424.

Stahl, S. A. (1999). *Vocabulary development*. Cambridge, MA: Brookline Books.

Stahl, S. A., & Kapinus, B. A. (1991). Possible sentences: Predicting word meaning to teach content area vocabulary. *The Reading Teacher, 45*, 36–43.

Stauffer, R. G. (1970). *The language experience approach to the teaching of reading*. New York: Harper & Row.

Stauffer, R. G. (1975). *Directing the reading-thinking process*. New York: Harper & Row.

Tierney, R. J., Readence, J. E., & Dishner, E. K. (1995). *Reading strategies and practices: A compendium* (4th ed.). Boston: Allyn & Bacon.

Tompkins, G. E. (2004). *Teaching writing: Balancing process and product* (4th ed.). Upper Saddle River, NJ: Merrill/Prentice Hall.

Tompkins, G. E., & Collom, S. (2004). *Sharing the pen: Interactive writing with young children*. Upper Saddle River, NJ: Merrill/Prentice Hall.

Children's Book References

Babbitt, N. (1975). *Tuck everlasting*. New York: Farrar, Straus & Giroux.

Brett, J. (1999). *Gingerbread Baby*. New York: Putnam.

Bunting, E. (1991). *Fly away home*. New York: Clarion.

Cheney, L. (2002). *America: A patriotic primer*. New York: Simon & Schuster.

Cushman, K. (1996). *The ballad of Lucy Whipple*. New York: Clarion.

Ellis, D. (2000). *The breadwinner*. Toronto, Canada: Groundwood Books.

Hunt, J. (1989). *Illuminations*. New York: Bradbury Press.

Hutchins, P. (1968). *Rosie's walk*. New York: Macmillan.

Kennedy, X. J., & Kennedy, D. M. (1999). *Knock at a star: A child's introduction to poetry* (rev. ed.), Boston: Little, Brown.

Lansky, B. (Sel.). (1991). *Kids pick the funniest poems: Poems that make kids laugh*. New York: Meadowbook Press.

Lewis, C. S. (1994). *The lion, the witch and the wardrobe*. New York: HarperCollins.

Lowry, L. (1993). *The giver*. Boston: Houghton Mifflin.

MacLachlan, P. (1983). *Sarah, plain and tall*. New York: Harper & Row.

Ness, E. (1966). *Sam, Bangs, and moonshine*. New York: Holt, Rinehart and Winston.

Prelutsky, J. (1996). *A pizza the size of the sun*. New York: Greenwillow.

Sachar, L. (1998). *Holes*. New York: Farrar, Straus & Giroux.

Shaw, N. (1986). *Sheep in a jeep*. Boston: Houghton Mifflin.

Shaw, N. (1989). *Sheep on a ship*. Boston: Houghton Mifflin.

Shaw, N. (1991). *Sheep in a shop*. Boston: Houghton Mifflin.

Soto, G. (1992). *Neighborhood odes*. San Diego, CA: Harcourt Brace.

Van Allsburg, C. (1984). *The mysteries of Harris Burdick*. Boston: Houghton Mifflin.

Yep, L. (1975). *Dragonwings*. New York: HarperCollins.

GLOSSARY

Aesthetic reading   Reading for pleasure.

Affix   A syllable added to the beginning (prefix) or end (suffix) of a word to change the word's meaning (e.g., *il-* in *illiterate* and *-al* in *national*).

Alphabetic principle   The assumption underlying alphabetical language systems that each sound has a corresponding graphic representation (or letter).

Antonyms   Words that mean the opposite (e.g., *good–bad*).

Applying   The fifth stage of the reading process, in which readers go beyond the text to use what they have learned in another literacy experience, often by making a project or reading another book.

Background knowledge   A student's knowledge or previous experiences about a topic.

Basal readers   Reading textbooks that are leveled according to grade.

Basal reading program   A collection of student textbooks, workbooks, teacher's manuals, and other materials and resources for reading instruction used in kindergarten through sixth grade.

Blend   To combine the sounds represented by letters to pronounce a word.

Bound morpheme   A morpheme that is not a word and cannot stand alone (e.g., *-s, tri-*).

Closed syllable   A syllable ending in a consonant sound (e.g., *make, duck*).

Cloze procedure   An informal assessment activity in which words are strategically omitted from a text; readers supply the missing words using context.

Cluster   A spiderlike diagram used to collect and organize ideas after reading or before writing; also called a map or a web.

Comprehension   The process of constructing meaning using both the author's text and the reader's background knowledge for a specific purpose.

Consonant   A speech sound characterized by friction or stoppage of the airflow as it passes through the vocal tract; usually any letter except *a, e, i, o,* and *u.*

Consonant digraph   Two adjacent consonants that represent a sound not represented by either consonant alone (e.g., *th–this, ch–chin, sh–wash, ph–telephone*).

Content-area reading   Reading in social studies, science, and other areas of the curriculum.

Context clue   Information from the words or sentences surrounding a word that helps to clarify the word's meaning.

Cueing systems   The phonological, semantic, syntactic, and pragmatic cues that students rely on as they read.

Decoding   Using word-identification strategies to pronounce and attach meaning to an unfamiliar word.

Diphthong   A sound produced when the tongue glides from one sound to another; it is represented by two vowels (e.g., *oy–boy, ou–house, ow–how*).

Drafting   The second stage of the writing process, in which writers pour out ideas in a rough draft.

Echo reading   The teacher or other reader reads a sentence and a group of students reread or "echo" what was read.

Editing   The fourth stage of the writing process, in which writers proofread to identify and correct spelling, capitalization, punctuation, and grammatical errors.

Efferent reading   Reading for information.

Elaborative processes   The component of comprehension that focuses on activating prior knowledge, making inferences, and connecting to the text being read.

Etymology   The origin and history of words; the etymological information is enclosed in brackets in dictionary entries.

Explicit instruction   Systematic instruction of concepts, strategies, and skills that builds from simple to complex.

Exploring   The fourth stage of the reading process, in which readers reread the text, study vocabulary words, and learn strategies and skills.

Expository text   Nonfiction writing.

Fluency   Reading smoothly, quickly, and with expression.

Free morpheme   A morpheme that can stand alone as a word (e.g., *book, cycle*).

Frustration level   The level of reading material that is too difficult for a student to read successfully.

Genre   A category of literature such as folklore, science fiction, biography, or historical fiction.

Goldilocks strategy An approach for choosing "just right" books.

Grand conversation A small-group or whole-class discussion about literature.

Grapheme A written representation of a sound using one or more letters.

Graphic organizers Diagrams that provide organized, visual representations of information from texts.

Guided reading Students work in small groups to read as independently as possible a text selected and introduced by the teacher.

High-frequency word A common English word, usually a word among the 100 or 300 most common words.

Homographic homophones Words that sound alike and are spelled alike but have different meanings (e.g., baseball *bat* and the animal *bat*).

Homographs Words that are spelled alike but are pronounced differently (e.g., a *present* and to *present*).

Homonyms Words that sound alike but are spelled differently (e.g., *sea–see, there–their–they're*); also called homophones.

Hyperbole A stylistic device involving obvious exaggerations.

Imagery The use of words and figurative language to create an impression.

Independent reading level The level of reading material that a student can read independently with high comprehension and an accuracy level of 95–100%.

Inferential comprehension Using background knowledge and determining relationships between objects and events in a text to draw conclusions not explicitly stated in the text.

Inflectional endings Suffixes that express plurality or possession when added to a noun (e.g., *girls, girl's*), tense when added to a verb (e.g., *walked, walking*), or comparison when added to an adjective (e.g., *happier, happiest*).

Informal Reading Inventory (IRI) An individually administered reading test composed of word lists and graded passages that is used to determine students' independent, instructional, and frustration levels and listening capacity levels.

Instructional reading level The level of reading material that a student can read with teacher support and instruction with 90–94% accuracy.

Integrative processes The component of comprehension that focuses on recognizing pronoun substitutions, synonyms, and cohesive ties between sentences in a paragraph.

Interactive writing A writing activity in which students and the teacher write a text together, with the students taking turns to do most of the writing themselves.

Invented spelling Students' attempts to spell words that reflect their developing knowledge about the spelling system.

K-W-L An activity to activate background knowledge and set purposes for reading an informational text and to bring closure after reading. The letters stand for What I (we) Know, What I (we) Wonder about, and What I (we) Learned.

Language Experience Approach (LEA) A student's oral composition is written by the teacher and used as a text for reading instruction; it is generally used with beginning readers.

Leveling books A method of estimating the difficulty level of a text.

Lexile scores A method of estimating the difficulty level of a text.

Listening comprehension level The highest level of graded passage that can be comprehended well when read aloud to the student.

Literacy The ability to read and write.

Literal comprehension The understanding of what is explicitly stated in a text.

Literature circle An instructional approach in which students meet in small groups to read and respond to a book.

Literature focus unit An approach to reading instruction in which the whole class reads and responds to a piece of literature.

Long vowels The vowel sounds that are also names of the alphabet letters: $/\bar{a}/$ as in *make*, $/\bar{e}/$ as in *feet*, $/\bar{i}/$ as in *ice*, $/\bar{o}/$ as in *coat*, and $/\bar{u}/$ as in *mule*.

Lowercase letters The letters in manuscript and cursive handwriting that are smaller and usually different from uppercase letters.

Macroprocesses The component of comprehension that focuses on the big ideas in the text.

Metacognition Students' thinking about their own thought and learning processes.

Metacognitive processes The component of comprehension that focuses on students' use of strategies.

Metaphor A comparison expressed directly, without using *like* or *as*.

Microprocesses The component of comprehension that focuses on fluency and chunking words into idea units when reading.

Minilesson Explicit instruction about literacy procedures, concepts, strategies, and skills that are taught to individual students, small groups, or the whole class, depending on students' needs.

Miscue analysis A strategy for categorizing and analyzing a student's oral reading errors.

Mood The tone of a story or poem.

Morpheme The smallest meaningful part of a word; sometimes it is a word (e.g., *cup, hope*), and sometimes it is not a whole word (e.g., *-ly, bi-*).

Narrative A story.

Onset The part of a syllable (or one-syllable word) that comes before the vowel (e.g., *str* in *string*).

Open syllable A syllable ending in a vowel sound (e.g., *sea*).

Orthography The spelling system.

Personification Figurative language in which objects and animals are represented as having human qualities.

Phoneme A sound; it is represented in print with slashes (e.g., /s/ and /th/).

Phoneme-grapheme correspondence The relationship between a sound and the letter that represents it.

Phonemic awareness The ability to manipulate the sounds in words orally.

Phonics Instruction about phoneme-grapheme correspondences and spelling rules.

Phonology The sound system of language.

Polysyllabic Words containing more than one syllable.

Pragmatics The social use system of language.

Prediction A strategy in which students state what they think will happen in a story and then read to verify their guesses.

Prefix A syllable added to the beginning of a word to change the word's meaning (e.g., *re-* in *reread*).

Prereading The first stage of the reading process, in which readers activate background knowledge, set purposes, and make plans for reading.

Prewriting The first stage of the writing process, in which writers gather and organize ideas for writing.

Proofreading Reading a composition to identify and correct spelling and other mechanical errors.

Publishing The fifth stage of the writing process, in which writers make the final copy of their writing and share it with an audience.

Quickwrite A writing activity in which students write on a topic for 5–10 minutes without stopping.

Readability formula A method of estimating the difficulty level of a text.

Reading The second stage of the reading process, in which readers read the text for the first time using independent reading, shared reading, or guided reading, or by listening to it read aloud.

Reading workshop An approach in which students read self-selected texts independently.

Responding The third stage of the reading process, in which readers respond to the text, often through grand conversations and by writing in reading logs.

Revising The third stage of the writing process, in which writers clarify meaning in the writing.

Rime The part of a syllable (or one-syllable word) that begins with the vowel (e.g., *ing* in *string*).

Scaffolding The support a teacher provides to students as they read and write.

Segment To pronounce a word slowly, saying each sound distinctly.

Semantics The meaning system of language.

Shared reading The teacher reads a book aloud with a group of students as they follow along in the text, often using a big book.

Short vowels The vowel sounds represented by /ă/ as in *cat*, /ĕ/ as in *bed*, /ĭ/ as in *big*, /ŏ/ as in *hop*, and /ŭ/ as in *cut*.

Simile A comparison expressed using *like* or *as*.

Strategy Problem-solving behaviors that students use in reading and writing, such as predicting, monitoring, visualizing, and summarizing.

Suffix A syllable added to the end of a word to change the word's meaning (e.g., *-y* in *hairy*, *-ful* in *careful*).

Sustained Silent Reading (SSR) Independent reading practice for 15–30 minutes in which everyone in the class or in the school stops what he or she is doing and spends time reading a self-selected book.

Syllable The written representation of an uninterrupted segment of speech that includes a vowel sound (e.g., *get, a-bout, but-ter-fly, con-sti-tu-tion*).

Symbol The author's use of an object to represent something else.

Synonyms Words that mean nearly the same thing (e.g., *road–street*).

Syntax The structural system of language or grammar.

Trade book A published book that is not a textbook; the type of books in bookstores and libraries.

Uppercase letters The letters in manuscript and cursive handwriting that are larger and are used as first letters in a name or at the beginning of a sentence.

Vowel A voiced speech sound made without friction or stoppage of the airflow as it passes through the vocal tract; the letters *a, e, i, o, u,* and sometimes *w* and *y*.

Vowel digraph Two or more adjacent vowels in a syllable that represent a single sound (e.g., *bread, eight, pain, saw*).

Whole-part-whole An instructional sequence that begins with reading or writing authentic texts (the first whole), continues with teaching concepts, strategies, or skills using examples drawn from the texts (the part), and ends with applying the newly learned information in more reading or writing activities (the second whole).

Word families Groups of words that rhyme (e.g., *ball, call, fall, hall, mall, tall,* and *wall*).

Word identification Strategies that students use to decode words, such as phonic analysis, analogies, syllabic analysis, and morphemic analysis.

Word sort A word study activity in which students group words into categories.

Word wall An alphabetized chart posted in the classroom listing words students are learning.

Writing process The process in which students use prewriting, drafting, revising, editing, and publishing to develop and refine a composition.

Writing workshop An approach in which students use the writing process to write books and other compositions on self-selected topics.

Zone of proximal development The distance between a child's actual developmental level and his or her potential developmental level that can be reached with scaffolding by the teacher or classmates.

INDEX OF AUTHORS AND TITLES

SUBJECT INDEX

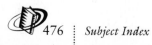